LAW AND RELIGION

CURRENT LEGAL ISSUES 2001

Volume 4

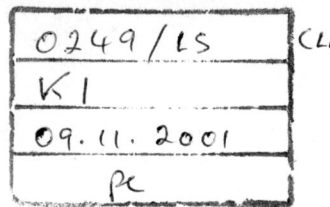
Current Legal Publications

Editor-in-chief **Michael D. A. Freeman**
Editor, *Current Legal Problems*
Associate Editor **Andrew Lewis**
General Editor, *Current Legal Issues*

Editorial Board

LAW AND RELIGION

CURRENT LEGAL ISSUES 2001
Volume 4

Edited by

RICHARD O'DAIR
Senior Lecturer in Laws
University College London

and

ANDREW LEWIS
Senior Lecturer in Laws
University College London

OXFORD
UNIVERSITY PRESS

OXFORD
UNIVERSITY PRESS

Great Clarendon Street, Oxford OX2 6DP

Oxford University Press is a department of the University of Oxford.
It furthers the University's objective of excellence in research, scholarship,
and education by publishing worldwide in

Oxford New York

Athens Auckland Bangkok Bogotá Buenos Aires Cape Town
Chennai Dar es Salaam Delhi Florence Hong Kong Istanbul Karachi
Kolkata Kuala Lumpur Madrid Melbourne Mexico City Mumbai Nairobi
Paris São Paulo Shanghai Singapore Taipei Tokyo Toronto Warsaw
with associated companies in Berlin Ibadan

Oxford is a registered trade mark of Oxford University Press
in the UK and in certain other countries

Published in the United States
by Oxford University Press Inc., New York

British Library Cataloguing in Publication Data

Data available

Library of Congress Cataloging in Publication Data
Law and religion/edited by Andrew Lewis and Richard O'Dair.
p. cm.—(Current legal issues; 2001, v. 4)
Includes index.
1. Law—Congresses. 2. Religion and law—Congresses. 3. Religion and law—Great
Britain—Congresses. I. Lewis, A.D.E. II. O'Dair, Richard. III. Current legal issues; v. 4.
K225. L368 2001   340—dc21   2001033854

ISBN 0-19-924660-2

1 3 5 7 9 10 8 6 4 2

Typeset in Sabon by
Cambrian Typesetters, Frimley, Surrey

Printed in Great Britain
on acid-free paper by
T.J. International, Padstow, Cornwall

CONTENTS

GENERAL EDITOR'S PREFACE

Following a now established pattern, the fourth Current Legal Issues Colloquium held at the Faculty of Laws, University College London, was focused on an interdisciplinary topic, Law and Religion. As a field of study this is well established, generating both specialized periodical publications and regular conferences of scholars. In keeping with the pattern of previous colloquia the organizers did not seek to constrain potential contributors within any predetermined limits, though they sought, as ever, to ensure that current issues of moment within the field were addressed. Some forty papers were presented over the two days of the colloquium, of which thirty are here published in fuller form. The hectic but intense atmosphere such a crowded programme generates provides its own rewards for participants. We hope that the published fruits will prove equally rewarding to a wider audience.

The colloquium was convened by Richard O'Dair of the Faculty of Laws, UCL, assisted by Andrew Lewis. Administrative assistance and secretarial support was provided, both before and after the colloquium, by Lisa Penfold, Jacqui Bennett, and Sue Galway. As ever the onlie begetter of this series, Michael Freeman, lent his considerable knowledge and support.

The Fifth CLI colloquium will be held on 2–3 July 2001 on the theme Law and Geography. Preparations are afoot for the July 2002 colloquium on Law and History. In 2003 the planned theme is Law and the Arts. Further general details of these future events may be obtained from Andrew Lewis (e-mail: a.d.e.lewis@ucl.ac.uk).

November 2000   Andrew Lewis

NOTES ON CONTRIBUTORS

Rex J. Ahdar is a Senior Lecturer in the Faculty of Law, University of Otago. He is the editor of *Competition Law and Policy in New Zealand* (Law Book Company, 1991); *God and Government: The New Zealand Experience* (with John Stenhouse) (University of Otago Press, 2000) and *Law and Religion* (Aldershot: Ashgate, 2000). His research interests include religious freedom, Church and State, family law, and antitrust law.

Edward M. Andries is a Professor of US and Comparative Law at the University of Montevideo, and has been a Visiting Professor of Comparative Constitutional Law at Austral University in Buenos Aires and at the National University of Rosario, Santa Fé, Argentina.

Paul Beaumont is Professor of European Union and Private International Law and Head of the Law School, University of Aberdeen. Recent publications include (as editor) *Christian Perspectives on Law Reform and Christian Perspectives on Human Rights and Legal Philosophy* (Carlisle, 1998). He has co-edited *Legal Framework of the Single European Currency* (Oxford, 1999) and *Christian Perspectives on Law and Relationism* (Paternoster 2000) and co-authored *EU Law* (Penguin, 1999) and *The Hague Convention on International Child Abduction* (Oxford University Press, 1999).

J. David Bleich is Professor of Law at the Benjamin N. Cardozo School of Law as well as the Herbert and Florence Tenzer Professor of Law and Ethics at Yeshiva University. He has served as visiting Gruss Professor at the University of Pennsylvania School of Law. Among his many publications are *Judaism and Healing* and the four-volume series *Contemporary Halakhic Problems*.

Matthijs de Blois studied law at Utrecht University, graduating in 1977, and joined the Law Faculty of Leiden University in the Department of International Law. His main fields of interest were the international protection of human rights and the law of the European Communities. In 1989 he received his doctorate on a thesis concerning the right to personal integrity in international law. Since 1990 he has been a member of the Department of Legal Theory of the Law Faculty of Utrecht University. His current research is in the field of the philosophical aspects of the law, especially of human rights law. Among his recent publications are 'The Fundamental Freedom of the European Court of Human Rights', in Rick Lawson and Matthijs de Blois, *The Dynamics of the Protection of Human Rights in Europe*, Essays in Honour of Henry G. Schermers, vol. iii (Dordrecht, 1994); and 'Self-Determination or Human Dignity, The Core

Principle of Human Rights', in Mielle Bulterman, Aart Hendriks, and Jacqueline Smith (eds.), *To Baehr in our Minds: Essays on Human Rights from the Heart of the Netherlands*, SIM Special No. 21 (Utrecht, 1998).

Anthony Bradney is Professor of Law in the Faculty of Law at the University of Leicester. He has written widely in the area of religion and law. His publications include *Living without Law: An Ethnography of Quaker decision-making, Dispute Avoidance and Dispute Resolution* (with Fiona Cownie) (2000) and *Religions, Rights and Laws* (1993).

Calum Carmichael is Professor of Comparative Literature and Adjunct Professor of Law at Cornell University. His recent books include *Law, Legend, and Incest in the Bible* (1997) and *The Spirit of Biblical Law* (1996). He is also the editor of the *Collected Works of David Daube* (Berkeley). His main research interests are Biblical Law, early Jewish Law and the New Testament, and law and literature in antiquity.

Peter Cumper is a Lecturer in Law at the University of Leicester, where he teaches Public Law and Human Rights. His recent publications include 'The Protection of Religious Rights under Section 13 of the Human Rights Act 1998' [2000] *Public Law* 254 and 'Religious Organisations under the Human Rights Act', in P. Edge and G. Harvey (eds.), *Law and Religion in Contemporary Society* (Aldershot: Ashgate, 2000).

Perry Dane is a Professor of Law and the Director of Faculty Development at the Rutgers School of Law, Camden. He was formerly a law clerk to the Honorable William J. Brennan, Jr., Associate Justice of the United States Supreme Court, and served on the faculty of the Yale Law School. His scholarly interests include religion and the law, constitutional law, choice of law, jurisdiction, American Indian law, the jurisprudence of Jewish Law, and legal theory. His publications include *The Public, the Private, and the Sacred: Variations on a Theme of Nomos and Narrative* (Cardozo Studies in Law and Literature); 'Jurisdictionality, Time, and the Legal Imagination', *Hofstra Law Review*; 'The Yoke of Heaven, The Question of Sinai, and the Life of Law', *University of Toronto Law Journal*; 'Maps of Sovereignty: A Meditation', *Cardozo Law Review*; and 'Vested Rights, "Vestedness", and Choice of Law', *Yale Law Journal*.

Norman Doe is a Professor and Director of the Centre for Law and Religion at Cardiff Law School. His books include *The Legal Framework of the Church of England* (Oxford, 1996) and *Canon Law in the Anglican Communion* (Oxford, 1998). He is a member of the European Consortium for Church and State Research, and is Deputy Chancellor of the Diocese of Manchester.

Howard M. Ducharme is Professor and Chair of Philosophy at the University of Akron, Ohio. He contributed 'Thrift-Euthanasia, in Theory and in Practice' to *Current Legal Issues 2000: Law and Medicine* (Oxford, 2000).

He is currently working on a book on the malleability of human life by gene therapy, embryonic stem cells, cloning, and artificial organs, and the enduring nature of a person.

Peter W. Edge is Reader in Law and Religion, Oxford Brookes University. His primary interests lie in the interaction of law and religion within the English jurisdiction, and under the European Convention on Human Rights. Recent publications include 'Male Circumcision after the Human Rights Act 1998', *Journal of Civil Liberties*, and 'Religious Rights and Choice under the European Convention on Human Rights', *Web Journal of Current Legal Issues*. With Graham Harvey he edited the collection *Law and Religion in Contemporary Society: Communities, Individualism, and the State* (Aldershot: Ashgate, 2000).

Malcolm D. Evans is Professor of Public International Law at the University of Bristol. His research interests concern the international protection of human rights (with particular interests in the freedom of religion and torture prevention) and the law of the sea. His principal publications include *Relevant Circumstances and Maritime Delimitation* (Oxford, 1989); *Religious Liberty and International Law in Europe* (Cambridge, 1997); and, with Professor Rod Morgan, *Preventing Torture* (Oxford, 1998) and *Protecting Prisoners* (Oxford, 1999). He has contributed chapters concerning religion and human rights to a number of edited collections, including most recently Peter Edge (ed.), *Law and Religion in Contemporary Society* (Aldershot, 2000) and Rex Adhar (ed.), *Law and Religion* (Aldershot, 2000). He is a member of the International Law Association Committee on International Human Rights Law and Practice and a Board Member of the Association for the Prevention of Torture.

Michael Freeman is Professor of English Law at University College London and Editor-in-Chief of *Current Legal Publications*, which includes *Current Legal Problems* and *Current Legal Issues*. He is the author of *Lloyd on Jurisprudence* and has interests in family law, private international law, and medical law. He has written extensively on the problem of the *agunah* and spearheaded the Chief Rabbi's Committee on the problem in the mid-1980s.

Jeanne Gaakeer received her Ph.D. from Erasmus University, Rotterdam. Her dissertation was a study of the history and development of the Law and Literature Movement, and, more specifically, of the works of James Boyd White. She is a Senior Lecturer in Jurisprudence and Legal Theory at Erasmus University, Rotterdam, and judge in the District Court of Middelburg. Her most recent publications in English include *Hope Springs Eternal* (Amsterdam, 1998); 'Translation and Judicial Ethos', in *Current Legal Issues 1999: Law and Literature* (Oxford, 1999); and ' "Ethos in Hollywood": A Reading of Bordewijk's Character, a Novel of Son and Father', *Trema* (May 2000).

Robert Gleave is Lecturer in Islamic Studies, University of Bristol. He received his doctorate in Islamic Law from the University of Manchester (1996), and now teaches Islamic Studies in the Department of Theology and Religious Studies (and Islamic Law in the Faculty of Law) of the University of Bristol. His publications include *Inevitable Doubt: Two Shi'i Theories of Jurisprudence* (Leiden, 2000) and he co-edited *Islamic Law: Theory and Practice* (London, 1997).

David Harte is a senior lecturer at Newcastle Law School in the University of Newcastle. His interests include environmental law with a particular emphasis on heritage conservation and in a number of aspects of religion and law, including the role of religion and churches in conservation and religion in schools. His recent publications on these topics include 'Religious Education and Worship in State Schools', in Norman Doe, Mark Hill, and Robert Ombres (eds.), *English Canon Law: Essays in Honour of Bishop Eric Kemp* (Cardiff, 1998); 'Legal Aspects of Development and the Church in the Countryside', in Nicholas Herbert-Young (ed.), *Law, Policy and Development in the Rural Environment* (Cardiff, 1999); and 'Establishment and Autonomy: The Church of England as a Voluntary Body', in Alison Dunn (ed.), *The Voluntary Sector, the State and the Law* (Hart Publishing 2000).

Mark Hill is Chancellor of the Diocese of Chichester and a Research Fellow at the Centre for Law and Religion at Cardiff Law School. He is the author of *Ecclesiastical Law* (London, 1995), a second edition of which will be published by Oxford University Press in 2001, and co-editor of *English Canon Law* (Cardiff, 1998). He is Case Notes Editor of the *Ecclesiastical Law Journal* and lately Visiting Fellow of Emmanuel College, Cambridge. He practises from chambers in the Middle Temple.

Bernard S. Jackson was appointed Alliance Professor of Modern Jewish Studies and Co-Director of the Centre for Jewish Studies at the University of Manchester in 1997, having previously held chairs in Law at Liverpool Polytechnic, the University of Kent at Canterbury, and the University of Liverpool. He has published widely in both Jewish Law and the semiotics of law, his most recent book being *Studies in the Semiotics of Biblical Law* (Sheffield Academic Press, 2000). In June 1998 he received the honorary degree of Doctor of Humane Letters from the Hebrew Union College, Cincinnati.

Anthony Jeremy is a solicitor and a Research Fellow at the Centre for Law and Religion, Cardiff University. His interests include Comparative Canon Law, particularly of the Anglican and Roman Catholic Communions. Recent publications include *Acts of the Colloquium of Roman Catholic and Anglican Canon Lawyers* (Rome, 1999; Windsor, 2000) and *The Impact of Canon Law on the Contractual Obligations of Good Faith Law and Justice* (2000).

Ian Leigh is Professor of Law at the University of Durham. He is author of *Law, Politics and Local Democracy* (Oxford, 2000) and co-author (with Laurence Lustgarten) of *In from the Cold: National Security and Parliamentary Democracy* (Oxford, 1994). He has written extensively in legal periodicals on public law and human rights and has advised religious groups on human rights questions. He is currently in receipt of a grant from the Arts and Human Research Board for a research project entitled 'Religious Liberty in a Liberal State: A Critical Appraisal'.

Javier Martínez-Torrón is Professor of Law at Complutense University, Madrid, and is a Doctor *utroque iure* (in Law and in Canon Law). He is a Corresponding Member of the Spanish Royal Academy of Jurisprudence and Legislation, and Vice-President of its Canon Law Section (1994), a Member of the International Academy for Freedom of Religion and Belief (1997), and a Member of the International Advisory Council of the Oslo Coalition on Freedom of Religion and Belief (1999). His publications include *Anglo-American Law and Canon Law* (Berlin: Duncker & Humblot, 1998) and he has also published on the future of the State law on religious affairs (Granada: Comares, 1999) and on some of the legal problems derived from the activity of Jehovah's Witnesses in Latin America (Mexico: UNAM, 2000).

Piotr Mazurkiewicz is an Assistant Professor in the Institute of Political Sciences at Cardinal Stefan Wyszyński University in Warsaw and the Papal Theological Faculty in Warsaw. His main area of the study and scientific interest cover history of social and political ideas, State–Church relations in a democratic system, European integration, axiology, and Catholic social thought. He is a co-author of *Ethik und Gesetzgebung. Ethics and Legislation* (1998); *Church–State Relations in Central and Eastern Europe* (1999), and (in Polish) *Society, Church, State (1945–2000)* (2000). He is a member of the European Society for Research in Ethics, 'Societas Ethica'.

Reid Mortensen is Senior Lecturer in Law at the University of Queensland, having previously practised as a commercial solicitor in Brisbane. His major research interests lie in law and religion in the Commonwealth and in conflict of laws, and he also writes on legal issues in the Pacific Islands. He has published widely in these areas, and is the author of *Private International Law* (2000).

Augur Pearce is a solicitor pursuing research at Cambridge into English and German Church legal history. He recently held the Kingsley Bye-Fellowship at Magdalene College. His recent articles published or awaiting publication include 'Public Religion in the English Colonies', 'The Christian Claims of the English Law of Marriage', and 'Sacred Time: An Historical Perspective'.

Steven H. Resnicoff is a Professor at DePaul University College of Law and he occupies its 2000–1 Wicklander Chair for Professional Ethics. His current research focuses on the interrelationship of religious and secular legal systems regarding commercial, legal, and medical ethics.

Julian Rivers has been a Lecturer in Law at the University of Bristol since 1993. His principal areas of research are in constitutional law and legal philosophy, with a particular interest in the relationship between law and religion. Recent publications include 'From Toleration to Pluralism: Religious Liberty and Religious Establishment under the United Kingdom's Human Rights Act' in Rex Ahdar (ed.), *Law and Religion* (Aldershot, 2000); 'The Virtue of Rights', *Studies in Christian Ethics*, 13/2 (Edinburgh, 2000); and 'Liberal Constitutionalism and Christian Political Thought', in Paul R. Beaumont (ed.), *Christian Perspectives on the Limits of Law* (Carlisle: Paternoster, 2001).

Danesh Sarooshi is a Senior Lecturer in Public International Law at University College London. He has published articles in a number of areas of international law, and his book *The United Nations and the Development of Collective Security* was published by Oxford University Press in its Oxford Monographs in International Law Series in 1999. He is currently completing a book entitled *The Theory of International Organizations*. He is a member of the International Law Association's International Committee on the Accountability of International Organizations.

Steven D. Smith, the Robert and Marion Short Professor at Notre Dame Law School, has published widely in the fields of American constitutional law, legal theory, and law and religion. His publications in the law and religion field include *Getting over Equality: A Critical Diagnosis of Religious Freedom in America* (New York University Press, forthcoming) and *Foreordained Failure: The Quest for a Constitutional Principle of Religious Freedom* (Oxford University Press, 1995, 1999).

Sophie C. van Bijsterveld is Associate Professor of Public International Law at Tilburg University (Katholieke Universiteit Brabant) in the Netherlands. She has written and edited various books in the field of fundamental rights and legislative developments, and further published on a wide range of topics of constitutional and international law, including issues of law and religion and higher education. Among her recent publications are *Godsdienstvrijheid in Europees perspectief* (Deventer: W. E. J. Tjeenk Willink, 1998) and 'Religious Liberty in European Perspective. Religion, International Law and Policy in the Wider European Arena: New dimensions and Developments', in Rex Ahdar (ed.), *Law and Religion* (Aldershot: Ashgate, 2000).

Gary Watt, solicitor, is a Lecturer in the Law School at the University of Warwick and the author of a number of articles and books in the areas of trusts, equity, and property. He has also written on the relationship between academic jurisprudence and legal practice.

TABLE OF CASES BEFORE NATIONAL AND INTERNATIONAL COURTS

European Court of Justice

Netherlands

Vanuatu

Western Samoa

TABLE OF NATIONAL LEGISLATION

TABLE OF INTERNATIONAL LEGISLATION

EDITORIAL INTRODUCTION

The fourth interdisciplinary colloquium at the Faculty of Laws, University College London, held on 3–4 July 2000 was devoted to law and religion. The convenors had approached their task with a number of aims in mind. Firstly, there was the desire to bring together scholars dealing with issues of law and religion in the broadest possible sense. In this the colloquium undoubtedly succeeded: speakers came from both common and civil law countries, from as far afield as New Zealand and with experience of diverse cultures—one speaker addressed freedom of religion in the Melanesian Isles. Much of what was achieved seems likely to have occurred as speakers reflected subsequently on conversations held and on the papers presented. Of course, this can never be demonstrated in a published volume.

Secondly, there was a desire to ascertain in a non-scientific and impressionistic way which of the many issues that might arise from the intersecting worlds of law and religion were attracting scholarly concern at this time. To this end, the convenors' 'Call for Papers' was deliberately broad and non-prescriptive. Thirdly, there was the desire to generate challenges to established ways of thinking on the questions raised.

It would not be appropriate in an editorial introduction to attempt to summarize all that was said over the two days of the colloquium. However, given our stated aims, an attempt will be made to convey a flavour of what was achieved by describing the programme which emerged. Considerations of space do not allow for consideration or even the mention of every paper presented.

Day 1 commenced with a session entitled 'First Principles'. Howard Ducharme began by arguing that many of the values considered fundamental by liberal legal systems, such as the intrinsic importance of the individual with all its legal implications, depended upon the coherence of the essentially religious notion of the soul. This notion has many contemporary critics, and Howard Ducharme mounted a vigorous defence. Gary Watt raised the provocative question of what, in a post-modern world, might be the scope and limits of our concept of a religion. In an intellectual climate which has come to acknowledge the existence of competing incommensurable rationalities, the State should impose only minimal limits on what counts as a religion in accordance with a minimalist concept of rationality.

Law, religion, and literature share a common need to interpret texts. It was thus to be expected that a number of papers would address questions of (to use the theologians' term) hermeneutics. These issues formed the focus of our second session. Here Steve Smith argued provocatively that the interpretative practices of lawyers share three important features with scriptural interpretation. These are the assumption that the text may contain meanings beyond those suggested by its ordinary language; the assumption that the text is authoritative; and the assumption that a number of texts with different authors should be read as being the product of a common mind. In the scriptural context, these practices are based on and seen as evidence for divine authorship. Professor Smith concluded with the thought that the similarities to which he points might perhaps indicate that law too should be seen as fundamentally religious. Given the secular assumptions which underlie so much of modern legal scholarship, it is clear that his views represent a highly provocative challenge to the status quo.

After lunch delegates were offered the choice between parallel sessions, one of which was entitled 'Religion and the Constitution'. The representation of religious leaders within a reformed second legislative chamber is clearly a pressing matter in the UK context, and Peter Edge offered a critical evaluation of the current position. In his view, the current arrangements are insufficiently inclusive and are in need of reform. The alternative session concerned religion and work. Steven Resnicoff and David Bleich brought a fresh Judaic perspective to some common questions of professional ethics which are normally considered only from a secular perspective. They argued in effect that a Jewish lawyer should be permitted to disclose client confidences when disclosure is required by Jewish law but not under current codes of ethics or the common law. Any other view fails to respect the lawyer's freedom of conscience. Nor can a client expect more if s/he employs a lawyer who has openly declared his or her allegiance to Jewish law. Peter Cumper presented the first of many papers touching on the European Convention on Human Rights (ECHR). He sounded a note of caution to those tempted to assume that the Human Rights Act 1998 (UK) inaugurates a new and golden age for the protection of human rights in the United Kingdom. On the contrary, Article 9 of the ECHR has in his view been interpreted much too narrowly by the European Court of Human Rights which, particularly in the workplace, has been slow to recognize behaviour as a 'manifestation' of religious belief so as to qualify for the protection of Article 9.

The last session of the first day focused directly upon human rights. From a historical perspective, Matthijs de Blois argued that the origins of legal protection of human rights (especially the right to freedom of religion) cannot be seen as lying solely in the Enlightenment and thus in a secular reaction to religious intolerance. De Blois demonstrated the existence of a radical Anabaptist stream within the Reformation which had influenced the writings of John Locke, whose influence on US constitutional history is well known. In similar vein, Malcolm Evans urged us to remember that the concept of human rights is not self-evidently the only value system around which society may be organized. Religion may be a competing source of fundamental values rather than, simply, a human right. Like Peter Cumper, Javier Martínez-Torrón, whose paper was presented by Professor Raphael Palomino, sounded a note of caution about the jurisprudence of the Court; he argued that the Court has been effective in preventing the infringement of religious freedom when the threat comes from those motivated by religious beliefs. It has been much less effective when the threat has come from the State acting upon a secular and therefore supposedly neutral non-religious ground. He warns that secularism can itself be seen as a creed, and an intolerant one at that.

As can be seen, a willingness to question the values inherent in the human rights movement quickly emerged as a theme of the colloquium. On Day 2 we began with a consideration of religious group autonomy in the human rights context. Rex Adhar argued that churches ought to be exempted from legal provisions prohibiting discrimination on the grounds of sexual orientation. This is not only a reflection of the fact that religious liberty requires freedom to associate (and is a collective as well as an individual right—a point emphasized by Julian Rivers). It also reflects the fact that liberal society is itself impoverished if it infringes upon the autonomy of private associations, for society is thus deprived of a potential source of new ideas and ways of living. In a memorable, if chilling, passage Adhar reminds us of the alternative view:

Theologian Paul Marshall once commented that 'in this liberal society, communities are not free: rather they are constrained to become liberal associations'. Some liberal theorists concede as much. Stephen Macedo, for example, reminds us the liberal citizens do not emerge 'naturally'. Rather, liberal democracies must act positively to shape its citizenry to appreciate and perpetuate liberal virtues. Thus, 'the transformative dimension of liberalism' needs to be recognized. If a liberal regime is to thrive, 'it must constitute the private realm in its image, and it must form citizens willing to observe its limits and able to pursue its aspirations'. Liberals ought not to be ashamed of defending a ' "moderate hegemony" of liberal public values'. 'The extinction of many, if not all, of the [religious] communities that pose truly radical alternatives to liberal democratic principles is to be welcomed.'

Ian Leigh also sought to challenge accepted wisdom in this area. Section 2A of the Local Government Act 1986 (England and Wales), popularly known as 'section 28', prohibits the promotion of homosexuality by local authorities. Eminent figures such as Lord Lester of Herne Hill and David Pannick have argued that this section is contrary to the ECHR. Leigh presents a powerful contrary argument. Among other things he asks whose human rights can be infringed when a public authority is prohibited from acting in this way.

The next session was entitled 'Secular Law and Religion' and considered the extent to which state law is and should be used to regulate the internal affairs of religious organizations. Norman Doe and Anthony Jeremy considered the differing but in their view complementary arguments for autonomy which emerge from secular and religious sources. Two further speakers, however, were prepared to question the autonomy thesis. Augur Pearce argued that whatever might be the case in relation to other churches, the Anglican Church is a public institution and cannot claim the same degree of autonomy. David Harte argued that all religious groups can be seen as performing public functions and that, as such, they should *seek* to be regulated according to the standards, especially the procedural standards, to be found within English public law. Such an approach, according to Harte, better equips them to carry out their mission than one in which they are treated as simply private associations governed solely by contract.

After lunch there followed a session entitled 'Perspectives of Diverse Faiths'. As we had hoped, a broad range of perspectives was represented. Danesh Sarooshi demonstrated the influence of the Baha'i community on the United Nations system of collective security. Moreover, he laid out a reformist vision for that system based on the Baha'i scriptures. Such a vision would involve a clear statement of the values, to be agreed between states, which collective security is meant to promote. This would facilitate the granting to the United Nations of increased powers, including the power to depose a government found to be threatening these fundamental values. Reid Mortensen considered the interplay of Christianity and traditional religions in Melanesia. He argued that though the path of an intolerant Christian state was always a possibility, it has not been followed. This is due in no small measure to the attitude of many of the Christian churches themselves. Robert Gleave took us back to the question of hermeneutics in an Islamic context. Noting that the Qu'rān is for Muslims a sacred text, but, problematically, contains little that is of obvious relevance to law, Gleave considered the (contrived?) interpretative devices to which scholars have had resort in order to make it a source of law. Thus the hermeneutical questions facing each of the major scriptural religions were considered in the colloquium. Smith's consideration of the Christian perspective has already been mentioned. Calum Carmichael (session 1) and Bernard Jackson (session 2) dealt with the hermeneutics of the Torah.

Our final session entitled 'Secular Enforcement of Religion' considered the justification, if any, for the adoption by the State of a social institution which is distinctively religious in origin. Thus Perry Dane considered the adoption by the state of Vermont of a statute which gives to same-sex unions all the incidents of marriage but not the name. Dane asks whether this makes sense. Is marriage anything more than the sum total of its incidents? And even if it does make sense, does the distinction serve any useful legitimate purpose? Michael Freeman's paper 'Is the Jewish *Get* Any Business of the State?' illustrates graphically the tensions between state law and religious freedom that seem to have emerged as a theme of the colloquium. On the one hand, there is Jewish law, under which a woman is not regarded as divorced unless her husband can be persuaded to grant her a religious divorce (the *get*). This discriminates against women and can even by used by their husbands as an instrument of extortion. The Jewish authorities seem, according to Freeman, unwilling to institute reforms. On the other hand, there is the possibility of state intervention, as has occurred in common law countries other than the United Kingdom. Yet this would infringe the autonomy of an apparently voluntary religious association. Writing as a member of the Jewish community and as a lawyer, Freeman finds the choice of the appropriate path for reform difficult. Ultimately, however, he opts for the preservation of autonomy and, in effect, appeals for reform from within the Jewish community.

What then was achieved by our fourth annual interdisciplinary colloquium? In a sense, of course, the reader will have to judge for him- or herself. From the editors' perspective, however, there emerged above all else a sense that human rights legislation is at best ambiguous in its implications for freedom of religion. At worst, it is dangerous.

Not all the papers given at the Colloquium are published here. In particular John Warwick Montgomery's paper entitled 'Can Blasphemy Law be Justified?' is published in *Law & Justice*, 146–7 (Trinity–Michaelmas 2000), and a paper by Derek O'Brien and Vaughan Carter on Rastafarianism and the Law is being submitted to the *Yale Journal of Law and Religion*.

Richard O'Dair

THE IMAGE OF GOD AND THE MORAL IDENTITY OF PERSONS: AN EVALUATION OF THE HOLISTIC THEOLOGY OF PERSONS

Howard M. Ducharme

Although advocates of the doctrine of the sanctity of human life now frequently try to give their position some secular justification, there can be no possible justification for making the boundary of sanctity run parallel with the boundary of our own species, unless we invoke some belief about immortal souls.

Peter Singer, 'Unsanctifying Human Life'

The No-Soul Dogma of Contemporary Academic Theology

There is no soul—no traditional, substantial, immaterial, irreducibly moral, common-to-all-world-religions soul—according to the dominant contemporary academic view, including contemporary academic theology. The soul—the mind, or one's person which makes the body precious by participation—cannot and does not exist *per se*. When the term is employed in an academic context today, it is assumed that it refers to a property of the physical brain, to an existential relationship of a functioning physical body, or to an ancient term with a story to tell—but it does not refer to a non-physical 'living substance'.[1] It is now presupposed that the existence of a physical substance is essential to the nature of a person, mind, or soul. In contemporary academic theology, this is the metaphysical assumption of the holistic theory of the soul—the dominant, king-of-the-hill position. It is a belief presumed to be beyond question.

All holistic theories are united on a *negative* claim, that a person is *not* an immaterial substance. Thus the substantial mind, soul, or person as defended and refined by Plato, St Augustine, St Thomas Aquinas, Descartes, and John Calvin, to pick a few major representatives of the common-sense and traditional understanding of the nature of a person, is

---

[1] Augustine, *Greatness of the Soul*, in *Ancient Christian Writers: The Works of the Fathers in Translation*, trans. Joseph M. Colleran (Westminster, Md., 1964), 16–19.

unequivocally false.[2] A brief description of some of their arguments for the immaterial, substantial, essentially moral self are noted below.

Augustine argues that we have direct access to, and immediate knowledge of, the substantial soul. Knowledge of the soul is not a religious belief that rests upon faith in divine or spiritual revelation: 'the mind knows itself, it knows its own substance'.[3] It is true, 'man's mind knows itself. The mind knows nothing so well as what is present to it, and nothing is more present to the mind than itself.'[4] Clearly then, 'when the mind views itself by thought, it understands and recognizes itself: thus it begets this understanding and self-recognition. *It is a non-bodily thing* that is being understood and viewed, and recognized in the understanding.'[5] It is a self-evident awareness that I am thinking and that I am not my functioning brain. In thinking, there is no experience or awareness of grey gelatinous convolutions, warm oxygenated blood flow, neurons firing, neo-cortical activity, pre-frontal lobe spatial location, and/or cognitive centres of the brain interacting with linguistic centres of the brain. To equate self-consciousness or thinking with brain activity therefore commits a fallacious equivocation. The common academic reply, that future empirical findings in neurobiology will some day prove such an identity claim, commits a faith-in-scientism fallacy. The other common reply here is that a biological activity can go on in the body without us having any awareness of it; for example, my liver, pancreas, and kidneys are functioning and I do not have an awareness of what they are doing. The problem with this objection to Augustine's point is that no one claims that thinking is liver, pancreas, or kidney function. So the second objection turns out to be a red herring fallacy.

Aquinas also argues that the human soul is an immaterial substance characterized by rational, intellectual, moral, and spiritual powers which are real, knowable, and non-physical.

God created man in his own image. Now it is by the soul that man is after God's image . . . [and] it is only substances that are properly and truly called beings . . . But the rational soul is a subsistent form, as we have seen. So it is properly said both to be and to come to be. And it cannot come to be out of matter already there, either of a bodily kind, because that would give it a bodily nature, or of a

---

[2] Although Aquinas adapted the form–matter schema of Aristotle—emphasizing the nature of a human being rather than the soul or person as emphasized in Augustine—both hold that the human soul or person as found in contemporary holistic theology is profoundly incorrect, as noted below. Also see John Calvin, *An Excellent Treatise of the Immortalytie of the Soule, by which is proved, that the soules, after their departure out of bodies, are awake and doe lyve, contrary to that erronious opinion of certain ignorant persons, who thinke them to lye a sleape untill the day of Judgement*, trans. from French by T. Stocker (1581).

[3] Augustine, *The Trinity*, book 10, ch. 10, sect. 16, trans. Edmund Hill (Brooklyn, 1991).

[4] Ibid., book 14, ch. 2, sect. 7, p. 375.

[5] Ibid., sect. 8, 376; my italics.

spiritual kind, because that would involve spiritual substances being transmuted into each other; so it has to be said that it can only come to be by creation.[6]

Therefore, the assertion of contemporary holistic anthropology that asserts the soul is a property or aspect of the body or functioning brain, or that it is an essentially physical, psychosomatic composition, is seriously wrong-headed. This is because 'the soul is not a composition . . . Nor is the soul a mode of composition . . . [Because if it were, then] each part of the body would have a distinct soul; since bone, flesh, and sinew are in each case composed according to a different proportion, each would possess a different soul. Now, this is patently false.'[7] The soul has no physical component and is an immaterial substance: the human soul is 'not composed of matter and form'.[8] The other common objection here is that divine creation of the soul is disallowed because it violates the contemporary doctrine of naturalism, i.e. only natural causes are permissible. However, if theism is the given assumption, then divine intervention in the world is not coherently or logically disallowed. It is presupposed as the principal distinctions between deistic and atheistic assumptions. Alternatively, if theism is not taken as a given, then naturalistic physicalism entails a creationist doctrine that is anti-realistic, i.e. constant creation and re-creation of persons by non-personal energy and/or neurons, as explained below. Thus, one-time creation of a soul is not as disruptive of reality as is its replacement theory.

Descartes provides the classic defence of substance dualism. What is commonly overlooked is that substance dualism does not deny that a functional unity may exist—that mind and body may function harmoniously, as in a healthy, conscious, alert human being:

Nature also teaches me, by these sensations of pain, hunger, thirst and so on, that I am not merely present in my body as a sailor is present in a ship, but that I am very closely joined and, as it were, intermingled with it, so that I and the body form a unit.[9]

Functional unity, however, is not proof of psychosomatic monism. This is because the

body is by its very nature always divisible, while the mind is utterly indivisible. For when I consider the mind, or myself . . . I am unable to distinguish any parts within myself [and] . . . I recognize that if a foot or arm or any other part of the body is cut off, nothing has thereby been taken away from the mind. As for faculties of

---

[6] St Thomas Aquinas, *Summa Theologiae*, Ia, Q. 90, Art. 2, trans. Edmund Hill, vol. 13 (London, 1964), 7, 9.

[7] St Thomas Aquinas, *Summa contra Gentiles*, book 2, Q. 64, trans. James F. Anderson as *Summa contra Gentiles, Book Two: Creation* (Notre Dame, Ind., 1975), 199.

[8] Aquinas, *Summa contra Gentiles*, book 2, ch. 87, pp. 293–4. See Victor E. Sleva, *The Separated Soul in the Philosophy of St. Thomas Aquinas* (Washington, DC, 1940).

[9] Descartes, *Meditations on First Philosophy*, in *The Philosophical Works of Descartes*, trans. John Cottingham, Robert Stoothoff, and Dugald Murdoch (Cambridge, 1988), ii. 56.

willing, of understanding, of sensory perception and so on, these cannot be termed parts of the mind, *since it is one and the same mind that wills, and understands and has sensory perceptions.*[10]

We know that a physical body is divisible, but 'we cannot conceive of half of a mind'.[11] A person, mind, or soul has either/or existence—there are no 6 per cent, 27 per cent, 93 per cent, or 110 per cent persons. Given the existence of a person or mind, only then can the development of intellect, conscience, virtue, relationships, and existential experiences occur—albeit variably, gradually, and alterably due to injury or disease. Holism has it just the other way round, i.e. that contingent properties of the brain, relationships, and/or subjectivity *create the person.* Such are some of the calamities of embracing an anti-realist theory of persons.

John Calvin asserts that the dualism of soul and body 'ought not to be controverted' because Scripture clearly teaches that the soul 'is an incorporeal substance', a position also defended in the 'heathen' philosophy of Plato.[12] Man is 'created in the image of God' and 'there is no doubt that the proper seat of his image is the soul'.[13] Calvin's rejection of the claims of contemporary holism are seen in his criticism of 'Osiander, whose perverse ingenuity in futile notions is proved by his writings, extending the image of God promiscuously to the body as well as the soul, [which] confounds heaven and earth together'.[14] In the history of biblical and Old Testament theology through the centuries—until the 1940s—the dominating interpretation of the image of God in Genesis 1:26–8 was 'without doubt the spiritual or immaterial interpretation', as in Philo, who emphasized the completely spiritual, non-material nature of God, hence the spiritual likeness of the soul as an immaterial substance.[15]

There is also a *positive* holistic definition of a person, in addition to the negative definition explained above. Given that a physical substance is essential, holism asserts that a person is a psychosomatic unity. There are innumerable species of holism on offer, but they can be organized into three types which differ on their emphasis: psychoSOMATIC unity, PSYCHOsomatic unity, and psychosomatic UNITY theories. Representative proponents of each of these species of holism are sketched out below.

Proponents of psychoSOMATIC unity holism include Arthur Peacocke, Adrian Thatcher, and Paul and John Feinberg. According to Peacocke and Thatcher, the material units of the universe are constituted in their physics,

[10] Ibid. 59. See also C. F. Fowler, *Descartes on the Human Soul: Philosophy and the Demands of Christian Doctrine* (Dordrecht, 1999); my italics.
[11] Descartes, *Meditations on First Philosophy*, 9.
[12] John Calvin, *Institutes of the Christian Religion*, book I, ch. 15, trans. John Allen, 7th edn. (Philadelphia, n.d.), 203, 211.   [13] Ibid. 206.
[14] Ibid. 203, 211. Also see Calvin, *An Excellent Treatise.*
[15] Gunnlaugur A. Jónsson, *The Image of God: Genesis 1: 26–28 in a Century of Old Testament Research* (Lund, 1988), 11.

in their 'matter-energy–space-time relationships' which have a 'built-in' potential to become a living 'human brain in the human body which displays conscious activity' and in 'man, the stuff of the universe has become cognizing and self-cognizing.'[16] A variant of this is seen in Paul and John Feinberg. They, however, prefer a *biochemical, genetic* psychoSO-MATIC unity holism: 'Personhood is grounded in biological considerations . . . genetic identity throughout life guarantees personhood in the fertilized egg and viable fetus . . . The *genetic code* is an objective basis for determining who qualifies as a person.'[17] If it is affirmed by these theologians that persons have an innate moral nature, it then follows that the Biochemical Image of God is somehow contained in matter-energy–space-time or human genetic code. In the Feinbergs' case, human DNA is assumed to be the essence of life and the criteria of the sanctity of life. There are two devastating problems here. Firstly, genetic code (human or otherwise) is not the essence of life. The fact is that DNA can be either dead (in a hair follicle on the floor) or alive (in a warm Petri dish medium or a human body). A human corpse has human genetic code, but it does not thereby have life or the intrinsic value of a person. Respect for a corpse is not equivalent to respect for a person. A corpse has genetic code but it does not have life. Secondly, it is a bald is/ought fallacy to equate ethical value with genetic code. Thus the Biochemical Image of God asserted by theologians commits both the DNA Blunder and an is/ought fallacy in the same stroke. DNA may be a blueprint for biological life as we know it, but it is not the essence of life or the essence of ethical worth.

The second type of holists are proponents of PSYCHOsomatic unity who emphasize subjectivity, existential, or relational notions. In *Defending the Soul* Keith Ward argues that the soul 'is truly material', being 'a point of subjectivity and transcendence'.[18] Warren S. Brown, Nancey Murphy, and H. Newton Malony argue that a 'person is defined by the potential for communication. Individuals *become* persons in relationship to God; thus personhood (the image of God) is based in relatedness and communication. The soul is discovered by going outside of oneself.'[19] The fallacy of person degrees present in all holistic theories is particularly clear here. A non-person entity gradually becomes a person, supposedly, as the quantity and quality of relationships and communication increases. Our ethical value literally depends upon the contingency of others relating to us. Their

[16] Adrian Thatcher, 'Christian Theism and the Concept of a Person', in A. Peacocke and Grant Gillett (eds.), *Persons and Personality* (Oxford, 1987), 186.
[17] John S. Feinberg and Paul D. Feinberg, *Ethics for a Brave New World* (Wheaton, Ill., 1993), 60, 61; my italics.
[18] Keith Ward, *Defending the Soul* (Oxford, 1992), 55, 148.
[19] Warren S. Brown, 'Conclusion: Reconciling Scientific and Biblical Portraits of Human Nature', in Warren S. Brown, Nancey Murphy, and H. Newton Malony (eds.), *Whatever Happened to the Soul? Scientific and Theological Portraits of Human Nature* (Minneapolis, 1998), 224–5; my italics.

relationships create persons. Just who is and who is not a person will depend upon who gets to stipulate the amount of relationships and communication necessary before an entity is allowed into the fraternity of persons. A hermit and an abandoned newborn would be prima facie instances of individuals that are not persons—or maybe 2 per cent persons or some other anti-realist concoction. Killing such entities would not be the killing of an innocent person—unless the holist wishes to argue that it is a 2 per cent or 17 per cent homicide. Laws of the land would obviously need to be amended to meet such anti-realist entailments of holism. The alternative, of course, is to reject a theory that produces such absurdities.

Another relational type of PSYCHOsomatic unity holism popular among theologians is the resonance field theory of persons found in Jürgen Moltmann. 'A person is the individual human being in the resonance field of the relationships of I–you–we, I–myself, I–it. Within this network of relationships, the person becomes the subject of giving and taking, hearing and doing, experiencing and touching, perceiving and responding . . . The person emerges through the call of God.'[20] Here, with a more refined explanation of the relationship criteria of personhood, the anti-realism escalates. Is a monk, living a solitary meditative life, a decomposing person in process of becoming a non-person? Is this a living suicide? Alternatively, is a Hollywood movie star (one to whom millions relate) a million times more a person than the monk? If I have an I–it relationship with my pet rock—me touching and it responding (or resisting)—does the relationship really turn the rock into a person? Is this a new form of asexual reproduction heretofore overlooked? Such absurdities reveal that something significant is missing here: hence the fallacy of resonance field creationism is committed when it is asserted that relationships create persons. The fallacy is avoided by affirming that you and I can have a personal relationship—given that we are persons. This common-sense view, however, rests upon a dualist concept of persons.

The third species of holism, psychosomatic UNITY holism, could also be called the amalgamation blur theory. Germain Grisez is a significant proponent of this view. He argues that dualism is inexplicable (there is no separable subject and owner of experiences). Alternatively, a person is a unifying principle of four orders of reality within experience. These are the physical, the intentional, the existential, and the cultural: 'A person is in all four of these orders, and he embraces all of them in himself.'[21] The assertion seems to be that I = a non-substantial principle and/or I = four orders of reality. The UNITY that is one's person = a bundle of physical organs in flux, plus a bundle of internal activities, plus a flux of existential aspects,

[20] Jürgen Moltmann, 'Christianity and the Values of Modernity and the Western World', Fuller Theological Seminary lecture (Apr. 1996), quoted in Brown, *et al.* (eds.), *Whatever Happened to the Soul?*, 225.
[21] Germain Grisez, *Beyond the New Theism* (Notre Dame, Ind., 1975), 349.

plus a contingent mix of ever changing cultural realities. I = a quadrant of multiple fluxes. It necessarily follows that I endure only momentarily because every change is a new and different quadrant of fluxes, i.e. a different person. But such a notion of the momentary existence of oneself is refuted by experience. My person is not replaced at the rate of the occurrence of any and all fluxes in the quadrant that constitutes myself. This claimed UNITY is the height of chaos and the depth of psychological disorder. It is certainly contradicted in the experience we have of being a person.

One entailment of holism that has now been shown is that a person is a perpetual flux—of four fleeting orders of reality (Grisez), of ephemeral and transitory relationships of experiencing and touching (Moltmann), of ever vanishing subjectivity and transcendence (Ward), and/or anti-personal matter-energy–space-time relationships (Peacocke and Thatcher) or genetic code (the Feinbergs). Thus, whatever type of holism one picks, the only choices available are impersonal, amoral, and anti-realist options, e.g. I = many perpetual fluxes of amoral components, I = transitory-fluctuating-psycho-bundles-of-somatic-material. A second entailment of holism shown above is that all species of holism are ultimately reductionistic. Persons are compound entities that reduce to the basic non-personal substances of reality: matter-energy, genetic code, or functioning neo-cortex. Moral standing (the image of God) reduces to contingent add-ons, e.g. subjective experiences and the occurrence of relationships. Because the substantial self of dualism is rejected, there are no persons with potential. Rather, there are partial persons with partial moral standing (or no moral standing until a stipulated developmental level has been reached) and everyone's moral worth is a contingent flux. If holism is true, reality is both impersonal and amoral.

It is important to recognize here that dualism is our common-sense, everyday understanding of the nature of a person and human being. This is readily acknowledged by the most explicit *opponents* of substance dualism. For example, David Lewis writes that dualism is the view 'of the common man'.[22] And J. J. C. Smart notes, 'there is in ordinary language a dualistic overtone: to some extent it enshrines the plain man's metaphysics which is dualism of body and soul'.[23] Even Daniel Dennett agrees that (at first glance) it seems plausible that there are minds with their mental events and bodies with their physical events.[24] Brian O'Shaughnessy recognizes that 'Something in us cannot but subscribe to the Cartesian account of the mind–body relation.'[25] John R. Searle acknowledges: 'I suppose

---

[22] David Lewis, 'An Argument for the Identity Theory', *Journal of Philosophy*, 63 (1966), 25.

[23] J. J. C. Smart, 'Materialism', *Journal of Philosophy*, 60 (1963), 661.

[24] Daniel Dennett, *Content and Consciousness* (London, 1969), 3–5.

[25] Brian O'Shaughnessy, *The Will*, 2 vols. (Cambridge, 1980), i. 29.

most people in our civilization accept some kind of dualism. They think they have both a mind and a body, or a soul and a body.'[26] And Derek Parfit explains this in book-length form: We believe ourselves to be a mind, separable from our body; the owner of all our experiences, feelings, and beliefs, the author and cause of free choices. But we are not what we believe ourselves to be, our identity is not what matters, and we ought not have such great personal concern about our own survival whether it be from day to day or from here into the hereafter.[27] So dualism is the everyday, common-sense view of a human being, as both materialists and dualists agree. This fact, however, only increases the rhetoric directed against dualism.

Dennett expresses the contemporary academic sentiment against dualism: 'This fundamentally anti-scientific stance of dualism is, to my mind, its most disqualifying feature and is the reason why . . . I adopt the apparently dogmatic rule that dualism is to be avoided at all costs.'[28] The obdurate king-of-the-hill attitude is best captured in Dennett's comment that 'dualism is not a serious view to contend with, but rather a cliff over which to push one's opponents'.[29] Similarly, Paul Churchland confidently assures us that: 'Our common-sense [dualistic] psychological framework is a false and radically misleading conception of the causes of human behavior and the nature of cognitive activity . . . it is an outright misrepresentation of our internal states and activities.'[30]

The same attitude is just as fervently held in contemporary academic theology. As John Hick wrote some twenty-five years ago, the 'prevailing view of man . . . is that he is an indissoluble psycho-physical unity . . . there is no room for the notion of soul in distinction from body'.[31] Adrian Thatcher extols the no-soul mentality in contemporary academic theology, as well as its metaphysical entailments: 'The blurring of the distinction between spirit and matter also blurs the distinction between God and the world and . . . theology is better for it.'[32]

The no-soul doctrine in academic theology is old news to those working in this field, but other academic disciplines—and certainly the general public—are surprised, if not shocked, to learn that the soul has been given up. Thus the following survey is offered as a brief catalogue of this surprising theological position.

In academic theology the anti-dualistic zeal is just as fervent and

---

[26] John R. Searle, 'Consciousness and the Philosophers', *New York Review*, 6 Mar. 1997.

[27] Derek Parfit, *Reasons and Persons* (Oxford, 1984), chs. 10–13.

[28] Daniel Dennett, *Consciousness Explained* (London, 1991), 37, 39.

[29] Daniel Dennett, 'Current Issues in the Philosophy of Mind', in Kenneth Lucey and T. R. Machan (eds.), *Recent Work in Philosophy* (Totowa, NJ, 1983), 157.

[30] Paul Churchland, *Matter and Consciousness* (Cambridge, Mass., 1984), 43.

[31] John Hick, *Death and Eternal Life* (San Francisco, 1976), 278.

[32] Thatcher, 'Christian Theism and the Concept of a Person', 183–4.

absolute as found anywhere. 'No form of dualism is rationally defensible,'[33] asserts Germain Grisez. George Carey affirms that 'it is a false trail to look within the human body for an immortal "soul," mind or residual self which somehow survives the destruction of the flesh'.[34] Fergus Kerr, in *Theology after Wittgenstein*, describes the two-step treatment for belief in the traditional soul. First, any contemporary Christian theologian who would retain the traditional soul 'needs to be taken to the cleaners', and if this does not get the stain out, then 'Therapy is required' to deal with the mental illness.[35] Joseph Fletcher also enlists medical metaphor rhetoric to explain that: 'This dualism of the physical and the spiritual has been, as we now commonly see, a canker at the heart of the Christian heritage.'[36]

Academic theologians began to adopt no-soul anthropology upon the publication of Darwin's *Origin of Species* in 1859.[37] In his *Notebooks* Darwin not only affirms that belief in the traditional soul is a false metaphysical belief; he scolds any who would retain it as holding a morally reprehensible belief. 'Man in his arrogance thinks himself a great work worthy the interposition of a deity. More humble and I think truer to consider him created from animals.'[38] Orthodox Darwinism leaves no difference in kind between man and animals; not even the worship of God is unique to man, because even the dog looks on its master as on a god, according to Darwin.[39]

The adoption of Darwinism into theology began immediately upon the publication of the *Origin*. The dualist nature of man that had been the dominant interpretation throughout the centuries now quickly converted the image of God into physical realities, even interpretations of the image of God as the upright posture of man.[40] Although general evolutionary theory does not require expulsion of the substantial soul, holistic anthropology concedes it and then works to add mental, ethical, and personal properties into the nature of matter.[41] By the 1950s the refinements of no-soul anthropology in New Testament theology began to draw heavily on

---

[33] Germain Grisez, 'Should Nutrition and Hydration be Provided to Permanently Unconscious and Other Mentally Disabled Persons?', (1989) 5 *Issues in Law and Medicine*, 173.

[34] George Carey, *I Believe in Man* (Grand Rapids, Mich., 1977), 171–2.

[35] Fergus Kerr, *Theology after Wittgenstein* (Oxford, 1988), 187.

[36] Joseph Fletcher, *Humanhood: Essays in Biomedical Ethics* (Buffalo, NY, 1979), 24.

[37] See Jónsson, *The Image of God*, 11.

[38] Charles Darwin, *Notebooks* ed. Paul H. Barrett *et al.* (Ithaca, NY, 1987), 300; quoted from James Rachels, *Created from Animals: The Moral Implications of Darwinism* (Oxford, 1990), 1.

[39] Charles Darwin, *The Descent of Man* (London, 1871), 68.

[40] Jónsson, *The Image of God*, 109.

[41] See John W. Yolton, *Thinking Matter: Materialism in Eighteenth-Century Britain* (Minneapolis, 1983) for the philosophical attempt at this which preceded the contemporary work of theological holism.

the existentialist theological work of Rudolf Bultmann, when it was then determined that Pauline anthropology is correctly understood to be holistic. 'The holistic definition has become so widely accepted that virtually all recent handbooks, dictionaries, and studies of Pauline theology take it for granted with little or no felt need for argumentative justification. W. D. Stacey writes of "Bultmann's conclusive treatment of this point." '[42]

The New Bible Dictionary is a standard theological student's reference work. In it we are confidently told that Bultmann's psychosomatic unity theory is, and the Greek soul–body dualism is not, the essence of man's being as taught throughout the entire Bible (except for one incidental Greek slip-up in one of the parables of Jesus).

As in the Old Testament, man's life and being, although viewed from different aspects, is a psycho-somatic unity (*cf.* Bultmann). The Gk. soul–body dualism is incidentally reflected in the parable of Lk. xvi.19 ff., but is not in accord with the general New Testament outlook or teaching.[43]

The penetration of physicalism into, and the expulsion of the immaterial from, academic theology are now thoroughgoing, to the point of paranoia. John Cooper observes that

The scholarly community has become highly suspicious—almost paranoid—of the presence of Platonic dualism in the traditional interpretation of Scripture. Nowadays most biblical scholars strive to outdo one another in emphasizing that Hebrew anthropology, like the Hebrew mind and Hebrew worldview in general, is decidedly antidualistic and enthusiastically holistic or monistic.[44]

Within the community of academic theologians, therefore, explicit rejection of substance dualism is not considered a controversial issue. 'It has become a dogma', Russell Aldwinckle notes, 'of much so-called biblical theology in our time to stress the sharp distinction between the Hebrew doctrine of man and the dualist Greek view which divides man into body and soul.'[45] It is now accepted without argument among theologians that the biblical view of man is a unitary being, commonly referred to as the Semitic totality concept. M. E. Dahl expresses the modern dogma in Old Testament language: 'It is not so much that man is *made* of "dust of the earth," he *is* dust.'[46] William May, using a variant of this mantra, recon-

---

[42] Robert H. Gundry, *Sōma in Biblical Theology, with Emphasis on Pauline Anthropology* (Cambridge, 1976), 5. Gundry is citing W. D. Stacy, *The Pauline View of Man* (London, 1956), 182.

[43] *The New Bible Dictionary*, ed. J. D. Douglas (Grand Rapids, Mich., 1973; repr. of 1st edn. 1962), s.v. E. E. Ellis, 'Life', 737.

[44] John W. Cooper, *Body, Soul and Life Everlasting: Biblical Anthropology and the Monism–Dualism Debate* (Grand Rapids, Mich., 1989), 37–8.

[45] Russell Aldwinckle, *Death in the Secular City* (Grand Rapids, Mich., 1974), 72; quoted from Cooper, *Body, Soul and Life Everlasting*, 38.

[46] M. E. Dahl, *The Resurrection of the Body* (London, 1962), 71; quoted from Cooper, *Body, Soul and Life Everlasting*, 39.

firms the commitment to physicalism: 'A man not only *has* a body, he is his body.'[47] Bruce Reichenbach confidently extends the no-soul metaphysic to the teaching of the entire New Testament: 'there is no continuously existing inner self or soul . . . [and] there is no New Testament warrant for holding that there is an interim existence between death and recreation'.[48] Thus, the scholarly consensus is that there is no soul and there is no metaphysical, ethical, or religious warrant for such a belief. 'Excise the canker' is their resounding demand.

THE ETHICAL IMPLICATION OF NO-SOUL THEOLOGY

The metaphysical relationship between the soul and the intrinsic value of persons is inherently dependent upon, and historically developed in, the doctrine of the soul found in Judaism and Christianity. The classic account of the history of the sanctity of human life is found in W. E. H. Lecky's *History of European Morals from Augustus to Charlemagne*. He explains that:

the first and most manifest duty of a Christian man was to look upon his fellow-men as sacred beings, and from this notion grew up the eminently Christian idea of the sanctity of all human life . . . a new standard higher than any which then existed in the world. The influence of Christianity in this respect began with the very earliest stage of human life . . . This minute and scrupulous care for human life and human virtue in the humblest forms, in the slave, the gladiator, the savage, or the infant, was indeed wholly foreign to the genius of Paganism. *It was produced by the Christian doctrine of the inestimable value of each immortal soul.* It is the distinguishing and transcendent characteristic of every society into which the spirit of Christianity has passed.[49]

Similarly, it has been argued that the history of the image of God is 'the history of the western understanding of man'.[50] Modern philosophical refinements of this connection can be found, for example, in the careful work of W. R. Sorley and C. A. Campbell.[51] Even the most staunch critics of the intrinsic value of persons (the traditional ethic), e.g. Peter Singer,

---

[47] William May, 'Attitudes toward the Newly Dead', (1973) *Hastings Center Report*, 3.

[48] Bruce Reichenbach, *Is Man the Phoenix? A Study of Immortality* (Grand Rapids, Mich., 1983), 181, 186.

[49] W. E. H. Lecky, *History of European Morals from Augustus to Charlemagne*, ii (New York, 1869), 19, 21–2, 36; my italics. It is relevant to add that Harold O. J. Brown, an evangelical theologian whose existential holism is commented upon later, cites this same passage without mention of the immortal soul. See Harold O. J. Brown, *Death before Birth* (Nashville, 1997), 123.

[50] Emil Brunner, 'Die andere Aufgabe der Theologie', *Zwischen den Zeiten*, 3 (1929), 264; trans. and quoted in Jónsson, *The Image of God*, 1.

[51] W. R. Sorley, *Moral Values and the Idea of God* (Cambridge, 1930) and C. A. Campbell, *On Selfhood and Godhood* (London, 1957). See also Timothy C. Potts, *Conscience in Medieval Philosophy* (Cambridge, 1980).

Helga Kuhse, and James Rachels, recognize this connection. Rachels acknowledges that

The traditional theory must be taken seriously; not only has its influence been enormous, but from a philosophical point of view it is the only fully worked out, systematically elaborated theory of the subject we have. Its development has been one of the great intellectual achievements of Western culture, accomplished by thinkers of great ingenuity and high moral purpose.[52]

Singer, the utilitarian, nearly salivates over the death of the soul and the death of the intrinsic value of persons. The modern mind has finally integrated biology and ethics: 'After ruling our thoughts and our decisions about life and death for nearly two thousand years, the traditional western ethic has collapsed.'[53] It has collapsed (more disastrously than Singer seems to know), and the traditional ethic—that all human beings have a special dignity and worth—is a 'transparent fiction no-one can really believe', weakened by the decline in religious authority and a better understanding of the origin of our species.[54] The disproof of the myth of creation undermined the belief that we were specially created by God, undermining the belief that we are made in the image of God.[55] Thus man is now known to be the same in substance and structure with the brutes. Singer explains that, historically, it has taken about a century to realize the ethical entailment of our equality with other species. But the 'final blow to the traditional western view . . . is now coming from new knowledge in genetics', i.e 'We now know that we share 98.4% of our DNA with chimpanzees. This is a very slight genetic difference.'[56] Because innate moral powers and moral capacities are essential powers of the mind, death of the soul is the death of the inherent moral nature of persons. Alternatively, if one seeks to retain the innate moral nature of persons as a physical property of the body, then the same ethical traits must be attributed to animals, hence to genetic code similarities, and ultimately to the inherent nature of matter-energy. This is not an attractive option. Thus the modern consensus is, as William Lycan explains, 'Moral facts are right up there with Cartesian egos . . . in the ranks of items uncordially despised by most contemporary philosophers.'[57] There simply are no moral facts about the world.

The collapse of the foundation of ethics has not gone unnoticed by theologians. In a survey of the breadth of this problem James M.

---

[52]   James Rachels, *The End of Life: Euthanasia and Morality* (Oxford, 1987), 4.
[53]   Peter Singer, *Rethinking Life and Death* (New York, 1994), 1.
[54]   Ibid. 4.   [55]   Ibid. 171.
[56]   Ibid. 177. The silent premiss here seems to be: If our genetic identity is 98.4% the same, then our moral identity must be 98.4% the same. This is a fallacious, hasty inference. A banana shares 40% of the genetic identity of humans. What inference follows from this fact?
[57]   William Lycan, *Judgement and Justification* (Cambridge, 1988), 198.

Gustafson writes that both Protestant and Catholic theological ethics 'currently share a quest, namely, for a philosophical foundation for Christian ethical thought and Christian moral activity'.[58] In a recent survey article Kevin Vanhoozer further refines the source of the crisis: ' "Know thyself." Socrates' exhortation is as urgent, and problematic, as ever: urgent, because the human race at the dawn of the third millennium, following the demise of the Christian paradigm [substance dualism with its ethical corollaries] and the break-up of modernity is suffering from a collective identity crisis.'[59] Thus, the intrinsic value of persons is debunked by critics outside the traditional ethic, and the foundation of the ethic is patently rejected by those inside the tradition. There is no doubt that a crisis exists in understanding of the value of persons.

A Non-Theological Argument for Dualism

Is it possible to conceive of a person as an immaterial substance, let alone know that a person is such? How can a moral agent possibly exist and not be composed of matter-energy, DNA, or neurons? Since dualism is now deemed to be intellectually incredible, an argument for dualism is offered below. It contains no religious or theistic premises. It is philosophically sound, and it matches fully with common sense.

The 'I Went to Kindergarten' Argument

(1) Assume materialism (psychosomatic holism; reductive, non-reductive, and/or dual aspect physicalism) is true: I = this psychosomatic unity; this physical, functioning body. What I am is what you see.

The concerted effort of nine holists is pulled together in an important work called *Whatever Happened to the Soul?* This work can be used as representative of refined forms of holism that clearly affirm premiss 1, e.g. 'the authors of this volume believe that non-reductive physicalism' is true. It is true that

humans are what you see; that is, there is not another invisible, nonmaterial part of the individual that must be factored into the formula of understanding. The person is he or she who physically stands before you . . . the human being is not divided into parts, such as body and soul . . . No part of human behavior or experience is prima facie excepted as nonmaterial and thus unobservable in principle.[60]

---

[58] James M. Gustafson, *Protestant and Roman Catholic Ethics* (London, 1978), 61.

[59] Kevin Vanhoozer, 'Human Being, Individual and Social', in Colin E. Gunton (ed.), *The Cambridge Companion to Christian Doctrine* (Cambridge, 1997), 158.

[60] Brown *et al.*, *Whatever Happened to the Soul?*, 228. Brown is speaking for 'the authors of this volume', who include its three contributing editors, together with Francisco J. Ayala, V. Elving Anderson, Malcolm Jeeves, Joel B. Green, Ray S. Anderson, and Stephen G. Post.

These writers fully recognize that this anthropology is directly at odds with the historical understanding of the soul within their theistic religious tradition. They readily acknowledge that the popular masses hold to dualism, but they believe non-reductive physicalism is required because of neuroscientific research done by various physicalists. They agree with Francis Crick: 'The idea that man has a disembodied soul is as unnecessary as the old idea that there was a Life Force. This is in head on contradiction to the religious belief of billions of human beings alive today.'[61]

(2) Make a true assertion about yourself: I went to kindergarten.

The reader need only make a similar first-person claim that is known to be true. Any such claim about yourself at any time in the past will do. The further back one can go yet still be certain of its truth, the greater the clarity that will arise upon questioning the first two premisses. If one can only affirm 'I went to college' or 'I went to bed last night', these assertions are adequate for the argument to proceed.

(3) If premiss 1 is true, then premiss 2 is false. Alternately, if premiss 2 is true, then premiss 1 is false.

That is, if I = this body which you see (or the body you could see if you were here), then I did not go to kindergarten because this 5 foot 8 inch, post-pubescent, 190-pound functioning body ≠ the 3 foot 6 inch, pre-pubescent, 48-pound functioning body that went to kindergarten in Elkton, Michigan, in 1955. There is no doubt that this 190-pound psychosomatic unity ≠ the 48-pound psychosomatic unity that went to kindergarten in 1955.

(4) I know I went to kindergarten, I know that this 190-pound body did not go to kindergarten, and I know the bundle of beliefs and relationships I now have did not exist in the kindergartener. Thus, I know premiss 1 is false and premiss 2 is true.

This is not a solipsistic conclusion because it is reproducible, falsifiable, and verifiable by others. You and I and every reader can verify the nature of one's own person. We can also falsify the criteria of personal identity of monism (holism) and the issues of enduring through time, and the bodily and psychological changes that occur through a lifetime. Memory, of course, is fallible and it is not asserted as the criterion of personal identity over time. It is merely employed, and its claims are open to verification and correction. It is not a memory or a bundle of memories that 'I' refers to in premiss 2. Neither is it claimed that a memory went to kindergarten. Rather, I—the self-conscious moral agent, subject and owner of memories

---

[61] Francis H. Crick, *The Astonishing Hypothesis: The Scientific Search for a Soul* (London, 1994), in Brown, *et al.*, *Whatever Happened to the Soul?*, 74.

and owner of a very different body—went to kindergarten in 1955. It is a clear, distinct, warranted truth-claim. I know I exist and that I endure through time, through an ever changing physical body, and through the ever changing contents of consciousness (beliefs, feeling, and desires). Each reader can attest to this same truth about one's own person. Hence we can know truths about the essential nature of persons.

(5) Therefore, psychosomatic holism, reductive, and non-reductive physicalism are demonstratively false.

(6) Therefore, person–body dualism is not only conceivable, but knowledge of one's person is immediately accessible in self-consciousness and is known to be non-identical with (non-reducible to) the contents of consciousness, let alone identical with the ever changing physical body.

PHYSICALIST OBJECTIONS: THESE BRAIN CELLS AND THIS UNIQUE GENETIC CODE WENT TO KINDERGARTEN

Owen Flanagan, in *The Science of the Mind*, recognizes the preceding type of argument for dualism and supplies the major objections to it. He acknowledges that 'It is this sort of thinking that . . . gives dualism some of its considerable plausibility, some of its great intuitive appeal. It is not decisive, however, because there are 'two sets of facts' that overturn the substance dualist explanation.[62]

First, *brain cells are atypical in that they can last a full lifetime*, and those that die are not replaced. Second, all ordinary cells are replaced in accordance with each person's unique genetic program. This program, *your genetic code, persists intact in each generation of cells*; it passes from cell to cell in the same way the rules of a game, like Scrabble or Monopoly, are passed on with each newly manufactured package. It is possible, therefore, that either the persisting neurons in the brain, or the persisting genetic program in the DNA or both, provide a physical basis for explaining personal identity over time.[63]

DUALIST REPLIES: BETTER BIOLOGY REFUTATIONS—NEUROGENESIS OF BRAIN CELLS IN ADULTS AND GENETIC CODE ALTERATIONS DURING LIFE

Flanagan's neurophysical objection to one's person being an immaterial substance are that the very same brain cells persist throughout the lifetime of an individual, that they do not die, and that they do not get replaced. Thus the physicalist explanation of the fact (and the meaning of) premiss 2 is that the neurons in the brain of the 190-pound body in 2001 = the neurons in the brain of the 48-pound body in 1955. Thus, I = these persist-

---

[62] Owen Flanagan, *The Science of the Mind*, 2nd edn. (Cambridge, Mass., 1984–93), 17.
[63] Ibid. 17–18; my italics.

ing neurons. The problem with Flanagan's neurophysical claim is that it is false. Recent neuroscience has discovered that there is a continuous neurogenesis of brain cells throughout the adult life of mammals.

Neurogenesis—new neuronal cell birth—has now been convincingly demonstrated to persist throughout the life of many higher mammalian species, including rodents, birds, tree shrews, cats, and most recently, new world monkeys (marmosets), old world monkeys (Rhesus), as well as humans . . . Among the steps that can be readily identified are proliferation, survival, migration, differentiation, and the establishment of functional connections.[64]

Neurons are in fact lost and new neurons are produced in the brain throughout the life of a human being. There are pools of immature, migrating neurons constantly produced in the brain, influenced by a wide variety of factors, including age, death of old neurons, gender, physical activity, learning activity, and stress. Therefore, Flanagan's neurophysical objection to dualism is false.

The remaining physicalist's assertion is that the unique genetic code of this 190-pound body = the same unique genetic code of the 48-pound body that went to kindergarten. Actually, Flanagan's genetic claim is twofold: (1) each person has a unique genetic code, and (2) an individual's genetic code persists without change throughout one's life. The problem with these two remaining objections to dualism is that they are false.

Firstly, every individual does not have a unique genetic code. Identical twins have identical genetic codes, and they are certainly not one and the same person. Cloning—either by artificial splitting of a multicellular fertilized egg or by somatic cell nuclear transfer into an enucleated egg from the nuclear donor, produces genetically identical individuals.[65]

Secondly, an individual's genetic code does not persist without change throughout one's lifetime. Various instances of this are readily known. Exposure to certain environmental mutagens changes the genetic sequence in one's DNA. Unintentional exposure to mutagenic radiation after the nuclear reactor explosion at the Chernobyl nuclear power station continues to show genetic alterations in those who lived in the

---

[64] Fred H. Gage, 'Science in an Uncertain Millennium', *American Association for the Advancement of Science, February 17–22, 2000, Annual Meeting Program* (2000), S20. Papers presented on this discovery at this conference were given by Pasko Rakic (Yale University), Fernando Nottebohm (Rockefeller University), Gage (Salk Institute), Elizabeth Gould (Princeton University), and Arturo Alvarez-Buylla (Rockefeller University). See Elizabeth Gould, Alison J. Reeves, Michael S. A. Graziano, and Charles Gross, 'Neurogenesis in the Neocortex of Adult Primates', *Science* (15 Oct. 1999), 548–52; Nicholas Wade, 'Brain may Grow New Cells Daily', *New York Times*, 15 Oct. 1999; Elizabeth N. Lashley, 'Death Leads to Brain Neurons Birth', *Science* (23 June 2000), 2111–12; J. Garcia-Verdugo, F. Doetsch, H. Wichterle, D. A. Lim and A. Alvarez-Buylla, 'Architecture and Cell Types of the Adult Subventricular Zone: In Search of the Stem Cells', *Journal of Neurobiology*, 36/2 (Aug. 1998), 234–48.

[65] See Report and Recommendations of the National Bioethics Advisory Commission, *Cloning Human Beings*, vol. ii (Rockville, Md., 1997).

area of the meltdown. Rates of thyroid cancer in children living nearby have risen tenfold. Drugs can cause changes in the individual's genetic sequence. Thalidomide was given to mothers as a mild tranquillizer early in pregnancy (after the genetic code was established), yet thousands of babies were born with genetic alterations resulting in incomplete or missing arms and legs. Cocaine, cigarettes, alcohol, and large amounts of vitamins can also alter the genetic code of a developing child—after its genome has been set at fertilization. Additionally, there is the phenomenon of gene-jumping or transposons—where genes jump from one site on a chromosome to another, thereby changing the genetic code of the individual. It is estimated that about '10 percent of the human genome is transposons. About half of these are called alu sequences, each consisting of three hundred bases.'[66] Together, then, 'the DNA in our cells undergoes an estimated 30 new mutations during our lifetime, either through mistakes during DNA copying or cell division or, more often, because of damage from the environment'.[67] Thus, the genetic code of the 5-year-old who went to kindergarten is not the genetic code of the 50-year-old writing this article. One's genetic code is a flux over time.

Hence each of the physicalist's or holist's objections to dualism are demonstratively false. Thus the dualist's evidence and explanation of who went to kindergarten is true, as it overcomes each of the physicalist's objections and substitutions for the enduring soul. The remaining objection that some holists posit is that the I in the kindergarten argument does not refer to anything—since the enduring soul is the only reasonable candidate if a referent must be picked. On this objection, there simply is no self who is self-conscious: I do not exist. The problem here is the contradiction in the affirmation. To assert 'I do not exist' entails and presupposes that I do exist, as in asserting that 'I know I do not exist'. It remains that person–body dualism is true and no-soul, holistic theories are false.

Particular Problems with Holism

PERSON, GOD, AND HOLISM

Adrian Thatcher is a theologian committed to a thoroughgoing defence of the holist theory of persons. In 'Christian Theism and the Concept of a Person' he argues that 'the credibility of theism suffers from a close association with Cartesian dualism . . . that neither the Christian concept of God nor the Christian understanding of the human person requires such a

---

[66] Ricki Lewis, *Human Genetics: Concepts and Applications*, 3rd edn. (Boston, 1999), 192.

[67] Maya Pines, 'Why so Many Errors in our DNA? 30 New Mutations per Lifetime', Howard Hughes Medical Institute, Blazing a Genetic Trail, on-line site: <http://www.hhmi.org/genetictrail/errors/wyso.htm>.

dualism in order to be credible'.[68] He offers arguments against dualism, followed by arguments for holism that 'draw on the new concept of matter, a gift of the physical sciences to theology'.[69]

The dualist concept of a non-embodied person is implausible, hence the concept of God as a person without a body is implausible, Thatcher argues. This flies in the face of the personalist consensus that exists between theists and atheists who 'have agreed to call God a "person," albeit a person without a body . . . [i.e.] "the personalist consensus" '.[70] A prime example of this consensus is seen in the work of Richard Swinburne and J. L. Mackie. Swinburne, the theist, affirms 'That God is a person, yet one without a body, seems the most elementary claim of theism.'[71] Mackie, the atheist, readily accepts the conceptual claim, adding that such a concept 'is "literally meaningful", readily conceivable, rightly immune to direct verification, and so on'.[72] Thatcher argues that both Swinburne and Mackie are wrong-headed on the concept of God as a person without a body, because Cartesian dualism is false and monistic holism is true. He argues that to allow God as a person without a body requires that 'we must adopt a Cartesian concept of a person. But there are good philosophical and theological grounds for steering clear of such a concept.'[73] The good philosophical reasons for rejecting Cartesian persons, we are told, are found in Derek Parfit's *Reasons and Persons*. Interestingly, Parfit (an atheist[74]) agrees with Swinburne and Mackie that dualism is not only conceptually valid, but it is also the common-sense view that we all use in everyday life, morality, and law. Nonetheless, Thatcher appeals to Parfit for a (holistic) definition of a person: 'the existence of a person, during any period, just consists in the existence of his brain and body, and the thinking of his thoughts, and the doing of his deeds, and the occurrence of many other physical and mental events'.[75] Parfit notes that this theory of persons is found in the atheistic arguments of David Hume and also in Buddhism.[76] The no-soul theological arguments developed by Thatcher, informed by Parfit, can now be considered.

---

[68]   Thatcher, 'Christian Theism and the Concept of a Person', 180.
[69]   Ibid.   [70]   Ibid. 181.
[71]   Ibid. 182; quoting Richard Swinburne, *The Coherence of Theism* (Oxford, 1977), 99.
[72]   Thatcher, 'Christian Theism and the Concept of a Person', 182; quoting J. L. Mackie, *The Miracle of Theism* (Oxford, 1982), 1–4, 12.
[73]   Thatcher, 'Christian Theism and the Concept of a Person', 182. The same logic is readily found among other modern theologians. John Macquarrie writes, 'If we have abandoned dualism when we are thinking about finite beings, does it make sense to retain it on the cosmic level in thinking of God and the world? It has no more plausibility there.' See John Macquarrie, foreword, in Grace Jansen *God's World, God's Body*, (Philadelphia, 1984), pp. ix–x.
[74]   Parfit, *Reasons and Persons*, 453.
[75]   Thatcher, 'Christian Theism and the Concept of a Person', 182–3, quoting Parfit, *Reasons and Persons*, 275.
[76]   Parfit, *Reasons and Persons*, 453: 'But, before the recent past, very few Atheists made Ethics their life's work. Buddha may be among this few, as may be Confucius, and a few Ancient Greeks and Romans . . . Hume was an Atheist who made Ethics part of his life's work. Sidgwick was another.'

The first reason why we should adopt holism, according to Thatcher, is because it is the unanimous view. He asserts that, 'among biblical scholars' there is 'a rare unanimity' that 'the biblical picture of the person is non-dualist, and that the Bible gives little or no support to the idea that a person is essentially a soul, or that the soul is separable from the body'.[77] Thatcher cites Lynn de Silva as authoritative on this claim.

> Biblical scholarship has established quite conclusively that there is no dichotomous concept of man in the Bible, such as is found in Greek and Hindu thought. The biblical view of man is holist, not dualistic. The notion of the soul as an immortal entity which enters the body at birth and leaves it at death is quite foreign to the biblical view of man. The biblical view of man is that man is a unity; he is a unity of soul, body, flesh, mind, etc. all together constituting the whole man. None of the constituent elements is capable of separating itself from the total structure and continuing to live after death.[78]

Thatcher acknowledges that the 'now fashionable holistic view of persons in biblical anthropology is not absolutely decisive', but the 'creatureliness and mortality' of man emphasized in the Bible are incompatible with dualism. The 'entire human being', in biblical thought, 'is subject to death and decay'. Theological evidence and support for this claim are some well-worn phrases: 'Dust you are, to dust you shall return' (Gen. 3: 19); 'All mankind is grass . . .' (Isa. 40: 6–8); 'You are no more than a mist, seen for a little while and then dispersing' (Jas. 4: 14). There are, however, acute problems with this argument.

Firstly, Thatcher argues (via de Silva) that all dualists, and certainly all theists, ought to reject dualism and adopt monism because it is 'now fashionable' and because here 'among biblical scholars' a 'rare unanimity' exists. This, by itself, is a bandwagon fallacy. Fashions come and go, and there are academic theological trends just as there are fashion trends. Just because tattoos, pierced tongues, and holistic theory are in vogue is not a sufficient reason to jump on the bandwagon. The criterion of truth, whether theological, metaphysical, or moral truth, is not academic consensus determined by the most recent popularity poll.

Secondly, Thatcher's claim that unanimity exists among biblical scholars on the no-soul nature of a human being fallaciously begs the question at issue and, at worst, is simply false. The hidden premiss in this supposed historical survey is that the time frame in which biblical scholars are counted as scholars is conveniently limited to the fashionable present, i.e. post-1940. The work of Rudolf Bultmann and J. A. T. Robinson after the Second World War seems to be the historical marker of the diversion into

---

[77] Thatcher, 'Christian Theism and the Concept of a Person', 183.
[78] Ibid.; quoting from Lynn de Silva, *The Problem of the Self in Buddhism and Christianity* (London, 1979), 75.

holism.[79] The fact is that there are biblical scholars who lived prior to the twentieth century. When an inclusive survey of theologians through the centuries is tallied, it shows that dualism is the dominant, consensus view for eighteen or more centuries and that no-soul theology is the dominant view only during the restricted period of the last fifty years or so. Prior to that, for eighteen or more centuries, 'The dominating interpretation [of the image of God and the nature of persons] is without doubt the spiritual or immaterial interpretation.'[80]

Thirdly, Thatcher argues that belief in the soul ought to be rejected because it is 'Greek and Hindu thought'. The argument rests upon an ethnocentric assumption—that Christian anthropology must not cross the ethnic boundary into Greek and Hindu anthropology. These are ethnic enemies of each other. This fallacy of guilt by association reasoning is common rhetoric used by many holistic theologians. However, if theistic holists insist on such rhetoric, then the dualist's rejoinder is that no-soul holism is Epicurean[81] and Buddhist.[82] It is the anthropology defended in the classic atheistic accounts of reality of Hobbes, Spinoza, Hume, and Nietzsche. Concerning basic truths of reality, atheism is the antithesis of theism. So Thatcher's negative arguments against dualism fail. This leaves two positive arguments for theological holism.

Thatcher's first positive argument for holism can be called his No-Soul, No-Pride Argument. He argues: 'Christian faith has nothing to fear from the suggestion that men and women lack a fixed non-bodily identity or essence. Indeed, that we have no permanent identity may well be why we seek the grace of God to confer unity and direction upon our lives.'[83] Thatcher is drawing on Parfit's no-self arguments here. If dualism is true,

[79] Gundry, *Sōma in Biblical Theology*, 5.

[80] See Jónsson, *The Image of God*, 11.

[81] The Epicurean view is that 'the soul is a body [made up of] fine parts' or 'atoms' that are scattered when the aggregate is destroyed. From 'Epicurus' Letter to Herodotus: Diogenes Laertius', 10. 63 and 10. 65, in Brad Inwood and L. P. Gerson (trans.), *Hellenistic Philosophy: Introductory Readings* (Indianapolis, 1988), 10–11.

[82] The Buddhist view is that there is no self, no owner or subject of experiences as in dualism. Thatcher acknowledges elsewhere that 'Christianity and Buddhism' (substitute: 'Holism and Buddhism') hold essentially the same view of the self. See Thatcher, 'Christian Theism and the Concept of a Person', 184, 188. Thatcher's philosophical authority on persons, Derek Parfit, makes the same connection between the materialist and the Buddhist view of persons. Parfit explains his position clearly: 'I claim that' the 'Reductionist View . . . is true . . . [and] *Buddha would have agreed.*' Elsewhere Parfit notes that 'before the recent past, very few atheists made Ethics their life's work. Buddha may be among this few . . . Hume was an Atheist who made Ethics part of his life's work.' Finally, Parfit quotes Buddhist teachings, showing that they are fully consistent with the reductionist, essential materialist, atheistic view of the person: 'Sir, I am known as "Nagasena" . . . [which] is just an appellation, a form of speech . . . "Nagasena" is only a name, for no person is found here.' Also, 'There exists no Individual, it is only a conventional name given to a set of elements . . . The Buddhist term for an individual . . . is *santana*, i.e. a "stream".' From Parfit, *Reasons and Persons*, 273, 453, 502–3.

[83] Thatcher, 'Christian Theism and the Concept of a Person', 184.

then there is a self who is the enduring moral agent, subject and owner of experiences. If holism is true, then there is no self, only a relational bundle of perceptions (a bundle of beliefs, feelings, and desires) that constitutes one's holistic self. These are un-owned, subjectless, ever fluctuating bundles, batches, and clumps of beliefs, feelings, and desires. This is the *no-self* view affirmed by Hume[84] and the Buddha;[85] it is a version of the PSYCHOsomatic unity theory. (Thatcher does add a non-verifiable theological suggestion—God is our glue—that is not considered here.) Problems with, and refutations of, this theory have already been explained above.

Thatcher now adds his no-pride, moral premiss—that Christian morality requires and teaches the no-self view found in Buddhism (by agreeing with de Silva) because Christianity teaches humility.

One writer, comparing the concept of 'self' in Christianity and Buddhism, even goes so far as to claim that 'Christianity goes beyond Buddhism in its doctrine of *annata*, denying both an "ego-entity" and "exclusive individuality" to the human person.' The modern concern, indeed obsession, with self, which issues in talk about self-analysis, self-knowledge, self-presentation, self-realization, self-esteem, and the like, can usually be contrasted with a Christian approach to these matters. In Christian teaching the self is supremely unimportant, for 'whoever cares for his own safety is lost; but if a man will let himself be lost for my sake, he will find his true self' (Matt. 16: 25). There is a surprising lack of emphasis on the self in Christian teaching, which actually liberates the individual from self-preoccupation and frees him or her for the love of God and of other people. *This is another example of a non-dualist understanding of the person actually advancing traditional Christian teaching.*[86]

According to Thatcher, the no-self entailment of the holist view is eminently compatible with, indeed present in, traditional Christian moral teachings. There are, however, a few pitfalls in these assertions.

The No-Soul, No-Pride Argument is a category mistake. It fallaciously equates the Christian ethical teaching on humility with the Buddhist ontological doctrine of being mindless. Christianity does teach an ethic of self-denial—but this is an ethical teaching about virtue—of denial of self-interests over the interests of others. This ethical instruction is not a

---

[84] See David Hume, *A Treatise of Human Nature*, I. iv. 6, ed. L. A. Selby-Bigge, 2nd edn. (Oxford, 1980), 251–2: 'There are some philosophers, who imagine we are every moment intimately conscious of what we call self; that we feel its existence and its continuance in existence . . . For my part, when I enter most intimately into what I call *myself*, I always stumble on some particular perception or other . . . I may venture to affirm of the rest of mankind, that they are nothing but a bundle or collection of different perceptions . . . in a perpetual flux and movement.'

[85] 'Buddha has spoken thus: "O Brethren, actions do exist, and also their consequences, but the person that acts does not . . . There exists no Individual, it is only a conventional name given to a set of elements." ' From *Cila Mara*, quoted in Parfit, *Reasons and Persons*, 502. For a critical evaluation of this doctrine, see Paul J. Griffiths, *On Being Mindless: Buddhist Meditation and the Mind–Body Problem* (La Salle, Ill., 1986).

[86] Thatcher, 'Christian Theism and the Concept of a Person', 184–5; my italics.

metaphysical teaching that we ought to annihilate ourselves, as Thatcher's interpretation would have it. Clearly, the ethic of self-denial presupposes and entails the existence of the dualist's metaphysical self because the goal is moral improvement of the enduring self, not annihilation. So Thatcher's No-Soul, No-Pride Argument for holism fails.

The remaining positive argument for the holist view that Thatcher offers can be called his Sub-Atomic Particle Argument. The old concept of matter as inert, dead stuff begged for powers in order to explain the movement of physical objects, like the stars moving through the heavens. Now, with the discoveries of modern science, matter is found to be a form of energy, a locus of activity. The implication is that just as we no longer require the existence of souls to explain the activities of the stars, neither do we require the existence of souls to explain the activities of persons. The modern theist must, Thatcher argues, incorporate the modern, subatomic concept of matter. This does not call for a minor adjustment to our concept of ourselves; it entails the radical affirmation that we are mindless. He appeals to the work of Arthur Peacocke to spell out this argument.

The *material units* of the universe—the sub-atomic particles, the atoms and molecules they form—are the fundamental entities constituted in their *matter-energy–space–time relationships*, and are such that they have *built in*, as it were, the potential of becoming organized in that special kind of system we call *living* and, in particular in the system of the human brain in the human body which displays conscious activity. *In man, the stuff of the universe has become cognizing and self-cognizing.*[87]

The new concept of matter necessitates 'enormous shifts of understanding'[88] of the soul. When Christianity does adopt these empirical truths— that the properties of matter are 'fathomless, emergent, and self-organizing'—then Christians will *not* be driven to

reify the soul or spirit in order to gain religious entry into the material world, for . . . [the mind is but] 'a new activity and function of the all-pervasive physico-chemical units that emerge when these units have evolved a particular kind of organized complexity.' This view of matter seems entirely consistent with Christian theology . . . and gives rise elsewhere to views of the person which are variously called 'holist', 'compositionalist', 'organicist', and so on.[89]

Here we see consciousness and self consciousness stipulated to be innate powers of subatomic particles. The essential nature of thinking matter is therefore present (but dormant?) in subatomic particles and actuated in the grey matter of the brain. So where dualism puts one ghost in the machine, holism puts a micro-ghost in every subatomic particle of the body, indeed

[87] Thatcher, 186; my italics.   [88] Ibid.
[89] Ibid. Thatcher is quoting from Arthur Peacocke, *Creation and the World of Science* (Oxford, 1979), 120.

in every bit of matter in the universe. Thus holistic theory excises the traditional soul from reality, only to compensate for its loss by adding untold
billions and billions of subatomic, dormant, minion souls into every
photon, electron, neuron, and toenail clipping. Is it really more scientific,
reasonable, and coherent to believe in holism?

Thatcher acknowledges that the annihilation of the traditional soul
required by the holist view of persons will take theology a little time to
accommodate, but when it does it must unavoidably 'recast the doctrine of
God's incorporeality'.[90] Such a recast, logically consistent, holistic theology will then upgrade theism to acceptable scientific standards. It replaces
inert matter with

the inclusive self-organizing one that becomes organized in the form of living
persons, [and] there are no reasons why we should not posit, within the inclusive
infinity of God, elements of matter. This is not to say that the material world
should be posited as God's body . . . only that God's corporeality is finite . . . [Such
divine corporeality will put] heightened emphasis on God's real presence in the
world.[91]

The consistent holist cannot believe that God is *a personal being* but that
God is *impersonal being–energy–corporeality itself.*

If God is not a person and Cartesian accounts of persons are not to be utilized in
speaking of him . . . God, then, is a real ontological subject, posited by faith, whom
we identify and praise with our term 'God' . . . [But to] think of God as a being is
to include him in a genus with other beings; better to call him being itself, from
whom all beings derive.[92]

There is no problem here with Thatcher's logic. Certainly, Augustine
agrees—a theologian must have a concept of persons that is circumspect of
both created persons and divine Person. The logic is sound. The problem is
that logically consistent holism mutates theism into pantheism, panenthe-
ism, Buddhism, and atheism.

*If the holistic theory of persons is true, then persons are extinguished
from reality or reduce to physico-chemical activity. God is extinguished or
reduces to impersonal, amoral energy. Theism is extinguished or its scientific substitute becomes indistinguishable from atheism.*[93]

THE REMAINING OPTION: THE IMAGE OF GOD AS EXTRINSIC VALUE

There remains one last holdout that many holistic theologians embrace as
the meaning of the image of God and the moral identity of persons.

---

[90] Thatcher, 'Christian Theism and the Concept of a Person', 187.
[91] Ibid.   [92] Ibid. 187–8.
[93] For critical evaluations of further theological problems in the holistic theory of
persons, see Cooper, *Body, Soul and Life Everlasting* and Charles Taliaferro, *Consciousness
and the Mind of God* (Cambridge, 1994).

The meaning of God's image in man is variously defined, but *most theologians agree* that it is only because he was made in God's image that man can relate to God. God takes some interest in the animals (see Jonah 4: 11) but he does not relate to them as he does to human beings. *If God relates in a personal way to a human creature, this is evidence that that creature is made in God's image.*[94]

God is said to relate to us in a personal way: 'in the creation, preservation, moral evaluation, and setting apart of his people for future service [as] is evident in these passages [Gen. 1: 27; Ps. 139: 13, 14; Jer. 1:5; Luke 1: 44; Ps. 55: 1]'.[95] So the claim is that *if God relates in a personal way to X, then X is made in the image of God.* The inherent moral capacity of the substantial soul is traded in for an existential relation. The image of God (ethical value) = being related to in a personal way by God. Therefore, there is no intrinsic value of persons—there are no moral facts about us— only a non-verifiable assertion about God. This is truly good news to secularists, utilitarians, and atheists alike, because such theologians agree on the facts—that there are no moral facts about persons. But the theological assertion itself fails on logical grounds.

The logical problem obtains for theologians who adopt a holistic view of human persons but retain the traditional concept of God as a Person without a body. Given this combination of beliefs, it follows that God can only act 'in a personal way' because God cannot act contrary to, or at odds with, himself. When God acts and whatever God does, it is an extrinsic, relational act of God in the world and to the world—independent of the object of the act. Thus, given that God 'relates in a personal way' to human beings (embodied persons or holistic persons) who need oxygen, food, and water, it follows that God 'relates in a personal way' to maintain oxygen, food, and water on the earth. If the extrinsic relation of God is the criteria of the image of God, it follows that oxygen, food, water, and human beings are all made in the image of God. This *reductio ad absurdum* (that water is made in the image of God) is unfalsifiable by the theologian because the existential relational claim about God (presumed to obtain uniquely to human beings) is unfalsifiable. Put another way, such an external, existential moral theology is not just meaningless, it is positively destructive of the value of persons.

Conclusion

It has been shown that contemporary academic theology rejects the traditional soul, and that it does so at its peril. Rejection of the traditional soul entails rejection of the substantial image of God, which entails rejection of the irreducible moral nature and intrinsic moral value of persons. The fact that persons are essentially characterized by an irreducible moral capacity

---

[94] Brown, *Death before Birth*, 126. Italics added.   [95] Ibid.

is the prerequisite for moral experience, moral development, conscience, ethical intuition, ethical principles, moral knowledge, moral responsibility, the moral sentiments, and personal relationships. As bearers of an inherent moral nature, we are beings that possess intrinsic moral value. Reason, ethics, and law therein have a first principle from which to work. Having an inescapable moral nature does not make a person inherently good— because goodness is a contingent, developmental character trait that results from the fitting exercise of one's moral agency. The holistic theory of persons rejects the substantial soul, believing that contemporary neuro-science and human genetics require as much. It has been shown that such scientific capitulation to physicalism is unwarranted and the reality of the moral identity of persons is utterly destroyed by the theologians' version of it—psychosomatic holism.

THE DIVINE IN THE LAW

Calum Carmichael

The archbishop of Canterbury recently condemned the view of the bishop of Edinburgh, who in his book *Godless Morality* had argued that God should be left out of the contemporary moral debate. The archbishop thought that the bishop was ignoring fundamental scriptural insights. I think that the archbishop is correct to insist that God be kept in any discussion of morality. However, his assumption that the idea of God he attributes to the Bible is one in which the deity is on the side of the good, the just, and the enlightened is, I shall argue, deeply flawed. In that the Bible figures so much in contemporary claims made about God, I shall focus my attention on it. I wish to show that the role of God is such a multifaceted one that to ignore its richness is not just to distort the sources but irresponsibly to cast aside profound insights about the human condition that are as valid today as they were in biblical antiquity.

What is Divine Law?

I begin with claims about divine law. Down through the centuries both Christians and Jews regard the laws of the Pentateuch as *lex Dei*. Even critical scholars claim that law in the Bible is inseparable from religion, and the following statement is typical.

If there be indeed a single and all-powerful creator of the universe, this divine being cannot but be sovereign over people and all living things. Sentient creatures such as human beings therefore seek to know whether this being makes any demands upon them. When such demands are discovered, whether through prophets or other channels of revelation, those demands necessarily constitute the law by which creatures are *ultimately* to be governed.[1]

Claims that base the authority of the law on a divine source are attributed to the biblical sources themselves. A more critical assessment of such notions is called for.

---

[1] Edwin B. Firmage, Bernard G. Weiss, and John W. Welch (eds.), *Religion and Law: Biblical-Judaic and Islamic Perspectives* (Winona Lake, Ind., 1990), p. vii. In his major 19th-century treatise on how judges ultimately decide cases, Joel Bishop claims that decisions are the result of God's direct involvement in the judicial process: 'Almighty God appears in the midst of the tribunal where it sits, and reveals the right way to the understandings of the judges, as surely as he appears in the tempest on the ocean, and teaches each water-drop where to lie when the wind goes down, so as to produce in the deep the same calm which has gone before in the sky. And, as the ocean-drops do not know the philosophy of this; so, oftentimes, the judges do not apprehend the true reasons of their decisions' (*The First Book of the Law* (Boston, 1868), 130).

It should first be pointed out that only in two instances does the deity speak rules directly. In almost all other instances God communicates rules to Moses, who then gives them to the Israelites. Very sophisticated thinking underlies the two modes by which the law is presented, direct communication from the deity and mediation through Moses. The suggestion that God spoke rules directly and also through a human intermediary is an attempt, found in all legal systems, to pursue the question of how law and ethics originate.

The two instances when the deity speaks rules directly are the giving of the Decalogue and the rules permitting the eating of meat and regulating homicide at the re-creation of the world after the Flood. The delivery of the Decalogue has a historical setting at the time after the people of Israel leave Egypt, when they are in the wilderness. This setting implies two ideas: the nation receives its laws at the time of its formation, and, equally important, there is evoked the very beginning of time so as to suggest that the Decalogue originated with the creation itself. Thus in the wilderness elemental forces of nature and supernatural powers are on display and those remind us of the creation of the world.

A number of other features in the text recapitulate aspects of the creation. The deity's voice speaks to no human audience, not even to Moses, suggesting that the voice that created the world also spoke the Decalogue.[2] Further, the people have to refrain at the sacred mountain from engaging in sexual intercourse. The implied reason is that symbolically they have to recapture the initial state of innocence of the first human couple, Adam and Eve, before they committed—from the deity's point of view—the first ever offence of eating the fruit of the tree of good and evil. When Adam and Eve became aware of sexuality, they acquired a sense of shame that is synonymous with the knowledge of good and evil—the knowledge of which the gods regard themselves as sole proprietors. Again, the rules in the second part of the Decalogue (Exod. 20: 12–17; Deut. 5: 16–21) come directly from the compiler's contemplation of the events that occurred among the first family ever, Adam, Eve, Cain, and Abel. He derives the rule about adultery, for example, from the statement about the institution of marriage after the birth of Eve from Adam's body. That statement has a son leave a father and his mother and cleave to his wife and become one flesh with her. The implication is that a marital union harks back to and reflects the origin of the first woman from the first man. The compiler of the Decalogue infers that any interference with such a union, adultery, offends against the order of creation.

---

[2] In the Apocrypha—books written between 250 BCE and 100 CE that are not included in the Hebrew canon of Scripture but for the most part turn up in the Septuagint (the translation of the Bible into Greek)—Ben Sira has the Decalogue delivered to the first humans (Sir. 17: 1, 11–13). On the link between the Decalogue and the creation of the world, see Calum Carmichael, 'The Ten Commandments—In what Sense Religious?', in Rex Ahdar (ed.), *Law and Religion* (Aldershot, 2000).

As for the rules that Noah receives directly from the deity after the destruction of the earth by floodwaters, the intent is to suggest that the deity has to accommodate himself to human evil in a re-created world whose existence he is nevertheless prepared to guarantee. He will no longer directly take steps himself to wipe out human wickedness but will require human beings themselves to attend to its removal. In this presentation of the Noachian rules we find also an idea that shows up in many different legal systems, namely, that the law will permit human ways and institutions even though they are perceived to be fundamentally evil.[3]

Most biblical rules come from Moses, who receives them from God. This mode of presentation is also a sophisticated fiction on the part of unknown scribes who formulate the rules in light of their nation's history and traditions. It is an imaginative attempt to trace rules back to a legendary lawgiver whose life coincides with the nation's beginning. In his laws Moses takes up problems in his own time (for example, Deut. 24: 8, 9, his sister's leprosy), problems that existed among his ancestors (for example, Exod. 21: 16, the kidnapping of Joseph; and Lev. 18: 9, 11; 20: 17, Abraham's marriage to his half-sister), and problems that arose long after he lived (for example, Deut. 17: 14–20, the appointment of a king in Israel). The recorders of this legal material engage in a process, the invention of their own legal traditions, which is a culture- and identity-building enterprise that occurs in the life of most nations.[4] A consequence of this process is that it is exceedingly difficult, if not impossible, to work out the laws that actually applied in a nation's early history.

The problem of working out what laws apply at any one time has its parallel in contemporary legal systems. The distinguished anthropologist of law Walter Weyrauch persuasively argues that the role of bargaining in the American legal system is at least as constitutive of it, if not more so, as the written law. One consequence is that we do not know the unwritten

---

[3] See David Daube, 'Concessions to Sinfulness in Jewish Law', in *Collected Works of David Daube*, i: *Talmudic Law*, ed. Calum Carmichael (Berkeley, 1992). Such concessions, for example, permitting people to eat meat, are quite different from the abolitions of laws on account of people's depravity. The abolition is not meant to support the sinners. An example is the removal in later Jewish law of the ordeal for women suspected of adultery because the men are so depraved sexually that it would be wrong to keep women under the statute (*Sifre* on Num. 5: 31; *Palestinian Sotah* 24a; *Babylonian Sotah* 74b).

[4] For Greek law, see Andrew Szegedy-Maszak, 'Legends of the Greek Lawgivers', *Greek, Roman, and Byzantine Studies*, 19 (1978), 199–209; for Roman Law, see H. F. Jolowicz, *Historical Introduction to Roman Law* (Cambridge, 1952), 4, 10; and for Scotland, Hector L. MacQueen, 'Regiam Majestatem, Scots Law and National Identity', *Scottish Historical Review*, 74 (1995), 1–20. The Vlax Rom (Gypsies) assert that their *kris* system of public assemblies to resolve disputes and formulate policies is an authentic, ancient form of Romany culture which may even go back to the Indian *panchajat* system. In fact, the origin of the *kris* system appears to be in the Romanian village assemblies of the 16th century at the time when the Vlax Rom became enslaved in Romanian neo-feudal society. See Thomas Acton, Susan Caffrey, and Gary Mundy, 'Theorizing Gypsy Law', (1997) 45 *American Journal of Comparative Law* 237, 247–9.

rules that apply when disputes, far and away the majority, in, for example, criminal law, divorce law, and personal injury are settled and not adjudicated. Even in cases that come to court, a straight, technical legal argument is unlikely to win. Required is communication usually by way of hints to judge and jury of unwritten rules and unarticulated social norms that 'ring a bell' with them and appeal to their sense of fairness. It is again often very difficult to articulate what these rules and norms might be.[5] If there is merit in this claim, we have a striking indication of how morality is not so much dependent on law but rather trumps it. Usually, morality is dependent on law in the sense that the moralist takes wrongs known to the law and treats them in an expansive way. In both Jewish and Christian teaching the notion of adultery is extended to the act of looking with desire on a woman and the label of murder to the feeling of anger (*Derekh Erets* 10; *Mekhilta de-Rabbi Shimeon* 111; Matt. 5: 21–9). In recent times legal terms for specific offences have been expanded to communicate moral ideas: property is theft and rape is any man's intercourse with a woman.

A unique feature of biblical law is that different bodies of legal material are incorporated at different points in a narrative history. For example, when Moses is about to die and the people of Israel are about to enter the land of Canaan, Moses looks both back and forward in time and delivers the laws of Deuteronomy. The scribes responsible for this merging of law and narrative history adopted a convention common in the ancient world. They made of Moses a legendary figure who judged past and contemporary developments in his nation's history as recorded in Genesis–Deuteronomy and anticipated future ones as recorded in Joshua–2 Kings. The literary traditions in these books of the Bible contain the same issues taken up in the laws. Law and storytelling are intimately linked. When we work out the links between the laws and the issues in the individual narratives, we can account, with remarkable precision, for the substance of the laws, the language of their formulations, and the bewildering sequence in which they are often set down. In the Decalogue, for example, a rule about murder comes after a rule about honour to parents with its promise of living long upon the ground (*'adamah*, not land, *'erets*). The explanation for the strange sequence is the lawgiver's focus on Cain's murder of the son Abel whom his parents had created and its consequence that he was no longer allowed to till the ground (*'adamah*).

---

[5] See Walter O. Weyrauch 'Aspiration and Reality in American Law', in Alan Watson (ed.), *Law, Morality, and Religion: Global Perspectives* (Berkeley, 1996), 222; also Lynn Lopucki and Walter O. Weyrauch, 'A Theory of Legal Strategy', (2000) 49 *Duke Law Journal*, 1405. T. M. McDonnell, 'Playing beyond the Rules: A Realist and Rhetoric-Based Approach to Researching the Law and Solving Legal Problems', (1998) 67 *University of Missouri–Kansas City Law Review*, 285–342, argues that law schools should teach students to research, less rules, than the judges, lawyers, and others who participate in litigation.

In what sense are the rules that Moses gives divine law? It is not along the lines that I cited at the beginning of this essay, namely, that a numinous awareness perceives some kind of ultimate sovereign who somehow through certain channels of revelation is able to make known his demands to human beings. Rather, the narrators of biblical events subject those events to critical evaluation, and their judgements are often expressed as if they come from the deity.[6] Moses, in turn, incorporates into his rules the spirit of the deity as it shows up in the narrative events. Sometimes, however, it has to be emphasized, Moses opposes the deity's judgement. A key issue, then, in understanding the nature of biblical law is to assess the role of the deity in those narratives in which he is mentioned.

Consider a story where the deity's role is major. The patriarch Abram travels to foreign parts, to Egypt, and his beautiful wife, Sarai, accompanies him. He fears that foreign eyes will fall on her and seek to acquire her—at the expense of his life. So he tells her to say to the Egyptians that she is his sister. The pharaoh himself chooses Sarai and he makes her his wife. Abram's life is spared and, indeed, the pharaoh treats him well on account of his sister. Untoward events take place, however, in the form of plagues afflicting Pharaoh and his house 'because of Sarai, Abram's wife' (Gen. 12: 17). The deity, that is, does not sanction the pharaoh's union with Sarai and treats it as adultery. The introduction of the deity into the story represents, in this instance, a universal standard. The reason why he is made to express that standard is the perception that no earthly power could exert authority in the matter, presumably on account of the pharaoh's elevated standing.[7]

If an earthly court were to be involved, it would perceive matters to be more complicated than the deity's response suggests. The court would have to weigh Abram's predicament of travelling in foreign parts with a beautiful wife against his life-saving ruse that Sarai is his sister. God's response, in fact, leaves much to be desired because it fails to recognize that the pharaoh, having been deceived into thinking that Sarai was a free woman, acted in good faith.

Inspired by the deity's stance, Moses, in Deut. 24: 1–4, devised a rule prohibiting the renovation of a marriage. Not surprisingly, he shed the story of some of its unique features. He posited a situation that might arise among Israelites on home territory, not one that might occur on foreign soil. He may, however, still have retained an aspect of the unequal power

[6] This particular fiction is a good example of Hans Vaihinger's philosophy of the 'as if' by which, in this instance, God is presented as if he were real. See *The Philosophy of 'As If': A System of the Theoretical, Practical and Religious Fictions of Mankind*, trans. C. K. Ogden, 2nd edn. (London, 1952). Taking up Vaihinger's views, Lon Fuller notes that most theories of law contain a good deal of fiction. One is the notion that law is the command of 'an intangible, undiscoverable sovereign'. See *Legal Fictions* (Stanford, Calif., 1967), 98.

[7] It is always important to ask why sometimes God is brought into a narrative and other times he is not. The Book of Esther, for example, has no reference to God.

relation among the parties. He has the first husband give up his wife on account of some gain that will accrue to him from letting her go to another man who, presumably, is in a position to grant a favour to the divorcing husband. Moses retained the moral stance in that his law states that should the second husband divorce the woman or die, the first husband cannot take her back. The law is understandable in that the first husband is judged to have been, in effect, pimping. In this regard the law adopts a stricter moral stance than the deity in the story in Genesis 12. In the law the woman cannot return to her first husband, whereas in the story Sarai is restored to Abram. To be sure, the lawgiver does not imagine a dilemma of the kind Abram confronted. More realistically he assumes, we can speculate, a situation where a husband stands to gain from the transaction that uses the institution of divorce to cover his tracks. The law is an example of how its spirit imitates—and improves on—the deity's response in a narrative. In this light, but only in this light, can the law be said to be divine law.

The Regressive Role of God

Time and again in biblical material the deity's involvement, in fact, does not bear too much critical scrutiny from the point of view of basic moral principles. David Daube often pointed to this major aspect. God is depicted as hostile to culture, including legal progress. The story of Adam and Eve is about God's unsuccessful attempt to prevent humans from having access to knowledge. He punishes them for winning out over his resistance (Genesis 2 and 3). At Babel, in a legend that touches on the concerns of law, God successfully opposes universal coexistence and mutual understanding (Gen. 11: 1–9).[8] In dealing with the inhabitants of Sodom, God is determined to apply the principle of collective responsibility and let innocent people suffer, and Abraham has to wrestle from him a more enlightened stance (Genesis 18).[9] Errors in the rules that God gives to Moses, about observing the inheritance rights of daughters, for example, have to be pointed out before he makes the desired alteration (Num. 27: 1–11; 36: 1–12).

Why is the deity linked with such shortcomings? One answer is that his portrayal brings out the frustrations and ambiguities human beings experience when striving to improve themselves. They do possess the knowledge of good and evil, but while affirming its importance and desirability they recognize that knowledge can be oppressive. 'For in much wisdom is much vexation, and he who increases knowledge increases sorrow' (Eccles. 1: 18). The punishments that the deity visits upon the actors in the Adam and

---

[8] See David Daube, *Civil Disobedience in Antiquity* (Edinburgh, 1972), 60–2.
[9] See David Daube, *Studies in Biblical Law* (Cambridge, 1947), 155–8.

Eve story convey the burdens that come from human enlightenment. Again, it is important and much to be welcomed that different groups of human beings come together to live in universal harmony as at Babel, but it proves impossible. Opposed to such a desirable outcome are monumental anti-progressive forces, in this context, God for short, standing for what is incomprehensible to us.

In dealing with the problems he encounters in Sodom, God applies the communal principle instead of what elementary justice demands, the application of the principle of individual responsibility. There is again the recognition of human limitation. However much these ancients might wish to apply the principle of individual responsibility, they find that the communal principle serves practical ends. If every member of a community is held accountable for an offence committed by one member, the outcome will be self-policing by all of them.[10] The role of the deity serves to point to those factors, often of a quite necessary kind for the functioning of society, that detract from the goals of achieving justice. Pragmatism trumps fairness. Note that the deity does not represent the ideal, rather the frustration of it. The perception is commendably realistic because, again, we are dealing with overwhelmingly negative forces at work in society. In those instances where God represents ideas that are opposed to human strivings or ideals, he represents a sensible recognition of severe human limitations. In some ways, the modern view about the role of genetics in relation to human behaviour is comparable.

No less complicated today is the intertwining of individual and collective responsibility. We need only think of such areas of conflict as sexual, racial, and international relations. The Western powers, for example, hold Saddam Hussein responsible for heinous offences, but in striking out at the Iraqi people their suffering raises disturbing questions about the nature of the punishment supposedly directed at him. It seems that the communal principle is being applied, whereas—so complex is the matter—it is individual responsibility that prevails; only the leader is being punished by the deprivations visited on his subjects.[11]

In light of the problematical role of the deity it is understandable why we might find that Moses sometimes stands opposed to God's judgement in the narrative history. When he does, it represents an advance. Here are two examples out of many. God strikes Onan dead for not giving conception to his dead and childless brother's widow, Tamar (Genesis 38). A son

---

[10] For an excellent discussion of the notion in modern times that responsibility for a crime rests not only on the offender but also on society as a whole, see Giorgio del Vecchio, *Justice: A Historical and Philosophical Essay*, trans. Lady Guthrie (Edinburgh, 1952).

[11] It is a form of punishment David Daube termed 'ruler punishment' (*Studies in Biblical Law*, 163). His statement (p. 158) made just after the Second World War as a German Jewish refugee in England is worth quoting: 'Both communal responsibility and ruler punishment are phenomena so near the vital interests of a society that it would be too much to expect the society concerned to be quite clear, or even outspoken, about them.'

born to her would, according to the levirate custom, re-establish the dead brother's estate. Onan acts as he does—it takes the form of withdrawing and ejaculating outside her—because if no heir is born, he will inherit his dead brother's share of the estate. His motivation, then, for avoiding his duty is greed. By any measure, however, his punishment for an act of disloyalty to his family is extreme. A major factor in accounting for the deity's harshness is that Onan represents Canaanite infusion into Jacob's line of descent. Onan's mother was a Canaanite and this group, more than any other in biblical material, epitomizes the lure to Israelites of other religions. The opposition to Canaanites is intense.

The fictional lawgiver Moses sets out a rule for precisely the issue in the narrative—what to do with a brother who refuses his honourable duty (Deut. 25: 5–10). Much more reasonably, Moses devises a more measured penalty that causes disgrace to be directed by the widow to the offending brother in front of bystanders. For his reprehensible passiveness in refusing to have intercourse with her, she likens him to the equally, in effect, passive Onan, whose deed of spilling his seed on the ground instead of inside Tamar would have been known to the rule's recipients. Thus in the law the widow removes the brother-in-law's shoe from his foot to signify withdrawal from intercourse and spits in his face to signify the misuse of his seed.[12]

The second example comes from the story about the aftermath of the seduction of Jacob's daughter Dinah by Shechem, the son of a Canaanite chieftain, Hamor (Genesis 34). Two of Jacob's sons, Simeon and Levi, are incensed about the disgraceful way in which Shechem treated their sister. Even more so, they are motivated to avenge his misdeed in furtherance of their religious principles. For them, and it is the narrator's position, there must be no truck whatsoever with the Canaanites. In other words, what the two brothers do in dealing with the problem has the divine stamp of approval.

The entire tribe to which the seducer Shechem belongs is tricked into becoming circumcised so that ostensibly its members might intermarry with the Israelites and also enter into commercial relations with them. On the third day, however, after all the males undergo circumcision, the two sons of Jacob set upon the debilitated men and kill all of them. The misdeed of one member of a group results in his death and the death of all of the men in their community, including Shechem's father, Hamor, the head of the group. Moses focuses on the injustice of what has occurred. A son's offence brings condign punishment not just on the actual offender but on his biological father too, and, further, on all other sons and fathers that owed their allegiance to Hamor and who might have entered into

---

[12] For the sexual symbolism in question, see Calum Carmichael, 'Gypsy Law and Jewish Law', (1997) 45 *American Journal of Comparative Law* 285–8.

negotiations for marriages with Israelite daughters. Moses sets out a law insisting on the principle that an offender, and only he, should be punished for a misdeed: 'The fathers shall not be put to death for the sons, neither shall the sons be put to death for the fathers: every man shall be put to death for his own sin' (Deut. 24: 16).

In both of the above incidents the actors appear on the international stage. This is significant because it is in an international setting that the purity of Israel is perceived to be most at threat. The divine harshness is a response to the problem of Israelite purity and results in the execution of Onan and the slaughter of the Shechemites. Moses' laws are more measured because they are meant for internal governance. It is generally true that rules that groups apply among themselves are more reasonable than those they apply to outsiders. Those interested in regulating relations between one nation and another typically lack the means to enact, even less to enforce, rules, and more often than not, should there arise a serious problem with the other, one nation in the name of its god resorts to an extreme measure. From an enlightened perspective it is lawlessness. The biblical rules that the lawgiver derives from his scanning of his nation's history are, unless otherwise indicated, intended for internal Israelite affairs.[13] Consequently, the rules are more in line with elementary standards of justice in that the means are more likely to exist to enact and enforce them.

New Testament material also illustrates the regressive role of God, and again the problem is the sharpness of division between, not one nation and another, but two internal groups. In his Gospel Matthew depicts the end of Judas's life in a favourable light. Judas repents of his grave misdeed of betraying a fellow Jew, Jesus, to a repressive regime (Matt. 27: 3–5). He does what the law requires of him. Having expressed his sorrow, he hands over his ill-gotten gain to the authorities and gives himself over to them to deal with his grave transgression. They, however, are not interested in him, and Judas, hanging himself, carries out a sentence of death that is appropriate to his crime. As David Daube has so well shown, Matthew would have regarded Judas as fully worthy to be in paradise because he repented.[14] In the Acts of the Apostles Luke takes a quite different approach to the end of Judas (Acts 1: 15–20). There is no repentance. Rather, falling headlong, swelling up, and bursting asunder, Judas is felled by heaven. The devastating divine judgement is unmistakable.

The different descriptions of Judas's end are revealing. Matthew's version represents a stance of forgiveness for someone who, like Judas, had believed in Jesus, lost confidence in him, saw the light again, and sought to

---

[13] Significantly, where relations with foreign groups are at stake, the rules can be fierce; e.g. Deut. 20: 16–18. In mitigation, they are often rules about engagement in war.

[14] See David Daube, 'Judas', in *Collected Works of David Daube*, ii: *New Testament Judaism*, ed. Calum Carmichael (Berkeley, 2000).

be readmitted to the community of believers. Luke's description, on the other hand, betrays a grim attitude to those who, once enlightened, then fall away. No hope of readmission to the Christian community is possible. The harsh attitude bespeaks a community that has settled into stable ways and has no need to receive back apostate members.

In the Matthean example Judas honourably pays the price the law required—repentance and punishment—and that settles the matter. He is free of his misdeed, forgiven, and, given the early Christian belief in the nature of the afterlife, accepted into the community of believers. In the Acts of the Apostles Judas is beyond the redemption granted by the law and a gruesome prospect awaits anyone who might follow the path of his broken faith. Judging with the utmost harshness any such backslider along the lines spelled out in Heb. 10: 20–31, the unforgiving community invokes the wrath of God to deal with the offender. It threatens damnation, a second-best means, to be sure, of visiting punishment.[15]

In the above examples law transcends religion in terms of desirable values. Similar problems with religion show up when it is indeed on the side of justice. Often the law is not in a position to punish for some offence, but religion insists on it. In a remarkable number of biblical accounts the narrator writes from the viewpoint of a supposed ideal religious and moral order because the legal order fails to visit consequences upon a culprit for his wrongdoing. The situations are typically ones within families where the law tends to keep out, for example when Jacob cheats his brother Esau out of his birthright, and ones in which powerful figures in society have offended, for example Kings David and Ahab.

The notion of mirroring punishment dominates those narratives where there is a passion for justice. Jacob is paid back in his own coin as retribution for cheating Esau out of his birthright when he, Jacob, the younger son, took over the rights of the elder one. In time Laban cheats Jacob, when the latter is about to acquire a wife. Laban substitutes in the wedding tent his older daughter, Leah, whom Jacob does not want, for the younger one, Rachel, whom he does want—the elder becomes the younger to Jacob's discomfort (Genesis 25, 27, 29).

King Ahab's son dies because Ahab is held culpable for causing Naboth to lose his ancestral property. It is mirroring punishment. Ahab's royal line comes to an end with the slaughter of his son because Ahab criminally stopped Naboth from having a member of his family perpetuate the family

---

[15] In reconciling the Lucan stance with the Matthean, the Church ruled in favour of the former so that, with singularly regrettable consequences, Judas's suicide was added to his offence of being an informer. 'With little exaggeration one can say that while for the past 1700 years or so Judas committed suicide because he was beyond the pale, in historical truth suicide, for Christians, got beyond the pale because he resorted to it' (ibid. 790). In New Testament times there was no prohibition of suicide. The error invades almost all discussions about Judas, e.g. Jorge Luis Borges, 'Three Versions of Judas', in D. A. Bates and J. E. Irby (eds.), *Labyrinths: Selected Stories and Other Writings* (New York, 1964).

property. Ahab himself dies in a battle to take back territory that rightfully belongs to his kingdom, but his death when attempting to acquire it is retribution for taking a man's property that did not belong to Ahab (1 Kings 21, 22).

King David is paid back in similar coin for his adultery with Bathsheba, the wife of Uriah, and his subsequent disposal of Uriah. In punishment for his adultery, David unwittingly sends his daughter Tamar to her brother Amnon, who rapes her. And in punishment for having Uriah deliberately killed in battle, David unwittingly sends Amnon to a sheepshearing festival where his brother Absalom has set him up to be murdered. Absalom himself, David's favourite son, meets death in battle in a way that the narrator has intentionally mirror Uriah's death in battle. In other words, David's offence against Uriah also predetermines Absalom's end (2 Samuel 11–18).[16] Heaven, we are to believe, works this way in the pursuit of justice. What might appear to be innocent, certainly unwitting, actions on the part of David are really predetermined by his preceding guilty actions. A modern reader is reminded of Freud's claim that what appear to be accidents, errors, and tragic occurrences are often but masks for what Freud calls semi-intentional harm on the part of those involved.[17] The Bible often lends support to the powerful notion that to overcome guilt we secretly punish ourselves in subtle ways that mirror our offences. The biblical perspective is well expressed in the classical Vietnamese saying (from the *Tale of Kieu*) 'Happiness or misfortune is prescribed by the law of heaven, but their source came from ourselves'. Heaven has David send Tamar to her seducer and heaven has David send the seducer to his death at the hands of his brother.

The historical fact that both Ahab and David get away with their offences determines the narrator's quest for other ways to suggest that wrongdoing will meet with its just deserts. Alas, in interpreting events as they do, the ancient writer(s) presents a view of justice that is profoundly unsatisfactory because innocent people are made to suffer in order to punish indirectly someone who has offended. The actors in the drama of unfolding retribution are but instruments in heaven's hands, mere objects to satisfy a craving for justice. Ahab's son dies on account of the heredity principle. Tamar is sexually violated in order to pay back David for his adultery. Her brother Amnon behaves in ways that are both morally and legally wrong, but not to the extent that he deserves to die, and certainly not that he should die in a quite lawless way at the hands of his brother Absalom. The fates of Amnon and Tamar are tied to David's action to cover up his adultery. The craving for justice reveals right values, rises to the heights in suggesting a unified view of all human action, but also

---

[16] See Calum Carmichael, *The Spirit of Biblical Law* (Athens, Ga., 1996), 149–61.
[17] See Sigmund Freud, *Psychopathology of Everyday Life* (London, 1966), 122–6.

depicts justice as cold, impersonal, and anti-human.[18] Charles Taylor notes that the scientific revolution in the sixteenth and seventeenth century saw how 'the ideal of *theōria*, of grasping the order of the cosmos through contemplation, came to be seen as being vain and misguided, as a presumptuous attempt to escape the hard work of detailed discovery'.[19] Francis Bacon was especially prominent in opposing this attempt to discover some overarching order in things. The same complaint can be levelled at attempts to seek unified views of justice.

The sensible conclusion to be drawn from the selected biblical material is that the human striving to achieve justice is more often than not beyond reach. Rather than furthering its quest, the role of God can serve to under-line the frustration in ever achieving it. Or, to put it more positively, his role helps to express the problems involved in seeking justice. One factor always to be borne in mind is that talk about God is invariably a transfer from human experience. When God is brought into the discussion, he can represent forces that either thwart or further the admirable human striving for justice and self-improvement. Theologians conceal the issues when they claim that 'God's revelation precedes and forestalls all human perception of God, all speech about God, and every attempt to experience anything about God or to know him.'[20] To the contrary, every mention of God in the text requires close scrutiny precisely because it reveals so much about the human enterprise.

Even in the matter of human beings experiencing a sense of God the position is similar to their use of language about God. Often in biblical law God is thought of as experiencing shame. He would look away from faeces within an army camp and, consequently, withhold his aid to the military should he find it present (Deut. 23: 19–14). He is appalled at the blot to his land because an unknown assailant has slain someone on it (Deut. 21: 1–9). He does not tolerate the sight of a hanged man after dark because on seeing such an abhorrent sight he would look away from the land of Israel (Deut. 21: 22, 23). At the human level the aim of shame and guilt is to further civilized behaviour. The desire to avoid the experience of the two emotions can lead to right conduct. Why then is God thought of as experiencing shame? The explanation is that we often use the language of shame when we are really talking about guilt, conscience.[21] Shame concerns the look of things, whereas guilt concerns the internal voice of

---

[18] On how legal reasoning has the potential at all times to dehumanize persons through the use of conceptual 'legal masks', see John Noonan, *Persons and Masks of the Law: Cardozo, Holmes, Jefferson, and Wythe as Makers of the Masks* (New York, 1976).

[19] Charles Taylor, *Sources of the Self: The Making of the Modern Identity* (Cambridge, Mass., 1989), 213.

[20] So part of the description of the volume Gerhard Sauter and John Barton (eds.), *Revelation and Story: Narrative Theology and the Centrality of Story* (Aldershot, 2000).

[21] A headline in *The Times* reads, ' "Children must Learn Shame": Teachers should Encourage Pupils to Develop Conscience' (19 May 2000).

authority. In so far as God works inside people's hearts and minds, he represents the force of guilt. The transfer of shame to God reflects the common phenomenon that we use the language of shame when we are speaking about guilt because the two emotions are so intertwined.

God can experience shame not just on account of human wrongdoing, that is, when he looks away from the ugly sight caused by it, but also because of his own unsatisfactory conduct. In Exodus 32 he is about to destroy all of the Israelites with the exception of Moses because they have angered him in creating the Golden Calf. Moses has to reason with God and point out that if he proceeds with his plan his reputation will suffer in the eyes of the Egyptians. One of the drawbacks of God's contemplated punishment is that his action would dishonour the patriarchs of the nation, Abraham, Isaac, and Israel, because it would show no respect for them as the progenitors of all the later Israelites. Reverence for ancestors is a value, Moses points out, that transcends national boundaries. The shame mechanism makes God see the problem, and the result is that he avoids it.

Concluding Remarks

1. I have focused attention on problematical aspects of divine law. For example, there are rules ostensibly coming from Moses that oppose the deity's judgements in narrative incidents. Such rules often assert a higher form of justice when, for example, they require that the consequences of an offence should be confined to the individual wrongdoer and not extended to those who are innocent. While divine justice works in its inscrutable and inexorable way, involving others as its instruments, Moses adheres strictly to the principle of individual responsibility. The correction can show up in the formulation of a rule, as the following example illustrates.

In Genesis 38 Judah's sons Er and Onan lose their lives in retaliation for their father, Judah's, bad treatment of Joseph (Genesis 37). The concern in the narrative to show that Judah is paid back for causing a father (Jacob) to lose his favourite son (Joseph) explains why the story of Judah and Tamar in Genesis 38 interrupts the Joseph story, which continues in Genesis 39. The rule about the goring ox in Exod. 21: 28–32 takes up the issue of how Joseph's brothers, the sons of the Ox, who constitute the house of Jacob, falsely claimed that an animal had killed Joseph.[22] The subject matter of the narrative prompts a consideration of the legal issue about an actual animal's responsibility for killing a person but with human culpability for its misdeed considered too. In the narrative Judah is the primary player in getting rid of Joseph, but it is his sons who suffer for his offence. Providence so arranges matters as to demonstrate that Judah is taught what it is like to lose sons. The law, however, in Exodus opposes

[22] See Calum Carmichael, *The Origins of Biblical Law* (Ithaca, NY, 1992), 132–5.

vicarious punishment. Unnecessarily, the rule states that should an ox gore a man's son or daughter, the same judgement applies. That is, the ox's owner alone is guilty for what is a capital offence. He, not his son or daughter, is to be held liable. The lawgiver is reacting against the divine retribution that caused a father's sons to lose their lives because he, Judah, offended against Jacob in disposing of his son Joseph.

2. The most common role ascribed to God is that of a powerful figure working inside people's minds and hearts. In a word, he can be the internal voice of authority and represent conscience. From the point of view of law, lacking as it does the means of visiting penalties on a whole range of offences, punishment sought from God represents but a second-best way of controlling human conduct. The list of curses in Deuteronomy 27 illustrates the kinds of offence inaccessible to ordinary legal remedy, the curse being an attempt to invoke divine power when human power is limited. The list contains heterogeneous offences: those committed by the powerful against the weak (removing a neighbour's boundary mark), ones that are committed in secret (sexual offences), ones that occur in a devious, unprovable manner (depriving the alien, the orphan, or a widow of justice), and ones that take place in the family (dishonouring a parent).

3. Divine law often reveals its shortcomings, but we can turn to aspects that offer a somewhat more positive evaluation—somewhat, because interesting problems again show up. Often the biblical lawgiver deduces a rule in a straightforward manner from the deity's action in a narrative. In the Decalogue, for example, he derives from the story of Cain and Abel a rule against murder. When God puts a mark on Cain, it is to prevent his murder because, it is implied, he is opposed to one human being arbitrarily killing another as Cain might have been after he had been sentenced to become a wanderer upon the earth. Although this is an example of the lawgiver concurring with the deity's judgement, it is nonetheless worth noting that in the narrative about Cain's fate God is cast in a helpful role for the human participants. The stance is contrary to the deity's hostile attitude to Adam and Eve's desire for the knowledge of good and evil in the preceding, related narrative. The narrator's aim is to reflect on the puzzle that human beings do possess the capacity to exercise judgement but frequently fail to do so. Thus God counsels Cain about controlling his anger and warns him—to no avail—about its bad consequences. What we have in both these accounts is a sober assessment of the human condition in which the narrator attempts to explore the mystery of the ambiguity in human nature. On the one hand, there are forces—identified with God or the gods—opposed to desirable human knowledge,[23] while, on the other

---

[23] The Greek perception was similar: 'While superior power was to the Greeks always a characteristic of the gods in relation to men, superior goodness was attributed to them only at a later stage and as an article of faith, often running counter to what seemed to be the facts of daily experience' (J. W. Jones, *Law and Legal Theory of the Greeks* (Oxford, 1956), 248).

hand, even when human beings are in a favourable position to act on such knowledge, because of counsel attributed to a divine source, they fail miserably.

4. Another type of law in which the deity appears is one that invokes historical memory. The rules establishing the Passover festival (Deut. 16: 1–8) and the Year of Jubilee (Leviticus 25) serve to recall the enslavement of the Israelites in Egypt and the subsequent exodus from there. These two rules and a number of others encapsulate history so that their observance will shape cultural and ethnic identity. They are like statues or emblems to be imprinted on the national consciousness.[24]

5. There are occasions when God appears to act in such a way as to give a perfect illustration of how a law should be observed. As usual, there are interesting features to be observed. What we have is not just an attempt to suggest that God and justice go hand in hand. In effect, he is making up for a previous instance where he is too closely allied with human chicanery. The narrative in Exodus 16 about how God provides manna to the starving Israelites in the wilderness is an example. The story is odd in that it shows how no matter the amount of food a family gathers each day, it miraculously turns out to be in accordance with exactly the quantity they should receive for their needs. Indeed, when measured with an *omer*, a technical means of measurement, the amounts conform to this degree of accuracy. God provides perfect weights and measures. Why should a narrator go to such lengths to demonstrate this kind of detailed conformity to a rule? The point of the narrative, I submit, is not just the general one of suggesting to hearers' minds a contrasting human scene in which all too common cheating shows up. Rather, it is a specific reaction to the example of such cheating in the first family of Israelites when, in fact, God is aligned with the chicanery. When the brothers of Joseph come to Egypt to obtain food because of famine in their own country, Joseph fills their sacks with grain but slips into them, without the brothers' knowledge, the money they had paid for it. When the brothers later return to Egypt to get more grain they hand over the money they had previously found in their sacks. They are told, however, that their money had been received and that 'God must have put treasure in your sacks' (Gen. 43: 23).

In effect, Joseph is cheating, albeit in a topsy-turvy manner, in the matter of giving correct weights and measures. Moreover, the deception is interpreted as God's doing. In terms of how the author of the entire Joseph story wishes to interpret the epic, there is truth in the claim. Joseph is

---

[24] Compare the current debate in New Mexico about the appropriateness of setting up a statue of the Spanish conquistador Don Juan de Oñate to celebrate 400 years of statehood. See Karen Michel, 'Propriety of Symbols', *Native Americas*, 17 (2000), 49–51. On constitutional legal issues in regard to public monuments and other historical artefacts in contemporary American society, see Sanford Levinson, *Written in Stone: Public Monuments in Changing Societies* (Durham, NC, 1998), 75–110.

tormenting his brothers in order to remind them of their original offence against him. According to his dream that foretold the family's future destiny, he is the sheaf of grain to whom they are to bow down. Angered by the thought of submitting to Joseph, the brothers seek to sell 'it'/him for money—unsuccessfully as it turns out. Having later to go to Egypt and obtain grain, not only do they bow down to the disguised Joseph, but also they receive money—a reminder of how they once sought money for 'grain' in the form of Joseph as the sheaf of grain in his dream. The intent of the development is to remind the brothers of their wrongdoing. From a broader perspective, however, the problem is that a grand scheme of how providence brings about justice leaves in its wake confusion about particular acts. Joseph's transaction with the food is not an act of generosity on his part, and to associate the deity with such human manipulation is decidedly problematic. The two stories are about starving Israelites, the later group of whom express a desire to return to Egypt because they had eaten well there. This second story about God's impeccably correct provision of food in the wilderness counters the impression in the first story that God was involved in a dubiously generous provision of grain to the starving brothers in Egypt.

6. The equation of God with what is perfect is often of a surprising nature. There is an incident recorded only in Matthew's Gospel that has bewildered and embarrassed interpreters (Matt. 17: 24–7).[25] The collectors of the temple tax ask Peter whether or not his teacher pays it. Peter says yes, but it appears that he does not really know. When he returns home, Jesus puts a question to him, 'What do you think, Simon? From whom do kings of the earth take toll or tribute? From their sons or from others?' Peter answers, 'From others.' Then says Jesus, 'The sons are free.' Now comes the bewildering part. Jesus says that, nonetheless, in order not to give offence to the authorities Peter should go to the sea, cast a hook, and the first fish that comes along will have in its mouth a shekel with which both of them can pay the tax.

Far from being a naive legend, such a brief tale turns out to be remarkably sophisticated. The money that will turn up in the mouth of the fish will constitute ownerless property. To pay it over to the taxing authorities will mean in effect that Jesus and Peter both pay the tax and do not pay it. They pay it in that it is their coinage; they do not pay it in that it did not come out of their pocket.

In the story a miracle is required to accomplish what is in fact a dodge. It is important to understand that the miracle in question is intended as an illustration of the principle that underlies Jesus' attitude. If the dodge can be effected in a way that does not require a miracle, well and good. The point is that the translation of the principle into practice is such a difficult

[25] See Daube, *New Testament Judaism*, 760–2, 771–81.

one it is little wonder that something on the scale of a miracle will be necessary. And what is the principle? Jesus and his band are sons of the temple's sovereign, God, and hence like the temple priesthood properly exempt from the temple tax.[26] Such a superior status, however, might not be understood, or even recognized, by the larger community and might alienate it if an open stand was taken on the matter. It is considered crucial, nonetheless, that they preserve their freedom to believe and act according to their elevated standing. So to cultivate that freedom it requires actions that will be informed by advice encapsulated in a saying found in another part of Matthew and unique to him. The enlightened elite must be 'as subtle as serpents and harmless as doves' (Matt. 10: 16). Incredibly, the conventional understanding of this story about the fish, no doubt influenced by Paul's contrary counsel about God and the payment of taxes in Romans 13, has it as a counsel of subservience to the authorities.[27] But it is far from that. In Daube's words it is rather a counsel of 'minimum performance': satisfy the authorities but give them nothing that is one's own. To accomplish such a tricky task requires what constitutes the essence of worldly wisdom, that is, deviousness, subtlety, and cleverness.

In the above example the perfect illustration of how to put into practice an important principle comes, it is implied, by means of God's assistance. What, in effect, is encouraged, however, is that human beings in some fundamental matters have to sail close to the wind, to walk a thin line between keeping the law and breaking it. God and deception are perilously close.

The common claim that God commands laws that should be obeyed is in need of qualification. Sometimes, from an enlightened perspective, there is truth in the claim. Other times, however, and they are far more common than has been recognized or admitted, the deity's diverse roles reveal a thoughtful, critical attitude to negative features that constantly show up in human affairs. In biblical sources such a stance is common enough among those authors who introduce talk about the deity into their narratives. In doing so, they use God in multifaceted ways to express a wide variety of ideas about law and morality. Over time the complexity of the position in the Bible is lost sight of, and with it there is a loss of depth and understanding. By the opening of the Christian era the Jewish philosopher Philo, like the rabbis of the period, cannot but view God as given to fair procedure and just ways. The fact, however, that Philo has to defend God against imputations of discrimination (against Cain and Er), for example,

---

[26] Priestly privileges have a long history. Compare how the priests in the Egypt of Joseph's time are exempt from the sovereign's repressive legislation (Gen. 47: 22).

[27] See M. D. Johnson, *The Gospel according to St Matthew*, in *The Interpreter's Bible*, vii (New York, 1951), 465.

points to some sensitivity in the matter.[28] The archbishop of Canterbury and the bishop of Edinburgh would have a more fruitful dialogue if each granted that discussion about the idea of God is a complex and sophisticated matter.

[28] *The Sacrifices of Abel and Cain*, 13. 52 ff.; *Allegorical Interpretation*, 3. 21. 65 ff.

GIVING UNTO CAESAR: RATIONALITY, RECIPROCITY, AND LEGAL RECOGNITION OF RELIGION

Gary Watt

Introduction

This paper is concerned with the relevance of rationality to the processes according to which groups, or particular behaviours of persons and groups, are determined to warrant exceptional treatment in law on account of their religious character. It will be observed that these processes are inevitably dominated by the particular rationalities of those groups and persons ('state agents') which have the power of legal recognition. One feature of this domination is the tendency of state agents in so-called pluralist, secular, democratic states to avoid or to 'privatize' the religious aspect of claims. Even when a claim is put on a religious basis, state agents tend instead to identify the essential question to be one of criminality or bodily integrity or conflict of rights or private international law[1] and so forth. In this way, state agents deny recognition to religions and religiously motivated behaviours without apparently infringing their expressed liberal ideal of neutrality between religions. However, even where the failure or success of a claim is acknowledged to turn upon a decision about its religious nature, legal recognition will typically be denied if the nature of the claim fails to correspond to a conception of the religious recognizable to the relevant state agents. Only in very rare instances has the ideal of neutrality been pursued to the point of accepting the claimants' own conceptions of the religious without reference to those of the state. Consideration of one such instance will occupy a significant section of this study.

In the light of these observations the aim of this paper must be a modest one. It is not to suggest that neutrality in the legal recognition of religious claims is achievable, still less how it is to be achieved. On the contrary, it will be argued that there is no neutral vantage point from which to adjudicate between incommensurable rationalities, religious or otherwise.

---

[1] See R. Freeland, 'The Islamic Law of Marriage and the English Courts', January [1999] *Fam. Law.* 44–45 and *Lee* v. *Lau* [1964] 2 All ER 248.

Rather, the purpose of this paper is to suggest that political will should not be directed towards neutrality between competing rationalities, but towards reciprocity between them. It must be admitted that reciprocity, if put too high, will exclude those for whom the object of their religion is the object of their ultimate concern, but if it is put low enough it will not.

The precise form that reciprocity should take will be worked out in practice in inscrutably subtle ways; all that can be offered here are some theoretical limits to its scope as between state agents and religious claimants. Certainly it should not be as high as this: that the State should only recognize those religions which recognize the state for all purposes all of the time. This would deify Caesar. Neither should it be lower than this: that the State should require as a precondition of legal recognition that religious claimants have the capacity to determine, according to their own rationalities, where the line is to be drawn between behaviour required by faith and behaviour required by state.[2] Thus any group or person claiming or desiring legal recognition on religious grounds must give unto Caesar (the State), not a particular rationality, but a basic rational capacity.[3] If the State demands more than this, it does so not because reciprocity requires it, still less because neutrality requires it, but because according to its own rationality it ought to, and because it has the power to do so.

In summary, then, the aim of this paper is to argue that, in a world of incommensurable rationalities, neutrality is impossible and reciprocity is desirable, and that a truly liberal account of reciprocity would put reciprocity at a minimum level. The minimum level of reciprocity justifies rational capacity as a precondition of legal recognition of religion, but nothing more. If anything more is demanded, it is demanded by an exercise of power, and expressions of liberality, neutrality, and objectivity that suggest otherwise are suspect and should be resisted or appropriately qualified.

Orientation

The territory bounded by the ideas of law, rationality, and religion remains to a great extent uncharted. It follows that the responsible guide,

---

[2] In *Thomas v. Review Board of the Indiana Employment Security Division* 450 US 707 (1981) a Jehovah's Witness refused to participate in his employer's new business of manufacturing military components, and claimed unemployment benefits. The Supreme Court held in his favour, stating (at 715) that 'Thomas drew a line, and it is not for us to say that the line he drew was an unreasonable one.'

[3] K. Greenawalt draws a similar distinction between 'rational grounds' and 'rational capacities' in 'Religious Convictions and Law Making', (1985) 84 *Mich. L Rev.* 352 at 369–70. See also Mitchell's distinction between 'rational procedures' and 'the adoption of 'rationalist' positions'. He says that 'We are committed by the traditions of a free society to accepting the former; we are not committed to the latter' (B. Mitchell, *Law, Morality, and Religion in a Secular Society* (Oxford, 1970), 125).

when asked for directions to the centre, ought not to respond in the manner of that old joke: 'Well, I wouldn't start from here if I were you'! The guide will acknowledge what Rorty refers to as 'the contingent character of starting-points'.[4] Rorty suggests that, having identified our starting point, the journey from there should be informed by pragmatism, namely to ask 'whether we ought to keep our present values, theories, and practices or try to replace them with others'.[5] A pragmatic approach fits well with the present task, which is to demonstrate that legal recognition of religion will never be ideal, but that state agents can nevertheless be encouraged to develop it along new, improved lines. Where I depart from Rorty's brand of philosophical pragmatism is at the point where it sets itself up as an alternative article of faith, as a version of what Leigh refers to as 'Liberal Fundamentalism',[6] and thereby oversteps the in-built limitations of its own project. Rorty transgressed in this way when he prescribed that people should give up their hope of 'becoming attuned to the voice of God in the heart',[7] and should abandon 'obedience to permanent nonhuman constraints'.[8] And, elsewhere, that citizens in a secular state 'must abandon or modify opinions on matters of ultimate importance, the opinions that may hitherto have given sense and point to their lives, if these opinions entail public actions that cannot be justified to most of their fellow citizens'.[9] It would have sufficed for Rorty to have observed that citizens must modify their behaviour *or* face the consequences of the power of the State. Pragmatists should acknowledge that one contingent characteristic of political and philosophical starting points is that, for persons with a strongly held religious faith, ultimate hope in and obedience to God (to the transcendent, to the divine) are not contingent features of their starting point, but inalienable features of their humanity. The devout will say that 'Whenever any other interest conflicts with loyalty to God, one must decide for God.'[10] Aside from this reservation, the pragmatic exercise is a useful one, to which end let us identify the significant features of our starting point. They are as follows.

[4] R. Rorty, 'Pragmatism, Relativism and Irrationalism', in his *Consequences of Pragmatism (Essays 1972–1980)* (Minneapolis, 1982), 166.
[5] R. Rorty, *Objectivity, Relativism and Truth, Philosophical Papers*, vol. i (Cambridge, 1991), 41.
[6] I. Leigh, 'Towards a Christian Approach to Religious Liberty', in P. Beaumont (ed.), *Christian Perspectives on Human Rights and Legal Philosophy* (Carlisle, 1998), 38.
[7] Rorty, *Consequences of Pragmatism*, 166.
[8] Ibid.
[9] Rorty, *Objectivity, Relativism and Truth*, 175. Even one of Rorty's supporters has criticized the inconsistency between two of Rorty's observations: on the one hand, that there is no neutral basis on which to judge between religious and political rationality, and, on the other, that the political is to be preferred (Y. Huang, 'Political Solidarity and Religious Plurality: A Rortian Alternative to Liberalism and Communitarianism' (1994–5) 11 *J L & Religion* 499).
[10] R. M. Adams, 'The Problem of Total Devotion', in R. Audi and W. J. Wainwright (eds.), *Rationality, Religious Belief and Moral Commitment* (Ithaca, NY, 1986), 178.

First, that there is such a thing as legal recognition of religion. Indeed, where legal recognition of religion is a present social fact, as it is in the United Kingdom, any attempt expressly to abolish it is bound to fail, for the statute of abolition would of itself recognize religion, albeit detrimentally. It is, of course, frequently suggested that the recognition of religion for the purpose of exceptionally *beneficial* treatment should be abolished in certain contexts so as to achieve equality of religions before the law.[11] The gist of such arguments is almost invariably this: the State cannot treat all religions equally favourably, so it should treat none of them at all. Not only does this tend to privatize, and thereby to trivialize, religious claims,[12] but there are also grounds to believe that equality before the law is actually threatened by abolitionist approaches. Legal recognition of religion does not exist in a vacuum. In England, for example, the law extends greater protection on grounds of race than it does on grounds of religion. It therefore extends greater protection to claims that can be framed in religious and racial terms than it does to those that can be framed only as religious. Thus, whereas a Sikh might succeed in establishing a claim to a religious holiday on grounds of race, Christians and Rastafarians[13] would probably fail to do the same.

Secondly, that there is something called rationality, being descriptive both of particular rationalities and of the collective or family-set of all rationalities. *Any* individual or group process according to which meaning is ascribed to past or future experience or action is a rationality as that term is used here.[14] It must be stressed, however, that where 'meaning' is retrospectively ascribed, it need not import instrumentality, and the ascription of meaning to future action (i.e. motivation) need be instrumental in only a limited sense.[15] Thus meaning might be symbolic,[16] or one might determine[17] to act entirely altruistically or in complete obedience to

---

[11]   See A. Bradney, *Religions, Rights and Laws* (Leicester, 1993) in relation to blasphemy (p. 97) and employment (p. 115). See also Peter Edge, 'Charitable Status for the Advancement of Religion: An Abolitionist's View', (1995–6) 3 *Charity Law and Practice Review* 29–35.

[12]   A consequence that Bradney himself is keen to avoid; see A. Bradney, 'Faced by Faith', in P. Oliver, S. Douglas Scott & V. Tadros (eds.), *Faith and Law* (Oxford, 2000).

[13]   In *Dawkins* v. *Crown Suppliers (PSA)* 1993 IRLR 284 the Court of Appeal held that Rastafarianism was not a racial group.

[14]   Even to bind oneself by the toss of a coin is a form of rationality. Compare M. J. Wreen, 'Autonomy, Religious Values, and Refusal of Life-Saving Medical Treatment', (1991) 17 *J Med. Ethics* 124, 125 §III.

[15]   See M. Hechter: 'The hallmark of rational action consists in its instrumentality. Thus, people are rational to the degree that they pursue the most efficient means available to attain their most preferred ends. These ends may be material or nonmaterial. People are irrational when they pursue a course of action regardless of its consequences' ('Religion and Rational Choice Theory', in L. A. Young (ed.), *Rational Choice Theory and Religion* (New York, 1997), 148. See also J. Rawls, *A Theory of Justice* (Oxford, 1972), 142.

[16]   R. Nozick, *The Nature of Rationality* (Princeton, 1993), 138–9.

[17]   Determination has been contrasted with reason. See e.g. J. Finnis, 'On the Practical Meaning of Secularism', (1998) 75 *Notre Dame Law Review* 491, 498. But both are rationalities as that term is used here.

another's command.[18] This brings us to another idea that needs explanation, that of group rationality.[19] An individual's rationalities might coincide with those of others on account of upbringing[20] or training or other formative influences, or simply by choice. Crucially, one does not cease to be rational simply because one's own preferred ends happen to coincide with those of others. Indeed, paradoxically, the opposite may be true. If one really thinks for oneself, in the sense that one's rationality coincides with the rationalities of none other, one is liable to be labelled 'irrational' or 'mad'.

Thirdly, that rationalities are incommensurable. They are incommensurable in that they 'have no common measure except unity',[21] which is to say that no two rationalities can establish common ground without thereby establishing a third rationality distinct from the other two in some respect. It follows from this that no rationality can claim to be neutral in the adjudication of other rationalities.[22] Accordingly, labels such as 'irrational' and 'non-rational', which can only be applied from the privileged perspective of a particular rationality, should be avoided unless appropriately qualified by the fact of their particularity.[23] Belief in bodily resurrection, for example, might be described as rational,[24] irrational,[25] or non-rational,[26] depending upon one's perspective. It should be stressed,

---

[18] See Oliver *et al.* (eds.), *Faith in Law*, editors' introduction, p. 5.

[19] See R. Trigg, *Rationality and Religion: Does Faith Need Reason?* (Oxford, 1998), 19.

[20] E. Evans-Pritchard observed of the Zande tribesman that 'he cannot think that his thought is wrong' (*Witchcraft, Oracles and Magic among the Azande* (Oxford, 1937), 195; cited in E. Gellner, *Legitimation of Belief* (Cambridge, 1974), 156).

[21] *Oxford English Dictionary*, s.v. 'arithmetic'.

[22] This echoes M. J. Perry, 'Comment on "The Limits of Rationality and the Place of Religious Conviction: Protecting Animals and the Environment" ', (1985–6) 27 *Wm. & Mary L Rev.* 1067, 1068: 'No privileged standpoint exists from which to adjudicate among competing conceptions of rationality—no standpoint that does not itself presuppose a particular conception of rationality.' Perry was commenting upon K. Greenawalt, 'The Limits of Rationality and the Place of Religious Conviction: Protecting Animals and the Environment', (1986) 27 *Wm. & Mary L Rev.* 1011, 1047 n. 89, where Greenawalt had referred with approval to Putnam's view that 'there is no neutral conception of rationality to which to appeal' (H. Putnam, *Reason, Truth and History* (Cambridge, 1981), 136).

[23] Perry ('Comment on "The Limits of Rationality" ', 1069) cautioned Greenawalt to rethink and abandon 'the putative distinction between rational judgments and nonrational ones'. Greenawalt does, in fact, introduce a note of caution in *Religious Convictions and Law Making*, 404.

[24] From, *inter alia*, some Christian and historical perspectives. '. . . those who hold religious beliefs will not, for the most part, concede that these beliefs, together with their moral implications, are non-rational' (Mitchell, *Law, Morality, and Religion*, 123.) See also Stephen Rocker, *Hegel's Rational Religion* (London, 1995). Contrast Rawls's suggestion that 'comprehensive doctrines' which are 'unreasonable and irrational and even mad' should be contained (*Political Liberalism* (New York, 1993), p. xvi). Rawls is surely over-confident in his ability to identify those 'comprehensive doctrines' which are 'unreasonable and irrational and even mad'.

[25] From, *inter alia*, some scientific and semantic perspectives (if 'death' *defines* an irreversible physical process, physical resurrection of a dead body is, by *definition*, impossible).

[26] From, *inter alia*, some Christian, some historical, and some scientific perspectives.

however, that if it is established that rationalities are incommensurable, it isn't by the same token established that exclusive claims to absolute truth must be invalid.[27] It is established merely that there is no neutral perspective from which to establish the superiority of claims to truth and that therefore such determinations cannot be the business of secular state.[28] If this means that 'Rationality has become relativized and suspect,'[29] then so be it. This will not lead to anarchy. Even at an interdisciplinary colloquium on law and religion, 'rational, intersubjectively controllable discourse'[30] is still a possibility. Some rationalities will continue to prevail in practice. They will work because they attract consensus, and vice versa.[31] Fish was surely correct to observe that, in politics, 'visions of life will never be on a par but always exist in some hierarchical relationship of precedence and subordination'.[32]

Fourthly, although it is a feature of our starting point that certain legal, political, and bureaucratic rationalities dominate legal recognition of religion, the persons who employ or exhibit those rationalities are unlikely to employ them to the exclusion of every other available rationality. Thus an observant Jew who is also an academic and a judge will understand claims framed in correspondingly Jewish, academic, and legal ways. It is in this fact that will be found our best hope of influencing the process of legal recognition from without legal rationality as well as from within. Rationalities are incommensurable, but people do not tend to see the world from an entirely unitary rational perspective. A major flaw of rationalism has been to suggest that they do. Of course, it is sometimes suggested that people are unable to transcend their particular rationalities, but the opposite is in fact the case. Human functioning depends upon a rational capacity that is more basic than (or transcends) any particular rationality or set of rationalities. Provided a person has rational capacity, he or she has the potential to establish preferences between rationalities.[33] Even if the preference for some rationalities might be so ingrained as to be

---

[27] Contrast C. G. Hall, ' "Aggiornomento": Reflections upon the Contemporary Legal Concept of Religion', (1997) 28 *Cambrian Law Review* 7, 12: 'There is no one faith or way to salvation. So we shun the exclusivist fallacy.'

[28] John Locke made much the same observation more than 300 years ago: 'every church is orthodox to itself; to others erroneous or heretical . . . the controversy between these churches about the truth of their doctrines . . . is on both sides equal; nor is there any judge . . . upon earth, by whose sentence it can be determined' (*A Letter concerning Toleration* (1689), repr. in *John Locke: A Letter concerning Toleration in Focus*, ed. J. Horton and S. Mendus (London, 1991), 12; cited in S. Fish, 'Mission Impossible: Settling the Just Bounds Between Church and State', (1997) 97 *Columbia Law Review* 2255, 2258.

[29] J. S. Jensen, in J. S. Jensen and L. H. Martin (eds.), *Rationality and the Study of Religion* (Aarhus, 1997), 14.

[30] Ibid. 13.

[31] See Rorty's suggestion that truth is found in 'unforced agreement' (*Objectivism, Relativism and Truth*, 38).

[32] See Fish, 'Mission Impossible', 2307.

[33] See R. Nozick, 'Rational Preferences', in his *The Nature of Rationality*, 139–51.

practically unalterable, state agents should not assume rational incapacity on the basis only of strong expressions of support for particular rationalities. Groups and corporations might incapacitate themselves by words, but a finding of individual rational incapacity must be based on additional evidence.

Fifthly, coherence, like rationality, cannot be judged from a neutral position. It is tempting to assume that a state agent, even if incompetent to determine the truth of religious claims,[34] is nevertheless competent to identify internal inconsistencies and incoherence in others' religious rationalities. This temptation must be resisted, as indeed the courts themselves have sometimes acknowledged.[35] The presumption should be that if a process is employed to ascribe meaning to facts or experience, the very fact that it is employable in this way suggests that it is at least coherent for practical purposes. What is inconsistent to the judge might be celebrated as paradox by the religious believer, or might simply be the believer's best attempt to live out his beliefs given the contingency of his secular environment.[36] We can expect others' rationalities to display at least a minimum level of consistency,[37] but we should not imagine that state agents are competent to judge whether or not that minimum level has been satisfied. Open up the Bible at the first page and you will quickly discover statements which, on a first reading, do not cohere. For some they will never cohere, for others any apparent inconsistency is easily resolved or explained. So, for instance, a literal reading of the first chapter of Genesis reveals that 'day' was not created until the fourth 'day'.[38]

There is a sense, too, in which 'incoherence' is the very hallmark of a rational mind, by which I mean a mind capable of ascribing meaning to future experience. This is because experiences may be wholly novel to us, and might be so inconsistent with our existing rationalities as to be for the time being unable to cohere with them completely, yet we cannot deny the experience of our senses.[39] With this observation Plantinga has stated that

---

[34] See F. Newark, 'Public Benefit and Religious Trusts', (1946) 62 *LQR* 234, 245, and Rawls, *A Theory of Justice*, 216–18.

[35] In *Thomas* it was noted (at 714) that 'religious beliefs need not be acceptable, logical, consistent, or comprehensible to others in order to merit First Amendment protection'. And in *Thornton* v. *Howe* (1862) 31 Beav 14 a bequest to advance religious teachings was upheld even though the teachings were described (at 20) as 'incoherent and confused'. (Although, in the event, the gift was void under the Mortmain and Charitable Uses Act 1736.)

[36] Bradney provides an excellent illustration of this in his discussion of *Chauhan* v. *Ford Motor Company* (Employment Appeals Tribunal 1985: *Lexis*): Bradney, 'Faced by Faith'.

[37] C. Cherniak, 'Minimal Consistency', *Minimal Rationality* (Cambridge, Mass., 1986), pt. 1.5, pp. 16–18.

[38] Verse 14.

[39] Even Locke acknowledged that 'an evident *Revelation* ought to determine our Assent even against probability' (*An Essay concerning Human Understanding*, IV. xviii. 9). Although, crucially, Locke would not permit a revelation to prevail over any *certainty* of reason. He also acknowledged the rationality of relying upon our own memories: *Essay*, IV. xvi. 1–3.

'Coherence . . . is neither necessary nor sufficient for warrant nondefective-ness.'[40] The mind with rational capacity is therefore an 'open mind' inas-much as it is capable of ascribing meaning to new experience and new meaning to past experience. It is with this observation that we can see the potential for common ground between rationality in the sense of 'reason-ableness'[41] and rationality as a description of individual and group processes.

Legal Recognition

There may be some heuristic benefit in seeking to distinguish two aspects of legal recognition, although it should be stressed that in practice they intermingle almost to the point of indistinction. The first aspect identifies that religion is the essence of a claim, that the question to be asked is 'Religious or not?' To acknowledge this aspect is to acknowledge that state agents, and adjudicators in particular, do not merely answer questions, they also influence the choice of question. To paraphrase (and reverse) a famous dictum of Lord Templeman, the law calls a spade a spade even if the claimant calls it a fork.[42] The second aspect is actual consideration of the question 'Religious or not?'

As has already been said, the tendency to privatize religious claims means that the first aspect is often a negative or 'default' form of recogni-tion, which is to say that the question will usually only be framed as 'Religious or not?' when no other (perhaps less controversial) form of question readily presents itself. The second aspect might also involve a similar negative approach, whereby the state agent, having acknowledged that the religious nature of the claim is the central issue, nevertheless asks itself whether the rationality which is claimed to be 'religion' should actu-ally be recognized instead as 'philosophy',[43] 'ethics',[44] 'superstition', 'science', and so on. Although this negative approach is probably at play, it is rarely referred to. Instead the second aspect of recognition usually involves the state agent in the positive process of comparing the 'religious'

[40] 'Coherentism and the evidentialist objection to belief in God', in Audi and Wainwright (eds.), *Rationality, Religious Belief and Moral Commitment*, 138.

[41] For Rorty 'to be rational is simply to discuss any topic—religious, literary or scien-tific—in a way which eschews dogmatism, defensiveness and righteous indignation' (*Consequences of Pragmatism*, 37). Reason in this sense was also central to Locke's thesis (*Essay concerning Human Understanding*, IV. xix. 2).

[42] *Street* v. *Mountford* [1985] 1 AC 809, 819 E–F.

[43] Lord Denning MR thought that Scientology was 'more' a philosophy than a religion: *R* v. *Registrar General, ex parte Segerdal* [1970] 2 QB 697 at 707 C–D.

[44] In *Barralett* v. *AG* [1980] 1 WLR 1565 the objects of the South Place Ethical Society included 'the study and dissemination of ethical principles and the cultivation of a rational religious sentiment'. Dillon J, rejecting its claim to charitable status, held (at 1571) that, 'Religion, as I see it, is concerned with man's relations with God, and ethics are concerned with man's relations with man.'

claim with the state agent's own conceptions of the religious. This is achieved by means of definition, indicia, paradigms, and so on.

The following extract from the Rt Hon Lord Justice Balcombe's account of his own judicial deliberations illustrates how he was able to avoid parents' religious claims in favour of a child welfare approach:

One tries conscientiously to approach the problem with objectivity, but one is inevitably conditioned by one's own cultural and religious (or indeed lack of religious) upbringing. A frequent experience was to be asked to make a child of parents who were Jehovah's Witnesses a ward of court, so as to give permission for a blood transfusion when medical evidence was to the effect that an operation was urgently required. I did so without hesitation—as did my colleagues. And yet by doing so we were making a value judgment that the child's welfare was best served by allowing a blood transfusion which was contrary to the fundamental tenets of the religious faith in which the child was being raised. I have no regrets at the decisions which I then took because I believe then, as I believe now, that what I did was to promote the child's welfare as the law required. But others—particularly Jehovah's Witnesses—might take a different view.[45]

This passage clearly demonstrates the critical self-reflection to which every state agent should subject itself when presented with claims of a religious nature. His Lordship acknowledges his despair of neutrality and his hope of objectivity. Most instructive of all, however, is that which he does not acknowledge. Namely that (contrary to his Lordship's assumption) Jehovah's Witnesses simply could not have taken a different view to his Lordship, because the debate had already been framed in terms of the child's welfare *as the law required*. This problem of framing the question is, as has been suggested, the problem of the first aspect of legal recognition. The problem is an inevitable feature of the sociology of law, as was apparent to the poet who observed that 'the Law upholds the Law, the Gospel over-ruling'.[46] Similar observations have been made in more sophisticated ways since.[47] It is difficult to see how it can be addressed apart from by appealing to the capacity of state agents to imagine[48] rationalities beyond their own.

Given the intransigence of the first aspect of legal recognition, it is unsurprising that most commentators have generally directed their efforts to influencing the second aspect of recognition, to addressing the question 'Is this movement, group, church etc. (or is this particular practice) religious or not?' When coming to this question the assertion by state agents

---

[45] 'The Attitude of the Law to Religion in a Secular Society' (1990) *Law and Justice* 5–19, 14.

[46] Law v. Gospel, *The Poetical Works of James Thomson*, ed. B. Dobell (London, 1895) vol. i, stanza I.

[47] See e.g., N. Luhmann, 'The Unity of the Legal System', in G. Teubner (ed.) *Autopoietic Law: A New Approach to Law and Society* (Berlin, 1988), 12–13.

[48] See R. Nozick, 'Rationality's Imagination', in his *The Nature of Rationality*, 172–81.

that 'as between religions the law stands neutral'[49] rings rather hollow. It merely confirms that neutral treatment is reserved to those who have been recognized as religions. The reality is that the law never 'stands neutral', because it cannot stand neutral as between religious and non-religious rationalities.[50]

The second aspect of legal recognition is dominated by the use of definitions, paradigms, and indicia derived by analogy to paradigms.[51] Much academic effort has therefore been directed to the formulation of alternative definitions, indicia, etc. or to the suggestion that such devices should be abandoned entirely. Whichever of these alternatives will better curb the inherent domination of the particular state agent in the particular context is the one that should be chosen. There are problems, however, with both approaches. Definitions, indicia, etc. are invariably conservative and confused, and have a low predictive value, but to accept all claims indiscriminately might be mere condescension.[52] On balance, however, the inclusive approach empowers, even if it condescends, and is therefore to be preferred.

In *Church of the New Faith* v. *Commissioner for Pay-Roll Tax (Vic)*[53] the High Court of Australia (and Murphy J in particular) came, in the manner of its recognition of the Church of Scientology, as close to the point of ultimate self-restraint as any state agent can be expected to come.[54] (Or, given that the late Mr Justice Lionel Murphy QC was a confirmed atheist, we might say that it came as close to the point of ultimate condescension as any state agent can be expected to come.) It is appropriate, therefore, that the remainder of this paper should be taken up with consideration of the approach of Murphy J, and with the question 'Did he go too far?' It will be seen that the principle of reciprocity, which can operate even as between incommensurable rationalities, suggests that he did, not necessarily in relation to the particular case of Scientology, but in his general statements of the law.

[49] Per Cross J in *Neville Estates* v. *Madden* [1962] Ch. 832, 853.
[50] W. Sadurski, *Moral Pluralism and Legal Neutrality* (Dordrecht, 1990), 193: 'it is impossible to preserve neutrality between religious and non-religious beliefs whilst accommodating religions' claims for special treatment and recognition'.
[51] 'The five most important and least ambiguous expressions of religion in the world have been Judaism, Christianity, Islam, Hinduism, and Buddhism. To the degree that anything is called "religious", it must in some way be analogous to the sorts of forms that are found within these major traditions' (W. Herbrechtsmeier, 'Buddhism and the Definition of Religion: One More Time', (1993) 32 *Journal for the Scientific Study of Religion* 1, 6).
[52] See C. Taylor, *Multiculturalism and the Politics of Recognition* (Princeton, 1992), 70, cited in M. Malik, 'Faith and the State of Jurisprudence', in Oliver *et al.* (eds.), *Faith in Law*, 141.
[53] (1983) 49 ALR 65
[54] See also Wilson and Deane JJ: 'Regardless of whether . . . the practices of Scientology are harmful or objectionable . . . Scientology must, for relevant purposes, be accepted as "a religion" in Victoria' (ibid. at 108).

Here, then, are the salient points of his judgment:

Administrators and judges must resist the temptation to hold that groups or institutions are not religious because claimed religious beliefs or practices seem absurd, fraudulent, evil or novel; or because the group or institution is new, the number of adherents small, the leaders hypocrites, or because they seek to obtain the financial or other privileges which come with religious status. In the eyes of the law religions are equal . . . any attempt to define religion exhaustively runs into difficulty. There is no single acceptable criterion, no essence of religion . . . Some claims to be religious are not serious but merely a hoax . . . but to reach this conclusion requires an extreme case . . . Any body which claims to be religious, and offers a way to find meaning and purpose in life, is religious.[55]

Four ideas appearing in this dictum call for special consideration. They are absurdity, fraud, evil, and novelty. To what extent should these ideas influence the legal recognition of religious groups and practices?

ABSURDITY

Murphy J would have found in English[56] and US[57] law a long history of judicial statements supporting his caution against the refusal of legal recognition on the ground merely that the religion appears absurd to the judicial (or 'reasonable') mind. It is a caveat that should be preserved. The judgement that another's religious viewpoint is 'absurd' is just as problematic as the judgement that another's religious viewpoint is 'irrational' or 'incoherent'. None of these judgements is neutral, and judges should resist them. If they cannot resist them, they should qualify them.

FRAUD

Concepts such as 'insincerity', 'want of probity', 'dishonesty', and 'fraud' are in frequent use by state agents, and state agents therefore *assume* a competence to recognize them in the behaviours of their subjects. It follows that state agents might recognize a religious claim if it is sincerely and honestly held, but refuse recognition if they suspect that the claim was framed in religious terms purely (or primarily) in order to secure non-religious benefits. This suspicion will be hardest to dispel where the non-religious benefit is most recognizable to the state agents. Thus, if a patient refuses life-saving medical treatment on religious grounds, the court, being unable to recognize the benefits of the afterlife, would have no basis to doubt the sincerity of the claim. If, on the other hand, a Hindu worker cites his faith as a ground for refusing to join a trade union, the suspicion

---

[55] Ibid. at 85–6.
[56] See e.g. *Thornton* v. *Howe* (1862) 31 Beav 14, 18–20.
[57] See e.g. *US* v. *Ballard* (1944) 322 US 78, 86–7.

might arise that he was merely trying to avoid paying his subscription fees, and the worker might feel under pressure to pay an equivalent sum to charity in order to deflect such suspicion.[58] The suspicion of insincerity is likely to be nowhere greater than when a group applies for charitable status on religious grounds, given the fiscal benefits that accompany charitable status and the fact that no recognized religion ordains non-payment of taxes.[59] There are of course many other reasons, apart from tax relief, to explain why a group might wish to be recognized as charitable. The group will acquire an increased capacity to attract donations, a degree of legitimacy that might assist in the future litigation of more fundamental aspects of their faith, and perhaps even a symbolic equality with other faiths which might improve their 'market position' in the competition for souls. For all this, the temptation will remain strong to suspect that religious claims to charitable status are insincere. Two questions therefore arise: does sincerity matter, and are state agents competent to judge the sincerity of a claim?

It has been argued that sincerity matters because it transcends particular rationalities, that 'without it neither matrimony, nor science would work'.[60] Let us assume that sincerity does matter, because matrimony and science would at least work *better* with sincerity than without, the next question is whether state agents are competent to identify when it is present. The problem is that sincerity, like coherence, is to a great extent a feature of a rationality that can only be adequately understood from the internal perspective. To judge sincerity from the outside depends upon imagination and supposition. Imagine and suppose for a moment that the tables are turned somewhat, and a devout religious believer has been called upon to judge the sincerity of a legal advocate or, for that matter, an academic. How well would their subjects fare? How would he or she regard the fact that an advocate can press opposing sides of the same argument in different cases on consecutive days in court? Only if the observer accepts that the advocate's own canons are plausible is he or she likely to be satisfied of the advocate's sincerity. It is not suggested that state agents should exclude sincerity from their deliberations—it clearly has value—but they should be slow to reach conclusions about sincerity based merely on externally observed phenomena. Murphy J acknowledged that some claims to legal recognition of religion might be hoax, but suggested that this conclusion should be reached in only the extreme case. Crucially, he did not

---

[58] Compare the facts of *Chauhan*.

[59] See P. W. Edge, 'The Legal Challenges of Paganism and Other Diffuse Faiths', (1996) 1 *Journal of Civil Liberties* 216–29, 226. (Edge is no doubt correct when he suggests that the abolition of religious recognition in this context would have the merit of removing fraudulent claims, but it is equally true that the abolition of the welfare system would remove fraudulent claims to welfare benefits.)

[60] J. S. Jensen, in Jensen and Martin (eds.) *Rationality and the Study of Religion*, 14.

think that Scientology was a hoax religion, even though it began life in the 1950s professing to be a science[61] and apparently sought legal recognition as a religion only after the medical professional establishment had sought, and in some places secured, the prohibition of its 'therapeutic' practices.[62] Murphy J was, perhaps, sympathetic to the pressures on any novel rationality to frame itself in terms generally understood, be it as philosophy or science or religion, in order to attract general consensus. His is an extreme example of restraint (or condescension), but it is an example that all state agents would do well to measure themselves against.

EVIL

In 1976 the Goodman Committee on Charity Law reported that 'however liberal or tolerant a society may be it has the duty to determine what is and what is not beneficial to it; accordingly between good and evil it cannot be neutral. It must exclude from charitable status what it regards as evil just as it can and does outlaw what it regards as detrimental to its moral welfare.'[63]

What is most fascinating about this statement is the distinction that it seeks to draw between evil and immorality. If they are not coextensive for the recognition of charitable status, then what, it might be asked, distinguishes them? When does 'society' consider purposes to be evil that are not immoral, and vice versa? One answer that appears from the law of charity is whenever they are 'adverse to the very foundation of all religion'.[64] However, this answer reduces the problem of legal recognition not one iota. If one is told that one's purposes are not religious *because* they subvert all religion, one will simply reply that they are religious and that therefore that they cannot subvert *all* religion. This answer creates a circle that the newcomer will find very difficult to break in upon, but it is the only answer that appears from the cases. And if there is no real distinction between evil and immorality for the purpose of denying legal recognition to religious claims, one is then thrown upon the age-old problem of assumed morality. What do state agents *mean* when they say that religious purposes should be presumed beneficial unless 'they are subversive of all morality'?[65] Whose morality establishes the paradigm? At what point does variation from the paradigm become subversion? Is Islam subversive of all morality because it permits polygamy? Is Christianity subversive of all

---

[61] L. Ron Hubbard, *Dianetics: The Modern Science of Mental Health* (New York, 1950).

[62] See R. Wallis, 'Dianetics: A Marginal Psychotherapy', in R. Wallis and P. Morley (eds.), *Marginal Medicine* (London, 1976), 77–109 (esp. 91–3).

[63] National Council of Social Service, *Charity Law and Voluntary Organisations: Report of the Goodman Committee* (London, 1976), 24.

[64] *Thornton* v. *Howe* (1862) 31 Beav 14, 20. *Re Watson* [1973] 3 All ER 678, 688 e–f.

[65] Ibid.

morality because its central sacrament is the representational[66] drinking of blood and eating of flesh? Is Hinduism subversive of all morality because belief in reincarnation admits the theoretical possibility that a person might marry deceased members of their immediate family?

If the concept of evil has no identifiable meaning in this context, apart from 'the subversion of morality' and 'the subversion of religion', and if these concepts are circular, then one suspects that Murphy J was right to reject them all. There is, however, one explanation for the presence of 'evil' as a ground of exclusion which does not immediately appear from the cases. Namely, to exclude the possibility that perceived 'anti-religions' such as Satanism might otherwise be granted legal recognition. In the United Kingdom one can confidently assert that if Christianity is not a religion, then nothing is. It follows logically that any rationality which is set up in *diametric opposition* to Christianity cannot be recognized as a religion. It matters not that such a religion might satisfy all the definitions and indicia that are used to identify religions; if it is the polar opposite of the key paradigm of religion, it cannot be recognized as a religion. The problem with this approach is, yet again, a practical one. Christianity, although the predominant paradigm, is not the only one. And even if Christianity were the only one, how would we identify what Christianity is and what is its opposite? Apart from the case of a group gauche enough to seek legal recognition for its avowed purpose of 'subverting Christianity in every way' or 'subverting all currently recognized religions in every way' state agents should be wary of recourse to exclusion on the ground of evil.

NOVELTY

When, on 17 November 1999, the Charity Commissioners for England and Wales refused to register the Church of Scientology (England and Wales) as a charity, one of the reasons they gave was 'the relative newness of Scientology'.[67] The Charity Commissioners took the usual approach, namely to compare Scientology to certain 'characteristics of religion which can be discerned from the legal authorities'.[68] This analogy- and precedent-based approach is inherently conservative, but that is, of course, the way that lawyers and laws tend to operate.[69] When Murphy J recognized the 'Church of the *New* Faith', he operated in a quite different way. He noted, instead, that religious movements are often, by their very nature, innovative. He doubted if Christianity would have been quite so successful

---

[66] Or real if *transubstantiatio* is accepted.

[67] Charity Commission, *Decision of the Charity Commissioners for England and Wales: Application for Registration as a Charity by the Church of Scientology (England and Wales)* (17 Nov. 1999), p. 1 §2 (b).

[68] Ibid. 13.

[69] See Edge, 'The Legal Challenges of Paganism', 223.

if it had been dismissed as novel. (Although, curiously, he omitted to acknowledge that thousands were martyred precisely because it *was* dismissed as novel, and that the success of Christianity arguably owed rather more to state persecution than it did to state recognition.) The charity commissioners were not, however, concerned solely with the religious character of Scientology. Their principal concern was, as ever, to determine whether the pursuit of its purposes would be beneficial to the public. In some cases the history of a group might be too short to make that assessment accurately, and the novelty of the group will for that reason be a relevant factor. However, one imagines that such cases will be rare and one doubts that novelty per se should be a factor in refusing to recognize Scientology, which, after all, described itself as a church as long ago as 1955.

To conclude this section we can say that the approach taken by Murphy J to the ideas of absurdity, fraud, evil, and novelty is enlightening, albeit prompted by his own professed secularism. However, his analysis can be criticized for what it omitted to address, in that it neglected to identify reciprocity as a necessary precondition to legal recognition. That will be the subject of the next section.

Reciprocity

One has to be careful when resorting to the idea of reciprocity that it does not descend to what Fish has called 'juvenile payback—"You won't give respect to us and we won't give it to you, so *there*" '.[70] As was stated in the introduction to this paper, reciprocity justifies a requirement of rational capacity, but it does not require that the citizen should hold a particular rationality. Rawls identified the link between capacity and reciprocity in the following terms: 'The only contingency which is decisive is that of having or not having the capacity for a sense of justice. By giving justice to those who can give justice in return, the principle of reciprocity is fulfilled at the highest level.'[71]

The problem with this vision of 'justice capacity' as opposed to 'rational capacity' is that it stacks capacity in favour of a particular rationality, Rawls's own liberal rationality, instead of allowing the religious believer to draw their own line. What is more, 'justice', for Rawls, imports the neutrality of the original position, and thus the distinctive merits of reciprocity as a pragmatic solution are lost by throwing it back upon the supposedly objective ideal of neutrality.[72]

---

[70] See Fish, 'Mission Impossible', 2283.

[71] Rawls, *A Theory of Justice*, 511.

[72] Naturally enough, some commentators regard this as a key *virtue* of Rawls's argument. See e.g. S. L. Darwall, *Impartial Reason* (Ithaca, NY 1983), 17. It should also be borne

It is Rorty, struggling free of neutral objective idealism, who suggests a more satisfying link between reciprocity and rationality. He presents a vision of a society in which

one's ultimate loyalty would be to the larger community which permitted and encouraged this kind of freedom and insouciance. This community would serve no higher end than its own preservation and self-improvement, the preservation and enhancement of civilisation. It would identify rationality with that effort, rather than with the desire for objectivity. So it would feel no need for a foundation more solid than reciprocal loyalty.[73]

Rorty is right to identify the preservation (and promotion) of the State as something that the State must protect,[74] but a maximal level of reciprocity is not required to achieve it. Certainly, there is no justification for prescribing that one's 'ultimate loyalty' must be to the State, or to society. To the devout religious believer such a statement is nonsensical. A minimum level of reciprocity would require nothing more than rational capacity.

Rational Capacity

'Rational capacity' is the capacity to ascribe *some* meaning to experience and action, and should be contrasted with 'rationality' which is used here as a description of *particular ways* of ascribing meaning to experience and action.[75] Thus it is not required that the State should actually be recognized, but only that the claimant be capable of recognizing state. The State should refuse legal recognition to claims where such recognition would entail recognition of rational incapacity. An entire religious group or corporation could, in theory, be denied legal recognition if its constitution or objects clause listed as one of its purposes 'the refusal for all purposes for all time to obey any demand of state', or some equivalent. In practice this is most unlikely, and rational capacity will probably only have a practical relevance in cases in which a particular religious practice arises for consideration. Consider, for instance, the Jewish practice of celebrating the feast (*mishteh*) of Purim. On that one night each year the observant Jew is exhorted to do a great many things, one of which is to 'drink until he can no longer tell the difference between "cursed be Haman" and "blessed be

in mind that the debate is ongoing as to whether reciprocity 'underlies or is derived from the concept of justice' (L. C. Becker, *Reciprocity* (London, 1986), 4). It must be doubtful that this version of the chicken-and-egg debate will ever be resolved. See, generally, B. Barry, 'Justice as Reciprocity', in E. Kamenka and A. Erh-Soon Tay (eds.), *Justice* (New York, 1980).

[73] See Rorty, *Objectivity, Relativism and Truth*, 45.

[74] '. . . the attitude of the law both civil and criminal towards all religions depends fundamentally on the safety of the State and not on the doctrines or metaphysics of those who profess them' (*Bowman* v. *Secular Society Ltd* [1917] AC 406, 467 per Lord Sumner).

[75] See n. 3 above.

Mordecai" '.[76] In other words, to drink until evil cannot be distinguished from good. Or, to put it another way, to drink until the mind lacks the capacity to ascribe meaning, by which is meant the capacity to make and maintain such distinctions as are necessary to provide a basis for choice between alternative meanings. If an extended liquor licence were sought in order to facilitate this aspect of the feast of Purim, and if the licence could not be granted on any non-religious ground, the religious nature of the celebration could not *of itself* justify the grant of the licence. This conclusion is unavoidable because the state agent would otherwise be required to recognize a particular religious practice which, even according to the claimant's own terms, is designed to create rational incapacity.

The example of Purim is chosen because the legal recognition of that festival will never, in practice, turn upon that one aspect of the festival, but what of those religions which ordain the use of drugs on a regular basis? In such cases it is suggested that the state agent should not recognize the religious character *of the drug-taking* for legal purposes, if the taking of the drugs is capable of undermining rational capacity and is intended by the taker to undermine rational capacity. This would mean that those who take proscribed drugs for religious reasons should not be exempted on religious grounds from the usual penalties that attend indictment and conviction for such use, always assuming that the drug is one which can destroy (or, perhaps, fundamentally impair) rational capacity. It would also mean that drugs counsellors who are dismissed from their employment because they use a proscribed drug should not be reinstated merely because the use of the drug is ordained by their religion.[77] However, it will seldom be a straightforward matter to determine whether the drug was intended by the taker to undermine their rational capacity. 'Intention' for this purpose should certainly include cases where rational incapacity is the professed desire or design of the drug-using devotee. In practice, however, one imagines that state agents would also include cases where rational incapacity, though claimed to have been unwished-for, was, in the opinion of the state agent, an inevitable, foreseeable consequence of the religious drug-taking or a significant risk inherent in the drug-taking, which risk the devotee had taken recklessly. Rastafarianism is a religion which ordains the use of the drug *Cannabis indica* ('ganja')[78] and is therefore a case in point. The state ('Babylon') should not presume that the use of ganja destroys rational capacity (it might actually increase it),[79] but if the conclusion were reached

[76] *Talmud, Megillah 7b.*
[77] Compare *Employment Division* v. *Smith*, 494 US 872 (1990), a case on similar facts involving members of the Native American Church who used peyote as a sacrament of their faith.
[78] E. Cashmore, *Rastaman* (London, 1979), 178.
[79] Ganja is considered by some users to produce 'lucidity' of mind. See K. Bilby, 'The Holy Herb: Notes on the Background of Cannabis in Jamaica', in R. Nettleford (ed.),

that the use of ganja is able to undermine, and was intended to undermine, rational capacity, Rastafarians would not be excepted on religious grounds from the criminal repercussions of cannabis use. In contrast, there is nothing in the principle of reciprocity between rationalities that would require a Rastafarian to wear a motorcycle crash helmet if to do so would necessitate the cutting of his dreadlocks in disobedience to Jah. If the state agent will not amend the regulations[80] so as to except Rastafarians from that rule, it is because it wishes to exercise its *power* to refuse legal recognition to that particular religion or religious practice. It is a power that might be challenged on the ground, if none other, of inequality.[81]

Aside from the drugs issue, an approach based on rational capacity clearly has something to say about claims brought by the mentally ill and by infants[82] and perhaps even by those whose rational capacities have been overborne by the oppressive influence of others.[83] There is not the space here to consider these in depth, but caution should be urged in each context so as to avoid as far as possible the unjustified privileging of particular rationalities, and if this cannot be avoided, then state agents should at least be alert to the particularized, compromised nature of the outcomes they endorse. If we do not heed this caution, there is a danger that we will merely replace the error of calling people 'mad' with the error of calling people 'irrational'.[84]

Conclusion

In relation to the drawing of boundaries between religion and State, Fish has suggested that 'that there can be no justification apart from the act of power performed by those who determine the boundaries and that therefore any regime of tolerance will be founded by an intolerant gesture of exclusion'.[85] Nevertheless, the aim of this paper has been to suggest that there is, in theory, a minimum level at which exclusion (the denial of legal

Rastafari (Kingston, Jamaica, 1985), 89; cited in N. J. Savishinsky, 'African Dimensions of the Rastafarian Movement', in N. S. Murrel, W. D. Spencer, and A. A. McFarlane (eds.), *Chanting down Babylon* (Kingston, Jamaica, 1998), 131.

[80] The Secretary of State has the power to do so; see Road Traffic Act 1988 s. 16(1).

[81] Sikhs wearing turbans are exempted from the requirement to wear a crash helmet (s. 16(2)).

[82] Children are a difficult case and deserving of a paper in their own right. A child's own claim can be admitted if the child has rational capacity (See *Re W (a minor)* [1992] 4 All ER 627 at 637). The problem is how far to recognize a parent's religious claim to treat their child in such-and-such a way. One suspects that the approach of Balcombe LJ in response to this problem is fairly typical (see 'The Attitude of the Law to Religion').

[83] See *Re T (An Adult: Refusal of Treatment)* [1993] Fam 95. Reciprocity will have something to say on the 'brain-washing' practices (so-called) that are attributed to certain religious movements, but there is not the space to say it here.

[84] See P. Wilson, 'The Law Commission's Report on Mental Incapacity: Medically Vulnerable Adults or Politically Vulnerable Law', (1996) 4 *Medical Law Review* 227, 247.

[85] See Fish, 'Mission Impossible', 2261.

recognition) is justified and is not merely the product of power. The fact that rationalities are incommensurable means that every idea of tolerance in the sense of neutrality will be flawed in principle, but it does not mean that every idea of tolerance in the sense of reciprocity must be similarly flawed. The State is justified in its refusal to recognize religious claims to exceptional treatment in law where such recognition would entail recognition of rational incapacity. Why? Because reciprocity requires that the state should not recognize that which is utterly incapable of recognizing it. Accordingly, the State should not recognize the right of a 5-year-old child to refuse life-saving medical treatment on religious grounds, not because the State must act as *parens patriae*, not because the child's particular rationality can be adjudged to be *wrong*, but because the 5-year-old child, by dint of minority, lacks the rational capacity necessary to draw a line between behaviour required by religion and behaviour required by State. However, even in this relatively uncontroversial example one cannot escape the fact that, ultimately, it is the state agents who have the power to fix reciprocity at a level deemed appropriate to them. Were we to absent entirely the paternalistic exercise of power, the child would simply be allowed to die. Likewise, all religious use of drugs would be permitted where the user claimed enhanced lucidity, and no amount of coercion by others would vitiate expressions of belief. At the edge of this abyss of anarchy it is the principle of reciprocity that holds us back, and we should have no objection (unless we prefer anarchy) to the State using power to establish reciprocity at the level justified by principle. Finding that level is the hard part, but a pragmatic moving towards it is easier. No academic comment upon the relevance of rationality to the legal recognition of religion can do much more than attempt to identify where the principled exercise of power ends and the unprincipled begins; and then to suggest in which direction we should move in order to restrain the unprincipled exercise of power. This paper has probably done more of the former, but hopefully it has done a little of both.[86]

[86] I wish to acknowledge the assistance I derived from informal discussions with colleagues in relation to this paper. I am especially grateful to Ralf Ragowski, John Harrington, Gavin Anderson, and the members of the Warwick Postgraduate Legal Theory Group led by Ken Foster.

POLITICS AND SOCIOLOGY: NEW RESEARCH AGENDAS FOR THE STUDY OF LAW AND RELIGION

Anthony Bradney

Introduction

The study of the relationship between religion and law in the United Kingdom has a long but, until recently, almost invisible history within British university law schools. Holdsworth's essay 'The State and Religious Nonconformity: An Historical Retrospect' was, for example, published as long ago as 1920.[1] Moreover, although an awareness on the part of legal academics of the potentially troubled relationship between British legal rules and religious sensibilities can sometimes seem to be a relatively recent phenomenon, in 1954, nearly half a century ago, Hanbury, in his introduction to Crowther's book on religious charitable trusts, commented, 'Fifty years have passed since Maitland told us that "Religious liberty and religious equality are complete". But this was true then, and is still true, only of the criminal law. As a statement of the law relating to charitable trusts, his remark can rank merely as an optimistic anticipation.'[2]

Long before this Blackstone had observed the way that religion can lead to unequal treatment in the law, stating in his *Commentaries* that 'The people, whether aliens, denizens, or natural-born subjects, are divisible into two kinds; the clergy and the laity,' and then noting that the clergy 'have . . . large privileges allowed them by our municipal laws'.[3] Yet this long history of writing about law and religion, of which the above are but illustrative examples, is not matched by a similar quantity of production. For many decades the writing that existed was spasmodic and disjointed. Equally, each essay or article that was published was a single item, neither developing a more general theme of argument by an individual author nor contributing to any wider line of intellectual development. Particular points were made, and authors and academic interest then moved on to

---

[1] W. Holdsworth, 'The State and Religious Nonconformity: An Historical Retrospect' (1920) 36 *Law Quarterly Review* 339.

[2] C. Crowther, *Religious Trusts* (Oxford, 1954).

[3] W. Blackstone, *Commentaries on the Laws of England*, 16th edn. (London, 1825), i. 376.

other concerns which were usually perceived as being more pressing. Furthermore, not only was there a failure to develop a discrete and sustained debate about the proper relationship between religion and legal rules, exploring the nature of religious liberty in the United Kingdom, but such articles and books as were produced failed to have an impact upon other more established areas of academic discourse. Crowther's book, for example, notwithstanding the fact that it was the only detailed account of religious charitable trusts in its time, received scant attention in the then current mainstream legal analyses of charitable trusts.[4] Writing was done, but the publications that resulted were pebbles that, having been cast into a pond, caused no ripples.

The fact that the Current Legal Issues Colloquium in 2000 is devoted to the relationship between religion and law is one piece of evidence that is indicative of a change in the place that this subject has within the research agendas of British university law schools. Further weight for the argument that the analysis of the relationship of religion and law within British legal systems now has a more substantial place within the British legal academy than it once did comes from the various specialist conferences that have been held on the subject and from the panels that have been devoted to the area at the annual conferences of both the Socio-Legal Studies Association and the Society for Public Teachers of Law.[5] The final two decades of the twentieth century saw the publication of a number of monographs devoted to this area of research.[6] The same period also saw the publication of a wide range of articles in a variety of journals. More people are now writing more about religion and law and, in some cases, this writing constitutes not just an occasional interest but is, rather, central to their research careers.[7]

Interest in the relationship between law and religion is likely to increase further with the implementation of the Human Rights Act 1998. How effective that Act will be in protecting religious sensibilities is open to question given, among other things, the relatively underdeveloped European Court of Human Rights jurisprudence on Article 9.[8] However,

[4] Thus, for example, the relevant edition of *Lewin on Trusts* makes no reference to Crowther (W. Mowbray, *Lewin on Trusts*, 16th edn. (London, 1964)). Crowther was not reviewed in either the *Law Quarterly Review* or the *Modern Law Review*.

[5] Thus, for example, a two-day conference on the subject was held Imperial College in Jan. 1999, the 1998 SPTL conference had a panel on religion and law in the main section of the conference, and panels on religion and law are a regular feature of SLSA annual conferences.

[6] See e.g. St John Robilliard, *Religion and the Law: Religious Liberty in Modern English Law* (Manchester, 1984); A. Bradney, *Religions, Rights and Laws* (Leicester, 1993); and C. Hamilton, *Family, Law and Religion* (London, 1995).

[7] Thus, for example, see Peter Edge's appointment as Reader in Law and Religion at Oxford Brookes University.

[8] See further A. Bradney, 'Religion and Law in Great Britain at the End of the Second Christian Millennium' in P. Edge and G. Harvey (eds.), *Law and Religion in Contemporary Society* (Aldershot, 2000).

even if the Act does not meet all or even many of the aspirations of some of its supporters, since it is the first Act to give a general right of action in the British domestic courts in relation to religious freedom, it is bound to increase litigation on this point. With this increase in litigation, there will be both an increase in academic literature which is designed to facilitate that litigation and an increase in academic literature which is written in response to the newly rising quantity of reported cases. An area of study to which law schools were once largely indifferent is thus now one where there is active and growing interest.

In the light of the change of the place of law and religion in the law school's agenda this essay will attempt to do two things. Firstly, it will seek to identify the focus of concern in relation to recent writing about religion and law in the United Kingdom, analysing the nature of the questions asked in the literature and seeking to establish both the intellectual foundations for the debate and the concerns that this debate has intended to foster. Research into religion and law, like any other area of research, does not exist in a vacuum. It finds its place in the confluence of detachment and integration which typifies the academy.[9] In the case of research originating in the law school the form of the research is influenced by the law school's historical relationship with legal practice, the law school's relationship with other parts of the university, and the law school's broader relationship with social, political, and cultural forces within British society. The precise place of religion and law in this confluence is of importance, influencing the role that the research can play. Secondly, the essay will argue that because of the direction that research into religion and law has taken there are both inherent limitations to, and misconceptions within, some of the debates that have been carried on in Great Britain hitherto: limitations and misconceptions that have both diminished the value of some of the work that has already been done and also diverted attention from questions which could have been asked and which are, arguably, of more fundamental significance than those questions which have, thus far, formed the centre of debate. This essay will contend that to date research into religion and law has mainly concerned itself with identifying incidences where law hampers the free exercise of religion or areas where, it is argued, legal rules can be created so as to allow such free exercise.[10] Law has been seen as a tool of social engineering which can 'solve' the problem of how religious freedom is to be facilitated within a modern

[9] P. Bourdieu, *Homo Academicus* (Cambridge, 1988), 40–62.

[10] This is not to say that other forms of work do not exist. Analysis of canon law is, for example, a long-standing tradition within English legal scholarship (see G. Moore, *English Canon Law* (Oxford, 1967) which is also being carried on in the current day (see N. Doe, *Canon Law in the Anglican Communion* (Oxford, 1998). Moreover, there is work which pursues very different themes from either those that I am examining here or other traditional analyses of law (see e.g. D. Cooper, 'Talmudic Territory? Space, Law and Modernist Discourse', (1996) 23 *JLS* 529).

or late modern state. This essay will argue that, in making this assumption, this kind of legal research has ignored the possibility that the relationship between law, modernity, and some religions should not be seen as a problem that is capable of solution but, instead, should be regarded as an area of intractable conflict, where the possibility of communication, let alone contact, compromise, or concord, between law and religion is prevented by the existence of competing epistemologies and ontologies.[11]

The Origins of Research into Law and Religion

For much of the twentieth century British university law schools, in the main, tacitly accepted Maitland's proposition 'religious liberty and religious equality are complete'.[12] Having noted this 'fact' the dominant view was that there was then nothing further left to say. Books, essays, and articles that were written on the subject were occasional acts of dissent from this general position. However, the silent response to these works has underscored the strength of the dominant view.

Given the long history of research noted above, any attempt to point to a particular moment when published research into law and religion became something consequential within British universities is doomed to failure. Any piece of work has its precursors and they too have their ancestors. However, the work of Robilliard and Poulter both seem to exemplify a change in the academy's attitude towards the relationship between religion and law. Robilliard, with his book *Religion and the Law: Religious Liberty in Modern English Law*, was the first person to devote a monograph explicitly to the relationship between religion and law in the United Kingdom. This book is the most important work by him on religion and law but it is, nevertheless, just one part of a small body of writing by him devoted to analysing the relationship between religion and law. Robilliard's work, with its wide-ranging treatment of issues relating to religion and law, is an implicit refutation of Maitland's assessment of the attainment of religious liberty and equality.[13] A non-exhaustive list of issues treated by Robilliard in which he sees possible conflict between British legal rules and the precepts of religions includes blasphemy and offences against religion, religious discrimination and unfair dismissal in

---

[11] The argument in this essay is that the importance of much previous research is diminished of its intellectual background. That which is of diminished value is still of value. This essay is not seeking to argue that such research has no value, nor that such research should not continue to be done. To say that a thing has limitations does not mean that it should not be done; to say that there are other questions to ask, even to say that these other questions are more important, does not mean that lesser questions should not still be put.

[12] See Maitland's statement cited in Crowther in n. 2.

[13] Sometimes it is an explicit refutation of the proposition. See Robilliard, *Religion and the Law*, p. ix.

labour law, and religious conscience and the criminal law.[14] Poulter's work, on its face, seems less germane to the subject matter of this essay. His early books and articles are explicitly concerned with the relationship between ethnic minorities and the law.[15] Even the title of his final book, *Ethnicity, Law and Human Rights*, seems to point more towards the analysis of the position of minority rights than any overt concern with the relationship between religion and law.[16] However, closer examination of his work, particularly his later work, suggests that it does indeed form part of the growing body of literature on law and religion, with his last book including, among other similar examples, chapters entitled 'Jews: The Controversy over Religious Methods of Slaughter' and 'Muslims: The Claim to a Separate System of Personal Law', and earlier works also discussing in detail the position of religious minorities.[17] Just as Robilliard's book forms part of a wider body of work, so Poulter's books are also only part of a much wider range of publications. In his case, issues raised in this larger corpus of work include Muslim headscarves in schools, blasphemy and racial hatred laws, and *talaq* divorces.[18] Again in Poulter's work, as in Robilliard's, there is an implicit refutation of the view that there is nothing of consequence to say about the relationship between religion and law in the United Kingdom.

Two things link the manner of analysis in the work of Robilliard and Poulter. First, neither writer was, in the purest sense of the word, a doctrinal writer. The body of work that they produced is not devoted to the purely internal analysis of the law using traditional theories of legal reasoning, searching for underlying legal principles, that Lord Goff sees as being the task of the doctrinal academic.[19] Indeed, had either been a doctrinal writer, in this pure sense, it seems likely that they would never have turned their attention to the study of law and religion in Great Britain. Because British law has historically lacked any wide-ranging statutory protection of religious liberty and freedom and because, more recently, British law has rarely, overtly referred to religion or religious

---

[14] 'Offences against Religion and Public Worship' (1981) 44 *MLR* 556; 'Discrimination and Indirect Discrimination: The Religious Dimension', *New Community* 8, (1980), 261; and 'Religion, Conscience and the Law' (1981) 32 *NILQ* 358.

[15] See e.g. S. Poulter, *English Law and Ethnic Minority Customs* (Butterworth, 1986); *Asian Traditions and English Law: A Handbook* (London, 1990).

[16] S. Poulter, *Ethnicity, Law and Human Rights* (Oxford, 1998).

[17] P. II of this book, entitled 'Case Studies in Relation to Particular Groups', contains six chapters, five of which deal with religious groups.

[18] 'Muslim Headscarves in School: Contrasting Legal Approaches in England and France' (1997) *Oxford Journal of Legal Studies* 43; 'Towards Legislative Reform of the Blasphemy and Racial Hatred Laws' (1991) *PL* 317; and 'Ethnic Minority Customs, English Law and Human Rights' (1987) 36 *ICLQ* 589.

[19] R. Goff, 'The Search for Principle', *Proceedings of the British Academy*, 69 (1983), 169. I use the past tense because Robilliard has left academic life for practice and Poulter died in 1998.

issues there has been little domestic case-law which has touched upon the matter.[20] A doctrinal writer thus finds comparatively little primary material which can serve as a basis for their writing. A further link between the work of Robilliard and Poulter is the fact that both have an explicit policy orientation to their writing. Their books and articles are concerned with issues of individual and social justice; with how law should treat people and how people should be able to live.[21] These points should neither be over-emphasized nor misinterpreted. In much of their work both Poulter and Robilliard largely restricted themselves to discussion of mainstream legal material in their work; their work may not be have been doctrinal but their sources were mainly statutes and cases.[22] In this sense, their writing is in keeping with the mainstream traditions of academic writing in British university law schools both at the time that they were writing and in the decades that had preceded their work. However, what they sought to do was not to clarify the stream of legal logic to be found in the primary material that they used or to render that material more tractable for the practitioner, as had been the historical practice of academics in British university law schools, but, rather, to examine its social effect and to compare that effect with what they thought ought to be the case.

In many senses Poulter and Robilliard's work is typical of a significant movement in the academic culture of British law schools in the period in which they were working. The 1970s onwards saw a change in the character of research work being done in British university law schools with an increasing disenchantment with purely doctrinal work.[23] At the same time law schools began to distance themselves from the legal professions, seeing their work not just as a service to the profession but, variously, as part of an attempt to secure wider social justice or to contribute to the advancement of knowledge.[24] The form that Robilliard and Poulter's work takes, not being purely doctrinal but at the same time not being wholly, or even largely, situated in some other non-law discipline, is characteristic of much work that came to be, and continues to be, done within the law school. Such work was, and is, 'socio-legal' both in the sense that the writers

[20] I use the term 'British law' to refer to the legal systems in Scotland on the one hand and England and Wales on the other hand. The situation in Northern Ireland has in recent decades been rather different. To say that there has been 'little domestic case-law' is, of course, a relative statement. The law reports reveal dozens, perhaps hundreds, of relevant cases. However, the numbers are slight when compared with the numbers of cases on even relatively obscure topics in areas such as contract, tort or company law.

[21] Thus, for example, see Robilliard, *Religion and the Law*, 37–41, and Poulter, *Ethnicity, Law and Human Rights*, ch. 10.

[22] This is not true of Poulter's final book which contains extensive references to works of history, sociology, theology, and philosophy.

[23] See e.g. J. Bridge, 'The Academic Lawyer: Mere Working Mason or Architect', (1975) 91 *LQR* 488, 496–7.

[24] See e.g. Z. Bankowski and G. Mungham, *Images of Law* (London, 1976).

refused to restrict themselves to the traditional tools and questions of doctrinal legal analysis and in the sense that their work was 'concerned with the policy of the law, and sometimes even the politics of the law'.[25]

The pattern established in the work of Robilliard and Poulter continues to be seen in much of the writing about religion and law published in the present day. A contemporary example of this form of writing is to be seen in the interim report of the inquiry into the extent of religious discrimination in England and Wales commissioned by the Home Office.[26] Although this report's main focus is on an empirical investigation into the incidence and nature of religious discrimination using mainstream social science methods, chapter 5 is devoted to an examination of the relevant law in this area. This legal treatment presumes the desirability of legal intervention, makes no attempt to justify the necessity of religious liberty or equality or even specify what this might mean, and merely records the legal rules which the authors see as being central to the area under review. References in this chapter of the report are largely limited to primary legal material.

The fact that much writing has been directed towards the protection of religious feelings has been both an implicit refutation of Maitland but, at the same time, it has also been an attempt to create policy changes that would make his proposition correct. However, this does not mean that writers have uncritically accepted the demands of all religions, creating a situation where the claim of religious freedom would act as a trump card, defeating all other arguments. On the contrary most writing in this area has sought to establish the 'proper' limitations of religious freedom. Thus, for example, in analysing decisions of the court in relation to child custody issues Walsh sought to distinguish religions where it would be appropriate to deprive adherents of custodial rights with respect to their children from other non-traditional but nevertheless acceptable religions whose parents should be treated in the same way as those parents belonging to mainstream religions.[27] However, both arguments about limitations to religious freedom and analyses of the way in which British legal systems have failed religious adherents continue the form of the analysis already noted in the work of Robilliard and Poulter; in both areas the arguments fail to make any substantial connection with any literature written outside the law school.

The fact that writers on religion and law have tended not to look outside the law school for intellectual stimulation to, and support for, their

---

[25] C. Campbell and P. Wiles, 'The Study of Law in Society in Britain' (1975–6) 10 *Law and Society Review* 547, 550. This is not to say that either Poulter or Robilliard would necessarily have characterized their work as being socio-legal.

[26] 'Religious Discrimination in England and Wales', <http://www.multifaithnet.org/projects/religdiscrim>.

[27] B. Walsh, 'Religious Considerations in Custody Disputes', (1988) 18 *Family Law* 198, 199–200.

writing is not because they are or were wholly unaware of the inherent limitations in using consideration of municipal law as a basis in itself for policy formulation. A critical analysis of judicial decisions or statutory provisions, especially if it is also a hostile analysis, plainly needs some assistance in establishing why those decisions or statutes are inappropriate. To show internal inconsistency in reasoning in decisions where religion is raised as an issue in either judgments or statutes, as some writers have done, of itself says nothing about which line of reasoning, if either, should, in the future, consistently be followed. Such an argument can show that a policy choice has to be made but not which choice is correct. Justifying policy choices, which are inevitably also value choices, needs something more than an examination of legal logic. However, British writers concerned with the analysis of religion and law frequently have tended to turn not to other academic disciplines in seeking this support but to supranational legal systems to which the United Kingdom is legally committed. Thus, for example, both Poulter in his wide-ranging analyses of matters relating to religion and law and Lee in his analysis of the particular issue of the *Satanic Verses* affair turn to international law as a source for the foundation for their arguments.[28] Other writers, in analysing the relationship between religion and law in the United Kingdom, have chosen to focus on cases which have come before the European Court of Human Rights.[29] The use of international law as a tool for explicitly or implicitly critiquing national law is indicative of an awareness of the need to move outside law in order to ground argument, yet, at the same time, it seems to betray an ambivalence about this necessity, with the shift of attention being not to something beyond law but, instead, to another, perhaps greater, law.

The use of international law as a vehicle for grounding policy arguments raises two problems: one general, whenever international law is used in debate in this way, and one specific to the use of international law in the examination of the relationship between religion and law. First, the dictates of international law are, in themselves, merely examples of policy choices, not justifications for those choices. International law creates a legal obligation for the United Kingdom, but whether that obligation is one which it is either politically expedient or ethically proper to acknowledge or act upon at any particular point in time is a separate matter. International law, like municipal law, is, in this sense, simply law. Whether it should be obeyed and whether it should be reformed are questions which can and should always be asked. In principle there is no reason why

---

[28] See e.g. S. Poulter, in a review of my own book *Religions, Rights and Laws*, in (1994) 110 *LQR* 159–60, and S. Poulter, 'Ethnic Minority Customs, English Law and Human Rights', (1987) 36 *ICLQ* 589. See also S. Lee, *The Cost of Free Speech* (London, 1990).

[29] See e.g. P. Cumper, 'A Path to a Bill of Rights', (1991) 141 *NLJ* 100.

the value choices that are inherent in international law should necessarily be superior to those that are to be found in municipal law. To show that there is an inconsistency between the demands of international law and those of municipal law is merely yet another example of inconsistency in legal logic in the same way that there can be inconsistencies of legal logic within municipal law. Where a conflict arises between the two, international law necessarily trumps municipal law only in terms of its own theory of validity. Some other source, outside international law, is needed to show why at a particular point in time the dictates of international law are of imperative concern. Secondly, international law, again like municipal law, is the result of the particular moments of its history. These moments have both their consequences and their causes. Thus Pogany writes that the 'growing recognition of individual and collective rights, in international law, reflects an essentially liberal outlook, characterised by political, social and religious pluralism, and a spirit of tolerance. This is, in effect, merely the ascendant political philosophy of Western (and increasingly Eastern) Europe and North America translated onto the international plane.'[30]

Among the long list of the consequences and causes for the particular moments of international law figures religion. Reisman writes that international law is imbued with 'the value assumptions of ... European, predominantly Christian, civilization'.[31] International law has made its own religious choices and there are in both its institutions and its structure of rights preferences for an ontology which is much closer to Christianity than it is to any other religion.[32] There is nothing that is necessarily objectionable about the place of Christian values in international law; there is still less anything that is surprising about the relationship between Christianity and international law. International law, like any other legal system, must make value choices and, given the politics of international law over the past centuries and the influence that Western nations have had on those politics, Christianity was always likely to exert more of an influence on international law than other religions. Moreover, too much must not be made of the thread of Christianity that runs through international law. International law is a long way from being a canonical law system. Nevertheless, a problem remains. The place of Christianity in

---

[30] I. Pogany, 'Religion, the Palestinian–Israeli Conflict and International Law', in A. Bradney (ed.), *International Law and Armed Conflict* (Stuttgart, 1992), 97.

[31] M. Reisman, 'Islamic Fundamentalism and its Impact on International Law and Politics', in M. Janis (ed.), *The Influence of Religion on the Development of International Law* (Dordrecht, 1991), 107.

[32] Exemplified, for example, in discussions about the right to freedom of religion in international law where 'there was an irreconcilable conflict between the Muslim states which were not prepared to accept the claim that all individuals were entitled to change their religious beliefs and others for whom this was an essential prerequisite' (M. Evans, *Religious Liberty and International Law in Europe* (Cambridge, 1997), 188).

international law is not *necessarily* objectionable but it *may* be objectionable. On analysis such Christian value choices as are to be found in international law may be seen to be appropriate and acceptable, but this analysis needs to be done so that this can be shown; and it may be that this cannot be shown. Prima facie, a legal system which purports to treat of all religions but which holds just one of those religions closer to its heart than it does the others may be seen to be objectionable. In this context, to use such a tainted source as an unproblematic basis for justifying policy choices with respect to issues relating to religion and legal rules in municipal law seems to be a move of questionable validity.

Even if the arguments above are correct and international law in fact lacks the intellectual weight that some writers have seen in it, using it does at least delineate the source of a writer's critique of domestic law. Why a writer thinks that the existing situation in municipal law is wrong and why the writer favours a particular new situation over other possibilities is made apparent. In the case of much writing on religion and law this source of critique is never made manifest either in the individual article or elsewhere in the author's work. Underlying the work is no more than an implicit and rather vague attachment to a liberalism that holds that religious freedom is desirable.[33] That this is unsatisfactory in itself is plain; that which is unexamined or underexamined may turn out also to be that which is false. More particularly, in relation to the analysis of religion and law, writing which does not make manifest the source of its critique leaves unanswered (and indeed unasked) a range of important questions. Why is religious freedom or equality important? Is religion something which is inherently valuable or is its value contingent on what the religion promotes either socially or individually?[34] Perhaps the most pressing question, in the light of the current Home Office research on religious discrimination, is what is the relationship between religious discrimination and forms of discrimination that have already been the subject of legislation. In the present era race, sex, and disability are seen as being unchosen human conditions for individuals, and individuals are therefore seen as being deserving of protection from discrimination because of such matters. Does religion take the same form, being for the believer an unchosen part of their identity, and do believers thus deserve the same legal protection as

---

[33] This would be true of, for example, a number of early articles on law and religion that I published. (See e.g. A. Bradney, 'Religious Questions and Custody Disputes', (1979) 9 *Family Law* 139–41 and 'Arranged Marriages and Duress', (1984) *Journal of Social Welfare Law* 278–81, (1985) *Journal of Social Welfare Law* 2.) I attempted to remedy this defect with ch. 2, 'A Statement of Method', in *Religions, Rights and Laws*, which sets out what I believe to be adequate foundational arguments for a schemata of rights pertaining to religious belief and religious freedom.

[34] This is not to say that these issues have not been examined; see e.g. T Macklem, 'Reason and Religion', in P. Oliver, S. Douglas Scott, and V. Tadros (eds.), *Faith in Law* (Oxford, 2000).

exist in relation to other parts of the human condition?[35] Questions such as these lurk in the background of much writing on religion and law, but until they come much more into the foreground, no matter what degree of diligence authors show, there will always be a limit to the progress that such writing can make.

As noted above, the implementation of the Human Rights Act 1998 will almost necessarily increase the amount of writing about the position of religious minorities in relation to a whole series of public regimes which can be seen as acting to their disadvantage. If this writing is to make substantial progress, if it is to do more than rehearse old arguments in new contexts, it will need to make explicit and clear connections with the theories that have, hitherto, largely implicitly underpinned the discourse. Here the challenge is not to change a research agenda, which has long been essentially a concern with the politics of law, but, rather, by making more manifest the basis of that politics, to identify more clearly both that which motivates us and that which divides us in that politics.

Religion, Modernity, and Law

Atiyah has commented on the way in which much British legal scholarship and analysis has tended to be pragmatic in character, concentrating on particular instances rather than on broad theoretical sweeps.[36] Thus commentators who work within the mainstream traditions of the law school must turn to individual examples of religions to ground their arguments. Looking at religion and law thus becomes not looking at religion and law, but looking at religions and laws and, more usually than not, looking at particular religions and particular laws.

Commentators looking at the contemporary situation in the United Kingdom can choose the religions they use for their examples from a rich variety of religions that are currently to be found within the United Kingdom. Yet, notwithstanding the dozens of religions that could be selected, writing concerned with religions and laws in the United Kingdom has frequently looked at only a very small number of the religions. The fact that discussion is limited to only a small number of religions raises the question, is this process of selection fortuitous, being either a matter of chance or at most no more than a matter of fashion within academic circles, or does the process of selection reflect wider pressures?

---

[35] Thus, for example, Dummett notes that, for the believer, religion is obligatory and given A. Dummett, 'Race, Culture and Moral Education', *Journal of Moral Education*, 15 (1986), 12–13. To accept such a view conflicts with those philosophical standpoints that see choice as being an inherent part of human nature and the acceptance of individual responsibility for those choices as being of the essence of ethics. (See A. Bradney, *Religions, Rights and Laws*, ch. 2).

[36] P. Atiyah, *Pragmatism and Theory in English Law* (London, 1987).

Religions that seem to recur in debate about religion and law in the United Kingdom include most notably Islam and New Religious Movements.[37] In relation to New Religious Movements, out of the many such religions, once again some examples seem to be selected more often than others: Scientology, the Unification Church, and, from an older generation, Jehovah's Witnesses.[38] What, if anything, do these religions have in common? What, if anything, separates them from other religions that could have been used as examples in debate? Conversely, there are religions that rarely feature in debate. In some cases the reasons for this absence is readily apparent. One would not, for example, expect to see the Church of England serve as a focus for debate on the difficulties that the law creates for the committed believer. The Church of England is the established church in England and its tenets of faith do not run counter to the mores of the country to the degree that is the case with some other religions. However, Hinduism, to take one example, is as 'alien' to the United Kingdom as is Islam, yet features far less frequently in the debate. Why does the debate largely ignore some religions?

Initial analysis suggests that the differences between the various religions that are commonly used in debate are more obvious than their similarities. Islam, for example, is the largest non-Christian religion within the United Kingdom, with a community membership of between 1 million and 1.5 million and an active membership of 580,000.[39] Figures for the number of members of individual New Religious Movements are somewhat speculative, but they rarely exceed the tens of thousands of British believers in any instance, and in many cases they will be much smaller.[40] Some large non-Christian religions have received scant attention in the literature. Hindus in the United Kingdom, for example, have a community membership of between 400,000 and 550,000 and an active membership of 155,000, but there seems to have been as much interest in the 600 members of the International Society of Krishna Consciousness, a variant of the Hindu faith largely but not entirely favoured by Western converts, as there has been in writing about the problems of more mainstream Hindu groups.[41]

---

[37]   At this point in this essay I am including in the term 'debate' not just published writing but also conference and seminar papers.

[38]   I am not, of course, suggesting that these are the only examples used. Rather, I am arguing that these examples recur more frequently than others.

[39]   'Religious Discrimination in England and Wales', paras. 3.4 and 3.6. See also P. Brieley and H. Wraight, *UK Christian Handbook 1996/97* (London, 1995), 283 and 284.

[40]   In 1995 the two biggest New Religious Movements in Great Britain were the Church of Scientology with 150,000 members and Jehovah's Witnessses with 131,000 members (Brieley and Wraight, *UK Christian Handbook*, 280 and 278). The Church of Jesus Christ of Latter-Day Saints (which many would not classify as a New Religious Movement) had 171,000 members (ibid. 279). No other New Religious Movement had more than 10,000 members, and in many cases membership was numbered in hundreds.

[41]   For figures on adherents, see 'Religious Discrimination in England and Wales'; Brieley

In part, writing about religion and law has plainly been driven by the interests of those outside the university law school. One source of these wider concerns has been the interests of those writing about the sociology of religion. Collections containing essays from both those working within the sociology of religion and those working within the field of law are usually unbalanced, with those from law finding themselves in the minority.[42] In such cases, the essays from legal scholars are, in effect, commentaries on issues and areas that have been raised for the authors by the wider group of sociologists of religion with whom they are working. The reasons for the choice of religion, by those from within the law school, lie wholly in the intellectual concerns of others outside their discipline.[43] Equally, writing about religion and law partially reflects the wider practical politics of some religious groups. The reason for writing about Islam may lie, in part, in the large number of Muslims that live within the United Kingdom who are, moreover, proportionately more likely to be active in their faith than many others in Christian faiths.[44] A large community that takes the tenets of its faith seriously generates a large number of problems that can be the subject of analysis. However, there are other faith groups who have a similar proportionate relationship between active and community membership.[45] The degree to which the Islamic community is politically organized and the way in which that organization manifests itself may also be important. To take only two of the more obvious examples, the Muslim community's response to the publication of *The Satanic Verses* involved concerted effort by a number of Islamic organizations as did the drive to gain state funding for Islamic schools.[46] It is not that the political

and Wraight, *UK Christian Handbook*, 282. Thus, for example, Poulter's chapter 'Hindus: A Dispute about Worship at a Temple' in his book *Ethnicity, Law and Human Rights* is largely devoted to ISKCON's dispute about the use of Bhaktivedanta Manor. On ISKCON, see K. Knott, *My Sweet Lord* (Wellingborough, 1986). This is not to say that there has been no writing about the position of Hindus. See e.g. W. Menski, 'Legal Pluralism in the Hindu Marriage', in R. Burghart (ed.), *Hinduism in Great Britain* (London, 1987).

[42] See e.g. S. Palmer and C. Hardman (eds.), *Children in New Religious Movements* (New Brunswick, NJ, 1999*)* and B. Wilson and J. Cresswell (ed.), *New Religious Movements: Challenge and Response* (London, 1999).

[43] Nevertheless, since the legal scholars have agreed to undertake the essays in the collection, they must also have taken on the intellectual concerns around which the collection revolves. These concerns, however, did not necessarily originate with them but, rather, with those outside the law school.

[44] Thus, for example, the research report 'Religious Discrimination in England and Wales' lists the community membership of Muslims as being between 1m. and 1.5m. while the active membership is listed as 500,000, i.e. 33% to 50% of the total (para. 3.4 and 3.61). By comparison the number of Catholics in the country in 1995 was 4,418,500, but the weekly mass attendance was only 1,192,000, i.e. 25% of the total (Brieley and Wraight, *UK Christian Handbook*, 250).

[45] The respective figures for Hindus are 400,000 to 550,000 as community membership but only 155,000 as active, i.e. 39% to 28% of the total membership ('Religious Discrimination in England and Wales').

[46] See e.g. S. Qureshi and J. Khan, *The Politics of the Satanic Verses* (Leicester, 1989) and J. Halstead, *The Case for Muslim Voluntary-Aided Schools* (Cambridge, 1986).

organizations of the Islamic community have created problems but, rather, that the organizations have taken problems and issues that already existed and have thrust them into the public arena; private griefs, through their work, have become public disputes. The move from the private to the public brought the issues to the attention of the academic community. In some instances members of the academic community became part of that effort to move the issues from being private, local affairs to matters of more general concern. Thus, for example, Poulter was one of those who was involved in debates about the publication of *The Satanic Verses* organized by the Commission for Racial Equality and the Runnymede Trust.[47] He was also one of the co-authors of *Islamophobia: A Challenge for us All*.[48] Here the argument is not that there is anything illicit or disreputable in either the political organization of the Islamic community, the attention that academics have paid to the work of such organization, or even the involvement of academics in their work. Instead, the argument is that the focusing of academic attention on a particular religion arises, at least in part, because of that political organization, not because the community is in any greater difficulties than other religious communities who either are not politically organized or have chosen to operate politically in a different manner.[49]

The way in which academic debate is swayed by influences from outside the academy, or by influences from outside that part of the academy which is ostensibly responsible for the literature which is being produced, is not necessarily a harmful thing. For those interested in the intellectual development of debate within the law school, and particularly for those who see merit in interdisciplinary work, evidence that the law school is influenced in its arguments by other academic disciplines will be seen in a positive light. For those who believe that the academy should, in whole or part, be concerned with political and legal reform, evidence that it is reacting to community politics will once again be seen positively. However, there is a danger inherent in these influences. The earlier part of this essay argued that part of the success of the last two decades of the twentieth century lay in the way in which spasmodic individual production became a sustained arena of academic debate. If debate is to be about *law and religion* it has to focus not on those religions which may be of intellectual interest in

---

[47] S. Poulter, 'Cultural Pluralism and its Limits: A Legal Perspective', in his *Britain: A Plural Society* (London, 1989).

[48] (London, 1997).

[49] Thus, one might contrast the Sikh campaign for a right not to wear crash helmets with the Muslim campaign with respect to *The Satanic Verses*. The former campaign generated little academic attention. Thus, for example, in his monograph on religion and law Robilliard devoted only part of one paragraph to the subject (*Religion and the Law*, 124) although Poulter dealt with the matter at greater length in his final book (Poulter, *Ethnicity, Law and Human Rights*, ch. 8). The Muslim campaign, a much more public affair, was, and continues to be, the subject of a considerable literature. (See e.g. Lee, *The Cost of Free Speech*, above.)

other areas of academic debate or be of political concern to some parties, organizations, or government, but on those which are of vital interest in the debate about law and religion.

A more fundamental factor may link those religions that figure pre-eminently in debate about religion and law than those factors mentioned above. The belief systems of frequently cited religions overtly reject not just late or post-modernity but modernity itself.[50] They insist upon detailed and total explanations of the world, prescribing behaviour and dominating the value horizons of their adherents.[51] As such, both their mode of thinking and the conclusions that they draw from that thinking are antithetical to that which lies at the heart of modernity. 'Modernity is essentially a post-traditional order . . . [where] most aspects of social activity, and material relations with nature, [are subject] to chronic revision in the light of new information and new knowledge.'[52] The legal rules of the United Kingdom spring from and are for this modernity. Modernity infuses not just what the rules dictate but the way in which the rules articulate the world. Reason, the promise of rationality, underwrites the law. Judges have a duty to give reasoned judgments and reason must justify the judgment.[53] But these religions are pre-eminently religions of faith. There

---

[50] Most religions reject modernity in the sense that they regard faith as having more value than (or equivalent value to) rationality. However, a religion that, for example, sees the frequency of earthquakes as a compelling argument in discussions about the nearness of the end of the world has a rather different relationship to that of a religion that, for example, takes most of its priests and bishops from the United Kingdom's better established universities. (Thus, for example, of the forty-two bishops and archbishops of the Church of England listed in *Dod's Parliamentary Companion* only four do not mention a degree from a traditional university in their entry in *Who's Who*; seven note that they hold a Ph.D. and two that they have a M.Phil. (*Dod's Parliamentary Companion 2000* (London, 2000), 366. It is religions of the former type that tend to take centre-stage in British arguments about religion and law.

[51] Rushdie captures this difference between the world-view of such religions and the modernity and post-modernity that he sees in the contemporary world with his much criticized description of Mahound 'spouting rules, rules, rules, until the faithful could scarcely bear the prospect of any more revelation . . . It was as if no aspect of human existence was to be left unregulated, free' (S. Rushdie, *The Satanic Verses* (London, 1988), 363–4). For a critical account of this aspect of Rushdie's work, see Z. Sardar and M. Wyn Davies, *Distorted Imaginations* (London, 1990), 158–65). Such rules are a long way from late or post-modernity. Thus, for example, of late modernity Giddens writes, 'radical doubt filters into most aspects of day-to-day life' and later, 'The more we reflexively "make ourselves" as persons, the more the very category of what a "person" or "human being" is comes to the fore' (A. Giddens, *Modernity and Self-Identity* (London, 1991), 181 and 217); while on post-modernity Bauman asserts 'Postmodernity has dashed modern ambitions of the universal and solidly grounded ethical legislation' (Z. Bauman, *Postmodern Ethics* (Oxford 1993), 223). But the true believer would accept neither Giddens nor Bauman.

[52] Giddens, *Modernity and Self-Identity*, 20.

[53] H. Ho, 'The Judicial Duty to Give Reasons', (2000) 20 *Legal Studies* 42. Of course judgments always fail to be reasoned, being built on faith and including great leaps in argument (W. Murphy and R. Rawlings, 'After the Ancien Regime: The Writing of Judgements in the House of Lords 1979/80' (1981) 44 *Modern Law Review* 617, (1982) 45 *MLR* 34). At the same time, judgments are always certain but also always subject to appeal, repeal, and

is thus a conflict not just between the demands of law and the demands of faith but between their ontologies.

These conflicts raise questions about the presumptions that underlie much of the mainstream approach to law and religion in Great Britain over the last three decades. The promise of this approach is a resolution to the position of the believer in the polity. Yet the fact of the conflict between the ontologies suggest that such a resolution is not possible. On this argument because these religions stand outside modernity their believers therefore stand outside the law.[54] Analysts of religion and law, on this view, thus need not to consider the possibilities of social engineering but to analyse the structures that divide society and forbid the possibility of conversation.[55] Statutes designed to improve the position of believers can do no more than camouflage the rifts within society. The Human Rights Act and other similar legislative acts are but placebos, calming the patient only if they fail to realize the form of their illness and the nature of the medicine. Here the challenge is to ignore, at least in the first analysis, the politics of law and religion and consider instead its sociology.

Conclusion

The signs of general improvement in British legal scholarship during the last decade of the twentieth century were one of the more hopeful features of British academic life. Wilson's comment that 'The words "English legal scholarship" though high sounding have a similar function to the words "disposable paper cup". Each adjective strengthens the message that one cannot expect much in terms of long term quality or utility from it'[56] still resonates over a decade after it was first made. Yet there are also now abundant examples of attempts to make solid and substantial connections with the major intellectual debates of the times, thus infusing legal scholarship with the vitality that is to be found elsewhere.[57] For research into law

revision; for believers in religions of this type, however, their beliefs are eternal, unchangeable, and unverifiable except through faith.

[54] See further A. Bradney, 'Faced by Faith', in Oliver *et al.* (eds.), *Faith in Law*.

[55] King argues that this position of conflict is not stable and that 'secular communication systems' which include law 'are firmly pushing religions [such as Islam] in the direction of a harmonization and secularization of their dogmas and of a trivialization which confines their distinctiveness to rites and rituals or to what we now call "culture" ' (M. King, 'The Muslim Identity in a Secular World', in M. King (ed.), *God's Law versus State Law* (London, 1995), 114.

[56] G. Wilson, 'English Legal Scholarship', (1987) 50 *MLR* 818, 819.

[57] Thus, for example, Goodrich, writing about the development of critical legal studies in Great Britain, observes the 'moves from early, Marxist inspired dismissal of law as an epiphenomenon, the expression of purely bourgeois rights, to recent evaluations of eros and alterity, of other laws and laws of the other, as the critical counterpoint to the intellectual sclerosis of the legal form' (P. Goodrich, 'The Critic's Love of the Law: Intimate Observations of an Insular Jurisdiction', (1999) 10 *Law and Critique*, 343, 344.

and religion the future lies in two directions. Firstly, that writing which concerns itself with attempts to facilitate a life of faith needs to consider why and whether such changes are desirable. Secondly, other writers, or the same writers in another mood, need to consider the structural relationships not between law and religion in society but between differing forms of religion and differing forms of law in differing forms of society, seeking not a solution to a problem but, rather, a description of a situation. Both this politics of law and religion and this sociology of law and religion will necessitate a clearer and more consistent use of the methods and concepts to be found elsewhere in the university.

LAW AS A RELIGIOUS ENTERPRISE: LEGAL INTERPRETATION AND SCRIPTURAL INTERPRETATION

Steven D. Smith

We live in a time that, according to social science prophecies over the last century or so, is supposed to see the decisive triumph of secularism;[1] and we in the academy are determined to honour the prophecies, even if the rest of humanity stiff-neckedly refuses to cooperate. James Boyd White notes that

in the academic world we tend to speak as though all participants in our conversations were purely rational actors engaged in rational debate; perhaps some people out there in the world are sufficiently benighted that they turn to religious beliefs or other superstitions, but that is not true of us or, if it is true, we hide it, and it ought not be true of them. Ours is a secular academy . . .[2]

These secular commitments powerfully influence—and restrict—the perspectives available to us in understanding law. Thus, Thomas Grey is more reporting than asserting when he says that in explaining and justifying law 'no ultimate mysteries [may] be invoked to legitimate its exercise—no transcendent authority, no Kierkegaardian leap of faith'.[3]

But this restriction may stand in the way of an accurate understanding of what law really is. For example, a special practice of interpreting texts is plainly central to law; and so legal scholars have naturally devoted enormous effort to understanding legal interpretation—how it works, what its presuppositions are, and so forth. These scholars could hardly overlook

---

[1] José Casanova explains: 'The theory of secularization may be the only theory which was able to attain a truly paradigmatic status within the modern social sciences. In one form or another, with the possible exception of Alexis de Tocqueville, Vilfredo Pareto, and William James, the thesis of secularization was shared by all the founding fathers: from Karl Marx to John Stuart Mill, from Auguste Comte to Herbert Spencer, from E. B. Tylor to James Frazer, from Ferdinand Tönnies to Georg Simmel, from Émile Durkheim to Max Weber, from Wilhelm Wundt to Sigmund Freud, from Lester Ward to William G. Sumner, from Robert Park to George H. Mead. Indeed, the consensus was such that not only did the theory remain uncontested but apparently it was not even necessary to test it, since everybody took it for granted' (J. Casanova, *Public Religions in the Modern World* (Chicago, 1994), 17).

[2] J. B. White, 'Response to Roger Cramton's Article', (1987) 37 *Journal of Legal Education* 533.

[3] T. C. Grey, 'The Constitution as Scripture', (1984) 37 *Stanford Law Review* 1, 6. Grey was discussing judicial review specifically, but his assumption derives from the legal culture at large.

the many similarities between the ways in which lawyers and judges interpret *legal* texts and the ways in which religious leaders and believers interpret what they regard as *sacred* texts. But the insistence on viewing modern law as a secular enterprise has typically forced these scholars to treat such similarities as merely intriguing 'analogies' or parallels, and hence to disavow any truly 'religious' quality in legal interpretation. In this vein, Bruce Ackerman suggests that 'a model of interpretation which can do justice to the complexity of American judicial practice . . . bears some striking resemblances to other great interpretive enterprises—most notably those that derive from the major religious traditions'. But Ackerman quickly adds that there is not and cannot be any sort of actual *faith* involved in legal interpretation: 'Most obviously, the American tradition is born in the spirit of the Enlightenment.'[4]

In my view, this disavowal in deference to secularism is unfortunate because it prevents us from acknowledging the real character of legal interpretation, and hence of law. Moreover, contrary to the intentions of secular scholars like Ackerman, the disavowal leaves legal interpretation, and hence law, looking bizarre and irrational. Religious interpretative practices 'make sense' only on religious presuppositions; deprived of the underlying faith, such practices seem merely silly or superstitious. If legal interpretation lacks any comparable faith, then it has no warrant or excuse for persisting in comparable practices. So law without faith comes to seem silly, or superstitious, or 'mindless'.[5]

In the domain of religion and religious scholarship, people seem to understand this point: when they abandon the faith that animated particular interpretative practices, they typically relinquish the practices as well. But in law it seems that as secular pretensions have become more insistent, the devotion to practices best understood as an expression of faith has if anything grown more intense. Ironically, it may be that a visitor to the university today will find a flourishing if embarrassed and self-effacing religious faith not so much in theology faculties or departments of religious studies as in law schools.[6]

In this paper I want to develop these suggestions by discussing three features that unite scriptural and legal interpretation. Firstly, both kinds of interpretation treat texts as repositories of *hidden or esoteric meanings*. Secondly, both kinds of interpretation treat texts as *authoritative* for our own decisions and conduct. Thirdly, both kinds of interpretation treat a diversity of seemingly disparate texts as forming a *harmonious, univocal whole*. Each of these features seems sensible *if* we suppose that the texts

  [4] B. Ackerman, *We the People: Foundations* (Cambridge, Mass., 1991), 159–60.
  [5] See S. D. Smith, 'Law without Mind', (1989) 88 *Michigan Law Review* 104.
  [6] This possibility is considered at length in J. Vining, *From Newton's Sleep* (Princeton, 1995).

under interpretation are the expressions of a divine or superhuman author; conversely, without some such assumptions the practices are an embarrassment.

At the outset I need to address one problem of method that might provoke an objection to my argument. I have been talking about 'scriptural interpretation' and 'legal interpretation' in the singular, as if each were a unified, coherent practice with an agreed method for interpreting texts. But of course there are millions of people who engage in these enterprises, and they do not all employ the same methods; often they disagree vehemently not only over the meanings of specific texts but also over *how* to go about interpreting texts. So how can I talk about common features uniting scriptural and legal interpretation?

My response is that though this is a real problem, it should not be exaggerated. Despite differences and disagreements, there are common features that can be observed in the way religious believers, ancient and modern, have treated sacred texts, at least within what are sometimes called the Jerusalem-based religions. And the same can be said, I believe, about at least a good deal of legal interpretation in the Anglo-American legal tradition. Our most passionate hermeneutical disputes may occur within agreed frameworks that we scarcely notice, but that to a detached observer not immersed in our culture would seem curious and remarkable and far more significant than the issues we argue about. Thus, James Kugel observes that 'the more one contemplates the whole corpus of ancient biblical interpretation, the more it becomes clear that, despite the great variety of styles and genres and even interpretive methods involved, underlying it all is a common approach, a common set of assumptions concerning the biblical text'.[7] With qualifications, the same is true, I think, in law. To be sure, prevailing practices growing out of a common law tradition have been repeatedly and powerfully criticized, especially over the last century, by legal theorists of various sorts; but as I have argued elsewhere,[8] the prevalence and force of such criticism simply makes it all the more remarkable that our legal practices have in fact maintained so much continuity with the past.

Still, for purposes of a short presentation the huge number of interpreters and schools of interpretation *is* a difficulty; space limits as well as severe constraints of competence force me to be selective. So this will be my method: in discussing the features of scriptural interpretation, I will draw primarily on a notable book I have quoted from already—Harvard professor James L. Kugel's *The Bible as it Was*. Kugel's study deals with the interpretation of Hebrew Scripture, mostly in the period between 200 BCE and 100 CE. I think the features he discerns in that context are

---

[7] J. L. Kugel, *The Bible as it Was* (Cambridge, Mass., 1997), 17.
[8] S. D. Smith, 'Believing Like a Lawyer', (1999) 40 *Boston College Law Review* 1041.

common in religious interpretation, and I will occasionally and very briefly notice similar features in other contexts; but I make no pretence of offering any general survey. Likewise, in discussing the features of legal interpretation, I will make frequent reference to the jurisprudential ideas of Ronald Dworkin, though again I will supplement the discussion with references to other sources. Dworkin's work is especially valuable for this purpose, I think, not only because he is probably the most prominent jurisprudential thinker of the last few decades (and one with a foot on both sides of the Atlantic) but also because his jurisprudence reflects a sustained effort to give a deep account of the way law actually works in the English and American systems. I realize that Dworkin has many critics—and indeed I make a conscientious effort to criticize Dworkin in nearly everything I write—but even if these criticisms are persuasive (as I think many of them are), they do not necessarily deprive Dworkin's jurisprudence of value as an explanatory account of the mindset implicit in Anglo-American law.

The Unity of Scriptural and Legal Interpretation

James Kugel observes that although biblical texts have always required interpretation, in the post-exile Jewish experience a number of features combined to give special importance to the practice of interpretation. For one thing, re-establishing a political and religious community after lengthy interruption was a challenging task, and 'Political differences among different groups within the returning exiles' prompted the competing groups to bolster their positions with sacred scripture; consequently, 'the Jews of this period turned to their own ancient writings to legitimate their political views'.[9] For various reasons the Jews of this period also emphasized the importance of 'law'—a law that was contained in the old texts.[10] As a result, cultural authority gravitated to a class of people specially learned in the arts of interpreting those texts. So 'the interpreters of Scripture enjoyed an increasing prominence and authority in the period following the Babylonian exile'; indeed, the interpreters 'ultimately came to encroach on territory that had previously belonged to another, rather different figure: the biblical prophet', whose authority did not derive from any supposed competence in reading and understanding ancient texts.[11] These developments (all of which have obvious modern parallels, I think, at least in American legal history) combined to support a practice of scriptural interpretation exhibiting reliance on four underlying assumptions.

THE ASSUMPTION OF ESOTERIC MEANING

The first assumption of the interpreters, Kugel explains, was that 'in place

---

[9] Kugel, *The Bible as it Was*, 6–7.   [10] Ibid. 8–10.   [11] Ibid. 10–12.

of, or beyond, the apparent meaning of the text is some hidden, esoteric message'. Thus, the text was viewed as 'fundamentally cryptic or esoteric'. Kugel points out that this way of viewing texts is 'hardly a natural thing. Whether we are reading a history book or a newspaper editorial or a rousing hymn, we generally assume that what the words seem to say is what they mean to say.' But scriptural interpreters worked from an opposite premiss. '. . . all interpreters are fond of maintaining', Kugel says, 'that although Scripture may appear to be saying X, what it really means is Y, or that while Y is not openly said by Scripture, it is somehow implied or hinted at in X'.[12]

Kugel notes, importantly, that this feature of interpretation went hand in hand with the growth of a special class of interpreters: hermeneutic assumptions and the political authority of this class reinforced each other.

The very fact that the Bible could be demonstrated time and again to contain some meaning other than the apparent one vouchsafed the necessity of specially trained interpreters who could reveal the Bible's secrets, and the interpretations that they put forward—precisely because they arose out of careful exegesis and would not appear to most readers at first blush—acquired an authority of their own.[13]

It is obvious, I think, that this particular and peculiar feature of scriptural interpretation is not limited to the context and culture that Kugel studies. Early Christians routinely found a figurative or spiritual dimension in scripture, which could be a source of surprising hidden meanings. Augustine was able to accept Christianity only after being persuaded that the scriptures, which often appeared on their face to be offensive and implausible, could be interpreted in non-literal ways, thus becoming a source of deep spiritual meanings. Indeed, the practice of non-literal interpretation in the early Christian Church became so extravagant that the Church eventually felt compelled to adopt stern measures to curb hermeneutical licentiousness.[14]

Again in the Reformation period the combination of a breakdown of ecclesiastical authority, the Protestant emphasis on the importance of scripture *(sola scriptura)*, and new philological and textual learning combined to produce an elaborate theorizing about the different kinds and dimensions of scriptural meaning.[15] Martin Luther, for instance, eventually distinguished eight levels of scriptural meaning; his overall approach served to ascribe Christological significance to all of scripture, even to Old Testament writings in which an ordinary reader would likely discern no

---

[12] Ibid. 18.   [13] Ibid. 18–19.

[14] On Augustine, see P. Brown, *Augustine of Hippo* (Berkeley and Los Angeles, 1967), 84, 252–5. On the prodigality of scriptural interpretation and its subsequent suppression in the early Christian Church, see E. Pagels, *Adam, Eve, and the Serpent* (New York, 1988), 62–77.

[15] See generally A. McGrath, *The Intellectual Origins of the European Reformation* (Oxford, 1987), 152–74.

reference to Christ at all.[16] And of course the challenge of correctly extracting these non-obvious meanings from scripture has provided a major reason for specialized training of ministers—and a basis for their resulting authority in religious matters.[17]

The assumption that the relevant texts contain hidden meanings not obvious upon ordinary or casual reading is hardly unique to scriptural interpretation; the assumption operates in literary criticism, for example, and it surely applies to law. To be sure, in recent years some American scholars and judges (most notably Justice Scalia) have been associated with a textualist or 'plain meaning' approach to enacted texts which seems calculated to resist the assumption of esoteric meaning. Consider in this respect Gary Lawson's statement that 'The Constitution of the United States is a recipe—a recipe for a particular form of government' and that 'interpreting the Constitution is no more difficult, and no different in principle, than interpreting a late-eighteenth-century recipe for fried chicken'. Lawson declares that 'Other approaches to interpretation are simply wrong.'[18] But although Lawson's pronouncement denies esoteric meaning in the constitutional text, it is crucial to recognize that his position is self-consciously offered as a *criticism* of what he acknowledges to be the actual, prevailing practices of constitutional interpretation. Those actual practices, as he well knows, proceed on a very different assumption.

That different assumption is voluminously defended in the theorizing of scholars like Ronald Dworkin, John Ely, Michael Perry—and, yes, even Robert Bork; such theorizing seeks in a variety of elaborate ways to explain and justify the assumption that the Constitution contains meanings that an ordinary reader unsocialized in the special arts of legal intepretation would be very unlikely to perceive there. In this respect, moreover, the theorists are not for the most part living out an academic fantasy (though they sometimes do that as well), but rather are attempting to account for the reality: the Supreme Court's decisions in a host of important areas from privacy rights to free speech to protection for women and minorities go well beyond what any ordinary reader would discern in the text itself.

If I emphasize American constitutional law, that is only because the disjunction between common-sense textual readings and the surprising or esoteric meanings often put forward by judges and scholars is perhaps most notorious in that domain. But a virtuoso interpreter like Dworkin is quite capable of extracting surprising or hidden meanings from law on all

---

[16] McGrath, *The Intellectual Origins of the European Reformation*, 158–60.

[17] See also S. Murata and W. C. Chittick, *The Vision of Islam* (St Paul, Minn., 1994), p. xxxvii: 'There were commentaries [on the Koran] that focused on grammar, historical background, juridical implications, theological teachings, moral edification, allegorical meanings, and so on. . . . But everyone recognized that the meanings of the Koran were inexhaustible.'

[18] G. Lawson, 'On Reading Recipes. . . and Constitutions', (1997) 85 *Georgetown Law Journal* 1823, 1833.

levels—statutory and common law as well as constitutional. And on a humbler level, the common law argumentation practised by ordinary lawyers and judges routinely presupposes hidden meanings in the relevant texts. Thus, in discussing a relevant precedent, lawyers and judges do not—and could not—simply read and follow what the case says. Instead, they search for the 'holding' of the case; this is to be distinguished from other, non-obligating features, described as the 'dicta', that may in fact make up nearly all of what is written in the decision. There is no consistent method or formula for sorting out these elements;[19] earnest efforts earlier in the last century to articulate the operative distinction have by now been largely abandoned.[20] Karl Llewellyn counted thirty-two 'impeccable' techniques for using or deflecting precedents, another twelve methods that he thought legitimate, an additional sixteen methods that are 'correct but less usual', and four techniques that he regarded as 'illegitimate' but that are nonetheless used.[21] This complex and shifting repertoire of techniques serves, we say, to extract the real meaning of the precedents—and of 'the law'—a meaning which can only be regarded as hidden in the raw textual materials.

All of this is perfectly familiar, and so may not seem noteworthy or strange. Nor is it novel to note that the assumption of hidden meaning in the texts supports the authority of a special class of people trained in the arts of legal interpretation—lawyers and judges. Understanding the law requires an 'artificial reason', as Coke said, acquired only through long, specialized training.

But although all of this is familiar enough, we should nonetheless appreciate that the assumption which supports these practices and their practitioners *would* seem incongruous and or flatly implausible in most contexts. Kugel remarks that the assumption in scriptural interpretation that texts have cryptic or esoteric meanings is 'hardly a natural thing': in

[19] See A. Scalia, *A Matter of Interpretation* (Princeton, 1997), 8 (asserting that 'what constitutes the "holding" of an earlier case is not well defined and can be adjusted to suit the occasion').

[20] The failure of the project can be discerned by comparing the 1st and 2nd editions of George Christie's *Jurisprudence* text. In the 1st edition Christie devoted a substantial block of text and materials to the problem of figuring out exactly how to extract the holding, or *ratio decidendi*, from a precedent (G. C. Christie, *Jurisprudence: Text and Readings on the Philosophy of Law*, 1st edn., (St Paul, Minn., 1973), 919–60). The included readings were already quite dated, and Christie acknowledged with palpable reluctance that 'one may be forced to conclude that there is no really satisfactory theory of the concept.' (ibid. 921). But Christie was unwilling to abandon the project because, as he cogently pointed out, without some account 'it is no longer possible to base one's explanation of the binding nature of precedent upon the concept of the *ratio decidendi* of a case' (ibid. 958). 'We therefore cannot avoid trying to make whatever sense we can of the concept' (ibid. 921). By the time of the 2nd edition, Christie had evidently conceded defeat: this entire section of the book was simply dropped. G. C. Christie and P. H. Martin, *Jurisprudence: Text and Readings on the Philosophy of Law*, 2nd edn., (St Paul, Minn., 1995).

[21] K. Llewellyn, *The Common Law Tradition: Deciding Appeals* (Boston, 1960), 77–91.

most areas of life we would not indulge any such assumption. In a similar but more overtly sceptical spirit (and in an essay trenchantly entitled 'Lies and Law'), Robert Nagel notices a 'strikingly similar impulse' uniting the jurisprudence of Ronald Dworkin, the Supreme Court's oft-quoted 'meaning and mystery of life' construction of the due process clause in *Planned Parenthood* v. *Casey*, and President Clinton's celebrated embellishments on words like 'is' and 'alone' in explaining why he was not guilty of perjury.[22] Dworkin, the Court, and Clinton are all engaged in the same practice, Nagel suggests—that is, 'to assign a surprising or counterintuitive meaning to an ordinary word'.[23]

Nagel quickly concedes that we do not typically regard 'President Clinton's laughable dodge' as being on a par with 'the most influential intellectual move of modern constitutional law'.[24] Clinton, we may say, was guilty of simple lying, or at best of rationalizing; Dworkin and the courts are engaged in a respectable and sophisticated project of 'interpretation'. Clinton was 'twisting' or 'distorting' or 'abusing' language; Dworkin and the courts, we think, are ascertaining the meanings that legal texts legitimately support or even require (even if the ordinary competent speaker of English would never have guessed it).

But what accounts for the difference? Why does the assignment of counter-intuitive or hidden meanings to words—meanings that an ordinary reader would never draw from the text—seem perfectly appropriate when we are reading sacred and legal texts, but dubious or even dishonest when we are speaking or reading in more ordinary contexts? We can defer this question until after we have noticed some other common features of scriptural and legal interpretation.

THE ASSUMPTION OF AUTHORITY

A second assumption in ancient biblical interpretation, Kugel explains, is that scripture is 'a fundamentally *relevant* text'. By 'relevant' he means that the text is treated as authoritative for present-day life and decisions, so that 'we ought to behave in keeping with what is written'. Once again, Kugel clarifies this assumption and calls attention to its unusual character by 'contrast[ing] it to the approach we normally take to the act of reading. If, for example, we were to open up *Gilgamesh* or the *Enuma Elish* or

---

[22] '[Clinton] proclaimed with a straight face', Nagel recalls, 'that a person might be thought not to be "alone" . . . if the relevant boundary line is expanded beyond the room he occupies to include his office, or beyond that, his suite of offices or, beyond that, a whole wing of the White House.' And Nagel wonders: 'Why not, inspired by the Court's poetic invocation of the most general interest in defining one's place in the universe, move the line out to include the entire heavily-populated East Coast or, indeed, this crowded planet itself?' (R. F. Nagel, 'Lies and Laws', (1999) 22 *Harvard Journal of Law and Public Policy*, 605, 607).

[23] Ibid. 607.   [24] Ibid.

some other ancient Near Eastern text, we might find the stories moving, the language stirring, but no one would likely suggest that we ought to behave in keeping with what is written there . . . '.[25] But precisely that assumption *was* operative in scriptural interpretation: 'Everything [in scripture] was held to apply to present-day readers and to contain within it an imperative for adoption and application to the readers' own lives.'[26]

This ascription of encompassing authority to the text distinguishes scriptural interpretation from the reading of many other kinds of texts—including, I think, literary texts (which we *do* sometimes treat like scripture in some other respects—most importantly in our assumption that literature contains layers of hidden meaning).[27] Conversely, the assumption of textual authority is plainly a feature that scriptural interpretation shares with legal interpretation. Thus, legal texts are routinely treated as authoritative—and are studied and interpreted precisely *because* they are authoritative. Legal decision-making in this respect makes a striking contrast with the more forward-looking, pragmatic costs-and-benefits decision-making that we employ in many areas of life. In the legal domain, in short, it is not only *a* reason to do something but a compelling or controlling reason that 'the Constitution' or 'the statute' (or, more generally, simply 'the law') so requires.[28]

Once again, we might wonder what justifies this ascription of authority to texts. There is no problem, of course, in explaining why we would *consult* a variety of texts in deciding how to live: from texts we can gain wisdom, or information, or assurance, or inspiration. But why should we treat texts as *authoritative* or, as we often say, 'binding'—as giving reasons for decisions that operate independently of and that may even override the conclusions that we would draw from our more pragmatic assessments of costs and benefits? The difficulty is evident, I think, in the fact that some prominent legal scholars seemingly *cannot* make sense of the notion of treating legal texts as authoritative in this sense. For example, Robin West argues that we ought to follow the Constitution; but to her this means

---

[25] Kugel, *The Bible as it Was*, 19.

[26] Ibid. 19–20.

[27] Just why this assumption of hidden meaning makes sense in the case of literature is an interesting question, I think, but one outside the scope of this paper. I should note, though, that the line between literature and scripture is sometimes quite thin; for some people or cultures, a revered author like Homer or Goethe or Shakespeare can be treated as an inspired source whose writings are treated as a kind of Scripture.

[28] The centrality of authority to law and the contrast between legal and pragmatic decision-making are both apparent in Ronald Dworkin's proposal regarding the fundamental point of law: 'the most abstract and fundamental point of legal practice is to guide and constrain the power of government in the following way. Law insists that force not be used or withheld, no matter how useful that would be to ends in view, no matter how noble and beneficial these ends, except as licensed or required by individual rights flowing from past political decisions about when collective force is justified' (Dworkin, *Law's Empire* (Cambridge, Mass., 1986), 93). Of course, this assumption about the point of law informs Dworkin's theories about the interpretation of legal texts.

using the Constitution as a 'source of insight' in the same way that we use 'the writings of Aristotle, John Stuart Mill, John Rawls, and Roberto Unger'[29]—which of course is *not* the way the Constitution is used in the American legal system. Richard Posner, perhaps the quintessential pragmatist in law, plainly finds the standard methods of legal decision-making in accordance with past authorities irrational and next to incomprehensible; so he increasingly views law as something to be 'overcome' in favour of a more sane, instrumentalist approach to decision-making. And in this respect Posner is merely re-enacting the position and mindset of his mentor, Holmes.[30]

It seems clear, however (as Posner himself complains[31]), that the standard methods of law *do* somehow suppose that decisions should be made in accordance with the authority embodied in legal texts. So what is it, if anything, that gives sense to this assumption of authority—an assumption which unites scriptural and legal interpretation?

THE ASSUMPTION OF UNITY

Once again, we can defer this question for a moment in order to consider a third feature that scriptural and legal interpretation have in common, though perhaps in different degrees. James Kugel explains that for ancient biblical interpreters Scripture was 'perfect and perfectly harmonious'. Their assumption

posits a perfect harmony between the Bible's various parts. Again, a comparison with other texts might be illuminating here. In an anthology of texts in English or Latin, for example, written by many authors over a period of more than a thousand years in diverse locales and under different political regimes and cultural norms, we would hardly expect to find absolute uniformity of views. One text would disagree with another not only in fundamental matters of orientation and belief, but even in its presentation of past events, since people's view of history tends to be colored by their own ideologies and, of course, to change radically over time. Yet with regard to Scripture—precisely because it was Scripture, a body of *sacred* writings—ancient interpreters adopted a different approach. They sought to discover the basic harmony underlying apparently discordant words, since all of Scripture, in their view, must speak with one voice.[32]

---

[29] Robin West, *Progressive Constitutionalism* (Durham, NC, 1994), 196.

[30] For a more detailed discussion of the point, see Smith, 'Believing Like a Lawyer', 1088–91.

[31] See e.g. R. A. Posner, *Overcoming Law* (Cambridge, Mass., 1995), 20: 'Yet most lawyers, judges, and law professors still believe that demonstrably correct rather than merely plausible or reasonable answers to most legal questions, even very difficult and contentious ones, can be found—and it is imperative that they be found—by reasoning from authoritative texts . . . and therefore without recourse to the theories, data, insights, or empirical methods of the social sciences.'

[32] Kugel, *The Bible as it Was*, 20. Compare Peter Brown's description of Augustine's remarkably similar assumptions: 'For Augustine and his hearers, the Bible was literally the

In law a similar assumption obtains, though perhaps in a less extreme form. To be sure, in law it is accepted that earlier enactments can be formally repealed, and it is also understood (now, I believe, in both England and the United States) that judicial decisions can occasionally be overruled. Moreover, in law a certain amount of pluralism is allowed for by the division of law into discrete subjects: so apparent discrepancies can sometimes be excused by observing, 'That was a contracts case, but this is a tort case.' Still, the prevailing assumption is that judicial decisions rendered by different judges divided by decades or even centuries, not to mention by temperament and class and training, and unrepealed statutes enacted by legislators similarly divided from each other, will somehow combine to form a harmonious whole.

Again, Dworkin's jurisprudence is perhaps the most eloquent testimony to this assumption. In Dworkin's view, in order for law to have authority we must be able to view it as constituting and reflecting a unified, coherent body of principles[33] and as the product of a 'single author'.[34] Dworkin's requirements in this respect may seem heroic, or rather herculean, but they are merely a dramatic way of presenting an assumption that is implicit in much ordinary lawyerly argumentation. Lawyers, that is, are constantly challenged to explain some seemingly contrary or incongruous precedent. 'But, counsellor, how do you account for this court's decision in *Cheddar v. Mozzarella?*' To a lay person, the answer to this question might seem straightforward: 'Obviously, the court was having a bad day', or 'Well, of course, the judges who decided that case were all Republican appointees'. As human beings, lawyers are perfectly capable of understanding this sort of explanation; but when acting *as lawyers* they also understand that such explanations are foreign to the assumptions of their discipline. Instead, they must show how the seemingly incongruous precedent fits into some overall coherent pattern. The law must—and therefore does—speak with one voice.[35]

So the assumption of harmony is perfectly routine in law; but that familiarity should not prevent us from noticing—as Kugel does in the scriptural context—that the assumption is also extraordinary. The law

"word" of God. It was regarded as a single communication, a single message in an intricate code, and not as an exceedingly heterogeneous collection of separate books.' And when 'seen in this light, the Bible became a gigantic puzzle—like a vast inscription in unknown characters'. (Brown, *Augustine of Hippo*, 252, 253.)

[33] Dworkin, *Law's Empire*, 225.

[34] These requirements are linked to Dworkin's view that law has authority only if it comes from a 'community of principle'—a notion that Dworkin explains (ibid. 211) in this way: 'people are members of a genuine political community only when they accept that their fates are linked in the following strong way: they accept that they are governed by common principles, not by rules hammered out in political compromise'.

[35] Pierre Schlag observes that the 'law is always announced in the singular: there is always, at the end . . . just one law' (P. Schlag, 'Clerks in the Maze', in P. F. Campos, P. Schlag, and S. D. Smith, *Against the Law* (Durham, NC, 1996), 218.

manifestly was *not* the product of a single author, so why on earth should we suppose that it was, as Dworkin insists?

The Religious Presupposition

Thus far I have discussed three features shared by scriptural and legal interpreters: an assumption that the relevant texts have hidden meanings to be brought out by specially trained interpreters, an assumption that the texts are authoritative for present-day decisions, and an assumption that apparently diverse texts speak with a single, harmonious voice. Each of these features contrasts markedly with the assumptions we indulge in more ordinary contexts. So at the end of each part of the discussion I have asked: What justifies this extraordinary assumption in the context of scriptural, and legal, interpretation?

Perhaps the easiest way to approach this question is by starting with scriptural interpretation, and with the last assumption. What justified biblical interpreters in treating the diverse books of scripture as if they came from a single, lucid author? The answer seems obvious: the interpreters treated the text in this way because they believed that the texts *were* in reality the expression of a single lucid and indeed omniscient author. They believed, that is, that God was in some sense the author of all scripture, and that the human, flesh-and-blood writers who were believed to have sponsored the texts were to some extent serving as scribes for the real, divine author. Thus, Kugel notes a fourth assumption in ancient biblical interpretation—'that all of Scripture is somehow divinely sanctioned, of divine provenance, or divinely inspired'.[36] The same assumption animated the complex practices of Christian biblical interpretation. As noted, for example, Protestant interpreters like Luther perceived a unified Christological message in all of scripture, including the Old Testament. They were able to attribute this theme to pre-Christian writings, as Alister McGrath explains, because for them the meaning of those texts 'ultimately derives from the fact that it is God himself who is the author of scripture'.[37]

If God is the author of all of scripture, then it is not surprising that scripture speaks with a single voice, even though its various chapters were penned by scribes separated by huge gaps of time, place, and culture. For the same reason, it is perfectly understandable that scripture would be authoritative for human conduct at all times and places, not merely for the

---

[36] Kugel, *The Bible as it Was*, 21–2.

[37] McGrath, *The Intellectual Origins of the European Reformation*, 123. See also Murata and Chittick, *The Vision of Islam*, 52: 'When Muslim scholars study the Koran, they look at every chapter, every verse, every word, and every letter as God's self-expression. There is nothing in the Koran that is not full of significance, because God has spoken with full awareness of what he is saying.'

particular context in which a particular text was written. Nor should it be surprising that scripture should contain hidden meanings not immediately obvious to the ordinary reader or even to the human beings who wrote the texts in the first place. That the human writer would not have perceived or intended a particular meaning is no more troublesome than is the fact that a lawyer's scrivener, or someone who takes dictation from a great poet or philosopher, does not begin to grasp the full significance of the words that he or she puts on paper. Why *should* the scrivener understand the meaning of the document?

So the seemingly extraordinary practices and assumptions of scriptural interpretation make very good sense if one assumes that scripture in all its manifestations is the expression of a single divine author. In the same way, the similar assumptions in legal interpretation *would* be readily understandable if we believed—or at least if the lawyers and judges who act on those assumptions believed—that legal texts are expressions of a superhuman author. So the sceptic who reads Dworkin and asks, '*Why* should we treat this messy conglomeration of diverse materials as the coherent product of a single author?' would be quickly silenced with the response: 'Because *they are*'. Likewise, it should not be hard to understand why legal texts would be treated as authoritative for us if they are supposed to express the will of God. And when a critic like Robert Nagel wonders what it is that leads us to say that when Bill Clinton uses words in a highly unconventional way he is *lying* but when Ronald Dworkin uses words in a highly unusual way he is *interpreting*, we have a ready answer: the words that Dworkin is construing (unlike those that Clinton is construing) are in some sense the expression of a divine semantic intention that transcends the mental states of their human scribes, so it is to be expected that those words will have deeper meanings.

But at this point, obviously, we encounter a problem. The practices and assumptions that pervade legal interpretation might make sense if we supposed that legal texts were in some sense a divine expression. And it may even be that at one time lawyers *did* suppose as much: quoting Richard Hooker's statement that law sits 'in the bosom of God, her voice the harmony of the world', Robert Gordon contends that until about the time of Holmes, lawyers 'had, as they saw it, a direct line to God's mind through their knowledge of the principles of legal science'.[38] I can't say whether this characterization is accurate or not. What *does* seem clear, though, is that most lawyers and judges over at least the last hundred years or so would emphatically disavow any such assumption.

In religion, when interpreters relax or abandon the assumption of the divine authorship of scripture, they typically abandon the related assumptions as well. Thus, in the modern academy scholars still study the Bible,

---

[38] R. Gordon, 'The Path of the Lawyer', (1997) 110 *Harvard Law Review* 1013.

but they typically do not seek to derive from it esoteric meanings that are supposed to be authoritative for our lives; nor do they suppose that the various biblical texts reflect a perfect harmony or speak with a single voice. Modern lawyers and legal scholars, on the other hand, disavow the assumption of divine authorship but—this is the strange part—continue to practise or even insist on the approach to interpretation that seems to presuppose some such assumption. Once again, Dworkin seems the perfect example.

So what should we make of this peculiar state of affairs? In my view, this is perhaps the most important problem with which contemporary jurisprudence should be struggling. For now, I will merely try to note three possible responses to that problem.

What we could call the 'critical response' would accept the description of our situation that I have just offered—the description which says that the practices of legal interpretation reflect a religious assumption that we routinely disavow—and then conclude that modern law is incoherent and irrational and is carried on in bad faith.[39] But even if this response is cogent—and for myself, I suspect there is at least *some* truth in it—the critical response does not really address the central puzzle: why do we persist in this incoherent or irrational practice?

A different response—we might call it the 'secular apologetic' response—would suggest that the three assumptions I have discussed can be explained and justified *without* invoking the fourth assumption that Kugel found in ancient biblical interpretation. The first three assumptions, that is, can be explained and justified on purely secular or perhaps pragmatic grounds. I admit to being sceptical of this response, and I have tried to criticize some versions of it elsewhere; but I can't try to evaluate the apologetic response here. However, I do want to try, very quickly, to anticipate and deflect one possible basis of complacency.

In my experience, lawyers confronted with an argument like the one I have made here will often respond by invoking a sort of nebulous pragmatism. 'There isn't anything so mysterious about it all,' they say. 'We continue to practise law in the prevailing way because *it works*—nothing fancier than that.' Now of course there is plenty of room to debate whether law as it currently operates 'works', or what it even means to say that it 'works'. But set those issues aside. even if you are confident that law 'works', I suggest that for present purposes, this observation is simply beside the point. That is because a successful apologetic response would need to show not *that* law 'works', but rather *how and why* it 'works'. Suppose it was once thought that automobile engines would run only on gasoline, or petrol, but it turns out that you can put water in them and they still go. That finding might be good enough reason for us to drive water-powered automobiles, but it would still leave a gaping hole in our understanding of how automobiles work; and merely saying 'Look, it works' would do nothing to fill that hole. In a similar way, the extraordinary assumptions evident in legal interpretation appear to make sense on the further assumption that law somehow emanates from a divine author; but if we think that legal interpretation 'works' in some pragmatic sense even without such an author, then we have some explaining to do.

So it is worth considering a third response—one that actually tries to suggest an explanation. Perhaps we really *do* believe that law in some sense emanates from a superhuman source, even though we think we don't. I am aware that on first hearing, this suggestion may seem not merely implausible but blatantly nonsensical. But perhaps the suggestion can be rendered worthy at least of consideration if we supplement it with two further observations. The first observation, insistently developed by Joseph Vining in his book *From Newton's Sleep*, is that we do not have immediate, perfectly reliable access to our own beliefs. Vining argues that what we *think* we believe is evidence—but *only* evidence—of what we *really* believe. The ways we use language (as opposed to what we explicitly assert) and the ways in which we act and plan and live are also evidence of what we believe.[40] So discovering what we believe entails a careful reflection upon what we think, say, and do in order to reveal our authentic, underlying beliefs.[41] These various kinds of evidence may often contradict each other—Vining frequently identifies statements or actions, for example, in which lawyers or scientists or philosophers tacitly deny what they explicitly assert, and vice versa[42]—so that the determination of belief is no easy task which we can know to be complete at any particular time.

The second observation returns to James Kugel's discussion of the fourth assumption underlying ancient biblical interpretation—the assumption, that is, of divine provenance or authorship. Kugel notes that the first three assumptions might seem to be derived from the fourth. We might imagine, in other words, that biblical interpreters *began* by believing that God was the author of scripture and proceeded to deduce that scripture would have hidden meanings, that it should be authoritative, and that it

---

[40] Vining, *From Newton's Sleep*, 128, 130, 189.

[41] Ibid. 60, 224, 331. In this respect, Vining's project is very much like that described by Michael Polanyi: 'I believe that the function of philosophic reflection consists in bringing to light, and affirming as my own, the beliefs implied in such of my thoughts and practices as I believe to be valid; that I must aim at discovering what I truly believe in and at formulating the convictions which I find myself holding; that I must conquer my self-doubts, so as to retain a firm hold on this programme of self-identification' (M. Polanyi, *Personal Knowledge: Towards a Post-Critical Philosophy* (Chicago, 1958; paperback edn. 1974), 267.

[42] Vining, *From Newton's Sleep*, 136, 140, 145, 176, 187, 249.

would be perfectly harmonious. But Kugel argues that the historical evidence does not support this depiction. It appears, on the contrary, that interpreters began with the first three assumptions and only over time came to appreciate that the fourth assumption was presupposed in their interpretative practices. So the assumption of divine provenance 'apparently did not come to be extended in homogeneous fashion to Scripture as a whole until a relatively late period'.[43] It seems that the biblical interpreters arrived at their belief in the divine authorship of scripture through the sort of reflective process Vining describes—that is, by examining their beliefs, words, and actions to bring to light what was presupposed in their overall practice.

What I am attempting is a similar sort of examination with respect to our current practices of legal interpretation;[44] and I am suggesting that such an examination points to a religious presupposition. But I do not expect modern lawyers to embrace this conclusion in the same way that Kugel's biblical interpreters evidently did. We face obstacles that those interpreters did not; among other things, we are burdened with a century or so of academic opinion that insists that the progress of human thought must be *away from* religion, not towards it. So for the immediate future, it seems most likely that we will simply have to endure the dissonance of engaging in a practice that seems to presuppose something we cannot acknowledge. We academic lawyers will continue to answer to Roberto Unger's famous description of the pre-Critical Legal Studies professoriate—'a priesthood that had lost their faith and kept their jobs'.[45]

Conclusion

We can end with a quotation from Mircea Eliade. The famous scholar of comparative religion observed that 'nonreligious man descends from *homo religiosus* and, whether he likes it or not, he is also the work of religious man'. And Eliade added that 'nonreligious man *in the pure state* is a comparatively rare phenomenon, even in the most desacralized of modern societies. The majority of the "irreligious" still behave religiously, even though they are not aware of the fact. . . . the modern man who feels and claims that he is nonreligious still retains a large stock of camouflaged myths and degenerated rituals.'[46] If Eliade was right, then I would submit that not least among this stock of myths and rituals is the massive enter-

---

[43] Kugel, *The Bible as it Was*, 23.

[44] Cf. Vining, *From Newton's Sleep*, 5 (asserting that 'it is too often overlooked that law is evidence of view and belief far stronger than academic statement and introspection can provide').

[45] R. M. Unger, 'The Critical Legal Studies Movement', (1983) 96 *Harvard Law Review* 561, 674–5.

[46] M. Eliade, *The Sacred and the Profane*, trans. W. R. Trask (New York, 1957), 203–5.

prise we call 'law'. And the fact that this enterprise not only survives but flourishes might lead us to wonder whether in reality, just beneath our aggressively secular pretensions, we have more old-fashioned faith than we are pleased to admit.[47]

[47] I thank Nicole Garnett, Rick Garnett, Vittorio Hosle, and Joseph Vining for helpful comments on an earlier draft of this essay.

HISTORICAL OBSERVATIONS ON THE RELATIONSHIP BETWEEN LETTER AND SPIRIT

Bernard S. Jackson

1. Introduction

Modern lawyers and theologians within the Judaeo-Christian tradition have tended to view the 'other' from within their own disciplinary framework. Lawyers used to be interested in broad questions of origins: were law and religion differentiated in early societies, and if so which came first?[1] More recently, does religion, in the West, provide the original form of legitimation for law, and in particular the model of a canonical text and its interpretation?[2] Theologians ask, What is the role of law within religion? In so far as the concerns of religion transcend mundane social life, does observance of divine law in this world (one possible definition of the 'good life') provide a ticket to the hereafter? Or, in more technical theological terms, is Justification by Works or Faith?

In this paper I shall try to disentangle these issues through a consideration of the famous opposition between 'letter' and 'spirit'. The dictum of Paul, famously rendered by the King James Version 'For the letter killeth, but the spirit giveth life,'[3] has itself been appropriated in their different ways by the lawyers and theologians. The former have often seen it as a piece of hermeneutic advice: as advocating interpretation of a written text according to *its* 'spirit' rather than its 'letter', thus favouring some form of 'free' or 'principled' interpretation over a 'literal' reading.[4] The latter more

---

[1] On Maine's views, see my 'Law and Language: A Metaphor for Maine, a Model for his Successors?', in A. Diamond (ed.), *The Victorian Achievement of Sir Henry Maine* (Cambridge, 1992), 288–92. A. S. Diamond strongly challenged prevailing assumptions. See my review of his *Primitive Law, Past and Present*, (1972) 88 *Law Quarterly Review* 161–70.

[2] See e.g. P. Goodrich, *Languages of Law* (London, 1990), 63–82.

[3] 2 Cor. 3: 6: 'The qualification we have comes from God; it is he who has qualified us to dispense his new covenant—a covenant expressed not in a written document but in a spiritual bond; for the written law condemns to death, but the spirit gives life' (RSV).

[4] In fact, the understanding of the distinction as one between literal and *allegorical* meaning goes back to the early Church. Calvin, in his commentary ad loc., was scathing of the use made of it: '*For the letter killeth*. This passage was mistakingly perverted, first by Origen, and afterwards by others, to a spurious signification. From this arose a very pernicious error—that of imagining that the perusal of Scripture would be not merely useless, but even injurious, unless it were drawn out into allegories. This error was the source of many evils. For there was not merely a liberty allowed of adulterating the genuine meaning of

typically see in it Paul's own endorsement of Justification by Faith ('spirit' = the Holy Spirit) rather than Works ('letter' = the Written Law).[5]

I shall argue, however, that the historical background indicates that the real dispute was one over the semiotics of revelation: through what means (text or inspiration) was the divine will made manifest, and to what extent was that form of communication both effective and accessible to human reason? The history of the division between Judaism and Christianity may be viewed as a conflict over the acceptable forms of communication of the divine message.

One methodological caveat before I begin. The 'historical' account I shall propose is an account of the claims made in the texts which have come down to us. When discussing biblical law, in particular, we must distinguish between the historical and social realities of the period (in so far as we may have access to them), and the claims of the authors of the biblical texts, which frequently reflect their own, normative views.[6] My focus is on the latter, rather than the former.

2. The Original Biblical Conception of Justice

The biblical authors had a radical view of the nature of justice, and offer some very specific accounts of the history of its development. For them, justice was divine—not merely in some ideological sense: that justice is a value mandated by God, and therefore that the administration of justice

---

Scripture, but the more of audacity any one had in this manner of acting, so much the more eminent an interpreter of Scripture was he accounted. Thus many of the ancients recklessly played with the sacred word of God, as if it had been a ball to be tossed to and fro. In consequence of this, too, heretics had it more in their power to trouble the Church; for as it had become general practice to make any passage whatever mean anything that one might choose, there was no frenzy so absurd or monstrous, as not to admit of being brought forward under some pretext of allegory. Even good men themselves were carried headlong, so as to contrive very many mistaken opinions, led astray through a fondness for allegory. The meaning of this passage, however, is as follows—that, if the word of God is simply uttered with the mouth, it is an occasion of death, and that it is *lifegiving,* only when it is received with the heart. The terms *letter* and *spirit,* therefore, do not refer to the exposition of the word, but to its influence and fruit. Why it is that the doctrine merely strikes upon the ear, without reaching the heart, we shall see presently' (available on internet at <http://www.ccel.org/c/calvin/comment2/2cor.htm>).

[5] Rom. 3: 19–20, 10: 1–4. See *The Sermons of Martin Luther* (Grand Rapids, Mich., 1909), viii. 225–6: 'Here man's heart is represented as a sheet, or slate, or page, whereon is written the preached Word; for the heart is to receive and securely keep the Word. In this sense Paul says: We have, by our ministry, written a booklet or letter upon your heart, which witnesses that you believe in God the Father, Son and Holy Ghost and have the assurance that through Christ you are redeemed and saved. This testimony is what is written on your heart. The letters are not characters traced with ink or crayon, but the living thoughts, the fire and force of the heart.' See further B. S. Jackson, 'Legalism', (1979) 30 *Journal of Jewish Studies* 1–22, 4–9.

[6] This has implications, *inter alia,* for the assessment of prophetic denunciation of economic practices which may have been quite legal under state law. See my ' "Law" and "Justice" in the Bible', (1998) 49/2 *Journal of Jewish Studies* 218–29, esp. 227–9.

was in the name of, or on behalf of, God (what we might term the theory of delegation).[7] Rather, justice was divine in a very direct sense: it belonged to (was an attribute of?) God,[8] and decisions on matters of justice were rendered by God himself.

How was this to be effected? Two answers are given. The first is that the judge is inspired by God at the level of the individual decision. The accounts of both early (royal) adjudication and the earliest charges given to the judges appointed by those kings coincide in stressing direct divine inspiration rather than recourse to a divine text. According to Proverbs 16:10: 'Inspired decisions are on the lips of a King; his mouth does not sin in judgement.' The famous adjudication by Solomon of the case of the two prostitutes (1 Kgs. 3: 16–28) concludes with the narrator's observation: 'And all Israel heard of the judgment which the king had rendered; and they stood in awe of the king, because they perceived that the wisdom of God was in him, to render justice.' Perhaps the most famous charge to the judges in the Bible is that of Deuteronomy 16, where they are commanded to deliver 'righteous judgment' (*mishpat tsedek*).[9] This is further explained in both negative and positive terms: negatively, that the judges must avoid both partiality and corruption; positively, that they must pursue justice.[10] The account of the 'judicial reform' of the ninth-century king Jehoshaphat is closely parallel: his charge to the first-instance judges he appoints makes no reference to their using a written law book; rather, he tells them to avoid partiality and corruption (as in Deuteronomy) and that '[God] is with you in giving judgment' (*ve'imakhem bidvar mishpat*).[11] In other words, judicial decisions were conceived to be inspired: we may understand this, from an external viewpoint, as a legitimation of the intuitive sense of justice.

---

[7] Though that is also claimed. The charge of Jehoshaphat to the judges includes: 'Consider what you do, for you judge not for man but for the LORD' (2 Chron. 19: 6).

[8] Deut. 1: 17, ' for the judgment is God's' (*ki hamishpat lelohim hu'*).

[9] Deut. 16: 18–20: 'You shall appoint judges and officers in all your towns which the LORD your God gives you, according to your tribes; and they shall judge the people with righteous judgment. You shall not pervert justice; you shall not show partiality; and you shall not take a bribe, for a bribe blinds the eyes of the wise and subverts the cause of the righteous. Justice, and only justice, you shall follow, that you may live and inherit the land which the LORD your God gives you.'

[10] *Tsedek tsedek tirdof.* But what is this *tsedek?* There is no suggestion that it consists in following the rules of a written law book; the noun *tsedek*, in its feminine form, *tsedakah*, means righteousness, and more concretely charity; it is difficult to grasp the sense of *tsedek* without being sensitive to this connotation. So it is possible to take the term most centrally translated 'justice' as having a non-positivist biblical connotation.

[11] 2 Chron. 19: 5–7: 'Consider what you do, for you judge not for man but for the LORD; he is with you in giving judgment. Now then, let the fear of the LORD be upon you; take heed what you do, for there is no perversion of justice with the LORD our God, or partiality, or taking bribes.' The fact that Jehoshaphat is elsewhere concerned with the use of a book of written *torah*, which he has used for public instruction (2 Chron. 17: 9), makes its absence from the judicial reform all the more striking. On these sources, see further B. S. Jackson, *Studies in the Semiotics of Biblical Law* (Sheffield, 2000), 116–19.

A second answer, perhaps reflecting a viewpoint closer to the interests of the priesthood, is that the oracle should be consulted in every case (and not simply in 'hard cases', as later sources seem to imply). That view emerges clearly from the narrative of the visit of Jethro, the father-in-law of Moses, to the Israelites immediately before the revelation on Sinai (Exod. 18). Recall the vivid picture in Exodus 18:13–15 of Moses as the overloaded first-instance judge:

> On the morrow Moses sat to judge the people, and the people stood about Moses from morning till evening. When Moses' father-in-law saw all that he was doing for the people, he said, 'What is this that you are doing for the people? Why do you sit alone, and all the people stand about you from morning till evening?' And Moses said to his father-in-law, 'Because the people come to me to inquire of God . . .'.

The problem, Moses explains, derives from the fact that the people expect him, in dealing with each and every case, 'to inquire of God' (*lidrosh elohim*—a term which here refers to oracular consultation[12]). Jethro, the story continues, advised Moses to create a system of judicial delegation, and to deal himself only with the 'great matters' which the judges bring to him.

3. From Spirit to Letter

The advice given by Jethro in Exodus 18—presented as a reaction to a purely practical problem—entails rejection of the idea of the direct inspiration of the first-instance judge. Instead, a system of delegation is to be introduced, the first-instance judges now making the decisions on the basis of rules which have been taught. Elsewhere, written law is specifically ascribed the function of a source of instruction.[13] So Exodus 18 itself presents a two-stage historical claim: at first, all adjudication was based upon the direct divine decision (through consultation of the oracle); later, 'easy cases' at least were to be decided by human agencies applying pre-existing rules.

A parallel historical development may be discerned in relation to the accounts of judges operating with direct divine inspiration. We read the following revealing notice regarding the sons of Samuel (1 Sam. 7: 15–8: 3):

> Samuel judged Israel all the days of his life. And he went on a circuit year by year to Bethel, Gilgal, and Mizpah; and he judged Israel in all these places. Then he would come back to Ramah, for his home was there, and there also he adminis-

---

[12] Cf. 1 Kgs. 22: 7–8; 2 Chron. 16: 6–7; 1 Chron. 10: 13–14, of Saul's consultation of a medium. See further S. Wagner, 'darash', in G. J. Botterweck and H. Ringgen (eds.), *Theological Dictionary of the Old Testament*, iii (Grand Rapids, Mich., 1978), 302–3.
[13] 2 Chron. 17: 9 (n. 11 above); see also Deut. 17: 18–20.

tered justice to Israel. And he built there an altar to the LORD. When Samuel became old, he made his sons judges over Israel. The name of his first-born son was Jo'el, and the name of his second, Abijah; they were judges in Beer-sheba. Yet his sons did not walk in his ways, but turned aside after gain; they took bribes and perverted justice.

The model of the inspired judge is thus found, in practice, to be incompatible with the hereditary principle: the sons of Samuel transgress precisely the forms of judicial behaviour prohibited in Deuteronomy 16. It is hardly coincidental that Samuel is the very prophet whom the people badgered, against his better judgement, for the appointment of a king. And it was Samuel who was responsible for what may well have been the first text of written law in the actual history of the Israelite kingdoms, namely the *mishpat hamelukhah*, which (presumably) defined and restricted the powers of the king (1 Sam. 10: 25). Thus, in the story of Samuel two themes are combined: on the one hand, the writing of law in order to restrain the powers of a king; on the other, the abuse of a hereditary *judicial* power. If written law was the remedy for the former, we may reasonably assume that it was also a remedy in relation to the latter. As in the traditions of the origins of law in Greece and Rome, written law is a response to the abuse of an earlier discretion, rather than discretion being the response to the supposed rigidities of an earlier written law.

4. The Bifurcation in Divine Justice

The effect of this is a bifurcation in divine justice. On the one hand, divine justice continues to operate directly, without any human intermediaries; on the other, those human agencies charged with implementation of divine justice are no longer acting directly at the instance of God (whether via inspiration or oracle). Divine justice, as operated through human means, thereby becomes that much less perfect. It is now subject to the limitations of human knowledge and judgement.

We see reflections of this in the handling of two major institutions associated with divine justice. The principle of measure for measure—a particular application of which is talionic punishment—could, it was assumed, be applied by God,[14] and was so applied, without arbitrariness and injustice. Not so, the Rabbis concluded, for human agencies. In the latter

---

[14] See e.g. B. Jacob, *Auge um Auge. Eine Untersuchung zum alten und neuen Testament* (Berlin, 1926), 93–100; on the earlier literature, see further Jackson, *Essays in Jewish and Comparative Legal History* (Leiden, 1975), 84 n. 58. For more recent discussion: T. A. Boogaart, 'Stone for Stone: Retribution in the Story of Abimelech and Shechem', (1985) 32 *Journal for the Study of the Old Testament* 45–56, 47–8; P. J. Nel, 'The Talion Principle in Old Testament Narratives', (1994) 20 *Journal of Northwest Semitic Languages* 21–9, esp. 22; B. S. Jackson, 'Talion and Purity: Some Glosses on Mary Douglas', in J. F. A. Sawyer (ed.), *Reading Leviticus: A Conversation with Mary Douglas* (Sheffield, 1996), 108.

hands, it had to be reduced to monetary compensation, for which measures of quantification were available in human society.[15] Similarly, the Decalogue threatens those who commit idolatry with transgenerational punishment:[16] You shall not bow down yourself to them, or serve them; for I the LORD your God am a jealous God, visiting the iniquity of the fathers upon the children to the third and fourth generation of them that hate me. And showing mercy to thousands of those who love me, and keep my commandments . . .'[17] The use of the first person shows, in context, that this is a measure reserved for the operation of direct divine justice. As far as the human operation of divine law was concerned, the principle adopted by Deuteronomy 24: 16 was to be that of individual responsibility: 'The fathers shall not be put to death for the children, nor shall the children be put to death for the fathers; every man shall be put to death for his own sin.' By the end of the First Jewish Commonwealth, however, the perceived consequences of the application by God of transgenerational punishment prompted a counsel of despair.[18] Experience showed that human beings could not voluntarily rise to the standards required by such direct application of divine justice. Jeremiah expresses this[19] in a famous passage (31: 29–34):

[15] One of the arguments deployed by the Rabbis against a literal interpretation of the biblical text is the following: 'What then will you say where a blind man put out the eye of another man, or where a cripple cut off the hand of another or where a lame person broke the leg of another. How can I carry out in this case [the principle of retaliation of] "*eye for eye*", seeing that the Torah says, *Ye shall have one manner of law*, implying that the manner of law should be the same in all cases.' See *Baba Kamma* 84a (*Talmud*, Soncino trans.), discussed further in 'The Original "Oral Law" ', in G. W. Brooke (ed.), *Jewish Ways of Reading the Bible* (Oxford, 2000); *Journal of Semitic Studies*, suppl. 10 3–19: 'Literal Meaning and Rabbinic Hermeneutics: A Response to Jan Broekman and Claudio Luzzati', *International Journal for the Semiotics of Law*, forthcoming. For the rabbinic system of assessment of damages for bodily injury, see Mishnah *Baba Kamma* 8: 1 (trans. in H. Danby, *The Mishnah* (Oxford, 1933), 342).

[16] Exod. 20: 5–6, cf. Deut. 5: 9–10. The love–hate theme is widely seen as originating in ancient Near Eastern treaties, referring to relationships of rebellion or loyalty. See M. Weinfeld, *Deuteronomy and the Deuteronomic School* (Oxford, 1972), 81–4; B. M. Levinson, 'The Human Voice in Divine Revelation: The Problem of Authority in Biblical Law', in M. A. Williams, C. Cox, and M. S. Jaffee (eds.), *Innovations in Religious Traditions* (Berlin, 1992), 46.

[17] A. Schenker has documented a strong ancient tradition seeking to avoid this conclusion by holding the sentence against the original sinning generation to be 'suspended' until the third or fourth generation (A. Schenker, 'La plus ancienne mention de la peine avec sursis dans l'histoire du droit: la notion de la peine avec sursis dans la Bible juive', Paper presented to the Institut des Études pour la Justice Hautes Colloquium *Genealogies de l'idée de justice: l'idée de justice dans la tradition juive*, Paris, 26–7 May 2000.

[18] Cf. M. Greenberg, 'Three Conceptions of the Torah in Hebrew Scriptures', in his *Studies in the Bible and Jewish Thought* (Philadelphia, 1995), 18–19, citing also Ezek. 36: 24–7 (pp. 19–20). See further B. S. Jackson, *Studies in the Semiotics of Biblical Law* (Sheffield, 2000), §9.1.

[19] On the importance of this issue as the context for Jeremiah's 'new covenant', cf. Levinson, 'Human Voice', 51.

In those days they shall no longer say: 'The fathers have eaten sour grapes, and the children's teeth are set on edge.' But every one shall die for his own sin; each man who eats sour grapes, his teeth shall be set on edge. Behold, the days are coming, says the LORD, when I will make a new covenant with the house of Israel and the house of Judah, not like the covenant which I made with their fathers when I took them by the hand to bring them out of the land of Egypt, my covenant which they broke, though I was their husband, says the LORD. But this is the covenant which I will make with the house of Israel after those days, says the LORD: I will put my law within them, and I will write it upon their hearts; and I will be their God, and they shall be my people. And no longer shall each man teach his neighbour and each his brother, saying, 'Know the LORD', for they shall all know me, from the least of them to the greatest, says the LORD; for I will forgive their iniquity, and I will remember their sin no more.

The substance of the opposition here is between a covenant, compliance with which was voluntary—and breach of which was visited by direct divine punishment—and a covenant compliance with which was automatic[20]—we might almost say, genetically programmed (perhaps a reversion to the guiltless—or at least shameless—state of nature before Adam and Eve ate of the tree of knowledge[21]). For the latter, Jeremiah still uses the metaphor of written law, but the covenant now is 'written in the heart', forming a spiritual bond between God and the believer.

5. Christian and Rabbinic Reactions

It is not difficult to see how the early Church could turn this into a doctrine of justification. First of all, concern for the afterlife was by this period much more pronounced than it had been in the time of Jeremiah. For most of the writers of the Hebrew Bible, man returned to the dust from which he was created;[22] divine punishment was focused on this

[20] Cf. G. von Rad, *Old Testament Theology*, ii (Edinburgh 1965), 212–15; W. McKane, *A Critical and Exegetical Commentary on Jeremiah*, ii: *The International Critical Commentary* (Edinburgh, 1966), 817–27 (noting Peake on the creation of an 'inerrant moral sense'; p. 820); H. McKeating, *The Book of Jeremiah* (Peterborough, 1999), 154–5.

[21] Gen. 2: 9, 17 (where God commands: 'But of the tree of the knowledge of good and evil, you shall not eat of it; for in the day that you eat of it you shall surely die,' which contributes to the Pauline doctrine that 'the letter killeth', since the law involves guilt and lack of the capacity fully to comply with its demands). For Jewish approaches to the problem of the tree of knowledge, see N. Leibowitz, *Studies in the Book of Genesis* (Jerusalem, 1972), 17–27. For a review of modern scholarship, see H. N. Wallace, *The Eden Narrative* (Atlanta, 1985), 115–30; G. J. Wenham, *Word Biblical Commentary*, i: *Genesis 1–15* (Waco, Tex., 1987), 62–4, arguing for understanding 'knowledge of good and evil' as 'moral autonomy' rather than 'moral discernment'.

[22] Notably Eccles. 12: 7: 'And the dust returns to the earth as it was; and the spirit returns to God who gave it'; cf. e.g. Ezek. 37; Pss. 22: 16, 44: 26, 103: 14, 104: 29, 119: 25; Job 10: 9, 17: 16 (equated with *She'ol*), 19: 25, 21: 26, 34: 15, Eccles. 3: 20. For discussion, see H. W. Wolff, *Anthropology of the Old Testament* (Philadelphia, 1974), ch. 12; more briefly, J. H. Neyrey, 'Eternal Life', in P. J. Achtemeier (ed.), *Harper's Bible Dictionary* (San Francisco, 1985), 282–3; *aliter*, W. T. Pitard, 'Afterlife and Immortality', in B. M. Metzger and M. D. Coogan (eds.), *The Oxford Companion to the Bible* (New York, 1993), 15–16.

world (including one's posterity within this world). By the time of Jesus, belief in the afterlife, and the divine judgement which preceded it, was much more widespread. To this extent, the effects of divine judgement (theodicy) were even more significant. The availability of a 'new covenant' through which human beings could be protected from sin was interpreted by Paul as referring to a spiritual bond (faith in Jesus) which dispensed with observance of Torah, rather than one which made such observance automatic. Even though the 'new covenant' was, according to Jeremiah, 'written' in the heart, the opposition was expressed by Paul more directly as one between 'Letter' and 'Spirit'.[23]

Naturally, a different approach was taken within the Jewish tradition. A variety of views are expressed on the role of Torah in the messianic age, and indeed of the kind of new covenant to which Jeremiah referred.[24] What was vital, however, from the rabbinic point of view, was that the messianic age had not yet arrived, and thus the promise of Jeremiah, whatever it meant, was deferred. The Rabbis had to grapple in a different way with the tensions between the different forms of revelation—direct personal inspiration on the one hand, textual transmission on the other—endorsed within the biblical texts. Nor was it open to them to distinguish between different historical phases of the development of the normative pentateuchal texts. Their response was to develop a new conception of the relationship between letter and spirit. The letter did, indeed, require interpretation. Though the Rabbis did not endorse a *concept* of 'literal meaning' comparable to ours,[25] they did—naturally enough—read the texts through the techniques of literacy rather than orality.[26] The techniques which they developed for this purpose did not oppose 'letter' and 'spirit' in the sense of modern legal hermeneutics. Rather, they attributed importance to those literary (as well as substantive) characteristics of the written

---

[23] In Rom. 2: 14–16 Paul adapts Jeremiah's image to his purpose: 'When Gentiles who have not the law do by nature what the law requires, they are a law to themselves, even though they do not have the law. They show that what the law requires is written on their hearts, while their conscience also bears witness and their conflicting thoughts accuse or perhaps excuse them on that day when, according to my gospel, God judges the secrets of men by Christ Jesus' (RSV).

[24] See esp. W. D. Davies, *Torah in the Messianic Age and/or the Age to Come* (Philadelphia, 1952), ch. IV.

[25] Their conception of ('simple meaning' *peshat,* as opposed often to *derash*) clearly included many interpretations we would regard as non-literal. Probably the earliest rabbinic reflection on this is that of R. Ishmael (*Mekhilta* ad Exod. 21: 19, Lauterbach iii. 53), who claimed that there were only three examples of interpretation according to (metaphorical, or parabolic, meaning *mashal*): the interpretation of 'an eye for an eye' as 'money' was *not* one of them! On the notion of *peshat,* see R. Loewe, 'The Plain Meaning of Scripture in Early Jewish Exegesis', (1965) 1 *Papers of the Institute of Jewish Studies* 140–85; L. I. Rabinowitz, 'Peshat', and 'Derash' in *Encyclopedia Judaica* (Jerusalem, 1972) and older literature there cited; S. Kamin, *Rashi's Exegetical Categorization: With Respect to the Distinction between Peshat and Derash* (Heb.) (Jerusalem, 1980); D. W. Halivni, *Peshat and Derash* (New York, 1991); Jackson, 'Literal Meaning and Rabbinic Hermeneutics'.

[26] See Jackson, 'The Original "Oral Law" '.

text[27] which a secular legal reading would ignore—precisely because the text, in their view, was not simply a secular legal text, but rather one dictated by God himself, and thus possessing semiotic characteristics beyond those of human draftsmanship.

How, then, could mere human interpreters perceive such meanings? The answer was to reattribute direct divine inspiration to the interpreters themselves. This is the significance of the original rabbinic institution of 'ordination' (*semikhah*), the continuation of the line of authority commencing with Moses, who 'laid hands' on the head of his successor, Joshua,[28] who in turn handed on the tradition of the 'Oral Law' (through which the written was interpreted) to the elders, etc.[29] A vivid illustration of the theological weight of such inspiration is to be found in a famous passage of the Talmud, which records a three-year-long dispute between the School of Hillel and that of Shammai on a point of law. In the end, a 'heavenly voice'[30] intervened to resolve the dispute, with the words:

R. Abba stated in the name of Samuel: For three years there was a dispute between Beth Shammai and Beth Hillel, the former asserting, 'The *halakha* is in agreement with our views' and the latter contending, 'The *halakha* is in agreement with our views'. Then a *bath kol* issued announcing, '[The utterances of] both are the words of the living God, but the *halakha* is in agreement with the rulings of Beth Hillel'. Since, however, 'both are the words of the living God' what was it that entitled Beth Hillel to have the *halakha* fixed in agreement with their rulings?—Because they were kindly and modest, they studied their own rulings and those of Beth Shammai, and were even so [humble] as to mention the action of Beth Shammai before theirs.[31]

This evocative passage has given rise to some discussion.[32] Is it intended as a divine endorsement of minority as well as majority opinion (since one generation's minority view may become the majority opinion of a later generation)? Does it suggest that divine law transcends the human logic of contradiction? However we may answer these questions, it is clear that the

---

[27] See B. S. Jackson, 'On the Nature of Analogical Argument in Early Jewish Law', (1993) II *The Jewish Law Annual* 137–68, esp. 151–2.

[28] Num. 27: 22–3; Deut. 34: 9. On the history of *semikhah*, see J. Newman, *Semikhah (Ordination): A Study of its Origin, History and Function in Rabbinic Literature* (Manchester, 1950); *Encyclopedia Judaica*, xiv (Jerusalem, 1972), 1140–7, and bibliography there cited.

[29] Mishnah *Avot* 1: 1; M. Elon, *Jewish Law, History, Sources, Principles* (Philadelphia, 1994), i. 192–3, 228–9.

[30] Despite the rejection of the *bat kol* as a source of *Halakhah* for other (substantive?) purposes, in the famous 'oven of Okhnai' passage: *Baba Metzia* 59b; see further Jackson, 'Literal Meaning and Rabbinic Hermeneutics'.

[31] Talmud *Eruvin* 13b.

[32] See further B. S. Jackson, 'Secular Jurisprudence and the Philosophy of Jewish Law: A Commentary on Some Recent Literature', (1987) VI *The Jewish Law Annual* 33–4; Hanina ben Menahem, 'Is there always One Uniquely Correct Answer to a Legal Question in the Talmud?', (1987) VI *The Jewish Law Annual* 167–8.

interpretation of the law is not a matter only of the meaning of its words, its letter. Even without the orality of the 'heavenly voice', the passage recognizes the pragmatics as well as the semantics of interpretation—the behaviour (and not merely the cognition) involved in meaning construction.

6. Conclusion

Modern jurisprudence continues to manifest these same tensions, between 'Rule of Law' positivists, who put their faith in a written text, and 'Legal Realists', who give primacy to oral interaction and the practical authority accorded to individuals and institutions. Particularly interesting, within this spectrum, are the models of judicial authority and activity proposed by Kelsen (the theory of normative alternatives)[33] and Dworkin (whose Hercules, we may recall, is described as a 'lawyer of superhuman skill, learning, patience and acumen',[34] and who indulges in a hermeneutic holism of truly rabbinic proportions[35]). But that is another story.

[33] See further B. S. Jackson, *Semiotics and Legal Theory* (London, 1985), 243–56, and *Making Sense in Jurisprudence* (Liverpool, 1996), 114–24.

[34] *Taking Rights Seriously* (London, 1978), 105.

[35] See further B. S. Jackson, in A. Soeteman (ed.), *Pluralism in Law* (Plenary Papers of the 2001 NR Conference (Dordrecht, 2001)).

'BATTER MY HEART':
ON THE THREE-DISCIPLINED
SEARCH FOR MEANING

Jeanne Gaakeer

The prologues are over. It is a question, now,
Of final belief. So, say that final belief
Must be in a fiction. It is time to choose.

Wallace Stevens, 'Asides on the Oboe'

In the Beginning

Was the word and the word became law. This scriptural metaphor draws
our attention to the relation between language and authoritative claims of
meaning. How does the word become law? What do people do with and
to language and what does language do to them? More importantly, what
do people do to one another with the help of language? When meaning is
claimed, the interrelation of law, literature, and religion reveals itself.
Ironically, we have come a long way since the days when this was obvious.
The origin of Greek tragedy is a case in point. Originally an act of
worship, the dithyramb sung round the altar of Dionysus quickly widened
its scope and began to include tales about the relationship between gods
and humans, culminating in plays about the essence of human life and
community, shown to be the result of conflict between god and man,
parent and child, rights and duties, or, basically, the eternal conflict
between good and evil. Thus, in plays such as Sophocles' *Antigone* religion's direct association with both law and literature went unchallenged. It
is important to note in this context that the story of Antigone's tragic
fate—and the same goes for the plots of the other Greek tragedies—was so
much part and parcel of the spectators' religious and cultural heritage that
attending the performances meant first and foremost learning how each
individual dramatist dealt with it, i.e. how he chose to present the story of
conflict. The spectators were theorists in the original sense of the word.
They were the *theoroi* who went to see the plays in order to learn the
lessons about the place of man in the cosmos, and, upon return in their
own villages, told and taught the moral lessons of what they had seen to
their families, friends, and neighbours.

But that was 2,500 years ago. As the original comprehensive view on
human and physical nature, on cosmos and human condition, underwent
dramatic changes, and law, literature, and religion ultimately developed

into separate disciplines, scholarly attention turned to their dissimilarities rather than their similarities. More specifically, the differentiation of both academic disciplines and social power structures that characterized the late nineteenth century engendered a form of autonomy for law and legal theory based on the positivist paradigm of natural scientific thought, which in turn tried to sever—and to a certain extent successfully—law's original ties to the evaluating attitude of morality and religion, of ethics and theology.[1] The rise of the dominant paradigm of the natural sciences which culminated in several forms of legal positivism did not augur well either for law's original practical relation to literature and religion. In the eighteenth century the Bible, the works of Shakespeare, and Blackstone's *Commentaries* were the main literary sources of the law, especially for lawyers in the United States, whose founders integrated Scripture and the demands of law and government. Study of this small yet all-encompassing canon, sometimes supplemented with the works of Cicero and Virgil, sufficed for professional success as well as professional satisfaction. Examples of the unity of the common law and Christianity abound.[2] The need to study moral values, human passions, and legal systematization by means of these canonical works soon came to an end. The ongoing process of professionalization and specialization of the practice of law led to a call to cast law in the mould of the natural sciences. When in 1870 Christopher Columbus Langdell, the dean of Harvard Law School, introduced the case-method, the original bond of law, literature, and religion came to an end. Langdell's ideal of law as a science with its logic of syllogistic reasoning drove the attention for the underlying norms and values of law, earlier on so often derived from the complexity of literary and religious narrative, into the background. The resulting dichotomy of law and the humanities sharpened as fact superseded fiction with the twentieth-century emphasis of the importance of the social sciences and their data based on empirical research. For the configuration of law and the humanities, this seemed the death blow.[3]

However, in the course of the twentieth century the positivist, rule-bound model of law came itself under severe attack when the horrors of the Holocaust showed the devastating effects of an ultimately formalistic legal hermeneutics.[4] Awareness of the danger inherent in the scientific approach to law of the reduction of legal problems to one dimension, and a call to offer a counterweight in the form of the study of law in the ethical

---

[1] Niklas Luhmann describes this process in *Ausdifferenzierung des Rechts* (Frankfurt am Main, 1981); for the Wallace Stevens motto, see *Collected Poems of Wallace Stevens* (New York, 1954).

[2] See S. B. Presser and J. S. Zainaldin (eds.), *Law and American History* (St Paul, Minn., 1980); P. Miller, *The Life of the Mind in America* (New York, 1965); R. v. *Woolston* (1729) Fitzg 64.

[3] See R. Ferguson, *Law and Letters in American Culture* (Cambridge, Mass., 1984).

[4] See R. H. Weisberg, *Vichy Law and the Holocaust in France* (New York, 1996).

and moral sense of Is and Ought resulted in a renaissance of the interest in the common bond of law, literature, and religion in the 1960s and 1970s. It took its first academic shape in the interdisciplinary movement of law and literature, soon followed by scholars who shared an interest in the relationship between legal discourse and law's societal roles but preferred to work on the intersection of law and theology.

Thus we should pause to reflect whether the long goodbye has finally come to an end with the rise of interdisciplinary fields of knowledge. For looked upon in retrospect, the tendency of scholarly fields to become autonomous disciplines has something of a paradox in it when we think of the fact that various fields of knowledge, the very formation of which into autonomous disciplines took place in the nineteenth century, are now brought on to counterbalance law's ongoing desire for autonomy. The claim uniting much of the work done within law and literature is that reading literature forces us to step back from the technicalities of law. On this view, works of fiction can illustrate a legal issue from a different perspective and enhance our understanding of law and the legal system and of our own performances as lawyers. The emphasis on positive law in the sense of precedents or statutory rules—all too often characteristic of legal education—thus finds its antidote in the study of literature. A reappraisal of the humanities both as a source of inspiration for a change in lawyers' understanding and use of written and spoken language, and as a source of values, is now in full swing. Reading works of fiction, or, more specifically, studying the portrayal of law and lawyers in a work of fiction, is claimed to promote awareness of questions of morals and values in law. As an experience of the imagination it also promotes our sensitivity by helping us develop our capacity for empathy or sympathetic understanding. This experience then, ideally, creates in us an awareness of the possibilities of meaning, especially when we pay careful attention to the form as well as to the content of what we read.[5] On this view, literary works with legal themes can give us insight in the struggles and tensions that are created by law as the regulation by society of the lives of individuals, precisely because literature differs from the abstract propositions that jurisprudence gives us on the subject, in that it always offers a particular experience.[6] This is, in short, the 'literature is edifying' view in the ideal sense of the word.

Following my interest in law and literature, I propose to extend one of its claims and to examine the interrelatedness of law, literature, and religion as ethical systems. Firstly, my focus will be on the congeniality of the views of Martha Nussbaum, James Boyd White, and Milner Ball, because the ethics of empathy proposed by these authors offers a valuable foundation

[5] For a detailed discussion, see my *Hope Springs Eternal* (Amsterdam, 1998).
[6] See also P. J. Heald (ed.), *Literature and Legal Problem Solving* (Durham, NC, 1998).

from which to pursue fundamental questions of law, literature, and religion alike in our contemporary pluralistic societies. If the success of any society or community depends for a large part on the capacity of its members to understand and acknowledge legal and moral or religious communities different from their own, and to act accordingly, we should turn to what literature, religion, and law teach us to ask: How should this person live? Am I my brother's keeper? Who is my brother, who is the other? Secondly, I will offer two illustrations of performances with language as ethical performances in order to clarify the idea of justice as reciprocity following from this.[7]

Words and Acts

ACTING WITH WORDS

James Boyd White has consistently argued that 'the justice that a judicial opinion achieves, or fails to achieve, can be seen as a matter of right relations—with one's language, with one's prior texts, with those one speaks to and about—at least as much as a matter of right results'.[8] On the assumption that a judicial opinion is a form of acting with words which has its effects on language as well as its readers, as lawyers we should consequently pay detailed attention to the ethical dimension of the meaning of texts, especially the texts of law, since 'the greatest power of law lies not in particular rules or decisions but in its language ... in the way it structures sensibility and vision'.[9]

On White's view of law as a cultural competence—the art of constituting culture and community—law is seen as an institution based on the idea of recognizing the other. Law offers opportunities to tell one's story and be heard. Thus, law is a method of translation as well as integration. It is a specific practice for understanding, dealing with, and, if possible, reconciling the opposite sides of a case. The work of lawyers is literary, for central to the enterprise of law is the idea of translating the stories of clients, parties in a lawsuit, into the language of the law, and where the judge is concerned, of translating these stories into a new reality for the parties involved, a reality which is at the same time a proposal for the form of the community shaped by law as the ordering force of society. On the view that people take the legal system to be legitimate only when they know themselves to belong to the legal community, we should therefore focus on the function and the value of the word, precisely because of the importance of the role of language in this process of transformation.

---

[7] J. B. White, *Justice as Translation* (Chicago, 1990).
[8] J. B. White, 'The Ethics of Meaning', in J. Neville Turner and P. Williams (eds.), *The Happy Couple: Law and Literature* (New South Wales, 1994), 269, 273.
[9] J. B. White, *The Legal Imagination*, abridged edn. (Chicago, 1985), p. xiii.

Central to White's view is also the idea of law as an argumentative process characterized by attention to the authoritative text. For lawyers as readers and writers of the texts of law this means that—in a normative, ethical sense, too—the right attitude to one's own language implies finding the right professional stance, both with respect to one's own use and understanding of the language of law and to one's response to other people, especially those one serves as an advocate or comes to adjudicate as a judge. Ideally, the lawyer should learn to '[use] a language and at the same time [express] a recognition of what it leaves out'.[10] Learning to do this requires an attitude of modesty and respect for one's fellow human beings, another aspect of the literary character of a lawyer's work. Thus the value for lawyers of the study of the humanities, and reading literature more specifically, is that it 'brings us to face two structural gaps. First: discontinuities of language and meaning between self and other. This . . . means that the concerns of the humanities are continuous with those of justice. Second: the discontinuities of language and meaning between parts of the self. This means that the concerns of the humanities are continuous with concerns for . . . integration.'[11] This idea of recognizing what can and cannot be said means that the dynamic process of change in language and culture is inherently uncertain. It also means that we cannot escape the question in what way this idea of acting with words can be a means of justification for the choices made in claiming meaning.

The relation between author and reader must then be studied. It comes into being because writing is a social activity meant to provoke response to the proposal that any text is. Essential in this process, especially because of the homology of law and literature White takes as his starting point, is his thesis with respect to a writer's ethos and its relation to both text and reader. As readers of legal texts we should always ask: What legal and social universe does the writer create? What attitude does he invite us to have towards the people and ideas, especially those with respect to the function and effect of law? What kind of character does he give himself in what he writes? What attitude towards the writer's ethos are we supposed to develop and do we actually develop?[12]

All texts thus have an ethical dimension in a double sense. The writer's ethos reveals itself in the text, and the relation constituted between text and reader is ethical. The reader, too, is a character in the world of the text, because the text elicits a reaction in the form of a judgement about the text, which in turn helps constitute the reader's character. This means that any text—a literary work, a judicial opinion, or a religious narrative—asks us to become its ideal reader. At the same time this implies the

---

[10] J. B. White, *The Legal Imagination* (Boston, 1973), 76.
[11] J. B. White, *From Expectation to Experience* (Ann Arbor, 1999), 101–2.
[12] J. B. White, *When Words Lose their Meaning* (Chicago, 1984), 15.

possibility of ethical criticism and the formation of a reader's character. Behind this is the presupposition that the reader is prepared to accept the world of the text as a real option and to reconstruct it as it were by reading. This reading by 'imaginary participation' helps educate the reader.[13] The result is a continuing emphasis on the need to recognize the similarity between law and literature since 'the central value of friendship—the recognition of others and the establishment of educative and reciprocal relations—can be stated as the central value of law and government too'.[14] That is why we should ask of any community we are called upon to judge whether or not it is a community of friendship, the essence of which, participation in deliberation and reciprocity, can be found not only in the willingness to reconsider one's views in the light of persuasive argument, but also in the capacity to recognize one's fellow humans and their needs and grievances. Law and literature are alike in that they both give voice to the voiceless and thus aim at 'the extension of our sympathies'.[15]

Our desire for meaning in law should therefore go beyond the mere search for intelligibility of words. This we can do only if in reading the texts of law we give an equal share to our capacity for analytical reasoning and our empathetic understanding. Thus, in imagining the law well, we are induced to develop a specific form of empathy. Reading fiction can contribute to this process in that the fictional narrative offers an experience that—while it is not ours—may resemble ours and in this way make us aware of similarities, or that may not resemble ours at all, and thus offer us a possibility to think about differences. The importance of the related activities of imagination, translation, and integration in law can be elucidated best when a fictional and a legal narrative are joined: 'When a real Captain Vere has the power to hang a real Billy Budd it becomes especially important that his methods of thought be ethically and intellectually good ones; and a text like *Billy Budd* itself, which teaches us much about false questions and the role of desire in judgment, is all the more valuable when brought to bear on a real opinion.'[16] Combined this way, the study of law and literature may ideally join cognitive insights of morals and values in law with empathetic understanding of the plight of those in whose lives the word of the law interferes deeply.

For Martha Nussbaum, too, literature is an indispensable medium to learn about law, for it provides us with a source of insight in the human condition. Reading literature, once this is incorporated in the professional lives of lawyers, can make valuable ethical and social contributions to the development of a professional ethos. Given the force of law as an institution, we may think of it like this: in law, too, social intercourse with fellow

[13] White, *When Words Lose their Meaning*, 8.   [14] Ibid. 220.
[15] *Heracles' Bow* (Madison, 1985), 104. The claim can, of course, be extended to (the texts of) religion.
[16] White, *From Expectation to Experiences*, 109.

human beings, especially in institutional settings where there are huge differences in power between the actors involved, forces us to recognize the needs of others. Literature promotes our sensitivity by helping us to develop our capacity for empathy. Nussbaum's proposed methodology is inductive. It starts from the particularity of the literary work and individual human experience rather than the generality of theory. The heart of the literary approach to portraying the complexity of human life in the texts of law is the ability 'to imagine the concrete ways in which people different from oneself grapple with disadvantage'.[17] An important part of this ability is the capacity of metaphorical imagination called fancy.[18] Ideally, fancy increases the capacity of judges, legislators, and policy-makers to imagine the needs of those whose lives they govern by their decisions. It enriches their imagination also in that it enables them to understand the effect of their acts on people's lives. At the same time it helps them to resist the negative sides of exclusively policy-oriented legal thought.

Nussbaum offers Dickens's *Hard Times* as an exemplary performance of her thesis. She shows that this novel invites us to a form of reading by imaginary participation, in Whitean terms, which accepts the textual world as a valid proposal of speaking about the actual world:

> For we are invited to concern ourselves with the fates of others like ourselves, attaching ourselves to them both by sympathetic friendship and by empathetic identification. . . . our natural response will be, if we have read well, to do unto other ordinary men and women as to ourselves, viewing the poorest as one whom we might be . . . (And by "reading well" . . . I mean, simply, reading with fancy and wonder, caring about the characters, being moved by their fate . . .).[19]

This ability of the imagination necessary for reading well is itself an empathic ability which is at once precondition for and product of reading well. It implies affective understanding of the other, and the capacity to act accordingly.[20] That is essential in the institutional discourse and practice of the law with its mechanisms of ordering society and individual human relations.

Like White, Nussbaum emphasizes the performative aspect and formative effect of literature on the reader's ethos. The experience of viewing the world of the text and its inhabitants empathically can and should be transformed into a norm for judging human relations, also in legal discourse. For many scholars in the field of law and literature, especially those in the field of feminist legal studies and law and theology, this means that alternative

---

[17] M. C. Nussbaum, *Poetic Justice* (Boston, 1995), p. xvi.

[18] Ibid. 36.

[19] M. C. Nussbaum, 'The Literary Imagination in Public Life', *New Literary History*, 22 (1991), 877, 894.

[20] Ibid. 907. For a similiar view, see Robin West, 'Economic Man and Literary Woman', (1988) 39 *Mercer Law Review*, 867, and *Caring for Justice* (New York, 1997).

discourses should be developed in which the voices of the disempowered can be heard. If the reader of literature and law, and I claim that the same goes in the context of religion, is able to develop this important character- istic of being able to see before his mind's eye, 'vividly what it is like to be each of the persons whose situations he imagines', then reading literary works can build a bridge between our view of justice and the actual effects of that view in social life.[21] Thus, for Nussbaum as much as for White, the norm from which to develop judgement about public life is to be found in the actual experience of reading and criticizing that can be translated and elevated to the level of interpersonal relations, because our actual knowl- edge and judgement of facts and values are inescapably the ground for any form of criticism.

What then does this literary–legal construction of a truly moral judge mean for the judge in practice? In *Love's Knowledge* Nussbaum lays the foundation for the image of the good Aristotelian judge, whose virtue lies correctly applying the equity of the flexible ruler. He is 'a judge of practi- cal wisdom, rather than being unreflectively subservient to law, [who] will apply it in accordance with his very own ethical judgment'.[22] Later Nussbaum mitigates this definition, the emphasis of which on subjective ethics will no doubt be indigestible to most lawyers. Then she says, 'I shall insist that technical legal reasoning, knowledge of law, and the constraints of precedent play a central role in good judging, supplying the bounds within which the imagination must work.'[23] The judicial characteristics exemplifying truly poetic justice are 'Intimate and impartial, loving with- out bias, thinking of and for the whole rather than as a partisan of some particular group or faction, comprehending in "fancy" the richness and complexity of each citizen's inner world . . .', and Nussbaum illustrates these with a number of cases.[24] In doing so, she associates herself with the tradition of analysing judicial opinions developed within law and litera- ture. Thus she rejects Justice Burger's (in)famous opinion in *Bowers* v. *Hardwick*, because it painfully shows the results of an abstraction from context and historicity when dealing with legal problems with a great impact on society and human relationships.[25] That is why, for Nussbaum, it is essential that judges develop a 'charity in the heart' to complement their technical-legal knowledge.[26]

THE WORD ACTS

Within the growing field of scholars interested in the intersection of law

---

[21] Nussbaum, *Poetic Justice*, 73.
[22] M. C. Nussbaum, *Love's Knowledge* (Oxford, 1990), 99.
[23] Nussbaum, *Poetic Justice*, 82.   [24] Ibid. 120.
[25] *Bowers* v. *Hardwick*, 476 U.S. 186 (1986).
[26] Nussbaum, *Poetic Justice*, 38.

and religion, or law and theology, Milner Ball takes a special place in that he includes literature in his search for meaning in a way congenial, though in different ways, to both White and Nussbaum. The question that has given direction to Ball's work since *The Promise of American Law* is, 'If law is a metaphor, what is it a metaphor of?'[27] Finding a metaphor for law using the insights drawn from literature, religion, and theology is Ball's leitmotiv. He elaborates the view that law can indeed be a medium for solidarity between people within a given community, thus making them a true community, or between different communities of people, thus promoting peace and mutual respect and understanding, if, and only if, law is able to offer a conceptual metaphor for humanity as a global community.[28] The attitude which Nussbaum describes as 'viewing the poorest as one whom we might be' can in Ball's opinion be promoted by reading the stories of the Bible because this contributes to the development of imagination and empathetic understanding, indispensable to lawyers. The metaphor offered is that of Christ's reign on earth as announced in Isaiah 11: 6–9, the Peaceable Kingdom, which occurs where and when, 'the Word of the biblical story intersects the world'.[29] In it Ball explicitly connects to law and literature.[30] For him, the study of the intersection of law and literature should pay more detailed attention to the stories and the trials and tribulations of minorities outside the mainstream of society. Law's actual violent effects on individual people's lives should be our concern. To this end, Ball proposes the combined study of literature and Scripture.

Ball does not offer a set of propositions. His text is itself a performance which—in the hermeneutic tradition—hopes to create in its readers understanding first, in that it enacts what cannot easily or completely be stated in propositional terms. Thus, Ball's methodology strongly resembles White's. Here too lies the point of congeniality with Nussbaum. Central to any reading should be a basic attitude of trust and respect, a charity of the heart. The performance of Ball's text starts with the stories of seven people who each in their own way represent an aspect of what Ball deems a desirable development in law and the legal profession, and aims to find out whether theology is able to shed a different light on what legal professionals (should) do. Theology as a discipline is the search for the meaning of the biblical Word. 'So from the biblical perspective, religion is unbelief,' says Ball, somewhat cryptically.[31] For him, religion is the epistemological pursuit of God, the desire for knowledge. The Word, on the other hand, 'generates faith rather than religion', in that in accepting the effect of the

[27] (Athens, Ga., 1981), 136.
[28] M. S. Ball, *Lying Down Together* (Madison, 1985).   [29] Ibid. 136.
[30] Ball's interest in law and literature dates back to 'The Play's the Thing', (1975) 28 *Stanford Law Review* 81.
[31] M. S. Ball, *The Word and the Law* (Chicago, 1993), 81.

Word in our lives and in caring about people we learn to let our hearts speak. As a search for knowledge, religion is 'centred on the self', while 'The Word directs to the other.'[32] This clearly shows Ball's focus on empathy as a basic attitude. He then calls upon literary works such as Toni Morrison's *Beloved* to show that religion, though itself in opposition to the Word, may nevertheless be the medium through which the Word shows itself. In the stories of Morrison's Baby Suggs, as well as in the work and lives of the legal professionals he discusses, Ball finds the core of his ethics, i.e. in the narratives 'that are types of specific, episodic service of the neighbour, including service of the neighbour by remaking dehumanizing institutions. These would be stories and examples of the Word taking form—action that is the responsibility and choice of humans, but action that is responsive to and engendered by the Word.'[33] Following Karl Barth, who emphasized the power of the Word to bring about belief, Ball explains his claim that the effect of the Word shows itself, with the text of Isaiah 6: 9–10 in which God tells Isaiah to tell the people, 'Hear ye indeed, but understand not' (AV). For Ball, this is *dabar*, the word which does what it says, i.e. the equivalent of a performative in analytical language philosophy.[34] This means that the Word 'bears its own possibilities for being known or not known by insiders or outsiders', and following the definition of *dabar*, it also means that, 'For both reader and nonreader . . . there is . . . no role for interpreters privileged or unprivileged. There is the word. The word does what it says as God performs mighty acts.'[35] He concludes that, 'We speak because we have been addressed by the Word.'[36] Rather than read in this a puritan call for a renewed predestinarian discourse, I understand this as a call to readers to look into their hearts and ask what the effect of a text is. That this is Ball's aim shows in the final chapter of *The Word and the Law*, entitled 'Morbidity and Viability in Law', where Ball discusses the theme of death in law. This is not just capital punishment, but first and foremost the subtle, textual form of death caused by the word of the lawyer which kills when it focuses on the letter rather than the spirit of the law and its societal context.[37] The pretence of neutral rule application is a doom, which is why Ball insists that we should pay careful attention to the way in which 'The life given law may be found in the lives of its performers.'[38] Only if lawyers take up

---

[32] Ball, *The Word and the Law*, 98.   [33] Ibid. 99–100.
[34] J. L. Austin, *How to Do Things with Words* (Oxford, 1962). See also M. S. Ball, 'Law and Prophets, Bridges and Judges', 7 (1989) *Journal of Law and Religion* 1, 17.
[35] Ball, *The Word and the Law*, 119.   [36] Ibid. 133.
[37] See also R. Cover, 'Violence and the Word', (1986) 95 *Yale Law Journal* 1601; and R. H. Weisberg, *The Failure of the Word* (New Haven, 1984).
[38] Ball, *The Word and the Law*, 150. I wish to add a personal note here. Since becoming a member of the Dutch judiciary it has been my experience that in order to create an image of neutrality many judges strongly favour writing in the passive voice, rather than by their grammar admit that it is they who decide.

their responsibilities and strive after justice rather than be mere officers of the legal system can law be the medium to constitute community, essential also to mankind's continued communal existence.[39] This also means—and here we see a congeniality with White's work—that when it comes to law in practice, 'We must risk ourselves, as well as our opinions, in the work of persuading and the surprise of being persuaded,' and that is a specific form of legal *dabar*, since 'the rule of law is for us the rule of persuasive argument performed in the language of the law'.[40] 'Does it work?' is the question in practice, then.

HABITS OF THE HEART

My conclusion at this point would be that the ideas of White, Nussbaum, and Ball converge on the point of an empathic model of law in which the minimum content of empathy is best described as the capacity to imagine oneself in the other person's situation in order to understand and feel one's way into the other person's experiences, so that one's attitude of empathy might form the basis for intersubjectivity in the sense of the individual's relation towards the totality of others. Now this does not necessarily mean that an unstipulated empathy with each and every actor within and without one's community is called for, but it does emphasize the need for a basic attitude of recognition of the other.[41] To this end the exemplary performances which these authors discuss in their works, as well as the exemplary performances that are their works, offer a powerful lesson to look at texts differently. They offer a mode for careful description of the value judgements provoked by our readings in order to hold them up to others for examination, and learn from that. On this view, we should not only reckon with the fact that the word has become law, but we should also fit the deed to the word in developing a new concept of justice. It is indeed truly a matter of religion, if we think of its Latin etymology. What joins us? That is, in the sense of *re ligere*, which means 'to be bound together as a community', whether for the purpose of serving a god, or of establishing a just society. And this joint existence itself is governed by that other derivative of the same stem, i.e. *lex*, or law, also from *ligo* or *lego*.

Following the related methodologies described above, I would say, firstly, that we should study the collective expressions of meaning in law, literature, and religion in terms of the resemblances rather than the differences of their relations, thus ending the long goodbye which has separated these disciplines. Secondly, that in doing so we may change or may have to

---

[39] Ibid. 153.
[40] M. S. Ball, 'All the Law's a Stage', (1999) 11 *Cardozo Studies in Law and Literature* 215.
[41] See also R. Alter, *The Art of Biblical Narrative* (New York, 1981). I borrow the phrase habits of the heart from Robert Bellah, *Habits of the Heart* (Berkeley, 1985).

change, depending on our initial position, the habits of our hearts. This in turn can only be accomplished if we are prepared to have our hearts battered by the word in all of the aspects discussed above.[42] That is why for a title I paraphrase the opening line of one of John Donne's Holy Sonnets in order to offer it as a metaphor for the interrelatedness of literature, law, and religion on the subject of making claims of meaning. The empathy necessary for that is the true combination of mind and heart.[43] The reflection of ethical, legal, and religious claims embedded in narratives or texts generally is what we should therefore study.

Job and Joshua

JOB

My first example is the Book of Job, which with its powerful motif of the determination of human fate in the divine council offers essential reading from a secular-legal point of view, too. Why? Because the questions the narrative raises—Why do good people suffer? What is justice?—are questions of retributive and distributive justice important to law. Not being a biblical scholar, my claims must and will be modest. I will not focus on the complex persona of Job and his case against God, nor on the theological aspects of wisdom literature, but on some of the others in the narrative, namely Satan and Job's friends. Careful attention to who they are and what they say will make us consider some of the pitfalls of the practice of law, as well as force us to think about who we might be. For as a literary work rather than a sacred text, Job challenges the reader to think about personal integrity and law as a human enterprise.[44] In focusing on Satan and Job's friends and reading well their arguments, we will see that this text elicits our judgement about both text and self. Thus the way in which a narrative itself imparts a way of looking at things offers a meaningful vantage point from which to resist an exclusionary doctrinal hermeneutics.

The facts in Job all point in one direction. The rule of law has gone

---

[42] See also T. S. Eliot's claim that our religion as well as the literature we read strongly affects our behaviour towards other people: 'Religion and Literature', in his *Essays Ancient and Modern* (London, 1936).

[43] The sonnet is entitled 'Batter my Heart, Three Person'd God'. Donne's poetic use of comparisons and sudden contrasts makes his work an ideal candidate for a metaphor to illustrate my point.

[44] My literary claim is modest too in that space does not permit me to pay attention to other aspects of the literary value of the Book of Job, as discussed, for example, by Northrop Frye, in *A Natural Perspective* (New York, 1965), and *The Great Code* (New York, 1981), and by J. William Whedbee, in *The Bible and the Comic Vision* (Cambridge, 1998). For similar reasons I cannot pay attention to either the seminal work of Harold Berman, George Anastaplo, and Thomas Shaffer in the field of law and religion, or such works as W. Fallers Sullivan, *Paying the Words Extra, Religious Discourse in the Supreme Court of the United States* (Cambridge, Mass., 1994). A literary work exploring the interpretative possibilities of Job is A. MacLeish, *J.B.* (London, 1959).

awry, for the righteous suffers, the wicked is successful. This already shows in the opening statement.

1: 6. Now there was a day when the sons of God came to present themselves before the Lord, and Satan came also among them.

1: 7. And the Lord said unto Satan, Whence comest thou? Then Satan answered the Lord, and said, From going to and fro in the earth, and from walking up and down in it.

1: 8. And the Lord said unto Satan, Hast thou considered my servant Job, that there is none like him in the earth, a perfect and an upright man, one that feareth God, and escheweth evil?

1: 9. Then Satan answered the Lord, and said, Doth Job fear God for nought?

1: 10. Hast thou not made an hedge about him, and about his house, and about all that he hath on every side? thou hast blessed the work of his hands, and his substance is increased in the land.

1: 11. But put forth thine hand now, and touch all that he hath, and he will curse thee to thy face.

1: 12. And the Lord said unto Satan, Behold, all that he hath is in thy power; only upon himself put not forth thine hand. So Satan went forth from the presence of the Lord. (AV)

Soon Job's servants and children are slain and when that does not make Job curse God, Satan is allowed a second strike. Job is smitten with sore boils. Satan's direct link between prosperity and goodness, suffering and sin, shows him to be a utilistic public attorney, who just cannot accept that man is good 'for nought'. His is an economic argument too. Job prefers God for the profit he brings. God's policy of letting his obedient servant Job prosper should therefore be tested. Satan's challenge to God is the challenge of a utilistic theology of the quid pro quo to a theology of benevolence and true justice. What should strike lawyers especially is that there is no presumption of innocence towards Job and the burden of proof is reversed. In being tested Job has to prove the obvious, namely his constant faith. Thus the first two chapters of Job set the scene for the refutation of Satan's accusation of God. This refutation takes the form of a game of question and answer in which the voices of Job's friends alternate with Job's own voice.

After being visited by Satan a second time, Job, who has neither uttered a complaint after the first series of disasters that befell him, nor followed his wife's advice to curse God and die, then has to face his friends. He asks to be given a reason for his present misfortune. Eliphaz the Temanite comforts him thus (4: 7): 'Remember, I pray thee, who ever perished, being innocent? or where were the righteous cut off?' Eliphaz's first argument is not an answer to Job's question, but a calm reproach, mirroring Satan's thesis. If the righteous man is cursed by evil, something must be wrong with him, or else God would not punish him this way. His thesis is simply that God is good; his conclusion that Job must have sinned. In a syllogistic manner typical of the legal formalist Eliphaz shies away from having to deal with Job's unbearable sorrow and despair, thus showing Job what kind of friend he is and reminding us what a flight into formalism may mean for human relations, a second lesson for lawyers to bear in mind. Driven to anger by Eliphaz's cool, doctrinal argument Job complains (6: 14): 'To him that is afflicted pity should be shewed from his friend.' It is unbearable for Job that a friend, a comforter, and a counsellor at that can say that something Job must have done wrong justifies his present agony.

Then Bildad the Shuhite joins in to give his answer, which again is not an answer to Job's question, for Bildad only reworks Eliphaz's argument (8: 6): 'If thou wert pure and upright; surely now he would awake for thee, and make the habitation of thy righteousness prosperous.' Repeating in part Eliphaz's argument, Bildad's monologue teaches lawyers yet another lesson. For Bildad does not really argue with Job. Although he does address Job's general thesis about the injustice of human fate, he does not refute Job's arguments about his particular misfortune. Bildad's thesis and answer also remain on the level of doctrine: one cannot argue with God, because man cannot rebel against the wisdom of experience; thus God must be good. Job's answer to Bildad and Eliphaz is an acknowledgement rather of God's power, when Job says that there is no possibility of a just fight between God and man, because God can do as he pleases (9: 19): 'If I speak of strength, lo, he is strong; and if of judgment, who shall set me a time to plead?' After having heard Eliphaz and Bildad declare that Job must be bad, the third friend, Zophar the Naamathite, directly jumps to the conclusion that Job must have sinned. His attitude should warn lawyers not to commit the same mistake professionally. For are we not sometimes prone to make Zophar's mistake? How many times do we not stop listening to a client's story when we come across something we can use—the professional déjà vu when all the facts and the evidence point in the direction of, say, a torts case, and we proceed to act immediately on this first impulse? How many times do we not do the same as judges burdened with a caseload when we base our opinion on the first applicable rule which presents itself?

Job's answer to his friends is that they only give him commonplaces, clichés, and he tells them that he knows how to use these too. (13: 1): 'Lo, mine eye hath seen all this, mine ear hath heard and understood it.' (13: 2): 'What ye know, the same do I know also: I am not inferior unto you.' Kierkegaard was right when he said that Job bore everything, until his friends came to comfort him. Then he lost patience! In the following exchanges of arguments between Job and his friends we see repetition only. Once more we are offered the circularity of the fallacious argument: Who is bad will be punished, therefore who is punished must be bad. Taken together, repetition and cliché point to a danger that looms large for lawyers, namely that of legal reification of human problems when lawyers are tempted to reduce human experience to legal cliché and people of flesh and blood to objects of discussion. Throughout the dialogues as the intensity of Job's complaint grows, he realizes that he has nothing in common with his friends nor with their arguments, a reaction that many people experience in the legal process. Job's friends do not really take him seriously; they see the effects of what they think must be Job's crimes, but they do not see Job. The caricature of the friends as counsellors offers us a powerful example of lack of true attention to the needs and grievances of the other. Thus the narrative vigorously reminds us of the significance of our professional legal attitude towards people and texts. For with respect to these counsellors' use of the language of the law—a language which should ideally prevent us from being the executioners of death in law—it is indeed as William Shakespeare later warned us in *The Merchant of Venice*, 'In law, what plea so tainted and corrupt, but being season'd with a gracious voice, obscures the show of evil? In religion, what damned error but some sober brow will bless it, and approve it with a text hiding the grossness with fair argument' (III. ii. 75–82).

When God finally answers Job out of the whirlwind, we see Job as the man who accepts the Word. For Job understanding is indeed a function of the Word as *dabar*. Not only is he battered by God in a literal sense, he also proclaims—in an almost Aristotelian fashion—that allowing ourselves to be battered in a figurative sense by the claims of fellow human beings should be our basic attitude, a precondition for brotherhood. Human vulnerability and dignity should be the key words in our legal discourse, if we are to see, no longer through a glass, darkly, but ultimately face to face. In the sense of 1 Corinthians 13: 12, as well as the almost literal sense, Levinas distinguishes which is immediately ethical in that it confronts both alterity and shared existence, autonomy and mutual dependence.[45] Is it a coincidence that Job is from the land of Uz, like the Good Samaritan?

JOSHUA

My second example is the story of Joshua. Not, however, the religious text about Moses' minister, who helped the tribes of Israel renew their covenant with God, but the lawsuit of 4-year-old Joshua DeShaney from Winnebago County, Wisconsin, who in 1984 was subjected by his father, with whom he lived after his parents had divorced, to a battering so severe that he suffered permanent brain damage and was profoundly retarded for the rest of his life. The evidence showed that the Winnebago Department of Social Services (DSS) involved in this case of child abuse knew what

[45] E. Levinas, *Totality and Infinity*. trans. A. Lingis (The Hague, 1979).

happened in the DeShaney home. After the final beating Joshua and his mother brought suit against the county, the DSS, and several of its workers. They complained that Joshua had been deprived of his liberty in the sense of bodily integrity without due process of law, in violation of his rights under the due process clause of the Fourteenth Amendment, because the DSS *et al.* had failed to intervene to protect Joshua against his father's beatings. I propose to read the DeShaney case as it came before the Supreme Court for the ethos emanating from, and the legal and social universe proposed in, the judicial opinions of Justices Rehnquist, Brennan, and Blackmun.[46]

Chief Justice Rehnquist delivered the opinion of the Court, holding that failure to protect an individual against private violence does not constitute a violation of the due process clause, because no affirmative obligation is imposed on the State to provide this type of protection. The Court also held that the State's knowledge of Joshua's dangerous situation did not itself establish a special relationship which might give rise to such an affirmative obligation either, since the State did not hold Joshua in its custody during the final beating, which, incidentally, was not by a State official but by his father.

Rehnquist's opening line, 'The facts are of this case are undeniably tragic' (191), seems to acknowledge Joshua's condition, but what then follows is a tale of the State's lack of action with respect to Joshua's welfare, which is itself law's tragedy in its lack of attention to this child's fate. Unmoved, cold, and to temptation slow, Rehnquist enumerates what the DSS did not do. In 1982 'the DSS interviewed the father, but he denied the accusations, and the DSS did not pursue them further' (192). When a child protection team is constituted to deal with Joshua's situation, 'the Team decided that there was insufficient evidence of child abuse to retain Joshua in the custody of the court' (192). After this,

the juvenile court dismissed the child protection case and returned Joshua to the custody of his father. A month later, emenergency room personnel called the DSS caseworker handling Joshua's case to report that he had once again been treated for suspicious injuries. The caseworker concluded that there was no basis for action. For the next six months, the caseworker made monthly visits to the DeShaney home, during which she observed a number of suspicious injuries on Joshua's head ... The caseworker dutifully reported these incidents in her files, along with her continuing suspicions that someone in the DeShaney household was physically abusing Joshua, but she did nothing more. In November 1983, the emergency room notified the DSS that Joshua had been treated once again for injuries they believed to be caused by child abuse. On the caseworker's next two visits to the DeShaney home, she was told that Joshua was too ill to see her. Still DSS took no action. (192–3)

---

[46] *DeShaney* v. *Winnebago County Department of Social Services*, 489 U.S. 189 (1989).

With this excruciatingly vivid tale of the State's inaction, Rehnquist gets the stepping stones to reject petitioners' claims that Joshua was entitled by law to protective services of the State and that

the State knew that Joshua faced a special danger of abuse at his father's hands, and specifically proclaimed, by word and by deed, its intention to protect him (197)

for

nothing in the language of the Due Process Clause itself requires the State to protect the life, liberty, and property of its citizens against invasion by private actors. The Clause is phrased as a limitation on the State's power to act, not as a guarantee of certain mimimum levels of safety and security. (195–6)

Since the State did not take Joshua into custody, did not, in short, institutionalize him, it had no duty whatsoever to assume responsibility for his safety. Rehnquist admits the possibility of the State having acquired a duty under state tort law to protect Joshua, once it started to gather information about Joshua's circumstances. He dismisses this at once, however, since petitioners base their claim on the due process clause. Mirroring his tale of the State's inaction, Rehnquist keeps telling us what he and the Court will not do as he adds,

Judges and lawyers, like other humans, are moved by natural sympathy in a case like this to find a way for Joshua and his mother to receive adequate compensation for the grievous harm inflicted upon them. But before yielding to that impulse, it is well to remember once again that the harm was inflicted not by the State of Wisconsin, but by Joshua's father. (203)

And besides, he claims, intrusion into the parent–child relationship too soon would be improper. In keeping close to legal doctrine and carefully setting the doctrinal scene with his enumeration of the State's inactions, Rehnquist can avoid the painful aspect of Joshua's suffering in a syllogistic manner, reminiscent of Job's friend Eliphaz. Rehnquist wears the formalist mask against which John Noonan warned us when he criticized lawyers, and judges especially, for their use of legal language solely for the purpose of avoiding having to deal with real people with real problems in real life.[47]

Justice Brennan's dissent jolts us out of this carefully created sense of legal normalcy. Brennan takes Rehnquist to task for his loading the legal dice, 'by leading off with a discussion (and rejection) of the idea that the Constitution imposes on the States an affirmative duty to take basic care of their citizens', because in doing so 'the Court foreshadows—perhaps

---

[47] J. Noonan, *Persons and Masks of the Law* (New York, 1976). See also Richard Posner's harsh cost-benefit analysis of Joshua's vegetative state in *Overcoming Law* (Cambridge, Mass., 1995).

even preordains—its conclusion that no duty existed even on the specific
facts before us'. Brennan's point is 'more than a quibble over dicta'; it is
'about perspective, having substantive ramifications'. For, 'in a constitutional setting that distinguishes sharply between action and inaction, one's
characterization of the misconduct alleged . . . may effectively decide the
case' (204), and this is even more so since Rehnquist, like Job's friend
Bildad, answers his own question, not the one raised by petitioners.

Rather than focusing on the State's inaction, which leads Rehnquist to
conclude that there was no State 'deed' establishing a right for Joshua,
Brennan extends the consequences of the State's intervening with a child's
life in the form of a child welfare system:

I would focus first on the action that Wisconsin has taken with respect to Joshua
and children like him . . . Wisconsin has established a child-welfare system specifically designed to help children like Joshua. Wisconsin law places upon the local
departments of social services such as respondent (DSS or Department) a duty to
investigate reported instances of child abuse . . . In this way, Wisconsin law
invites—indeed, directs—citizens and other governmental entities to depend on
local departments of social services such as respondent to protect children from
abuse. (208)

Brennan enumerates the people who did take action in referring to the
DSS: Joshua's stepmother, the neighbours, the police, and the caseworker
who informed her boss. Therefore,

Through its child-welfare program . . . the State of Wisconsin has relieved ordinary
citizens and governmental bodies other than the department of any sense of obligation to do anything more than report their suspicions of child abuse to DSS. If DSS
ignores or dismisses these suspicions, no one will step in to fill the gap. Wisconsin's
child-protection program thus effectively confined Joshua DeShaney within the
walls of Randy DeShaney's violent home until such time as DSS took action to
remove him. (210)

This leads Brennan to the conclusion, 'I would allow Joshua and his
mother the opportunity to show that respondents' failure to help him
arose . . . from the kind of arbitrariness we have in the past condemned'
(211). He reads the due process clause legally as well as truly empathically
for its spirit when he claims that the Constitution is not and should not be
indifferent to the indifference shown to Joshua by the DSS.

Justice Blackmun, joining Brennan, adds a dissent in his own voice too:

Today, the Court purports to be the dispassionate oracle of the law, unmoved by
'natural sympathy' . . . But, in this pretense, the Court itself retreats into a sterile
formalism which prevents it from recognizing either the facts of the case before it
or the legal norms that should apply to those facts. . . . the Court today claims that
its decision, however harsh, is compelled by existing legal doctrine. . . . I would
adopt a 'sympathetic reading', one which comports with the dictates of fundamental justice and recognizes that compassion need not be exiled from the province of

judging. . . . Poor Joshua . . . It is a sad commentary upon American life, and institutional principles that this child, Joshua DeShaney, is now assigned to live out the remainder of his life profoundly retarded . . . (212–13)

Taken together, the opinions of Brennan, Blackmun, and Rehnquist show that legal justice need not be divorced from compassion, and that lack of compassion can lead to injustice in the sense of a violation of a legal and judicial duty of care in every sense of the word. Reading them not only to learn who won, but especially in the sense White, Nussbaum, and Ball distinguish, namely for the road taken to come to the decision and to achieve justice, can make us truly and mutually cognizant of the requirements of our own disciplines and professions, in law, religion, and literature.

A Sense of Obligation

In their focus on the human condition law, literature, and religion find a common ground. I have tried to show that cultural disciplines like these operate best by empathetic participation in other people's lives and actions. For law and religion this is especially important now that they both contain the authority and the formal means to order human life and society. These ordering orders may and often do clash when the individual's religious claims which constitute his being led to actionable behaviour which cannot be reconciled with the demands of law.[48] Therefore, if law is not found but made, legal interpretation is an ethical–moral undertaking per se. There lies the problem of final justification, too, for beyond the institutional authoritative force of law lies the question of what actually makes us truly believe that a judicial decision is right. If the written justification of a court's holding is to persuade us, in the sense that we are moved to accept and live by its authority, can this be done other than by appealing to our heart as well as to our intellect? Can we, for example, at all agree that Joshua's fate was tragic and not be at least a bit uncomfortable with Rehnquist's opinion? Can we believe this is justice if our hearts tell us it is not? Can the opinion make us believe or is it make-belief? The question of the morality of a discourse and a practice itself then comes to the fore, and, extending Bourdieu's claim that belief is an inherent part of belonging to a field, or rather the precondition of entry, I would say that in law as well as religion justice depends on the way in which we enact our beliefs, against the background of a shared world-view. Thus, if truth is relative to an audience, convincing justification is what matters.[49] As lawyers especially we represent people. Should we then not truly re-present

---

[48] See e.g. *Bob Jones University* v. *United States*, 103 S.Ct 2017 (1983), *Wisconsin* v. *Yoder*, 405 U.S. 205 (1972), and *Valsamis* v. *Greece*, ECHR 74/1995/580/666.

[49] P. Bourdieu, *The Logic of Practice*, trans. R. Nice, (Cambridge, 1990), 67–8.

them, i.e. make them present again and show that a sense of what befell
them is present in what we do as their representatives in law? When this
ethic of empathy is made translatable and is indeed translated into a
collective standard in which men are treated as persons rather than objects
to be manipulated, we may finally arrive at conditions which make true
respect for the other in our pluralist societies possible. The Roman jurist
Ulpian was right. Law is a matter of *suum cuique tribuere*, but this presupposes careful attention to the other, my brother.[50] So the justice of any
society depends on whether we as its individual members care. The ethics
of empathy proposed by White, Nussbaum, and Ball can be the dynamic
of creative justice in this sense too. As lawyers and readers of texts we
should once again become *theoroi* in the classical Greek meaning of the
word. Not only theorists who bring what knowledge they have of the
requirements of their own disciplines to a better understanding of the
common bond of law, literature, and religion, but theorists especially who
truly care about 'the weightier matters of the law, judgment, mercy, and
faith' (Matthew 23: 23 AV). That will be a matter of experience reflected
in action.[51] Whether or not this happens because the Word speaks in us in
a biblical sense, we should at least realize that the Word of the law speaks
through us. We should therefore not be its mouthpieces or *bouches de la
loi* in a mere formalist sense. Now, my conclusion may be speculative,
controversial, or downright unsophisticated, but I maintain that the literary–legal methodology can be propaedeutic to further inquiry from which
law, literature, and religion may benefit. In one of Stephen Crane's poems
'A man said to the universe, "Sir, I exist!", "However," said the universe,
"the fact has not created in me a sense of obligation".' I maintain that it
should.

[50] Justinian, *Corpus Iuris Civilis, Digesta*, Dig. 1. 2. 10.
[51] For an example of the success of the literary–legal methodology, see J. C. Sheldon,
'Shylock, Cordelia, and the Maine District Court', (1999) 51 *Maine Law Review*, 10–13, a
personal account of a judge's professional disappointment and the cure found in literature.

POST-MODERNISM, HERMENEUTICS, AND AUTHENTICITY: INTERPRETING LEGAL AND THEOLOGICAL TEXTS IN THE TWENTY-FIRST CENTURY

Edward M. Andries

If the title of this paper is a bit curious, it could be either because the terms themselves—post-modernism, hermeneutics, and authenticity—raise an eyebrow, or perhaps because the relation of the terms to one another is in no way self-evident. It would therefore seem appropriate to start with some preliminary definitions. This strategy presents an immediate problem, however, because to define post-modernism one must disavow post-modernism: a definition would reduce post-modernism to some fundamental core or essence, which would be too foundationalist, too essentialist. Post-modernism rejects the very possibility of essences, cores, or foundations that undergird modernist, or even pre-modern, definitions.

Assuming for the moment that there may be such a thing as the essence of post-modernism, one can nevertheless agree with Peter Schanck's observation that there is no single principle on which post-modernism is grounded or which comprises its essence.

Instead, several interrelated concepts do so, each of which in a sense undergirds the others. Each depends on the others for its existence and each is a precondition of the others. These concepts may be summarized as follows: (1) The self is not, and cannot be, an autonomous, self generating entity; it is purely a social, cultural, historical and linguistic creation. (2) There are no foundational principles from which other assertions can be derived; hence, certainty as the result of either empirical verification or deductive reasoning is impossible. (3) There can be no such thing as knowledge of reality; what we think is knowledge is always belief and can apply only to the context within which it is asserted. (4) Because language is socially and culturally constituted, it is inherently incapable of representing or corresponding to reality; all propositions and all interpretations of texts, are themselves merely social constructions.[1]

---

[1] Peter C. Schank, 'Understanding Postmodernism Thought and its Implications for Statutory Interpretation', (1992) 65 *Southern California Law Review* 2505, 2508–9.

For our purposes, it is most important to note that for the post-moderns, the meaning of a text is never grounded or stable, and therefore one can always find multiple meanings or truths.

Furthermore, post-modernism rejects the role of reason itself, and with it all philosophy, as a foundation for social criticism. Jean-François Lyotard defines the post-modern condition as one in which the 'grand narratives' of legitimization including narratives of historical progress, scientific rationalism, reason, and justice are no longer credible.[2] No longer anchored philosophically, the very shape or character of social criticism changes; it becomes more pragmatic, ad hoc, contextual, and local. This wide-ranging attack on metaphysics has led to a general scepticism of overarching theories and integrating principles, and, as a partial consequence, has led to disordered interpretations of theological texts as well as legal codes and constitutions. Looking more carefully at the implications in the field of law, one can immediately see at least one problem, namely, that 'overarching theories and principles' are the backbone of codes and constitutions.[3]

Turning now to the term 'hermeneutics', one observes that traditionally, whether in theology or law, the word has referred to rules, guidelines, and criteria for proper interpretation. Accordingly, hermeneutics does not investigate the objective truth of a writer's meaning; it does not inquire what is true or false, but only what the author intended to say. In its narrowest definition, it does not inquire into the special character of a writing—for instance, whether it be sacred or profane. Accordingly, biblical hermeneutics would presuppose a knowledge of the history of the canon of both Old and New Testament, an acquaintance with the results of lower or textual criticism and related philological and historical scholarship, and a study of the relevant treatises on inspiration.

When speaking of hermeneutics in its traditional sense, it is helpful to distinguish three types of interpretation: authentic, legal, and scientific. The most direct and simple way of determining the meaning of an author consists in the latter's statement of the sense he intended to convey. Such a statement, whether it proceeds from the author himself or from another person who has certain knowledge of the author's mind, is called an *authentic* interpretation. The *legal* interpretation differs from the authentic in that it proceeds, not from the lawgiver himself but from his successor, or from his equal in legislative power, or from the supreme legal authority. To the extent that there may be a transition from authentic to legal inter-

---

2 Jean-François Lyotard, *The Postmodern Condition: A Report on Knowledge*, trans. G. Bennington and B. Massumi, (Manchester, 1984), 27–41.

3 As explained later in the paper, even if one doesn't believe in their legitimacy, one would still have to entertain their existence in order properly to interpret the original meaning of the code.

pretation, the nature of this transition may vary depending on whether one is interpreting in the field of law or in the field of theology.[4]

Finally, the *scientific* interpretation differs from both the authentic and the legal; its value is not derived from authority, but from the trustworthiness and the learning of the commentator, from the weight of his arguments, and from his faithful adherence to the rules of hermeneutics, which may be of either universal or particular application depending on the nature of the writings to be interpreted. The Bible, for example, may demand additional rules of hermeneutics which are not applicable to profane writings. Scientific interpretation is closely aligned with what can be considered the focal meaning of hermeneutics. Here the interpreter must be guided by the quasi-criteria of the author's meaning: his language, his train of thought or the context, and his psychological and historical condition at the time of writing. In the case of Scripture, considerations of inspiration and authority may be added to these three criteria.

A distinction exists between 'context' within the framework and method of scientific interpretation, and context within the framework of authentic or legal interpretation. In the latter, the authority of the interpreters arises in part by virtue of the fact that they, more than any others, share the same context, in its essentials, as the author(s). They themselves are insiders—inside the same tradition, or at least the same world-view in so far as it might relate to the text. Scientific interpretation is open to outsiders (and insiders) whereas authentic or legal interpretation is open to insiders only. However, post-modernism would deny the possibility of scientific interpretation, claiming that context cannot really be understood by an outsider. In partial response, the following story may be illustrative: An old man is on the beach in the evening with a friend. He sees an incredible reflection from the stars across the water and says to his friend, 'Look at that; it is beautiful.' The friend replies: 'Look at what? I see nothing.' The old man says, 'Ah yes, well stand over here, where I am standing, and you will also see it.' The friend stands where the old man was standing and then sees the reflection. In this way, we can see how in some instances proper context, condition, or position can be essential to having any understanding of what the author is talking about. In a sense, this is the

---

[4] In theology, those who are the most 'inside' the tradition, or more specifically, most inside the author's mind, may themselves select those to be newly included as the next generation of authoritative 'insiders' tasked with continuing the transmission of authentic interpretations. In so-called revealed religions in particular, namely, Judaism, Christianity, and Islam, authority is necessarily implicated in the transmission of the message and its meaning, particularly given the complex and occasionally analogical use of language in the tradition and text. The meaning of this language has been transmitted from the time of the revelation itself up to the present day. By contrast, in law, e.g. constitutional law, there is no formal mechanism of succession whereby the framers of the Constitution would be able to appoint the authentic insiders (as judges) in a top-down fashion, and whereby those insiders would themselves be responsible for selecting the next generation of the same.

equivalent of a conversion. One can be made an insider, but as with the old man's friend, it would seem possible only under the direction of one who is already there. So, it seems we have a double meaning of 'authority'. Firstly, the authority of others is necessary so that one can be led inside. Secondly, once inside, it is the basis for asserting one's own authority with respect to interpretation. Scientific interpretation requires a consideration of context, and thereby may require, to the extent possible, standing where the author stood, at least as a temporary exercise, in order to do justice to the author's meaning. If one chooses to ignore the author's perspective, either believing it impossible to understand or ignoring it simply because one disagrees with it, then the element of context will be lacking and proper scientific interpretation becomes impossible.

Therefore, it is safe to say that if post-modern presuppositions are generally accepted, then the possibility of purely scientific interpretation is eliminated and authentic or legal interpretation becomes our only hope for ascertaining the meaning of an author. And if one dispenses entirely with the goal of determining the author's meaning (rather than simply reading possibilities in the text from which the reader can create his or her own meaning), then the very act of writing a text for posterity itself becomes absurd and no written text could legitimately have any real authority— whether Scriptures, codes, or constitutions.

Taking a closer look at the effects of post-modernism, one finds that 'hermeneutics' taken in its more current sense refers less to rules or criteria for determining an author's intent, and more to the process of interpreta- tion and the role of the subject—the interpreter—in that process. Cartesian or Kantian epistemology is at the root of much current thought on hermeneutics. Furthermore, the shift from the traditional to the more current usage of the term hermeneutics parallels, and in fact is a part of, the shift from historical to literary criticism. The literary-hermeneutical approach includes such non-contextual approaches as structuralism and deconstruction, and a variety of contextual approaches such as rhetorical criticism, sociological and psychoanalytic criticism, and phenomenological criticism, the latter best represented by the work of Ricœur. It is of course true that both Heidegger's and Gadamer's consideration of hermeneutics from the standpoint of ontology and Husserl's and Ricoeur's phenomeno- logical approach to hermeneutics have made significant philosophical contributions to the language-centred approach to the understanding of texts. Central to contemporary hermeneutical theory is the conviction that all historical (as opposed to mathematical or scientific) understanding is dialogical in nature. Under this approach, the interpretation of texts involves a 'dialogue' between reader and text about the subject matter with which the text is concerned.

For post-Heideggerian philosophers, it may be said that hermeneutics is an inquiry into the modalities of 'being in the world' that allow all meaning to emerge, and is thus ontological. Gadamer's purpose, for example, is not to develop a procedure of understanding, but to clarify the conditions in which understanding takes place. Much of this so-called 'ontological' school of hermeneutics in many ways presupposes and manifests Kant's transcendental idealism, while at the same time attempting to overcome it. Gadamer focuses on the problem of aesthetics, for example, because he sees Kant's contention that aesthetic appreciation is merely subjective as symptomatic of the ascendance of the Enlightenment's scientific method as the paradigm of all knowledge.[5] Gadamer insists on the importance of truth that is beyond scientific methodology. His thought is consistent with the so-called first principle of post-modernism—that the self is not, and cannot be, an autonomous, self-generating entity; rather, it is a social, cultural, historical, and linguistic creation. He builds on Vico's challenge to the unitary Cartesian paradigm of knowledge, and points to the classical rhetorical tradition as a way of understanding no less legitimate or important than the methodological model of the natural sciences.[6] Gadamer views textual interpretation as a dialogue wherein the text 'speaks'.[7] The text engages the reader's horizon before the reader is able to question it consciously. The interpreter comes to the text with his own horizon, or 'forestructure of meaning',[8] which is a 'meaning and a possibility that one brings into play and puts at risk'[9] before the horizon of meaning that is the text. Reading involves the fusion of these indeterminate horizons and approaches 'the full realization of conversation in which something is expressed that is not only mine or my author's, but common'.[10] The important question is whether that 'common something' can properly be called the meaning of the text, and if so, under what conditions?[11]

Paul Ricœur develops Gadamer's notion of text as potential meaning and, like Gadamer, regards the text as an artefact that is distinct from the subjective intentions of its author. The author's discourse has been 'fixed' by his act of writing down his words; as such, the matter of the text supersedes the author's intention. In fact, Ricœur views the text as wholly autonomous, with no support from the intentions of the author, and thereby hands writing over to the sole interpretation of the reader. Thus,

[5] For Kant, however, 'knowledge' does not proceed from any merely objective foundation either. It is rather the result of the subsumption of the material of intuition under the formal framework of the categories.

[6] However, as with Kantian scientific knowledge, Gadamer's historically embedded dialogical (and rhetorical) knowledge cannot claim to be objective knowledge of the reality of the object per se, but rather, for Gadamer, a third thing resulting from the convergence of object and perceiver in a so-called playful encounter.

[7] H.-G. Gadamer, *Warheit und Methode* (1960), trans. as *Truth and Method*, 2nd edn., (New York, 1975), 340.

[8] Ibid. 236. [9] Ibid. 350. [10] Ibid.

[11] The answer to this question is not unrelated to the insider–outsider distinction explained above.

the emphasis is on the interaction of reader with text in the reading process, by which the text is being actualized or realized by the reader. It implies that 'the potential text is infinitely richer than any of its individual realizations'.[12]

In the area of theology, Scriptures do not frequently mediate their truth in propositional terms, but rather through narrative. Various interpretative methodologies have developed to address the narrative nature of Scriptures, but what is important to note is that these so-called narrative methodologies, anchored in the world of literary criticism, have invaded the so-called propositional universe of the law. With respect to narratives, Ricœur has distinguished three so-called *worlds*: that *behind* the text, namely the milieu impinging on the author;[13] that *within* the text, namely the environment created by the system of interlocking signs that make the text; and that *in front of* the text, by which he means the vision of what is possible opened up for the reader, which enables one to realize one's 'ownmost powers'.[14] This later world is for Ricœur the significance of literature. It is achieved by the effacement of the descriptive referent of the text, that is, the world it is talking about, in order to redescribe reality in terms of its possibilities for the individual. Ricœur's primary concern throughout his various discussions of literature is with the possibilities of human existence, and not with literature as an act of communication. This is a deficiency he owes to aspects of Kantian thought. Trapped in a Kantian dichotomy between the sensible and the intelligible, Ricœur must nonetheless find a way of accounting for the mind's ability to grasp the potential abundance of what is presented to it, i.e. the text. He does this, as he says himself, by having recourse to the notion of the *productive* imagination as Kant develops it in the third Critique, *The Critique of Judgment*. Imagination, therefore does what the mind cannot do, that is, it must move ecstatically in an act that, rather than assimilate the particular to the universality of the categories (as in a determinant judgement),[15] finds a universal for a given particular.[16] The redescription or configuration proposed by Ricœur is a move through the play of images from something determined by the structure of the world to something discovered by the creative ordering of the productive imagination, thus pointing to the subjectivist outcome in Ricœur.[17]

---

[12] See W. Iser, 'The Reading Process: A Phenomenological Approach', in his *The Implied Reader* (Baltimore, 1974), 280.

[13] Cartesian thought might categorically dismiss this *world* as 'tradition', unworthy of the status of knowledge. However, here it is not claiming to be knowledge only in a qualified way, i.e. only as information contributing to knowledge of what the author meant.

[14] P. Ricœur, *Time and Narrative*, trans. K. McLaughlin and D. Pellauer, 3 vols. (Chicago, 1984–88), 81.

[15] Note the parallel to traditional civil or code law methodology.

[16] Note the parallel to typical common law methodology.

[17] Ricœur, *Time and Narrative*, i, 39 ('the ideas of beginning, middle and end are not taken from experience. They are not features of some real action but the effects of the ordering of the poem').

One aspect of this subjectivist tendency is clearly problematic: How is it possible in any way whatever to conceive of an ideal sense of a text without reference to reality? It would seem more accurate to say that any text has an internal texture of references which, by reason of the nature of the act of reading, build up simultaneously a textuality of reference to the world. This bond between the world created by the text and the world referred to by the text, coupled with the fact that the referential statements within the text continue to function as such, provides the ground for rejecting the split between text and world presupposed by Ricœur and many others.

The variety of *literary* hermeneutical approaches to the interpretation of texts has precluded totalitarian claims for any one approach. What all of these recently developed schools have in common is their operation within the linguistic–literary rather than the historical paradigm. They all deal with the text in its final form rather than with its genesis, and they are concerned with the literary world projected *in front of* the text rather than with the historical world *behind* the text. Their hermeneutical interests are in present meaning mediated by language through interpretation rather than in historical meanings uncovered by exegesis which are then inserted into contemporary contexts by a process of application.

From an Anglo-American legal perspective, interpretation is further complicated by the competing methodologies of the common law and civil law systems. We call the legal systems of the United Kingdom and the United States common law systems, but of course we know that today, speaking at least with respect to the US system, it is really a mixed system of common law and codes, not to mention constitutions, state and federal. In recent years, some, especially within the critical legal studies movement, have focused more on the common law aspects of the Anglo-American system. In contrast with European codes, in which the aspiration to logical coherence is central, the common law tradition is frequently acknowledged by even some of the most conventional of legal theorists to be a rather loose and not particularly logical system of interpretation and practice. Accordingly, some have embraced the common law as a fully post-modern set of practices, taking the least logical part of law, and exploring it for its radical potentials. As with other texts, even common law holdings *may* be considered 'autonomous' in the sense that they are subject to use apart from any reasoning behind them. The fact that a court decided one way versus another in a particular factual context is more determinative for future cases than why the court decided the way it did. Here, even the common law can be taken as an artefact and divorced from the context and tradition that produced it. Such a practice, employed by many post-moderns and/or those with a somewhat radical political agenda, should not be surprising considering that legal scholars from the founding era of the United States generally viewed the common law as a system more or less grounded in natural law. With this in mind, one can understand why a post-modern would want to, or be compelled to, divorce the common law from the world behind it.

Although it may evidence a certain intellectual dishonesty to interpret codes as if the rules found therein were not really specified in legislated text, but rather gleaned from the collection of judge-made rules from prior cases, the over-application of common law methodology is subject to more serious criticism when it is used as the method of choice for interpreting written constitutions containing a separation of powers structure such as that found in most modern constitutions. In the United States we do not need *Marbury* v. *Madison*[18] to understand that the Constitution is more akin to a code than to common law rules. The very fact that it is written is enough. A written constitution presupposes that future interpreters will attempt to read and understand the meaning of the text, the meaning that the framers intended to express, by virtue of writing it. Furthermore, this focus on the text traditionally has been the hallmark of interpretative practices in code law systems.

It is clear that if the world behind the text is thought to be either unknowable or irrelevant, the text itself is thought to be autonomous, and the world in front of the text and the possibilities for human existence are thought to be the real determinants of meaning, then common law methodology is not only perfectly suited for the task of interpreting codes and constitutions, but really is the only possibility. However, such assumptions, which would justify the application of common law methodology to codes and constitutions, are themselves not justified, and furthermore, they are inconsistent with the separation of powers structure of the US Constitution. The first assumption, that the world behind the text is either unknowable or irrelevant, is not justified for the reasons previously alluded to—namely, at the philosophical level, the problematic yet widely accepted Kantian dichotomy between the sensible and the intelligible. At the more practical level, this assumption is also betrayed by the common-sense understanding of the framers that by adopting a *written* constitution, future interpreters would attempt to ascertain what they meant by the words they used—not what future interpreters wanted the words to mean, but what the framers wanted the words to mean. The last assumption for justifying a common law approach to constitutional interpretation—that the world in front of the text and the possibilities for human existence are the real determinants of meaning—might be a perfectly harmless assumption with respect to interpreting literature, but it has no place in the interpretation of written constitutional text where the judges' very authority to interpret that text and strike down actions of other branches of government as inconsistent with it rests on the perception underlying the holding of *Marbury* v.

---

[18] *Marbury* v. *Madison*, 5 U.S. (1 Cranch) 137, 2 L.Ed. 60 (1803).

Madison that judges are naturally appropriate expositors of the law—that 'it is emphatically the province and duty of the judicial department to say what the law is'.[19] 'What the law is' is written in the constitution and was meant to be interpreted according to the meaning that was put in the text by the framers, not according to the meaning created by future interpreters. If, however, one insists that the meaning of this written text is unknowable and wholly dependent on the subjective preferences of the reader, then the distinction between a written and unwritten constitution evaporates,[20] and so does the basis for the judicial review power given to courts in *Marbury*. Moreover, if the meaning of the more determinate provisions of the constitution *can* be worked out in accordance with a process leaving little room for subjective preferences and value choices by the interpreters, then even if the process sometimes seems tedious, it should nevertheless provide results that are sufficiently certain to begin to legitimize the separation of powers system giving courts the power of judicial review. Clearly, historical evidence is not lacking that indicates the framers intended judicial review.[21]

If one opts for the continued viability of judicial review, and therefore implicitly concedes the possibility of knowing the meaning, the original meaning, of a constitutional text, then one has the opportunity to address yet another problem—specifically, which sense of the term 'original meaning' is to be used? To borrow from Ronald Dworkin, the disagreement is over whether the rules should implement the framers' broad conceptions of constitutional meaning or their narrow conceptions of the same.[22] Of course, this issue is only truly problematic when examining facially vague, ambiguous, or equivocal text.

When interpreting seemingly ambiguous and open-ended text, one must keep in mind that 'original meaning' is not necessarily indicated by what the drafters' actual social or ethical practices were, but perhaps instead by the meaning of the text for them in the broader context of the principles from which they sought to order the republic. Furthermore, with respect to facially vague or open-ended provisions, they are necessarily principled, and the principle must be coherent and consistent with the constitution as a whole.[23]

---

[19] Also, this assumption is highly problematic with respect to theological texts to the extent that these texts announce a message that has been *revealed* by an event in history and is not self-evident. The knowledge of this particular meaning comes from those events and as such is more dependent on an authentic 'insider' interpretation of those events.

[20] This is not to say that the meaning of an unwritten constitution is wholly dependent on the reader's subjective preference.

[21] See e.g. *Federalist*, no. 78 in G. W. Carey and J. McClellan (eds.), *The Federalist* (Dubuque, Ia., 1990).

[22] See R. Dworkin, *Taking Rights Seriously* (London, 1977), 134–6; and, 'The Forum of Principle', (1981) 56 *New York University Law Review* 469, 471–500.

[23] Also, with respect to theology, the text must be interpreted as a part of a whole, which must be coherent in the context of the whole. The part must be seen in the context of its position in a larger array of meaning.

More specifically, one can recognize two essential criteria or requirements for the discernment of legitimate interpretative principles.[24] The first requirement is that the principle must have been historically present in the ideological tradition(s) to which the framers belonged. This criteria addresses the world *behind* the text and aims to do full justice to the consideration of context in the interpretative effort. Accordingly, a philosophical realist might find it easier to interpret the US Constitution since such a person could enter into a scientific interpretative effort with the confidence of personally acknowledging and understanding the principles setting the context within which the framers wrote. Alternatively, for a post-modern, such a realist world-view replete with natural law principles would not be convincing from their personal perspective, which would seek to replace all universal or eternal principles with hermeneutical fluidity and historic contingency. Nonetheless, if post-moderns wish to reasonably support the institution of judicial review, themselves not admitting their ability to engage in scientific interpretation as outsiders, they would be forced to support authentic, or at least legal, interpretation. In doing so, they would be forced to concede that certain world-views grounded in philosophical realism, including, for example, aspects of traditional natural law theory, informed the world-view of the framers and in this respect are relevant to the task of interpreting their words. Because post-moderns would proclaim their inability to understand these principles as the authors understood them, however, the interpretative task would have to be handed over to others—to insiders.

The second criteria for the discernment of top-level principles is that the principle must be coherent in itself and in relation to the entire body of the text to which the specific provision belongs. Here it should be recognized that there is a process of interpreting and integrating original principles for purposes of arriving at coherency among and between these principles, some of which, depending on how they are construed, may seem to be at tension with others.[25]

Inevitably, anyone advocating an originalist methodology today will face an assault on that methodology by those who claim that the *Brown* v. *Board of Education* case could not have reached the result it did—the end of state-sponsored segregation in public schools—without that court's explicit rejection of the original meaning of the Fourteenth Amendment's equal protection clause. In response, many originalists have invoked the *principle* behind the equal protection clause of this amendment as justifying the *result* in *Brown*, despite the fact that the Court used a different

[24] These same criteria or requirements are also useful, and perhaps essential, for purposes of evaluating the extent to which potentially erroneous constitutional precedent is or should be binding.

[25] e.g. potential conflicts between the two religion clauses of the First Amendment, or more generally, between principles such as respect for life and respect for liberty.

justification.[26] The problem is that if the social and ethical practices of the drafters and ratifiers of the Fourteenth Amendment are taken to indicate that they did not intend that amendment to exclude the possibility of state-sponsored segregation in schools, but if a general principle of equality is simultaneously extracted from the text and taken to exclude such segregation, then we may be inclined to give an extracted principle, divorced from the intentions of the authors, i.e. divorced from the world behind the text, priority over a historically ascertainable original 'meaning' of the text. And if we extract a principle from a text without regard to the world behind the text, then we run into the same problems as previously mentioned regarding judicial review and its requirement that judges state what the law is and not create the law themselves. However, this is not to say that judges ought not to use principles *within* the text in determining the meaning of that text in a current setting. The resolution of this tension between the original so-called narrow meaning of a text, and the principle extracted from a text, to the extent that there is to be any resolution, will be found by making further distinctions when speaking of principles within and behind the text.

It is difficult to justify an appeal to a principle detached from the history and context of the text to defeat a historically ascertainable meaning of a text at the time it was written. If the appeal to principle is to be legitimate within our separation of powers system, which has implied the power and authority of judicial review, then the governing principle must also be historically present at some level in the world behind the text, the world from which the text was generated. In this respect it is important not to get stuck at the principle extracted from the text, arrived at through some inductive process. Rather, this principle which is inductively generated, or perhaps in more Kantian terms 'creatively imagined', from the text should be supplemented with the broader principles presupposed in the context of the time the text was written. These broader principles are linked directly to the Constitution as a whole, and then via deductive application, to the specific provisions. In this way, a hierarchy of principles or contexts must be recognized in order to more properly come to an organic interpretation of the text where the part is read in the context of the whole, the entire whole, not just a larger sub-part.

We can therefore distinguish three types of input into our textual-originalist search for meaning: (1) the specific applicable meaning of the text at the time it was written, gathered from the framers' own practices, taken to indicate their specific views on how the issue should be resolved at that time; (2) the prima facie principle specifically relating to and taken from the text at issue; and (3) the broader principle or principles behind the text, behind the amendment as a whole, and the Constitution as a whole.

---

[26] See e.g. R. Bork, *The Tempting of America* (New York, 1990), 81–3.

According to the so-called historical requirement for the discernment of principles, if a principle from the second category—one specifically relating to the text at issue and generated by reference to that text—is to defeat the alleged historical 'meaning' from the first category, then it will need the support of the broader historically rooted principle(s) from the third category. Otherwise, for the reasons previously mentioned, it would remain difficult to say that judges are in fact 'stating what the law is' if they have no reference to the world behind the text. Adopting an interpretation that is consistent with the principles from both the second and third categories, while perhaps inconsistent with the imputed meaning from the first category, allows for the conclusion that the principle adopted by the framers may have been loftier from a moral point of view than the framers' own social and ethical practices.

Furthermore, as previously noted, we must assume that the Constitution is a coherent and consistent document. Such a document would necessarily have within it some hierarchy of principles structuring it and allowing for coherent and consistent resolution of tensions that may appear to exist when simply looking at the face of the text. The fact is, judges will always formulate some similar type of hierarchy in their own minds, regardless of whether or not they would admit to it, or make their presupposed hierarchy of principles explicit. Regardless of what one thinks of 'reading principles' from the text, it will always occur. Therefore, it is best to proceed by focusing and refining the debate on exactly what those principles are and in what hierarchy they are arranged—as a matter of both history and coherency.

It is clear that this sort of interpretative scheme is much more akin to traditional code law or civil law interpretation, which generally starts with a contextual whole, containing general and unifying principles, and moves down to making particular determinations that are coherent in the context of this whole.[27] Whether post-moderns like it or not, this is a more deductive approach to reasoning, starting with the general and moving to the specific and concrete. However, just as the US legal system is a mixed system of common law, code law, and constitutional law, the approach advocated herein integrates both the inductive reasoning elements of the common law with the deductive methodology of the civil or code law. Again, the principle generated by reference to the specific text may be arrived at through inductive reasoning moving from the specific to the general, i.e. from text to principle, whereas the more general principles behind the article or amendment and the Constitution as a whole are deductively applied to the more specific and textually linked principle in

---

[27] Emphasis should be given to the word 'traditional' in the phrase 'traditional code law or civil law interpretation'. Today many code-law-based countries have informally and unofficially adopted common law interpretative methodologies.

order to properly align it and set its permissible boundaries. This higher principle is deductively applied to help us understand the lower and otherwise somewhat generic principle and to give it the proper connotation.

With respect to the notion of proper and permissible boundaries for otherwise open principles, the equal protection clause of the Fourteenth Amendment is again a useful example. No reasonable definition or interpretation of 'equal protection', whether historically grounded or not, would permit discrimination against any group or class of persons that would have the effect of denying them 'equal protection of the laws'—but that still leaves open the question of what *constitutes* a denial of equal protection. We have the text, the meaning of which some might argue is indicated by the framers' own practices with respect to the question at issue, e.g. segregation. We have an extracted or inductively generated principle of 'equality'. And finally, we have a general principle (or principles) behind the amendment as a whole and behind the Constitution as a whole which can help us to understand what 'equality' can and cannot mean. What sense of equality was meant by the framers? Equality in opportunity? Equality in results? Or, perhaps, at a more fundamental level, equality in dignity? Going even further, how and why would equality in dignity be a coherent principle? The answer to the latter question might provide the top ordering principle for virtually every controversial rights question arising under the US Constitution and many others.[28]

Admittedly, looking for a higher and broader level of historically grounded principle(s) expands our inquiry into the meaning of a given text in the Constitution, requiring a careful study of the cultural, legal, and philosophical tradition within which the framers lived so that their words, and principles taken from their words, can be interpreted with reference to this context. Fortunately, it would seem that with respect to the so-called world behind the text, it is often easier to have general knowledge of that world than specific historical knowledge related to the particular textual provision at issue. Even those advocating the complete autonomy of the text, divorcing it from the intent behind it, and looking more at the current possibilities of meaning for the text using 'principles' as a mere surrogate for current and supposedly shared national 'values', will recognize the many possible ways of seeing these values. For example, the values may be seen as permanent and universal features of human social arrangements— natural law principles—as they typically were in the eighteenth and nineteenth centuries, i.e. the world *behind* and *within* the constitutional text.

[28] See Edward M. Andries, 'On the German Constitution's 50th Anniversary: Jacques Maritain and the 1949 German Basic Law (*Grundgesetz*)', 13 *Emory International Law Review* 1, 49–60. See also Edward M. Andries, 'Religious and Philosophical Norms in the Constitutions of Germany and the United States', in Proceedings of 2nd Annual European and American Conference on Church Autonomy and Religious Liberty, Trier, Germany (Frankfurt, forthcoming).

Or, they may be seen as relative to our particular civilization, and subject to growth and change, as they typically are today.[29] If judges are looking for principles to aid their legitimate interpretative efforts, the choice between these two types or categories of principles is obvious. For purposes of the judiciary, values (as opposed to facts) from the world *in front of* the text but not *behind* the text or *within* the text should be largely irrelevant.[30]

In order to use the original intent or original meaning of a text, we must have epistemological access to this meaning, the author's meaning, not our own. Scientific interpretation, which approaches the focal meaning of hermeneutics, can assist us greatly in this task, taking into account as it does the world behind and within the text. If a post-modern categorically rejects the possibility of scientific interpretation, while continuing to respect the distinction between written text and unwritten tradition, as well as the institution of judicial review, authentic and/or legal interpretation remain the only possibilities.

With respect to scientific interpretation, for a post-modern, understanding someone else's horizon (principles, context, world-view) exactly as that other person understands it is impossible. According to post-modern thought, which one must presuppose if one were to reject scientific interpretation, the meaning for the interpreter that emerges is a fusion or a synthesis of his own horizon with the referent or author's horizon. Therefore, only those most 'inside' the referent horizon already would be capable of accurately interpreting or knowing the author's meaning, and this interpretation would not be scientific, but based on authority.

If, as in most legal systems, there is no formal mechanism for the selection and inclusion of 'insiders' in the same way that there may be in theology, the question of who is inside and who is not will be left for substantive debate. Naturally, the debate will focus on the compatibility and coherency of one's espoused principles with the principles demonstrated to be in the world behind and within the text, keeping in mind that we have contemporaneous expositions of what these principles were, and *qua* principles, presumably continue to be. Finally, it is worth noting that any such debate must be a reasoned one, which, at least in theory, could exclude true post-moderns from participation.

[29] In contrast, true natural law principles do not change, but their generality allows for change via application of the principles to current facts and circumstances.
[30] Current and shared national values, as distinct from historical principles, are properly the concern of the legislature, not the judiciary.

THE 'FIRST SOURCE' OF ISLAMIC LAW: MUSLIM LEGAL EXEGESIS OF THE QURʾĀN

Robert Gleave

Introduction

A defining characteristic of Muslim legal discourse is the assumption that the Qurʾān represents God's communication with humanity. There were debates about the integrity of the text itself,[1] and extensive disputes concerning its interpretation, but the affirmation that God communicated to humankind through a revelatory process, and that the Prophet Muḥammad was the initial recipient of that revelation, is taken as axiomatic for Muslim jurists.[2] God speaks in the Qurʾān, and among the issues he addresses is the law he has commanded his community to obey. The laws which the Qurʾān proclaims enjoy a privileged, sacred status, and can only be ignored or set aside if God himself has given a subsequent law, abrogating the former ruling, or allowing an exception. A divine law may only be abrogated (or provided with an exception) by a law of similar status.[3]

The limited nature, both in number and subject matter, of the legal rulings in the Quranic text was recognized by early Muslim jurists, and this limitation was overcome by supplementary means of deducing God's law (Sharīʿa).

One such supplementary means was to posit additional sources, outside the Qurʾān, which contribute to our knowledge of the Sharīʿa. Prime among these was the Sunna—the example of the Prophet Muḥammad himself, who is said to have led a sinless life from the beginning of his Prophetic mission until his death (dated as the years 610–32). His actions were in perfect obedience to the law of God (both that which is mentioned in the Qurʾān, and that which is not). This supplementary source was given status on the basis of various Quranic verses which exhort the

---

[1] See J. Eliash, 'The Shiʿite Qurʾān: A Reconsideration of Goldziher's Interpretation', *Arabica*, 16 (1969), 15–24; E. Kohlberg, 'Some Notes on the Imāmī Attitude towards the Qurʾān', in S. M. Stern, A. Hourani, and Y. Brown (eds.), *Islamic Philosophy and the Classical Tradition: Essays Presented to R. Walzer* (Oxford, 1972); B. Todd Lawson, 'A Note for the Study of a "Shīʿī Qurʾān" ', *Journal of Semitic Studies* (*JSS*), 36 (1991), 279–95.

[2] See e.g. W. Hallaq, 'The Primacy of the Qurʾān in Shāṭibī's Legal Theory', in W. Hallaq and D. Little (eds.), *Islamic Studies Presented to Charles J. Adams* (Leiden, 1991), and B. Weiss, 'The Primacy of Revelation in Classical Islamic Legal Theory as Expounded by Sayf al-Dīn al-Āmidī', *Studia Islamica* (*SI*), 59 (1984), 79–109.

[3] On the theory of abrogation, see generally the work of J. Burton cited in n. 33 below.

believers to follow both God and his Prophet. The Sunna, then, is theoretically validated as a source of law by the Qurʾān, and is to be found in
collections of aphorisms attributed to the Prophet (*hadīth*).[4] Another
supplementary source was community consensus (*ijmāʿ*) on a legal ruling,
which was also (with some debate) validated by (suitably interpreted)
Quranic verses and Prophetic *hadīth*.[5]

The second means of deducing God s law was through a complex
hermeneutic theory, whereby jurists were able to interpret the Qurʾān (and
the words of the Prophet) in as extensive a manner as was possible,
thereby making the limited legal content of the Quranic text useful in the
derivation of a much wider set of legal rulings than might be thought from
a cursory reading. The theory was primarily 'intentionalist' in emphasis.[6]
It was designed to provide a jurist with the tools whereby he might
discover God s intended meaning in the Qurʾān. This hermeneutic was a
matter of great discussion in works of legal theory (*uṣūl al-fiqh*), and it is
this second means of deducing the law with which I am primarily
concerned in this paper.[7]

Exegetical Methodology in Muslim Legal Theory

The principal exegetical process which facilitated the extension of (limited)
Quranic rulings (beyond what might be considered their immediate application) was analogical reasoning. This process is often termed *qiyās* in the
secondary literature, though it is not wholly identical with the term in the
juristic tradition.[8]

Analogical reasoning first proceeded by identifying the ratio (*al-ʿilla*)
behind a divine command found in the Qurʾān. Once discovered, the
ruling is thereby transferred to all occasions when the ratio is present. For
example, if the ratio behind the prohibition on the consumption of grape-
wine is discovered to be that grape-wine is intoxicating, then the consumption of all intoxicating substances is also prohibited. Discovering the ratio,

---

[4]   This source was given literary form in these collections, the earliest of which date from
the late 9th century CE. The legal validity of the ruling found in the *hadīth* was, to an extent,
dependent upon their historicity (assessed by additional criteria). See W. Hallaq, 'The
Authenticity of Prophetic Ḥadīth: A Pseudo-Problem', *SI* 74 (1999), 75–90.

[5]   See W. Hallaq, 'On the Authoritativeness of Sunni Consensus', *International Journal
of Middle Eastern Studies*, 18 (1986), 427–54; D. Stewart, *Islamic Legal Orthodoxy: Twelver
Shiʿite Responses to the Sunni Legal System* (Salt Lake City, 1998), 25–60.

[6]   For an excellent summary, see B. Weiss, *The Spirit of Islamic Law* (Athens, Ga.,
1998), 38–65.

[7]   There are extensive scholarly debates about the early development of Islamic Law, and
the influence of the Qurʾān on its content. See e.g. J. Burton, *The Sources of Islamic Law*
(Edinburgh, 1990), 30, 70; N. Calder, *Studies in Early Muslim Jurisprudence* (Oxford,
1993), 217–19; Y. Dutton, *The Origins of Islamic Law: The Qurʾān, the Muwatta' and
Madinan Amal* (Richmond, 1999).

[8]   On this point, see W. Hallaq, 'Non-Analogical Arguments in Sunni Juridical *Qiyās*',
Arabica, 36 (1989), 286–306.

then, became of critical importance, and Muslim theorists wrote at length on this topic.

At times, God actually informs the reader of the ratio: 'Perform the prayer on account of the setting of the sun' (Q 17. 78). The phrase 'on account of' (*li*) is taken as an indicator, from God, of the ratio, and hence on any occasion when the sun sets, the prayer should be performed.

Such a revelation of the ratio (*manṣūṣ al-ʿilla*) was, unfortunately, rare, and one of the prolonged and complex debates in Muslim legal theory concerned the determination of the ratio when it was not immediately known from the revealed texts (Qurʾān or Sunna).[9] Underlying the acceptance of analogical reasoning was a presumption that God's law is a consistent law, in which commands and prohibitions are justified according to a discernible and coherent logic. For some, this bound the Almighty to the constraints of human reason in an unacceptable manner, but for most, it seemed a natural way of extending explicit rulings in the revealed texts to novel situations.[10]

Analogical reasoning was not, however, the only exegetical technique used. Other modes of argumentation, familiar to logicians, were also described and legitimized in works of legal theory. For example, God says, in the Qurʾān: 'Do not say "fie" to [your parents]' (Q 17. 23). The legal theorists, with almost near unanimity, agreed that a prohibition such as this meant more than simply prohibiting the use of 'fie' between child and parent. Other words of insult were included in the prohibition. The ruling was made to prohibit (generally) a child's impertinence to their parents.

Muslim legal scholars, also with near unanimity, agreed that this prohibition referred to more than a child insulting his or her parents. It implied that an action of greater severity (such as hitting one's parents) was also forbidden. In a sense it meant 'Do not *even* say "fie" to one's parents, such is the respect due to them'. This type of argument is termed 'hinting at the higher by means of the lower', and is identical with the *a minori ad maius* of Western philosophical discourse. However, since it requires the reader to extend a ruling beyond an explicit wording of the Quranic text, it is considered an 'implication' (*mafhūm*). The extension, though, is by common consent perfectly legitimate. God is viewed as intending, in this prohibition, to convey a ruling not found in the text.[11]

Other means of extending the rulings found in the Qurʾān were also

---

[9] A flavour of the Muslim discussions concerning the discovery of a ratio in a revealed rule can be gained from B. Weiss, *The Search for God's Law: Islamic Jurisprudence in the Writings of Sayf al-Dīn al-Āmidī* (Salt Lake City, 1992), 593–632.

[10] For those who rejected analogy, see I. Goldziher, *The Zahiris: Their Doctrine and their History* (Leiden, 1971); R. Gleave, 'Imāmī Shīʿī Refutations of *qiyās*', in B. Weiss (ed.), *The Alta Papers* (Leiden, forthcoming).

[11] For an examination of implication, see Weiss, *The Search for God's Law*, 481–501. Some jurists considered this reasoning a type of analogy (see Hallaq, 'Non-Analogical Arguments in Sunni Juridical *Qiyās*', 289–96).

legitimized by legal theorists. For example, among the statements in the Qurʾān concerning pregnancy, the following two are to be found: '[The mother] weans him [the child] for two years' (Q 31. 14): '[The mother] carries him, both in pregnancy and weaning, for a period of thirty months' (Q 46. 15). From these two statements the jurists calculated that the minimum period of pregnancy is six months. Thirty months less two years (i.e. 24 months) is six months. The jurists are not concerned here with biology, but with legality. The legal importance of setting a minimum period for pregnancy becomes clear when considering the prohibition on extramarital sexual relations. Pregnancy is viewed as evidence of such relations, and hence evidence of a contravention of the prohibition. If a woman marries a man, and six months or more later gives birth to a child, no accusation of extramarital relations can be made on the basis of this evidence. If the birth occurs within a six-month period, then the pregnancy is counted as evidence of illicit sexual intercourse (*zinā*).

Whether or not God intended the ruling concerning the minimum period of pregnancy is, legally speaking, irrelevant. An unavoidable consequence of combining God's statements is this ruling. Though the legal theorists do not dwell on this 'unintended' consequence of God's words, they view such implications as forming part of the legal context in which God speaks. That legal context is the Sharīʿa, and hence even though the ruling is not integral to God's intention, it is nonetheless an accepted element of the Sharīʿa. God spoke against the background of a legal minimum period of pregnancy, and one can deduce this even when he does not state it explicitly.

There are many other examples of the extension of Quranic rulings through analogy and implication, and hence many other methods of interpreting the Qurʾān. Some were more debated than others. There were so-called literalists who argued that verses such as 'Do not say "fie" to one's parents' meant nothing more than a prohibition on saying 'fie'. In the absence of other rulings, it may be permitted to bombard one's parents with abuse, as long the word 'fie' is not used. The literalists faced ridicule from the majority of legal theorists: do they mean 'fie' in the Arabic language alone? Can one legitimately use the equivalent of 'fie' in other languages? These literalists were marginalized, and eventually died out. They played a part in mainstream jurisprudence as 'straw men', or they became the subject of juristic humour.

To what extent these arguments were utilized in the elaboration of the law is part of a general debate among Islamic legal scholars concerning the relationship between legal theory (*uṣūl al-fiqh*) and substantive law (*furū al-fiqh*). The presumption on the part of most Muslim jurists was that the relationship was derivative (legal rulings are derived from the sources according to the methods legitimized in works of theory). Some also have ascribed a descriptive role to legal theory (theory describes the manner in which rulings, which are already known, were derived, even though the argumentation process was not made explicit in the text). Some Western Islamicists have proposed that legal theory and positive law were separate literary traditions, which only occasionally interacted. This discussion has not yet reached a scholarly consensus.[12]

Exegetical Techniques in Works of Quranic Commentary (*tafsīr*)

The need for a theory of exegesis which encompassed the above examples, and other similar instances, emerged due to an apparent contradiction.[13] Theologically speaking, the Qur'ān must be the communication of God's will to humanity. Practically speaking, it is not worded with the (supposed) clarity of a legal draughtsman, nor does it contain much of legal import. In short, as a legal document, it has severe limitations, though owing to its theological position, its content must be observed in any formulation of the law. The classical exegetes' task was to interpret the Quranic text in such a manner that its relevance to the law was prominently displayed. Wherever possible, the law must be shown to have been derived from the Qur'ān, even if, historically speaking, the origin of much of Islamic law lay outside the Qur'ān. The limitations of the text restricted the number of occasions when this was possible, and this has led to a prevalent description of Islamic law, particularly in the formative period, as uninfluenced by the Qur'ān. When the opportunity did arise, the exegetes exploited it with dedication in order to demonstrate both their theological orthodoxy and that the Qur'ān is a mine of legal knowledge, provided by God for the benefit of humankind.

One example of this exploitation can be seen in the formulation of the Muslim law of taxation. Perhaps the most important tax is termed, in legal compendia, *zakāt*, and refers to an income–holdings tax, obligatory on all adult Muslims. The Qur'ān, it is generally agreed, establishes the obligatory

---

[12] On these debates, see the case-studies: W. Hallaq, 'Murder in Cordoba: *Ijtihād, Iftā'* and the Evolution of Substantive Law in Medieval Islam', *Acta Orientalia*, 55 (1994), 55–83; M. Fadel, 'Rules, Judicial Discretion and the Rule of Law in Eighth-Ninth/Fourteenth-Fifteenth Century Granada', in R. Gleave and E. Kermeli (eds.), *Islamic Law: Theory and Practice* (London, 1997); R. Gleave, 'Marrying Fatimid Women: Legal Theory and Substantive Law in Shīʿī Jurisprudence', (1999) 6/1 *Islamic Law and Society* 38–68.

[13] The use of the Qur'ān in works of *furūʿ al-fiqh* deserves a separate study. Works of *furūʿ* are normally structured according to (fairly) fixed chapter headings, in a compendium style. These features, it might be argued, developed with little influence from the Quranic text. In works of *tafsīr* (Quranic commentary) the writers reflect directly on the Quranic text (in theory). This discussion, as least formally, is dictated by the Qur'ān and consists not only of legal matters. This privileging of the Quranic text is the reason for my selecting *tafsīr* works rather than *furūʿ* works as my main sources in what follows. For a detailed exposition of the development of *tafsīr*, see N. Calder, '*Tafsīr* from Ṭabarī to Ibn Kathīr: Problems in the Description of a Genre, Illustrated with Reference to the Story of Abraham', in G. R. Hawting and Abdul-Kader A. Shareef (eds.), *Approaches to the Qur'ān* (London, 1993).

nature of *zakāt*. It is a religious duty to pay one's *zakāt*, but it is also an enforced acquisition by the Muslim state. Muslim jurists did not conceive of an ideal state which would offer its Muslim subjects a choice over paying this tax; rather the state had the right to acquire the *zakāt* payment (by force if necessary). Conversely, by paying one's *zakāt* to a Muslim state, one was not thereby responsible for its distribution. The religious duty was fulfilled however the state used the tax revenue.[14]

The issue I wish to concentrate on concerns the distribution of *zakāt*, on which the Qurʾān is apparently silent (except in very general terms), though there is this verse: 'Alms (*ṣadaqāt*) are for the poor, the destitute, those who work with them [i.e. the alms, meaning the tax collectors], those whose hearts have been reconciled (*al-muʾallafa qulūbuhum*), those in slavery, debtors, the path of God and the traveller, as a duty to God. God is knowing and wise.'

The problems associated with the usage of this verse in constructing a system of *zakāt* distribution is that God, in this verse, does not employ the term *zakāt* to describe the revenue. He uses the term *ṣadaqāt*, which in classical jurisprudence refers to voluntary (or supererogatory) payments to charity, rather than compulsory taxation.[15] Such a verse would aid considerably in the development of *zakāt* law, limiting the causes and categories of persons who can legitimately receive the revenue. However, the verse refers to *ṣadaqāt*, not *zakāt*. Despite this initial problem, Muslim exegetes and legal writers (with unanimity, to my knowledge) have identified this verse with *zakāt* distribution. Many, particularly later writers, do not even consider the possible irrelevance of the verse, and the problematic non-employment of the term *zakāt*. It appears that the verse has been so intimately associated with *zakāt* distribution that the tradition no longer felt the need to justify its relevance. Those exegetes who did discuss the *zakāt–ṣadaqāt* issue normally resolved the problem by arguing that *ṣadaqāt* in the Qurʾān is used as a general term, both for the compulsory tax and the voluntary alms donations. They provided several (suitably interpreted) examples of this usage, and claimed that voluntary donations were, strictly speaking, termed *ṣadaqāt al-taṭawwuᶜ* (voluntary alms). The pivotal role this verse occupied in the law of *zakāt* compelled an adjustment in the legal lexicon.

Before moving on to other legal issues relating to this verse, it is perhaps worth considering what the *zakāt–ṣadaqāt* issue indicates concerning

---

[14] Examples of how the issue of *zakāt* and *zakāt* distribution were discussed in Muslim legal literature can be found in N. Calder, 'Zakāt in Imāmī Shīʿī Jurisprudence from the Tenth to the Sixteenth Century AD', *Bulletin of the School of Oriental and African Studies* (*BSOAS*), 46 (1982), 468–80, and 'Exploring God's Law: Muḥammad ibn Aḥmad ibn Abū Sahl al-Sarakhsī on *zakāt*', in Christopher Toll and J. Skovgaard-Petersen (eds.), *Law in the Islamic World: Past and Present* (Copenhagen, 1995).

[15] See T. H. Wier and A. Zyzow, 'Ṣadaḳa', in *Encyclopedia of Islam*, 8 vols. to date, 2nd edn. (Leiden, 1960–), viii. 708–16.

Muslim conceptions of the Qurʾān as a legal document. The Qurʾān is the speech of God, it consists of God s utterances to humanity. I use the term 'utterance' aware of its importance in linguistic studies, in particular those of Mikhail Bakhtin. For Bakhtin, an utterance emitted by an individual must be considered part of a 'dialogue'.[16] A characterization of an utterance based purely on grammatical and linguistic analysis is bound to be not only limited, but positively misleading. An utterance exists both as a response and as a response-prompt. Bakhtin conceives of utterances as ranging from 'a single-word, everyday rejoinder to large, complex works of science or literature'.[17] The Qurʾān could be classified as the latter, when taken as a whole, and as the former when considering individual verses. Any utterance exists in a dialogic relationship with other utterances which involve a relationship between 'speakers' in dialogue, even if one party is silent. Under a Bakhtinian scheme, the Qurʾān is a response to a (possibly unspoken, or even unauthored) question, and this, I feel, accurately portrays the respected place accorded to the Qurʾān in Muslim legal exegesis. It is, both as a whole and in atomized chunks (such as Q 9. 60), a response to an (as yet unknown) question, and humanity s response is, in part, the exegetical tradition known as *tafsīr*. The Qurʾān contains the answers, and it is the exegete's task to discover (for which, one might read 'formulate') the question, and then understand the answer. In this case, the question is formulated (implicitly) as 'How does one distribute *zakāt*?', and the answer is Q 9. 60. The postulated divine authorship of the Qurʾān enables this dialogic relationship to emerge (at times, explicitly, but mainly implicitly) in the exegesis, and the manner of its presentation, as in this case, locks the reader into this, rather than that, particular understanding of the verse.[18] The success of this technique is demonstrated by the fact that this verse, despite the initial terminological difficulty, structured classical (and modern) legal discussions on the distribution of *zakāt*.

There are a number of (surmountable) exegetical and linguistic barriers to a straightforward identification of the contents of this verse with *zakāt* distribution. Most I can consign to a footnote;[19] however one is of particular interest. All of the categories appear to designate a clear recipient cause

---

[16] See M. Bakhtin, 'The Problem of Speech Genres', in his *Speech Genres and Other Late Essays*, trans. Vern W. McGee, ed. Caryl Emerson and Michael Holquist (Austin, Tex., 1986). For a more extensive (though earlier) explanation of dialogue, see Bakhtin's discussion in [pseudo-]Voloshinov, *Marxism and the Philosophy of Language*, trans. Ladislav Matejka and I. R. Titunik (New York, 1997).

[17] Bakhtin, 'The Problem of Speech Genres', 77.

[18] Works of *tafsīr* were (and are), of course, in a dialogic relationship with other 'questions' posed by tradition or environment.

[19] The grammatical problem relates to an ellipsis. The particle *hum* or *alladhīna* should be present before the phrase. The phrase can then be considered an adjectival relative clause. For other examples of this rare grammatical construction, see A. Beeston, *Written Arabic* (Cambridge, 1969), sect. 8. 14–17. I thank Dr Y. Dutton for directing me to this reference.

or class of persons (though obviously with some need of refinement: Who counts as poor? How do they differ from the destitute? Which activities fall into God's path?). *Al-muʾallafa qulūbuhum*, translated here as 'those whose hearts have been reconciled', presents a more problematic identity. What exactly this phrase means, and to whom it might refer, has been the object of some discussion.

Returning once more to Bakhtin, his concept of the utterance includes an emphasis, not only on its dialogic role (already examined), but also on its circumstantial role, or, as Bakhtin words it, its place in 'real life dialogue'.[20] The words of a sacred text are necessarily disconnected from the circumstance of their utterance, and for some Muslim exegetes this disconnection posed no problem (one might compare them with the Saussurean linguists, who, as Bakhtin argued, analyse the sentence but not the utterance).[21] However, for most, a major method of exegesis was locating the dislocated verse in a context (i.e. an episode in Muḥammad's life in response to which it was revealed). Once positioned, the exegetes became unable to envisage a meaning for this verse outside this context. By setting the verse in a context the exegetes truncate many possible lines of interpretation. These 'circumstances of revelation' (*asbāb al-nuzūl*)[22] are presented as both exegetical aids, and historical events. The phrase *al-muʾallafa qulūbuhum* is unanimously associated (by the exegetes) with the battle at Ḥunayn in 630 between the Muslims (led by the Prophet) and the Hawāzin tribal federation. In order to conquer the Hawāzin, the Prophet recruited a number of non-Muslim mercenary tribes. After the victory these tribes received a share of the booty. Some Muslims objected to this payment, on the grounds that the recipients were not dedicated to the cause of Islam but merely hired hands. However, the Prophet explained that he had given them shares of the booty in order to 'reconcile their hearts' (to Islam?).[23] This phrase, said to have been spoken by the Prophet, provides the background to any interpretation of the phrase 'those whose hearts have been reconciled' in Q 9. 60. They were given shares not just as rewards for their military efforts, but also in order to attract them to Islam. The legitimacy of this practice was confirmed in Q 9. 60 through God's explanation that *zakāt* revenue can be used to attract people to Islam.

The immediate exegetical problem is that the background story does not refer to *zakāt*, but to war booty (*farāʾiʿ*). The distribution of *zakāt* and

[20] Bakhtin, 'The Problem of Speech Genres', 75.
[21] Ibid. 80–1.
[22] See A. Rippin, 'The Function of *asbāb al-nuzūl* in Quranic Exegesis', *BSOAS*, 51 (1988), 1–21.
[23] For historical accounts of this event, see Ibn Hishām, *Kitāb sīrat rasūl allāh*, ed. F. Wüstenfeld, 2 vols. (Gottingen, 1859–60), ii. 880; al-Wāqidī, *Kitāb al-maghāzī* (Berlin, 1882), 367.

that of *farāʾiᶜ* are governed by different rules in Islamic law, and this has prompted one (non-Muslim) commentator to argue that Muslims have interpreted the verse incorrectly.[24] I, however, am unconvinced that 'incorrect' is an appropriate term to employ when describing an exegetical tradition, since I am unsure what might constitute a 'correct' interpretation of a verse in such a context (what criteria might be used?).[25] I do concede that it is initially puzzling how a verse referring to the distribution of *zakāt* (or more accurately *ṣadaqāt*) was associated with a story referring to the distribution of war booty. No exegete I have consulted has tackled the apparent irrelevance of the story to the verse (an irrelevance apparent to me, but obviously not to them). The fact that the association has not been questioned is, possibly, a testament to the power of a tradition of scholarship in both forming an exegetical method and limiting the interpretations which appear plausible. A possible response to my puzzlement is that the relevance of the story demonstrates (at a deeper level) that revenue gained by the state in a legitimate manner (i.e. through taxes or war) can be used to attract potentially hostile parties to the Muslim cause. In essence, the exegetes would be proposing an analogy between booty and tax on this matter. However, this line of discussion has not been explored. One reason why this does not appear to have been a popular line of reasoning may have been the strict regulations regarding the analogical process discussed above.

To summarize so far: the initially puzzling phrase *al-muʾallafa qulūbuhum* is interpreted by means of setting the verse against the general conception of the Qurʾān as God's utterance. Since it is an utterance, it can be viewed as a response in dialogue (*pace* Bakhtin) with a previous utterance (i.e. the question 'What do we do with *zakāt*?'). The uncertainty in meaning of God's utterance is dissolved through a contextualization of the utterance (making it part of 'real life communication'). That the context appears (to me) irrelevant to the distribution of *zakāt*, did not trouble the Muslim exegetes. The controlling influence of their (and my) interpretative traditions limits what is considered plausible or rational (by either party).[26] The assumption for any exegete is that the Qurʾān, being God's word, is legally relevant. God does not utter nonsense, and something that appears to be nonsense or incongruous (e.g. *al-muʾallafa*

---

[24] See W. M. Watt, *Muḥammad at Medina* (Oxford, 1956), 348–53.

[25] Watt's argument is based on an appeal to the literal meaning of the verse, coupled with other contextual factors, as if a text such as the Qurʾān can have an undisputed literal meaning. 'What is obvious is only obvious because we have a system whereby we separate the obvious from the obscure, the unambiguous from the ambiguous. There is nothing inherently obvious about the meaning of this text—its obviousness is made by our perceiving it as such' (S. Fish, *Is there a Text in this Class? The Authority of Interpretive Communities* (Cambridge, Mass., 1980), 313).

[26] Tradition (which enables any hermeneutics to begin) 'has a justification outside of reason' (H.-G. Gadamer, *Truth and Method* (London, 1975), 153, 235–41).

qulūbuhum) must have a legal referent in the Sharī‘a. We know the answer; we are merely unsure about the question. This assumption of relevance behaves rather like Grice's proposal that underlying communication there are a number of (unspoken) maxims, one of which concerns the assumption of the relevance of one utterance to the previous utterance.[27] God is in communication with humankind in the Qur’ān, and the meaning of God's speech can only be understood if that dialogue is re-created. It is assumed throughout the discussions that the model dialogue is human–human communication; the maxims of relevance, economy, order, and information which are operative in human conversation (working according to Grice's cooperative principle) being operative in divine–human communication.

Having stabilized (at least provisionally) the meaning of the verse, the exegetes turn to its contemporary relevance. It is established that expenditure on *al-mu’allafa qulūbuhum* from tax revenue was justified by the Prophet, but is such expenditure legitimate in the post-Muhammadan era? In short, can we still cajole, entice, and even bribe people to become Muslims, or join the Muslim cause? It is here that the exegetes begin to part company.

The argument for suspending the share of *al-mu’allafa qulūbuhum* was based on the rise to power of the Muslim empire. The Prophet had paid the mercenaries because he needed their support. Islam (in its classical expression) no longer needs such support, and therefore need not employ such tactics. The position is summed up by the great tenth-century exegete al-Ṭabarī: 'Today we do not give them [i.e. *al-mu’allafa qulūbuhum*] anything because Islam is strong.'[28] On the other hand, the argument for the continued validity of the *al-mu’allafa qulūbuhum* share is based on the continued need for it. The ratio (*‘illa*) for God ruling that *zakāt* could be given to *al-mu’allafa qulūbuhum* was its benefit to the Muslim community. As long as the community might benefit from such a policy, the share remains legally valid. The eleventh-century al-Tha‘alabī puts it thus: '[The purpose] of seeking their [*al-mu’allafa qulūbuhum*'s] friendship was only to bring Islam benefit or protect it from harm. The sound opinion is that the ruling [concerning the *al-mu’allafa qulūbuhum* share] remains if it is

---

[27] See H. Paul Grice, 'Logic and Conversation', in P. Cole and J. L. Morgan (eds.), *Syntax and Semantics*, iii: *Speech Acts* (New York, 1975). A fascinating application of Grice's theory is found in A. Samely, 'Scripture's Implicature: The Midrashic Assumptions of Relevance and Consistency', *JSS* 37/2 (1992), 167–205.

[28] Abū Ja‘far Muḥammad b. Jarīr al-Ṭabarī (d. 922), *Jāmi‘ al-bayān ‘an ta’wīl ay al-qur’ān*, ed. M. Shakur, 10 vols. (Cairo, 1955), x. 116. See also Muqātil b. Sulaymān (d. 767), *Kitāb tafsīr al-khams mā’a āya min al-qur’ān al-karīm*, ed. I. Goldfeld (Tel Aviv, 1984), 47, and ‘Abdallāh b. ‘Umar al-Bayḍāwī (d. 1286), *Anwār al-tanzīl wa asrār al-ta’wīl* (Beirut, n.d.), 258. Shī‘ī jurists also declare the share redundant, but for a different reason. The only person authorized to utilize the share is the Imam, and he is in hiding. See e.g. Muḥammad b. Ḥasan al-Ṭūsī (d. 1067), *al-Tibyān fi tafsīr al-qur’ān*, 10 vols. (Beirut, n.d.), v. 243.

needed.'[29] There were also those who argued that since God has said the Muslims should spend money on *al-mu'allafa qulūbuhum*, then we must do so (even if it appears unnecessary). These were identified as the literalist interpreters and not given much credence by mainstream Muslim jurists. For the literalists, identifying the ratio, and thereby deciding when the share can, and cannot, be utilized is an unjustified intrusion into God's sovereignty.

A compromise between these positions was proposed by the exegetes. The *al-mu'allafa qulūbuhum* share is, it was proposed, divisible into different subcategories. For some categories the expenditure is still valid; for others it is no longer valid owing to the disappearance of the ratio. The commentary of al-Maḥallī and his pupil al-Suyūṭī (known as Jalalayn) states: '[The *al-mu'allafa qulūbuhum* share is given] in order that they might become Muslims, or to strengthen their Islam, or that their people might become Muslims, or that they might defend the Muslims. The first and last categories are not given today . . . on account of the strength of Islam, unlike the other two categories, which should be given.'[30]

The division of the class *al-mu'allafa qulūbuhum* into subcategories became a popular means of exploring the meaning of the phrase in Q 9. 60. As a general trend, the early exegetes posited a unified definitive class of people, while from al-Ṭabarī onwards the trend was to list an increasing number of subcategories, until one reaches the great commentary of the twentieth-century reformer Rashīd Riḍā. In his work he lists six subclasses of people, both Muslim and non-Muslim, who can qualify for a share of *zakāt* under the rubric of *al-mu'allafa qulūbuhum*.[31]

The major dislocation of the categories from the story of the Prophet's battle at Ḥunayn is the acceptance that the share can be given to both Muslims and non-Muslims (not only the latter, as implied by the story). The Muslim recipients 'whose hearts are reconciled' are variously defined as 'those with weak intention' whose faith might be strengthened by the gift, or Muslim leaders who might convert their tribes to Islam, or those living on the edge of the Muslim polity who can usefully defend Islam from attack.[32] Originally applied to non-Muslims alone, the Quranic

---

[29] Aḥmad b. Muḥammad al-Thaʿalabī (d. 1035), *Jawāhir al-ḥisān fi tafsīr al-qurʾān*, 5 vols. (Beirut, 1997), ii. 136–7. See also Fakhr al-dīn al-Rāzī (d. 1209), *Mafātiḥ al-ghayb*, 16 vols. (Cairo, 1906–9), iv. 679, and Abū Bakr Muḥammad Ibn ʿArabī (d. 1148), *Aḥkām al-qurʾān* (Tunis, 1988), 950–4.

[30] Jalāl al-dīn al-Maḥallī (d. 1459) and Jalāl al-dīn al-Suyūṭī (d. 1505), *Tafsīr al-jalālayn* (Beirut, 1987), 251.

[31] Rashīd Riḍā (d. 1935), *Tafsīr al-manār* (Cairo, 1935), 23. See also Mawlana Mawdudi (d. 1979), *Tafhim al-Qurʾān: Towards an Understanding of the Qurʾān*, trans. and ed. Z. I. Ansari 5 vols. (Leicester, 1990), iii. 222–5.

[32] See e.g. Muḥammad b. Aḥmad al-Qurṭubī (d. 1272), *al-Jāmiʿ li-aḥkām al-qurʾān*, 10 vols. (Beirut, 1997), v. 178–9; al-Ḥusayn b. Masʿūd al-Baghawī (d. 1117/1122), *Maʿālim al-tanzīl*, 5 vols. (Beirut, 1993), ii. 303–5; Abū Farāj ʿAbd al-Raḥmān Ibn Jawzī (d. 1200), *Zād al-masīr fi ʿilm al-tafsīr*, 10 vols. (Beirut, 1994), iii. 498–9; Maḥmūd b. ʿAbdallāh al-Ālūsī (d. 1854), *Rūḥ al-maʿānī*, 16 vols. (Beirut, 1994–6), ix. 122–3.

phrase is expanded to refer to certain classes of Muslim. This expansion is justified through historical references to the Prophet's gifts to Muslims (though rarely with the accompanying phrase *al-muʾallafa qulūbuhum*, or anything similar) and demonstrates that the initial limitation of the above Quranic phrase did not restrict the exegetes. The dogmatic position of the Quranic text (as legal source) inspired the writers to extend its reference (over time) and thereby overcome any 'inherent' limitation dictated by syntax and grammar. They all agree that the share of *al-muʾallafa qulūbuhum* is still valid. They were also able to legitimize the employment of this share to many more causes than previous exegetes, through a (seemingly innocuous) expansion of subcategories of recipients.

The example of *al-muʾallafa qulūbuhum* and Q 9. 60 demonstrates, then, not only the doctrinal position of the Qurʾān in Muslim legal writings, but also the techniques used by the exegetes in a determined effort to draw from the text the maximum available legal information (in a sense, there was no maximum, save that imposed by the institutional limitations of Muslim scholarship).

The exegetes' attempts to overcome the limitations of the Quranic text occasionally led them to entertain possible changes in the text itself. Contrary to the impression given in some introductory books on Islam, the Quranic text was not seen as a perfectly stable document in either the formative or the classical periods. Muslim commentators recognized variants of the text (called *qirāʾat*, and normally numbered at seven). Some also recognized passages which had (somehow) been revealed by God, but omitted from the text.

Concerning the latter phenomenon (the omitted passages), these verses were thought (by oversight or other means) to have been omitted from the Qurʾān. I limit myself to one famous example: the punishment for adultery. In the Qurʾān the punishment for extramarital intercourse is decreed to be 100 lashes (Q 24. 2). There are, however, a number of *ḥadīths* in which the Prophet is said to have stoned to death those guilty of this crime. This conflict between Qurʾān and Sunna led to prolonged and protracted discussions about the relationship between the two sources. One solution, favoured by many jurists, was to postulate a verse in the Qurʾān, in which the stoning penalty was enunciated. This verse, they proposed, had been lost, but the ruling had survived in the form of a Prophetic injunction (to stone adulterers). The Quranic ruling referring to 100 lashes was, then, reinterpreted as referring only to instances of premarital sexual relations (i.e. fornication), while the stoning penalty referred to adultery. The problem, it appears, had arisen because jurists knew what the penalty for adultery was (that is, stoning), but found no evidence for it in the Qurʾān. The solution was to contemplate a lost verse. The solution came with the risk of devaluing the legal status of the Quranic text. It is important to remember that the devaluing of the text did not, however, imply the devaluing of the Word of God itself. It merely enforced a cleavage between the Qurʾān as source and the existent text.[33]

Regarding the variants, these were traditionally attributed to pious, prominent early Muslims. There was an agreed text (the *muṣḥaf ʿuthmān*, the Uthmanic recension, named after the third caliph who is reported to have ordered its collection). There were also additions and alterations to that text, which though not universally accepted, did enjoy a lesser, 'explanatory' authority. Western scholars have debated the authenticity of both the attribution and the existence of these variants.[34] For some, they are not variants, but exegetical glosses, current in the later Muslim community, presented as variants of the Uthmanic recension in order to elevate each gloss from (human) interpretation to (potentially divine) revelatory variant. Most of the variants are 'corrections' of 'mistakes' in Quranic Arabic, or explications of ellipses within the text by the addition of words or phrases. Most do not impact on legal matters.[35]

On occasions, however, the so-called textual variants of the Qurʾān could be used to provide legal rulings which were (apparently) unavailable in the agreed text. One example of this involves an issue of Muslim marriage law. Sunni Muslims accept only one kind of marriage (*nikāḥ*): a contract between two parties (usually the suitor and the bride's father) that on payment of a dowry (either in full, immediately, or divided into payments) and subsequent maintenance to the bride, the man will enjoy sexual access to the woman, and have paternal rights over any resultant children. This contract is terminated by divorce (*ṭalāq*; for which there are many and various regulations).

Many Shīʿī Muslim jurists, however, add an additional form of marriage: the marriage of pleasure (*nikāḥ al-mutʿa*), in which a man contracts with a woman to pay her a dowry (usually without subsequent maintenance payments) in order to enjoy sexual access to the woman for a limited period of time. Once this period of time has elapsed, the contract is no longer valid. Sunni Muslims have, generally, viewed this type of marriage as a highly reprehensible form of prostitution. Shīʿī Muslims, however, consider it a valid contract.

One of the arguments in support of *mutʿa* marriage, used by the Shīʿī jurists, involves a textual variant.[36] The verse Q 4. 24 reads (after a list of

---

[33] See the extensive work on *naskh* by Professor J. Burton: *The Collection of the Kurʾān* (Cambridge, 1977), 72–86; 'The Origin of the Islamic Penalty for Adultery', *Transactions of the Glasgow Oriental Society*, 26 (1975–6), 16–27; *The Sources of Islamic Law*.

[34] J. Wansbrough, *Quranic Studies* (Oxford, 1977), 205–6. See also Burton, *The Collection of the Kurʾān*, 29–45.

[35] For an examination of the significance of the two transmissions in currency today, see A. Brockett, 'The Value of *ḥafṣ* and *warsh*: Transmissions for the Textual History of the Qurʾān', in A. Rippin (ed.), *Approaches to the History of the Interpretation of the Qurʾān* (Oxford, 1988).

[36] I have dealt with this variant, and the ensuing exegetical debate around *mutʿa* marriage, in R. Gleave, 'Shiʿite Exegesis and the Interpretation of Q4.24', in A. Jones (ed.), *University Lectures in Islamic Studies* (London, 1998).

women forbidden in marriage): 'All other women are permitted to you. . . . For that which you have enjoyed from them, give them their due as a duty.' Though the Shīʿī cite and utilize an identical Qurʾān to the Sunnis, in their works of exegesis a variant of this verse is mentioned. The variant does not share the same authority as the agreed text, which has been subject to generations of community agreement. However, the variant has obtained the status of 'possible revelation', and hence can (and is) used as evidence of the validity of the *mutʿa* marriage. The variant reads: 'All other women are permitted to you . . . For that which you have enjoyed from them *for a stipulated period (ilā ajal musamman)*, give them their due as a duty.' The variant (given in italics above) explains the reference of the verse as, unambiguously, the 'marriage of pleasure', not merely because the word enjoy comes from the same Arabic root as the word *mutʿa*, but also because it states that the marriage is for 'a limited period'.

This variant was much discussed and debated. Shīʿī exegetes, in their debates with Sunnis, maintained that it was not just the Shi'a who accepted the variant as possible revelation. As al-Kāshānī states, 'The Sunnis also relate this reading from a group of companions.'[37]

The Sunni response was that even if the verse was revealed in this way, the ruling was subsequently abrogated by Prophetic Sunna.[38] The evidence for abrogation (*naskh*) involved the prohibition of *mutʿa* marriage by the second caliph and companion of the Prophet, Umar. Umar, since he was a close companion of the Prophet Muḥammad, is believed to have acted in conformity with the Prophet's Sunna. Hence his prohibition on *mutʿa* is taken as an indicator of the Prophet's views when these are unavailable in the collections of *ḥadīth*.

Abrogation itself is a contentious issue in Islamic legal theory, in particular the abrogation of the Qurʾān by the Sunna. In theory, a divine ruling can be abrogated by a later divine ruling. The earlier ruling is perceived as a preparatory law, revealed to train the Prophet's community for the full and complete law revealed to the Prophet before his death. This procedure was used to explain the apparent contradictions in the Qurʾān, and hence the date of revelation of each verse (a matter of not inconsiderable controversy) inevitably contributed to a jurist's view regarding the validity, or otherwise, of a ruling. Whether the Qurʾān could abrogate the Sunna (and vice versa) depended (to an extent) on the jurist's views concerning the status of Sunna (was the Sunna revelation equal to the Qurʾān, or was it of lower revelatory status?). With respect to this verse, the discussion was even more complicated. That the verse was revealed with the addition ('for a stipulated period'), is itself dubitable. That Umar's actions can be taken

---

[37] Muḥsin Fayḍ al-Kāshānī, *Tafsīr al-Ṣāfī*, 5 vols. (Tehran, 1994), ii. 438–9.
[38] e.g. al-Rāzī, *Mafātīḥ*, vi. 49–54. A good summary of this debate is found in A. Gribetz, *Strange Bedfellows: Mutʿat al-nisāʾ and Mutʿat al-ḥajj* (Berlin, 1994), 158–80.

as an indicator of the Prophet's Sunna is also disputed (merely because he was a trusted companion, does this mean he always acted in accordance with the Prophet's wishes?). Even if these objections are resolved, there is the wider debate about whether the Qur'ān can abrogate the Sunna, and vice versa. These ambiguities and debates provided a rich vein of subject matter, mined in subsequent exegetical works over the centuries. The dispute continues into the modern period in the *tafsīr* of the famous Lebanese Shī'ī scholar Faḍlallāh, who writes:

The justification for allowing this type of marriage (*mut'a*) is to be found in the unusual circumstances of [the verse's] revelation. . . . We know that abrogation (*naskh*) refers to ending [the applicability] of a ruling *because there is a benefit for society in the ruling coming to an end*. . . . In light of this, we can see that illegitimate sexual relations exist side by side with permanent marriage in every period and in every part of the world. . . . Permanent marriage does not appear to be the solution to the problem of the sexes. This is what we understand from Imam 'Alī's ['Alī was the first Shī'ī leader, termed *imām*] words, 'If 'Umar had not prohibited *mut'a*, only the wretched would perform *zinā*.'[39]

For Faḍlallāh, abrogation occurs for a reason. If there is a debate over whether or not a verse is abrogated, the matter can be settled by examining the benefit for society accruing from the two possible scenarios: abrogation or non-abrogation. The reason for non-abrogation in this case is that the earlier ruling (on the legitimacy of *mut'a*, found in the variant) is of greater benefit (*maṣlaḥa*) to society than the later ruling (of Umar). If there is no benefit in abrogating a verse (and, conversely, a benefit in maintaining its validity), then it cannot (rationally speaking) have been abrogated (since this would thwart God's greater plan of providing a law which benefits society). In Faḍllallāh's view, the benefit from maintaining the ruling found in the variant verse and according *mut'a* marriage legal validity is that *mut'a* prevents the proliferation of illegitimate sexual relations. Since this is beneficial for society, the ruling (and hence the variant verse) cannot have been abrogated.

The importance of Faḍlallāh's contribution to the abrogation debate lies in his use of the term 'benefit' (*maṣlaḥa*), and signals a general trend in modern Quranic exegesis. Quranic rulings need to be tested against the needs of society, and their benefits analysed. They are no longer simply obeyed as unquestionable rules. If there appears to be a harmful effect resulting from the application of a Quranic ruling, the relevant verse or verses must be reinterpreted, and the ruling reformulated in order to produce the desired result. This trend, which is evident in the works of a number of modern exegetes, is in part due to the impact of enlightenment rationalism on the Muslim world, and the adjustment of Muslim legal

---

[39] al-Shaykh Muḥammad Ḥusayn Faḍlallāh, *Min waḥy al-qur'ān*, 8 vols. (Beirut, 1983), iv. 125–6.

thinking under its influence. In these matters, it might be argued that the Shīᶜa have an advantage over the Sunnis: their standard position has been the validity of reason (ᶜaql), alongside revelation (naql), as a source of knowledge. The Sunnis have, in the main, privileged the latter over the former.[40]

The example of the (entertained, but not incorporated) alteration of the Quranic text ('for a stipulated period') enabled jurists and exegetes to validate a ruling not 'explicitly' (if such a term can be used) mentioned in the text. The variant provides evidence for a particular legal interpretation of the verse, even though it is agreed that it does not form part of the canonical text. Once the referent of the verse is secured (as it has been for Shīᶜī writers in the discussions over mutᶜa marriage), other discussions over abrogation can be pursued. This adds another possible method of Quranic legal exegesis: the (potential) plasticity of the canon's limits can be exploited for legal ends.

Conclusion

Most of the exegetical techniques outlined in the above analysis were not only available for the interpretation of the Qurʾān. For most jurists, the Qurʾān and the Sunna enjoyed a (near) equal status as revelation. While the Qurʾān represented a (relatively) stable text, the Sunna had to be constructed from reports of the Prophet's life (mainly found in collections of ḥadīth). The latter had the added obstacle of a test for authenticity far more rigorous than that applied to the Quranic text in the classical period. Variant ḥadīth reports were much more numerous than variants of the Quranic text, and presented many more exegetical issues (which were also, in truth, opportunities).

The techniques of exegesis were validated in works of legal theory. Analogy (through the discovery of the ratio) and implication (both intended and unintended) are just two examples of such techniques. In works of Quranic exegesis (tafsīr) and positive law (furūᶜ al-fiqh), one finds additional techniques such as historical contextualization and consideration of possible Quranic variants. Employing these techniques enabled the jurists to expand the legal significance of the Qurʾān by extending the law found in the Qurʾān.

The latitude allowed jurists in their explanation of rulings derived from verses found in the Qurʾān was not inconsiderable, as I hope the above analysis has shown. However, it was a matter of debate. Unacceptable interpretation (referred to as taʾwīl baᶜīd) was a frequent accusation between jurists, when it was felt that the limits of interpretation had been

---

[40] I discuss the reason–revelation debate in Shīᶜī law in R. Gleave, *Inevitable Doubt: Two Shīᶜī Theories of Jurisprudence* (Leiden, 2000), 183–219.

overstepped (or, as Eco has put it, 'over-interpretation' had occurred).[41] This was primarily used as a polemic device to discredit sectarian opponents rather than bring errant colleagues into line. It was not that there was a free-for-all when interpreting the Quranic text. The tradition of scholarship, in which certain methods of exegesis were permitted and others were prohibited, together with developing and sophisticated linguistic studies of the Arabic language, provided restraints.[42] As I hope I have shown, these restraints did not ensure a monovalent presentation of God s message in the Qurʾān.[43] With regard to legal matters, they were (perhaps intentionally) designed to allow diversity (*ikhtilāf*), thereby ensuring difference (over the interpretation of a particular verse) within unity. This must form part of the explanation for the impressive coherence of the Islamic juristic tradition up to the early modern period. This coherence has (to an extent) broken down in the face of modernism, where the demand for unambiguous interpretations of the Quranic text has partially ended the acceptance of diversity of opinion in legal matters.

[41] See U. Eco, *Interpretation and Over-Interpretation* (Cambridge, 1992), 45–66.
[42] See K. Versteegh, *Arabic Grammar and Early Quranic Exegesis* (Leiden, 1993).
[43] This can be said generally of the exegetical tradition, though it was not without its monovalent exponents. See Calder, '*Tafsīr*', 123–7.

FREEDOM OF RELIGION AS THE FRUIT OF THE RADICAL REFORMATION

Matthijs de Blois

Introduction

Students in my philosophy of human rights classes are sometimes surprised when I use for the historical introduction to the discussion of the roots of human rights a text which takes the Reformation as its point of departure.[1] They have in most cases been trained in academic environments where the notion prevails that the basic structures of Western democratic states are the product of the ideas of the Enlightenment, thereby neglecting other sources which have contributed to the development of freedom, the rule of law, and human rights. For many people the history of human rights starts with the Enlightenment's creed *par excellence*, the French *Déclaration des droits de l'homme et du citoyen* of 1789. It is therefore not a surprise that the interpretation of human rights often tends to be in line with the French Revolution—rather anticlerical or at least not very positive to religion in general, and the Christian religion in particular. Has not the Enlightenment for good reasons been characterized as a

shared mood or temper, or attitude to the world, in which the dominant note was one of profound scepticism towards traditional systems of authority or orthodoxy (especially those of religion), and a strong faith in the power of human reason and intelligence to make unlimited advances in the sciences and conducive to human welfare?[2]

Another approach is, however, possible. It is submitted that the roots of human rights are not exclusively to be found in the Enlightenment. Alongside that movement the theology of at least one of the four currents of the Reformation should be mentioned. I have in mind the Radical or (Ana-)Baptist wing of the Reformation, which next to the Lutheran, Calvinist, and Anglican exerted an influence both in Europe (from 1525) and America.[3] It provided the theological alternative for the intertwinement of State and Church in the Middle Ages, which was also defended

---

[1] J. H. Burns, 'The Rights of Man since the Reformation: An Historical Survey', in Francis Vallat (ed.), *An Introduction to the Study of Human Rights* (London, 1970).

[2] J. M. Kelly, *A Short History of Western Legal Theory* (Oxford, 1992), 249–50.

[3] The terms 'Radical' and '(Ana-)Baptist' will be explained below.

with theological arguments. Not scepticism but an interpretation of the Bible led the Radical Reformation to the separation of Church and State and the freedom of religion and belief, the oldest of the human rights enacted in legal texts. The general idea of restricting the competences of the government also prepared the ground for other freedoms, such as the freedom of expression and the right to privacy.

Outline

I start with the relationship between Christians, the Christian Church, and the State from the beginnings of Christianity. This is important because both the New Testament and church history play an important role in the theological arguments presented by the representatives of the Radical Reformation for the separation of Church and State and religious freedom, which form the central part of this paper. Thereafter I will indicate the influence they have had also outside the scope of the theological debate in legal texts and especially in the writings of one of the most important human rights philosophers, John Locke. Finally, I will make some concluding remarks.

The New Testament

In the Gospel of Matthew we find the intriguing passage where Jesus is confronted with the question whether it is lawful to pay taxes to Caesar. He asked for a sample of the tax money. They brought him a *denarius*. 'And He said to them, "Whose image and inscription is this?" They said to Him, "Caesar's." And He said to them, "Render therefore to Caesar the things that are Caesar's, and to God the things that are God's." '[4]

Apparently there are two spheres: the sphere of the government and the sphere of religion. Jesus accepts as legitimate the authority of the pagan Roman government in regard to the levying of taxes next to the service of the true God. This position set the stage for the early Christian Church, which came into being on the Day of Pentecost, ten days after the Ascension of Jesus. It consisted of those who accepted the gospel message and came to believe in Jesus and who underwent baptism as the outward sign of their faith.[5] The Church, which grew as a result of the missionary activities which followed Pentecost, initially consisted of Jews. It did not take long, however, before the Greeks also came to believe in Jesus. That meant that the Church had no longer a specific ethnic identity. The message of the gospel was for mankind as such and was not restricted to a special group. Christianity spread rapidly over the Roman empire.

[4] Matt. 22: 20–1. Bible quotations are from the King James Version.
[5] See Acts 2: 41.

Churches consisted of members of Jewish as well as Greek or Roman origin. They came from different strata in society. It is interesting to see what their position was vis-à-vis the governmental authorities. First of all, Christians were exhorted to be obedient to the government. The *locus classicus* is the thirteenth chapter of Paul's Letter to the Romans: 'Let every soul be subject to the governing authorities. For there is no authority except from God, and the authorities that exist are appointed by God.'[6] This Letter was written during the reign of Emperor Nero, when the Christians were only a small minority and the governing authorities in the empire were pagans.[7] The Apostle Peter appealed in his first letter for Christians, who where apparently subject to persecution, to assume the same attitude: 'submit yourselves to every ordinance of man for the Lord's sake, whether to the king as supreme, or to governors, as to those who are sent by him for the punishment of evildoers and for the praise of those who do good'.[8]

The obligation to obey the government was not absolute, however. We find in the New Testament one clear exception, which was expressed by the Apostles when they stood before the Sanhedrin: 'We ought to obey God rather than men.'[9] This led to great difficulties in the Roman empire when Christians refused to take part in the rituals of the official state religion.

Finally, it is clear from the New Testament that Christians should pray for the government. Paul wrote to his assistant Timothy: 'I exhort first of all that supplications, prayers, intercessions and giving of thanks be made for all men, for kings and all who are in authority, that we may lead a quiet and peaceable life in all godliness and reverence. For this is good and acceptable in the sight of God our Saviour.'[10] The ambition of the early Church was no more than a peaceable life, which enabled it to serve its Lord. We do not read of political strategies or blueprints of something like a 'Christian State'. The distinction between the order of the Church and the order of the State seemed to be the consequence of the existence of the Church as a body to be separate from the world.[11] We find a clear illustration of what this meant in practice in a passage concerning the application of discipline in the Church in the First Letter of Paul to the Corinthians, where a distinction is made between the order of the Church and the order of the State. The Corinthian Church is admonished to apply church discipline to one of its members, but it is made clear that it can do so only to members. 'For what have I to do with judging those also who are outside [the Church]? Do you not judge those who are inside [the Church]? But

---

[6] Rom. 13: 1.
[7] F. F. Bruce, *The Spreading Flame: The Rise and Progress of Christianity from its First Beginnings to the Conversion of the English* (Grand Rapids, Mich., 1995), 137.
[8] 1 Pet. 2: 13–14.   [9] Acts 5: 29; see also Acts 4: 19.
[10] 1 Tim. 2: 1–3.   [11] See Rom. 12: 2 etc.

those who are outside God judges. Therefore "put away from yourselves an evil person." '[12]

The Turning Point

This espousal of separation was very different from the ideas on the position of religion current in ancient society. The religion was part of public life *par excellence*. The Pontifex Maximus was one the highest functions in the empire, held since Augustus by the emperors themselves. The performance of religious duties was enforced by severe legal sanctions. Performance, not belief, was what the Roman state religion required. So the empire could accept all kinds of other religions, if only their adherents complied with public acts of worship, which was impossible for Christians. This led from time to time to their persecution by the Roman authorities. An example is the severe persecution by Scapula, the proconsul of Africa (211–13), when many believers were thrown to the lions and others burned to death. This caused Tertullian (*c.* 160–220), the lawyer who became a Church Father, to write Scapula a letter in which he in unequivocal terms and in line with the New Testament stressed freedom of belief: 'It is a fundamental human right, a privilege of nature, that every man should worship according to his own convictions: one man's religion neither harms nor helps another man. It . . . is certainly no part of religion to compel religion.'[13] This plea for legal recognition of religious freedom was written as early as 212! It was, however, not upheld by the official representatives of the Christian Church in the ages to come.

A turning point came when after the severe persecutions under Diocletian (284–305) his successor, Constantine (306–37), accepted Christianity as one of the religions of the empire, in the Edict of Milan (313). Both pagans and Christians were free to confess and practise their religion.[14] This toleration did not last very long. Constantine thought it wise to seek the support of the impressive number of Christian citizens for his policies. From a persecuted minority they became a privileged majority. This was not without effect for both the Church and the State. The idea of separation lost its practical significance for many members of the Church when the State began to embrace Christianity as the religion of the State, which it officially became under Theodosius I in 380.[15] Citizenship and membership of the church became almost identical. Theodosius I ruled:

---

[12] 1 Cor. 5: 12–13.

[13] Quoted in Johannes Quasten, *Patrology*, vol. ii (Utrecht, 1964), 266–7.

[14] Compare on the Edict of Milan (and the preceding Toleration Edict of Galerius of 311) in Périclès-Pierre Joannou, *La Législation impériale et la christianisation de l'empire Romain* (Rome, 1972), 19–22, and J. Westbury-Jones, *Roman and Christian Imperialism* (London. 1939), 198–207.

[15] Compare Joannou, *La Législation impériale*, 43–52.

all peoples over whom our rule extends shall live in that religion which was revealed to St. Peter ... We give orders that all these are to adopt the name of 'Catholic Christians'; the rest we shall let pass for fools and they will have to bear the reproach of being called heretics. They must come first under the wrath of God and then also under ours.'[16]

In the Codex of Justinian we find a compilation of legislation against heretics.[17] Its intention was very clear: 'Let all heresies forbidden by Divine Law and the Imperial Constitution be forever suppressed.'[18] It will be clear that this approach to the relationship between the Christian religion and the public authorities differed completely from the position of the early Church as it appears in the writings of the New Testament. It seems to be more akin to the place of ancient pagan religion in the Roman empire. The intertwinement of Church and State was nevertheless provided with a theological foundation by, for example, Augustine.[19] The new approach was not, however, acceptable to all Christians.[20] A number of them clung to the idea of separation. As a consequence they were considered to be heretics, even when they adhered to all the other basic theological tenets of the Catholic Church. There is good reason to see the history of Christianity as having two phases. The first describes the official line, which developed in close relationship with the society and the political authorities of the day. The second involves the underground current, a term which because of a permanent threat of persecution should be taken not only figuratively but also almost literally. It is this current which came to the surface at the time of the Reformation as its Radical or (Ana-)Baptist wing.

The Reformation

The Protestant Reformation at the beginning of the sixteenth century marked the end of the official unity of the Church of Christendom. For all their diversity the mainstream of the different movements which fall under the heading of Protestantism share a number of principles, which indicate their common points of disagreement with the medieval Catholic Church.

[16] *Codex Theodosianus*, 16. 1. 2, trans. in Leonard Verduin, *The Reformers and their Stepchildren* (Grand Rapids, Mich., 1964), 34.
[17] See on Justinian, who reigned from 527 to 565, in Westbury-Jones, *Roman and Christian Imperialism*, 230–49.
[18] *Codex Justinianus*, 1. 5. 2, trans. in S. P. Scott, *Corpus Iuris Civilis: The Civil Law*, vol. xii (New York, 1973), 63.
[19] See P. R. L. Brown, 'St. Augustine's Attitude to Religious Coercion', and Michael Wilks, 'Roman Empire and Christian State in the De Civitate Dei', in John Dunn and Ian Harris (eds.), *Augustine*, vol. i (Cheltenham, 1997), 382–91, 512–33.
[20] Compare E. H. Broadbent, *The Pilgrim Church* (1931, repr. Southampton, 1989), 20–6; R. A. Markus, *Christianity in the Roman World* (New York, 1974), 105–6; Bruce, *The Spreading Flame*, 337–9; Verduin, *The Reformers and their Stepchildren*.

First, the doctrine of the direct responsibility of the individual to God and therefore the emphasis on the importance of personal belief, without the need of an intermediary function of a priest. In the second place, the acceptance of the Bible as the single authority in matters of doctrine and morality, thereby rejecting the authority of the ecclesiastical tradition. Further, the doctrine of salvation by grace and not by works. The final point to be mentioned is the rejection of papal authority and the Roman Church hierarchy.

The Radical or (Ana-)Baptist wing of the Reformation had opinions which deviated on a number of other issues from those of Lutherans, Calvinists, and Anglicans. These opinions had important consequences for the position of the Christian in society and the role of the State. Before moving on to an analysis of these points, I first have to make clear what is understood here by the terms 'Radical' and '(Ana-)Baptist'. The term 'Radical' indicates that Reformers of this persuasion went further in the rejection of the principles and practices of the undivided medieval Catholic Church than did the other Protestant reformers. As far as the term (Ana)Baptist is concerned, the following can be said. It refers of course to the practice of believers' baptism, one of the tenets of the Radical Reformation. The prefix 'Ana' is placed between brackets both because the idea of rebaptism was rejected by those who underwent believers' baptism and because in the English-speaking world the term 'Baptist' became more and more familiar from the seventeenth century onwards.

The terms 'Radical Reformation' and '(Ana-)Baptism' and the forms derived therefrom are here used interchangeably. They cover a diversity of persons, groups, and ideas. The terms are used to refer to the fanatics trying to establish the New Zion by force in Münster (1533–5), but also to the pacifist followers of Menno Simons (1496–1559), who relentlessly condemned the Münster experiment, and was in that respect more representative of the ideas of the Radical Reformation as a whole. As indicated, the terms also refer to the Baptists in the British Isles and in the American colonies, who shared many theological ideas with the Calvinists. For example, they were in many cases less reluctant to assume public office, compared to their brethren on the European continent.

Radical or (Ana-)Baptist principles

Notwithstanding all the diversity within the Radical wing of the Reformation, I think there is sufficient ground to discern a number of common theological principles which, taken together, have important consequences as regards religious freedom and the relationship between Church and State. I will restrict myself to the following five points, which at the same time illustrate the distinctions between the Anabaptists and other Protestants.

The differences find their roots in a different interpretation of the Bible, especially with respect to the relationship between the Old and the New Testament.[21] It should be noted that since the times of Constantine and Theodosius arguments concerning a role of the public authorities in the enforcement of the true Christian religion were *inter alia* derived from the example of the theocracy we find in the Old Testament. These arguments were also used by Protestant reformers. Calvin, for example, derived the obligation of the Christian magistrate in Geneva to punish heretics from the rule in Deuteronomy 13: 5, where the people of Israel are instructed to put to death the prophet who seduces the people to worship idols.[22] Therefore, it has to be noted that the (Ana-)Baptists were more than the other Reformers convinced of the fact that the coming of Christ in this world marked a new period in the history of God with mankind. The position of the Christian Church in society in their view differed in many respects from the position of the people of Israel under the Old Testament. Under the Old Testament 'Church' and 'society' were inseparably connected. The theocracy for the people of the Abrahamic covenant embodied rules for worship and sacrifices, but also matters which nowadays belong to the sphere of private or public law. The New Testament situation was typified by a Church of believers living in a society consisting of many non-believers. The believers were united not on the basis of their descent from a common ancestor but by their personal belief in Jesus Christ. The public authorities could not forthwith be considered to be 'Christian magistrates'; they should not be compared with the rulers of Israel under the Old Testament dispensation. An early (Ana-)Baptist treatise on the relationship of the Christian and the State (written before 1535) emphasized in this connection: 'But Christ and His own have another office.'[23] Another representative of the Radical Reformation held:

for although we were to grant that it was commanded to some rulers in Israel to punish idol worship and such like, this was because Israel was a servile people of the law . . . among which everything was by constraint, also their religion. Now however in the free doctrine of the Gospel of Christ all coercion has ceased, so that it is not proper either by the use of force or the secular rule to saddle anyone with the faith against his will; nor is it proper for the magistrate to penalize anyone for

---

[21] See O. H. de Vries, *Leer en praxis van de vroege dopers, uitgelegd als een theologie van de geschiedenis* ('Teaching and Institutions of the Early Anabaptists Interpreted as a Theology of History') (Leeuwarden, 1982).

[22] J. W. Allen, *A History of Political Thought in the Sixteenth Century* (London, 1929), 86–7.

[23] See Hans J. Hillerbrand, 'An Early Anabaptist Treatise on the Christian and the State', *Mennonite Quarterly Review*, 32/1 (Jan. 1958), 32. Compare also H. Bonger, *De motivering van de godsdienstvrijheid bij Dirk Volckertszoon Coornhert* (Arnhem, 1954).

the lack of faith; for this is the prerogative exclusively of the Son of God and of no creature on earth. . .[24]

We find a similar approach in the booklet *The Bloody Tenent of Persecution* (1644) by Roger Williams (to whom we will return later). He defended universal religious freedom with a reference to the will and command of God 'since the coming of his Son the Lord Jesus'.[25] In other words, under the New Testament the position of the government in respect of the defence of the true religion has been radically changed compared to the Old Testament.

Not only was a different view of biblical history at stake. The Radicals also had a different view of church history.[26] While in the official Christendom the era of Constantine was considered to be the beginning of a triumphant period in church history, they saw it as the beginning of the decline. This concerned *inter alia* the tendency of the Christian Church after Constantine to let the public authorities defend spiritual truths with public force. Time and again we find the name of Constantine as the one who deprived the Christian Church of its purity. In the early tract quoted previously it is said that 'There was not among the Christians of old at the time of the apostles until the Emperor Constantine any temporal power or sword among the Christians.'[27] This change turned, in the words of Roger Williams, 'the Gardens of the Churches of Saints . . . into the Wilderness of whole Nations'.[28]

BELIEVERS AND NON-BELIEVERS

This brings us to the second point, the sharp distinction between believers and non-believers in society. One of the main tenets of the first confessional document from (Ana-)Baptist circles, the *Brüderliche Vereinigung* (or the Schleitheim Confession of Faith) of 1527, was the separation of the believers from the world. The decisive importance of personal faith was taken to its uttermost consequences. Only those who, through repentance and personal faith in Jesus Christ, had experienced a renewal of their lives could be counted as believers. The believers' baptism was the outward sign of this. It also marked the separation from non-believers, who were in society almost without exception considered to be Christians because of their nominal membership of the institutional Church. The biblical motives for this separation were found in passages in the Epistles where it is stated that there cannot be fellowship between righteousness and

[24] In Verduin, *The Reformers and their Stepchildren*, 78–9.
[25] See for the text Leo Pfeffer, *Religious Freedom* (Skokie, Ill., 1979), 10–11.
[26] Verduin, *The Reformers and their Stepchildren*, 21–62.
[27] Quoted by Hillerbrand, 'An Early Anabaptist Treatise', 31.
[28] Quoted by Edwin S. Gaustad, *Liberty of Conscience: Roger Williams in America* (Grand Rapids, Mich., 1991), 79.

lawlessness, no communion of light with darkness, no accord of Christ with Belial, no part of a believer with an unbeliever, and no agreement of the temple of God with idols.[29] The Christian was supposed to withdraw from every non-Christian institution or person.[30] For many this had as a consequence the rejection of participation in public office or the army. The other side of the coin was that in many countries it was made impossible for adherents to the Radical Reformation to obtain public office. In the Protestant countries in general membership of the 'national' or the state Church was a prerequisite for any function in government. It should be noted, however, that many Baptists in the English-speaking world held different views on the compatibility of the Christian faith with public office.[31] It appears that even in Cromwell's army there were a number of Baptists.[32] Another example is Roger Williams, who was chief officer of Providence.[33] In general, however, a life separated from the world was characteristic of the (Ana-)Baptists.

THE CHURCH

This latter point is directly related to the (Ana-)Baptist concept of the Church.[34] The conflict between the mainstreams of the Reformation and its radical branch was before all other things a conflict on the delineation of the Church.[35] The Church was seen by the representatives of the Radical Reformation as the body of Christ, the Corpus Christi, composed only of believers, that is persons who explicitly confessed their belief in Christ. For example, in the Dordrecht Confession of Faith of 1623 we find in Article VIII the Church defined as the body constituted by those who by repentance have become true believers and have been baptized. It is a body redeemed by the blood of Christ, preserved by him, and protected until the end of the world.[36]

The true Church is in this view a visible body, clearly separated from the rest of society.[37] It can, according to the Dordrecht Confession, be

---

[29] 2 Cor. 6: 14–16. See De Vries, *Leer en praxis*, 35.

[30] *The Mennonite Encyclopedia*, i: *A-C* (Scottdale, Pa., 1955), 447.

[31] Compare the Baptist Confession of Faith 1689, which held in Article 24 that 'It is lawful for Christians to accept and carry out the duties of a magistrate when called upon.' The quotation is from the updated edition by Peter Masters (London, 1989).

[32] See Ernest A. Payne, *The Free Church Tradition in the Life of England* (London, 1944), 43.

[33] Gaustad, *Liberty of Conscience*, 123.

[34] Compare the analysis of the sect by Max Weber, *Wirtschaft und Gesellschaft. Grundriss der verstehenden Soziologie* (Tübingen, 1972), 721–3.

[35] Verduin, *The Reformers and their Stepchildren*, 16.

[36] The full title of the first English translation of this Confession was *The Christian Confession of the Faith of the Harmless Christians, in the Netherlands Known by the Name of Mennonists*. See *The Mennonite Encyclopedia*, ii: *D–H* (Scottdale, Pa., 1956), 91.

[37] Compare Allen, *A History of Political Thought*, 38.

recognized by its evangelical faith, its Christian love, the godly manner of life of its members, and the observance of the ordinances of Christ (baptism and the Lord's Supper).

The idea of the Church being composed of true believers has as a consequence that its membership is voluntary. People cannot be forced to believe, nor can it be assumed that they automatically inherit the faith of their parents. Only those who have freely accepted the faith are considered to be members.

It is this idea of the Church which was unacceptable for the other reformers, such as Luther, Zwingli, and Calvin, although Luther and Zwingli initially hesitated. They realized that accepting the ideas of the Radical Reformation would mean that the greater part of society could not be considered to be part of the Church. The idea of a Christian society, a Corpus Christianum, would be lost, having regard to the fact that also in those days the number of true believers was limited.[38] That would have important consequences, also in the political field. It would no longer be possible for Christian leaders to see the population as such as a Christian nation. In the view of the other reformers the Church was a body, indeed with a clear written confession, but including all living in a certain area. Their idea was to replace the Roman Catholic Christendom of the Middle Ages by a Protestant—Lutheran or Calvinistic—society. It should therefore not come as a surprise that as a result of the mainstream Reformation national Protestant state churches were instituted, a fact officially acknowledged in the *cuius regio eius religio* principle, confirmed by the Religious Peace of Augsburg in 1555. It is in the same line of thinking that the infant baptism remained a fundamental issue for the Protestant official or semi-state churches. In the early times of the Reformation the baptism of children was enforced by the law. The Protestant city of Strasbourg, for example, ordered in 1534 that no child was to be left unbaptized and that if necessary it should be baptized by officers of the law.[39]

The tension between the necessity of personal faith for salvation, which was accepted also by Luther, Calvin, and Zwingli, and the idea of national churches consisting of both true believers and others, was solved by the introduction of concepts like the visible Church (the citizens of a Protestant nation) and the invisible Church (of believers) or the *ecclesiola in ecclesia*, that is the (small) body of believers in the large institution of the Church.[40]

CHURCH DISCIPLINE

The controversy concerning the nature of the Church also had important

---

[38] Verduin, *The Reformers and their Stepchildren*, 17–20.
[39] Ibid. 120.   [40] Ibid. 82.

consequences for the maintenance of church discipline, which touches upon the relationship between Church and State. The (Ana-)Baptists took very seriously the idea of not being of this world as far as the quality of their lives as Christians was concerned. Living a holy life was expected of all believers. The Church should be pure. If necessary disciplinary measures should be applied to members of the Church, but only by the Church itself. It has been said that the (Ana-)Baptists could be seen as those who had restored the New Testament model of church discipline.[41] Konrad Grebel, one of the early leaders of the Radical Reformation, wrote as early as 1524:

Try with the Word to create a Christian congregation, with the help of Christ and his rule, as found in Matthew 18 and as we see in practice in the Epistles . . . He who refuses to reform . . . resisting the Word and the work of God, and who continues in that way, such a man, after Christ and His Word and rule have been preached and after he has been admonished by two or three witnesses and the congregation . . . such a man must not be put to death but classified as a heathen man and a publican and be let alone.[42]

The procedure is one of admonition, with excommunication as the ultimate sanction. In other documents it was made clear that even in the cases where the social fellowship with the apostates must be broken, the ultimate purpose was to bring them to acknowledge their sin and to repent.[43] It is important to underline that there should be no involvement of the public authorities. The *Brüderliche Vereinigung* of 1527 made a sharp distinction between the respective responsibilities of the government and the Church: 'The sword is an ordinance of God outside the perfection of Christ; the Princes and Rulers of the world are ordained for the punishment of evil-doers and for putting them to death. But within the perfection of Christ excommunication is the ultimate in the way of punishment, physical death being not included.'[44] Prosecution of 'heretics' was not considered to be part of the office of government.

   Most other Protestants saw on the contrary a role for the public authorities in upholding church discipline. This was very clearly put forward during the Disputation at Emden between the representatives of the Reformed churches in the Netherlands and the representatives of the Radical Reformation in 1578. Menso Alting, who spoke on behalf of the Reformed churches, and referred to his opponents as 'the men', held: 'Our view of the church of God is diverse from that of "the men"; they exclude the office of the magistrate from the Church and they refuse to ascribe to the civil power any punitive function in the Church of God. But we, in

---

[41] Ibid. 120.   [42] Trans. ibid. 121.
[43] See Article XVII of the Dordrecht Confession of Faith, *Mennonite Encyclopedia*, ii: 93.
[44] Trans. in Verduin, *The Reformers and their Stepchildren*, 57.

keeping with the Word of God include the office of the magistracy in the church of God.'[45] As a consequence even after the Reformation, not only in Roman Catholic countries but also in countries with Protestant rulers, those who deviated from the official religion had to fear persecution by the public authorities on the initiative of the Church.

CHURCH AND STATE

The logical consequence of the foregoing is to deny the State (that is, the governmental authorities) powers in respect of religion. The task of the government since the genesis of the Christian Church was in the eyes of the (Ana-)Baptists necessarily restricted to 'earthly' things. This, in those days, unusual view of a restricted role for the government led frequently to the accusation that they rejected governmental authority as such. That is not true, at least not for their main representatives. Time and again the biblical foundations of government and the obligation to obey were underlined. In the early tract already quoted above it was said that

The gracious God has set the magistrate (from above) on earth to maintain outward peace. . . . The magistrate, set by God, Romans 13, to carry the sword according to God's order and instruction. . . . To preserve those who walk in the flesh through the might of the sword to the punishment and revenge of malice, for otherwise there would not be peace in property as one can feel everywhere. All this stems from God's goodness and grace who knows and wants only man's good and not evil.[46]

The English Baptist Thomas Helwys was of the opinion that the magistracy was a holy ordinance of God and that it was a sin to speak evil of the government or to despise it.[47] Along the same lines the Dordrecht Confession of Faith (1632) held in Article XIII that the government was established by God for the punishment of the wicked and the protection of the good. It declared that Christians should recognize rulers as ministers of God and honour them, and that they should pay taxes and pray for the rulers.[48]

The task of the government was, however, considered to be in principle a restricted one. This is, for example, explained in Helwys's book *The Mystery of Iniquity*, written in 1612, which is the first plea in England for universal religious liberty.

Our Lord the King is but an earthly king, and he hath no aucthority as a King but

[45] Trans., in Verduin, *The Reformers and their Stepchildren*, 130.

[46] See for the translation Hillerbrand, 'An Early Anabaptist Treatise', 30. Compare on the view of the (Ana-)Baptists on the government also Harold Schaff, 'The Anabaptists, the Reformers and the Civil Government', *Church History*, 1 (1932), 27–46.

[47] See Henry Cook, *What Baptists Stand For* (London, 1947), 166.

[48] *Mennonite Encyclopedia*, ii. 92–3.

in earthly causes, and if the King's people be obedient and true subjects, obeying all human laws made by the King, our Lord the King can require no more: for men's religion to God is betwixt God and themselves: the King shall not answere for it, neither may the King be judg betwene God and Man. Let them be heretikes, Turcks, Jewes, or whatsoever, it apperteynes not to the earthly power to punish them in the last measure.[49]

The circulation of his book with these radical words led to his imprisonment in Newgate prison.

The approach of Helwys was characteristic for the (Ana-)Baptists. Sometimes they used as an argument put forward against the application of public force in respect of religion the example of Jesus Christ, who did want to assume governmental powers, but fled when the crowd wanted to make him king and who was willing to suffer innocently.[50] Many pointed out, against those who referred to the Old Testament to justify the use of public force in respect of religion, the decisive change under the New Testament. We have already seen that above. The Frisian Reformer Menno Simons, whose followers are known as Mennonites up to this day, wrote that the Church should not depend for its protection on political power. It could only be saved and protected by the Lord Jesus Christ with his powerful word and the Holy Spirit.[51] He referred to the biblical parable of the wheat and the tares in Matthew 13: 24–30 to explain that it is not up to the political authorities to sift out the true believers and the heretics.[52] This parable was an important motive also in other (Ana-)Baptist writings on the freedom of religion and it still serves as an argument in Christian theology to defend religious freedom.[53] It is therefore worth while to summarize it here. In the parable Jesus compares the Kingdom of God to a man who sowed good seeds in his field. While men slept, his enemy came to sow tares among the weed. When both the good and the bad seed sprung up, the servants wanted to gather the tares from between the wheat. The householder did not permit this 'lest while you gather up the tares you also uproot the wheat with them. Let both grow together until the harvest, and at the time of the harvest I will say to the reapers, "First gather together the tares and bind them in bundles to burn them, but

[49] Quoted by Payne, *The Free Church Tradition*, 35.

[50] See Hillerbrand, 'An Early Anabaptist Treatise', 31.

[51] See H. W. Meihuizen, *Menno Simons* (Haarlem, 1961), 120. See also Broadbent, *The Pilgrim Church*, 185–97.

[52] See M. C. Postema, *Het spoor van Menno Simonsz gedachten* (Kampen, 1986), 29–30. See also Ronald J. Sider, 'An Evangelical Vision for American Democracy: The Anabaptist Perspective', in *The Bible, Politics and Democracy* (Grand Rapids, Mich., 1987), 41.

[53] See e.g. J. Verkuyl, 'Over de theologische fundering van mensenrechten en de praktische effectuering ervan in de context van deze tijd', *Wereld en Zending, tijdschrift voor missiologie* (1974), 244–64. See on the role of this parable in church history Roland H. Bainton, 'The Parable of the Tares as the Proof Text for Religious Liberty to the End of the Sixteenth Century', *Church History*, (1932), 67–89.

gather the wheat into my barn".'[54] The opponents of the (Ana-)Baptists used this parable to criticize their idea of a pure Church. They followed Augustine, who saw the tares growing in the Church side by side with the wheat.[55] The (Ana-)Baptists, on the other hand, used the parable to show that no public force should be used against non-believers in society in general in anticipation of God's final judgement. This idea seems to correspond with the explanation by Jesus that the field is the *world* (and not the Church).[56]

We also find a reference to this parable in the booklet *The Bloody Tenent of Persecution, for cause of Conscience*, published in 1644 and addressed to 'both Houses of the High Court of Parliament' by Roger Williams, probably the most famous of the (Ana-)Baptist writers on the freedom of religion, because of his role in American constitutional history.[57] In 1630 he left England for the New World. After a number of years he was banished from Massachusetts, again because of his religious opinions, and settled on Rhode Island.[58] He formulated the theological basis of freedom of religion and the separation of Church and State in the following terms:

Sixthly, It is the will and command of God, that (since the coming of his Son the Lord Jesus) a permission of the most Paganish, Jewish, Turkish, or Antichristian consciences and worships, be granted to all men in all Nations and Countries: and that they are only to be fought against with that Sword which is only (in Soul matters) able to conquer, to wit, the Sword of Gods' Spirit, the Word of God . . .

Tenthly, An inforced uniformity of Religion throughout a Nation or civil state, confounds the Civil and Religious, denies the principles of Christianity and civility, and that Jesus Christ is come in the Flesh.[59]

What is striking in this text as well as in the one quoted earlier from Helwys is the radical character of the religious freedom. It includes not only the different Christian denominations, but also Jews and pagans of different persuasions. It makes explicit that the civil and the religious should not be mixed up. The foundation of the freedom is nevertheless explicitly a Christian one, in that it refers to a command of God for the phase of God's history which started with the Incarnation of Jesus. Next, that it assumes the necessity of the use of the Word of God to contradict other opinions.

This last point draws our attention to the fact that in addition to the lack of competence for the public authorities in the field of religion, there

---

[54] Matt. 13: 29–30.
[55] Augustine, *City of God*, ed. David Knowles (Harmondsworth, 1972), 915.
[56] See Matt. 13: 38. Compare Verduin, *The Reformers and their Stepchildren*, 116–17.
[57] See on this publication, Gaustad, *Liberty of Conscience*, 69–87.
[58] See ibid.
[59] Text in Pfeffer, *Religious Freedom*, 10–11.

was another argument against the involvement of the government in this field. That is the point that it is impossible for the government to force people to accept the true religion. In an English pamphlet of 1614 we read that 'As kings and bishops cannot command the wind . . . so they cannot command faith.' The only way to combat spiritual error was by 'the Spirit of Christ and doctrine of the Word of God'.[60] The saving faith cannot be forced upon anybody. It is interesting to note that also Luther at a certain phase in his development made the same point. He wrote in his *Von Weltlicher Uberkeyt* in 1523: 'But the thoughts and meanings of the soul can be clear to none but God. Therefore it is futile and impossible to command or to force any man to believe this or that . . . Thus is it each man's own business what he believes.'[61] Shortly afterwards he adopted the opposite view that it was the task of the magistrate to persecute both Catholics and (Ana-)Baptists.[62]

Radical Principles Turned into Law

Roger Williams's point of view was not to remain mere theory. His ideas were included in the *Charter of Rhode Island and Providence Plantations* granted in 1663 by King Charles II to the population of this colony. It provided for an unprecedented freedom of religion, stating that

no person within the said colony, at any time hereafter, shall be in any wise molested, punished, disquieted, or called in question, for any differences of opinion in matters of religion, and do not actually disturb the civil peace of our said colony; but that all and every person and persons may, from time to time, and at all times hereafter, freely and fully have and enjoy his and their own judgments and consciences, in matters of religious concernments . . . they behaving themselves peacefully and quietly, and not using this liberty to licentiousness and profaneness, nor to the civil injury or outward disturbance of others. . .[63]

This can be seen as the first legal fruit of the (Ana-)Baptist theology of the rejection of the power of the public authorities in the field of religion. The Charter of Rhode Island was the first of a number of colonial charters respecting to a lesser or greater extent the freedom of religion. For quite a long time it remained the most radical one.[64] It illustrates that a political

---

[60] Quotation from Leonard Busher, *Religious Peace, or, A Plea for Liberty of Conscience*, in Cook, *What Baptists Stand For*, 167.

[61] Trans. in Allen, *A History of Political Thought*, 25. Compare also Schaff, 'The Anabaptists', 32–4.

[62] Allen, *A History of Political Thought*, 26.

[63] Text in Pfeffer, *Religious Freedom*, 12.

[64] Compare Georg Jellinek, 'Die Erklärung der Menschen- und Bürgerrechte', in Roman Schnur (ed.), *Zur Geschichte der Erklärung der Menschenrechte* (Darmstadt, 1964), 46–54. See, for an excellent analysis of the historical development of the religious freedom in America, Michael W. McConnell, 'The Origins and Historical Understanding of the Free Exercise of Religion', (1990) 103 *Harvard Law Review*, 1409–517.

community which was established by committed Christians was the first to accept the principle of tolerance.[65]

Gradually and with different degrees of radicalism the same principle was included in other colonial charters. This was the basis for the recognition of the freedom of religion in the Bills of Rights of the independent American states, such as Article 16 of the Virginia Declaration (1776), which held that

religion, or the duty we owe to our Creator, and the manner of discharging it, can be directed only by reason and conviction, not by force or violence; and therefore all men are equally entitled to the free exercise of religion, according to the dictates of conscience; and that it is the mutual duty of all to practise Christian forbearance, love, and charity towards each other.

The process of constitutional development in the United States culminated in the adoption of the First Amendment to the Constitution (in 1791) holding that

Congress shall make no law respecting an establishment of religion, or prohibiting the free exercise thereof . . . The American experience was an important source of inspiration for the later development towards the protection of human rights in both national and international law.

Locke on Toleration

It is not only the constitutional development in the United States as such which bears the clear imprints of the theology of the Radical Reformation. Also in the work of the philosopher who is seen as the *auctor intellectualis* of the American Revolution, John Locke, we come across striking resemblances to the principles of the (Ana-)Baptists.

John Locke (1632–1704) grew up in a Puritan family who stood at the side of the Parliamentarians in the English Civil War. He was no doubt familiar with the teachings of the (Ana-)Baptists. As an Oxford undergraduate he heard the Independent John Owen, who was dean of Christ Church.[66] Owen used biblical arguments against the repression of heretics by the government, most likely similar to those of the (Ana-)Baptists.[67] The Independents and the (Ana-)Baptists had many aspects of the idea of the Church in common. Locke was not himself in religious terms of a persuasion which could be classified under the heading of the Radical Reformation. He always remained a member of the Anglican Church; his

---

[65] Compare Emil Brunner, *Die Menschenrechte nach reformierter Lehre*, Conference, University of Zürich, 29 Apr. 1942, 7. It should be noted that Brunner not completely correctly qualifies Williams as an Independentist Calvinist.

[66] See Payne, *The Free Church Tradition*, 58, and Maurice Cranston, *John Locke* (London, 1957), 41.

[67] Cranston, *Locke*, 41.

opinions in his later life have been qualified as 'latitudinarian Anglicanism'.[68] Locke was not even particularly sympathetic towards representatives of the Radical Reformation, as can be concluded from his report of 1684 on a visit to one of the Dutch radical sects, the Labadists. He appeared to be rather critical of at least the way they practised their separation from the world.[69] Notwithstanding this, we find in several of his writings a defence of religious liberty and a restriction of the role of the government in respect of churches based on arguments similar to those used by the representatives of the Radical Reformation.

What is at first striking when we read his writings on the freedom of religion and the separation of Church and State is that this philosopher, who is seen as an exponent of the Enlightenment, used theological arguments derived directly from the New Testament, in a way which is in line with the Radical Reformation. His arguments are not presented as the result of a kind of scepticism regarding theological truth, but on the contrary because of a concern for the true nature of Christianity.[70] This is made very clear in *A Letter concerning Toleration*, which was written in 1686 in Utrecht and was published in 1689.[71] It starts with the statement that toleration is the chief characteristic of the true Church.[72] Locke refers in that connection to the words of Jesus to his disciples in Luke 22: 25 that 'The kings of the Gentiles exercise lordship over them, but you shall not do so.' True Christianity implies love and a holy way of life. It is contrary to the Gospel to use arms in order to convert erroneous people. He confronted his contemporaries who wanted to wield the worldly sword for Christian warfare with the following very characteristic statement:

If, like the Captain of our salvation, they sincerely desired the good of souls, they would tread in the steps and follow the perfect example of that Prince of peace, who sent out his soldiers to the subduing of nations, and gathering them into his church, not armed with the sword, or other instruments of force, but prepared with the Gospel of peace, and with the exemplary holiness of their conversation.[73]

We find aspects of the (Ana-)Baptist theology in *A Letter* as well as in other writings. The first example concerns the relationship between the

---

[68] Mark Goldie, introd. to Locke, *Political Essays*, ed. Mark Goldie (Cambridge, 1997), p. xiv. See, on his religious connections, Herbert D. Foster, 'International Calvinism through Locke and the Revolution of 1688', in John Dunn and Ian Harris (eds.), *Locke* (Cheltenham, 1997), i. 1–25. Cranston points out that some of Locke's writings even led to a suspicion of Unitarianism or Socianism, labels which Locke rejected (*Locke*, 390).

[69] Locke, *Political Essays*, 293–6.

[70] See also Jeremy Waldron, 'Locke, Toleration and the Rationality of Persecution', in Dunn and Harris, *Locke*, ii. 350–74. Maybe in his Third Letter for Toleration, which is not discussed here, he demonstrated some scepticism concerning theological truth. See Cranston, *Locke*, 367.

[71] Cranston, *Locke*, 259.

[72] Locke, *A Letter concerning Toleration*, ed. Mario Montouri (The Hague, 1963), 7.

[73] Ibid. 13.

Old and the New Testament. Having explained that the powers of the magistrate did not extend to the sphere of religion and therefore also not to the punishment of idolatry (we will come back to this), he comes to the point that in the Law of Moses idolaters were to be rooted out.[74] Locke agrees that this was a fact, but stresses that this was the law for Israel, being a theocracy, where there was no difference between commonwealth and Church. Under the Gospel, however, no Christian commonwealth was instituted. There are cities and kingdoms which have accepted the Christian faith (a thing not so easily admitted by the (Ana-)Baptists), but they have retained their ancient form of government.

There are also indications that he shared the view of the Radical Reformation on the development of Christianity since Constantine. In an untitled paper against a proposal for legislative imposition of Anglican conformity, written in 1681, we find references to the 'Christian religion . . . as it was in the beginning [where it was] left to the real convictions of men's minds and their free submission to the doctrine and discipline that they thought right without any force or compulsion.' He refers to a time 'When the temporal authority came to be mixed with ecclesiastical juris-diction'.[75]

Locke subsequently underlines the importance of the distinction of the business of civil government, which is the care of the commonwealth, from that of religion, which is the care of men's souls. The care of the common-wealth is restricted to the civil interests of its citizens, which are 'life, liberty, health and indolency of the body', an enumeration which reminds us of the natural rights mentioned in the *Second Treatise of Government*.[76] It is, however, also in conformity with the view of the (Ana-)Baptists of a restricted government. In a brief paper written in 1676 Locke held that the Gospel did not alter civil affairs in the least, so that, *inter alia*, the magistrate had not more, but also not less, power than he had before the spreading of the Gospel over his heathen subjects.[77]

Returning to *A Letter concerning Toleration*, we find three arguments there to demonstrate that the civil magistrate has no authority in the field of religion.[78] In a nutshell they can already be found in his *An Essay on Toleration*, which dates from 1667.[79]

The first such argument is that this power had not been entrusted to

---

[74] Locke, *A Letter concerning Toleration*, 71–5.

[75] The paper is referred to as 'Critical Notes on Stillingfleet' (who was the divine who proposed the conformity); a fragment is printed in Locke, *Political Essays*, 373.

[76] John Locke, *Two Treatises of Government*, Everyman's Library (London, 1978), 119. See also the tract 'Of the Differences between Civil and Ecclesiastical Power', written in 1674, in Locke, *Political Essays*, 216–21.

[77] In the paper 'Obligation of Penal Laws', with a reference to Col. 3: 18–22, in Locke, *Political Essays*, 235–7.

[78] Locke, *A Letter concerning Toleration*, 17 ff.

[79] Locke, *Political Essays*, 134–59.

him either by God or by the people. God has not given any man the power to compel another man to follow his religion. Next to that no man can transfer this power to another (the civil magistrate). True religion consists of a persuasion of the mind. 'Faith is not faith without believing.'[80] It is not difficult to hear in this statement the echo of the idea of the personal character of faith, which dominated the approach of the Radical Reformers.

Also the second argument has its predecessors in the (Ana-)Baptist writings. It is that the civil magistrate not only has no competence in religious matters, but it is also impossible for him to influence the inward persuasion with outward force. Force can bring about outward conformity, but not saving faith, 'the way of salvation not being any forced exterior performance, but the voluntary and secret choice of the mind'.[81]

Finally, even if it would be possible for the magistrate to change minds by the use of force (*quod non*), then it would depend on the religion of the magistrate himself whether or not his subjects would be saved for eternity, because rulers differ as to religious opinions. It would be tragic if the faith of the subjects would depend on them 'For there being but one truth'.[82] In other words, faith is much too important to be left to the magistrates; 'salvation . . . is too great to give away'.[83] It is interesting to see that for Locke the idea that there is but one truth, the acceptance of which is decisive for eternal salvation, leads him to reject the power of the government in religious affairs.

Having explained the role of the government, Locke then turns to that of the Church. He defines it as a 'voluntary society of men, joining themselves together of their own accord in order to the public worshipping of God in such manner as they judge acceptable to him, and effectual to the salvation of their souls'.[84] This is precisely the concept of the Church we find in the writings of the (Ana-)Baptists. It is underlined by the remark made by Locke that nobody is born a member of any Church. The Church is composed of those who by their own will decide to join it. The Church should be free to make its own rules. As far as Locke is concerned, these rules should be restricted to what the Holy Spirit has explicitly declared in the Holy Scriptures to be necessary for salvation. But if churches like to impose other rules (such as the application of the principle of apostolic succession for the appointment of ecclesiastical functionaries), they are free to do so. The rules concerning church discipline are to be confined to the

---

[80] Locke, *A Letter concerning Toleration*, 17.
[81] Locke, *Political Essays*, 138.
[82] Locke, *A Letter concerning Toleration*, 21.
[83] Locke, *Political Essays*, 138.
[84] Locke, *A Letter concerning Toleration*, 23. See also his 'Of the Difference between Civil and Ecclesiastical Power', where it is stated that 'The end of religious society is the attaining happiness after this life in another world' (Locke, *Political Essays*, 216).

end of a religious society, that is the public worship of God and the acquisition of eternal life. Here again Locke seeks to prevent a mixture of spiritual and worldly power. He excludes the application of force with effects
for the wordly goods of citizens in order to impose the order of the
Church. The Church may only operate with the means which fit its nature,
that is exhortation, admonition, and advice, the ultimate sanction being
excommunication. Excommunication dissolves the ties between the person
concerned and the Church, but does not have any effect on that person's
civil goods. In *A Letter concerning Toleration* Locke refers to the text
already quoted that the Church 'judgeth not those that are without' (1
Cor. 5: 12) to underline that it does not want exclusion from civil rights
for religious reasons.[85] In the untitled paper of 1681 already mentioned,
Locke refers to the 'true discipline of Christ, which was either by preach-
ing and persuasion to make men truly Christians, or else by expulsion to
shut them out from church communion . . .'[86] This is exactly the notion of
church discipline propagated by the (Ana-)Baptists.

If we continue to read *A Letter* and other writings by Locke, it becomes
clear that he did not himself draw on all the consequences of his own
theory. The exclusion of Roman Catholics and atheists from the liberty of
conscience is well known.[87] He was not as radical as Roger Williams in his
Bloody Tenent. There is no doubt, however, that the ideas of Locke on
toleration were influential as regards the development of the liberty of
conscience and the separation of Church and State, which became one of
the hallmarks of first and foremost the United States Constitution and
later also of other constitutions in the Western world. It has been made
clear that much of Locke's ideas were based on the Bible. Locke's understanding of the New Testament is on many points similar to the interpretations of the representatives of the Radical Reformation. It can therefore be
concluded that Locke's writings, perhaps more than the theological tracts
of the (Ana-)Baptists themselves, have been a vehicle by which to influence
the development of the law in the Western world in the direction of the
Radical ideal of a free Church in a free State.

Concluding Remarks

It has become clear that the most ancient human right, religious freedom,
has been defended at least by some, throughout the history of Christianity
on the basis of the teachings of the New Testament. At the time of the
Reformation this approach was advanced in the writings of the representatives of its Radical or (Ana-)Baptist wing, in many cases against the ideas

---

[85] Locke, *A Letter concerning Toleration*, 103.
[86] Locke, *Political Essays*, 373.
[87] Locke, *A Letter concerning Toleration*, 89–93.

and practices of Roman Catholic and mainstream Protestant scholars and authorities. We have seen how their views on the relationship between the Old and the New Testament, the separation of believers from the world, the concept of the Church and the exclusive role of the Church itself in regard to discipline of its members led to the idea of a separation of Church and State and the freedom of religion and belief. This idea gained ground both in the law and in theories which prepared the way for human rights. By these means its influence is recognizable to the present day. Alongside this, it can be said that the (Ana-)Baptist approach has officially or at least in practice been embraced by other Christian denominations in our time.

What has been said shows that the political philosophies brought together under the umbrella of the Enlightenment's rationalism cannot be held to be the only ideological source of human rights. There are sufficient reasons to assume that the biblical arguments played their part in the construction of an important aspect of the modern State. As such the foregoing is an illustration of the influence of religion on the law.

THE EUROPEAN COURT OF HUMAN RIGHTS AND RELIGION

Javier Martínez-Torrón

Introduction

The international protection of freedom of religion and belief improved substantially during the second half of the twentieth century.[1] Religious liberty has travelled a long way since it was recognized by the Universal Declaration of Human Rights in 1948. Together with various United National initiatives,[2] and impelled by the 1948 Universal Declaration, other important steps have been taken by international organizations with a more limited geographical reach.

Among them, the European Convention on Human Rights is especially significant.[3] The European Convention was created by the Council of Europe in 1950, and has often been presented as a model of efficiency in relation to the international protection of human rights, especially because of the judicial machinery created to enforce its provisions: the European Court of Human Rights, located in Strasbourg. By comparison with the pre-existing international systems for the protection of human rights, this evaluation is probably justified. The European system, however, is not perfect, at least as far as the protection of freedom of thought, conscience, and religion is concerned.

---

[1] A good exposition of the history of international efforts to guarantee the protection of religious freedom can be found in B. G. Tahzib, *Freedom of Religion or Belief: Ensuring Effective International Legal Protection* (Dordrecht, 1995), 63–247; and M. D. Evans, *Religious Liberty and International Law in Europe* (Cambridge, 1997), 6–171. For a summary description of the concept of religious freedom present in international documents, see J. Duffar, 'La Liberté religieuse dans les textes internationaux', in *La libertad religiosa: memoria del IX Congreso Internacional de Derecho Canónico* (Mexico, 1996), 471–97.

[2] After the Universal Declaration, there have been two main milestones in the history of the UN's efforts to promote the respect of religious liberty around the world. The first is the 1966 International Covenant on Civil and Political Rights (esp. Art. 18). The second is the 1981 Declaration on the Elimination of All Forms of Intolerance and of Discrimination Based on Religion or Belief.

[3] I could also mention the 1969 American Convention on Human Rights (esp. Art. 12); the 1981 African Charter on Human and Peoples' Rights (esp. Art. 12); and some of the documents produced by the Organization (formerly Conference) for Security and Cooperation in Europe, in particular the Vienna Concluding Document of 1989 (esp. principles 16–17). For a more detailed analysis of these documents, see J. Martínez-Torrón, 'La protección internacional de la libertad religiosa', in *Tratado de Derecho Eclesiástico* (Pamplona, 1994), as well as the bibliography there cited. For the purposes of this essay, I have reduced the bibliographical references to a minimum. Further references can be found also in Tahzib, *Freedom of Religion or Belief*, and Evans, *Religious Liberty and International Law*.

In the following pages I will explain the basic features of the European Court, especially its composition and procedures (in the next section). Thereafter I will attempt to describe what are, in my opinion, the main strengths and weaknesses of the case-law of the European Court in relation to freedom of religion and belief (in the following two sections).[4] I conclude by identifying those aspects of the European Court's jurisprudence that will need to be modified if this jurisprudence is to be considered as an example that should be followed in the international context.

The European Court of Human Rights

The Council of Europe was founded in 1949 as part of a post-war movement towards European unity. Its principal objective was the bringing together of the efforts already being made by the European democratic countries to protect human rights. Membership of the Council of Europe has been steadily expanding—there were initially ten members[5]—as democracy had itself spread throughout Europe.[6] Acceptance as a member of the Council of Europe has become a measure of democratic credentials.

The first and principal achievement of the Council of Europe—its masterpiece, as some have said—is the European Convention on Human Rights, which was signed in Rome on 4 November 1950 and came into force on 3 September 1953. The European Convention has been successively amended by several protocols. The Convention has three provisions dealing with religion. Freedom of thought, conscience, and religion is recognized by Article 9 of the Convention.[7] Article 14 enshrines the principle of

---

[4] In this essay I will use the term 'religious freedom' or 'freedom of religion and belief' with essentially the same meaning as 'freedom of thought, conscience, and religion' (the latter is the expression utilized by the European Convention). The reason is that, in my opinion, the reference to thought, conscience, and religion was not meant to separate three different rights but merely highlight diverse aspects of the same fundamental right. On the other hand, as religion seems to be—historically as well as conceptually—the centre around which this right has been construed, the wording 'religious freedom' may be considered sufficiently expressive. For a more extensive explanation of this idea, see Martínez-Torrón *La protección internacional*, 186–93.

[5] The Statute of the Council of Europe was signed in London on 5 May 1949 by the representatives of Belgium, Denmark, France, Ireland, Italy, Luxembourg, the Netherlands, Norway, the United Kingdom, and Sweden.

[6] There are currently forty-one member states of the Council of Europe, after the large-scale incorporation of post-socialist countries. Information about the Council of Europe, its organization, activities, documentation, etc. can be obtained on-line at <http://www.coe.fr/index.asp> (June 2000).

[7] Article 9: '1. Everyone has the right to freedom of thought, conscience and religion; this right includes freedom to change his religion or belief and freedom, either alone or in community with others and in public or private, to manifest his religion or belief, in worship, teaching, practice and observance. 2. Freedom to manifest one's religion or beliefs shall be subject only to such limitations as are prescribed by law and are necessary in a democratic society in the interests of public safety, for the protection of public order, health or morals, or for the protection of the rights and freedoms of others.'

equality and prohibits discrimination on the grounds of religion.[8] Article 2 of the First Protocol (1952) endorses the right of parents to choose the religious or ideological orientation of their children's education.[9]

As stated, the main reason for the success of the European Convention is that a specific judicial body—the European Court of Human Rights— was created to guarantee the efficient protection of the rights and freedoms recognized in the text. This has made the European Convention a unique instrument for the advancement of human rights in the international sphere. It is therefore worth describing the structure and procedures of the European Court before analysing its case-law on religious freedom.

The European Convention functions as a 'bill of rights' for democratic Europe, and the European Court of Human Rights acts as its constitutional court and interprets the text. The Court began its activities in January 1959. Its structure and procedure have been substantially changed by Protocol 11 to the Convention, which came into force in November 1998.[10]

The Court is now in permanent session. It has as many judges as there are states who have signed the European Convention and consequently accepted the jurisdiction of the Court. Each state nominates three candidates. The Parliamentary Assembly of the Council of Europe then elects one judge from each list for a period of six years.

One of the most interesting and important modifications introduced by Protocol 11 is that individuals have been granted the right of direct access to the Court. Before 1998, when individuals considered that their Convention rights had been infringed, they were entitled only to file an application against the relevant member state at the European Commission of Human Rights. The Commission acted as a filter; it decided which applications were worthy of a hearing on the merits and transmitted these applications to the Court, accompanied by a report on the merits of the case.

Protocol 11 eliminated this filter. Today, the Court may receive applications directly from any person, non-governmental organization, or group of individuals. All applications are first examined by a committee of three

---

[8] Article 14: 'The enjoyment of the rights and freedoms set forth in this Convention shall be secured without discrimination on any ground such as sex, race, colour, language, religion, political or other opinion, national or social origin, association with a national minority, property, birth or other status.'

[9] Article 2 of the Protocol: 'No person shall be denied the right to education. In the exercise of any functions which it assumes in relation to education and to teaching, the State shall respect the right of parents to ensure such education and teaching in conformity with their own religious and philosophical convictions.'

[10] The full text Protocol 11, and the rest of the basic texts of the Convention, can be obtained from the web site of the European Court; <http://www.echr.coe.int/>(June 2000). All the decisions of the Court are now available—with a useful search tool—on the web pages quoted above.

judges. Provided it is unanimous, the committee may declare an individual application inadmissible, either for procedural reasons or because it considers the application 'manifestly ill-founded'. Otherwise, the admissibility and merits of the case will be decided by a Chamber of seven judges. The Court may also sit in a Grand Chamber of seventeen judges if a case raises an issue of general importance—especially when a serious question concerning the interpretation of the Convention is involved, or when the decision of a Chamber might be inconsistent with the case-law of the Court. In Chambers as well as in the Grand Chamber the judge nominated by the state which is the subject of the application sits as an ex officio member.

The Court, in accordance with the text of the Convention, has traditionally preferred to dispose of an application by way of a friendly settlement, provided that human rights are duly respected. If this is not possible, the Court will follow its ordinary judicial procedures and deliver a judgment that is final and has binding force for the states. If the Court finds that there has been a violation of the Convention, the party injured may be afforded a just satisfaction. The Committee of Ministers will ensure that it is duly rendered. The experience of more than forty years reveals that member states normally accept and execute the decisions of the Court.

Until 1993 the Court did not take much interest in questions of religious freedom.[11] Applications based on Article 9 of the Convention were usually declared inadmissible by the Commission as manifestly ill-founded. Sometimes its decisions were more broad-ranging than one would expect of a non-judicial body. The Commission's reasoning was not always cogent.

The situation has changed remarkably in recent years. It is not altogether clear why this change has occurred, but the recent expansion of the Council of Europe to eastern Europe may be partly responsible. For several decades most member states carefully protected religious freedom. The accession of a large number of post-communist countries to the system of the European Convention may have led the Court to consider more carefully the content and limits of the right to freedom of thought, conscience, and religion. In any event, the decisions of the European Court

---

[11] Indeed, the first case decided on the basis of Article 9 was *Kokkinakis* v. *Greece*, 25 May 1993. Until then the Court had decided only one case in which a religious or conscience issue was involved, and the decision was taken with reference to Article 2 of the First Protocol: *Kjeldsen, Busk Madsen and Pedersen* v. *Denmark*, 7 Dec. 1976. A recent and succinct analysis of the case-law of the European Court and Commission of Human Rights can be found in F. Margiotta Broglio, 'Religione e stato in alcuni sistemi constituzionali atipici: il caso della Convenzione Europea del 1950', in J. Martínez-Torrón (ed.), *La libertad religiosa y de conciencia ante la justicia constitucional: Actas del VIII Congreso Internacional de Derecho Eclesiástico del Estado* (Granada, 1998). See also N. Blum, *Die Gedanken-, Gewissens- und Religionsfreiheit nach Art.9 der Europäischen Menschenrechtskonvention* (Berlin, 1990).

of Human Rights represent the only aspect of the Council of Europe system which binds member states. Therefore, it is important to analyse the case-law of the Court concerning religious freedom in its individual as well as in its institutional aspects. This study will necessarily be brief and will consider also the doctrine previously developed by the European Commission of Human Rights, which was abolished in 1998. The Commission did not have any formal adjudicatory power. Nevertheless, the reasoning contained in many of its decisions and reports is such that they can be said to constitute a sort of case-law which parallels that of the Court. Moreover, the Commission's understanding of religious freedom has, generally speaking, been adopted in the jurisprudence of the Court after 1993.

The Secular State and the Churches

Freedom of thought, conscience, and religion is most naturally seen as an individual right, but it has a very significant institutional or 'collective' dimension. In international law it is widely accepted that every religious group is entitled to religious freedom, no matter whether it is a traditional major Church or a recent and atypical group.[12] All religious denominations must have freedom to act in any country, without being the object of unjustified restriction or persecution. This freedom extends to minority groups even if they defend moral values conflicting with those which are widely accepted in the society in question.

The case-law of the European Commission and the European Court of Human Rights has set out the specific legal consequences of the right to collective religious freedom.

THE POSITION OF THE MAJOR CHURCHES

One of the most important aspects of the Strasbourg jurisprudence concerns the principles governing the system of relations between Church and State.

The Court has implicitly admitted that the State may collaborate with one or more religious groups. It does not have to collaborate with all groups equally. Equality (Article 14 of the European Convention) must be applied rigorously in relation to religious freedom, but is not necessarily required in relation to collaboration. The Court has accepted the privileged

---

[12] As far as the European Convention is concerned, the European Commission affirmed in 1979 that it is 'artificial' to differentiate between the religious freedom of a Church and that of its followers. A religious organization actually acts on behalf of its members when it presents an application, and is consequently fully entitled to claim a violation of Article 9. Cf. Dec. Adm. 7805/77, 16 *Decisions and Reports* 70 (the decision regarded an application filed by the Church of Scientology against Sweden).

collaboration between Church and State which exists where there is an established Church as in England or in some Scandinavian countries. It has also accepted such collaboration when it takes the form of a covert adoption by the State of a particular creed, as in the case of Greece. The important thing—in the Court's opinion—is that these relationships of privileged collaboration do not produce, as a side effect, any unjustified harm to the freedom that other groups or individuals must enjoy in religious and ideological matters. In other words, Article 9 of the European Convention is aimed at providing an adequate guarantee of freedom of religion and belief. Its purpose is not to establish certain uniform criteria for Church–State relations in the Council of Europe states, nor—even less—to impose a compulsory secularism (*laïcité*). Underlying this approach is the idea that the State's attitude towards religion is primarily a political issue and is the result, to a large extent, of the historical tradition and the social circumstances of each country.

Thus in the *Kokkinakis* case,[13] after a careful scrutiny of the legal restrictions on religious proselytism in Greece—and notwithstanding the fact that the Greek government were in breach of the Convention—the European Court did not deny that the close connection between the Greek Orthodox Church and the State was a legitimate political choice.

Furthermore, the Commission has explicitly affirmed that the creation or maintenance of an established Church does not itself constitute a violation of Article 9 of the Convention provided that membership of the official Church is not mandatory.[14] The Commission has also accepted as compatible with the European Convention other expressions of state collaboration with religious bodies that do not treat all such bodies equally. For instance: the granting of financial aid to particular churches in the form of tax exemptions;[15] the assigning of some of the taxes collected by the State to the maintenance of the official Church[16] or the Church to which the taxpayer belongs;[17] the granting to the churches of standing to sue their followers before the state courts in order to enforce the payment

[13] *Kokkinakis* v. *Greece*, 25 May 1993. The same conclusion can be drawn from the report of the commission in the case of *The Holy Monasteries* v. *Greece*, which ended with a friendly settlement (Rep. Com. 13092/87 and 13984/88, 14 Jan. 1993; the decision of the Court, accepting the fairness of the agreement, was delivered on 1 Sept. 1997).

[14] Rep. Com. 11581/85 (*Darby* case), n. 45. It has even been admitted that in a system with a state Church such as Sweden, the government can dismiss a minister for intentionally neglecting the civil duties attached to his religious office (Dec. Adm. 11045/84, 42 *Decisions and Reports* 247).

[15] Dec. Adm. 17522/90 (the 'El Salvador' Baptist Church argued that it suffered a discriminatory treatment because its places of worship were not exempted from the real property taxes in Spain, as Catholic premises were).

[16] Rep. Com. 11581/85 (*Darby* case, concerning the payment of local taxes aimed at financially supporting the Swedish Lutheran Church).

[17] Dec. Adm. 10616/83, 40 *Decisions and Reports* 284 ff. (concerning the ecclesiastical tax in a Swiss town, aimed at financially supporting the churches which were legally recognized; the tax had to be paid by members of the respective churches in the civil registry).

of religious taxes;[18] and allowing the teaching of Christian doctrine by the official Church in public schools, provided that this teaching is done in an objective and pluralist manner, and assuming that the collaboration of the State cannot be regarded as 'indoctrination'.[19]

The position of the traditional major churches has been so strikingly respected that the European Court has held that the protection of the religious feelings of their faithful must prevail over certain forms of freedom of expression which have been characterized as blasphemy. In the recent cases of *Otto-Preminger-Institut* and *Wingrove*, the Court upheld the ban on the commercial distribution of certain films that had been held to be offensive to the feelings of Christian people by the Austrian and British authorities respectively.[20]

MINORITY RELIGIOUS GROUPS

In recent years the Strasbourg Court has paid increasing attention to the rights which Article 9 of the European Convention grants to minority religious groups. Its approach can be summarized in this way: minority religious groups are entitled to a true freedom to act, and not merely to toleration. I will try to summarize the main implications of this notion as they emerge from the case-law of the Court.

Some of these implications flow from the principle of equality enshrined in Article 14 of the European Convention. Under Article 14 discrimination on religious grounds is forbidden. Therefore, individuals have a right not to be subject to discrimination on account of their membership of a minority religion, even if their belief and behaviour contrasts sharply with commonly accepted social customs. Thus, in *Hoffmann* the European Court held that when a national court decides the custody of children following a divorce, differential treatment on the basis of religion was unacceptable.[21] Similarly, members of minority religious groups must not

---

[18] Dec. Adm. 9781/82, 37 *Decisions and Reports* 42 ff. (the Catholic Church in Austria took a Catholic married couple to the civil courts to claim the payment of the ecclesiastical tax that Catholics must pay in every Austrian diocese).

[19] Dec. Adm. 4733/71, 14 *Yearbook of the European Convention* 664 ff., and Dec. Adm. 10491/83, 51 *Decisions and Reports* 41 ff. (concerning religious education in Swedish public schools).

[20] *Otto-Preminger-Institut* v. *Austria*, 13 July 1995, and *Wingrove* v. *United Kingdom*, 25 Nov. 1996. The former related to a satiric movie entitled *Council in Heaven*, in which God was presented as a senile man prostrated before the devil and Jesus Christ as a mentally retarded person; an erotic relationship between the devil and the Virgin was also insinuated. The latter referred to a video of eighteen minutes' duration containing a peculiar interpretation of St Teresa of Avila's ecstasy, in a pornographic setting with homosexual connotations.

[21] *Hoffmann* v. *Austria*, 23 June 1993. The case was decided in the light of Article 14 in conjunction with Article 8 of the Convention (right to respect for private and family life). A housewife had converted to Jehovah's Witnesses and taken the children with her when the divorce proceedings were still pending. The European Court reversed the decisions of Austrian national courts, which had granted the children's custody to the father. In my opinion,

be kept under surveillance in the absence of a compelling justification other than their religious affiliation, though the Court's jurisprudence on this point is not totally clear.[22] It has also been held that individuals may not be subject to compulsory confinement in order to subject them to a process of 'deprogramming' in order to free them from their adherence to a 'sect'.[23]

The prohibition of discrimination contained in Article 14 of the Convention is, in principle, applicable not only to discrimination against individuals but also to discrimination against religious groups as such. However, the European Court does not seem to have interpreted this principle in a consistent fashion.

An expansive interpretation of the principle of equality was adopted in the case of *Canea Catholic Church*. There the Court held that every religious denomination has not only the right to be accepted as existing de facto but also the right to be considered for the grant of legal personality on a basis which is fair and similar to that applied to other denominations. National governments cannot unreasonably discriminate between religious faiths with regard to the requirements that they—or their institutions—must fulfil in order to be acknowledged as legal persons in the secular sphere. This is particularly the case when legal personality is indispensable for the enforcement of civil rights in the state courts. Otherwise, in addition to the implications for the right for freedom of religion, there would be a violation of the right to a hearing by a tribunal, which is an integral part of the right to a fair trial (Article 6 of the European Convention).[24]

---

although the principles stated by the European Court are right, the decision was wrong: the wife had unilaterally broken the marital agreement, according to which children had to be brought up according to the common religion of spouses (they were both Roman Catholics at the time). It is very significant that the decision was adopted by five votes to four. See the dissenting opinion of Judge Mifsud Bonnici.

[22] *Tsavachidis* v. *Greece*, 21 Jan. 1999. The case related to the surveillance of Jehovah's Witnesses by the National Intelligence Service. It ended in a friendly settlement in which the Greek government agreed to pay a sum of money for the costs and submitted a formal statement declaring that 'the Jehovah's Witnesses are not, and will not in the future be, subject to any surveillance on account of their religious beliefs'. By then the European Commission had already elaborated its report on the merits of the case, and expressed the opinion that there had been a violation of Article 8 (thirteen votes to four) and there had been no violation of Article 9 (nine votes to eight).

[23] *Riera Blume and others* v. *Spain*, 14 Oct. 1999. The case referred to some members of the so-called Centro Esotérico de Investigaciones. The applicants' homes were searched following a judicial order, and the applicants were subsequently confined in a nearby hotel against their will for 'deprogramming'; the confinement did not follow any judicial order, and was carried out by a private 'anti-sects' association with a degree of participation by the Catalan police. The Court avoided pronouncing any opinion under Article 9, and decided in favour of the applicants in the light of Article 5.1 (right to liberty and security).

[24] *Canea Catholic Church* v. *Greece*, 16 Dec. 1997. The case related to the Roman Catholic Church of the Virgin Mary in Canea, built in the 13th century, which is the cathedral of the Roman Catholic diocese of Crete. Two people living next to the church had demolished one of the surrounding walls, and opened a window looking onto the church in the wall of their own building. The Greek courts denied legal standing to the church, as it had

By contrast, the Court's decision in *Cha'are Shalom Ve Tsedek*, which concerned the ritual slaughter of animals, provides a very recent example of a restrictive interpretation of the equality principle.[25] A seriously divided court held by ten votes to seven that national authorities enjoy a margin of appreciation which permits them to give different legal treatment to religious denominations, as long as individuals' freedom to practise their religion has not been impaired. More precisely, it was held that neither the right to freedom of religion nor the equality principle was violated when the French authorities granted an administrative permit for ritual slaughter exclusively to the Jewish Consistorial Association of Paris. This institution represented most of the main denominations within Judaism, and no permit was given to a minority Jewish association of ultra-Orthodox orientation which considered that the examination performed by the inspectors of the Consistorial Association was insufficiently rigorous to guarantee the necessary religious purity of the food.[26] According to the Court, religious freedom was respected in that members of the applicant association could obtain meat that satisfied their religious scruples—that is to say, they could buy the required food in a small number of butchers' shops or, alternatively, import it from Belgium. Nor was the principle of equality infringed; the French authorities had a margin of appreciation which allowed them to grant permits to only one Jewish community institution in order to safeguard public health (by ensuring the necessary hygienic conditions) and public order (by fostering reciprocal

not complied with the formal requirements generally stated by the Civil Code to acquire legal personality. This denial contradicted an abundant administrative and judicial practice in Greece in relation to the Roman Catholic Church. Furthermore, it constituted discrimination with regard to the Greek Orthodox Church and to the Jewish communities, which were granted legal personality and standing to sue without having to follow the civil formalities common to all associations. It is worth noting that the case was decided in the light of Article 6 (right to a fair trial), taken alone and together with Article 14; as a violation of Article 6 had been found, the Court declined to decide on the alleged violation of Article 9.

[25] The *Jewish Liturgical Association Cha'are Shalom Ve Tsedek* v. *France*, 27 June 2000.

[26] According to the French legislation and the European Union directives, ritual slaughter constitutes an exception to the general rules designed to guarantee the due hygienic conditions and to avoid unnecessary suffering to animals. This exception is granted in order to respect the ritual laws of some religions, especially Judaism and Islam. Ritual slaughter may be performed only by those persons who have been authorized by the religious bodies specifically approved by the French administration. In France only the Joint Rabbinical Committee (Commission Rabbinique Intercommunautaire) has received the administrative approval necessary to grant permits regarding ritual slaughter according to the Torah and the Talmud. That Committee is part of the Jewish Consistorial Association of Paris, an institution representing most Jewish communities in France and most of the main denominations within Judaism, with the exception of the liberals and the ultra-Orthodox. The applicant Jewish liturgical association, which is of ultra-Orthodox orientation, considered that the persons appointed by the Joint Rabbinical Committee performed an excessively liberal revision of the requisites established by the divine law, and consequently the purity of food was not sufficiently certified. For that reason, the applicant association had asked, unsuccessfully, for a specific administrative permit for its own slaughterers.

toleration between different religious groups). Indeed, the Court noted that the applicant association had had an opportunity to reach an agreement with the Consistorial Association of Paris which might have allowed them to have the ritual slaughter performed by its own personnel. The negotiations had failed because of differences relating to the levying of religious tax on the buyers of the certified food. As stated, the *Cha'are Shalom Ve Tsedek* decision was strongly contested by a remarkable number of the justices, who considered that, in this case, the Court had interpreted the equality principle in an unacceptably restrictive way. In their view, the Court had failed to give sufficient weight to the State's obligation to provide equal legal treatment in order to guarantee pluralism, which is an indispensable precondition to exercise of freedom of religion.[27]

In the recent *Thlimmenos* case, the Court added a further and interesting twist to its interpretation of the equality principle. Article 14 is violated not only when states treat differently persons in analogous situations without providing an objective and reasonable justification for the different treatment. The Court stated that 'The right not to be discriminated against in the enjoyment of the rights guaranteed under the Convention is also violated when States without an objective and reasonable justification fail to treat differently persons whose situations are significantly different.'[28]

In this respect, it was relevant when determining the consequences of a criminal conviction that the conduct in question could be characterized as an act of conscience. In particular, it was held that, when a person has been convicted of felony for refusing to perform military service on account of his religious beliefs, he has a legitimate claim to be exempted

---

[27] Seven justices affirmed, in a joint dissenting opinion, that the Court had omitted to analyse whether the applicant association—a minority Jewish association—was in a situation analogous to the Jewish Consistorial Association of Paris, as far as the legislation on religious bodies was concerned: i.e. whether it was a body of religious nature, and whether it pursued religious aims and utilized equivalent means. If that was the case, as it seemed to be, the right approach would have been to examine whether the French administration had an 'objective and reasonable justification' to grant the requested administrative permit for ritual slaughter to one Jewish association, and to deny the same permit to the other. Apparently, that justification did not exist, and consequently—the dissenting opinion concluded—the association of Cha'are Shalom Ve Tsedek had been a victim of discrimination. The French State could not take into account the different number of followers, the doctrinal discrepancies in the religious requirements for 'pure' food, or the inability of both associations to reach an agreement. On the contrary, the State was obliged to provide an analogous legal treatment as a means to guarantee pluralism, which is an indispensable condition to the exercise of freedom. Moreover, the European Court did not attach enough importance to two facts: firstly, administrative French praxis had been very different with regard to the Muslims—there was a remarkable diversity of representative bodies approved by the French administration to grant permits for ritual slaughter—and secondly, it was inaccurate to invoke reasons of public health in this case, because the hygienic conditions required by the applicant association were stricter than the ones usually existing in the slaughterhouses of the Consistorial Association.

[28] *Thlimmenos* v. *Greece*, 6 Apr. 2000, n. 44.

from the general rule which disqualifies those convicted of felony from entering the Civil Service.[29]

On the other hand, religious groups have gained recognition of their right to possess and manage their own places of worship and meeting. To deny this right without due justification is incompatible with the European Convention, according to the decisions of the Court in *Manoussakis* and *Pentidis*. Both cases were the result of applications submitted by Jehovah's Witnesses, who claimed that Greek law on places of worship had been applied to them in a discriminatory and hostile manner. The Greek legislation provides that explicit permission must be granted by the civil authorities for the opening of a public place of worship. The alleged aim of this provision is to ensure that places of worship are not run by secret sects, that there is no danger to public order or morals, and that places of worship will not be used as a cover for proselytism, which is explicitly forbidden by the Greek Constitution. The European Court concluded that the legislation gave to the Greek authorities an excessive discretion and that it did not provide any basis for ensuring that decisions were made in an objective way.[30]

The proselytism of religious minorities was the focus of attention for the European Court in two further cases involving the state of Greece. In the *Kokkinakis* case, the Court held that Article 9 of the Convention

---

[29] The applicant in the *Thlimmenos* case was a Jehovah's Witness who had been convicted of insubordination in 1983 for refusing to perform unarmed military service on account of his religious beliefs, at a time of general mobilization; he was sentenced to four years' imprisonment, and was released on parole after two years. In 1988 he passed a public examination to become a chartered accountant, a liberal profession which, until 1993, could be exercised only by those who became members of the Greek Institute of Chartered Accountants. In spite of his successful examination—he came second among sixty candidates—the Executive Board of the Institute refused to appoint him because, according to the law, a person who did not qualify for the Civil Service could not be appointed a chartered accountant, and conviction of felony constituted a disqualification for the Civil Service. The European Court considered that the Greek State had violated Article 14 of the Convention in conjunction with Article 9. It was true that the authorities were bound to apply the law in force and deny the applicant's appointment, but the legislation itself had failed to make the appropriate distinctions: there existed no objective and reasonable justification for not treating the applicant differently from other persons convicted of a felony, and his exclusion from the profession of chartered accountants did not pursue a legitimate aim.

[30] *Manoussakis and others* v. *Greece*, 26 Sept. 1996; *Pentidis and others* v. *Greece*, 9 June 1997. In *Manoussakis* the applicants had asked for government permission to set up a place of worship, and they began to utilize the place as the permit had not been granted within a period of time that they considered to be excessive. Criminal proceedings were initiated against them in the Greek courts. The European Court held that there had been a violation of Article 9, after evaluating especially three facts: the Greek authorities had an excessive discretion to estimate the need to open a place of worship; there was no time limit to the decision-making process in relation to the decision concerning the permit—which could perpetuate the proceedings indefinitely; and the Greek Orthodox Church intervened in the decision-making process. The *Pentidis* case ended with a friendly settlement: after the condemnatory judgment received in *Manoussakis*, the Greek government granted the administrative authorization required by the Jehovah's Witnesses.

includes the right of individuals and religious groups to spread their doctrines and to gain new followers through proselytism, provided that they do not use abusive, fraudulent, or violent means.[31] More recently, in the *Larissis* case, the Court added a new and interesting twist to this doctrine as it relates to proselytism carried out in exceptional environments, such as the armed forces. More precisely, it was held that restrictions on proselytism are legitimate when applied to a superior–subordinate relationship; i.e. when a superior tries to convert a subordinate, even if it has been done merely through respectful conversations on religious matters. Such restrictions are justified by the need to ensure that the relationship is not abused as will be the case when subordinates act because of improper pressure from their superiors. However, restrictions on proselytism are not justified when the same kind of religious conversation takes place between an officer and a civilian, even if the latter is also situated within the military environment, because the two are not linked by any subordinate relationship.[32]

Lately the European Court's decision in the *Serif* case has reinforced the need for religious groups to be allowed autonomy over their own internal affairs. Except when there is a 'pressing social need', the State cannot legitimately interfere in a decision made by a religious community on a purely religious question, even when that religious community is sharply divided over the issue leading to the possibility of 'social tension'. This is one of the unavoidable effects of pluralism, which is in turn inseparable from democracy.[33] In particular, 'the Court does not consider that, in democratic societies, the State needs to take measures to ensure that religious communities remain or are brought under a unified leadership'.[34]

---

[31] *Kokkinakis* v. *Greece*, 25 May 1993. An elderly man, a follower of the Jehovah's Witnesses, had been arrested and subsequently sentenced by the Greek courts, under the law that declares proselytism a crime, which in turn responds to the constitutional ban on proselytism. Both provisions are aimed at protecting the social status of the Greek Orthodox Church. The Court concluded that the Greek government did not supply enough evidence to prove that Mr. Kokkinakis was engaged in improper proselytism. For a detailed comment on this decision, see J. Martínez-Torrón, 'Libertad de proselitismo en Europe: a propósito de una reciente sentencia del Tribunal europeo de derechos humanos', (1994/1) *Quaderni di diritto e política eclesiástica* 59–71. See also J. Gunn, 'Adjudicating Rights of Conscience under the European Convention on Human Rights', in S. D. van der Vyver and J. Witte (eds.), *Religious Human Rights in Global Perspective* (The Hague, 1996). On the problems involved in defining the concept of proselytism in international law, see N. Lerner, 'Proselytism, Change of Religion, and International Human Rights', (1998) 12 *Emory International Law Review* 477–561.

[32] *Larissis and others* v. *Greece*, 24 Feb. 1998. This case involved three officers of the Greek Air Force who belonged to the Pentecostal Church.

[33] See also recently, among other cases, *Freedom and Democracy Party (ÖZDEP)* v. *Turkey*, 8 Dec. 1999, n. 37.

[34] *Serif* v. *Greece*, 14 Dec. 1999. The case regarded the appointment of a religious Islamic leader (mufti) in a region of Greece (Thrace) with a significant Muslim population of Turkish origin. He had been elected by the Muslim community without the participation of the state authorities as prescribed by the Greek law governing the election and appointment

These principles seem all the stronger if they are viewed in the light of the case of *United Communist Party of Turkey*.[35] The Court declared that there is a close connection between freedom of association (Article 11) and freedom of expression (Article 10). In a pluralistic society the freedom to express an opinion, even when it may 'offend, shock or disturb', is one of the objectives of freedom of assembly and association. Naturally, this reasoning is equally applicable to freedom of thought, conscience, and religion, as enshrined in Article 9. It follows that religious freedom must be construed as widely as the jurisprudence of the European Court on freedom of association suggests. The same is probably true with regard to the connection between freedom of religion and freedom of expression, because these provisions of the European Convention are all aimed at protecting pluralism, without which, as the Court has repeatedly emphasized, democracy cannot exist.

Deficiencies in the Protection of the Religious Liberty of Individuals and of Some Religious Minorities

The European Convention is like all other international documents on human rights in that it treats freedom of thought, conscience, and religion as a right that belongs primarily to individuals. On a conceptual level, any right of a religious association appears as a 'product' derived from the individual's right. However, the strictly individual dimension of this freedom is the one that, paradoxically, has been under-protected in the jurisprudence of the European Court.

THE MEANING OF THE TERM 'PRACTICE' IN THE EUROPEAN CONVENTION

The problem arises from the terminology utilized by the European Convention of Human Rights, as well as by most international texts that explain the meaning of freedom of religion and belief. Among the aspects of the freedom that deserve protection, Article 9.1 mentions the right to manifest one's religion or belief in worship, teaching, practice, and observance. If we direct our attention to the term 'practice', the most obvious interpretation seems to be that Article 9 guarantees the right of individuals to behave in accordance with the dictates of their conscience. This guaran-

---

of muftis (it must be noted that the law had been changed a few days before the election took place and once it had been organized). The Greek government justified the intervention of the State on account of the administrative and judicial functions that muftis exercise. The case involved also some interesting issues concerning a number of international treaties signed by Greece in the 1910s and 1920s, but the Court decided not to express any opinion on the subject.

[35] *United Communist Party of Turkey and others* v. *Turkey*, 30 Jan. 1998, nn. 42–3. The case was decided in favour of the applicants under Article 11.

tee should apply whether the individual is practising an institutionalized religion or, alternatively, simply acting upon a personal belief system. It should be irrelevant whether the individual's conscience is grounded on religious or non-religious beliefs.[36] Of course, this guarantee is necessarily limited (Article 9.2) because the freedom to act is never absolute.

This broad construction of freedom of conscience has been proposed by the General Comment of the Committee of Human Rights on Article 18 of the 1966 UN International Covenant on Human Rights.[37] I am afraid, however, that the attitude of the European Court and Commission has been rather different with regard to Article 9 of the European Convention. What follows is an attempt to summarize their approach to the issue.[38]

The Strasbourg case-law has stressed that it is necessary to distinguish between the internal and external aspects of religious liberty. The former, the freedom to believe, includes the freedom to choose one's beliefs—whether religious or non-religious—and the freedom to change one's religion. The latter consists of the freedom to manifest one's religion or belief. The internal dimension of religious freedom is *absolute* and may not be restricted, while the freedom to act is by its very nature *relative* and may accordingly be subjected to the restrictions specified in Article 9.2.[39]

All this seems indisputable. It is obvious that public authorities should not take or permit direct action to compel citizens to believe or not to believe in something. For the same reason, the Court held in the 1976 case of *Kjeldsen, Busk Madsen and Pederson* that the State, when organizing the educational system, is not allowed to foster activities which amount to the indoctrination of pupils with a particular religious or moral view of life contrary to the convictions of their parents.[40]

---

[36] It does not seem accurate to interpret the term 'practice' as the mere practice of rites, considering that the ritual dimension of religious freedom is alluded to in other words used in Article 9, in particular the terms 'worship' and 'observance'.

[37] The General Comment on Article 18 was adopted by the Committee on 20 July 1993. For an analysis of the text, see Tahzib, *Freedom of Religion or Belief*, 307–75.

[38] See also, on this subject, Evans, *Religious Liberty and International Law*, 293–314.

[39] Dec. Adm. 10358/83, 37 *Decisions and Reports* 147, in which the Commission utilizes the expression 'forum internum'. The same doctrine is reiterated in Dec. Adm. 10678/83, 39 *Decisions and Reports* 268 and Dec. Adm. 14049/88. See also Rep. Com. 11581/85 (*Darby* case), n. 44. The Court, following the Commission's approach, has subsequently alluded to this double side of religious freedom, and has emphasized that the limits stated in Article 9.2 are applicable only to the freedom to *manifest* one's religion or belief, but not to the freedom to *choose* one's religion or belief (*Kokkinakis* v. *Greece*, 25 May 1993, nn. 31 and 33).

[40] *Kjeldsen, Busk Madsen and Pedersen* v. *Denmark*, 7 Dec. 1976. The case related to the implementation of a new system of sex education in public schools, with the purpose of preventing undesired pregnancies among teenagers. Some parents alleged conscientious objection to this teaching, as they considered that sex education was the exclusive domain of parents. *Kjeldsen* was the first case decided by the Court in which religious beliefs were concerned, and the only one until *Kokkinakis* in 1993. The decision focused on the interpretation of Article 2 of the First Protocol (right to education, and right of parents concerning their children's education).

However, the crucial question is how to understand the relative character of the freedom of individuals to act according to the dictates of their own conscience. This is an issue closely connected with the problem of conflict between law and conscience between legal and moral duties. In my view, the solution proposed by the European Court is inadequate.

Its approach has been based on drawing a line between the concepts of *manifestation* and *motivation*. The European Convention does not confer an unrestricted right to behave in accordance with one's beliefs. The term 'practice' has thus been understood as not including each and every act motivated or influenced by a religion or belief.[41]

NEUTRAL LAWS AND MORAL OBLIGATIONS: THE INDIRECT RESTRICTION OF RELIGIOUS FREEDOM

This approach seems reasonable in the abstract. Behaviour *obliged* by conscience—which seems to be what Article 9 has in mind—is different from behaviour which is simply *permitted* by conscience. Nevertheless, the truth is that the case-law of the Commission and the Court reveals that they have adopted a fairly restrictive attitude. They have gone one step further and held that the protective umbrella of Article 9 does not even extend to the individual's behaviour when it is *required* by his conscience.[42]

In this view, the European Convention protects only against an interference of the State that is *directly* aimed at restricting either worship practices or the attempt to attract new members (this was in fact the situation in *Kokkinakis*, cited above[43]). By contrast, Article 9 offers no protection against interference that is the result of a 'neutral' law, i.e. a law that pursues legitimate secular goals. The problems arise when the legal duties imposed by a 'neutral' law collide with the moral obligations of certain individuals, who see their right to practise their religion or belief as being *indirectly* and nonetheless unavoidably restricted.[44] The immediate consequence is that a

---

[41] This doctrine has been repeatedly stated by the Commission and implicitly assumed by the Court. See Rep. Com. 7050/75, 19 *Decisions and Reports* 19–20 (*Arrowsmith* case, concerning a British pacifist sentenced to a term of imprisonment for having distributed illegal leaflets among English soldiers in Northern Ireland); Dec. Adm. 10358/83, 37 *Decisions and Reports* 147 (conscientious objection to paying taxes, in the percentage of the State budget aimed at military costs); Dec. Adm. 10678/83, 39 *Decisions and Reports* 268 (conscientious objection to contributing to the public system of pensions); Dec. Adm. 11579/85, 48 *Decisions and Reports* 255 (conflict between the laws governing religious and civil marriages); Dec. Adm. 14049/88 (conscientious objection to paying taxes, in the percentage of the state budget aimed at financing legal abortions in France).

[42] For further details on this approach of the Strasbourg jurisdiction, see J. Martínez-Torrón, 'La giurisprudenza degli organi di Strasburgo sulla libertà religiosa', (1993) *Rivista internazionale di diritti dell'uomo* 335–79.

[43] See n. 31 above and accompanying text.

[44] This is the case of the different types of conscientious objection (which go far beyond the most well-known type, i.e. conscientious objection to military service). An extensive

moral burden is placed upon the shoulders of these people, as they are required to choose between disobedience to the law and disobedience to their own conscience—one choice leads to a secular sanction, the other to a spiritual sanction.

As early as 1976 this mode of reasoning can be seen in the *Kjeldsen* decision, where the Court held that the State is free to organize the educational system, and particularly the curricula of state schools in a particular way, even if the religious or philosophical convictions of parents are thus ignored. As noted above, the only limit is that indoctrination will not be permitted.[45]

The same criteria were reaffirmed twenty years later in two cases which also concerned problems arising within an educational context. The twin decisions of *Efstratiou* and *Valsamis*[46] arose from the applications of two Greek secondary school students, both Jehovah's Witnesses, who refused, for religious reasons, to participate in school parades organized to commemorate the outbreak of war between Greece and Italy in 1940. The students argued that their conscience forbade them attending a civic celebration in which a war was commemorated and in which military and ecclesiastical authorities took part. They had been denied permission to be absent from the parade, and their failure to attend was punished by a one-day suspension from school. The European Court sustained the punishment, considering that Article 9 does not grant any right to be exempted from rules which apply generally and in a neutral manner.

In my opinion, this interpretation of Article 9 distorts the appropriate conceptual approach to the problem. It is universally accepted that human rights must be construed broadly. Therefore, in order to understand the exact meaning of freedom to manifest one's religion or belief in 'practice', it seems that we should approach the question via a two-stage process: (1) freedom to practise one's religion or belief must be understood as protecting, in principle, every act of the individual when he obeys the dictates of his own conscience; (2) paragraph 2 of Article 9—the limits to religious liberty—will be used, when necessary, as a corrective element for a freedom which, by its own nature, tends to be exercised in an undefined and unpredictable way.

---

analysis of conscientious objections in international and comparative law, with numerous bibliographical and case-law references, can be found in R. Navarro-Valls and J. Martínez-Torrón, *La objeciones de conciencia en el derecho español y comparado* (Madrid, 1997); there is an Italian version: *Le obiezioni di coscienza: profili di diritto comparato* (Turin, 1995). The case-law of the United States is especially rich in dealing with these situations. There is an interesting and comprehensive study of it elaborated by a Spanish scholar, with abundant bibliographical reference: R. Palomino, *Las objeciones de conciencia: conflictos entre conciencia y ley en el derecho norteamericano* (Madrid, 1994).

[45] See n. 40 above and accompanying text.

[46] *Efstratiou v. Greece*, 18 Dec. 1996, and *Valsamis v. Greece*, 18 Dec. 1996. The texts of both sentences are almost identical, as indeed were the facts in issue.

In this way, we can reconcile two important interests that are inclined to conflict with each other: the maximum degree of initial protection for freedom of belief, and the security that the legal order demands. Furthermore, we introduce an important assumption: the State has the burden of proof with regard to the need for a restrictive measure, i.e. it must affirmatively prove that in a particular case of conflict it is necessary 'in a democratic society' to restrict the exercise of religious freedom. If this approach is taken, it is possible to prevent the development of policies which ignore the need for religious freedom and which are especially harmful for minority groups.

SUBSTITUTING THE COURT'S JUDGMENT FOR THAT OF THE INDIVIDUAL ON MATTERS OF CONSCIENCE

The decisions *Efstratiou* and *Valsamis* are deficient in a further respect. When the Court examined the arguments of the applicants, it declared that the parades which the Jehovah's Witnesses found morally offensive were merely civic acts without any particular or ideological connotation and held that, consequently, these parades could not offend the pacifist convictions of the students.[47] In this way, the Court in effect substituted its own judgment on a matter of conscience for that of the persons concerned. The Court was, in effect, presuming to define what it was 'reasonable' for the applicants to believe with regard to their participation in a national commemorative ceremony. In my opinion, this was a grave and dangerous mistake. It might mark the beginning of a process leading to the Courts determining which beliefs are 'reasonable' and which are not. Naturally, it is necessary to verify—as far as possible—that nobody is using fabricated allegations about their moral convictions in order to avoid fulfilling their legal duty. But this does not mean that a secular court is competent to elucidate when a person's beliefs are sufficiently consistent from an 'objective' point of view. This is a slippery slope. In Western legal culture there is a deeply rooted conviction that public authorities within the secular State must refrain from pronouncing on the truth or otherwise of religious or moral beliefs.

In these decisions the European Court did not seem to be aware of something which is quite essential to the protection of religious liberty in our civilization. Our desire to protect an individual's freedom of conscience is not contingent upon the objective truth of his beliefs. If it were, the Courts would have to judge the truth of any alleged beliefs, leading to what might perhaps be called a new Inquisition. Freedom of conscience must be respected because it is considered a fundamental aspect

---

[47] See esp. nn. 31 and 37 of the *Valsamis* decision, and nn. 32 and 38 of the *Efstratiou* decision.

of the individual's autonomy in democratic societies and consequently the legal system has determined that nobody may interfere in the individual's conscience provided that other relevant juridical interests are not endangered. What freedom of religion and belief protects is the right to choose the truths in which one is willing to believe. Hence, Article 9.2 of the European Convention provides that state control has to be limited to restricting the exercise of that freedom when it is 'necessary in a democratic society'.

In other words, the government is not obliged to protect religious freedom because it considers that the convictions of its citizens are correct or, perhaps, useful. It is obliged to protect the freedom to believe and the freedom to act accordingly because they constitute an essential element of a democratic system. The protection of that freedom is a paramount *public* interest, and not just a *private* interest of individuals and groups. This is something that is easily understood with respect to other liberties—for instance, freedom of expression, or freedom of association—but it is, for some reason, sometimes ignored when dealing with religious liberty.[48]

On the other hand, it is important to note that the outcome of the aforementioned approach of the European Court of Human Rights is bound to transcend the individual sphere. I have already said that the European Court has positively required the acknowledgement of the rights of minority groups.[49] This must now be seen as subject to the qualification that the Court's restrictive doctrine to individual rights is bound to have a negative impact on the rights of some religious minorities, particularly those which hold to ideas which represent a sharp contrast with the ethical choices assumed by the majority of people in the relevant society.

In effect, legal provisions which are considered as 'neutral' usually conform—as does any law—to the ethical values prevalent in the society in question. 'Neutral' laws will rarely conflict with the morals of the major churches,[50] but they will sometimes lead to conflict with minority religious groups that are socially atypical.[51] If we accept that a 'neutral' law must automatically prevail, and that the State is under no obligation to justify its refusal to grant exemption from such a law by reference to what is 'necessary in a democratic society', we are imperilling the rights of minorities.

[48] Indeed the European Court has repeatedly stated, in regard to the freedom of expression and the freedom of association, that pluralism is indispensable for democracy. See, recently, *United Communist Party of Turkey and others* v. *Turkey*, 30 Jan. 1998, nn. 42–3; and *Freedom and Democracy Party (ÖZDEP)* v. *Turkey*, 8 Dec. 1999, n. 37.

[49] In the previous subsection of this essay.

[50] Naturally, there are exceptions, especially when the party or parties in power are determined to change some of the ethical patterns of society through legislation—they often succeed after a few years. The laws decriminalizing abortion in the Western world constitute a good example of it.

[51] This is the reason why Muslims and Jehovah's Witnesses, for instance, experience frequent problems in European countries.

Conclusion: Religious and Secular Intolerance

If we analyse the different threats to religious liberty, we come to see that as regards the law of the State, the main problem is likely to be intolerance. In this regard, it is important that we distinguish between two sorts of intolerance.

One is religious intolerance. The legal and constitutional structure of the State is designed according to the dictates of a particular religion, and other religions or belief systems are either disregarded or persecuted, depending on how hostile the government and the hierarchy of the official religion are. This is currently the case, for example, in many Islamic countries and in some countries where a strong Christian Orthodox Church is established (as, for example, in a great part of eastern Europe).

The other is secular intolerance. The State decides to be positively secular and draws a line of separation between State and religion. This choice is normally justified either by reference to historical factors (e.g. France), or by arguing that it is necessary to preserve the reciprocal autonomy of the State and the churches (e.g. the United States), or by claiming that it is indispensable to keep the State free from the religious intolerance of a significant part of the population (e.g. Turkey). In any event, experience shows that these states frequently adopt an aggressive secularism and endeavour to remove any actual reference to religious beliefs and practice from public life. Secularism then becomes a sort of official 'religion'.

Religious intolerance transforms a religious dogma into the law of the State. Secular intolerance transforms the law of the State into a religious dogma. Neither of these seems to be an adequate solution to the question of freedom of religion and belief.

If we examine the case-law of the European Court of Human Rights, we can see that it has been willing to condemn religious intolerance, but it has failed to realize that, in its doctrine of the automatic superiority of 'neutral' laws over freedom of conscience, there may be an implied and dangerous espousal of secular intolerance.

We Europeans are usually proud of the system we have built for the protection of human rights. We tend to think that ours is not only a good system but that it is the *best* system, and it is a model that should be followed elsewhere. This view is justifiable in relation to the supranational judicial machinery for the enforcement of Convention rights. But our judgement may be less positive when we begin to focus on the interpretation given to some of the Convention rights in the case-law of the European Court.

As far as religious liberty is concerned, the case-law certainly has a positive aspect: for example, its emphasis on the idea that the granting of privileges to the major churches must be accompanied by an acknowledgement

and a real protection of the rights of religious minorities.[52] State cooperation with the churches can vary in its extent, but the freedom of religious
groups must be understood in terms of strict equality. The level of cooperation may vary, but the level of freedom cannot. The European Court
seems to be very conscious of the need to emphasize this general principle
after the enlargement of the Council of Europe with the incorporation of
post-communist countries. Moreover, this is an idea that can be 'exported'
to other countries and to other cultures.

The negative side of the case-law is, as we have seen,[53] the tendency to
accord absolute supremacy to 'neutral' laws as against the rights of the
individual and his conscience. The effects of this approach are harmful not
only for individuals, but also for those minority religious groups which
defend moral values which do not fully respond to the Western heritage—
i.e. the values of the Judaeo-Christian tradition, which is now mixed with
some of the values typical of secularism. One of the main problems we
have in this regard is the increasing Islamic population of Europe due to
migration.

This is, of course, an idea which it is difficult to 'export', and which
should not be exported, to other countries. It seems that our supranational
judicial system has failed to design an appropriate legal framework to
make possible the integration of non-Western cultures and religions into
Europe. Furthermore, it is an example of how not to proceed. If the
European Court affirms the unconditional supremacy of 'neutral' laws as
against freedom of conscience, it may prove difficult rationally to object to
the parallel supremacy of 'religious' laws in states where we find intolerance. After all, in both cases, the laws in question are backed by the
legislative authority of the State.

Certainly, we need to discuss whether it is possible to integrate non-
Western religions and cultures into Europe without rupturing the social
and physical framework which is characteristic of our concept of democracy. Most people think that this can be achieved, although some think
that it can not. In any event, if we Europeans really do want to be an
example to other continents of how to respect human rights, the least we
can do is to try.[54]

---

[52] See the earlier section of this essay, 'The Case-Law of the European Court on
Treatment by the Secular State of the Churches'.

[53] See the previous section of this essay.

[54] Funding for this essay has been provided by Project PB96–0633, granted by the
Spanish Ministry of Education. The ideas developed here are based upon the chapter written
for the volume *Facilitating Freedom of Religion and Belief: Perspectives, Impulses and
Recommendations from the Oslo Coalition* (with Rafael Navarro-Valls), forthcoming. I
would like to thank Professor Rafael Palomino, Complutense University Law School, for his
valuable contribution to it.

HUMAN RIGHTS, RELIGIOUS LIBERTY, AND THE UNIVERSALITY DEBATE

Malcolm D. Evans

Insisting on the necessarily universal character of rights . . . is seen and will continue to be seen as a modern form of imperialism, using the same old private means. Universal rights are simply another form of universalizing the truths of a particular tradition. It is being illiberal about being liberal, forcing people to be free.

H. P. Glenn, *Legal Traditions of the World*

Introduction

Few issues seem to arouse human rights activists more than the claim that the attempt to apply human rights standards on a universal basis is neo-imperialism or cultural hegemony. For many, the universality of human rights has become a watchword and attempts to suggest otherwise can engender reactions ranging from a cautious suspicion[1] to outright contempt. Much of the debate surrounding the universality of human rights rather suggests that one is dealing with a clash of absolute values: a conflict of titans that will set the path of human destiny towards the light or into the darkness of the abyss.

The universality debate has also generated an extensive body of literature which has done much to shed light on the issues at the heart of that debate and has certainly revealed the essentially Western origins of the currently dominant conceptions of human rights.[2] Yet as that debate shows, other forms of values flowing from the wellspring of humanity have emerged which have taken their place alongside 'Western human

---

[1] For a good example of this form of response, see R. Higgins, *Problems and Process: International Law and how we Use It* (Oxford, 1994), 96–9, who argues at p. 96 that 'it is sometimes suggested that there can be no fully universal concept of human rights, for it is necessary to take into account the diverse cultures and political systems of the world. In my view this is a point advanced mostly by states, and by liberal scholars anxious not to impose the Western view on others. It is rarely advanced by the oppressed, who are only to anxious to benefit from perceived universal standards.'

[2] See e.g. C. Brown, 'Universal Human Rights: A Critique', in T. Dunne and N. J. Wheeler (eds.), *Human Rights in Global Politics* (Cambridge, 1999), 103. For a recent and robust reaffirmation of this, see H. P. Glenn, *Legal Traditions of the World* (Oxford, 2000), 244: 'Human rights are inextricably bound up with the western legal tradition and exist as such only within it.'

rights' thinking.[3] Particular 'challenges' have come from Africa and, most recently, in the high-profile debate concerning so-called 'Asian values'.[4] As a result, much of what now comprises the common corpus of contemporary international human rights standards lies well beyond the conceptions of its first compilers while their global reach suggests that just because a vision of the ordering of society originates within one place or political system does not mean that it is inappropriate for others.[5] It is too often assumed that it is the Western origins of contemporary human rights standards that renders their application in a non-Western context a matter for legitimate concern and, perhaps unintentionally, this spurious line of reasoning receives support from those who seek to discern a 'non-Western' origin for the same phenomena, as if an indigenous grounding for essentially alien human rights thinking will be sufficient to justify its acceptance.

Nevertheless, the inability to find a consensus on the basis for the universalism of human rights might legitimately prompt some reflection on the a priori nature of the assumption that human rights *are* universal.[6] The triumph of human rights-speak has, however, had the effect of transforming the question of whether a human rights approach is appropriate into the question of how to make the outcome of adopting a human rights approach acceptable.[7] This can be achieved both by modulating the manner in which human rights are applied so as to reflect local or personal

[3] See e.g. J. Donnelly, *Universal Human Rights in Theory and Practice* (Ithaca, NY, 1989), 49–65; M. Ritter, 'Universal Rights Talk/Plurality of Voices: A Philosophical–Theological Hearing', in M. Janis and C. Evans (eds.), *Religion and International Law* (The Hague, 2000), 431–52.

[4] This has generated an extensive literature. For an excellent sampler of contributions to the debate, see H. J. Steiner and P. Alston, *International Human Rights in Context*, 2nd edn. (Oxford, 2000), 366–402, 538–53. For an impressive recent addition to this literature, see J. R. Bauer and D. A. Bell (eds.), *The East Asian Challenge for Human Rights* (Cambridge, 1999). It has been argued that the 'debate' is flawed in that it fails to recognize the diversity within Asian cultures (see e.g. Y. Ghai, 'Human Rights and Governance: The Asia Debate', (1994) 15 *Australian Year Book of International Law* 1) and, more radically, that the entire idea of 'Asian values' is parasitic upon the 'West-centric' framework that it is seeking to oppose and, as such, is 'misguided and wrong' (see I. Tatsuo, 'Liberal Democracy and Asian Orientalism', in Bauer and Bell (eds.), *The East Asian Challenge*, 29–42). But cf. Glenn, *Legal Traditions of the World*, 279, who argues that despite this diversity, there 'appear to be underlying, common attitudes [although] we may have to climb rather high to see common features'. The human rights debate is conducted on such a pinnacle.

[5] Thus Glenn (*Legal Traditions of the World*, 312) argues in the context of Asian legal traditions that 'If you are a westerner arguing the human rights case, you will be met by opposition which is either Confucian, or communist, or both subtly combined. You may also find a surprising amount of agreement on what you are arguing for.'

[6] One of the most pointless observations in the entire universality debate is that the universal validity of the human rights ideal is demonstrated by the (near) universal adherence of states to the major international human rights instruments. This is—or should be—entirely irrelevant (though doubtless gratifying) to those who seek to establish the universal applicability of the idea of human rights as a framework.

[7] See Ritter, 'Universal Rights Talk', 419, who observes that 'Although the international community may well agree upon the recognition of human rights, there remains disturbing disagreement as to *why* and *how* they should be recognized'.

interests, or by seeking to influence the manner in which a particular outcome will be viewed. Although the substance of the issue remains the same—how acceptable is the application of the human rights framework— the manner in which it is addressed is transformed by this change of focus. Thus the question of the relevance of the human rights approach has become all but inextricably linked with the question of its application in diverse settings which, strictly speaking, has nothing to do with the universality of human rights at all. This, then, is at least in part responsible for the confusion surrounding the universality debate that was noted above.

The process that culminated in the 1993 World Conference on Human Rights and the Vienna Declaration and Programme of Action[8] provided the ideal diplomatic and political framework within which to play out the tensions and confusions between differing conceptions of the place of human rights in the international community and the differing facets of universalism. If the tradition growing out of the Universal Declaration on Human Rights[9] has been one of the civil and political rights of individuals, successively supplemented by economic and social rights and 'solidarity' rights, the chief legacy of Vienna has been its formal recognition and affirmation of the interrelated nature of these various elements of the human rights canon, a *mélange* of norms, principles, and concepts which provide a fertile breeding ground for substantive obfuscation. In a sense, the Vienna process was a micro-rendition of the involvement of international law in human rights protection: an essentially 'Western liberal' starting point coming into contact with, and being challenged by, other conceptions of human rights protection and resulting in an intellectually incoherent but internationally acceptable web of normative opportunities. Thus in a key passage the Vienna Declaration says that:

All human rights are universal, indivisible and interdependent and interrelated. The international community must treat human rights globally in a fair and equal manner, on the same footing, and with the same emphasis. While the significance of national and regional particularities and various historical, cultural and religious backgrounds must be borne in mind, it is the duty of States, regardless of their political, economic and cultural systems, to promote and protect all human rights and fundamental freedoms.[10]

This statement appears to be a ringing endorsement of the universality of human rights[11] but the response of the Conference to the 'universality' debate, which it both reflected and engendered, is so difficult to engage

---

[8] For an overview of the process and the Declaration text, see (1993) 14 *Human Rights Law Journal* (HRLJ) 346; (1993) 32 *International Legal Materials* (ILM) 1661.

[9] UN General Assembly Res. 217A (III), 10 Dec. 1948.

[10] Vienna Declaration and Programme of Action, para. 5.

[11] This was described as 'a decisive defeat for the advocates of strong cultural relativism' by J. Donnelly, 'The Social Construction of Human Rights', in Dunne and Wheeler (eds.), *Human Rights in Global Politics*, 89.

with since, on reflection, it becomes apparent that it was not really about the universality of human rights at all (or at best was only addressing a number of issues that are better considered as foreign to that debate). What was lacking was questioning of the presupposition that the idea of human rights is universally applicable.[12]

The United Nations decided that as part of the preparatory work for the Conference 'regional meetings shall be convened for each region that so desires'[13] and those that took place demonstrated distinctive approaches to the human rights enterprise.[14] Having opened the process out to regional influence, it was inevitable that points of divergence would come to be seen in regional terms and that disagreements would be seen as evidence of a threat to the 'universality' of human rights. It then simply remained for the Conference to put back together the package which it had caused to be taken apart. It is difficult to re-read the Vienna Declaration today without wondering whether its ritual incantations of the universal validity of the human rights ideal were not purchased at too high a price, particularly as it was never under any real threat in the first place.[15] Despite first impressions, the real problem did not concern the question of whose understanding of human rights was to be 'universal': it concerned the manner in which competing visions of human rights norms—generally accepted as valid in their own right—would interact with each other to produce a common 'universal' corpus, and this remained as intractable as ever.[16]

---

[12] It is, of course, hardly surprising that a World Conference on Human Rights convened in order to breathe new impetus into the human rights movement at the very highest of levels should fail to engage with its *raison d'être*. It was not what it was there to do. The very fact that it was a UN enterprise underscores the point that even this exercise was conducted within the constraints of a particular vision of the ordering of affairs, a vision that places a primacy upon the State as the creator and bearer of 'international obligations', including 'human rights' obligations.

[13] UN General Assembly Res. 46/116, 17 Dec. 1991, para. 4(d).

[14] See the Final Declaration of the regional meeting for Africa of the World Conference on Human Rights, the Tunis Declaration of 6 Nov. 1992, (1993) 14 *HRLJ* 367; Final Declaration of the Regional Meeting for Latin America and the Caribbean of the World Conference on Human Rights, the San José Declaration of 22 Jan. 1993, (1993) *HRLJ* 368; Final Declaration of the Regional Meeting for Asia of the World Conference on Human Rights, the Bangkok Declaration of 2 Apr.1993, (1993) 14 *HRLJ* 370.

[15] None of the regional declarations purported to question universality: indeed, they all went out of their way to stress their adherence to it. See e.g. the Tunis Declaration, para. 2, 'The universal nature of human rights is beyond question: their protection and promotion are the duty of all States, regardless of the political, economic or cultural system'; the San José Declaration, Preamble, '*Bearing in mind* that the guiding principles of the study and implementation of international human rights instruments in the United Nations system should be interdependence, universality, objectivity, non-selectivity and the responsibility of States to fulfil their obligations'; Bangkok Declaration, para. 7, 'Stress[ing] the universality, objectivity and non-selectivity of all human rights and the need to avoid the application of double standards in the implementation of human rights and its politicization, and that no violation of human rights can be justified'.

[16] Thus the Tunis Declaration, para. 5, argues that 'no ready-made model can be

Considered in the abstract, consensus on the universal acceptance of a given formulation of a human rights norm can be achieved relatively easily by subscribing to an ever more complex and contradictory matrix of relevant but competing concerns that bear upon the application of that right.[17] To complicate matters further, it is evident that some potential components of that matrix will themselves be human rights while others will not, and the actual components of that matrix will vary with the human right in question. Couched in the language of universality, one might say that a particular vision of a human right approaches universality in its application (as opposed to its applicability) when the number of factors that can legitimately be included within that matrix in a given situation is as few as possible.

It is now possible to separate out a number of different elements of the universality debate which are often confused and conflated. The first concerns the case for the universal relevance of the idea of human rights as a dominant concept in the ordering of society. The second concerns the universal acceptance of particular formulations of human rights. The third concerns the question whether a universally accepted formulation of a human right is to be interpreted and applied in a fashion which reflects and responds to diverse cultural, regional, and personal factors.[18]

The purpose of this chapter is to consider how religion stands in relation to these questions. The second of these three questions will be considered first, and in the next section it will be shown that there is in fact no universally accepted formulation of the freedom of religion as a human right. In consequence, it becomes unnecessary for the purposes of this chapter to address the third of the questions posed above.[19] Even if this

---

prescribed at the universal level since the historical and cultural realities of each nation and the traditions, standards and values of each people cannot be disregarded'. The Bangkok Declaration, para. 8, argues that 'while human rights are universal in nature, they must be considered in the context of a dynamic and evolving process of international norm-setting, bearing in mind the significance of national and regional peculiarities and various historical, cultural and religious backgrounds'.

[17] Whether an outcome of this nature can be achieved will ultimately depend upon the willingness of participants in a negotiation to compromise in order to produce an agreed outcome. If the dominant aim is to develop a formula that commands widespread (universal) support, the problems can be glossed over and left to be addressed if the formula comes to be applied. If, however, the dominant aim is to propagate a particular conception of religion or religious order, then it is less likely that the participants will make such compromises.

[18] Cf. the three forms of relativism identified in M. Perry, *The Idea of Human Rights* (Oxford, 1998), ch. 3: 'Are Human Rights Universal?', these being 'anthropological', 'epistemological', and 'cultural'. By anthropological relativism, Perry means the claim that there is no common human nature to which universal rights can adhere, rather than the claim that the idea of human rights is of universal significance, which for Perry is grounded in the ineliminably religious nature of human rights themselves. He thus avoids the question of the potential clash of value systems altogether. See further n. 78 below.

[19] This third question is particularly complex and can itself be broken down into two elements. As far human rights and religion are concerned, the first element of the question becomes 'To what extent is religion seen as a "human right" which is to be interpreted and

Malcolm D. Evans

conclusion was disputed and it was thought that there was a universally accepted formulation, or that the practice revealed a common approach, the first of the three questions would still need to be addressed, that is, whether it is legitimate to accord to any such universal formulation of a human right a dominant position in the ordering of society. This question is considered in the penultimate section, where the approach to this question from within a human rights perspective is contrasted with that taken by religious traditions that also make universalist claims. The moment at which the claim for universality is won or lost is contingent upon one's views of what universality comprises. That debate is beyond the scope of this chapter, which limits itself to identifying and considering the questions that should be addressed. It also needs to be stressed that a chapter of this length cannot hope to consider these questions in detail, and its purpose is merely to sketch the contours of the issues raised.

Is there a Universally Accepted Formulation of the Freedom of Religion in International Human Rights Law?

The starting point for considering this question must be the texts of international human rights instruments which, as will be seen, show that there is a general consensus based around a tripartite structure: Firstly, there is the assertion of the right to the freedom of 'thought, conscience and religion'. Secondly, it is provided that the freedom of 'religion or belief' may be manifested in 'teaching, practice, worship and observance', both individually or collectively and in public or in private. Thirdly, the exercise of the freedom of religion may be restricted on a number of specified grounds. The widespread adoption of this pattern is hardly surprising since it was established by Article 18 of the Universal Declaration of Human Rights[20] (UDHR) in 1948 and has influenced those texts which have come after, including at the UN level Article 18 of the 1966 International Covenant on Civil and Political Rights (ICCPR)[21] and Article 1 of the 1981 Declaration on the Elimination of All Forms of Intolerance and of Discrimination Based on Religion or Belief (1981 Declaration).[22] There

---

applied in the light of other relevant concerns?' (or, 'How extensive is the matrix to which its application is subject?'). The second becomes 'To what extent is religion seen as a factor which bears upon the interpretation of other human rights?' (or, 'What role does religion play as a component of the matrices relating to other human rights?').

[20] For an examination of the background to Article 18 of the UDHR, see M. Scheinin, 'Article 18', in A. Eide (ed.), *The Universal Declaration of Human Rights: A Commentary* (Oslo, 1992), 263–6; M. D. Evans, *Religious Liberty and International Law in Europe* (Cambridge, 1997), 183–93.

[21] 999 *United Nations Treaty Series* 171. For the background to Article 18 of the International Covenant, see M. J. Bossuyt, *Guide to the Travaux Préparatoires of the International Covenant on Civil and Political Rights* (Dordrecht, 1987), 351–71; Evans, *Religious Liberty and International Law*, 194–207.

[22] UN General Assembly Res. 36/55, 25 Nov. 1981. For an examination of the

are, however, significant variations of detail between these instruments, and it is by no means clear that any one particular version of this formula should be accorded primacy over others. Some differences are either semantic or trivial, but others are of greater significance. For the purposes of this chapter, what is more important than the disparities between the various texts adopted at the global UN level are the disparities between them and the various regional convention texts that address the freedom of religion. Those considered in this chapter will be Article 9 of the 1950 European Convention on Human Rights and Fundamental Freedoms (ECHR),[23] Article 12 of the 1969 American Convention on Human Rights (ACHR),[24] Article 8 of the 1986 African Charter on Human and Peoples' Rights,[25] Articles 26 and 27 of the 1994 Arab Charter on Human Rights,[26] and Article 10 of the 1995 Commonwealth of Independent States Convention on Human Rights and Fundamental Freedoms (CIS Convention).[27] These will be explored below, using the three basic elements as a framework for presentation.[28]

THE ASSERTION OF THE RIGHT

All three of the principal UN instruments adopt the common formulation that 'Everyone has the right to freedom of thought, conscience and religion.'[29] Among the regional instruments this is found only in Article 9 of

Declaration, see N. Lerner, 'Toward a Draft Declaration against Religious Intolerance and Discrimination', (1981) 11 *Israeli Yearbook of Human Rights* 82 and 'The Final Text of the UN Declaration against Intolerance and Discrimination Based on Religion or Belief', (1982) 12 *Israeli Yearbook of Human Rights* 185; D. J. Sullivan, 'Advancing the Freedom of Religion or Belief through the UN Declaration on the Elimination of Religious Intolerance and Discrimination', (1988) 81 *American Journal of International Law* 487; B. G. Tahzib, *Freedom of Religion or Belief* (The Hague, 1996), 165–212; Evans, *Religious Liberty and International Law*, 227–61.

[23] 213 *United Nations Treaty Series* 221; *European Treaty Series* 5. For the drafting of Article 9, see Evans, *Religious Liberty and International Law*, 262–72.

[24] *Organisation of American States Treaty Series* 36; (1970) 9 *ILM* 673.

[25] See (1982) 21 *ILM* 58; (1986) 7 *HRLJ* 403.

[26] Adopted by the Council of the League of Arab States in Res. 5437 of 8 Sept. 1994. For an English translation of the text, see (1997) 18 *HRLJ* 151.

[27] See (1996) 17 *HRLJ* 157–62. The implementation of the Convention is overseen by a Human Rights Commission of the Commonwealth on Independent States which was established pursuant to Article 33 of its 1993 Charter (for which see (1995) 34 *ILM* 1279), the Regulations of which are found in (1996) 17 *HRLJ* 163–4. For analysis of the relationship between the CIS Convention and the ECHR (and arguing for the primacy of the latter), see A. A. Cançado Trindade, (1996) 17 *HRLJ* 164–80 and J. A. Frowein, (1996) 17 *HRLJ* 181–4.

[28] A proper comparative analysis of these texts would require a detailed exploration of the interpretation placed upon them by the various mechanisms established to oversee their implementation, and this is beyond the scope of this paper.

[29] UDHR, Art. 18; ICCPR, Art. 18; 1981 Declaration, Art. 1. The sole draft article of the proposed UN Convention to be adopted by the 3rd Committee in 1967 was also couched in this form. See J. Claydon, 'The Treaty Protection of Religious Rights: UN Draft Convention in the Elimination of All Forms of Intolerance and of Discrimination Based on Religion or Belief', (1972) 12 *Santa Clara Lawyer* 403.

the ECHR, although the CIS Convention differs only to the extent that it substitutes the word 'faith' for 'religion'.[30] Outside the UN and European theatre, the approach is less consistent. The ACHR reflects the tripartite structure of the UN instruments but limits itself to proclaiming that 'Everyone has the right to freedom of conscience and of religion,'[31] the freedom of thought being located alongside the freedom of expression in Article 13, which provides that 'Everyone shall have the freedom of thought and expression.' Other regional instruments are more obviously divergent. The Arab Charter is consonant with the tripartite approach, and provides that 'Everyone has a guaranteed right to freedom of belief, thought and opinion.'[32] It is the African Charter which veers furthest from the pattern of the other instruments, simply providing that 'freedom of conscience, the profession and free practice of religion shall be guaranteed'.[33]

It might be argued that the essential point lies in the recognition given to the freedom of religion by all of these human rights instruments, and whether they do so in conjunction with 'thought' and 'conscience' is secondary. There is truth in this. However, these opening affirmations are not to be read in isolation, and the significance of the variations lies in the manner in which it feeds into the vexed question of what 'counts' as a form of religion for the purposes of the remainder of the articles. Linking the freedom of religion with patterns of thought and conscience holds open the possibility of adopting an inclusive, latitudinous approach, and it was certainly the intention of the drafters of the UN instruments that patterns of atheistic thought were to be placed alongside forms of religious belief within the scheme of protection.[34] The American Convention implies a somewhat different approach. It links conscience with religion and separates them off from thought and expression. This suggests a distinction between those patterns of thought which are of a spiritual, moral, and ethical nature and those which are not, and identifies the former as a kind of *lex specialis* which are to be accorded a different and higher degree of protection within the Convention system than other patterns of thought.

The texts of the Arab and African Charters also indicate a similar diver-

---

[30] CIS Convention, Art. 10(1).   [31] ACHR, Art. 12(1).
[32] Arab Charter, Art. 26.   [33] African Charter, Art. 8.
[34] Although employing the same language, the practice under the ECHR and the ICCPR has taken divergent paths, the ECHR taking a liberal approach (see C. Evans, Religious Freedom in European Human Rights Law', in Janis and Evans (eds.), *Religion and International Law*, 392, where she describes it as adopting 'a philosophy of openness') whilst the Human Rights Committee seems to take a fairly restrictive approach (see M. D. Evans, 'The United Nations and the Freedom of Religion: The Work of the Human Rights Committee', in R. Adhar (ed.), *Law and Religion* (Aldershot, 2000), 39–45, where the difference between the form and substance of the practice is explored, and paradoxical signals noted).

gence. The African Charter again links conscience with religion and could be taken to suggest that the freedom of conscience represents the internal dimension of a belief, the outward expression of which is religious in nature. In other words, they are each other's alter ego and conscience and religion are to be understood in mutually referring and reinforcing terms. Whether or not this is true, the formulation, once again, is clearly anchored in spiritual, moral, and ethical values. This is even clearer in the case of the Arab Charter. At first sight, the linkage between 'belief, thought and opinion' in Article 26 of the Arab Charter and the freedom to 'practise religious observances' in the following Article 27 seems to mirror the approach of the UN instruments and the ECHR. However, the context is very different since the Preamble to the Charter roots the entire text within an Islamic religious tradition, the paramountcy of which is evident.

There are, then, signs of different approaches to the range of beliefs which fall to be considered within the general rubric of the international protection of religion as a human right at the regional level, and the significance of this is not to be underestimated. Nor is it to be devalued by pointing to the fact that many of those states party to the regional instruments are also party to the UN Covenant[35] or did not oppose the adoption of the 1981 Declaration within the UN General Assembly.[36] The point is that at a regional level states have chosen to place the emphasis in a different place, while conforming to the general idea of the protection of religion as a human right. At the level of the affirmation of that right, these nuances are slight, but attain a greater potency when considered in conjunction with the remainder of their schemes of protection.

THE MANIFESTATION OF RELIGION

Once again, the UN and the ECHR adopt a common approach, though with some variation in detail, to the question of manifesting the freedom of religion. In substance, they all follow Article 18 of the UDHR, which provides that 'this right includes . . .[37] freedom, either alone[38] or in community with others and in public or private, to manifest his religion or

---

[35] As at 15 May 2000, 144 states were a party to the ICCPR. It is notable that the majority of those member states of the UN which are not party to the ICCPR come from the Asia–Pacific region and include Brunei, Fiji, Indonesia, Lao People's Democratic Republic, Malaysia, Myanmar, Papua New Guinea, and Singapore, as well as many smaller island nations. China has signed, but at the time of writing has not yet ratified, the ICCPR. Other non-parties include Bahrain, Botswana, Cuba, Eritrea, Ghana, Guinea-Bissau, Mauritania, Oman, Pakistan, Qatar, Swaziland, Turkey, and the UAE, as well as a number of smaller Caribbean island states.

[36] The 1981 Declaration was adopted without a vote.

[37] The deleted material concerns the freedom to change one's religious belief. There is no real consensus on this and it will be considered separately below.

[38] In the ICCPR and the1981 Declaration 'individually' replaces 'alone'.

belief in teaching practice, worship and observance'.[39] This formula raises many questions, the most significant being as follows. Firstly, does the use of the term 'belief' extend the freedom of manifestation beyond the scope of religion and apply it to other patterns of 'thought and conscience' referred to in the opening affirmation of the right? Secondly, what are the range of practical activities which might legitimately qualify as a form of manifestation for the purposes of this formula? Thirdly, are the forms of manifestation listed a closed list? These questions are not easily answered, but it is evident that the UN instruments and the ECHR are flexible enough to embrace a very broad range of patterns of belief and related activities, even if in fact they are applied in a more restrictive fashion.[40]

The other regional instruments adopt a very different approach. The CIS Convention, in other ways so similar to the UN and ECHR pattern, speaks of 'freedom either alone or in community with others, to engage in religious worship, attend and perform religious and ritual ceremonies and act in accordance with [one's religion or belief]'. As with the UN and ECHR texts, it is not made clear whether 'belief' is to be understood as a synonym for 'religion' (remembering that the opening statement of the right mentioned neither, but referred to 'faith'). As to the forms of manifestation, the forms expressly stated are narrow and inward-looking, focused upon the conduct of religious worship, rites, and ceremonies and excluding teaching. However, they are accompanied by the very broad idea of a right to act 'in accordance with' one's religion or belief. This can be interpreted in a much broader fashion than any of the four forms of manifestation listed in the other instruments. It is, therefore, not an obviously more restrictive text, despite perhaps appearing so on a first reading.

Article 10 of the American Convention is rather ambiguously drafted. It provides that the freedom of conscience and religion 'includes . . . freedom to profess or disseminate one's religion or beliefs either individually or together with others, in public or in private'. On the face of it, this is an extremely limited range of expressly protected activities, but it is clear that the scope of the right is considerably more extensive. As will be seen below, Article 12(3) addresses the question of the extent to which manifestations of religion and belief can be subjected to legitimate restrictions. At this point, it must be noted that Article 12(1) does not describe the freedom to profess or disseminate as a particular form of manifestation at all. In other words, whereas the UN instruments and the ECHR set out various heads of protected forms of manifestation, which are potentially subject to legitimate restriction, the ACHR accepts that manifestations

---

[39] The order in which these four forms of manifestation are listed varies: in the ECHR 'worship' is brought to the head of the list, while in the ICCPR and the 1981 Declaration the order is 'worship, observance, practice and teaching'.

[40] See Evans, 'Religious Freedom in European Human Rights Law', 394–6, and Evans, 'The United Nations and the Freedom of Religion', 44–8.

may be subject to limitation, but does not mention a substantive right to manifest at all. This rather suggests, and practice seems to confirm,[41] that there is a freedom to manifest religion or belief under the ACHR but that, unlike the UN instruments and the ECHR, the forms that a manifestation might take are not indicated at all.[42] Turning to the other regional instruments under consideration, Article 27 of the Arab Charter provides that 'Adherents of every religion have the right to practice their religious observances and to manifest their views through expression, practice or teaching . . .'. Once again, the scope of these freedoms is obviously unclear and open to various interpretations[43] but it does endorse the approach of identifying defined forms of manifestation. This is not dissimilar to the position under the African Charter, which in Article 8 laconically provides that 'the profession and free practice of religion shall be guaranteed'.

It might be concluded that there is a general recognition that the freedom of religion must be complemented by a right to manifest that religion. Regional practice departs from the UN instruments in the forms and degrees of specificity offered. Non-European regional models tend to focus on aspects of religious ritual and ceremony while holding open the door for a range of other legitimate forms of manifestation, the rationales for which would presumably be made out on a case-by-case basis. As with the affirmation of the right, the differences that flow from these nuances should not be trivialized, but, as before, there does seem to be a general consensus around the approach, if not the manner in which it is to be given expression. And, as before, the evidence comes from the disparities between the regional models when compared to the UN instruments.

RESTRICTIONS ON THE RIGHT

It is in the area of restrictions upon the exercise of the right to freedom of religion that there is the most disparity between the various formulations, including disparities within the family of UN instruments. Article 29(2) of the UDHR provides a general limitation applicable to all Declaration

---

[41] See S. Davidson, 'Civil and Political Rights Protected in the Inter-American Human Rights System', in D. Harris and S. Livingstone, *The Inter-American System of Human Rights* (Oxford, 1998), 258.

[42] This conclusion is supported by the wording of Article III of the American Declaration on the Rights and Duties of Man, adopted on 2 May 1948 and on which the American Convention is based, which provides that 'Every person has the right freely to profess a religious faith, and to manifest and practice it both in public and private.'

[43] One interesting point concerns the inclusion of expression in the forms of manifestation. It is presumably the expression of the religious views of adherents of religion that is referred to, although this is not clear from the text. The significance is that the Charter contains no other provision relating to freedom of expression. It is difficult to decide whether it is more problematic to argue that the general freedom of expression is at least offered to adherents of religion or whether it is better to accept that there is no such freedom on non-religious matters granted at all.

rights, including both the 'freedom of thought, conscience and religion' and the right to manifest religion or belief found in Article 18. This was not followed in subsequent UN instruments, and the ICCPR and the 1981 Declaration only permit restrictions to be placed upon the manifestation of religion or belief, and not upon the right itself. This is also true of the ECHR, the ACHR, and the CIS Convention.

The Arab Charter is more equivocal. It follows the UDHR in having in Article 4(a) a general derogation clause which applies to all convention rights, but the potential impact of this may be offset by Article 3(a), which provides that 'No restriction upon or derogation from any of the fundamental human rights recognized or existing in any State Party to the present Charter in virtue of law, conventions or customs shall be admitted on the pretext that the present Charter does not recognize such rights or that it recognizes them to a lesser extent.' The African Charter also seems to permit restrictions upon the freedom of religion as well as on the freedom to profess and practise religion,[44] but it must be recalled that Article 8 of this instrument does not separate out the right to freedom of religion from the freedom of manifestation and so it may well be inappropriate to draw this conclusion.

The ICCPR[45] and the ACHR[46] also include the freedom of religion among those articles that cannot be derogated from in times of war or national emergency, but it is not included in the list of non-derogable rights in the ECHR,[47] the CIS Convention,[48] and the Arab Charter. This would seem to be a significant disparity. However, it must be borne in mind that under the ECHR the enjoyment of this freedom is restricted to the so-called *forum internum*, the realm of the inner self, and any form of pressure sufficient to violate this would almost certainly entail violation of other Convention provisions, notably Article 3 concerning torture and inhuman or degrading treatment or punishment which is itself non-derogable.[49] Thus in practice, if not in form, the position under the ECHR, and

---

[44] African Charter, Art. 8, providing that 'the profession and free practice of religion shall be guaranteed. No one may, subject to law and order, be submitted to measures restricting the exercise of these freedoms'.   [45] ICCPR, Art. 4(2).

[46] ACHR, Art. 27(2). Unlike under the ICCPR, the freedom of 'thought' is not non-derogable since it is found in Article 13 alongside the freedom of expression, which, unsurprisingly, may be subject to derogation.

[47] ECHR, Art. 15(2).

[48] CIS Convention, Arts. 35(1) and (2). However, as with the Arab Charter, the CIS Convention only permits derogations 'provided such measures are not inconsistent with other obligations under international law'.

[49] In fact, the position adopted is somewhat broader and requires that the individual is not required to act in a way which prejudices their inner beliefs, although the thresholds are by no means obvious. See further Evans, *Religious Liberty and International Law*, 294–5 and 315–18; Evans, 'Religious Freedom in European Human Rights Law', 393–4. The approach is buttressed by ICCPR Article 18(2) and the 1981 UN Declaration, Article 1(2), both of which provide that 'No one shall be subject to coercion that would impair his freedom to have a religion or belief or his choice.'

probably the CIS Convention which is modelled on it,[50] should be seen as according to the ICCPR and ACHR in this regard. If the non-derogable nature of the freedom of religion is accepted, then the saving provision in Article 3(a) of the Arab Charter and, if necessary, its equivalent in the CIS Convention have the potential to harmonize the approach, although it cannot be assumed. The African Charter does not deal with this situation at all.

It might, then, be concluded that the freedom of thought, conscience, and religion is seen as an absolute right. Although it must be accepted that this does not mean that religious believers are ensured an absolute freedom of, say, worship, it is still not insignificant that individuals are to be accorded absolute protection from subjection to forms of coercion or indoctrination in order to force them to espouse[51] other forms of belief, religious or otherwise.

This, however, is not the end of the question since all of the texts permit a range of restrictions to be placed upon the manifestations of religion and there is considerable diversity here. The requirement that restrictions must be provided for by law is found in all the other instruments. The key differences concern the various legitimate grounds of restriction and whether the particular restriction is *necessary* to order to attain the stated ends. The UDHR has adopts a rather open-ended approach, providing that

In the exercise of his rights and freedoms, everyone shall be subject only to such limitations as are determined by law solely for the purpose of securing due recognition and respect for the rights and freedoms of others and of meeting the just requirements of morality, public order and the general welfare in a democratic society.[52]

This suggests a rather broadly conceived balancing exercise, the 'general welfare in a democratic society' offering a particularly generous ground for restriction. The subsequent UN instruments adopt a much tighter approach, both the ICCPR and the 1981 Declaration using the same formula, that the freedom 'may be subject only to such limitations as are prescribed by law and are necessary to protect public safety, order, health or morals or the fundamental rights and freedoms others'.[53]

Article 12(3) of the ACHR is essentially the same but without the qualification that the rights and freedoms of others that may justify a restriction be 'fundamental'. This is also true of the ECHR and the CIS Convention, which also are similar, but both require that restrictions be necessary 'in a

---

[50] CIS Convention Article 3, which addressed torture and inhuman or degrading treatment or punishment, is non-derogable (Art. 35(2)).

[51] It might be wondered whether it is possible to force anyone to truly adhere to a form of belief, even if it is possible to induce outward compliance.

[52] UDHR, Art. 29(2).

[53] ICCPR, Art. 18(2); 1981 UN Declaration, Article 1(3).

democratic society'. The CIS Convention allows restrictions for the protection of public order and public heath or morals, whereas the ECHR only extends the 'public' dimension to 'order'. The CIS Convention, however, also includes 'national security' as a legitimate head of restriction. The Arab Charter offers a further variant, permitting restrictions 'provided by law and deemed necessary to protect the national security and economy, public order, health or morals or the rights and freedoms of others'.[54] The African Charter merely provides that 'No one may, subject to law and order, be submitted to measures restricting the exercise of these freedoms.'[55]

Once again, there appears to be a degree of consensus within this textual diversity. Although no one formulation predominates, the ICCPR and the 1981 Declaration seem to reflect the essence of the approach, with regional conventions offering greater (in the case of the Arab and African and CIS instrument) or lesser (in the case of the ECHR[56]) weight to the interests of society as a whole.

CHANGE OF RELIGION

No matter what degree of consensus can be built around the various elements of the tripartite structure considered in the previous subsections, it is simply disingenuous to claim that there is a consensus concerning the freedom to change one's religion or belief, although it is routine to do so.[57] The UN instruments themselves bear testimony to the lack of consensus on this issue. Article 18 of the UDHR expressly provides that the freedom of religion 'includes freedom to change his religion or belief'. This was contested by a number of Islamic states and Article 18 of the ICCPR is deliberately more equivocal, providing that 'This right shall include freedom to have or to adopt a religion or belief of his choice.'[58] In the 1981 Declaration the words 'or to adopt' were dropped, the resulting phrase being 'This right shall include freedom to have a religion or whatever

---

[54] Arab Charter, Art. 4(a).

[55] African Charter, Art. 8.

[56] To the extent that the ECHR can be construed as permitting restrictions on the grounds of 'private' as opposed to 'public' health or morals it is, however, the more potentially intrusive instrument.

[57] It has been authoritatively asserted on numerous occasions that the freedom of religion does indeed embrace the freedom to change religion. See e.g. the 1987 Odio Benito Report, commissioned by the UN Sub-Commission, which argued that, despite the differences in wording, all three instruments meant the same thing (E/CN.4/1987/Sub.2/1987/26, para. 200; Human Rights Committee, General Comment No. 23, para. 5; and the Reports of the UN Special Rapporteur on his visits to Pakistan, E/CN.4/19996/95/Add.1, para. 84, and Iran, E/CN.4/1996/95/Add.2, para. 91; and his most recent Annual Report, E/CN.4/1999/58, para. 107).

[58] See e.g. Tahzib, *Freedom of Religion or Belief*, 84–7; Evans, *Religious Liberty and International Law*, 196–202.

belief of his choice.'[59] These changes were not cosmetic and although a compensating saving clause was introduced,[60] its sufficiency to preserve the right as previously conceived is open to doubt.[61] Among the regional instruments the ECHR follows the text of the UDHR while the ACHR also provides that the freedom of religion 'includes freedom to maintain or to change one's religion or belief'.[62] The CIS Convention departs from the ECHR model, recognizing the 'freedom to choose' rather than 'change' one's religion or belief. This is capable of bearing a more restrictive interpretation. Perhaps unsurprisingly, neither the African nor Arab Charters allude to a right to choose, change, or adopt a religion, and in the light of the pressure exerted by states from within these regions on the matter, it would be unwarranted to see this as stemming from disinterest rather than from rejection. There can be little doubt that this is one of the most problematic components of the international formulation and presents serious problems for any who might seek to maintain that any single formulation of the right enjoys universal acceptance.

CONCLUSION

While different formulations may indicate certain preferences for more restrictive or more expansive approaches, it is probably true to say that all texts are capable of bearing similar interpretations and delivering similar outcomes, although the language within which such outcomes could be achieved would vary. It seems that it is also possible to build a consensus around the tripartite structure of the principal UN instruments, though it would be unwise to claim that any one particular version is truly reflective of a general consensus. It may, then, be concluded that, for the purposes of the discussion of universality and the freedom of religion as an international human right, there is as yet no formulation that can legitimately be offered as having a universal legitimacy, although there is a predominantly accepted international *approach* that is subject to regional variation.

One consequence of this conclusion is that it becomes unnecessary to pursue in any detail the final of the three potential questions posed concerning the universality of religion as an international human right. To recap, this concerns the question of whether a universally accepted formu-

---

[59] See e.g. Tahzib, *Freedom of Religion or Belief*, 168; Evans, *Religious Liberty and International Law*, 237–8; N. Lerner, 'Religious Human Rights under the United Nations', in J. D. van de Vyver and J. Witte Jr. (eds.), *Religious Human Rights in Global Perspective: Legal Perspectives* (The Hague, 1996), 116, accurately describes as 'a weakened text'.

[60] Article 8 provides that 'Nothing in the present Declaration shall be construed as restricting or derogating from any right defined in the UDHR or ICCPR.'

[61] See Evans, *Religious Liberty and International Law*, 238, but cf. Sullivan, 'Advancing the Freedom of Religion or Belief', 495, who argues that Article 8 of the Declaration has the effect of preserving the UDHR and ICCPR position.

[62] ACHR, Art. 10(1).

lation of a human right is to be interpreted and applied in a fashion which reflects and responds to diverse cultural, regional, and personal factors. Since there is no such universally accepted formulation, this task cannot be undertaken. It must already be apparent from the preceding sections that there must be space for differential application of what is no more than an emergent common approach rather than a common norm.

Of course, this is only half an answer. It might be objected that an examination of the practice under the various global and regional systems could indicate that there is in fact a greater degree of universality than the examination of the texts themselves suggests. This is certainly possible, but it is insufficient to prove the case that a given formulation of the norm has a universal potency.[63] It would not be surprising to discover that bodies established to oversee the implementation of human rights commitments might draw on each other's work and adopt mutually reinforcing interpretations. This, however, does not mean that those who are the recipients of that interpretative work—the states party to the Conventions—need necessarily accept its validity,[64] and it is this which, ultimately, is critical to the emergence or adoption of a 'universal' formulation. Unless or until that hurdle is overcome, examinations of the work of human rights treaty bodies can only indicate what the acceptance of particular formulations might entail.[65] A quite different but equally compelling reason for not pursuing the interpretative work any further here lies in the dearth of relevant material generated under those instruments which least conform to the dominant UN and ECHR model. To ignore this and proceed to

---

[63] Cf. C. Taylor, 'Conditions for an Unforced Consensus on Human Rights', in Bauer and Bell (eds.), *The East Asian Challenge*, 124, argues for a tripartite distinction between 'norms, legal forms, and background justifications' (p. 143). Taylor argues that there can be an unforced consensus on the content of norms (human rights) despite their being grounded in quite different conceptual frameworks. This seems unproblematic. He also believes that they might legitimately take a variety of legal forms. This would suggest that universal human rights can indeed exist despite the lack of a 'universally' recognized formulation. The difficulty with this is that, as he accepts (p. 137), there will also be room for differences in the practice of interpreting and applying these norms. It is somewhat unclear whether a variety of legal forms embraces both diversity in its formulation as well as diversity in its application. If, as seems likely, he is arguing for both, it would seem very difficult to identify a common norm without the existence of a common formulation since there would be too many variables to trace back through. If, however, the difference in legal form is meant only to embrace variations in application, one is still left looking for a common normative statement, which Taylor does not seem to consider necessary.

[64] The negative responses to Human Rights Committee General Comment No. 24 on Reservations to Human Rights Treaties stands as a salutary warning to those who would urge treaty monitoring bodies to adopt overly expansive approaches. See generally J. P. Gardner (ed.), *Human Rights as General Norms and a State's Right to Opt Out: Reservations and Objections to Human Rights Conventions* (London, 1997).

[65] It might, of course, indicate that it makes no real difference to the outcome which formulation is adopted and this might certainly assist in the task of encouraging states to move towards the acceptance of a common formula but that is a different exercise from that being undertaken in this paper.

consider whether the output under those instruments supports a claim for a universal formulation or application of the freedom of religion would be to ride roughshod over the evidence of disparate regional thinking and simply lend credence to claims of neo-imperialism and cultural hegemony.

A further objection might be that while a substantial uniformity in practice would not be sufficient to demonstrate that there was a consensus around a particular formulation, there would be no need for such a consensus if the practice was uniform. That is to say, the only purpose of seeking a universally accepted formulation of the right is in order to progress to the stage of developing a uniformity of application and if this is achieved, then universality is proven. There is force in this argument and such a study would indeed be worth while. Nevertheless, it still falls short of the mark. Even if there was a common approach, one must be cautious when translating practice into prescription, and particularly so when there is a lack of uniformity at the prescriptive level: the textual divergences would remain and hold open the possibility that the convergent stream of practice may legitimately part company in the future as the interpretative possibilities are explored and exploited, a mere temporary alignment of moving bodies. Moreover, it is simply not consonant with the manner in which the human rights canon has developed to look to practice in order to perfect an understanding of the normative web. Time and time again the force of human rights declarations are deployed against the manifestly contradictory practice of states.[66] To suggest that practice should take precedence over the language of the instruments themselves would risk upsetting the entire structure of international human rights protection.

Religion and the Universality of the Idea of Human Rights as a Dominant Concept in the Ordering of Society

The all-pervading influence of human rights in the international sphere is now manifested in many ways, and most of the fundamental building blocks of the international legal order have been influenced by it[67] and

---

[66] For robust criticism of the tendency to ignore the manifest realities of state practice in constructing norms of customary international law pertaining to human rights, see J. Shand Watson, *Theory and Reality in the International Protection of Human Rights* (New York, 1999).

[67] It has long since triumphed over the principle established in Article 2(7) of the UN Charter, of non-interference in the domestic affairs of states. It influences the recognition of new states. Domestic courts are permitted to exercise civil and criminal jurisdiction with regard to human rights abuses that have no direct connection with their territory; ex-heads of state may lose their immunity before domestic courts for such proceedings and it may not be long before states can themselves be subject to civil actions in respect of serious violations of human rights before the courts of third states. Human rights concerns have fuelled the process culminating in the adoption of the 1998 Rome Statute of the International Criminal Court. They provide examples of norms of *ius cogens*— principles carrying a higher normative weight than others—and of *erga omnes* obligations—the breach of which is a wrong

compatibility with human rights is fast becoming the touchstone by which nearly all else is assessed.[68] Moreover, it should not be forgotten that the title of the founding instrument of contemporary international human rights instruments is the *Universal* Declaration of Human Rights. Drafted by a small conclave and dominated by those steeped in the traditions of Western thought,[69] the Declaration nevertheless claims to be a 'common standard of achievement for all peoples and all nations' and calls on 'every individual and every organ of society' through teaching and progressive measures 'to secure their universal and effective recognition and observance'.[70] This was reaffirmed in the Tehran Proclamation adopted at the 1968 International Conference on Human Rights,[71] and the opening paragraph of the Vienna Declaration and Programme of Action says that 'the universal nature of these rights and freedoms is beyond question'.

Yet it must be open to question, and proponents of human rights do themselves no favours by intolerantly foreclosing debate.[72] Nevertheless, a serious debate on this question appears to be currently beyond the reach of the international community of states, which seems unable to recognize

against the entire international community. The UN Human Rights Committee (HRC) has argued that treaties dealing with human rights are not subject to the usual operation of the rules concerning the treaties (see HRC General Comment No. 24) and that human rights obligations pertain to the inhabitants of a territory and once granted cannot be lost, even in cases of a change of sovereign (see HRC General Comment No. 26). Most dramatically, human rights concerns increasingly figure among the reasons given in justification for the recourse to the use of force within the international community, and it may not be too much of an exaggeration to say that 'wars for the protection of human rights' are now well within the contemplation of the international community of states.

[68] Cf. M. de Blois, 'The Foundations of Human Rights', in P. R. Beaumont (ed.), *Christian Perspectives on Human Rights and Legal Philosophy* (Carlisle, 1998), 28–9, who claims that 'human rights have for many people almost the significance of a religious belief . . . [and] the basis of a new creed'. Put in those terms, it is not surprising to find that he concludes, 'Christians should not be found among the followers of this religion.'

[69] Revealed most clearly in the writings of John Humphrey, director of the Human Rights Division at the time. See J. P. Humphrey, *Human Rights and the United Nations: A Great Adventure* (Dobbs Ferry, NY, 1984) and 'The UN Charter and the Universal Declaration on Human Rights', in E. Luard (ed.), *The International Protection of Human Rights* (London, 1967), 48.

[70] UDHR, Preamble.

[71] Final Act of the International Conference on Human Rights, Tehran, 22 Apr.–13 May 1968, UN Doc. A/CONF.32/41.

[72] See Brown, 'Universal Human Rights', 121: 'Even judged in its own terms, the international human rights regime has not been particularly effective partly because of the blithe unwillingness of some activists to recognize that there are philosophical and cultural problems associated with their position.' For a good example of this form of a priori rejection of the claims of competing value systems, see C. Loh, 'The Importance of Universal Standards in Asia', in M. Davies (ed.), *Human Rights and Chinese Values* (Hong Kong, 1995), 155, who argues that 'If the argument that cultural, social or religious factors give rise to different and yet equally valid conceptions of human rights is accepted, then the most despicable acts . . . could be excused under the pretext of cultural pluralism and/or sovereign rights.' For an exploration of the interaction between these concepts, see M. D. Evans, 'Law, Religion and Human Rights: Locating the Debate', in P. Edge and G. Harvey, *Law and Religion in Contemporary Society* (Aldershot, 2000), ch. 10.

that the espousal of human rights values merely represents a contemporary approach to issues that in previous ages have been addressed through other conceptual apparatus.[73] Rather than engage with this question of why the idea of human rights as a conceptual model of universal validity should take preference over any other competing models of global order-ing, the general response is to hunt for justifications of universality which are capable of universal endorsement.[74] This misses the point. There are any number of potential theories that can plausibly support the conclusion that the idea of human rights is of universal relevance. But even if one agrees that such theories do sustain the case of universalism, this does not mean that there cannot be other conceptions which may be equally convincing and with which the idea of human rights must engage.[75] To be sure, each will be equally convinced of its superiority, but the key lies in recognizing that this does not necessarily entail intolerance of other univer-salist claims.[76]

[73] See e.g. R. Tuck, *The Rights of War and Peace* (Oxford, 1999), who traces the legal and political discussions of 16th- and 17th-century colonialism by Victoria, Gentili, Grotius, and Hobbes within the framework of humanist and scholastic thinking. Today these debates would be conducted within the language of human rights. The issues are timeless: it is the form in which they are expressed that changes.

[74] See e.g. Dunne and Wheeler (eds.), *Human Rights in Global Politics*, which includes a number of alternative strategies; e.g. B. Parekh, 'Non Ethnocentric Universalism', 128, who argues for identifying a set of universal *values* (rather than *rights*) through cross-cultural dialogue, but accepts that 'Universal values form the basis of universal human rights, which are a subcategory of, and represent a particular manner of realizing, these values' (p. 150). K. Booth, 'Three Tyrannies', ibid. 31, argues for a 'bottom-up' approach that sources the univer-sality human rights in 'the universality of human wrongs' (p. 62). Many other examples of this approach could be given.

[75] See e.g. Donnelly, 'The Social Construction of Human Rights', who, while a keen advo-cate of the human rights enterprise, accepts that 'Human rights are an eminently contestable basis for ordering social and political life (pp. 81–2) and that 'there is nothing natural, let alone inevitable, about ordering social and political life around the idea of human rights' (p. 84). In consequence, he can accept that 'it would be a limiting and potentially dangerous delusion to see current human rights ideas and practices as fixed, let alone the final and perfect unfolding of a comprehensive, timeless visions of human rights and wrongs. We must remain open to alterna-tive strategies and practices for realizing human dignity' (p. 88). Writing in the context of the 'Asian values' debate itself, he has recently observed that 'Whether this late-twentieth-century human rights approach is best in every contemporary society is a matter of legitimate debate, but unless the distinctive nature of that approach is recognized, that debate will be, at best, vacuous or misguided' (J. Donnelly, 'Human Rights and Asian Values: A Defense of "Western" Universalism', in Bauer and Bell (eds.), *The East Asian Challenge*, 68.

[76] The essential intolerance of liberal-inspired human rights doctrine is particularly trou-blesome since the very idea of liberalism is predicated upon tolerance. Yet as Rawls graphi-cally illustrates, liberal toleration is reserved for tolerant liberals; see J. Rawls, *The Law of Peoples* (Cambridge, Mass., 1999), 59 ('we recognize that a liberal society is to respect its citizens' comprehensive doctrines—religious, philosophical, and moral—provided that these doctrines are pursued in ways compatible with a reasonable political conception of justice and its public reason'). Non-liberal peoples who, *inter alia*, demonstrate religious tolerance, but not religious equality, may qualify as 'decent' peoples and therefore come within the purview of his 'law of peoples' and qualify for toleration by liberal peoples (pp. 121–3). 'Outlaw states', including those basing themselves on comprehensive doctrines, are simply not to be tolerated (p. 81).

The consequences of failing to address the general question of the universality of the idea of human rights is that it becomes very difficult—if not impossible—for serious debate to take place between human rights adherents and those who espouse other forms of universalist conceptions of the ordering of society. The latter are offered a stark choice: either enter into dialogue within the human rights framework, or be marginalized by it. It seems that this is the position that the religious community has found itself in[77] and has tended to opt for the latter option. Is it, however, a cuckoo in the human rights nest?[78]

The problem which religion poses for any non-religious ordering of society is that it offers a set of values, goals, and imperatives which have an absolute quality, even if the manner in which they are to be interpreted and applied is a matter of legitimate debate within the various religious traditions themselves. Put in this way, it is immediately apparent that there is a parallel with the 'universality' debate in the human rights context. The universality of religion may find expression in a general belief that the created order must be subject to forms of governance which reflect its divine origins. This is the equivalent of the first of the questions posed in relation to the 'universality' debate. The equivalent of the second question would be whether there is a generally accepted formulation of religious belief that is accepted 'universally'. The equivalent of the third question would be that of how a religion responds to various cultural or other diversities that bear upon it.

When the questions posed in relation to the idea of human rights are applied to religion, it produces a set of answers that may seen paradoxical. Not all believers actually subscribe to the form of universalism that demands that religion be placed at the centre of the ordering of society.[79] Indeed, the transcendental nature of much theology positively eschews such concern with worldly governance and so yields the field to others without a contest. Christianity, for example, is more generally associated with democracy than theocracy. It may be concerned with the legal and

---

[77] See e.g. H. Charlesworth, 'The Challenges of Human Rights for Religious Traditions', in Janis and Evans (eds.), *Religion and International Law*, 412: 'All religious traditions need to acknowledge and discuss the full range of human rights treaties and to develop their doctrines, through debate and dialogue, in their light.'

[78] Cf. those who argue that the very stuff of human rights is in fact 'religious' in nature, thus turning the entire subject—as seen from a classic liberal perspective—on its head. See e.g. Perry, *The Idea of Human Rights*, 11–41 ('Is the Idea of Human Rights Ineliminably Religious?'); J. E. Wood Jr., 'An Apologia for Human Rights', in J. Witte Jr. and J. van der Vyver (eds.), *Religious Human Rights in Global Perspective: Religious Perspective* (The Hague, 1996). Ritter, 'Universal Rights Talk', 452, recalling Nietzsche, argues that 'Absent religious authorization, rights talk is reduced to a self-proclaimed moralism, the authority of which resounds no further than the authority of its speaker: The advocacy of human rights has consequently become culturally imperialistic and normatively impotent.'

[79] See e.g. Glenn, *Legal Traditions of the World*, 279–80, commenting on the attitudes of Asian religions.

moral consequences of governance but not more generally with its structure. Strands of Islamic thought and practice take a different view. Be that as it may, the idea that religion provides a starting point for the structuring of one's being and one's relationship to others can be taken as an accepted premiss for religious believers. This being so, religionists should be slow to reject the legitimacy of a religious ordering of society, albeit that many believers would dispute the need or extent to which this was necessary to give effect to a given pattern of religious belief.

Disagreements on the form of religious ordering equate to the second and third of our questions. It is not difficult to see that there is no generally accepted form of religion that is accepted on a 'universal' basis since there are, of course, many religions which compete for adherents. This observable fact is not affected by the claims of some religions to have unique and universal legitimacy or by others that no religion has universal legitimacy. Indeed, this merely reinforces the point. Similarly, it is equally clear that particular religious traditions that make claims to 'universality' are capable of adopting flexible approaches to the application of their religion in the light of regional, cultural, and other relevant factors.[80] In other words, the universalist claims of a particular religion do not seem to be threatened in any way by its not being 'universally' accepted as the only legitimate form of religious belief, even if it claims to be so.[81] Nor do religions that make such claims consider themselves threatened by their being interpreted and applied in a different fashion in different contexts. On the contrary, it is noteworthy that many religions see their ability to adapt to regional and cultural factors as a sign of their 'universal' appeal: their universality is made manifest in their diversity rather than in their homogeneity.

If, then, these are some of the general lessons that can be learned from a cursory glance at the experience of another universalist conception of the ordering of society, they show how impoverished—some might say immature—the 'universality' debate in the human rights context actually is. The problem seems to me to lie in the nature of its universal claim. The argument that the idea of human rights is of universal relevance tends to be seen by many in the human rights community as excluding any other forms of potentially universal and equally valid touchstones of legitimacy. In other words, there is a battle to be fought for the ground covered by our first question. The focus of religious universalism is, however, different.

---

[80] This takes place at many levels, such as in the use of local imagery in the presentation of the tenets of religious belief, in the performance of religious rites and ceremonies and in the response to broader questions of social relevance.

[81] Cf. I. Leigh, 'Towards a Christian Approach to Religious Liberty', in Beaumont (ed.), *Christian Perspectives on Human Rights*, 38, who points out that it is liberals who find this phenomenon disconcerting and that they 'can only succeed in reconciling mutually contradictory religious claims by stifling or diluting them in a way which they may find convincing but their adherents will not'.

The very substance of religious belief may leave open the possibility of there being other forms of principles which may legitimately bear upon the ordering of society. Indeed, religious believers might voluntarily concede this, choosing to place their emphasis on other aspects of religious belief, such as private spirituality, morality, or a focus on an afterlife. In short, although some religious believers might be disappointed or shocked by the lack of commitment to a religious conception of the ordering of society, many would be quite untroubled by it. On either view, believers would not see this as in any way threatening any claims they might hold for the 'universality' of their religious beliefs. While accepting the truth of their own religion—and rejecting that of others—universalist religions tend to make their universalism manifest through proselytism and the conversion of non-believers. This is best likened to attempts within a human rights framework to establish a uniform formulation of a right—our second question. Thus the essential thrust of the universalism of a religious believer lies in the propagation of their beliefs in the face of competing beliefs, rather than in the a priori exclusion of competing ideologies which may provide the motivation.[82]

Conclusion

It now becomes apparent why international human rights, religion, and the universality debate seem to have an uneasy relationship. As far as international human rights are concerned, religious beliefs present competing universalist ideologies which, by posing alternative approaches, do indeed threaten the universality of the idea of human rights. Religious belief must therefore be made subordinate to the human rights framework. Religious believers, however, rarely see it this way since they do not see diversity as a threat to the universality of their beliefs. If, as was argued at the start of this section, international human rights does itself no real favours by foreclosing debate on the legitimacy of its foundational claims to universality, religious believers do neither themselves nor the human rights framework any favours by not contesting that claim at the outset. For although it need not be contested in order to preserve their own claim to universality, that failure inevitably means that the role of religious belief becomes transmuted into the enjoyment of religious liberty as a human right, a very much more restricted and qualified thing.

---

[82] It must, of course, be recognized that this is a benign construction and there are many other possible manifestations of this impulse. Proselytism and conversion can take many different forms, ranging from the setting of examples and reasoned debate through various degrees of inducement and coercion, to extreme forms of violence and persecution. Similarly, the universalism in religion can easily be related to homogeneity in religion, leading to expulsions of non-believers from territories, all of which is seen as inimical from a human rights perspective. Whether it is inimical to the religious tradition is a question that can only be addressed from within that tradition.

RELIGIOUS LIBERTY AS A COLLECTIVE RIGHT

Julian Rivers

Introduction

The passage of the Human Rights Act 1998 in the United Kingdom provoked unexpected and vigorous opposition from a number of religious groups.[1] The government sought to placate the opposition by a single clause, which has now become section 13(1) of the Act: 'If a court's determination of any question arising under this Act might affect the exercise by a religious organisation (itself or its members collectively) of the Convention right to freedom of thought, conscience and religion, it must have particular regard to the importance of that right.'

The argument that this section is meaningless,[2] because it simply draws attention to a pre-existing right, ignores the dynamic nature of human rights jurisprudence. Section 13 requires the judiciary in the process of developing the case-law to pay particular attention to the collective aspects of religious liberty and to ensure that they are protected. Where there is a conflict between this interest and another, the presumption must be that the interest in collective religious liberty will prevail. The purpose of this paper is quite simply to address the obvious question: what is religious liberty as a collective right?[3]

Individualism and Collectivism under the European Convention on Human Rights

Aspects of collective religious liberty are protected under the European Convention on Human Rights (ECHR).[4] It is clear that religious associations can be 'non-governmental organisations' for the purposes of Article

---

[1] The debate and issues are considered in Julian Rivers, 'From Toleration to Pluralism: Religious Liberty and Religious Establishment under the United Kingdom's Human Rights Act', in R. Ahdar (ed.), *Law and Religion* (Aldershot, 2000). See also Peter Cumper, 'The Protection of Religious Rights under Section 13 of the Human Rights Act 1998', [2000] *Public Law* 254.

[2] See e.g. J. Wadham and H. Mountfield, *Blackstone's Guide to the Human Rights Act 1998* (London, 1998), 55.

[3] The classic argument for collective religious liberty is, of course, that of J. N. Figgis, *Churches in the Modern State*, 2nd edn., (London, 1914).

[4] See also, in respect of national minorities, Article 8 of the Council of Europe Framework Convention for the Protection of National Minorities (1995), which includes the right to establish 'religious institutions, organisations and associations'.

34 ECHR and thus as 'victims' have the right to bring individual applications alleging breaches of their human rights.[5] This is true, even if they are
part of an established Church, since these are treated as exercising non-
governmental functions.[6] It is also irrelevant whether the association has
legal personality or not.[7] This means that parts of larger organizations can
bring applications.[8] Where individuals have brought actions alleging that
states have failed to protect them from their own religious associations, the
Commission has consistently held that individual religious liberty is
protected by the ability to join and leave religious associations.[9] This effectively protects the liberty of the association to maintain its own religious
ethos. However, in spite of the recognition of collective religious liberty,
the case-law of the Convention organs has demonstrated an individualist
bias, at times to the neglect of serious issues of religious liberty.

THE ADMISSIBILITY OF COLLECTIVE APPLICATIONS

The Commission had initially taken the view that applications from religious organizations were inadmissible.[10] Since Article 9 only protected
individual interests in religious liberty, they could not be victims for the
purposes of Article 34. This untenable position was soon changed, but the
reasoning for allowing applications by religious associations is still
ambiguous: 'a church body is capable of possessing and exercising the
rights contained in Article 9(1) in its own capacity as a representative of its
members'. This formula reappears at regular intervals, but it is not clear
whether religious liberty is a right of the association itself, or whether the
association simply represents the common individual interests of its
members. In cases involving religious property, the collective element is
unavoidable, since in most cases such property is held by a religious organization as a legal person, or on trust for religious purposes. Thus in the
Holy Monasteries[11] case there was no question that the applicants were
the monasteries as corporate bodies. In *Serbo-Greek Orthodox Church in
Vienna v. Austria*,[12] which concerned the occupation of church premises in

---

[5] *X & Church of Scientology v. Sweden*, No. 7805/77, 16 DR 68 (5.5.79) and subsequent cases.
[6] *Holy Monasteries v. Greece* A 310 (9.12.94), para. 49.
[7] *Christian Association of Jehovah's Witnesses v. Bulgaria*, No. 28626/95, 90 DR 77
(3.7.97).
[8] See e.g. *Spetz v. Sweden*, No. 20402/92 (12.10.94).
[9] *X v. Denmark*, No. 7374/76 5 DR 157 (8.3.76); *E. & G.R. v. Austria*, 9781/82, 37
DR 42 (14.5.84); *Gottesmann v. Sweden*, No. 10616/83, 40 DR 284 (4.12.84); *Knudsen v.
Norway*, No. 11045/84, 42 DR 247 (8.3.85); *Karlsson v. Sweden* No. 12356/86, 57 DR 172
(8.9.88).
[10] *Church of X v. UK*, No. 3798/68, 29 CD 70 (17.12.68), 75. The Commission has
maintained its view that freedom of conscience could not be enjoyed by a collective body:
Verein Kontakt-Information-Therapie v. Austria, No. 11921/86, 57 DR 81 (12.10.88), 88.
[11] See n. 6.   [12] No. 13712/88 (2.4.90).

the aftermath of a church schism, the Commission accepted that the victim was the Church itself, and not the particular priests who would be the beneficiaries of the tenancy agreement in issue. In *ISKCON* v. *United Kingdom*[13] the reasoning of the Commission shows that it considered the primary victim of planning constraints on Bhaktivedanta Manor to be the International Society for Krishna Consciousness, and not the individual priests who also applied.

The distinction between individual and collective religious liberty at the admissibility stage would be trivial enough were it not for the fact that in some admissibility decisions the Commission has relied on the existence of breaches of individual liberty to deny standing to an association. This occurred in the recent *Scientology* decision,[14] in which the Commission reaffirmed a strand in the case-law stating that 'a corporate applicant cannot claim to be itself a victim of measures alleged to have interfered with the Convention rights of its individual members'. Where an association claimed to represent its members, it had to identify them and show it had received specific instructions from each of them, as their agent. This should be contrasted with *Christian Association of Jehovah's Witnesses* v. *Bulgaria*.[15] The Bulgarian government had refused to register the Jehovah's Witnesses as a recognized religion in Bulgaria, and various Jehovah's Witnesses suffered serious injustices as a result. The Association made an application in its own name, and the Bulgarian government tried to argue that standing should be denied, because the individuals claiming injustice were the real victims. However, the Commission was quite happy to accept the argument that the individual injustices were examples of the consequences of the failure to register the Association, which could plead a breach of religious liberty in its own right.

The root of the admissibility problem is that there will be many cases in which both the association and specific individuals will be directly affected by alleged breaches of human rights. In principle, it is wrong to strike out a good case at the admissibility stage simply because there may be a more appropriate victim, so long as the applicant is itself also sufficiently directly affected to be a victim. In other cases the Commission has shown much more appropriate flexibility. Thus in *Hautaniemi* v. *Sweden*,[16] which concerned the right of a Finnish-speaking congregation in the Church of Sweden to use a liturgy of the Finnish Lutheran Church, the Commission accepted that both the congregation (parish) and the minister were victims. The fact that the minister was a victim did not prevent the congregation's own application. Practically, of course, the best advice must be to join an association and the most directly affected individuals together.

---

[13] No. 20490/92, 76 DR 90 (8.3.94).
[14] *Scientology Kirche Deutschland e.V.* v. *Germany*, No. 36283/97 (7.4.97).
[15] No. 28626/95, 90 DR 77 (3.7.97).
[16] No. 24019/94, 85 DR 94 (11.4.96).

INDIVIDUALISM IN SUBSTANTIVE RELIGIOUS LIBERTY

The individualist bias affects not only issues of standing, but also matters of substance. Judge Martens drew attention to this in a concurring opinion in *Manoussakis*.[17] The Court had held that the conviction of the Jehovah's Witness applicants for operating a place of religious worship without government consent was unjustified in the circumstances. Martens pointed out that the issue was not so much that of injustice to these particular applicants, but the injustice caused to Jehovah's Witnesses and other religious minorities by the entire system for registering places of religious worship. Subsequent applications from Jehovah's Witnesses in Greece have shown the truth of this comment.[18]

The refusal of the Commission to entertain an application alleging a breach of Article 9 in *Kustannus* v. *Sweden*[19] is a clear example of a failure to recognize collective religious liberty. In this case the Swedish Freethinkers' Association had established a limited liability company to carry on its publishing and distribution function. The Association remained a majority shareholder in the new company. The company maintained that it had a humanist and atheist ethos, and that the provision under Swedish law that only individuals could be exempt from paying church tax on religious grounds was a breach of its Convention rights. It is clear that individuals required to pay church tax against their conscience enjoy the protection of Article 9.[20] The Commission held that it could not benefit from the protection of Article 9 because it was not a religious community and not a non-profit organization.[21] But why should not a group of like-minded people form a commercial company and seek to operate it according to their (and hence the organization's) corporate ethos?

However, perhaps the most conspicuous example of a neglect of collective religious liberty is the recent decision in *Serif* v. *Greece*.[22] Serif claimed to be the elected and true chief mufti of Rodopi in Thrace, in

[17] *Manoussakis* v. *Greece*, No. 18748/91 RJD 1996-IV 1346 (26.9.96), Concurring Opinion at para. 2.
[18] *Pentidis* v. *Greece*, No. 23238/94 (9.6.97); *Tsavachidis* v. *Greece*, No. 28802/95 (4.3.97).
[19] No. 20471/92 (15.4.96).
[20] *Darby* v. *Sweden* A 187. The Commission found a breach of Article 9; the Court preferred to deal with the case as impermissible discrimination in property law on grounds of residence (Art. 14 in connection with Art. 1 First Protocol) since non-members resident in Sweden were exempt from the tax. A state that gave no exemptions at all from a church tax would be in breach of Article 9.
[21] Thus reaffirming a consistent line in its decisions that religion and commerce are quite distinct. See *X and Church of Scientology* v. *Sweden*, 16 DR 68 (5.5.79); *Company X* v. *Switzerland*, 16 DR 85 (27.2.79).
[22] No. 38178/97 (14.12.99).

opposition to the government-appointed chief mufti. He was convicted of various criminal offences including usurping the functions of a minister of a known religion. He argued that this was a breach of his religious liberty and that of the Muslim community in Thrace who had elected him as their chief mufti. The Greek government's response was that in law the chief mufti was government-appointed. The Court of Human Rights accepted that Serif's religious liberty was infringed, and approached the problem by asking whether his conviction was necessary in a democratic society. They held that since allegations of his performing administrative functions (such as conducting weddings) were unsubstantiated, the only ground for his conviction was his wearing the clothes traditionally associated with the office, and issuing messages of spiritual guidance and encouragement. Even if he were not chief mufti, to convict somebody in those circumstances would be an unjustifiable breach of their liberty. In short, people have the right to pretend to be clergy if they wish. This misses the point entirely. The issue at the heart of this dispute was rather, who had the right in Greek law to appoint the chief mufti of Rodopi, and then, regardless of Greek domestic law, whether the Muslim community had the right under the European Convention collectively to elect their spiritual leader if they so wished. The Court ducked that central issue.

The Structure of Collective Religious Liberty

It is easy enough to notice that collective religious liberty is being under-emphasized within any given legal system; it is much harder to define the proper scope of collective religious liberty. The problem is partially obscured by the fact that Article 9 ECHR offers only a minimum level of protection, and that elements of the freedom of religious communities in a practical sense may be more properly protected by other articles instead. For this reason, it is more fruitful to focus primarily on domestic law, while keeping international obligations in mind. The problem can also be obscured by the need to reach decisions on specific controversial questions concerning the content and extent of collective religious rights. The primary purpose of this paper is rather to suggest an analytical framework for the discussion of collective religious liberty.

Collective religious liberty is not simply an aggregation of individual members' interests. Rather, it is the set of rights, immunities, privileges, and powers held by a religious association as such. Collective religious liberty in this sense is the liberty of a community of people sharing a common religious faith to organize themselves and structure their corporate life according to their own ethical and religious precepts. There are four basic elements in the protection of collective religious liberty.

RELIGIOUS COMMUNITIES AS ORDINARY LEGAL ASSOCIATIONS

If collective religious liberty is to be recognized at all, religious communities must be able to take the form of legal associations, whether incorporated or unincorporated. They must be able to benefit from all the powers that legal persons usually enjoy, such as owning property, trading for the purposes of the organization, employing people, suing and being sued. Problems with the legal status of the Catholic Church in Greece arose in the case of *Canea Catholic Church* v. *Greece*.[23] The Church was in dispute with neighbours over the demolition of a party wall and the construction of a window overlooking its property. The Appeal Court and the Court of Cassation denied the Church a remedy on the grounds that it had failed to fulfil the formalities for acquiring legal personality under Greek law. The ECtI IR held that in the light of the long-standing judicial and administrative practice assuming that the Catholic Church had legal personality without formal registration, there had been a breach of Article 6, and that any requirement that the Catholic Church register forthwith would be unreasonable as it might imply that the Church lacked personality before the date of incorporation. Given that the Church in question had existed since 1879 and the diocese (of Crete) since 1213, the Court could not see 'any plausible reason for the fact that in 1996 the Greek Catholic Church still does not enjoy a precise legal status'.[24]

A number of interesting issues are raised by the *Canea* case. There was considerable disagreement about whether the case fell under Article 9 or Article 6. A majority of the Commission went for Article 9 on the grounds that the ability to protect property associated with a manifestation of religion was a means of exercising that right. Since there was the possibility of acquiring legal personality under Greek law, there was no breach of Article 9 per se, but the insistence that the Catholic Church should now fulfil those formalities was, in the circumstances, discriminatory and a breach of Article 14 in connection with Article 9. While one can accept the general point about the relevance of Article 9 to the acquisition of legal personality and civil rights by religious associations, this was an ordinary property dispute between two neighbours, and the minority view on the Commission, subsequently adopted by the Court, that this was more properly an issue of civil rights (Article 6) is to be preferred.

Another interesting issue was whether the failure to recognize the Catholic Church as having public law (as distinct from private law) personality was discriminatory. Although, in general, the Commission and Court are prepared to accept that established majority churches may have special rights and privileges, the Jewish community in Greece also has public law status. Both the Commission and the Court took the view that

---

[23] No. 25528/94, RJD 1997-VIII 2843 (16.12.97).   [24] Para. 61.

Catholicism was one of three principal and long-standing forms of religious belief in Greece, and that the position of the Catholic Church was thus anomalous. However, the Court would go no further than 'noting' this fact, and explicitly left the choice of legal form for the Catholic Church open.[25]

Under English law, this core of collective religious liberty is in principle unproblematic. If a religious community is not content to remain an unincorporated association, it can become a company limited by guarantee, or it can generally establish trusts of the property for the purposes of the community. Some countries have schemes of special registration for religious associations, either as a prerequisite for the recognition of their legal status, or as a condition for the exercise of some of their functions. Where the community simply wants to exercise (collectively) the normal legal powers of any individual, it is hard to see that such schemes are justified.[26] At any rate, they must be no less onerous than for equivalent bodies with recreational or commercial objects.[27]

EXEMPTIONS FROM THE GENERAL LAW

In practice, disputes concerning the liberty of religious associations do not often turn on their being treated more restrictively than commercial, recreational, or other charitable associations. Rather, the disputes concern a claim for exemptions to be made on grounds of religious belief. The ethic that governs the general law is in some way at odds with the ethic of the religious community, and the general law is thereby experienced as oppressive. Recognizing religious liberty as a special human and constitutional right requires exemptions from the application of the general law to accommodate religious belief and practice. This does not mean that exemptions must always be granted whenever the religious interest is raised, because there will be times when society will want to insist on certain standards regardless of their incompatibility with some minority religious practice. This middle path approach of granting exemptions from the general law unless 'necessary in a democratic society' for the protection of certain important interests is exemplified by the structure of Article 9 ECHR. It is a way of steering a course between assimilation and accommodation.[28]

The decision to grant planning permission provides a good example of

[25] Para. 47.

[26] This appears to be the situation in some east European countries. Under the (English) Places of Worship Registration Act 1855, registration is not compulsory, but is a condition for the enjoyment of special privileges and powers.

[27] This does not mean that states may not on occasion be justified in banning certain religious organizations if their objects are fraudulent or oppressive.

[28] On the conflicting arguments for assimilation and accommodation, see S. Poulter, *Ethnicity, Law and Human Rights* (Oxford, 1998), esp. ch. 1.

the shift in reasoning brought about by the Human Rights Act. In deciding to grant planning permission,[29] planning authorities have to take into account 'any . . . material considerations'.[30] There are many relevant criteria,[31] and it would appear that in practice planning authorities take into account the religious needs of associations. Under the Human Rights Act 1998, planning authorities will certainly be required to take into account rights under Article 9 ECHR, whether by the section 3 route of an interpretation of the words 'material consideration' or by the section 6 route of the direct duty on public bodies.

In the case of *ISKCON* v. *Secretary of State for the Environment*,[32] the European Commission rejected an application of the International Society for Krishna Consciousness alleging a breach of Convention rights in respect of planning control over the development of Bhaktivedanta Manor. The manor had been acquired in 1973 as a theological college for Hindu priests, but over the years had become a centre for Hindu worship, attracting numbers far in excess of the original agreement. The planning authority issued an enforcement notice which, together with a refusal to grant planning permission for the new use, was upheld on appeal at every level.

The European Commission held that the religious liberty of ISKCON was restricted by the enforcement notice,[33] and that the issue was whether such a restriction was 'necessary in a democratic society'. That resolved itself into the question of whether adequate weight was given to the interest in religious liberty, and whether the decision of the planning authority was proportionate to the legitimate interest upheld. Since detailed consideration had been given to the special religious circumstances of the case, the application failed on the facts at this point.

The decision of the European Commission in ISKCON makes clear what is implicit in the structure of the ECHR. Once an interest has been identified as falling within a Convention right, it is not simply one consideration to be taken into account with all other valid considerations; rather it is given privileged status. In terms of planning law, the interest of a religious community in being able lawfully to carry out religious activities on its premises is not simply one material consideration to be balanced

---

[29] It should be obvious that religious considerations are not relevant to the question of whether there has been a material change of use for the purposes of s. 55(1) Town and Country Planning Act 1990. Thus in *Hussain* v. *Secretary of State for the Environment* (1971) 23 P & CR 330 (ritual slaughter of chickens not incidental to use as retail shop) the dispute should not have been whether planning permission was necessary—it clearly was—but whether it should be granted.

[30] Town and Country Planning Act 1990 s. 70(2).

[31] See e.g. the exposition in M. Grant (ed.), *Encyclopaedia of Planning Law and Practice* (London, 2000), paras. 10.01–70.22/1/1.

[32] No. 20490/92, 76 DR 90 (8.3.94).

[33] Strictly speaking, it was infringed by the failure to grant permission for a change of use.

against all the others, but is to be limited only to the extent necessary to protect the rights and interests of others as expressed in the other ordinary planning considerations. Decision-taking is restructured to create a presumption in favour of the enjoyment of Convention rights, with other legitimate interests only pursuable in proportionate manner.

In the context of employment, religious liberty—both individual and collective—is protected in principle by freedom of contract.[34] For example, ministers of religion are not treated as being appointed under a contract of employment, but may bring an ordinary private law action for breach of contract.[35] The content of that contract is determined by the rules of the employer organization. But as employment law increasingly imposes ethical standards on employers that can conflict with their own religious ethos, collective religious liberty as a distinct right becomes significant. Thus the Sex Discrimination Act 1975 contains an exemption for posts and qualifications restricted to one sex in the cases of employment for the purposes of an organized religion.[36]

However, the limited nature of this exemption was made apparent by the case of *O'Neill* v. *Governors of St. Thomas More School*.[37] A religious education teacher at a Roman Catholic school had become pregnant by a priest, and she was dismissed from her post. The school conceded unfair dismissal, and the Employment Appeals Tribunal also found that there had been sex discrimination. This appears to take inadequate account of the desire of the school to maintain a certain religious ethos, and should be contrasted with *Board of Governors of St. Matthias Church of England School* v. *Crizzle*.[38] The Employment Appeal Tribunal accepted that a requirement that the head teacher be a 'committed communicant Christian' was potentially discriminatory but justified for the purposes of section 1(1)(b) of the Race Relations Act.[39] In this case, the policy of the education system to preserve schools with a distinct religious ethos made it relatively easy for the governors to establish a good reason for the discrimination. As

---

[34] The Convention organs have increasingly relied on freedom of contract to protect individual religious liberty: compare *Ahmad* v. *United Kingdom* (1982) 4 EHRR 126 with *Stedman* v. *United Kingdom* (1997) 23 EHRR CD 168.

[35] *Davies* v. *Presbyterian Church of Wales* [1986] 1 WLR 323, *Santokh Singh* v. *Guru Nanak Gurdwara* [1990] ICR 309.

[36] S. 19. This section has been amended by the Sex Discrimination (Gender Reassignment) Regulations 1999 to take account of the decision of the ECJ in *R.* v. *S & Cornwall County Council* C-13/94 [1996] IRLR 347 that the Equal Treatment Directive covered discrimination on the grounds of transsexualism. Organized religions may refuse to employ a female–male transsexual on the same grounds that they may refuse to employ a woman.

[37] [1997] ICR 33.

[38] [1993] ICR 401. The matter is now clearly regulated by statute; see School Standards and Framework Act 1998, s. 60(4).

[39] The weakness of *Mandla* v. *Dowell Lee* [1983] 2 AC 548, is that there may be cases not covered by the Race Relations Act where direct religious discrimination is justified.

far as employment in schools is concerned, the matter is now clearly regulated by a complex and careful statutory regime.[40]

The European Commission's current proposal for a directive establishing a General Framework for Equal Treatment in Employment and Occupation represents a potentially serious threat to collective religious liberty. It forbids all discrimination, direct, indirect, or potential, on grounds of racial or ethnic origin, religion or belief, disability, age, or sexual orientation. Article 4(1) creates a general exemption for 'genuine occupational qualifications', and Article 4(2) creates a specific exemption for 'public or private organisations which pursue directly and essentially the aim of ideological guidance in the field of religion or belief with respect to education, information and the expression of opinions'. For such organizations, a difference of treatment based on a relevant characteristic related to religion or belief does not constitute discrimination where the particular occupational activity within the organization is directly and essentially related to its aim, and where it constitutes a genuine occupational qualification.

It is hard to see why Article 4(2) is necessary at all, because it appears that religious organizations are being put under a more restrictive regime than other organizations. A single exemption for genuine occupational qualifications would cover all necessary exemptions. Furthermore, Article 4(2) is incredibly narrowly drawn. It would appear to be incompatible with section 60(5) School Standards and Framework Act 1998; it would make it difficult to insist that a church secretary be a Christian or the cleaner of a mosque a Muslim. Human rights are an integral part of the general principles of law of the European Union, whose observance the European Court of Justice ensures. Respect for human rights is a condition of the lawfulness of all Community acts.[41] The European Human Rights Commission has consistently and correctly held that where an individual is in dispute with their Church, the liberty of the individual is protected by their freedom to leave the organization.[42] Even if one shares the refusal of the European Human Rights Commission to extend the benefits of religious liberty to commercial organizations, at least non-profit-making organizations have the right under Article 9 ECHR to employ people consistently with their collective religious ethos. A good case can be made that Article 4(2) is unlawful as it stands.

THE PRIVILEGES OF RELIGIOUS ASSOCIATIONS

The new protection of human rights contained in the Human Rights Act

---

[40] School Standards and Framework Act 1998, s. 60.
[41] Opinion 2/94 on Accession by the Community to the ECHR [1996] ECR I-1759.
[42] See n. 8.

1998 is not to jeopardize existing rights and freedoms already enjoyed in the United Kingdom.[43] The scope of collective religious liberty is not limited to the rights enjoyed under Article 9, but also embraces further aspects protected by English law. As well as privileges such as access to prisons, hospitals, and educational chaplaincies, religious associations are granted tax exemptions, and may soon have formal representation in the legislature.

The key privilege associated with charitable status is its attendant financial advantages. Of course, a religious association need not be a religion for the purposes of the relevant law, so long as it can satisfy one of the other recognized heads of charity law, but cases in which plausibly religious trusts or associations have been denied charitable status are familiar from the case-law. One thinks of the trust for private masses in *Gilmour* v. *Coats*,[44] and most recently the denial of charitable status to the Scientologists by the Charity Commissioners.[45]

The case-law on the third head of charitable status, 'advancement of religion', demonstrates a commitment to a fairly narrow view of religion, although just how narrow is disputed. To have a religion you have to believe in a supreme being[46] and you have to worship it.[47] In short, your God must be infinite and personal, and to the extent that your God is not infinite and personal, you are going to have difficulty showing that you have a religion. So, animism, ancestor-worship, and various forms of paganism are going to struggle, because their gods are personal, but not infinite—they don't worship *a supreme being*. And scientology, freemasonry, theosophy, Zen Buddhism, and humanism are going to struggle because their gods are infinite and not personal—they don't *worship* a supreme being. In short, the test presupposes a Christian conception of religion, or at least, an Islamo-Judaeo-Christian conception of religion.

It is assumed that trusts with charitable objects confer a public benefit unless the contrary is shown, but there is some dispute as to what amounts to a public benefit. It has been suggested that the element of public benefit is provided by the mixing of members of religious associations with the general public,[48] and there is some support in the case-law for this rationale.[49] While this explains the outcome in *Gilmour* v. *Coats*, it does not explain the refusal of charitable status to private religious ceremonies. The drift of reasoning in the cases since *Gilmour* v. *Coats* is to require public

---

[43] Human Rights Act 1998, s. 11.   [44] [1949] AC 426.
[45] Decision of 17 Nov. 1999.
[46] *Re South Place Ethical Society* [1980] 1 WLR 1565.
[47] *R.* v. *Registrar General, ex parte Segerdal* [1970] 1 QB 430.
[48] J. Martin, in Hanbury and Martin, *Modern Equity*, 15th edn., (London, 1997), 418.
[49] Wickens V-C in *Cocks* v. *Manners* (1871) LR 12 Eq 574, 585, referred to both direct and indirect public edification. See also Cross J in *Neville Estates* v. *Madden* [1962] Ch. 832, 853.

access to the practices of the religious association, because the law assumes that a religious service is beneficial to all those who attend it.

In theory, it is possible for a religious association to be charitable under the fourth head, other purposes beneficial to the community, but where the benefit is intangible, the courts require a reasonable consensus of fair-minded people to accept the beneficial nature of the practice. This test is unlikely to be satisfied by new religious movements. In the case of Scientology's rejected application, the Charity Commissioners held that it did not engage in worship or veneration, it was not entitled to the presumption of public benefit because of the newness of its practices and public concern about their impact, and that the core activities were private rather than public. There was no consensus that its practice of 'auditing' was generally beneficial.

The House of Lords is unique among democracies in providing formal representation of an established Church in a legislative chamber. In practice, the representation of religious concerns in the House of Lords has been expanded by ad hoc appointments of leaders from other denominations[50] and the willingness of individual peers to speak, unofficially, for the community of which they are a member. Clearly there is no way in which Article 9 ECHR can be read to include a right of all religious communities to such representation, and while the existence of twenty-six bishops of the Church of England is seen simply as a matter of establishment, it is arguable that the issue is not even within the ambit of Article 9 for the purposes of Article 14. However, it is clear that the bishops see their role not as narrowly Anglican, but as bringing a broadly Christian, even generally religious, perspective to bear on debate.[51]

The first stage of reform[52] to the House of Lords has left the position of the Church of England bishops unchanged, with the government referring the whole matter of religious representation to the Royal Commission.[53] In its report, the Commission emphasized the importance of including people capable of articulating a range of philosophical, moral, and religious viewpoints, both religious and secular, and it suggested that the proposed Appointments Commission should have regard to that principle.[54] A substantial majority of the Royal Commission considered that in addition there should continue formal religious representation, but that it should be broadened beyond the Church of England.[55] In their view, there should be at least five members explicitly appointed to represent non-Christian

---

[50] e.g. Lord Jacobovitz, former chief rabbi, and the late Lord Soper, former convener of the Methodist Conference.

[51] Church of England's submission to the Royal Commission on the House of Lords, cited at para.15.10 of the Report.

[52] House of Lords Act 1999.

[53] Royal Commission on Reform of the House of Lords, Cm. 4534 (Jan. 2000).

[54] Paras. 15.4–15.6; Recommendation 107.

[55] Paras. 15.7–15.9; Recommendation 108.

religious communities in the United Kingdom and the twenty-six seats currently allocated to bishops of the Church of England should be redistributed among all Christian denominations. Five seats would go to representatives from Scotland, Wales, and Northern Ireland, five to non-Anglican English denominations, leaving sixteen to the Church of England.[56]

Of course, the selection of individuals is not entirely straightforward; some religions do not have a hierarchical structure, and both the Roman Catholic Church and the Church of Scotland have difficulties with clergy holding public office. The Royal Commission recognized these difficulties, but suggested that the Appointments Commission would be able to negotiate an acceptable solution with the groups concerned. There will be no formal right of representation on the part of any one religious group, but a duty on the Appointments Commission to secure equable representation, which means that in practice (for example) Roman Catholics in England and Muslims generally are guaranteed a couple of representatives each. The Church of England will also need to rethink its representation, in that application of the seniority rule to the eleven[57] remaining seats would give each diocesan bishop only a couple of years or so in the House. The Royal Commission encouraged the Church of England to rethink its representation with the aim of ensuring the standard fifteen-year term of office.[58]

The Royal Commission recognized that demographic changes and patterns of adherence should be reflected in adjustments to the pattern of religious representation proposed.[59] This raises the vexed question of what equality means in this context. The statistical basis of the Royal Commission's report is far from clear, but it contains two tables, one suggesting that there are 2–3 million non-Christian religious believers in the United Kingdom and just under 32 million baptized Christians in England. Given that England's Christians are to have twenty-one members (or roughly one per 1.5 million) it is hard to see the basis on which non-Christians have five members (or roughly one per 500,000). Jews and Sikhs are certain to be represented, the Greek Orthodox, with a community only marginally smaller, almost certainly not. The division of Christian representation between the four countries is based on population, not membership of churches, which is curious, since membership (on the basis of baptism) is probably higher in Northern Ireland and lower in Scotland. If they had based the division on church membership, they might have found it easier to justify the obvious political need for two representatives from Northern Ireland.[60]

---

[56] Paras. 15.10–15.23; Recommendations 109–13.

[57] The archbishops of Canterbury and York, and the bishops of London, Durham, and Winchester, sit by right.

[58] Paras. 15.27–15.28; Recommendation 115.　　　　[59] Recommendation 114.

[60] Para. 15.23.

All this assumes that equality is to be understood in the sense of proportionality, and this is arguably inappropriate, given the small numbers
involved. Even if it were accepted in principle, the concept of membership
varies from religion to religion. The Commission makes a brief attempt to
justify using baptism as the criterion for Christian representation;[61] it does
not begin to analyse on what basis it considers there to be 300,000 Jews or
1–1.5 million Muslims. However, the purpose of the reform is to ensure
that religious communities have a voice, and this could have been better
ensured by establishing a minimum threshold for representation, with the
remainder of the seats split roughly proportionately. A threshold of (say)
100,000 would bring Buddhists into the House, as it would the smaller
Christian denominations.

RELIGIOUS COMMUNITIES AND PUBLIC FUNCTIONS

Many religious communities carry out social functions now also regulated
by the state. They educate, marry, and bury people. They resolve disputes
and run hospitals. This raises questions about the relationship between
the 'religious' and the 'secular' activity. On one model, the two forms
exist in parallel—a neutral legal form precedes or follows the religious
ceremony. However, the right to collective religious liberty is better
protected in general by granting legal effect to the religious form itself,
since the law is then taking seriously the spiritual significance attached to
the activity by believers. The final level of collective religious liberty
involves the recognition that at times religious communities carry out the
same functions as the state, and that their performance of those functions
should be granted the same legal status and effect as the equivalent state
performance.

One of the more arcane corners of English law is the status granted to
Christian names. A Christian name is a forename given in the course of
Christian baptism.[62] In *Re Parrott*,[63] it was held by Vaisey J that a gift in a
will conditional on the beneficiary's changing his name was void, because
a Christian name could only be changed on confirmation by a bishop, by
Act of Parliament, or by addition on adoption. Thus a Christian name,
unlike any other name, cannot be changed by deed poll. All this is in practice irrelevant, since any name assumed by use and reputation is valid for
the purposes of legal identification, and if one wishes to register a change
of name, a certificate is filed on the register to the effect that
'Notwithstanding the decision of Vaisey J. in *re Parrott* . . . the applicant

---

[61] Para. 15.19.
[62] What follows probably applies to names given in the course of any baptism by water
in the name of the Trinity. See *Kemp* v. *Wickes* 3 Phill 264, 276.
[63] *In re Parrott, Cox* v. *Parrott* [1946] 1 Ch. 183.

desires the enrolment to proceed.'[64] The system of birth registration and the possibility of executing a deed poll function as a neutral system of name allocation applicable to all regardless of belief.[65] It is hard to see that collective religious liberty requires special recognition to be given to religious naming ceremonies.

Marriage is, of course, the central issue demanding consideration under this head. The problems are well canvassed in the literature.[66] In theory, it is possible for people to get married according to their own religious rites; in practice, the system only appears to work well for Christian denominations and Jews. One of the causes may have been the definition of religious worship under the Places of Worship Registration Act 1855, which raises similar issues as the definition of religion for purposes of charity law. This problem has not existed for the last decade, in that marriages can now be celebrated in a wide variety of places.[67]

The law relating to burial and cremation raises a few questions of religious liberty, both the liberty of the Church of England[68] and of other religions. There are no restrictions on the right to operate a private burial ground other than those arising from the law of nuisance along with health and safety regulations. Indeed, a gift to maintain a Quaker burial ground has been held a valid charitable gift,[69] and one can assume that the same would apply to any other religion recognized by charities law. An element of religious pluralism was introduced by the Burial Act 1853, which required burial authorities to maintain part of their land as unconsecrated, and to allot part of the unconsecrated land for the use of other religious denominations. The current legal regime is governed by the Local Authorities Cemetery Order 1977, which follows the same principle of allotting portions of cemeteries according to religious beliefs,[70] and includes a power on the part of a religious group to specify that ashes not be scattered in 'their' area.[71] Two areas of discrimination still appear on the face of the legislation. Article 5(5) appears only to permit the use of Christian burial rites outside of any allotted area, and Article 13 gives the relevant diocesan bishop a veto over inappropriate memorials in consecrated areas, but no equivalent powers to other denominations or religions with respect to allotted areas.

---

[64] *Personal Property* para. 1273 N. 8 in *Halsbury's Laws of England*, 4th edn., vol. 35 (London, 1994). It is hard to see why that should not suffice as a change of name for the purposes of a conditional testamentary gift.

[65] In any case, it is arguable whether Christian baptism is essentially a ceremony of name allocation.

[66] See C. Hamilton, *Family, Law and Religion* (London, 1995), ch. 2; A. Bradney, *Religion, Rights and Laws* (Leicester, 1993), ch. 3.

[67] See the Marriage (Registration of Buildings) Act 1990.

[68] Space prevents a discussion of the Church of England's powers and duties regarding burial. See N. Doe, *The Legal Framework of the Church of England* (Oxford, 1996), ch. 14.

[69] *In re Manser, AG v. Lucas* [1905] 1 Ch. 68.   [70] Art. 5(1)(b).

[71] Art. 5(6).

The right to establish and operate a school is essentially a matter of private law, and many religious groups make use of this right to run schools according to their own ethos. Assuming that the school is approved by HM Inspectors, parents can fulfil their duty to send their school-age children to school by sending them to such a private school. Problems in getting approval are rarely litigated.[72]

In theory, there is nothing to stop a school established by a private individual being subsequently brought into the state system.[73] However, the practical requirement that the secretary of state be satisfied of the need for the new school will mean that only larger groups of like-minded people will be able to achieve state funding. In that sense, the ability to run a school according to a certain religious ethos is a matter of collective liberty.

The long-running campaign to bring some Islamic primary schools within the system was finally successful in January 1998, and that year also saw the creation of a new statutory framework for the regulation of state schools with a religious character. The School Standards and Framework Act 1998, together with relevant regulations, contains a new designation procedure whereby the secretary of state can identify a school as having a religious character.[74] The designation procedure does not affect the religious character of a school, which is a matter of fact, but it impacts in a number of ways on the life of the school. In particular it affects the form of religious education[75] and collective worship,[76] staffing matters,[77] pupil admission,[78] and the official description of school ethos.[79]

The regulations contain a number of criteria by which a school may be designated religious, principally the presence of a foundation governor specifically to represent the interests of one or more religions or religious denominations,[80] or the fact that the premises were initially provided for the school on trust for the provision of education in accordance with the tenets of one or more religions or religious denominations.[81] The regulations contain a two-phase designation scheme. By 1 September 1999 the secretary of state was to have prepared a list designating all existing schools appropriately, and then a similar procedure applies for the desig-

---

[72] An exception concerns the failure of a Belz Hasidic Jewish school at Clapton Common to get approval. See R. v. *The Secretary of State for Education and Science, ex parte Talmud Torah Machzikei Hadass School Trust* (1985) *The Times* 12 Apr., Lexis transcript.

[73] This is more or less what happened with the Islamia school in Brent established by Yusuf Islam (aka Cat Stevens).

[74] School Standards and Framework Act 1998 s. 69 and the Religious Character of Schools (Designation Procedure) Regulations 1998 SI 1998, 2535.

[75] SSFA 1998, s. 69 and Schedule 19.

[76] SSFA 1998, s. 70 and Schedule 20.

[77] SSFA 1998, ss. 58–60. Some of these issues were also determined by the course of the debate on the Human Rights Bill 1997–8.

[78] SSFA 1998, s. 91.

[79] SSFA 1998, Schedule 12.

[80] Regulations 5(1)(a) and 9(6)(a).

[81] Regulations 5(1)(c) and 9(6)(c).

nation of new schools and correction of errors and omissions in the original designation.

The regulations contain consultation requirements with the Church of England, the Church in Wales, the Roman Catholic Church, the Methodist Church, the Free Church Federal Council, the Seventh-Day Adventist Church, the Board of Deputies of British Jews, and the Association of Muslim Schools. Furthermore, the current lists of designated schools only contain Christian, Jewish, and Muslim schools.[82] However, there is nothing in the new statutory scheme to prevent a school with a different religious ethos from being designated as such, the only limit being that one must be able to identify the religion or religious denomination in question. It is possible that disputes about the meaning of religion may arise in this context, although the practical requirements of establishing sufficient parental demand may prevent this.

The Privileges and Powers of Religious Associations under the European Convention on Human Rights

The paucity of case-law under the ECHR means that any attempt to map its requirements onto the structure of collective religious liberty must proceed with some caution. It is suggested, however, that the basic contours of the ECHR's requirements are tolerably plain. The right to form a legal person and to be exempt from onerous general laws is governed by Article 9. This raises a threshold question: what counts as a religion and a manifestation of religion for the purposes of Article 9, paragraph 1? It also raises a justification question: when is it 'necessary' to limit such activity in the public interest as set out in Article 9, paragraph 2?

Article 9 does not give religious associations a substantive right to any particular privilege or power, which is within the discretion of states, and varies considerably. However, Article 14 in connection with Article 9 requires religious non-discrimination in the grant of these privileges. In fact, cases are extremely rare on this point.[83] One exception is *Iglesia Bautista El Salvador* v. *Spain*.[84] In this case a Protestant church in Valencia claimed that the imposition of property tax on its premises while Catholic churches were exempted from such requirements was a breach of its religious liberty and the requirement of non-discrimination. The

---

[82] Designation of Schools having a Religious Character (England) Order 1999, SI 1999, 2432; Designation of Schools having a Religious Character (Wales) Order 1999, SI 1999, 1814.

[83] *Spetz* v. *Sweden* No. 20402/92 (12.10.94) indirectly concerned the right of a Pentecostal Church to carry out legally effective marriages, but the case was not argued on the basis of Article 14 in connection with Article 9, and the matter was not discussed from this aspect.

[84] No. 17522/90, 72 DR 256 (11.1.92).

Catholic exemption arose from a concordat between Spain and the Holy See. The Commission rejected the application on the grounds, firstly, that Article 9 gives no right to special tax exemptions for religious bodies. Secondly, they held that the distinction in treatment between Protestants and Catholics did not amount to discrimination since the Catholic Church represented a majority of the population, and the tax exemption was part of an agreement whereby the Catholic Church would make its cultural heritage available to the general population. For current purposes it is significant that the Commission appears to assume that the tax exemption was within the broad ambit of Article 9 for the purposes of non-discrimination; the only real issue was whether discrimination had actually taken place. Once again, threshold questions arise as to what counts as a religion for the purposes of non-discrimination. The justification question is somewhat different. Article 14 does not prevent the drawing of all religious distinctions; it does require that such distinctions be 'objective and reasonable'.[85]

As we have seen, English law tends to be restrictive in the variety of religious associations it grants special privileges and powers to. It is by no means clear that this is inconsistent with the ECHR. On one hand, there seems to be a determined refusal by Convention organs to consider whether New Religious Movements are religions for the purposes of Articles 9 or 14;[86] on the other hand humanism and pacifism are included, at least for the purposes of individual right.[87] Since the mere definition of religion is never conclusive of an issue (except for the activity of the illimitable *forum internum*), there is no reason for not adopting a broad initial definition. The question then becomes whether restrictive laws fulfil a 'pressing social need' and whether the rules that control access to privileges and public law powers are 'objective and reasonable'.

When it comes to distinguishing between religious groups, the least problematic criterion of all is size. Where the right in question depends on the allocation of a limited resource, such as seats in a legislature, or determining the ethos of an entire school, then requiring the religion to have a certain membership is practically indispensable. Another criterion found more commonly in continental Europe is formal representativeness and hence hierarchy. The issue with Islamic education in France and Germany, for example, is who can speak authoritatively and enter into legal relations for the Islamic community. In the United Kingdom we tend—quite

---

[85] It should be noted that the provision of education is also affected by Article 2 First Protocol.

[86] The issue has been avoided in the case of Scientology, Druidism, and the 'Divine Light Centre'. See D. J. Harris, M. O'Boyle and C. Warbrick, *Law of the European Convention on Human Rights* (London, 1995), 357–8. It was assumed that freedom of religion was in issue in the case of 'Universal Life' (*Universelles Leben* v. *Germany*, No. 29745/96 (7.11.96)), which, however, sees itself as a Christian group.

[87] *Arrowsmith* v. *UK*, No. 7050/75 19 DR 5 (12.10.78).

correctly—to seek pragmatic solutions to such problems of organizational structure. This is particularly apparent in the Wakeham Commission's report, and is also implicit in the system for designating schools with a religious character.

Another criterion that appears regularly in this area is that of public access. The definition of public benefit for the purposes of charitable status and the requirements for registration as a place of religious worship mean that members of the public must be able to attend and observe ceremonies without themselves being committed to the religion they are observing. This requirement of public accessibility seems unobjectionable from the point of view of Article 14 ECHR. It is a quid pro quo for the grant of fiscal privileges, and is not specific to any one religion. But what are the reasons for adopting it? Firstly, instead of simply assuming that the impact of any religion on general society will be beneficial, it enables the public to make up their own mind about the value of the practices in question. It enables individuals to be eclectic in their choice of religious commitment. Secondly, it imposes a measure of potential accountability on the organization, since outsiders can look to see what is going on.

None of these criteria is religiously neutral. Not every belief system has large numbers of adherents; not every belief system has a hierarchical organization; not every belief system accepts that it is good for individuals to make up their own mind about each element of the religion in question; not every belief system accepts that the discipline of public scrutiny is a good thing. The difficulty facing liberal democracies is that while wanting to avoid questions of religious truth, they are forced to make judgements about the relative value of religious beliefs. A commitment to the first two elements of collective religious liberty simply requires a refusal to use state force to modify the behaviour of those who sincerely believe in the rightness of their actions, unless such force is strictly necessary 'in the interests of public safety, for the protection of public order, health or morals, or for the protection of the rights and freedoms of others' (Article 9 paragraph 2 ECHR). By contrast, the granting of special privileges requires a positive assessment of the value of the religion's impact on society, while the right to exercise public law powers presupposes a certain consistency between the ethos of the religious community and that of society at large. In that sense, as one moves through the different elements of collective religious liberty identified here, so the criteria to be adopted in determining the application of each right become themselves more obviously religious in character.

Conclusions

There is a tendency in both the theoretical literature and the case-law to conceive of religious liberty as an individual right. This paper has suggested that an important part of religious liberty is the freedom to join and leave religious communities, which have their own collective identity, their own legal personality, their own legal privileges and powers. The attempt to translate issues of religious liberty into issues of individual liberty alone denatures the subject matter. Furthermore, we should be particularly cautious that the introduction of the ECHR through the mechanism of the Human Rights Act 1998 does not result in a devaluing of elements of religious liberty not protected by Article 9 or the other rights. The ECHR contains a set of minimum standards. In the area of collective religious liberty, the United Kingdom has, in some respects, gone beyond those minimum standards. The practical difficulty is to know how far to extend existing privileges and powers. And the problem with the Human Rights Act is that it imposes a structure of rationality on such an exercise which may be impossible to satisfy.

CLASHING RIGHTS, EXEMPTIONS, AND OPT-OUTS: RELIGIOUS LIBERTY AND 'HOMOPHOBIA'

Ian Leigh

Introduction

The purpose of this paper is to consider the means of resolving the potential clash between two emergent rights: the rights to equal respect and non-discrimination irrespective of sexual orientation and freedom of religious belief. The need for such resolution is pressing in view of current demands in the United Kingdom to legislate on both issues.

The rate of change, especially in public pronouncements on (and, perhaps, in public attitudes to) homosexuality risks leaving people with traditional religious objections to the morality of same-sex intercourse exposed to legal and informal sanctions for holding or expressing those views. In a short space of time British society has moved from the official position where homosexual behaviour was not approved but was officially tolerated in private between consenting adults, to the present climate in which public expression of the view that homosexual behaviour is morally wrong is likely to be condemned as 'homophobia'. In the process the subtle distinctions within the range of graduated responses that a liberal society might adopt to questions of sexual orientation are in danger of being neglected.

In legal terms those graduated responses can perhaps be categorized in the following way: decriminalization of homosexual behaviour;[1] removal of public discrimination;[2] legal recognition of same-sex unions;[3] prohibition of private discrimination; discrimination or sanctions permitted by public authorities against individuals professing or holding 'homophobic' views; criminalization of 'homophobic hate speech' or sexual orientation equality 'denial'.[4] This is a scale which progresses from treating sexual orientation as a private matter towards regarding the elimination of

---

[1] Sexual Offences Act 1967; see further n. 16 below.
[2] e.g. the lifting of the ban on homosexuals and lesbians serving in the armed forces following the ruling from the European Court of Human Rights in *Smith and Grady* v. *UK* (2000) 29 EHRR 493; *Lustig-Prean and Beckett* v. *UK* (2000) 29 EHRR 548.
[3] Only the Liberal Democrats among major UK political parties favour such a move: *The Times*, 19 Sept. 2000.
[4] This phase is highly conjectural and, in view of the antipathy of the United Kingdom to hate speech laws in the realm of race and Holocaust denial, it seems unnecessary to discuss it further. The Netherlands, however, has taken this step in its General Equal Treatment Act 1994.

perceived prejudice and discrimination against homosexuals and lesbians as a goal of public policy requiring the coercive and symbolic use of law. Different considerations arise at each stage: arguments which may justify decriminalization, for example, do not necessarily justify legal recognition of same-sex unions or the introduction of sexual orientation discrimination legislation. Similarly, opposition to some of these measures can be consistent with acquiescence in others. The label 'homophobic' is far too monochrome to capture these nuances.

Attempts, whether by a public authority or a private employer, to deal with what it perceives to be 'homophobia' can too easily be perceived by the persons affected as oppressive discrimination against their religious beliefs.[5] Nothing in UK law currently requires public authorities to impose sanctions against private individuals professing or holding 'homophobic' views or, conversely, prevents them (or private individuals) from doing so. Although the decriminalization of dissent and non-conformity and the abolition of legislative religious discrimination were completed by the end of the nineteenth century, religious discrimination, whether by public authorities or by private organizations, has yet to be made unlawful (except in Northern Ireland). Several current developments raise the possibility, however: the implementation of the Human Rights Act, the signature of the Twelfth Protocol to the Convention, proposals for the reform of discrimination law, and a recent European directive.

It is not hard to see how, when we move beyond simple decriminalization and the removal of public discrimination in the cases of religious liberty and equal treatment irrespective of sexual orientation, the possibility may arise of conflict between these rights. The potential for conflict can be seen in the contemporary controversy over two recent law reform proposals, which are discussed in greater depth below. The first is the proposed abolition of the prohibition on the promotion of homosexuality by local education authorities—the notorious 'section 28'. Secondly, following enlargement of its powers under the Amsterdam Treaty, the European Council of Ministers has passed an equal treatment directive, to be implemented by member states by December 2003.[6] This directive aims

---

[5] For example, in Dec. 1999 a Christian cable and satellite television channel (the 'God Channel') was fined £20,000 by the Independent Television Commission (ITC) for four breaches of the Commission's Advertising Code. One of the infringements involved a passage (of fifteen seconds' duration in a presentation of twenty-eight minutes promoting a forthcoming conference) in which homosexuality was referred to as 'an abomination' (quoting from the Book of Leviticus in the King James Version). The Channel argued that, however unpopular such a view might be, it was a protected manifestation of religious belief under Article 9 of the ECHR and, moreover, that its freedom of expression under Article 10 was at stake. The ITC found that the passage was 'grossly offensive' to public feeling (ITC Determination, 20 Dec. 1999).

[6] Council Directive 2000/78/EC of 27 Nov. 2000 Establishing a General Framework for Equal Treatment in Employment and Occupation. For the Commission's earlier draft, see 25.11.99 COM (1999) 565 final 1999/02225 (CNS).

to combat discrimination in employment based on racial or ethnic origin, religion or belief, disability, age, or sexual orientation. The directive again raises the issue of 'clashing rights'.

Before we reach detailed examination of these issues, however, it is helpful to clarify the basis on which sexual orientation equality rights are claimed and how this gives rise to potential conflict.

Sexual Orientation and Human Rights

Those who claim that there is a human right to pursue one's sexual orientation commonly do so on one (or both) of two grounds: personal autonomy and privacy or equality.[7] Each of these is, of course, disputed by opponents of such rights, and the cause of disagreement goes to the heart of the contested nature of sexual orientation.[8] Proponents of rights not to be discriminated against on grounds of sexual orientation are also, however, to some extent locked in the same dilemma about the contested nature of orientation, and this is reflected in their espousal of two partially inconsistent grounds.[9]

The heart of the dispute is about whether sexual orientation is a fixed and immutable personal characteristic. If so, the principle that homosexuals and lesbians should not suffer discrimination can be seen as comparable to the legal regulation of sex and race discrimination, and the equality ground for sexual orientation rights is given credence.

However, the 'immutable characteristic' argument does not enjoy widespread popularity even among those sympathetic to 'gay rights'—among academic writers a socially constitutive view of sexuality is dominant.[10]

---

[7] See generally E. Heinze, *Sexual Orientation: A Human Right* (Dordrecht, 1995); N. Bamforth, *Sexuality, Morals and Justice* (London, 1996); R. Wintemute, *Sexual Orientation and Human Rights: The US Constitution, the ECHR and the Canadian Charter* (Oxford, 1995).

[8] Unfortunately, it is rare for commentators, legislators, and judges to define the sense in which they are referring to 'homosexuals' or 'lesbians'. The most common implicit usage seems to be that someone is homosexual or lesbian if either they have been in a same-sex romantic relationship or have engaged in same-sex acts of intercourse or sexual arousal. Most people who fall into these categories are bisexual, at least in terms of their sexual experience and history: see n. 12 below. The failure to define terms leads to fundamental confusion with regard to the immutability argument. For rare examples of recognition of the difficulty, see Wintemute, *Sexual Orientation and Human Rights*, 6–18, and N. Bamforth, 'Sexual Orientation Discrimination after *Grant* v. *South West Trains*', (2000) 63 *MLR* 694, 696–7.

[9] A possible third argument—that sexual orientation deserves respect as an aspect of personal identity (which may not be immutable)—seems to me to add little to the privacy–autonomy argument.

[10] The literature is reviewed in D. Munsey, 'The Love that Need not Name its Speaker', (1996) 2(1) *National Journal of Sexual Orientation Law*, <http://www.ibiblio.org/gaylaw/issue3 munsey.htm', arguing for a 'constructivist' rather than an 'essentialist' view. See also Stychin, pointing out the paradox that it was opponents of section 28 (see below) who were forced to rely on unconvincing arguments about the fixed nature of sexual orientation in order to oppose the idea that homosexuality could be 'promoted' (C. Stychin, *Law's Desire* (London, 1995), 43–4).

Nor is it borne out by the best available research evidence on sexual preferences and experience. This suggests that the overwhelming proportion of the comparatively small number of people in the population who have engaged in a homosexual intercourse are 'bisexual' rather than exclusively homosexual in the choice of their partners.[11]

Even if one accepted the 'immutable characteristic' thesis, that does not conclude the argument. The assumption that people either have no choice but to act according to their 'orientation' or always have a right to do so is not without its critics either. The former view is opposed by those who reject a Humean conception of human nature in favour of natural law.[12]

Alternatively, even if sexual orientation is a matter of personal preference and behaviour, it may be argued, nevertheless, that such choices lie in the private realm, which is not the law's concern.[13] J. S. Mill and H. L. A. Hart may be cited to the effect that consensual same-sex intercourse is none of the business of the State.[14]

It does not much matter which of these two arguments is used when discussing whether certain forms of homosexual behaviour should be decriminalized if the objective is to achieve parity with legal regulation of heterosexual behaviour, as in the debate in the United Kingdom in recent years over equalizing the age of consent.[15] The difference does, however, become significant in dealing with those issues where conflicts with other

---

[11] A major study of sexual behaviour in Britain found that 6.1% of men and 3.1% of women interviewed by questionnaire reported any incident of 'homosexual contact' in their lifetimes; when genital contact was specified, these figures reduced to 3.6% and 1.7% respectively. Over 90% of the men and 95% of the women who had a partner of the same sex had also had a partner of the opposite sex. Thus, 0.3% of men and 0.1% women in Great Britain are exclusively homosexual or lesbian throughout their lives. Of those who reported having had same-sex intercourse (i.e. genital contact) for half of all such men and two-thirds of all such women they only ever do so with a single partner, on an experimental basis (K. Wellings, *Sexual Behaviour in Britain: The National Survey of Sexual Attitudes and Lifestyles* (Oxford, 1994), 213–14).

[12] see e.g. Robert George, *In Defence of Natural Law* (Oxford, 1999), ch. 15; John Finnis, 'Law, Morality, and "Sexual Orientation"' (1994) 69 *Notre Dame Law Review* 1049.

[13] Liberals may argue that this is the basis for protecting religious liberty also. For an alternative perspective, see I. Leigh, 'Towards a Christian Approach to Religious Liberty', in P. Beaumont (ed.), *Christian Perspectives on Human Rights and Legal Philosophy* (Carlisle, 1998).

[14] J. S. Mill, *On Liberty* (London, 1859); H. L. A. Hart, *Law, Liberty and Morality* (Oxford, 1963). And in this context, see *Report of the Departmental Committee on Homosexual Offences and Prostitution*, Cmnd. 247, 1957.

[15] The age of consent for homosexual intercourse was lowered from 21 to 18 by the Criminal Justice and Public Order Act 1994. Proposals to equalize it with the age of consent for heterosexual intercourse at 16 are contained in the Sexual Offences (Amendment) Act 2000. A recent Home Office White Paper suggests the complete harmonization of the criminal law to remove any elements which treat offenders differently because of the sex of the victim (Home Office, *Setting the Boundaries: Reforming the Law on Sex Offences* (July 2000), para. 6.53). This will also be a requirement as regards homosexual intercourse in private between more than two consenting men, following the ruling of the European Court of Human Rights in *ADT* v. *UK*, Appl. No. 00035765 (31 July 2000).

rights are most likely to occur, namely over the ambit of anti-discrimination legislation. Here, the equality ground can be seen as justifying legal measures which a respect for personal autonomy and privacy could not support without self-contradiction.

The problem is that very similar arguments can be used by critics of sexual orientation equality legislation. It could be argued that private individuals and organizations ought not to be legally compelled to sanction or condone conduct or lifestyles which they regard as immoral. To force them to act contrary to their belief about the immorality of same-sex sexual conduct can itself be seen as an interference with their privacy, autonomy, and equality.[16]

How are such disputes over freedom of religion and sexual orientation to be resolved? What weight is to be given to the view that some religious people hold that homosexual *conduct* (rather than inclination) is immoral?

Liberal legislators may argue that a view of this kind should not form the basis for public policy because to do so would give state backing to moral judgements. A variant on this advanced by Rawls is that in a liberal society public appeals to 'comprehensive views' should not be allowed and that constitutional discourse should be conducted by 'public reason'.[17] A view is 'comprehensive' if it comprises an overarching philosophy of life. This would certainly debar choice on the basis of religious conviction; for example, opposition to sexual orientation rights because homosexual practice is against the tenets of a particular religion. However, Rawls appears to accept that at least some versions of liberalism (for example, Millian liberalism) are also 'comprehensive' in this sense. For Rawls, principles of justice within a liberal society and fundamental issues, such as constitutional procedures, are sustained by an 'overlapping consensus' of political (i.e. non-comprehensive) liberalism among people of different 'comprehensive views'.[18] This supposedly gives those with mutually opposed world-

16 Such objections might be overcome if it was demonstrated that there was a clear societal interest in righting any disadvantage faced by homosexuals and lesbians. Similar arguments prevailed in the 1960s when it became abundantly clear that the failure to combat racial discrimination was leading to the creation of an economically and socially excluded underclass. For a study (based on self-reporting) of suspected sexual orientation discrimination in employment, see A. Palmer, *Less Equal than Others* (London, 1993) (cited by Bamforth, 'Sexual Orientation Discrimination'). However, there is also some evidence that a higher proportion of homosexuals and lesbians than heterosexuals are educated to degree level and that, on average, they have higher incomes and disposable incomes (Christian Institute, *Bankrolling Gay Proselytism: The Case for Extending Section 28* (Newcastle, 1999), 34–5).

17 Rawls's original formulation of principles of justice in *A Theory of Justice* (Oxford, 1971) has been criticized as a 'comprehensive' view of its own so that he has now adopted the more modest position described (J. Rawls, *Political Liberalism* (New York, 1993)).

18 '. . . citizens are to conduct their public political discussions of constitutional essentials and matters of basic justice within the framework of what each sincerely regards as a reasonable political conception of justice, a conception that expresses political values that others as free and equal also might reasonably be expected reasonably to endorse' (Rawls, *Political Liberalism*, 1).

views sufficient common ground, while debarring resort to 'non-public' reasons, i.e. reasons for the adoption of public policy or legislation which fall outside the shared understanding and reasonable balance of political views.[19] For Rawls the restriction of argument to public reasons of this kind is characteristic of constitutional adjudication by courts and it is a limitation which should also be embraced by legislators and proponents of public policy.

Even if one were to accept, with Rawls, that the constitutional essentials within this overlapping consensus comprise the equal basic rights and liberties of citizenship, including freedom of conscience, freedom of thought, and of association, this by no means determines all aspects of the issue. Plainly it might demonstrate that denial of constitutional rights, such as the right to vote, on grounds of religion or sexual orientation should not be based on 'comprehensive' views. However, it is a matter of interpretation whether equality requires, for example, a remedy to be granted for discrimination in the enjoyment of other public benefits or against non-state actors or, indeed, whether freedom of conscience is to be overridden by such remedies, and the part played by other 'comprehensive' views in reaching such decisions. It is these more focused questions that we are concerned with here.

Some advocates of religious liberty embrace Rawls's qualification or something broadly similar. Thus, Kent Greenawalt argues that religious objections to homosexual conduct cannot in a liberal society justify prohibition. However, he claims that religious liberty is implicated if private employers are prevented from acting on their moral judgements on sexual behaviour and, likewise, if religious institutions are prevented from discriminating as they as regard appropriate on religious grounds. 'Since protection of religious freedom and autonomy and promotion of equal opportunity against socially unwarranted discrimination are both legitimate governmental objectives in a liberal society, the model of liberal democracy yields no easy resolution to this legislative dilemma.'[20]

Other commentators see appeal to the 'overlapping consensus' as a ruse to privilege liberalism over other comprehensive views by an argumentative sleight of hand. This calls into question the feasibility of a distinction between 'comprehensive' and 'political' liberalism or, alternatively, suggests that the 'overlapping consensus' unduly favours 'comprehensive'

---

[19] Rawls, *Political Liberalism*, 137. The circularity of this formulation appears conceptually sterile, while in practice allowing sufficient space for Rawls to interject his own comprehensive views; see the penetrating criticism of Paul Campos, 'Secular Fundamentalism', (1994) 100 *Columbia LR* 1814, 1820–1 and 1824–5.

[20] K. Greenawalt, *Religious Convictions and Political Choice* (New York, 1987), 93–4. He argues further that parents of children in state schools 'may have a legitimate interest in not having their children taught by role models that they regard as abhorrent' so that non-discrimination on grounds of sexual activities or preferences of teachers is 'troublesome'.

liberalism.[21] In similar vein the natural lawyer Robert George rejects as unconvincing attempts by liberal scholars to appeal to political liberalism to foreclose debate over issues such as abortion and homosexuality. Thus he argues that Stephen Macedo's supposedly 'non-comprehensive' defence of state recognition of same-sex unions in fact depends on 'comprehensive' liberalism.[22] Rather than accepting Rawls's narrow limitation on public argument, Robert George prefers to debar only argument based on comprehensive views appealing to sheer authority or secret knowledge.[23]

Enough has been said to demonstrate that given the contested nature of sexual orientation liberals are unlikely to be able to resolve the problem posed by the clash with religious liberty by appeal to some supposedly neutral concept of equality which rules religious objections out of bounds.

Reform of Section 28

Kent Greenawalt has perceptively remarked that it is difficult to see how a government can take a 'neutral' stance on the portrayal of gay and lesbian lifestyles in state-funded schools.[24] His point is that any position taken must either tend to validate or disapprove such lifestyles, which is the very issue in contention in public debate. If heterosexuality is presented as the norm, this may appear to reinforce the minority status of homosexuals and lesbians and be perceived as discriminatory. Ignoring the issue altogether would equally, in the current climate, be seen either as an implicit criticism of a 'deviant' lifestyle or as a failure to tackle social prejudice. Alternatively, if children are presented with apparently even-handed information about heterosexuality and homosexuality, moral conservatives will argue that this is not 'neutral' since it carries the implicit message that what they see as immoral behaviour is acceptable.

Recent controversy in the United Kingdom over the proposed reform of 'section 28' (more accurately, section 2A Local Government Act 1986) which prohibits local authorities from promoting homosexuality, demonstrates Greenawalt's point only too clearly. In England and Wales the

---

[21] Greenawalt argues that the overlapping consensus makes it easier for comprehensive liberals to offer public reasons for their proposals than it does for people with religious 'comprehensive' views (K. Greenawalt, *Private Consciences and Public Reasons* (Oxford, 1995), 83–4 and 119; and see Campos, 'Secular Fundamentalism').

[22] R. George, *In Defence of Natural Law* (Oxford, 1999), 213–18.

[23] Ibid. 221.

[24] Greenawalt, *Private Consciences and Public Reasons*, 80. See also *Chamberlain* v. *Surrey School District*, Court of Appeal for British Columbia, 20 Sept. 2000, 2000 BCCA 519, Docket CA025465, reversing the decision of the BC Supreme Court ruling to allow books on same-sex relationships into kindergarten and grade-one classrooms against the wishes of a majority of parents. The Court of Appeal held that refusal of permission to use the books did not violate a statutory requirement that education be on strictly secular lines: 'A religiously informed conscience should not be accorded any privilege, but neither should it be placed under a disability' (Mackenzie J).

repeal of section 28 was (unsuccessfully) proposed by the government under the Local Government Bill 1999/2000 (clause 61). The House of Lords twice amended the bill to preserve section 28: on the second occasion ministers conceded defeat in order to prevent the remainder of the bill from being lost.[25] In Scotland, however, repeal went ahead under the Ethical Standards in Public Life etc. (Scotland) Act.[26] Section 25 of that Act effects the repeal and section 26 introduces a duty on councils in relation to their functions affecting children to have regard to the value of a stable family life.

To critics section 28 'enshrines' discrimination against homosexuals in the field of education,[27] and amounts to a state endorsement of bigotry and prejudice.[28] It has been claimed that it prevents teachers from dealing frankly with issues of sexuality, that it impedes efforts to tackle bullying of pupils on grounds of their sexual orientation (actual or perceived), and that it is an infringement of free speech. To supporters the provision acts as a safeguard against the exposure of children to inappropriate teaching materials, some bordering on the pornographic, and against attempts to indoctrinate children into political correctness. It is unnecessary to enter into the detail of the claims and counter-claims here except to make the obvious point that for both sides section 28 has assumed a symbolic significance greatly exceeding any possible practical effect it could be demonstrated to have. Opponents perceive it as a symbolic statement that homosexual orientation implies second-class citizenship. Supporters perceive it as upholding the conventional family and the institution of marriage. For both, the campaigns around the provision have been instrumental in developing group identity.

In view of the near mythological status of section 28 it is wise to refer to the salient provisions in full:

A local authority shall not:

    (a) intentionally promote homosexuality or publish materials with the intention of promoting homosexuality;

    (b) promote the teaching in any maintained school of the acceptability of homosexuality as a pretended family relationship.

---

[25] See HL Debs., vol. 616, cols. 97–130, 24 July 2000.

[26] The Scottish Executive published its proposals for the repeal of section 2A in a consultation paper *Standards in Public Life: Consultation on the Ethical Standards in Public Life etc. (Scotland) Bill.*

[27] H. Fenwick, *Civil Liberties*, 2nd edn., (London, 1998), 618.

[28] For critical accounts, see Stychin, *Law's Desire*, ch. 3; D. Cooper and D. Herman, 'Getting "the Family Right": Legislating Heterosexuality in Britain 1986–91', in D. Herman and C. Stychin (eds.), *Legal Inversions: Lesbians, Gay Men and the Politics of the Law* (Philadelphia, 1995); D. Monk, 'Beyond Section 28: Law, Governance and Sex Education', in L. J. Moran, D. Monk and S. Beresford (eds.), *Legal Queeries: Lesbian, Gay and Transgender Legal Studies* (London, 1998).

Referring to the text, several popular misconceptions can be cleared up immediately. The legislation does not bind the governing bodies of individual schools or teachers: when Parliament wishes to address them in education legislation, the current practice is to do so directly.[29] Subsection (b) refers instead to the local authority's role in *promoting* teaching and subsection (a) clearly covers material that a council may prepare for use in schools in its area.[30] An individual teacher, therefore, has no legal reason to refrain from discussing homosexuality in class or with individual pupils. This is also the view of the Department for Education.[31] Still less is a teacher required to express disapproval of homosexuality, or indeed to refrain from expressing a personal view about it, whatever that might be. It follows that the provision does not present a legal obstacle to teachers in dealing with bullying of pupils perceived to be homosexual, despite the perception of teachers and teaching unions that it does. Indeed, to the contrary, there is the statutory duty of head teachers and school governors to prevent 'all forms of bullying'.[32] Nor does section 28 amount to a formal legislative endorsement of discrimination by local authorities since it is not concerned with the treatment of individuals according to their merits or conduct, but rather with prohibiting the publication of certain views at public expense. Theoretically, a council could use section 28 as a reason for withholding a grant from some body that promotes homosexuality, but even here it could be argued that the 'promotion' would be by the grant recipient, not by the council.[33] Moreover, it would have to be shown that any promotion by the council was 'intentional'. In practice, many councils routinely fund gay and lesbian voluntary groups through community grants.[34] On close analysis it turns out, then, that it is the

[29] Hilary Armstrong (local government minister) conceded that it does not apply to schools in the Second Reading debate on the Local Government Bill 2000: HC Debs., vol. 348, col. 214, 11 Apr. 2000.

[30] It does not, however, prevent use of materials prepared by others, leading critics to argue that councils have exploited a 'loophole' by encouraging the use of materials prepared by health authorities that they would have been prohibited from publishing (Christian Institute, *Bankrolling Gay Proselytism: The Case for Extending Section 28* (Newcastle, 1999)). Concern about the 'avoidance' of restrictions was recognized by the government: the ministerial guidance under section 148(4) of the Learning and Skills Act 2000 (n. 49 below) extends to the use of 'any material which may be produced by NHS bodies for use for the purposes of sex education in schools'.

[31] Circular 12/88, para. 21.

[32] Schools Standards and Framework Act 1998, s. 16(4). The Local Government Act 2000, s. 104 amends section 2A to remove any uncertainty and make clear that it is not intended to prevent head teachers, the governing bodies, or individual teachers of maintained schools from taking steps to tackle any form of bullying.

[33] The Department of the Environment has advised councils that to fund arts projects with a homosexual theme would not infringe the section (Circular 12/88, para. 19).

[34] While the debates over reform were raging a challenge was mounted in the Court of Session to the funding by Glasgow City Council of groups allegedly promoting homosexuality. The case was settled with the council giving an undertaking to comply with section 28 (*The Scotsman*, 13 May 2000).

symbolism of the provision which is much more significant than its true legal impact.[35]

Notwithstanding these limitations, two leading human rights lawyers have argued that section 28 may breach the European Convention on Human Rights (ECHR).[36] They suggest that the provision is discriminatory and impinges on freedom of expression. Both points, however, seem to involve giving a reading to section 28 that is wider than the text and an interpretation to the ECHR jurisprudence that is more protective of homosexual practice than can be supported from the cases as a whole. It is helpful to begin with the attitude of the ECHR.

The ECHR does not recognize homosexual relationships as 'family relationships'. Indeed, the case-law is clearly to the contrary under Article 12 (the right to marry and found a family). In *Rees* v. *UK* (one of the transsexuals cases) the Court of Human Rights stated that Article 12 referred to the traditional marriage between persons of the opposite biological sex and cited the fact that the article was 'concerned to protect marriage as the basis of the family'.[37] Thus, in *Kerkoven* v. *Netherlands*[38] the long-term lesbian partner of the mother of a child born by artificial insemination had no ECHR claim for violation of her rights under Article 12, nor protection of her 'family life' under Article 8. If anything, this supports the point that homosexual relationships are not to be treated as genuine families, which underlies section 28.[39] Indeed, it is because of the failure to recognize their partnerships as marriages and families under Article 12 that homosexuals and lesbians have phrased their subsequent Convention challenges under Articles 8 and 14. These have been more successful. It has been held that

---

[35] For a discussion of the effectiveness and symbolic nature of law in combating discrimination on grounds of sexual orientation, see N. Bamforth, 'Human Rights, Sexual Orientation and the Social and Legal Impact of Law and Law Reform', in C. Gearty and A. Tomkins (eds.), *Understanding Human Rights* (London, 1996).

[36] Lord Lester of Herne Hill, HL Debs., vol. 609, cols. 465–7, 7 Feb. 2000; David Pannick QC, 'Europe will have the Final Word in Section 28 Debate', *The Times*, 29 Feb. 2000.

[37] Series A, no. 106, 17 Oct.1986, see paras. 49 and 50.

[38] *Appl. No. 15666/89* (19 May 1992); and see *Sheffield and Horsham* v. *UK* (1999) 27 EHRR 163 (as regards Art. 12) and (as regards 'family life' under Art. 8) *X* v. *UK* (1983) 32 D & R 220 and *S* v. *UK* (1986) 47 D & R 274, para. 2.

[39] Lord Lester (HL Debs., vol. 609, col. 465) cited *Salgueiro da Silva Mouta* v. *Portugal*, European Court of Human Rights, 21 Dec. 1999, as establishing the principle that homosexual relationships are real family relationships. The ECHR found a violation of Article 14, in conjunction with Article 8 because the applicant had suffered *discrimination* at the hands of the Portuguese courts which he would not have suffered had he been heterosexual, with regard to respect for his family and private life (custody of his natural child). It is well established that custody issues between a parent and child concern 'family life' under Article 8. The decision does not, therefore, give any recognition to the homosexual relationship in which the father was living so as to treat it as a 'family'. Instead, the process of reasoning is strikingly similar to that used in *Hoffman* v. *Austria* (1994) 17 EHRR 293, where the European Court found that Austrian judges had discriminated in denying custody to a mother because she was a Jehovah's Witness.

Article 8 may be infringed where the State criminalizes private consenting homosexual intercourse[40] or inquires intrusively into the sexual orientation and behaviour of service personnel.[41] Critics may argue that the difference of approach under Articles 12, 8, and 14 is inconsistent. It can, however, be rationally explained on the basis that the Convention treats people engaging in homosexual and lesbian behaviour as acting within the protected area of private choice where they are not to be penalized, but, on the other hand, the State is not required to give such relationships public recognition, or to compel others to do so. It could be argued, therefore, that in outcome, if not by conscious design, the European Court of Human Rights has thus shown itself to be sensitive to the graduated response to sexual orientation described earlier.[42]

Lord Lester of Herne Hill has argued that section 28 breaches Article 10 of the ECHR, which protects freedom of expression, describing it as piece of 'clumsy state censorship and illiberal social engineering'.[43] The free speech argument is ingenious but unconvincing. It is built on the foundation that section 28 compels local education authorities (LEAs) to ensure that teachers teach that homosexual partnerships are of lesser status than heterosexual ones. As we have seen, however, on a plain reading of the provision it does not require *teachers* to deny that homosexuality is a pretended family relationship since it is not addressed to teachers (or schools) at all, but rather to LEAs. Nor does it require LEAs to forbid their teachers from treating homosexuality as a pretended family relationship.[44] Instead, the plain prohibition under section 28 is on the active promotion of homosexuality by an *LEA*—it would be breached, for example, if a council *required* its teachers to teach that homosexual relations are equal in status to heterosexual relations. Lord Lester's point about its 'chilling' speech therefore looks improbable. It might, perhaps, be argued that it is the free speech of local authorities themselves which is restricted by the prohibition on promotion under section 28. It is doubtful, however, whether as a governmental body a local authority could be a victim for the purposes of the ECHR, Article 34, or under section 7 of the Human Rights Act (HRA). Even if it could, it would be permissible to restrict its rights to protect the rights and freedoms of others—notably the parents and children, provided the restriction was necessary in a democratic society and prescribed by law.[45] Although Article 10 recognizes the right to receive

---

[40] And Article 14 if there is discrimination between the age of consent for heterosexual and homosexual intercourse (*Sutherland* v. *UK* (1997) 24 EHRR (CD) 22; [1998] EHRLR 117).

[41] *Smith and Grady* v. *UK*.   [42] See Introduction.

[43] David Pannick QC likewise believes Article 10 to be infringed, for reasons that are not fully explained.

[44] Contrary to what Lord Lester argues at col. 465.

[45] More convincingly, David Pannick argues that section 28 would not pass these tests since it is not formulated with reasonable precision (criticizing the vagueness of 'promotion'

ideas, this does not imply a right to receive them from a particular body, such as a local authority. This is not a case of a blanket legal ban.

Lester and Pannick's arguments about discrimination are built in each instance on the back of the free speech arguments. But this is puzzling: if there is any discriminatory impact (which I have already disputed above), it is in the content of the message, and not in who may exercise putative Convention rights to impart and receive ideas. Yet what Article 14 prohibits is discrimination in the *enjoyment* of other Convention rights. The rhetorical argument that section 28 'singles out one sexual preference for ostracism' (Pannick) fails to point to a category of persons whose enjoyment of Convention rights has been discriminated against in this way. Nevertheless, the government apparently also believes that section 28 is discriminatory, as the reaction of Hilary Armstrong, the local government minister, to the defeat in the House of Lords made clear.[46]

These points ought to be fatal also to any domestic attempt to have section 28 declared to be incompatible with the ECHR, since a domestic court could only issue a Declaration of Incompatibility under section 4 of the HRA if it were impossible to adopt a 'Convention-friendly' reading as required under section 3 HRA. It leaves open the possibility, however, that an LEA which instructed its teachers, as a matter of the exercise of its discretion, to teach that homosexual relationships are of lesser status might be alleged to be acting unlawfully under section 6 HRA. Any such argument would involve complex issues about the extent to which public employees have Convention rights in the workplace[47] and, if so, whether those rights can be restricted for the protection of the rights and freedom of others—to prevent the indoctrination of children[48] or violation of parental rights to have their children educated in accordance with their religious and philosophical convictions. In any event, if such a claim were possible, the argument would be reversible with the removal of section 28. In that context, if some LEAs were to compel their teachers to teach that homosexual partnerships were of equal status contrary to the teachers' beliefs, then, arguably, those teachers too would have Convention claims under Article 10. This is a reason for giving recognition to the teacher's freedom of conscience in any reform.

Indeed, it is difficult to see any situation in which section 28, as

---

and 'a pretended family relationship') and in view of the fact that in the *Fitzpatrick* case the House of Lords recognized a homosexual partnership as a family relationship for the purposes of succession to a tenancy under the Rent Act 1977.

[46] BBC Radio 4, *Today* programme, 25 July 2000.

[47] See *Halford* v. *UK* (1997) 24 EHRR 523; *Ahmed* v. *UK* (2000) 29 EHRR 1; [1999] IRLR 188.

[48] The need for protection of the rights of others has been recognized in Article 10 cases concerning public officials, e.g *Ahmed* (above). In *Rommelfanger* v. *Germany* (1989) 62 DR 151 the Commission rejected an Article 10 claim by a doctor at a Catholic hospital who was dismissed for making public statements on abortion.

presently worded, could raise a live Convention issue under the Human Rights Act. LEAs will of course be 'public authorities' under section 6 HRA. But it is doubtful if section 28 requires them to do anything which contravenes another person's Convention rights. The only people who could claim to be affected by it are teachers, pupils, or parents. We have seen that a teacher who positively wishes to teach that homosexuality is of equal (or higher status) than marriage is not prevented from so doing by section 28. Any claim by parents who wished this message to be conveyed to their children would be problematic—the parent is free to teach this, or to find someone else who will, but has no right to compel a state school or teacher to do so under Article 10. Perhaps the strongest claim would be if a parent whose religious or philosophical views comprised the position that homosexuality was of equal status could claim that the right to have his or her child educated in accordance with these convictions was violated. It is doubtful that an omission would suffice—there would have to be positive teaching of the superiority of marriage which the parent found offensive. This is not (as we have seen) a requirement of section 28, but a school or LEA which behaved in that fashion might find itself challenged for the way that its discretion had been used. In practice, as in the converse situation, the right to withdraw the child might safeguard the parent's Convention rights.

Since section 28 does not clearly compel any behaviour by an LEA affecting another person's Convention rights, it would certainly not be held incompatible under section 4 HRA and, equally, it is hard to see how it would be necessary in any context to give the section a Convention-friendly reading under section 3 HRA to protect someone's rights.

Does the repeal of the provision in Scotland and its proposed repeal in England and Wales threaten the ECHR rights of parents who do not wish their children to be taught that homosexuality is of equal status? Firstly, for the converse of the reasons discussed earlier, simply repealing the provision does not of itself effect a change in teaching. Where teaching advocating an equal status view of homosexuality has been erroneously held back by section 28, it perhaps would become more likely as a result of repeal. Nevertheless, the prospect that LEAs would be free to promote homosexuality if they chose led critics to extract concessions from the government and the Scottish Executive by arguing that safeguards were necessary—in both cases these take the form of guidance affirming the social importance of marriage, at least as a context for raising children.[49]

---

[49] The Learning and Skills Act 2000 (s. 148) amends the Education Act 1996, s. 351. The secretary of state is required to issue guidance which is binding on the governing bodies of schools. The guidance must be 'designed to secure that when sex education is given to registered pupils at maintained schools—(a) they learn the nature of marriage and its importance for family life and the bringing up of children, and (b) they are protected from teaching and materials which are inappropriate having regard to the age and the religious and cultural

They were able to argue that without such safeguards there was a risk that their right to have their children educated in accordance with their religious and philosophical convictions would be violated and that an individual school or LEA might be challenged under section 6 HRA or that the government might be liable for failure to protect these rights at Strasbourg.[50]

Two further domestic protections are relevant. First, in England and Wales (though not in Scotland) parents have a statutory right to withdraw their children from sex education classes, other than parts contained in the National Curriculum.[51] At present the National Curriculum provides for purely biological aspects of human sexual behaviour to be taught in science. Plainly, if homosexuality were taught as a cross-curricular theme, as has been advocated by one Health Authority,[52] and this became included in the National Curriculum, any protection of parental views from the right of withdrawal would be significantly diluted.

It is at this point that it could be argued that in failing to provide a more general statutory right of withdrawal the United Kingdom would be in violation of Article 2 of the First Protocol. This provides that everyone has the right to education and that the State, in exercising its functions in relation to education, must respect the right of parents to ensure that education and teaching is in conformity with their own religious and philosophical convictions.[53] One of the few cases decided under the article concerned sex education in Denmark and provides useful guidance.[54] The Court held that the 'information or knowledge must be conveyed in an

background of the pupils concerned' (s. 148(3)). The scope of the proposed guidance was a political battleground. Opponents argued that the guidance gave marriage insufficient weight as against alternative family arrangements; government amendments were defeated in the House of Lords at the Third Reading, only to be restored in a modified form by the Commons and then endorsed by their Lordships: HL Debs., vol. 615, cols. 849–72, 18 July 2000. In Scotland: draft circular under s. 26 of the Ethical Standards in Public Life (Scotland) Act; and see the Scottish Executive, Report of the Working Group on Sex Education in Scottish Schools (June 2000).

[50] There was less possibility that the repealing legislation would itself be found to be incompatible with the ECHR under HRA s. 4 or *ultra vires* the Scottish Parliament on Convention grounds.

[51] Education Act 1996, s. 405.

[52] Camden and Islington Health Promotion Trust, *Colours of the Rainbow: Exploring Issues of Sexuality and Difference* (London, 1995).

[53] A reservation has been entered by the United Kingdom, which only accepts the article in so far as is compatible with the provision of efficient instruction and training, and the avoidance of unreasonable public expenditure. The reservation takes effect also in domestic law (Human Rights Act 1998, Schedule 3, Pt. II). However, it has been suggested that the reservation may not be valid (see *SP* v. *UK* (1997) 23 EHRR CD 139, application inadmissible on other grounds). Moreover, even if the reservation applies, in the comparable example of parental objections to corporal punishment, the Court of Human Rights has found that a system allowing parents to exempt individual pupils would not be unduly onerous (*Campbell and Cosans* v. *UK* (1982) 4 EHRR 293).

[54] *Kjeldsen, Busk, Madsen and Pedersen* v. *Denmark* (1976) 1 EHRR 711.

objective, critical and pluralistic manner'. It found that warning children of the dangers and disadvantages of sexually transmitted disease, abortion, and unmarried parenthood constitute objective advice. On the other hand: 'exalting sex or inciting pupils to indulge precociously in practices that are dangerous for their stability, health or future or that many parents consider reprehensible' would not.[55] Individual schools and local authorities (which will both be 'public authorities' under the Human Rights Act) would act unlawfully if they breached the rights of parents under this article. The potential liability of the government for the contents of circulars to educational authorities, either domestically or at Strasbourg, would be more conjectural since, plainly, these operate at some remove from classroom.

A second argument concerns teachers themselves. Teachers have a right not to be disqualified from teaching or discriminated against through promotion or pay because of their religious opinions.[56] Bearing in mind the broad reach of Article 9, a Convention-friendly reading of this provision under section 3 of the HRA could extend its reach to those with objections of conscience to teaching that homosexuality is of equal status, whether or not grounded on their religious beliefs.

All of this demonstrates abundantly the difficulty that the State faces in reconciling the conflicting human rights arguments of parents, pupils, and teachers in the contested territory of sexual orientation. As Greenawalt observed, it seems to be virtually impossible in the context of a public education system for a State to maintain a strictly neutral stance when opinions are strongly opposed.[57] The position is further complicated by the divided responsibility of differing layers of government for education. Probably the best that can be achieved is to allow those whose convictions are offended by a particular syllabus or type of teaching to withdraw from it, disruptive as it may be to the educational programme. If, as it has stated, the government revisits the repeal of section 28, this alternative may yet be found to have merit.

Discrimination Law

The growing reach of equality law may soon raise the serious prospect of clashing rights in legislation eliminating discrimination on grounds of religion and belief and sexual orientation. Should a person whose religious beliefs include the assertion that same-sex intercourse is immoral have equal protection when this is contrary to the equal opportunities policy of a public sector employer? Should a religious institution be able to act on

[55] Ibid., para. 54.
[56] School Standards and Framework Act 1998, s. 59(2).
[57] See n. 24 above.

that premiss in recruiting staff? Conversely, should a gay rights group such as Stonewall or Outrage! be permitted to reject job applicants who hold such beliefs? These questions may soon pass from the realm of the hypothetical to the practical.

Discrimination on grounds of sexual orientation or behaviour is not generally unlawful[58] in the United Kingdom at present. Sexual orientation discrimination does not fall under the Sex Discrimination Act 1975[59] and the European Court of Justice (ECJ) has ruled that employers whose benefits favour employees with heterosexual partners do not breach the current equal pay directive governing sex discrimination.[60] Domestic challenges by way of judicial review to the actions of public bodies have also failed[61] but might well succeed now that the Human Rights Act is in force, in view of recent ECHR jurisprudence on Article 8.[62]

Equally, except in Northern Ireland (where the Fair Employment (Northern Ireland) Act 1989 prohibits some forms of discrimination[63]), religious discrimination is generally not unlawful in the United Kingdom.[64] Here again the Human Rights Act may have some impact, especially in precipitating reconsideration of cases holding that religious discrimination

---

[58] e.g. *Saunders* v. *National Camps Association* [1980] IRLR 174; see also *Boychuk* v. *Symons Holdings Ltd* [1977] IRLR 395 (dismissal of employee for wearing Gay Liberation badge held to be fair); contrast *Bell* v. *Devon and Cornwall Police Authority* [1978] IRLR 283. The House of Lords has held that a surviving homosexual partner can succeed to a tenancy as a member of the 'tenant's' 'family' (*Fitzgerald* v. *Sterling Housing Association* [1999] 3 WLR 1113). The Independent Review recommends the introduction of legislation concerning both direct and indirect discrimination on grounds of sexual orientation (Report of the Independent Review of UK Anti-Discrimination Law; publ. as B. Hepple, M. Coussey, and T. Choudhury, *Equality: A New Framework* (Oxford 2000)).

[59] *Smith* v. *Gardner Merchant* [1998] IRLR 510, CA (dismissal of homosexual barman). The Court of Appeal remitted the issue, however, to the Industrial Tribunal for consideration of less favourable treatment whether a lesbian would have been treated in the same way.

[60] *Grant* v. *South Western Trains* (1998) 3 BHRC 578; [1998] IRLR 206, ECJ (for critical analysis see Bamforth, 'Sexual Orientation Discrimination'). Subsequently, the High Court held that in the light of the interpretation of 'sex' in *Grant* dismissal on grounds of sexual orientation clearly did not breach the equal treatment directive either and, accordingly, it rescinded its reference of the issue to the ECJ: *R.* v. *SS for Defence, ex parte Perkins* [1998] IRLR 508. Notably, Lightman J refused (at 510) to distinguish *Grant* on the basis that it concerned an active relationship whereas the armed forces ban at issue in *Perkins* concerned merely orientation. See also *Smith* v. *Gardner Merchant* [1996] ICR 790.

[61] *R.* v. *Director of GCHQ, ex parte Hodges, The Times*, 26 July 1988, and *R.* v. *Secretary of State for Defence, ex parte Lustig-Prean, Smith and Others* [1996] 1 All ER 257; *R.* v. *SS for Defence, ex parte Perkins* [1998] IRLR 508.

[62] See further S. Palmer, 'Human Rights: Implications for Labour Law', [2000] CLJ 168, 188–90.

[63] And see Northern Ireland Act 1998, ss. 76 (prohibiting discrimination by public authorities on grounds of religious belief) and 75 (duty on public authorities to promote equality of opportunity between persons on various grounds, including both religious belief and sexual orientation).

[64] For a valuable study of the issues surrounding the introduction of legislation concerning religious discrimination, see T. Choudhury, Working Paper on Religious Discrimination for the Independent Review of the Enforcement of UK Anti-Discrimination Law.

falls outside the Race Relations Act 1976.[65] In future the courts would be bound to interpret the Act as far as possible consistently with the parties' Convention rights, including Articles 9 and 14. Proposals for the introduction of religious discrimination legislation have come from the Commission for Racial Equality[66] and are under consideration by the Home Office following an independent review commissioned by the Nuffield Trust.[67] A recent European directive (discussed below) requires the United Kingdom to introduce legislation on both sexual orientation and religious discrimination in employment.

In addition, Article 14 of the ECHR prevents states from discriminating on any ground including religion and any 'other status' (which, although it is not expressly mentioned, can cover sexual orientation) in the enjoyment of rights under the Convention. Protocol 12 of the Convention, which the United Kingdom has not ratified and which is not yet in force,[68] requires states to secure that 'any right set forth by law' is enjoyed without discrimination on such grounds.[69] Article 2 of the protocol provides that 'No one shall be discriminated against by any public authority' on any such ground.

As the grounds of discrimination are multiplied, the possibility of conflict between them arises. The potential conflict between clashing rights of religious liberty and of non-discrimination law can be resolved in one of several ways.[70]

Exemptions or Exceptions?

Firstly, there is the possibility of exempting religious organizations from the operation of aspects of discrimination law. Examples of this approach

---

[65] In *Mandla* v. *Dowell Lee* [1983] 2 AC 548 it was held that Sikhs constitute a 'racial group'; cf. *Seide* v. *Gillette Industries* [1980] Industrial Relations Law Reports (IRLR) 427 as regards Jews. However, Rastafarians have been held not to be a 'racial group' in *Crown Suppliers* v. *Dawkins* [1991] IRLR 327; likewise Muslims have been held not to constitute an ethnic group but rather an (unprotected) religious one: *JH Walker* v. *Hussain* [1996] IRLR 11.

[66] Commission for Racial Equality, *Second Review of the Race Relations Act* (London 1992).

[67] Report of the Independent Review of the Enforcement of UK Anti-Discrimination Law.

[68] For brief analysis: G. Moon, 'The Draft Discrimination Directive to the European Convention on Human Rights: A Progress Report', [2000] EHRLR 49. As a matter of domestic law the protocol may be added to the 'Convention Rights' protected under the Human Rights Act 1998, by secondary legislation made under sections 1(4) and (5) of that Act, although by section 1(6) this is not operative until the protocol itself comes into force.

[69] Twelfth Protocol, Art. 1.

[70] In addition to the two possibilities discussed below, if a sexual orientation discrimination statute applied to indirectly discriminatory action (as in the Sex Discrimination Act 1975 and Race Relations Act 1976) the question of possible justification on religious grounds might also arise.

include the General Equal Treatment Act of 1994 of the Netherlands, which contains exemptions allowing preachers to characterisze homosexuality as immoral provided this occurs in the context of a church service and not outside. The same legislation permits religious schools to discriminate where necessary for fulfilment of their functions. A similar approach has been followed in the Massachusetts Gay Civil Rights Act and in the Republic of Ireland's Employment Equality Act, both of which contain wide exemptions for religious institutions from the general principle of non-discrimination.[71] A domestic precedent for this approach exists under the Sex Discrimination Act 1975, section 19 of which allows a religious body to restrict employment to one sex in order to comply with doctrines of the religion or avoid offending the religious susceptibilities of a significant number of its followers. This allows some churches, for example, to maintain their objections to the ordination of women.[72]

The exemption approach has several advantages. Firstly, it states the position clearly in advance, rather than by requiring the justification for exemption to be considered on a case-by-case basis. It therefore gives an exempted organization greater certainty of its position so that recruitment practices can be formulated clearly ahead. Secondly, it gives legislative underpinning to the public–private divide in a way that may seem naturally attractive to liberal exponents of religious liberty. In this approach a religious institution is permitted to select according to its beliefs because it is treated as operating in the private sphere of life. Whether religious bodies should be so regarded, particularly when exercising functions with a clear secular parallel which fall on the public side of the divide, is of course controversial—as demonstrated recently in the United Kingdom by the debates over whether the Human Rights Act should extend to churches when acting as 'public authorities'. Advocates of non-discrimination may well question why religious institutions should be permitted to operate in a way that would otherwise be regarded as discriminatory. We face here in effect a conflict between group rights (to associate with others of similar belief) and individual rights (to be treated fairly and not according to some discriminatory factor). The exemption route creates what Esau has described as 'Islands of Exclusivity'.[73] Freedom to associate with others of

---

[71] General Laws of Massachusetts, Ch. 151B, s. 1; Employment Equality Act 1998, s. 37.

[72] In the recent independent review of discrimination legislation chaired by Professor Bob Hepple it was suggested that an exemption for 'small private associations' might be made to proposed legislation on sexual orientation. Religious susceptibilities were not specifically acknowledged; however, for a proposal of this kind by one of the Commission's consultants, see R. Wintemute, 'Gay and Lesbian Inequality 2000', (2000) 6 EHRLR 603, 625. In the case of proposed legislation on religious discrimination, however, the Commission suggested that there might be an exemption for an organized religion where the 'essential functions' of a job require it to be done by persons of a particular sexual orientation and the purpose is to avoid offending the religious susceptibilities of a significant number of its followers (n. 67 above).

[73] A. Esau, 'Islands of Exclusivity: Religious Organizations and Employment Discrimination', (2000) 33 *Univ. of British Columbia LR* 719.

like mind necessarily involves freedom to exclude people who do not share the beliefs in question. In a liberal society in which those so excluded are free to join other religious groups or to form their own on the same basis, this should not be seen as harmful. Indeed, conversely, if the State were to prevent exclusivity through its non-discrimination laws, it would be tantamount to denial of a basic aspect of religious liberty. Paradoxically, perhaps, exclusive societies can be seen as adding to the diversity of society.

Although not specifically in the context of the rights of a religious body, the United States Supreme Court has recently affirmed associational rights in a case brought by a gay activist following his exclusion as a deputy scout leader.[74] The New Jersey Supreme Court found that Boy Scouts of America had violated the state 'public accommodations' statute which made it unlawful to discriminate on grounds of sexual orientation. The US Supreme Court ruled that to apply the state law to require the Boy Scouts to admit the Respondent would be to violate its First Amendment right of 'expressive association'. By being forced to admit a member that it did not desire the association's ability to advocate public or private viewpoints critical of homosexual behaviour would be significantly impaired. Rehnquist CJ, giving the majority opinion, argued that the right of expressive association 'is crucial in preventing the majority from imposing its views on groups that would rather express other, perhaps unpopular, ideas' and 'the fact that an idea may be embraced and advocated by increasing numbers of people is all the more reason to protect the First Amendment rights of those who wish to voice a different view'.

A second possible approach is provide exceptions for particular *activities* (which may or may not be limited to a particular class of defendants). The key is that the defendant has the onus to establish the necessity of an activity being excepted having regard to the goals or the nature of the post in question and the organization concerned. Such exceptions are commonly referred to in the UK literature as Genuine Occupational Qualifications (GOQs) and in North America as Bona Fide Occupational Requirements (BFORs). In the United Kingdom race and sex discrimination legislation[75] each contains examples, although it is the former which are perhaps most comparable to protections for religious groups. The nearest analogy is with section 5(2)(d) of the Race Relations Act 1976, which allows a job to be reserved for a member of a particular racial group where the post in question provides persons of that racial group with personal services and those services can most effectively be provided by a person of that racial group. Decisions under this exemption have

---

[74] *Boy Scouts Association of America* v. *Dale*, US Supreme Ct. No. 99–699, Decided 28 June 2000.
[75] Sex Discrimination Act 1975, s. 7.

stressed that to qualify the postholder must have direct contact with the service users, rather than acting in an executive capacity.[76]

European law affords another example. Under the Equal Treatment Directive Article 2 exempts occupational activities where by reason of the nature or context in which they are carried out the sex of the worker constitutes a determining factor. The ECJ has stressed the duty of national courts to assess the proportionality of any such exemptions in domestic law.[77] It has also held that respect for private life must be taken into account in qualifying the right to equality.[78]

GOQ requirements have the advantage of proportionality: they allow a court to test the need for privileged treatment against the duties of the post in question and the objectives of the body seeking an exception. From the point of view of the body concerned, however, this may involve judging the 'work' to be done from a fundamentally secular perspective. Alvin Esau describes this as an 'instrumental' approach—focusing on the specific task of the person concerned—rather than an 'organic' approach where the employee is expected to participate in the mission of the organization as a whole in a way that cannot be confined to a job description.[79] According to the instrumental approach it may be judged that the duties of a church secretary could be performed adequately by a Muslim, but adopting an organic approach such a person would be unable to assent to the fundamental tenets of the employing institution. In a sense the GOQ–BFOR approach involves denial of 'associational rights': the employer is not free to define itself as a religious body in the way that it chooses. There is a further disadvantage in that it may be hard to predict where a GOQ will be found to apply and much may depend on the subjective assessment of whoever adjudicates on the claim for an exception.

Detailed consideration to the scope of exemptions on religious grounds to anti-discrimination legislation was given by the Australian Commonwealth Human Rights and Equal Opportunity Commission in a report in which it advocated the introduction of a Federal Religious Freedom Act cover religious discrimination.[80] The Commission received arguments from a number of 'fundamentalist Christians' (its terminology)

---

[76] In *London Borough of Lambeth* v. *CRE* [1990] IRLR 231, CA; *Tottenham Green Under-Fives Centre* v. *Marshall* [1989] IRLR 147, EAT. In the latter case, it was held that an Industrial Tribunal had erred in concluding that a GOQ for an Afro-Caribbean nursery worker was not made out where the nursery was attended by many children of Afro-Caribbean descent. The Employment Appeal Tribunal was impressed by evidence of the need for the worker to understand the children's needs, to empathize with them, and to read to them in their own dialect, and stressed the direct connection between the post and the provision of services (ibid. 148–9).

[77] *Johnstone* v. *Chief Constable of the RUC* [1986] IRLR 263.

[78] *Commission of the EC* v. *UK* [1984] IRLR 29.

[79] Esau, 'Islands of Exclusivity'.

[80] Human Rights and Equal Opportunity Commission, *Article 18: Freedom of Religion and Belief* (Sydney, 1998), 74–8.

that they saw the conduct of a private or family business as matter of personal moral responsibility or conscience and that this entitled them to follow a policy of not employing practising homosexuals or lesbians. While acknowledging the sincerity of these beliefs, and the right of individuals to follow them in the private sphere, the Commission rejected the claim for a general conscience exemption. It argued instead that discrimination in employment affecting another person was in the public sphere of life.

It did, however, acknowledge that religious organizations were in a special position. It recognized that:

accommodating the distinct identity of religious organisations is an important element in any society which respects and values diversity in all its forms.

and that

It is reasonable for employees of these institutions to be expected to have a degree of commitment to and identification with the beliefs, values and teachings of the particular religion.

But on the other hand:

To allow religious organisations an absolute exemption could encourage prejudice and unfair treatment of certain individuals.

In their case it proposed an exemption containing a number of safeguards:

A distinction, exclusion or preference in connection with employment as a member of the staff of an institution that is conducted in accordance with the doctrines, tenets, beliefs or teachings of a particular religion or creed, being a distinction, exclusion or preference required by those doctrines, tenets, beliefs or teachings made in good faith and necessary to avoid injury to the religious susceptibilities of adherents of that particular religion or that creed should not be unlawful provided that it is not arbitrary and is consistently applied.

The exemption was intended to apply in addition to further exceptions for a 'distinction, exclusion or preference in respect of a particular job based on the inherent requirements of the job' and a 'preference in employment for a person holding a particular religious or other belief' which was established to be a GOQ. Neither of these was to be limited to particular categories of jobs or institutions.

The European Directive

Extended powers for the European Community to legislate to combat discrimination on grounds including sexual orientation and religion or belief were included in the Amsterdam Treaty.[81] The Council has recently

---

[81] Art. 13 of the Treaty establishing the Community, as modified, provides: 'Without prejudice to the other provisions of this Treaty and within limits of the powers conferred on

passed a directive,[82] to be implemented by member states by December 2003, to 'put into effect . . . the principle of equal treatment as regards access to employment and occupation, including promotion, vocational training, employment conditions and membership of certain organisations' (Article 1).·

Article 4 of the directive gives limited exceptions which may be relevant. Article 4(1) allows member states to exempt difference of treatment based on an otherwise discriminatory characteristic if 'by reason of activities concerned or the context in which they are carried out, such a characteristic constitutes a genuine occupational qualification'.[83] Taken by itself this might open the possibility for a religious body to argue that a lifestyle condition related to its doctrines and should be exempted, despite its effect on practising homosexuals and lesbians. However, a more restrictive second exception (Article 4(2)) has been included in the text which may have the effect of excluding such arguments.

As originally drafted, Article 4(2) applied to religious institutions which could satisfy a narrow and genuine occupational qualification test.[84] The proposed exception only applied to organizations directly and essentially pursuing the aim of or ideological guidance in the field of religion or belief with respect to education, information, and the expression of opinions. A church or religious school clearly could bring themselves within this definition but the business or partnership (such as doctors or solicitors) whose working ethos is based on a shared faith commitment could not. Moreover, even within the organization concerned it was only the 'particular occupational activities within those organisations which are directly and essentially related to [the] aim' which were to be excepted. It could easily be argued that clerical, secretarial, and other support staff were not

it by the Community, the Council, acting unanimously on a proposal from the Commission and after consulting Parliament, may take appropriate action to combat discrimination based on sex, a racial or ethnic origin, religion or belief, disability, age or sexual orientation.'

[82] Council Directive 2000/78/EC of 27 Nov. 2000 Establishing a General Framework for Equal Treatment in Employment and Occupation; for the Commission's proposals (referred to below), see 25 Nov. 1989 COM (1999) 565 final, 1999/02225 (CNS). For discussion in the UK, see *Ninth Report of the European Union Committee, EU Proposals to Combat Discrimination*, HL Paper 68 (1999–2000), debated at HL Debs., vol. 614, cols. 1177 ff., 30 June 2000. For critical analysis of the directive, see Christian Institute, *The European Threat to Religious Liberties: A Response to the European Union's Proposed Employment Directive* (Newcastle, 2000).

[83] A similar exemption appears in the Directive Implementing the Principle of Equal Treatment between Persons Irrespective of Racial or Ethnic Origin, COM (99) 566 final, Council 6 June 2000, Art. 4.

[84] '. . . member States may provide that, in the case of public or private organisations which pursue directly and essentially the aim of ideological guidance in the field of religion or belief with respect to education, information and the expression of opinions, and for the particular occupational activities within those organisations which are directly and essentially related to that aim, a difference of treatment based on a relevant characteristic related to religion or belief shall not constitute discrimination where, by reason of the nature of these activities, the characteristic constitutes a genuine occupational qualification' (Art. 4(2)).

within this. The relevant European Commissioner has argued, for example, that within a church school (contrary to the existing UK law)[85] teaching posts generally would not be exempted but that a religious commitment might be lawfully required of a teacher responsible for religious education. The difference in treatment had to be based on a relevant characteristic related to religion or belief not to constitute discrimination. A narrow reading of this provision (such as that apparently intended) would have disabled religious institutions from applying 'lifestyle' qualifications (for example, not to engage in extramarital sexual intercourse, including homosexual intercourse) on their staff in accordance with what they took to be their mission and ministry. On such a reading religion or belief might easily be taken to exclude aspects of 'private' behaviour.[86]

In view of these limitations a vigorous campaign was mounted by those concerned about the potential effect on the employment practices of churches, mosques, synagogues, and Sikh temples (especially as regards clerical and secretarial appointments), of religious schools, and of religious charities, such as relief agencies, housing associations, children's and old people's homes, and hospices.[87] Opponents of the directive doubted whether it would permit these bodies to continue to employ only staff who shared their religious commitment. When similar concerns were earlier raised in relation to the Human Rights Act 1998, Section 13 was introduced, requiring a court or tribunal to have 'particular regard' to freedom of belief, to mollify opponents, especially those concerned over religious charities.[88] In addition explicit statutory protection was given for teaching appointments in religious schools. It seemed probable that these safeguards would now be trumped by domestic anti-discrimination legislation implementing the directive.[89] In the event, however, some attempt was made in

---

[85] School Standards and Framework Act 1998, s. 60.

[86] See statements by Commissioner Demetriou, European Parliament, Verbatim Report of Proceedings, 18 Jan. 2000.

[87] Baroness Young: HL Debs., vol. 614, col. 1188, 30 June 2000; Lord Bishop of Southwark, ibid., cols. 1199–1200; Lord Pilkington of Oxenford, ibid., cols. 1201–2; Lord Griffiths of Fforestfach, ibid., cols. 1208–10.

[88] S. 13 makes specific reference to 'religious organisations'. The home secretary made clear that this was intended to be interpreted as wider than churches, to cover bodies with 'religious objectives' (HC Debs., vol. 312, col. 1021 (20 May 1998)). Hence he rejected as unnecessary an amendment designed to allow religious charities to exclude from employment people who did not share their beliefs (ibid., col. 1024. See further P. Cumper, 'The Protection of Religious Rights under Section 13 of the Human Rights Act 1998', [2000] *PL* 254, 260–1; Leigh, 'Towards a Christian Approach to Religious Liberty', 69–71).

[89] At least if, as is probable, implementation is by primary legislation. If secondary legislation were utilized under section 2(2) European Communities Act 1972 the statutory instrument might be challengeable for incompatibility with Convention rights under sections 3 and 6(1) of the Human Rights Act 1998. It is not clear whether secondary legislation made under the 1972 Act to implement a directive is saved by section 3(2)(c) HRA, nor how UK courts would resolve two potentially conflicting duties under the 1972 and 1998 Acts.

the Council of Ministers to accommodate religious critics by amending the text of Article 4(2) in several important respects.

Firstly, the scope of organizations entitled to exemption was broadened: as amended, Article 4(2) can apply to 'churches and other public or private organisations the ethos of which is based on religion or belief'. This could certainly include religiously motivated schools and charities. It is questionable, though, whether it extends to private businesses owned by or comprised solely of persons of a particular faith group—it would depend perhaps on whether the basic purpose was taken to be the carrying on of the business or profession (in the same way as any other—non-religious—business people or practitioners), or whether the shared religious commitment of the participants was judged to be fundamental. Secondly, the nexus between the qualifying organization and the exempted position was loosened somewhat: the amended text refers to 'where, by reason of the nature of these activities or of the context in which they are carried out, a person's religion or belief constitute a genuine, legitimate and justifiable occupational requirement, having regard to the organisation's ethos'. While this deletes the reference in the draft text to the duties of the post being 'directly and essentially related' to the aim of the body concerned, it may, nevertheless, still allow argument as to whether a particular post is sufficiently central to warrant exemption. Finally, limited permission is given for exemption for 'lifestyle' conditions—obligations on individuals to 'act in good faith and with loyalty to the organisation's ethos'. Any such exemptions are, however, subject to the other provisions of the directive (since these prohibit sexual orientation discrimination it is therefore doubtful if a requirement of abstinence from same-sex activity could be exempted) and must be in conformity with the national constitution.

In theory religious objections to homosexual behaviour might be accommodated under the directive by distinguishing it from inclination or sexual orientation. The explanatory memorandum to the directive states that 'a clear dividing line should be drawn between sexual orientation, which is covered by this proposal, and sexual behaviour, which is not'. On its face the first of these qualifications might allow employers to continue to exclude persons engaging in homosexual acts, without focusing on orientation as such. But it seems (quite apart from practicality) to raise further questions about possible indirect discrimination.[90] Notwithstanding that most people engaging in same-sex sexual acts have some heterosexual experience, a higher proportion of homosexuals and lesbians engage in same-sex acts than do heterosexuals, since a large majority of the population is exclusively heterosexual.[91] Any such condition, therefore, has

[90] Under Articles 1(1) and (2)(b) indirect discrimination would be impermissible. On justification, see n. 70 above.
[91] n. 11 above.

an adverse impact on homosexuals, however 'homosexual' and 'heterosexual' are delineated.[92]

The difficulty which employers or religious organizations might face in trying to uphold a distinction between mere homosexual or lesbian preference and attraction, on the one hand, and activities and behaviour, on the other, is illustrated by a case from Australia.[93] The Federal Human Rights and Equal Opportunity Commission found that the Catholic Education Office (CEO) of the archdiocese of Sydney had breached the New South Wales Anti-Discrimination Act of 1977 by denying teaching accreditation to work in a Catholic school to a lesbian, Jacqui Griffin. The CEO defended its decision on the basis that Ms Griffin's high-profile public position and statements in support of homosexual and lesbian teachers and students, personal lifestyle, and advocacy of homosexual behaviour were incompatible with the Church's teaching. However, it was unable to substantiate its allegations of Ms Griffin's advocacy of homosexual or lesbian behaviour or concerning her private life. The Commission found that her public advocacy of toleration and understanding towards homosexual and lesbian teachers and students, far from being incompatible with Catholic teaching (and so bringing the CEO within an exception under the legislation), was consistent with it. The assumption that because Ms Griffin acknowledged her sexual orientation she therefore acted upon it was contrary to the Catholic Church's own teaching that people of homosexual or lesbian orientation should remain celibate.

Overall, it is clear that the draft directive gives very little space to those with religious objections to sexual orientation equality. An exception (Article 4(2)) which was inserted in part apparently to meet the concerns of religious institutions is more restrictive than the GOQ exception in Article 4(1). It appears that in this respect, although perhaps not generally, religious groups might be better protected if Article 4(2) were removed altogether, therefore.[94] More radical alternatives would be to recognize these concerns by an exception along the lines proposed in Australia or to exempt the private sector entirely. The latter would leave member states with a freer hand to shape their own religious and sexual orientation legislation to balance the conflicting arguments in a way that fitted national religious and social attitudes.

The proposed directive demonstrates how religious liberty can be at risk

[92] If 'homosexual' means people who have (any) same-sex sexual experience, then for this purpose reference to indirect discrimination would be tautologous, of course.

[93] Human Rights and Equal Opportunity Commission, *Report of Inquiry into a Complaint of Discrimination in Employment and Occupation: Discrimination on the Ground of a Sexual Preference*, HRC Report No. 6.

[94] The House of Lords Select Committee urged the deletion of Article 4(2) because of its 'narrow and convoluted' drafting and the likelihood that it would operate unintentionally to limit the ability of religious organizations to claim GOQs (*Ninth Report of the European Union Committee*, para. 111).

from the privileging of a particular conception of equality and non-discrimination, especially where private action and belief are subordinated. It embodies a refusal to accept that private individuals are entitled to act on or form private moral judgements about homosexual conduct which depart from the 'correct' non-judgemental official position. This is characteristic of an unfortunately strident and intolerant form of 'comprehensive' liberalism—one so confident of its own moral judgements that it is unmoved at trampling over those of religious minorities—an approach which I have labelled elsewhere as 'Liberal fundamentalism'.[95] Despite amendments which were more sympathetic to the concerns of religious groups, the directive places a low value on 'associational' religious liberty as compared to individual rights.

Conclusion

'Fundamentalist' and 'homophobic' are two of the most powerful derogatory labels in contemporary discourse, carrying immediate connotations of intolerance, prejudice, and closed-mindedness. Too often, however, their mere deployment serves to excuse those using the labels from engaging in reasoned debate about why their own preferred 'comprehensive views' concerning equality or non-discrimination should trump those of the person or group so labelled.

It might be argued, of course, that the social goal of eliminating prejudice justifies using the law in a symbolic and educative fashion to make private individuals behave in an 'unprejudiced' way. This view would simply refuse to accept that private individuals are entitled to act on or form private moral judgements about homosexual conduct which depart from the 'correct' non-judgemental official position. Here again we face the contested nature of sexual orientation. For liberals to rule religious 'comprehensive views' out of bounds while enforcing their own preferred views cannot be passed off as morally 'neutral', however.

The preferred solution advanced in this paper is to suggest that in practice some of the difficulties of conflicting rights could be resolved through use of the public–private boundary—that is, by confining the operation of sexual orientation equality law to public authorities and leaving individuals free to act on their own moral judgements. In the case of reform of section 28 this would mean guaranteeing effective opt-out provisions protective of parental rights to have their children educated in accordance with their religious convictions. In the case of sexual orientation discrimination legislation it requires either legislation to stop at the public sector or granting generous exemption for religious institutions, rather than the GOQ approach.

[95] Leigh, 'Towards a Christian Approach to Religious Liberty'.

Delineating the public–private boundary in this way will not satisfy those holding a religious position contrary to sexual orientation equality that such legislation is 'neutral'. They may still reject Rawls's limitation on public debate and wish to oppose such laws as damaging to society and individuals. However, if they lose the democratic debate, it at least provides some protection for a minority position. It is paradoxical perhaps that religious groups whose world-view ultimately rejects the liberal public–private divide should find within it their best hope of preserving their distinctiveness.

Nor will exclusion of the 'private' sphere persuade 'comprehensive' liberals that what they see as bigotry and prejudice deserve to be ring-fenced. Nevertheless, their goal of elimination of discrimination will have been advanced in the public arena and it may be claimed that the law will have a symbolic and educative effect beyond its immediate ambit.

Compromises are, of course, intellectually unsatisfactory, but they are sometimes practical. This one may be the least divisive solution to one of the most contentious issues our society faces.[96]

[96] I am grateful to Helen Fenwick and Richard O'Dair for critical comments on an earlier draft. I benefited also from discussions with Paul Beaumont, Simon Calvert, Colin Hart, Mark Mullins, and Colin Warbrick, although none has commented on the text. Thanks also to Rex Ahdar, Tafyul Choudhury, and Alvin Esau for supplying and suggesting materials. I acknowledge gratefully the support of the Arts and Humanities Research Board under its Research Leave scheme.

RELIGIOUS GROUP AUTONOMY, GAY ORDINATION, AND HUMAN RIGHTS LAW

Rex J. Ahdar

Should churches be allowed to refuse to ordain openly practising homosexual or lesbian candidates for the ministry? This is a test case of the wider issue of the appropriate application of human rights norms to religious groups. I argue 'no' to state interference with ordination matters, drawing from lessons learned from the acrimonious New Zealand debate on the topic. The New Zealand battles are, of course, mirrored in similar protracted and heated denominational controversies in other nations: for example, those in the Presbyterian Church, the Episcopal Church and the United Methodist Church, in the United States.[1]

First, I discuss the case for religious group autonomy. Liberal political theory supports it. Furthermore, both courts and the promulgators of international human rights instruments acknowledge the importance of deferring to the decisions of the religious organizations themselves when it comes to matters of leadership and internal governance.

The protection of religious freedom and the furtherance of a policy of non-discrimination are worth while and largely harmonious social goals. But a conflict between these objectives can sometimes arise. One specific danger is that human rights or anti-discrimination laws may have a 'chilling effect' upon religious groups' determinations on leadership and, in turn, subvert those groups' very vision. The experience of the New Zealand Methodist and Presbyterian Churches, debating in the shadow of the Human Rights Act 1993, illustrates this. That statute bans 'sexual orientation' discrimination in certain activities (employment, accommodation, and so on). Those churches, at least in part, have acted with an eye to avoiding litigation and bureaucratic entanglement rather than solely upon the basis of their own assessments of who would best serve their spiritual needs.

Theologian Paul Marshall once commented that 'in this liberal society,

---

[1] See J. D. Small, 'Signs of the Postdenominational Future', *Christian Century*, 5 May 1999, 506; 'PCUSA Opts for Further Study of Gay Ordination', *Christian Century*, 14 July 1999, 704 (two-year moratorium on the gay clergy issue passed by the General Assembly of the 3.6m. member denomination); B. Ghent, 'Breach of Faith', *The Advocate*, 6 July 1999, 25 (debate on gay priests in 2.4m. member Episcopal Church of America); 'UMC Pastors Launch Gay Rights Campaign', *Christian Century*, 29 Jan. 1997, 93 (faction within the 8.6m. member UMC dissent from that denomination's ban on gay ordination).

communities are not free: rather they are constrained to become liberal associations'.[2] Some liberal theorists concede as much. Stephen Macedo, for example, reminds us that liberal citizens do not emerge 'naturally'. Rather, liberal democracies must act positively to shape their citizenry to appreciate and perpetuate liberal virtues. Thus, 'the transformative dimension of liberalism' needs to be recognized. If a liberal regime is to thrive, 'it must constitute the private realm in its image, and it must form citizens willing to observe its limits and able to pursue its aspirations'.[3] Liberals ought not to be ashamed of defending a ' "moderate hegemony" of liberal public values'.[4]

Yet, by insisting that civil associations 'mirror the principles of the overarching political community' a dull homogeneity may result.[5] The things we treasure from civil associations generally, and religious groups especially—new ways of thinking, the development of concepts of the good life, the inculcation of virtue, respect, loyalty, sacrifice, and so on—may be jeopardized by state conformity to public juridical norms of behaviour. The liberal state may be cutting off its nose to spite its face. 'It is not obvious as an empirical matter', maintains William Galston, 'that civil society organizations within liberal democracies must be organized along liberal democratic lines' to perform their valuable societal functions. I agree with Galston that the 'burden of proof' ought to lie with 'those who seek to shape or restrict the internal life of nonpublic associations'.[6] Galston urges:

A liberal polity guided . . . by a commitment to moral and political pluralism will be parsimonious in specifying binding public principles and cautious about employing such principles to intervene in the internal affairs of civil associations. It rather will pursue a policy of *maximum feasible accommodation*, limited only by the core requirements of individual security and civic unity. That there are costs to such a policy cannot reasonably be denied. It will permit internal associational practices (e.g., patriarchal gender relations) of which many strongly disapprove. It will allow many associations to define their membership in ways that may be viewed as restraints on individual liberty . . . Unless liberty—individual and associational—is to be narrowed dramatically, however, we must accept these costs.[7]

There exists an ironic possibility that human rights laws may operate to stifle the very liberty they seek to foster. Laws designed to preserve freedom may be turn out to be intolerant, repressive codes. David Smolin puts

---

[2] Paul Marshall, 'Liberalism, Pluralism and Christianity: A Reconceptualization', *Fides et Historia*, 21 (1989), 4, 9.

[3] Stephen Macedo, 'Transformative Constitutionalism and the Case of Religion: Defending the Moderate Hegemony of Liberalism', *Political Theory*, 26 (1998), 56, 58.

[4] Ibid. 76.

[5] William A. Galston, 'Expressive Liberty, Moral Pluralism, Political Pluralism: Three Sources of Liberal Theory', (1999) 40 *William and Mary Law Review* 869, 875.

[6] Ibid. 871.   [7] Ibid. 875–6.

the case against blind acceptance of international human rights norms in the strongest terms (perhaps to shock the reader): 'Will International Human Rights be Used as a Tool of Cultural Genocide?' is the provocative title of a recent essay.[8] If totalitarianism comprises 'an attempt to place all aspects of life of a people under the control of a centralized political authority',[9] then mediating groups, such as families and religious organizations, pose a threat. They provide a different locus for citizens' affections, a different loyalty. Ironically, argues Smolin, human rights theory, having evolved out of efforts to curb the horrendous abuses of totalitarian governments, both left and right, is itself in danger of falling into the same trap: 'the modern human rights movement . . . mistook the establishment of human rights as an ultimate good, and thus yearned (however comically, given its impotence) to constitute a new form of totalism'.[10]

If law is fundamentally religious in origin,[11] then conservative religionists become disturbed when they hear human rights norms sometimes being referred to in quasi-religious terms. Human rights standards have been described as constituting 'a large normative canon'[12] or a 'set of secular ethics'.[13] Some human rights advocates appear to share an unequivocal 'belief in the redemptive quality and power of human rights law'.[14] When human rights scholars refer to this being 'the age of rights' and 'human rights being the idea of our time',[15] they effectively elevate human rights (universal, omnipotent) 'to a near-mythical, almost biblical plateau'.[16] However, the Universal Declaration of Human Rights 1948 and its progeny can, if one is not careful, become false idols, another ill-fated tower of Babel.[17]

---

[8] David M. Smolin, 'Will International Human Rights be Used as a Tool of Cultural Genocide? The Interaction of Human Rights Norms, Religion, Culture and Gender', (1996) 12 *Journal of Law and Religion* 143.

[9] Ibid.

[10] Ibid. 144. Smolin illustrates his thesis by exploring the potentially devastating effect the United Nations Convention on the Elimination of All Forms of Discrimination Against Women would have upon a traditional religious community, such as Hasidic and Orthodox Jews, if coercively implemented. Groups such as these apparently perpetuate 'stereotyped roles for men and women' (Art. 5) in violation of the Convention's norm of sexual equality.

[11] See e.g. R. J. Rushdoony, *The Institutes of Biblical Law* (Nutley, NJ, 1973), 4–5.

[12] Thomas M. Franck, 'The Emerging Right to Democratic Governance', (1992) 86 *American Journal of International Law* 46, 79.

[13] Francesca Klug, 'A Bill of Rights as Secular Ethics', in R. Gordon and R. Wilmot-Smith (eds.), *Human Rights in the United Kingdom* (Oxford, 1996), 37, 53: 'International human rights standards provide a set of secular ethics which, whilst drawing upon the moral teachings of all the major religions, attempt to express universal and timeless values.'

[14] Makau wa Mutua, 'The Ideology of Human Rights', (1996) 36 *Virginia Journal of International Law* 589, 595.

[15] Louis Henkin, *The Age of Rights* (New York, 1990) p. ix; quoted in Mutua, 'The Ideology of Human Rights', 627.

[16] Mutua, 'The Ideology of Human Rights', 627.

[17] Mary Ann Glendon, 'Knowing the Universal Declaration of Human Rights', (1998) 73 *Notre Dame Law Review* 1153, 1154.

Liberal Respect for Religious Group Autonomy

Liberal political theory provides at least three justifications for religious group autonomy.

Firstly, religious organizations are—along with neighbourhoods, families, and voluntary associations—'mediating structures'. This term, coined by Berger and Neuhaus, refers to 'institutions standing between the individual in his private life and the large institutions of public life'.[18] Such structures help the individual to mediate between the two spheres of public and private. Furthermore, they socialize individuals, enabling them to see that their self-interest is connected with the interests of others, that their actions have consequences.[19] They may also function as a counterweight to potential totalitarian tendencies of the modern, powerful state.[20] In *The Culture of Disbelief* Stephen Carter argues that religions, at their best, can serve a valuable role as a 'bulwark against government tyranny'.[21] He explains:

> Religions are in effect independent centers of power, with bona fide claims on the allegiance of their members, claims that exist alongside, are not identical to, and will sometimes trump the claims of obedience that the state makes. A religion speaks to its members in a voice different from that of the state, and when the voice moves the faithful to action, a religion may act as a counterweight to the authority of the state.[22]

As Carter colourfully puts it, 'Democracy needs its nose-thumbers'[23] and religions can—due to their allegiance to something other than, and higher than, the state—operate to resist tyranny.[24] The principle that one institution, such as the Church, ought not to be dominated by other, such as the State, is referred to in Christian social and political theory as 'sphere

---

[18] Michael Novak (ed.), Peter Berger, and Richard John Neuhaus, *To Empower People: From State to Civil Society*, 2nd edn. (Washington, 1996), 158. The original essay was published in 1977 and the Novak collection reproduces that seminal pamphlet, together with eleven essays exploring the original argument.

[19] 'Mediating structures teach that we cannot simply have things our own way . . . In voluntary associations, individuals learn to compromise, persuade, and sublimate narrow self-interest for the greater good of the group . . . mediating institutions teach that one's welfare is tied to the welfare of one's community. Without such training, the impetus will be for individuals to pursue self-interest without regard to others' (Timothy Fort, 'The First Man and the Company Man: The Common Good, Transcendence and Mediating Institutions', (1999) 36 *American Business Law Journal* 391, 428).

[20] This thesis is developed by Stephen Carter, *The Culture of Disbelief* (New York, 1993), ch. 2.

[21] Ibid. 36. See similarly John H. Garvey, *What are Freedoms For?* (Cambridge, Mass., 1996), 153.

[22] Carter, *The Culture of Disbelief*, 35.   [23] Ibid.

[24] 'Religion makes us aware that the civil order is but part of the timeless moral order ordained by the universal sovereign, and not the mere choice of passing majorities' (Michael W. McConnell, 'Establishment and Toleration in Edmund Burke's "Constitution of Freedom" ', (1995) *Supreme Court Review* 393, 423).

sovereignty' (in neo-Calvinism)[25] or 'subsidiarity' (in Catholic social thought).[26]

Not all religious communities are of the 'nose-thumbing' kind, of course. Carter's conception of religion is very much that of the dissenting Church. There are faint echoes of Luther's remonstrance, 'Ich kan nicht anderst, hie stehe ich' ('I cannot do otherwise, here I stand') here.[27] Some religious communities, however, may be thoroughly acculturated and see the state's policies as consistent with and furthering their religious objectives. Alternatively, some religious groups may have such an extreme separationist attitude that they completely eschew participation in this-worldly public affairs. They make no pretence of acting as a bulwark against tyranny.[28]

Secondly, man is a social being. Groups provide a context for personal growth, expression, and fulfilment: 'An individual's definition and sense of self depends to a significant extent on the character of the recognition granted by others.'[29] Groups formed on the basis of spiritual beliefs are no exception. A religious community, par excellence, affords its members the opportunity to interact, to find a sense of identity and meaning.[30]

Thirdly, religious groups, among other types of association, may be a wellspring for new ideas, arguments, and methods of reasoning outside the prevailing concepts and ways of thinking of liberal democracy.[31] Fred Gedicks explains:

In liberal society, the government has no competence to determine moral ends. In theory, at least, the goals of liberal democratic government must depend on the values held by those it governs—values that originate outside of government in churches, families, political parties, trade unions, private schools, and other voluntary associations. In the absence of these groups, government and society would be deprived of the enriching world-views that these groups contribute to . . . culture and politics.[32]

Some theorists also believe there is a crucial link between religion and the fostering of important civic virtues, such as law-abidingness, honesty,

---

[25] See L. Kalsbeek, *Contours of a Christian Philosophy* (Toronto, 1975), ch. 28.
[26] See *Catechism of the Catholic Church* (*Liberia Editrice Vaticana*), CEPAC edn. (Kuala Lumpur, 1994), para. 1883.
[27] Quoted in Scott C. Idleman, 'The Sacred, the Profane, and the Instrumental: Valuing Religion in the Culture of Disbelief', (1994) 142 *University of Pennsylvania Law Review* 1313, 1334.
[28] See ibid. 1348–9.
[29] Frederick Mark Gedicks, 'Toward a Constitutional Jurisprudence of Religious Group Rights', [1989] *Wisconsin Law Review* 99, 116.
[30] Paul Horwitz, 'The Sources and Limits of Freedom of Religion in a Liberal Democracy', (1996) 54 *University of Toronto Faculty of Law Review* 1, 53–4.
[31] Ibid. 52–3.
[32] Gedicks, 'Toward a Constitutional Jurisprudence of Religious Group Rights', 116.

thrift, and self-restraint.[33] But to speak of the virtue-enhancing propensities of religion generally is sweeping. It is 'religious communities *of the
right sort*'[34] that liberal democracy needs. There are religions and religions: 'To ask about religion's value-inculcating role at the close of the
twentieth century one must speak not only of high-church Presbyterians,
but of snake-handling fundamentalist Christians, Shiite Moslems, and
Santerians, to mention only a handful of examples.'[35] Moreover, while
religious groups may prescribe valuable moral norms and civic virtues,
other institutions also fulfil this function.[36]

The Courts' Traditional Deference to Religious Group Autonomy

The incompetence of any human authority to evaluate religion correctly as
true or false has been described as a 'common Protestant conviction': 'no
mortal man and no human institution can be regarded as infallible'.[37] John
Locke in his *Letter concerning Toleration* argued:

For every church is orthodox to itself; to others erroneous or heretical . . . So that
the controversy between these churches about the truth of their doctrines, and the
purity of their worship, is on both sides equal; nor is there any judge, either at
Constantinople, or elsewhere upon earth, by whose sentence it can be determined.
The decision of that question belongs only to the Supreme Judge of all men, to
whom also alone belongs the punishment of the erroneous.[38]

Courts in the common law world are notoriously reluctant to determine
disputes of a religiously sensitive nature. There is not an absolute barrier
to civil adjudication of church disputes—courts have, for example, long
been called upon to resolve questions of property division following
schism within a denomination—but the jurisdiction is exercised circumspectly. Recently the New Zealand Court of Appeal in *Mabon* v.

---

[33] John Locke insisted religious belief was needed to foster moral values such as law-
abidingness and self-restraint (see Sanford Kessler, 'John Locke's Legacy of Religious
Freedom', *Polity*, 17 (1984–5), 484, 495). A recent comprehensive exposition of the civic
virtue rationale for religious freedom is that by Timothy L. Hall, 'Religion and Civic Virtue:
A Justification of Free Exercise', (1992) 67 *Tulane Law Review* 87.

[34] Macedo, 'Transformative Constitutionalism', 65.

[35] Hall, 'Religion and Civic Virtue', 108. Steven D. Smith, *Foreordained Failure: The
Quest for a Constitutional Principle of Religious Freedom* (New York, 1995), 102,
comments: 'Are the social fruits of religion sweet or bitter? Upon reflection it should be plain,
I think, that these questions not susceptible of any general or uniform response. The only
plausible answer, rather, is "It depends . . .".'

[36] Schools, universities, families, service clubs, debating societies, and sporting organizations are other mediating institutions which contribute to the virtues thought vital to a liberal
democracy. See Hall, 'Religion and Civic Virtue', 112–13; Smith, *Foreordained Failure*, 103.

[37] Winthrop S. Hudson, 'The Theological Basis for Religious Freedom', *Journal of
Church and State*, 3 (1961), 130, 133.

[38] John Locke, *Epistola de tolerantia (A Letter concerning Toleration)* (1689), in John
Horton and Susan Mendus (eds.), *John Locke, A Letter concerning Toleration—In Focus*
(London, 1991), 24.

Conference of the Methodist Church of New Zealand endorsed the received view: 'Clearly, and reflecting the separation of church and state, Courts must be reluctant to determine what are at heart ecclesiastical disputes where matters of faith and doctrine are at issue. But the Courts will intervene where civil or property rights are involved.'[39]

English courts too are loath to determine matters of internal church governance. A recent example is *Wachmann*.[40] The chief rabbi disciplined the applicant Wachmann, an Orthodox rabbi, declaring him religiously and morally unfit to hold office. This ruling followed an internal commission of inquiry that substantiated allegations of adultery by the applicant with members of his congregation. Wachmann's employment was terminated and he sought judicial review. The High Court refused this in forthright terms. Despite judicial review extending to bodies 'which in earlier days would have surely have been thought beyond its reach',[41] further extension to this body was unwarranted. The chief rabbi's discharge of his religious functions was simply not of a public law character. The entanglement of Church and State occasioned by permitting review added further force to this conclusion. Simon Brown J observed:

the court would never be prepared to rule on questions of Jewish law. Mr Carus [counsel for Wachmann], recognising this prospective difficulty, says in advancing his challenge here the applicant would be prepared to rely solely upon the common law concept of natural justice. But it would not always be easy to separate out procedural complaints from consideration of substantive principles of Jewish law which may underlie them . . . the court is hardly in a position to regulate what is essentially a religious function—the determination whether someone is morally and religiously fit to carry out the spiritual and pastoral duties of his office. The court must inevitably be wary of entering so self-evidently sensitive an area, straying across the well-recognised divide between church and state. One cannot, therefore, escape the conclusion that, if judicial review lies here, then one way or another this secular court must inevitably be drawn into adjudicating upon matters intimate to a religious community.[42]

I mentioned at the outset the potential conflict between a state policy to safeguard religious freedom and a public policy to eliminate discrimination based upon objectionable grounds. A good illustration of the resolution of the clash between anti-discrimination law and church autonomy is the American case *Rayburn* v. *General Conference of Seventh-Day Adventists*.[43]

The plaintiff was denied a pastoral position in the Seventh-Day Adventist Church and brought an action alleging sexual and racial

---

[39] [1998] 3 NZLR 513, 523.
[40] R. v. *Chief Rabbi of the United Hebrew Congregations of Great Britain and the Commonwealth, ex parte Wachmann* [1993] 2 All ER 249.
[41] Ibid. 253.   [42] Ibid. 255.
[43] 772 F. 2d 1164 (1985).

discrimination. The Court of Appeals held that the suit was barred by the
First Amendment. It repeated the Supreme Court's long-standing recognition of the constitutional right of churches to select their own clergy free
from state interference, 'for perpetuation of a church's existence may
depend upon those whom it selects to preach its values, teach its message,
and interpret its doctrines both to its own membership and to the world at
large'.[44] Was the State's interest in eradicating discrimination of sufficient
magnitude to override the interests of religious freedom guaranteed under
the First Amendment? The Court was in no doubt:

Here the balance weighs in favor of free exercise of religion. The role of an associate in pastoral care [the position Rayburn sought] is so significant in the expression
and realization of Seventh-day Adventist beliefs that state intervention in the
appointment process would excessively inhibit religious liberty.[45]

Judicial review here would also impermissibly entangle secular courts
with church authority resulting in 'an intolerably close relationship
between church and state both on a substantive and procedural level'.[46] At
a substantive level, conformity due to governmental pressure was not an
imaginary risk:

It is axiomatic that the guidance of the state cannot substitute for that of the Holy
Spirit and that a courtroom is not the place to review a church's determination of
'God's appointed' . . . The danger is that *choices of clergy which conform to the
preferences of public agencies may be favored* over those which are neutral or
opposed.[47]

At a procedural level, state entanglement by way of protracted and
expensive legal proceedings would be likely if suits such as the plaintiff's
were entertained. Church personnel and records would, said the Court,
inevitably become subject to subpoena, discovery, and cross-examination,
remedies dispensed might have far-reaching implications, and continued
court monitoring to ensure compliance might be required.[48] Thus, once
more,

There is the danger that churches, wary of EEOC [Equal Employment Opportunity
Commission] or judicial review of their decisions, might make them *with an eye to
avoiding litigation or bureaucratic entanglement* rather than upon the basis of their
own personal and doctrinal assessments of who would best serve the pastoral
needs of their members.[49]

A case squarely in point is *Walker* v. *First Presbyterian Church.*[50] A

[44] *Rayburn* v. *General Conference of Seventh-Day Adventists*, 1168 per Wilkinson J,
applying the Supreme Court decisions, *Kedroff* v. *St. Nicholas Cathedral*, 344 U.S. 94, 116
(1952), and *Serbian Eastern Orthodox Diocese* v. *Milivojevich*, 426 U.S. 696, 713 (1976).
[45] 772 F. 2d 1164, 1168.   [4] Ibid. 1170.
[47] Ibid.; my italics.   [48] Ibid. 1171.   [49] Ibid.; my italics.
[50] 22 FEP Cases 762 (1980).

Californian court upheld the right of the Church to discharge the plaintiff, its Church organist and a practising, 'unrepentant' homosexual. The ban upon sexual orientation in employment in the San Francisco Police Code had to yield to the First Amendment free exercise right of the Church to determine who should be a member of its worship team.

Religious Group Autonomy in Human Rights Legislation

Modern human rights legislation customarily defers to church autonomy on matters of clergy selection and the like. For example, in the United States, discrimination in employment on the usual bases (sex, race, national origin, etc.) is prohibited under Title VII of the Civil Rights Act 1964. Section 702 of that Act provides an exemption for religious bodies where they discriminate in employment on the basis of religion.[51] Anti-discrimination statutes in several Australian states contain exemptions for religious organizations designed to preserve their religious autonomy.[52] An example is section 32 of the Australian Capital Territory's Discrimination Act 1991, which reads:

32. Nothing in Part III applies in relation to—(a) the ordination or appointment of priests, ministers of religion or members of any religious order; (b) the training or education of persons seeking ordination or appointment as priests, ministers of religion or members of a religious order; (c) the selection or appointment of persons to perform duties or functions for the purposes of, or in connection with, any religious observance or practice; or (d) any other act or practice of a body established for religious purposes, being an act or practice that conforms to the doctrines, tenets or beliefs of that religion and is necessary to avoid injury to the religious susceptibilities of adherents of that religion.[53]

The United Kingdom Human Rights Act 1998 was substantially amended during its passage (following intensive lobbying by British churches designed to safeguard their religious freedoms[54]) and now contains section 13(1), which reads: 'If a court's determination of any question arising under this Act might affect the exercise by a religious organisation (itself or its members collectively) of the Convention right to freedom of thought, conscience and religion it must have particular regard to the importance of that right.'

---

[51] It reads: 'This subchapter [i.e. Title VII of the Civil Rights Act 1964] shall not apply ... to a religious corporation, association, educational institution or society with respect to the employment of individuals of a particular religion to perform work connected with the carrying on by such corporation, association, educational institution or society of its activities.'

[52] See generally Reid Mortensen, 'Rendering to God and Caesar: Religion in Australian Discrimination Law' (1995) 18 *University of Queensland Law Journal* 208.

[53] For a similar exemption, see e.g. s. 75 of the Equal Opportunity Act 1995 (WA).

[54] See Julian Rivers, 'From Toleration to Pluralism: Religious Liberty and Religious Establishment under the United Kingdom's Human Rights Act', in R. Ahdar (ed.), *Law and Religion* (Aldershot, 2000), ch. 7.

International human rights instruments also reinforce this deference to religious group autonomy. Article 9(1) of the European Convention on Human Rights accords organized religious communities the right to determine their choice of clergy.[55] In similar fashion, Article 18(1) of the International Covenant on Civil and Political Rights 1966 (ICCPR) makes it clear that the right of religious freedom applies 'individually or in community with others'. In its exegesis of Article 18 the UN's Human Rights Committee stated:

In addition, the practice and teaching of religion or belief includes acts integral to the conduct by religious groups of their basic affairs, such as the freedom to choose their religious leaders, priests and teachers, the freedom to establish seminaries and religious schools and the freedom to prepare and distribute religious texts or publications.[56]

This statement is in the Committee's 1993 General Comment No. 22; a pronouncement described as 'an authoritative statement'[57] of the Committee's understanding of the article. The Human Rights Committee's observation on church autonomy simply echoes the mention made in the UN Declaration on the Elimination of All Forms of Intolerance and of Discrimination Based on Religion or Belief 1981.[58] Article 6 provides a non-exhaustive catalogue of particular freedoms within the rubric of religious freedom, including paragraph (g): freedom 'To train, appoint, elect, or designate by succession, appropriate leaders called for by the requirements and standards of any religion or belief'. Unlike the ICCPR, the 1981 Declaration is not strictly speaking binding as a source of direct legal obligation on states.[59] Nevertheless, such declarations still carry weight.

A Danger

A danger looms when human rights norms collide with certain religious group practices. Some judges have discerned that the mere prospect of state intrusion into a religious organization's decision-making on matters of leadership or membership may intrude upon that group's process of 'self-definition' and thus entail a 'chilling effect' upon religious group autonomy.

---

[55] See e.g. *Prussner* v. *Germany* (1987) 8 EHRR 79, and *Serif* v. *Greece*, app. no. 38178/97, 14 Dec. 1999.
[56] General Comment No. 22, para. 4. The Human Rights Committee adopted the General Comment (CCPR/C/21/Rev 1/Add 4) on 20 July 1993.
[57] Malcolm Evans, *Religious Liberty and International Law in Europe* (Cambridge, 1997), 208.
[58] Adopted without vote by the General Assembly on 25 Nov. 1981 (GA Res. 36/55).
[59] Since it was adopted as a General Assembly Resolution which under the UN Charter has only a recommendatory status (UN Charter, Art. 10). See Evans, *Religious Liberty and International Law in Europe*, 257.

Justice Brennan in *Corporation of the Presiding Bishop of the Church of Jesus Christ of Latter-Day Saints* v. *Amos*[60] put the case for judicial deference to religious organizations' control over their internal governance in terms of the importance of self-definition. Any group, but especially a religious one, must be able to define its purpose or 'mission'. It has, as Gedicks puts it, a 'narrative' or 'vision' of itself.[61] It should have the ultimate say over who is a member or not, what are its core concerns, who should lead it.[62] Justice Brennan explained that a religious community

represents an ongoing tradition of shared beliefs, an organic entity not reducible to a mere aggregation of individuals. Determining that certain activities are in furtherance of an organization's religious mission, and that only those committed to that mission should conduct them, is thus a means by which a religious community defines itself. Solicitude for a church's ability to do so reflects the idea that furtherance of the autonomy of religious organizations often furthers individual religious freedom as well.[63]

Religious group self-definition may trammel individual rights. The organization may 'condition employment in certain activities on subscription to particular religious tenets'.[64] (In *Amos* the non-profit gymnasium owned and operated by the Church of Jesus Christ of Latter-Day Saints discharged a building engineer who failed to maintain his 'temple recommend', a certification of his Mormon membership. The Supreme Court held that the case fell within the exemption for religious organizations from the ban on religious discrimination under Title VII of the Civil Rights Act 1964.) The process of self-definition, the control over one's own narrative, was, however, important enough for Justice Brennan to countenance infringement of individual liberty and the thwarting of the government's interest in a societal policy of non-discrimination.[65] Judicial determination of whether an activity is 'secular' or 'religious' (let alone clergy selection) may require 'a searching case-by-case analysis'[66] resulting in the very sort of government 'entanglement' in religious affairs which is best avoided. As equally disturbing was the 'chilling effect' of state intervention in religious organization governance: '[The] prospect of government intrusion raises concern that a religious organization may be chilled in its free exercise activity.'[67] Once more, the Church may make its decision with an eye as much on state standards and bureaucratic intervention

---

[60] 483 U.S. 327 (1987).
[61] Gedicks, 'Toward a Constitutional Jurisprudence of Religious Group Rights', 108.
[62] 'We are willing to countenance [religious groups discrimination in employment] because we deem it vital that, if certain activities constitute part of a religious community's practice, then a religious organization should be able to require that only members of its community perform those activities' (*Amos*, 483 U.S. 327, 342–3).
[63] 483 U.S. 327, 342. See also Garvey, *What are Freedoms For?*, 149–50.
[64] 483 U.S. 327, 342.   [65] Ibid. 342–3.   [66] Ibid.   [67] Ibid.

as on its own religious convictions: 'the community's process of self-definition would be shaped in part by the prospects of litigation'.[68]

Vindication of group rights over individual liberty (and the societal goal
of non-discrimination) is not something to be done lightly. Individuals
sacrificed in the name of church autonomy are entitled to feel disgruntled.
In mitigation two things can be said. Firstly, when the individuals joined,
they voluntarily gave up their personal religious liberty.[69] Now they are
part of a dynamic, organic whole. Secondly, if they are unhappy, they are
free to leave and join with those with more congenial beliefs. It is not
apparent that they should be able to invoke the State to force the group to
conform to *their* vision. Admittedly, the opportunity to exit must be
'meaningful', and should leaving the group be practically impossible (for
financial or other reasons) a case for state intervention arises.[70] But this
would seldom be so, for there is usually no shortage of social, religious,
and economic alternatives available for those expelled or denied admission.[71]

The Gay Clergy Debate in New Zealand

The ordination of openly practising homosexual or lesbian candidates for
the ministry (OPHM) has been a matter of sharp controversy within
certain New Zealand denominations. Controversy has been confined
primary to two churches, the Presbyterian and Methodist Churches (with
some smouldering debate in the Anglican Church as well).

For some churches OPHM is not an issue. Thoroughgoing conservative
denominations—the Pentecostal churches, Open Brethren, Seventh-Day
Adventists, the Salvation Army, etc.—have not, at least publicly, debated
the issue. Lacking liberal theological factions within those churches, such
debate is unlikely to arise. However, these churches take a keen interest in
the subject, for it is a matter which 'affect[s] the entire church not just part
of it'.[72] For the Catholic Church, the requirement of celibacy for priests
officially rules out the possibility of gay clergy.[73]

The Anglican Church has been reluctant to state firmly its position on
OPHM. Recently, the Tikanga Pakeha (the Pakeha section of the Church)
established a commission to study human sexuality issues. In its 1998
report the commission refused to rule out OPHM and argued instead for a
local case-by-case approach:

---

[68] 483 U.S. 327, 343–4.

[69] See e.g. *Prussner* v. *Germany*.

[70] Galston, 'Expressive Liberty', 906; Gedicks, 'Toward a Constitutional Jursiprudence
of Religious Group Rights', 151–3.

[71] Gedicks, 'Toward a Constitutional Jurisprudence of Religious Group Rights', 152–3.

[72] Dean Comerford, 'Homosexual Issues Affect Entire Christian Church', *Challenge
Weekly*, 21 July 1998, 3.

[73] *Catechism of the Catholic Church*, para. 1579.

Given that in the Anglican Church in Aotearoa, New Zealand and Polynesia, the decision to ordain a person deacon or priest lies with the Bishop after due consultation and advice from others . . . it is the view of the Commission that each application for ordination should be dealt with on an individual basis regardless of the candidate's marital status, gender, sexual orientation, or sexual preference.[74]

The question of gay clergy has divided Methodists.[75] The catalyst for the polarizing debate between liberal and conservative Methodists was the effort by a Dr David Bromell to achieve ordination. Bromell had been a Baptist minister but was asked to resign in 1986 when he declared he was a practising homosexual. Bromell was appointed as a supply (relieving) minister in a Dunedin Methodist parish. He applied for 'full connexion' into the ministry in 1990, but the annual Methodist Conference rejected his bid. Eventually, influenced by the Human Rights Act 1993, the 1997 Annual Conference voted to receive Bromell into full connexion. The vote was not unanimous, with about a third of the Conference expressing strong disapproval. Disgruntled evangelical Methodists—including many Pacific Island congregations—quickly formed the Wesleyan Methodist Movement with a view to breaking away from the Church. OPHM was not the only concern prompting the proposed split, but it was, as one conservative put it, 'the straw that broke the camel's back'.[76] Bromell was duly appointed as superintendent of the Christchurch Methodist City Mission. In an effort to avoid a wholesale schism caused by conservative Methodists breaking off to join like-minded brethren from the Presbyterian fold, the 1998 Conference agreed in principle to an Evangelical Synod. Opposition by liberal elements to the creation of such a synod at the 1999 Conference left conservative Methodists frustrated and pondering their future.

The most acrimonious and protracted debate on gay clergy has been that of the Presbyterian Church of Aotearoa New Zealand (PCANZ). A series of General Assemblies since 1985 has grappled with the issue. At the time of writing the saga has still not been concluded. The 1985 Assembly distinguished between homosexual orientation and practice, affirmed that 'homosexual acts [were] sinful', but added the rider that God loved and accepted homosexuals as people. The Church was urged to initiate compassionate ministry to those in a homosexual lifestyle. In 1991 a Special Committee was appointed by the Assembly to investigate OPHM and report back. Presbyteries were instructed not to proceed to the licensing,

---

[74] Tikanga Pakeha Commission on Sexuality of the Anglican Church in Aotearoa, New Zealand and Polynesia (May 1998), 14.

[75] The following narrative of the Methodist and Presbyterian debates omits precise references to resolutions, statements, and so on, in the interest of brevity. For the full citations and extended analysis, see R. J. Ahdar, 'Worlds Colliding: Aspects of New Zealand Conservative Christians' Encounter with the Law', University of Otago Ph. D. thesis, 2000, ch. 9.

[76] Frith Rayner, 'The Other Side', *Crosslink* (June 1999), 8–9.

ordination, or induction of any self-avowed active homosexual until that time. The 1991 Assembly passed a carefully worded resolution affirming that 'God's intention for sexual relationships, as affirmed by Jesus Christ, is loving, mutual and faithful marriage between a man and a woman, and that intimate sexual expressions outside of that context fall short of God's standard.' While echoing again the need for 'compassionate ministry, forgiveness and restoration' of those who fall short in this area, it was clear on OPHM: 'those who continue in sexual acts in any context outside of heterosexual marriage are not appropriate persons to be in the leadership of this Church'.

In 1993 the Assembly deferred the vote on OPHM, thereby allowing the prohibition on presbyteries (imposed by the 1991 Assembly) to lapse. This was to establish 'a neutral environment' and defuse deepening division until the Special Committee reported. One presbytery was impatient. In 1995 a Dunedin church attempted to license Martin Dickson, a self-avowed practising homosexual living with a partner. A Judicial Commission of the PCANZ found that the Dunedin presbytery had failed to observe procedural fairness and had pre-empted the 1995 Assembly decision.[77] It decided, however, that in the particular circumstances of this case Dickson ought to be licensed. He had commenced his four-year training at Knox College (the national seminary) with the assurance from senior personnel that his homosexuality would not be an impediment to his being licensed. Although such an assurance was wrong, his legitimate expectations had now to be recognized. Invoking a regulation giving the Church power to dispose of cases in exceptional circumstances where justice so required, it approved the licensing. The Human Rights Act 1993 featured prominently in its report. Dickson's lawyer, Judith Medlicott, was later to remark that the Act had played a prominent role and that 'without the existence of the Act the outcome may have been different'.[78] Dickson was licensed, which meant he could now accept a 'call' from a parish or act as a chaplain. Ordination would be another step again, however. Many evangelicals within the PCANZ were outraged.

Matters again came to a head at the 1996 General Assembly. The following resolution was adopted by 172 votes to 142:

That Assembly, recognising the need for a clear ruling on practising homosexuals in leadership in the Church, rules that its courts shall not license, ordain or induct practising homosexuals. At the same time, Assembly recognises the deep diversity of convictions in the Church on issues relating to homosexuality generally and calls

---

[77] See *Report of Decision of the Assembly Judicial Commission re Nine Dissents with Complaint Against Decision of Dunedin Presbytery Dated 1 November 1994 to License a Candidate* (25 Aug. 1995), 1.

[78] 'The Presbytery of Dunedin Licenses Gay Student to the Ministry,' *Crosslink* (Dec. 1995), 1; S. Lippert, 'Homosexual Minister Licensed,' *Otago Daily Times*, 13 Nov. 1995, 3, for comment from Mrs Medlicott.

the Church to move ahead in a spirit of gracious respect and compassion for one another.

Conservative Presbyterians were pleased, but OPHM supporters such as Galaxies (Gay and Lesbian Christians in Every Sphere) were dismayed. 'I'm sad', commented a homosexual elder at a central Wellington church, 'at the stony hearts of so many people at the assembly.' In 1997 that congregation flouted that 1996 ruling and licensed a Ms Alyson Murrie-West, a lesbian elder. Presbyterian churches in Eastern Southland publicly dissociated themselves from this pre-emptive decision.

Hopes for a definitive verdict in 1998 were again to be frustrated. The attempt to ratify the 1996 ban on homosexual leadership failed to gain the necessary majority. The Assembly now required a 60 per cent vote for successful ratification, and thus the simple majority in favour of the 1996 ruling (54.5 per cent) fell short. The 1998 Assembly voted instead to impose a one-year ban on OPHM, a similar ban on advocacy of views on the subject, and for the establishment of a Commission on Diversity. The Commission heard submissions and prepared plans for separate synods or streams within the PCANZ to accommodate the differing convictions of members on this vexed topic.

The Extra General Assembly in 1999 saw a majority of members reject proposals in favour of gay clergy. The vote of 146 (46 per cent) in favour versus 171 (54 per cent) against OPHM was interpreted as an impasse by some commentators but as a victory by Presbyterian AFFIRM, an umbrella group for conservative and evangelical Presbyterians.[79] Both sides failed to gain the necessary 60 per cent needed to carry the day. What it did mean was that the issue lay on the table—both camps resigned to battling on—with another Assembly scheduled for September 2000 to wrestle with the issue again.

The Shadow of the Human Rights Act

A key premiss in the church debates has been the belief that a clear ruling from the church authorities on gay clergy was required. The PCANZ, for instance, took the understandably cautious approach that nothing short of a clear edict from the General Assembly would guarantee that congregations would enjoy immunity from suit under the Act. Presbyterian AFFIRM, whose affiliates had most to lose, articulated their concern thus:

In the absence of specific [church] regulations, the church is vulnerable to be forced to accept practising homosexuals as ministers by the provisions of the Human Rights Act, through either a ruling from the Human Rights Commission, or by a decision of the High Court in a test case. The lawyer [Judith Medlicott] who was

---

[79] See Stuart Lange, 'A View from the Assembly Trenches', *Crosslink* (Aug. 1999), 9.

acting for the practising homosexual who was licensed [Dickson] has publicly threatened that 'it ill behoves' anyone to oppose his ordination. A 'non-decision' by this Assembly would expose the PCANZ—and potentially *any* congregation— to expensive litigation.[80]

But the prospect of costly lawsuits was not the principal reason why conservatives within these Protestant churches sought a definitive answer on gay clergy. For them the issue was pivotal. Acceptance of homosexual or lesbian leadership was a watershed—would conservatives or liberals control the direction of the narrative henceforth?

Liberal Christians' response was twofold. Firstly, they questioned what all the fuss was about. One mused, 'Some day we will look back and wonder why we struggled . . . It may be a surprise to discover the wheels do not fall off the Church when a parish appoints a homosexual minister.'[81] Their second strategy was to strongly support OPHM as a matter of 'justice' and the Church 'working for the human rights of all people'. For them, one's sexual orientation or practice was as much an irrelevant requirement for leadership as it was for membership. God's love and mercy mandated 'inclusiveness' and 'tolerance'.

Conservatives replied by emphasizing the holiness as well as the mercy of God and reaffirming the continued relevance of the unchanging moral law. It was not an issue of justice, since no one had an inalienable right to be a church leader, nor was it a matter of inclusiveness, for the Gospel was about repentance, grace, and transformation. The distinction between membership, where inclusiveness could rightly pertain, versus leadership, which called for more exacting exclusive standards, was reiterated. OPHM was not even a matter of competing interpretations since the Scriptures, properly read, were 'very clear'.[82] No, it was matter of truth and a question of authority: would the Church take its lead and be subservient to the Scriptures or to mere human secular opinion? The Church was in danger of making 'liberalism' its authority. But, retorted one evangelical Methodist minister, 'where does liberalism find its authority? Is it the Scriptures, sermons of Wesley, or somewhere else?' Liberalism was endeavouring to impose justifications for homosexuality upon the Scriptures, 'making Scripture subject to liberalism'. This was, he continued, plainly wrong. It ought to be God above Caesar and never the other way round.[83] The failure of liberal Christians to appreciate the significance of OPHM simply demonstrated to conservatives that there 'are two world views, two spirits, two logical choices'. Accepting homosexual leadership would be a graphic succumbing to the *Zeitgeist*. In the conservative understanding, just as the

[80] Presbyterian AFFIRM, *Should the Presbyterian Church Ordain Practising Homosexuals? A Position Paper*, (Auckland, June 1996), 8.

[81] The Revd Norman West, quoted in 'Te Hahi Hits "the Issue" ', *Crosslink* (Oct. 1997), 5.

[82] The Revd Chris Dombroski, quoted ibid.   [83] Ibid.

state is under God, likewise Caesar's law is subservient to God's law. When the state exceeds its delegated authority and trespasses in spheres properly not its domain, civil disobedience may be the reluctant last resort. The belligerent streak in conservatives eschews 'supine yielding to the pressures of secularisation'. Presbyterian AFFIRM hinted at possible disobedience if the Human Rights Act were construed to force them to ordain practising homosexuals as ministers. It reminded its members of its Reformation roots: 'even if the Ruling [banning OPHM] *were* illegal (and we do not believe that it is), the Assembly would have ultimate responsibility not to the secular law but to the law of God'.

Liberal Christians, by contrast, harboured real reservations on flouting the law, at least on this issue. Liberals had been prepared to risk breaking the law on matters of social justice such as apartheid and Springbok rugby tour protests. But this issue was different. Liberal Christians supported the Human Rights Act. They had furnished submissions to Parliament in favour of sexual orientation being added as a ground of prohibited discrimination just a few years earlier. Some denominations, where the liberals' sway was stronger, were content to comply with the Act. The Methodist Annual Conference 1993 decided that the Methodist Church ought to 'order its life and practice within the intent of the [Human Rights] Act'. The then Methodist president, the Revd Mervyn Dine, said the Church 'won't be trying to find clauses in the act to get them out' of abiding by the statute. For supporters of gay clergy, the Act was a valuable tool in changing church policy. It is idle to suggest the Act was supported by liberal Christians solely to allow and advance the cause of OPHM, but, once in place, it could nonetheless be usefully invoked.

The experience of the churches debating in the shadow of the Human Rights Act illustrates, I suggest, that the mere prospect of state intrusion may intrude upon a Church's process of self-definition and thus entail a 'chilling effect' upon its religious autonomy. It is difficult not to conclude that the PCANZ's process of self-definition was shaped, at least in part, by the prospects of litigation. To paraphrase *Rayburn*, the Methodist and Presbyterian Churches made their decisions with an eye to avoiding litigation and bureaucratic entanglement rather than solely on the basis of their own doctrinal assessments of who would best serve their pastoral needs. At the very least, the spectre of the Act gave a heightened sense of urgency and anxiety to what was already a simmering division. The influence of the Act is all the more problematic since it is by no means clear it applied to OPHM in the first place.

Are Ordination Decisions Caught?

Some conservative Christians were concerned at their religious liberties being curtailed should sexual orientation be added as a ground of prohibited discrimination in the human rights legislation. In her speech in the House of Representatives the associate minister of health, Mrs Katherine O'Regan (the parliamentarian responsible for introducing the sexual orientation amendment to the Human Rights Bill), endeavoured to assuage such fears: 'it is not my intention that the legislation should force churches to accept homosexual ministers'.[84] Many conservatives were, nonetheless, not assured.

The impact of the ban upon sexual orientation in the Human Rights Act 1993 upon the gay clergy question is complex. The Act's import cannot be considered in the round, for its prohibitions (and exemptions) apply at different stages in the ordination process —training, licensing and ordination, and appointment—with potentially different outcomes.

I wish to concentrate upon the middle, ordination phase, but, as for the other two, a brief comment is merited. At the training stage, questions about a candidate's sexual orientation might be suspect (as indicating an intention to discriminate[85]), as would refusals to enrol a candidate for training at a Bible college or seminary because of his or her sexual orientation.[86] Here we see a 'chilling effect' at work again—selection of future leaders occurs with an eye to prospective litigation under secular law.

Following the Court of Appeal's judgment in *Mabon*,[87] a minister will not usually be deemed to be 'employed' by the Church concerned. In the infrequent and exceptional cases where ministerial appointments are found to constitute 'employment contracts' the churches must avail themselves of the exemption allowing different treatment based on religious or ethical belief 'where the sole or principal duties of the position are, or are substantially the same as, those of a clergyman, priest, pastor, official, or teacher among adherents of that belief'.[88] To secure immunity the religious institution would be obliged to satisfy the tribunal that the applicant's beliefs about homosexual conduct are 'religious beliefs' at odds with its (the institution's) own religious tenets.

A crucial threshold question is whether there is discrimination occurring at all. As we have seen, conservatives consistently maintain a distinction be drawn between 'orientation' and 'practice'. For them the objection is practising homosexuals, not those who seek to be leaders and who harbour a sexual 'leaning' or 'propensity' towards persons of the same gender. One's leaning or 'orientation' to commit sin (as conservatives view it) is to be expected. Persons with sinful propensities (which is everyone) cannot be condemned and cannot be ruled out of leadership because of such weakness or vulnerability alone. Persons who unashamedly give vent to their

[84] (1992) 532 *New Zealand Parliamentary Debates* 13208.

[85] S. 23.

[86] See s. 40 (discrimination by vocation training bodies) and s. 57 (discrimination by educational establishments).

[87] [1998] 3 NZLR 513.   [88] S. 28(2).

weaknesses and refuse to refrain from sinful acts, however, are not fit for leadership. No one who knowingly, openly, and habitually commits sinful acts is fit for the ministry.

Is the refusal to ordain a homosexual or lesbian candidate by reason of his or her sexual 'practice', discrimination by reason of sexual orientation?[89] If a Church were to ordain a candidate with a homosexual orientation who pledged to remain celibate, i.e. refrain from sexual relations with another member of his or her sex, then the operative reason would indeed appear to be sexual practice and not orientation.[90] There is, nonetheless, the argument that 'practice' necessarily includes an 'orientation' to that effect also. Of course some churches might ostensibly reject candidates on the ground of homosexual practice when they are in reality basing the refusal upon homosexual orientation alone. But that would be a question of fact.[91]

The Ordination Exemption Analysed

Section 38 of the Act stipulates that it is unlawful for a qualifying body (one empowered to confer an 'approval, authorisation or qualification' that is needed for engagement in a 'profession, trade or calling') to discriminate on any of the prohibited grounds. Section 39(1) provides an exemption for religious organizations, but, and herein lies the problem, it is not a model of clarity:

39. Exemptions in relation to qualifying bodies —

(1) Nothing in section 38 of this Act shall apply where the authorisation or qualification is needed for, or facilitates engagement in, a profession or calling for the purposes of an organised religion, and is limited to one sex or to persons of that religious belief so as to comply with the doctrines or rules or established customs of that religion.

Several readings of section 39 are possible.[92] Firstly, it could mean that religious bodies can restrict authorizations to persons of one sex or religious

---

[89] S. 21(1)(m). That provision declares sexual orientation 'means a heterosexual, homosexual, lesbian, or bisexual orientation'. For clarification, see Robert Wintemute, 'Sexual Orientation Discrimination', in C. McCrudden and G. Chambers (eds.), *Individual Rights and the Law in Britain* (Oxford, 1994), 494.

[90] But some conservatives question whether a celibate homosexual would pass muster. See e.g. the Revd Stuart Lange, *Homosexuality and the Church* (Auckland, 1998), 15–16: 'A "celibate homosexual" whose mind is swimming with inappropriate sexual thoughts and desires is hardly a suitable person to be a spiritual leader.'

[91] See the Opinion for the Human Rights Commission by Associate Professor Paul Rishworth, Professor Margaret Bedggood, and Colin Pidgeon QC, May 1988 (on file with author). I should disclose I had input into a draft version of this opinion.

[92] I am indebted to the Rishworth, Bedggood, Pidgeon Opinion here. A greatly condensed discussion is in P. Rishworth, 'Bill of Rights, Human Rights' [1998] *New Zealand Law Review* 585, 601–2.

belief but cannot withhold approvals by reason of the candidate's *other* attributes—race, colour, age, marital status, national origin, sexual orientation, etc. This construction seems unlikely. It would mean that churches could not decline to ordain a candidate who was married, nor one who was 'living in a relationship in the nature of a marriage'.[93] The Catholic Church would have difficulty with the former and most denominations would oppose the latter.

Secondly, the widest reading of the section would afford religious organizations a categorical exemption from section 38 because of the *type* of qualification they confer rather than simply immunizing particular decisions of the religious body based on nominated grounds. The section states tha 'Nothing in section 38 . . . shall apply' (thus rendering the section 38 prohibition otiose) 'where the authorisation is needed for a calling for the purposes of an organised religion' (ordination is invariably restricted to adherents of that Church so as to fulfil the tenets of that faith). This construction accords with the statement of Katherine O'Regan in the parliamentary debates, the protection afforded clergy ordination decisions by the United Nations Human Rights Committee's General Comment No. 22, and the immunity recognized in many common law jurisdictions. Here the Church would not need to point to a rule, doctrine, or custom holding that ordination of practising homosexuals is impermissible. The reference to rules, doctrines, and customs in the closing words of section 39(1) is simply to make the obvious point that any restriction upon ordination must necessarily be due to the religious institution's desire only to admit leaders who share the aims and mission of that institution. The wide reading does render redundant the closing words of section 39(1), namely, 'and is limited to one sex [onwards]'. But this strained construction is required to preserve church autonomy in such a sensitive area as leadership selection. The wide construction would mean that churches would be able to restrict approvals on *any* of the thirteen prohibited grounds in section 21(1). Thus, a denomination would be free, for example, to ordain only persons of one race or ethnic origin. Such a ramification is certainly unpalatable in many people's eyes but is part and parcel of recognizing the principle of church autonomy. Churches should be free to select leaders on bases the majority of people in society would abhor. The Human Rights Act's norms do not govern the life of *all* private associations; the Act, for example, already exempts clubs from its coverage.[94] Presumably churches, clubs, and other voluntary associations face public disapproval and evaporating patronage if their leadership decisions are unpopular. A social rather than legal sanction should suffice.

---

[93] S. 21(1)(b)(vi).
[94] S. 44(4). See further Mai Chen, 'Self-Regulation or State Regulation? Discrimination in Clubs', (1993) 15 *New Zealand Universities Law Review* 421.

A third construction is possible. Much denominational debate has assumed that the section 39(1) exemption requires churches to point to a rule, doctrine, or custom precluding practising homosexuals from becoming ministers. Once in place, the institution can then refuse ordination of the basis of the applicant's[95] unacceptable 'religious belief'. The relevant religious belief here is the candidate's belief that 'sexual intercourse between people of the same sex is not a sin', 'practising homosexuals are fit to be ministers', or some similar variant. This argument requires one to attribute to a practising homosexual the belief that his or her own actions are appropriate—surely not a difficult equation. It also requires beliefs about sexual morality and practice to be characterized as a species of religious belief. Again, this is not difficult for if beliefs about what to eat or wear can be classified as religious beliefs, beliefs about sexual behaviour can likewise. Given these premisses, the conclusion follows: the candidate's religious belief (about homosexual acts or gay leadership) do not correspond with those of the religious institution. 'Religious belief' has to be 'stretched' somewhat to accommodate church autonomy. The end result (no practising homosexuals are ordained) is the same as the second interpretation above, but the route is tortuous. The onus of proving this exemption (as with all exemptions under the Act[96]) lies upon the defendant institution. It must establish, on the balance of probabilities, that there exists a 'doctrine, rule or established custom' of their Church to the effect that homosexual leadership is impermissible. In practical terms, what ought to suffice here?

There ought to be no need for the institution to have an express, written rule promulgated by its governing body.[97] Evangelicals within the PCANZ have sought such a ruling (out of an understandable abundance of caution) but it ought to not be strictly necessary. Where it exists, it is clearly ample evidence, but the institution ought to be able to glean its position on such a matter from its general principles and tradition. The thrust of the Scriptures and the traditions of Christian sexual ethics mandate that no practising homosexual be a pastor. If churches can point to existing general doctrines on celibacy or intimate sexual expression only within marriage, that ought to suffice. Besides, section 39(1) does not require a specific written rule. It refers also to 'established customs'. Customs are typically unwritten and must be discerned by those following them.

---

[95] Or, on the basis of the institution's religious belief. The same end result is achieved due to incompatibility of the two parties' views.

[96] See s. 85.

[97] See Gedicks, 'Toward a Constitutional Jurisprudence of Religious Group Rights', 142–4, who criticizes the law's demand for such a discrete tenet or doctrine: 'narrow categories like doctrine, practice or administration do not capture all or even most of the essential intentions, commitments, beliefs, settings and stories that create the narratives of a religious group, that is, those very things that bind individuals together into a community of belief' (ibid. 144)

If general custom or tradition suffice, then an authoritative statement from the institution on the matter ought likewise to suffice. If the church leadership or national body proffer the view that their 'rules, doctrines or established customs' dictate that practising homosexuals be denied (or allowed) ordination, that should be enough. To go behind the assertion of the institution would be dangerous. It would risk the sort of 'entanglement' by secular tribunals with ecclesiastical affairs which has been universally decried. The tribunal ought to take at face value the authoritative statement, even amidst internal friction within the Church concerned. Otherwise, it risks embarking upon a task it is ill equipped to undertake—resolving matters of theological controversy. Of course, much turns upon what is an 'authoritative' statement. The secular tribunal cannot simply take at face value *any* proffered statement of custom and tradition from *anyone* in that body. The point at issue may be hotly contested, with various factions claiming to be the authentic voice of the institution. To this extent, the tribunal may be required to evaluate competing evidence from opposing 'camps'. Hopefully, where this situation arises, the tribunal would act circumspectly and limit its assessment to deciding who is the authoritative spokesperson without becoming embroiled in the substance of the complaint. Where the denomination has a devolved structure with autonomous local congregations and no authoritative national body, it is possible that each congregation may need to be an 'organised religion' for the purpose of the section.

The very fact that the third interpretation can give rise to testing questions such as 'Does a rule or custom exist?' 'Who is in a position to state it?' 'Do such persons speak for the institution?' indicates the improbability that this construction was the one intended by Parliament.

Conclusion

Conservative Christians opposed the addition of 'sexual orientation' to the prohibited grounds of discrimination under the Human Rights Act 1993. They foresaw that their religious freedom would be curtailed by the State preventing them from rejecting openly practising gay candidates for the ministry. Whether there is any truth to this concern is still unclear. The Human Rights Commission is still pondering the point as the debates within certain denominations continue to rage. The uncertain application of the Human Rights Act has contributed to the increasing complexity and urgency of church debates. For many, the Act's prohibition against sexual orientation discrimination, and the cryptic wording of the exemption for churches, has played too significant a part in what should be a quintessential matter of self-definition. The potential application of secular law has, for conservatives, had a 'chilling effect' on resolution of a critical ecclesiastical issue: the control over its own narrative, its vision of itself, has been impinged upon.

Reflecting liberal democratic ideals, the State has sought to accommodate religious conviction by inserting exemptions for religious organizations in the Human Rights Act. Parliament's aspiration that church autonomy and clergy selection be preserved may yet be foiled by clumsy drafting and a Commission determined to vindicate gay rights. If the result of a test case should turn against conservatives and they should lose their freedom to refuse to ordain avowedly gay candidates for the ministry, the intolerant, totalitarian propensities of human rights laws will have been revealed. I suspect civil disobedience by many conservative congregations would follow. If the Church chooses to abandon its sexual ethic for leadership to conform with state requirements, it will have been effectively transformed into a different entity. Having lost the authority to define itself, 'In a very real sense, the group ceases to exist.'[98]

If churches are exempt, peaceful coexistence will have been restored. Nonetheless, Christians, and religionists generally, cannot afford to be sanguine. They will need to remind the liberal State of its own professed tenets, those such as the value of religious communities as mediating institutions and their enriching role in fostering moral and civic virtue. Perhaps the conservative Christian conception of the good life may no longer be one that a liberal democratic society values, nor tolerates—it is too intolerant, bigoted, and disruptive of the discourse shaped by ideological pluralism. From the liberal standpoint, 'The extinction of many, if not all, of the [religious] communities that pose truly radical alternatives to liberal democratic political principles is to be welcomed.' [99] Christians, and indeed all believers, may need to work that much harder to remind the State of the merits of religious group autonomy.

[98] Ibid. 114.
[99] Macedo, 'Transformative Constitutionalism', 75.

FREEDOM OF RELIGION: LEGAL PERSPECTIVES

Sophie C. van Bijsterveld

Introduction

Questions relating to freedom of religion are receiving renewed interest. Over the last few years a variety of issues relating to freedom of religion in west European countries have succeeded in attracting national and even international attention. Although concrete incidents vary from country to country, there are some patterns to be discerned. Issues such as the wearing of a headscarf or headgear in school (by pupil or teacher) or at the workplace, the presence of religious symbols such as a crucifix in public institutions, and the observance of religious holidays have caused friction and debate, and have set in motion judicial machinery.[1] Also, religiously inspired expressions offensive to particular groups or persons or expressions that are offensive to adherents of particular beliefs have caused legal and societal disapproval and debate.[2] This is also true for conflicts relating to (institutional) procedures or (material) norms that function within religious organizations such as churches but differ from the mainstream societal ones. It is clear that all these issues contain a high degree of controversy, and that they raise questions as to the content and limits of freedom of religion and religious expression. In line with these issues and incidents, there is attention in the scholarly literature for freedom of religion, its scope and limits. Repeatedly and probably increasingly the question of the scope and limits of religious liberty will be discussed and legal solutions that define these in the various cases will be taken up in the scholarly debate.

This essay, too, deals with freedom of religion, albeit from a different perspective. Its aim is not to give an answer to questions concerning the range of religious freedom issues such as those mentioned above. It is not meant to determine whether particular expressions of religion fall within or rather outside a constitutionally guaranteed freedom of religion. This essay is intended to pose a prior, more fundamental question concerning

---

[1] For these and other examples, see the annual country reports in *European Journal for Church and State Research*.

[2] At the level of the Council of Europe, see *Otto-Preminger-Institut* v. *Austria* ECHR 20 Sept. 1994, appl. no. 13470/87; and *Wingrove* v. *The United Kingdom* ECHR 25 Nov. 1996, appl. no. 17419/90. Both rulings are available on the web site of the European Court of Human Rights: <http://www.echr.coe.int>.

the *function* of a constitutionally guaranteed freedom of religion. This enables us to create a broader horizon for assessing the way in which the law deals with religion, and it enables us to subject to critical evaluation the way in which the right to freedom of religion actually functions. The thoughts developed in this essay have relevance for the west European context in general; they are, however, more specifically related to developments in the Netherlands.[3]

Firstly, I will sketch how the fundamental rights perspective on religion implicitly provides us with a very particular perception of religion and how, in line with this, in the Netherlands the implementation of the fundamental rights perspective in the field of legislation has focused on subtleties and legal refinements rather than on fundamental issues. Subsequently, I will show how the complex relation between religion, law, and culture leads to a remarkable paradox, which also tends to leave us with a particular image of religion.

Next, a broader perspective on religion is presented, a perspective that is closer to the phenomenon of religion itself. From this broader perspective I will show, by way of examples from the Dutch point of view, where the real dynamics and developments in the field of religion are. After a discussion of these developments in the light of social reality, I explore the meaning and role freedom of religion should have for these developments. The conclusion is that freedom of religion as it is often understood in court rulings and legislation tends to direct our attention to rather specific and traditional aspects of religion, while the more fundamental aspects— aspects that are and will be of major importance in the future—are under- exposed.

Freedom of Religion: The Fundamental Rights Perspective

Legal conflicts with an element of religion tend to be dealt with in the context of fundamental rights. This fundamental rights perspective determines to a large extent the way in which religion is perceived in law and by lawyers, and how the discussion on the relation between religion and law is conducted. At least three aspects inherent to the fundamental rights approach determine the dominant legal view on religious issues.

Firstly, fundamental rights—classic liberties—as they are listed in the Dutch Constitution are predominantly formulated from the perspective of the private individual. Religion, then, tends to be approached as a mere *personal characteristic*, rather than as a social phenomenon as well.

Secondly, inherent to the fundamental rights approach is the dichotomy between State and individual. This means, first of all, in terms

---

[3] This essay draws in part on S. C. van Bijsterveld, 'Vrijheid van godsdienst geherdefinieerd', (1999) 24 *NJCM-Bulletin* 1023–37.

of fundamental rights, that there is the underlying distinction between the realm of the 'public' and the 'private'. Religion, then, belongs to the *private sphere*, separate from the public sphere. Although reality is much more complex, constitutional law is shaped along the lines of this dichotomy between State and individual, and abstracts to a large degree from the social reality with its range of intermediate structures.

Thirdly, there is the classic conception of fundamental freedoms, liberties of private individuals, corresponding with the duty of *non-interference* by public authority. This means that religion is seen as a hands-off area for public authorities.

This set of presuppositions inherent to the fundamental rights approach provides the frame of reference for the way in which religion as a phenomenon is perceived in policy and law. Even though the fundamental rights doctrine itself is much further developed and richer than the enumeration of these three characteristics suggests, and has moved beyond the simple model it entails, it seems justified to say that the fundamental rights approach to religion is to a large extent determined by these contrasts.

The focus on fundamental rights, rights backed by courts, has another implication as well. The setting of rights backed by courts also tends to focus our attention to *certain aspects of religion*. It is evident, or at least not surprising, that when an appeal to freedom of religion is made, courts need to link up with a *clear, recognizable, and commonly accepted concept of religion*. It is exactly liturgical aspects and aspects relating to the expression (in writing or otherwise) of religion that meet this requirement. Thus, an administrative court in the Netherlands has ruled that for a (potentially successful) appeal to freedom of religion there should be an immediate expression of religion that is manifest according to objective standards.[4]

In short, the above seems to culminate in a specific concept of religion, safeguarded by a private individual's claims to religious liberty to be realized by non-interference of public authorities.

Legal Fine-Tunings

Of course, in current Western thought there are nuances and countercurrents that challenge the patterns presented above. Furthermore, the actual relation between religion and law is much more varied and complex, differing from country to country, and changing and developing in time. In fact, in practically all west European countries religion is firmly embedded, constitutionally as well as in its structural and institutional setting. Especially in countries with systems of established churches or systems of cooperation between Church and State, there is more to the

---

[4] Afdeling Rechtspraak Raad van State, 7 Apr. 1983, *AB* 1983, 430 [antroposofische arts].

relation between religion and law than the fundamental rights approach alone. Even in systems where Church and State are separated, the law in fact deals with religion in a variety of ways and in a variety of aspects.[5] Despite the generality and simplicity of the analysis above, however, it seems justified to conclude that the popular outlook tends to perceive religion as the private asset functioning in a private sphere, an outlook that is congruent with the classic liberty approach.

In the Netherlands the fundamental rights approach has also led to a focus on particular aspects of religion in the *domain of legislation*. The 1983 general revision of the Constitution itself and, in line with this, its implementation in legislation stressed the legal equality of religion and belief, and made an issue of requiring very specific authority by Act of Parliament for restrictions of fundamental rights by subordinate legislation or through the exercise of administrative power. Subsequently, relevant legislation was reformulated with great precision. With that, the changes in the law with regard to religion and belief were first and foremost fine-tunings.

It is no exaggeration to say that the revision of the Dutch Constitution and its implementation focused on certain aspects of freedom of religion and belief. Equal treatment of religion and belief was realized to the extent that the legislative provision allowing church bell-ringing (or its equivalent) was reformulated to apply not only to religious gatherings but also to convening meetings of non-religious belief. Sunday legislation was adapted with great care to meet equal treatment requirements and to limit the few discretionary powers the existing law provided for. A few years later, however, a rigorous liberalization of Sunday laws on working hours and shop opening was to take place, setting the fine-tunings in the shade.

Although an examination of religion and belief from the perspective of the 'new' elements in the Dutch Constitution had and still has its value, the developments with regard to guaranteed freedom must be looked at solely from that perspective, or the really fundamental developments and questions will be overlooked. Thus, for example, the Constitution played a substantial role in the implementation of fine-tuning legislation concerning Sunday as a day of rest, but hardly played a role in the near abolition of the protection of Sunday as a day of rest a few years later.

An analogy can be made with the functioning of the constitutionally guaranteed freedom of press and freedom of opinion. For a long time legal constitutional literature paid disproportionate attention to subtleties in the formulations of municipal regulations concerning the distribution of

---

[5] For the systems of Church and State relationships within the countries of the European Union, see Gerhard Robbers (ed.), *State and Church in the European Union* (Baden-Baden, 1995). See also S. C. van Bijsterveld, *Godsdienstvrijheid in Europees perspectief* (Deventer, 1998).

pamphlets in streets, while the real developments in the field of freedom of opinion, expression, and the press were taking place elsewhere, namely in the field of mass media and ICT issues, thus not at the micro-level, but rather at the meso- and macro-levels. Intrinsic developments in the legal arrangements concerning the object of the guarantee and the scientific fundamental rights discussion can thus easily follow separate tracks. This is also the case with regard to the subject of this essay. It is, in other words, important to ensure that legal discussions do not start to go off on their own track, but keep their focus on the issue they were actually addressing.

Religion, Law, and Culture: A Paradox

From a different perspective, the position of religion in the law deserves our attention. There is also a certain embarrassment inherent in dealing with religion in the law, which becomes clear when we include the cultural element.

The relationship between religion, law, and culture is a complex one. Usually, they are in line with each other, that is, they are in a certain harmony. They influence each other, and the developments that take place in one sector are usually within the space that other sectors provide. In a free, open, and religiously pluralistic society this balance is, to a certain extent, elastic and flexible. Therefore, their mutual relationship often remains invisible and below the surface.

This may result in the following situation with respect to the perception of religion. Expressions of religion and religious practice of traditional religions present in society traditionally run more or less parallel to society's mainstream culture and they tend to be embedded in the organizational structures of society. Thus, expressions of religion and religious practice are common and accepted, and not perceived as 'different' from the ordinary.

This may lead to a remarkable paradox. At the basis of this paradox lies the difficulty of finding an adequate place for religion in the context of law and politics, even if its practice is completely embedded in society. When it concerns very manifest expressions of religion, expressions that are clearly recognizable as 'different', these are often experienced as problematic in the context of law and politics; when this is not the case, they are often seen as dilutions.

That this may have practical consequences has been shown more than once. At least some of the issues and incidents mentioned in the introduction can be seen in this way. Even though the particular expressions of religion (that are seen as 'different') can be legally protected in the context of freedom of religion, their problematic character stands out. Let us consider another example from the Dutch experience. The paradox was clearly shown in the discussions surrounding the Equal Treatment Act[6] and, more specifically, with respect to the positions of religiously oriented institutions. When for admission to an institution, for example, religion is used as a ground for refusal, this quickly leads to highly controversial situations (for example, the refusal to admit a liberal Jewish boy to an Orthodox Jewish secondary school).[7] If an open admissions policy is followed by institutions (which is usually the case, and sometimes even prescribed by law), then the identity and thus the ideological ground of existence of such an institution often comes into question. In this light, the current debate on the religious identity of schools with a pupils having different religious backgrounds can be mentioned. Thus, religion in such a context runs the risk of being either negated or identified with highly problematic situations.

The analyses above relating to the perception of religion are not solely restricted to the way in which the law deals with religion. There is also a more general sociological dimension to this insular approach to religion. We are all aware of the fact that our Western society is fundamentally characterized by differentiation and segmentation. In this mindset religion, too, is just one of the segments of our lives, distinct and separated from others such as politics, culture, labour, health care, education, and so on. Processes of secularization and individualization, whatever precise meaning these concepts have, only tend to reinforce this awareness.

   These almost delusively simple approaches to religion in the law and the equally simple concepts of religion may have functioned adequately in the recent past. For at least some decades the fictions and constructs upon which they rested may have been acceptable. Furthermore, processes such as secularization and individualization as they started to manifest themselves may have distracted the general attention from the issue of religion as a social phenomenon and may have placed issues relating to religion and law in the shadow of others. This then took place in the self-evident situation in which the national state and the law were the first and foremost integration frame for its citizens not only politically, but also socially and ethically. Circumstances, however, have changed.

Religion and the Interpretation of Social Reality

For a balanced and realistic examination of current legal developments with regard to religion, however, it is necessary in the first place to explore the phenomenon of religion itself. It is important to realize that religion refers to more than just an individual having a particular set of opinions or

---

   [6] The full text of this Act is available (including in English) at <http://www/cgb.nl>.
   [7] HR 22 Jan. 1988, *AB* 1988, 96 [Maimonideslyceum].

the expression of such opinions in a liturgical context, however important these aspects are. The way in which religion manifests itself in society is complex. Religion influences culture, convictions, organizational structures, and social relations. Religion has *social, educational, communicative*, and *institutional dimensions* as well. In order to understand legal developments with regard to religion it is important also to see religion within these phenomena, in the way it is actually expressed in society, including its *legal infrastructure*.[8] These aspects are essential to religion and its presence in society, but to a large extent they also remain implicit expressions of religion. We may think of areas such as the transfer of 'implicit' religion through mass media, education, charities, and voluntary work.

In various societal fields sweeping developments are taking place, ideologically and socially: changing patterns of work, new communication technologies, reduction in numbers of pupils. It is in itself not surprising that these developments find their translation into legislation. With reference to secularization, individualization, and value pluralism (in the Netherlands), the place of religion in the framework of that legislation is put under pressure.

It is well known that our concepts and ways of expressing ourselves are determined by the way in which we approach and experience reality. Notions, concepts, and modes of expression not only are means to label the world around us, but also influence our view of reality to a certain extent. This is no different for legal and sociological notions, concepts, and expressions.

Many government measures that are put forward or implemented and that have consequences for the legal 'space' available for exercising religion[9] at least party appeal to 'individualization' and 'secularization', 'religious and belief' pluralism, and, even if implicitly 'depillarization'. Even if these have a function as 'sensitizing' concepts, they have only a restricted value as a description of the situation in society or as a final point society is moving towards. Reality is much more complex. Individualization, for instance, does not mean the end of social life or of participation in common frameworks. Secularization is no prelude to the 'end of religion'. The importance of religion in society is not diminishing, as the examples mentioned in the introduction show. Instead of making us sensitive to certain changes in society, a dogmatic treatment of these and similar notions may inhibit a realistic view of society. Emphasis on the decrease in church attendance, for instance, may conceal that the number of church visitors, nevertheless, is remarkably high.

---

[8] First and foremost expressed in the formal relationship with the State (separation, cooperation, and establishment); these include the social, educational, and communicative dimensions just mentioned. These dimensions and their significance, however, are often underexposed in the legal debate.

[9] Notably in the field of education, in the mass media, and in collective moments of rest.

The report 'God in the Netherlands, 1966–1996'[10] offers a striking insight into the complexity of the relation of people to churches, religions, and belief systems. Apart from the well-known figures of decrease of membership of Christian churches, the report contains a wealth of information on the attitude of people towards religion and belief, and their expectations with regard to their institutional and social dimensions. These facts put the trends just mentioned into perspective, as does the presence of non-Christian religions.

When the concepts and notions mentioned above are taken as a yardstick by the legislature and are followed by accompanying initiatives, they easily become self-fulfilling prophecies. For instance, when it becomes (socially and legally) more difficult to hold on to the day of rest, fewer people will do so. When keeping the ideological identity of schools becomes more difficult, fewer schools will do so. The religious dimension in the media will decrease quantiatively, when there is less space for religious media.[11]

The Function of Freedom of Religion

Taking the Dutch situation and developments as a point of reference, the degree of attention paid to legislative projects implementing the 1983 constitutional revision, which labelled as legal fine-tunings, strongly contrasts with the absence of such attention to developments that have much more drastic consequences for the place of religion. Often this legislation is defended, including where it concerns religion, by referring to the changing social circumstances. In the last section such references were put into perspective. In any case, such references should not be made too easily and should not function as stereotypes.

Secondly, numbers have limited significance in the context of fundamental rights. Just as the importance of the freedom of association would not decrease if there were fewer associations, the importance of freedom of religion does not decrease where fewer people adhere to a religion.

Apart from the sociological context of the interpretation of societal developments, one may ask oneself—at a more fundamental level, of course—if, from the point of view of freedom of religion, these broader developments are relevant. In other words, are we still speaking of freedom of religion as a fundamental right? To answer this question, it is necessary to analyse the function of freedom of religion and, relatedly, the object of this freedom.

---

[10] G. Dekker, I. de Hart, and J. Peters, *God in Nederland, 1966–1996* (Amsterdam, 1997).
[11] These examples relate to developments in the Netherlands. I shall not elaborate on them here.

What, ultimately, is the function of freedom of religion? Does it only concern certain guarantees for a sphere of freedom of expression and a certain (liturgical) practice?[12] Or does it imply a certain openness in the way religion manifests itself in its social, educational, communicative, and institutional dimensions? The answer says something about the State and its attitude towards religions, belief systems, ideologies, or, more generally, in discussions of values and norms, and the answer is contained in the question. Three elements seem to me to be of special importance. These concern the underlying reason for protecting religious freedom, the nature of fundamental rights, and the relation between the legislature and the courts. I will briefly address each of these elements.

Liturgical and other explicit and visible expressions of religion have an important place in the guarantee of freedom of religion, and in legal discussions this is also the case. This is not surprising, as it is these expressions that are the most apparent. They are not, however, the whole of religion; they are expressions of deeper convictions and insights. Religions offer coherent patterns of values and norms, visions of humanity, visions of the world; they concern ways of associating with others and of dealing with fundamental life questions, and provide ethical insights and approaches. Religious experience and celebration, expression and communication with others, take place in all sorts of socialization and communication processes. Guarantees of the freedom of religion and belief that leant too heavily towards one aspect of religion would deprive it of a great part of its importance.

As to the nature of fundamental rights, these are not easily encapsulated in one-dimensional terms. From the development of a modern fundamental rights theory and codified fundamental rights, attention is increasingly being paid to the various levels at which fundamental rights function: not only at the (micro-)level of the individual but also at the (meso-)level of organizations and at the (macro-)level of the organization of society as a whole. This characterization in terms of levels also makes clear that fundamental rights protection has aspects that go beyond the level of the single individual. It is evident that its acceptance has consequences for the effective protection of these rights by government.

The third element concerns the relationship between legislature and judge. I referred above to the ruling of a Dutch administrative court that required as a precondition for a potentially successful appeal to this right an immediate expression of religion that is manifest according to objective standards. This implies a restricted interpretation of the freedom of

---

[12] This would be the case, for example—to take an area already mentioned in this essay—if a request not to work on Sunday had to be made in the form of an appeal to conscientious objection, as a newly introduced bill proposes. However good its intentions to protect Sunday observance, the bill would make it an *abnormality*.

religion, and one may wonder whether the dimensions just mentioned fall within this category.

Whatever this restrictive interpretation, it is perfectly comprehensible by a court and must be understood in the context of the special position of the court, which in individual cases, i.e. at the micro-level, needs to make freedom of religion operational and manageable. The legislature—and government more generally—do not function only at the level of guaranteeing a sphere of freedom for the individual, but also have a responsibility to create an atmosphere of freedom at the meso- and macro-levels. In other words, the legislature must facilitate freedom of religion in the broader context of the law. An awareness of this, coupled with a fair understanding of religion itself, makes the need for such a broader interpretation evident, and such an interpretation can be given especially through legislation and policy.

Making a choice for a broader and, therefore, more realistic interpretation of the freedom of religion and belief, and one that also comprises social and societal expressions of it, does not mean that legislative concretizations of this freedom are always given and fixed. As legislation changes and develops, so will its concretizations be subject to change, though not as a random historical or cultural fact. This is not to suggest that there are easy solutions. It does mean that in the context of legislative processes a genuine discussion is needed about the consequences for religion and belief, a discussion that goes beyond the more technical questions.

It may be clear that this leads to the conclusion that government or other public authority needs to take a frank and realistic approach to religion, based on a realistic understanding of religion. It is exactly such an approach that slowly emerges at the international level, not inhibited so much by tradition.[13] This includes three aspects, all of which have to do with and recognize religion in its *public dimensions*.[14] The first is the public dimension of religion in its *potentially problematic* aspect. The second is the public dimension of religion in its *positive* aspect; I mean to refer here to the contribution of religion to *ethical understanding* and to its part in the construction of *civil society*. The third is the awareness that the public dimension of religion in the context of *protection of fundamental rights* requires more than a simple absence of public authority interference.

Let me add a few more words with regard to the second aspect, the

---

[13] For legal and policy developments with regard to religion at the international level, see S. C. van Bijsterveld, 'Religion, International Law and Policy in the Wider European Arena: New Dimensions and Developments', in Rex Ahdar (ed.), *Religion and Law* (Dartmouth, 2000).

[14] At the constitutional level, of course, the public dimension of religion is recognized notably in systems with an established Church and in systems of cooperation between Church and State.

positive aspect of religion—religion in its integrating function and role in community-building. At a deeper level, obviously, the contribution of religions to 'value' discussions and ethical approaches to contemporary legal and ethical problems come to the fore. It is exactly this dimension that has been taken for granted or neglected in the legal and policy debate, but that obviously is of increasing importance at present. It also coincides with the general openness that is emerging for intermediary institutions and non-governmental organizations, and with an (even if implicit) awareness of the changing role of the State as a natural focus for orientation and identification for its citizens, as I have already said, not only politically, but also socially and ethically.

Of course, the plea for a more realistic approach to religion in the context of law is not a plea to make religion an overt policy issue. It is meant to warn against a one-sided and outdated approach. The hands-off and individually oriented fundamental rights approach mentioned at the beginning of the essay will continue to have its value and will remain important. However, as I have hoped to show, it is not in itself the complete and final approach to questions of how to deal with religion in the context of law.

Conclusion

Freedom of religion is one of the showpieces in treatises on the history of the development of fundamental rights. Dutch constitutional history shows us that guaranteeing freedom of religion is a sign of progressiveness and tolerance. Since its initial recognition freedom of religion is a firmly entrenched fundamental right.

However important this perspective is, it may easily lead to a one-sided approach to religion, which does not do justice to religion itself and the role of religion in society. A more realistic and future-oriented approach is needed. Especially in a time of individualization, globalization, and value pluralism, leading to changes in the nature of law, the State, and society itself, the hitherto dominant approach to religion needs to be counterbalanced.

As in the value discussions that are being conducted, the stress is easily on either very theoretical and abstract notions or on very concrete solutions; in the more legally oriented discussion on freedom of religion sometimes a link is skipped, that of the social, communicative, educational dimension, that of 'space' for the mediation of religion in society. This is an element of religion and law that should not be lost.

THE PUBLIC MANIFESTATION OF RELIGION OR BELIEF: CHALLENGES FOR A MULTI-FAITH SOCIETY IN THE TWENTY-FIRST CENTURY

Peter Cumper

Introduction

For many people the right to share their beliefs with others, or to live publicly according to their religious convictions, is not merely a basic human right but also a sacred duty.[1] The European Court has accepted that religious freedom 'implies, inter alia, freedom to manifest [one]'s religion [and that] . . . Bearing witness in words and deeds is bound up with the existence of religious convictions.'[2] These 'words' and 'deeds' often take a wide variety of forms. For example, faith can be manifested through an abstention from work on a particular day,[3] the celebration of important religious festivals,[4] the observance of certain rituals,[5] the acceptance of a distinctive appearance,[6] the wearing of certain clothes,[7] the rejection of various foods,[8] the refusal to perform military service,[9] and the duty to make pilgrimages to holy places of worship.[10] Of course, the manifestation of these practices, rites, and rituals is never absolute. The State can, on occasion, intervene to protect the *general* public interest, by imposing curbs on the exercise or expression of a religion or belief. The European Convention on Human Rights (1950) (ECHR) adopts this approach. While Article 9(1) of the ECHR guarantees the general principle of freedom of thought, conscience, and religion, Article 9(2) places limits on the

---

[1] For example, Jesus said that 'whoever declares publicly that he belongs to me, the Son of Man will do the same for him before the angels of God' (Luke 12: 8).

[2] *Kokkinakis* v. *Greece* (1994) 17 EHRR 397.

[3] e.g. Saturdays for Jews, Sundays for Christians, and Fridays for Muslims.

[4] e.g. Christmas for Christians, Diwali for Hindus, Eid for Muslims, and Passover for Jews.

[5] For example, this can range from circumcision or christening at birth, to marriage sacraments and ultimately through to burial ceremonies.

[6] e.g. growing a beard for some Sikh and Muslim males, or the decision to wear one's hair as locks by Rastafarians.

[7] e.g. the wearing of a turban by Sikh males or the hijab by Muslim women.

[8] e.g. halal food for Muslims and kosher food for Jews.

[9] e.g. the opposition of Quakers and Jehovah's Witnesses to compulsory military service.

[10] e.g. the haj for Muslims or visits to Lourdes for some Catholics.

manifestation of religion or belief.[11] Given that the European Convention has now been incorporated into UK law, by way of the Human Rights Act 1998,[12] British judges will have to interpret these rights[13] and, in particular, fix the parameters of Articles 9(1) and 9(2) of the ECHR.

The courts will not only have to take account of the interests of 'believers' and 'non-believers', but will also be required to accord proper recognition to the diverse traditions of the many different 'religions' in contemporary multi-faith Britain. One of the greatest challenges for judges in interpreting the Human Rights Act will be the duty of fixing the boundaries which govern the proper manifestation of religion and belief. In this paper I will advance the argument that all bona fide religious groups in the United Kingdom will only enjoy equal rights if, when considering questions relating to the manifestation of religion or belief, British judges adopt a more imaginative and radical approach than that which has hitherto been employed by both the European Commission and the Court of Human Rights.[14] In addressing this issue I will: examine the constituent elements of Article 9(1) of the ECHR;[15] consider what is meant by *freedom* of religion and belief, with particular emphasis on the individual's rights in the workplace; and, finally, discuss some of the factors which the courts are likely to take into account when determining what constitutes a lawful manifestation of religion or belief.

Article 9 of the European Convention on Human Rights

There are two elements to Article 9(1) of the Convention.[16] First, it has an

---

[11] Article 9(1): Everyone has the right to freedom of thought, conscience and religion; the right includes the freedom to change his religion or belief, and freedom, either alone or in community with others and in public and private, to manifest his religion or belief, in worship, teaching, practice and observance.' Article 9(2): 'Freedom to manifest one's religion or beliefs shall be subject only to such limitations as are prescribed by law and are necessary in a democratic society in the interests of public safety, for the protection of public order, health or morals, or for the protection of the rights and freedoms of others.'

[12] The Human Rights Act 1998 came into force on 2 Oct. 2000. The Human Rights Act requires that the actions of public authorities must be compatible with the Convention (s. 6) and that 'So far as it is possible to do so, primary and secondary legislation must be read and given effect in a way which is compatible with the Convention rights' (s. 3(1)).

[13] For a complete list of the Convention rights which are incorporated into UK law, see Schedule 1 of the Human Rights Act 1998.

[14] Under the Human Rights Act, British judges will 'not be bound by previous interpretations' of the European Commission and Court of Human Rights but 'will be able to build a new body of case law, taking into account Convention rights' (White Paper, *Rights Brought Home*, Cm. 3782, para. 2.8).

[15] For the purposes of this paper I will concentrate on Article 9(1) and avoid any detailed analysis of Article 9(2) of the ECHR.

[16] Notwithstanding the fact that the ECHR prohibits discrimination on religious grounds (Article 14) and guarantees the right of parents to ensure the education and teaching of their children in conformity with their own religious and philosophical convictions (Art. 2,

'internal' dimension, since it guarantees an individual's 'freedom of thought, conscience and religion'.[17] This right, which is 'largely exercised inside an individual's heart and mind',[18] is absolute, in so far as the State is prohibited from seeking to indoctrinate its citizens,[19] or forcing them to deny,[20] or even reveal[21] their faith. Secondly, Article 9(1) has an 'external' dimension, since it recognizes that one has the right to manifest a 'religion or belief' in 'worship, teaching, practice and observance'. Unlike the former, the latter is subject to a number of limitations: thus, where a restriction is 'prescribed by law' and 'necessary in a democratic society', curbs can be placed on the *manifestation* of religion or belief on the grounds of public safety, public order, health, or morals, and 'for the protection of the rights and freedoms of others'.[22]

The differences between the 'internal' and the 'external' elements of Article 9(1) are also apparent in the way in which they have been handled by the Strasbourg human rights organs. The absolute guarantees of freedom of 'thought, conscience and religion' which relate to an individual's 'inner state of mind'[23] have been extended[24] to cover long-established religions (e.g., Buddhism,[25] Christianity,[26] Islam,[27] Judaism,[28] and Sikhism[29]) and newer faiths (eg. Jehovah's Witnesses,[30] the Divine Light Zentrum,[31] and the Church of Scientology[32]) as well as a wide range of philosophical

Protocol 1), I will limit my analysis to an examination of the challenges posed by the incorporation of Article 9 into British law.

[17] Articles 18 of the UN Declaration on Human Rights (1948) and the International Covenant on Civil and Political Rights (1966) are also drafted according to this model.

[18] D. Gomien, *Short Guide to the European Convention on Human Rights* (Strasbourg, 1991), 69.

[19] *C.J., and J.J. and E.J.* v. *Poland* (1996) Application No. 23380/94, 84A DR 46.

[20] See *Recueil des travaux préparatoires*, vol. i (The Hague, 1975), 223.

[21] See P. van Dijk and G. van Hoof, *Theory and Practice of the European Convention on Human Rights*, 3rd edn. (The Hague, 1998), 542.

[22] Art. 9(2).

[23] This term is used by M. Sheinin, 'Article 18', in A Eide *et al.* (eds.), *The Universal Declaration of Human Rights: A Commentary* (Oslo, 1992), 266.

[24] The Strasbourg Human Rights organs have adopted an approach which is similar to that taken by UN bodies working in this area. Neither the UN Declaration of Human Rights (1948), nor the International Covenant on Civil and Political Rights (1966), specifically provide a definition of the terms 'thought', 'conscience', and 'religion'. However, the Krishnaswami Study has suggested that the term 'religion or belief' would 'include, in addition to various theistic creeds, such other beliefs as agnosticism, free thought, atheism and rationalism' (E/CN.4/Sub.2/200/Rev.1, 1).

[25] *X* v. *UK*, No. 6886/75, 5 DR 100.

[26] *Steadman* v. *UK*, Application No. 29107/95, 23 EHRR CD 168 (1997).

[27] *Ahmad* v. *UK*, Application No. 8160/78, 4 EHRR 126 (1982).

[28] *D* v. *France*, Application No. 10180/82, 35 DR 199.

[29] *X* v. *UK*, Application No. 8160/78, 22 DR 27.

[30] *Kokkinakis* v. *Greece*, Application No. 14307/88, (1994) 17 EHRR 397.

[31] *Omkarananda and the DLZ* v. *Switzerland*, Application No. 8118/77, 25 DR 105 (1981).

[32] *X and the Church of Scientology*, Application No. 7805/77, 16 DR 68 (1979).

and ideological convictions (e.g. veganism[33] and pacifism[34]). Indeed, the European Court of Human Rights has even accepted that the rights in Article 9 are not merely for the benefit of 'believers'[35] but are also a 'precious asset for atheists, agnostics, sceptics, and the unconcerned'.[36] In contrast to this, however, in matters relating to the *manifestation* of religion or belief, the Strasbourg human rights organs have adopted a much more rigid approach. This has tended to involve a distinction being drawn between conduct which is only motivated by religion or belief, and that which is a direct manifestation of a religion or belief.[37] Only the latter has been deemed worthy of protection, and in proceeding to analyse the approach of the European Commission and Court I will examine the pivotal word in Article 9 of the ECHR: 'freedom'.

'Freedom' of Religion and Belief

It is a truism that *freedom* of religion or belief is a fundamental right. The ECHR guarantees it to 'everyone',[38] and the European Commission on Human Rights has even been prepared to extend it not merely to individuals, but also to churches,[39] and 'associations with religious and philosophical objects'.[40] Yet the breadth of this 'freedom' to manifest one's faith should perhaps not be exaggerated. There are a number of occasions, particularly at the workplace, when individuals may willingly forfeit some of their religious freedom. Perhaps the clearest example of this is the position of clergy and office-holders in a Church or religious organization. For example, when the Church of Denmark prevented one of its priests from imposing conditions on the christening of children which were contrary to official church policy, the European Commission held that the Church had acted lawfully.[41] The Commission held that the servants of religious organizations 'are employed for the purpose of applying and teaching a specific religion'[42] and that 'Their individual freedom of thought, conscience and religion is exercised at the moment they accept or refuse employment as clergymen.'[43] In spite of the priest's opposition to the teachings of the Danish Church, he was nevertheless free to leave the Church in protest at its teachings.

   This interpretation has long been accepted by the European

---

[33]   *X* v. *UK*, Application No. 18187/91 (10 Feb. 1993).
[34]   *Arrowsmith* v. *UK*, Application No. 7050/75, 19 DR 5 (1978).
[35]   *Kokkinakis* v. *Greece* (1994) 17 EHRR 397, 418.
[36]   Ibid.
[37]   See *Arrowsmith* v. *UK*, Application No. 7050/75, 19 DR 5 (1978).
[38]   See Art. 9(1) of the ECHR.
[39]   *X and the Church of Scientology* v. *Sweden*, Application No. 7805/77, 16 DR 68.
[40]   *Omkarananda and the DLZ* v. *Switzerland*, Application No. 8118/77, 25 DR 105.
[41]   *X* v. *Denmark*, Application No. 7374/76, 5 DR 157.
[42]   Ibid.   [43]   Ibid. at 158.

Commission,[44] and with the enactment of the Human Rights Act it seems inevitable that it will also be accepted by British judges.[45] After all, the spiritual autonomy of churches and religious organizations demands both that they retain their doctrinal independence and that those who are employed in their service abide by certain tenets of belief. To accept otherwise would risk jeopardizing the discipline which underpins the authority of ecclesiastical bodies. In the same way, it could be argued that the strict obedience of military discipline is essential for the efficient running of the armed forces. For example, in *Kalac* v. *Turkey*,[46] the European Court held that the dismissal of the director of legal affairs in the Turkish air force on account of his close ties with a controversial Muslim sect had not breached Article 9(1) of the ECHR.[47] Thus, those who enter the priesthood or freely sign up for one of the armed services are taken to have joined in the knowledge that, as a consequence of the relevant ecclesiastical and military discipline,[48] they may face restrictions on the exercise of their religion or belief.[49]

The unusual nature of a religious vocation and the rigid, formalized structure of service life are the principles which underpin this policy. Yet it is submitted that the special benefits and burdens of service in those areas[50] tend to distinguish them from most other positions of employment.[51] What of the freedom of people to manifest their faith in areas which, on the face of it, require much less discipline and uniformity—say, someone employed

[44] See also *Knudsen* v. *Norway*, Application No. 12356/86, 42 DR 247, and *Karlsson* v. *Sweden*, Application No. 12356/86, 57 DR 172.

[45] The UK courts have long taken the view that the decisions of non-statutory bodies exercising non-governmental functions in the area of doctrinal matters are not subject to judicial review (*R.* v. *Chief Rabbi, ex parte Wachmann* [1992] 1 WLR 1036).

[46] 27 EHRR 552.

[47] The European Court held that 'in choosing to pursue a military career Kalac was accepting of his own accord a system of military discipline [which meant accepting] limitations incapable of being imposed on civilians' (ibid., at 564).

[48] Arguments relating to military discipline were not accepted by the European Court in *Smith and Grady* v. *UK*, 29 EHRR 493, where the European Court held that the Ministry of Defence's policy of banning gays and lesbians from the armed forces was in violation of Article 8 of the ECHR.

[49] See *Yanasik* v. *Turkey*, 74 DR 14.

[50] The most obvious 'benefit' of being an office-holder either in a religious organization or in the armed services is that one is given power directly by the state (e.g. to conduct marriage ceremonies or to take life, respectively). The 'burdens' include the strict discipline and the anti-social hours of such positions of employment.

[51] The European Court of Human Rights distinguished between service personnel and civilians in *Larissis* v. *Greece* (1999) 27 EHRR 329. The Court held that Greece had acted lawfully in prohibiting three Pentecostal airmen from seeking to proselytize other service personnel, but accepted that there had been a violation of Article 9 in so far as they had been prevented from proselytizing civilians. Similarly, in *Goldman* v. *Weinberger* 106 S. Ct 1310 (1986), the US Supreme Court upheld a regulation which forbade an Orthodox Jew, who was a captain in the US Air Force, from wearing a yarmulke while on duty. In contrast to this, Sikhs serving in the British army and in the police service are permitted to wear their turbans.

in a high street shop? This was the issue in *Steadman* v. *UK*[52] where Louise Steadman, an assistant manager at a branch of a travel agency, refused to sign an amended contract of employment on the ground that Sunday would have been included as a normal working day. She was subsequently dismissed and argued that her refusal to work on a holy day constituted a violation of her freedom to manifest her Christian faith in worship, practice, and observance.

The *Steadman* decision is of interest because the European Commission recognized that it had jurisdiction even though Steadman had been employed in a private company and the State had not been directly responsible for her dismissal. Although it remains to be seen whether the Human Rights Act will have horizontal effect,[53] the *Steadman* case adds weight to the argument that Article 9 of the Convention may be extended to cover not merely the actions of public authorities, but also those of certain private bodies and individuals. In addition, *Steadman* illustrates the narrow interpretation of the term 'freedom' under Article 9 of the Convention. The European Commission regarded Steadman's complaint as being less an issue of religious freedom and more a matter of contractual liability, holding that she had been dismissed as a result of her failure 'to agree to work certain hours rather than for her religious belief as such'.[54] The Commission justified its decision on the basis that Steadman 'was free to resign and did in effect resign from her employment'.[55] It is submitted that this interpretation of Article 9 is dangerously narrow since it presupposes that the market will be sufficiently healthy for an applicant to move on to another job of comparable worth without unnecessary hardship. This will often not be the case. In fact many who feel that they are being forced to compromise or even act contrary to their faith will have to suffer in silence, since they cannot afford to exercise their religious *freedom* by resigning from their present employment.

But perhaps the most interesting facet of the *Steadman* case is that if the applicant, as a practising Christian, encountered problems in the course of her employment, one would assume those coming from different religious traditions are likely to face even greater difficulties when they seek to manifest their faith at the workplace. After all, in Britain public holidays are based on the Christian calendar and minority faiths enjoy no such privileges for their holy days and festivals. These problems were illustrated in *Ahmad* v. *ILEA*,[56] where a Muslim teacher started taking an extra

---

[52] *Steadman* v. *UK* (1997) 23 EHRR CD 168.

[53] For example, on the question of whether the Human Rights Act will, in the future, be limited to actions against public bodies, compare the views of Sydney Kentridge QC in *Constitutional Reform in the United Kingdom: Practice and Principles* (Oxford, 1998), 70, with those of Sir William Wade, ibid. 62, 63.

[54] *Steadman* v. *UK* (1997) 23 EHRR CD 168, 169.   [55] Ibid.

[56] [1978] 1 All ER 574.

seventy-five minutes after his Friday lunch break to attend the nearest mosque for prayers. After his colleagues objected that this disrupted work in school, his employers (the Inner London Education Authority) offered him a four-and-a-half-day weekly contract. Ahmad refused and left claiming unfair dismissal. By a two to one majority the Court of Appeal held that this dismissal was fair. Lord Scarman (dissenting) focused on the breadth of Article 9(1) of the Convention and was adamant that the relevant human rights issues in the case meant that it 'did not end with the law of contract'.[57] Instead, he argued that the educational system must accommodate the beliefs of both teachers and children and warned that to reject Ahmad's appeal would 'mean that a Muslim, who took his religious duties seriously, could never accept employment as a full-time teacher'.[58] On the other hand Lord Denning (Orr LJ concurring) stressed the limitations under Article 9(2) of the Convention and asserted that Ahmad's 'right to manifest his religion . . . must be subject to the rights of the education authorities under the contract'.[59] This latter approach was the one adopted by the European Commission on Human Rights when it considered, and subsequently rejected, Ahmad's complaint.[60] The Commission emphasized the binding nature of Ahmad's contractual obligations[61] and was even unwilling to find a violation of Article 9(1) since 'the applicant remained free to resign if and when he found that his teaching obligations conflicted with his religious duties'.[62] The right of the applicant to resign has been described by the European Commission as 'the ultimate guarantee of . . . freedom of religion',[63] and the Commission has employed this approach to dismiss an application from a Seventh-Day Adventist railway worker who had wanted to celebrate his sabbath on a Friday afternoon rather than on a Sunday.[64] Thus, while Article 9 certainly protects an existing employee from being compelled, on threat of dismissal, to change his or her beliefs,[65] such a person enjoys much less freedom to *manifest* these beliefs at the workplace.[66]

There are a number of reasons why the UK courts would be well advised not to follow the European Commission's approach.[67] For a start

---

[57] Ibid., at 585.   [58] Ibid.   [59] Ibid., at 578.
[60] *Ahmad* v. *UK* (1982) 4 EHRR 126.   [61] Ibid., at 133.
[62] Ibid., at 135.
[63] *Konttinen* v. *Finland*, Application No. 24949/94, 87A DR 68.
[64] '. . . having found his working hours to conflict with his religious convictions, the applicant was free to relinquish his post' (ibid., at 75).
[65] See *Knudsen* v. *Sweden* (1985) 42 DR 247.
[66] For example, the European Commission has held that 'even if motivated by religious convictions [a person who has refuses to work generally applicable hours] cannot as such be considered protected by Article 9, para 1.' (*Konttinen* v. *Finland*, at 75).
[67] This approach was also taken in *Karaduman* v. *Turkey*, Application No. 16278/90, 74 DR 93, where the European Commission held that since a Muslim woman had chosen to study at a secular university, she had to abide by a university regulation which forbade the wearing of Muslim headscarves.

it is irrational in so far as it presupposes that everyone has a real choice to find alternative employment. As was noted earlier, economic factors, housing costs, and family ties all militate against the proper exercise of this 'freedom'. It is also inequitable to the extent that it discriminates against members of minority faiths.[68] Because Britain is at least nominally a Christian country, and employers tend to fix their working week around the Christian calendar, the 'Christian' employee who 'chooses' to seek alternative employment is likely to have considerably more choice when searching for a 'sympathetic' working environment compared to someone from a different religious tradition.[69] And finally, the European Commission's approach in *Ahmad* is illogical in the sense that it is based on the Western premiss that religion, unlike race, is only a matter of choice—that if one has the benefit of 'choosing' to hold a particular set of beliefs, one must accept the burden of certain restrictions on one's faith at work. Yet for many people their religion is inextricably bound up with both their race and their culture[70]—to disentangle these elements would be impossible, and to accept employment which would force them to deny their faith is therefore not a viable option.

In the light of these criticisms, one might ask why the Strasbourg human rights organs have interpreted the manifestation of faith at the workplace so narrowly? The most obvious explanation would appear to be that both the European Commission and the Court have been wary of imposing unreasonable financial burdens on states.[71] In spite of the fact that it has already been well accepted that positive obligations may be created by Article 9 of the Convention,[72] the duty on the State to recognize the manifestation of one's religion or belief at the workplace is not absolute. If this were the case, not merely would there be a real risk of administrative chaos,[73] but there might also be an erosion of the rights of

---

[68] It remains to be seen whether Parliament will rectify the anomaly that Northern Ireland is the only part of the United Kingdom where religious discrimination is expressly forbidden by law. On this generally, see *Religious Discrimination in England and Wales*, Interim Report, Jan. 2000, University of Derby (London, 2000).

[69] Under the ECHR a state is not forbidden from basing its religious holidays on the religion of the majority: *X* v. *UK*, Application No. 8160/78, para. 28.

[70] On this generally, see B. Parekh, 'The Concept of National Identity', *New Community*, 21 (1995), 255–68, and T. Modood, ' "Black", Racial Equality and Asian Identity', *New Community*, 14 (1988), 280–4.

[71] For example, in *M* v. *Austria* (1993) 16 EHRR CD 25, the European Commission accepted that while the applicants had been unable to attend a trial because its date had conflicted with their celebration of an important Jewish holiday, their application would still be rejected as the case had been complex and there was insufficient time for the State to arrange an adjournment.

[72] See *Otto-Preminger-Institut* v. *Austria* (1995) 19 EHRR 34, 47, and *Dubowska and Skup* v. *Poland* (1997) 24 EHRR CD 75.

[73] This argument was accepted by Lord Denning in *Ahmad* v. *ILEA* [1978] 1 All ER 574, 578.

members of the 'secular' majority.[74] Yet in a multi-faith society should an employee not be accorded something more than the 'right' to resign should a contractual term conflict with his or her religious belief?[75] As a result of the Human Rights Act, the courts will have the task of determining the extent to which individuals are guaranteed the right to manifest their religion or belief at the workplace. Unless British judges interpret Article 9(1) of the European Convention more boldly than has hitherto been the case, there will be a danger that 'all employees will be equal but some will be more equal than others'.[76]

Regulating the Manifestation of Religion or Belief

The incorporation of the ECHR into UK law will demand that British judges develop their own criteria for determining the extent to which the law should recognize the manifestation of religion and belief. I will suggest three factors in particular which are worthy of detailed consideration: the 'motive' underpinning the actions of those claiming to manifest their religion or belief; the 'necessity' of the relevant activity; and the 'sincerity' of individual or group members. In spite of the difficulties associated with each of these tests, I will argue that, on occasion, they may be of assistance to judges when they come to interpret the Human Rights Act.

'MOTIVE' AND THE MANIFESTATION OF RELIGION OR BELIEF

For the purposes of Article 9 of the European Convention, 'manifestation' only covers forms of expression which relate specifically to two factors: 'religion' or 'belief'.[77] Every major religious tradition has come within the remit of the former,[78] while the latter has been held to include pacifism,[79] atheism,[80] and even communism.[81] Thus, while it might be assumed that one's remit to manifest religion or belief in 'worship, teaching, practice

---

[74] See A. Bradney, 'Faced by Faith', in P. Oliver, S. Douglas Scott, and V. Tadros (eds.), *Faith in Law* (Oxford, 2000), 104.

[75] For example, the European Commission against Racism and Intolerance has recently suggested that states should implement codes of conduct 'to combat religious discrimination in access to employment and at the workplace' (General Policy Recommendation No. 5: *Combating Intolerance and Discrimination against Muslims*: <http://www.ecri.coe.int/en/02/02/14/e02021401.htm>).

[76] Adapted from G. Orwell, *Animal Farm* (London, 1945), 105 ('All animals are equal, but some animals are more equal than others').

[77] This is in contrast to freedom of expression generally, which is covered by Article 10 of the ECHR.

[78] For example, see nn. 25–9.

[79] *Arrowsmith* v. *UK*, Application No. 7050/75, 19 DR 5, 19.

[80] *Angeleni* v. *Sweden*, Application No. 10491/83, 40 DR 41.

[81] *Hazar, Hazar and Acik* v. *Turkey*, Application Nos. 16311/90, 16312/90, and 16313/90, 72 DR 200.

and observance' is wide-ranging, it soon becomes clear that this is actually not the case.

The European Commission has held that 'the term "practice" as employed in Article 9(1) does not cover each act which is motivated or influenced by a religion or belief'.[82] In *Arrowsmith* v. *UK*[83] the question was whether the distribution of leaflets at an army camp calling on British soldiers to refuse to serve in Northern Ireland would constitute a lawful manifestation of pacifist beliefs. The Commission held that, in principle, 'public declarations proclaiming generally the idea of pacifism and urging the acceptance of a commitment to non-violence'[84] would be a 'normal and recognised manifestation of pacifist belief'.[85] However, the Commission distinguished between the latter and situations where 'the actions of individuals do not actually express ... belief [which is] protected by Article 9(1), even when they are motivated or influenced by it'.[86] Notwithstanding the fact that Arrowsmith was clearly a 'convinced pacifist',[87] the fact that her leaflets 'did not express pacifist views'[88] meant simply that they would not come within the remit of Article 9(1) of the Convention.

The Commission's test, of focusing on the nature of the *manifestation* of a religion or belief rather than the *motivation* underpinning it, has been employed to reject a number of applications, ranging from the objections of a Quaker that a proportion of his taxes should not fund defence expenditure,[89] to complaints relating to compulsory participation in professional associations,[90] pension schemes,[91] and the payment of car insurance.[92] It was also used in *X and the Church of Scientology* v. *Sweden*,[93] where it had been claimed that advertising restrictions on the sale of a religious artefact called an E-Meter violated Scientologists' rights to manifest their religion. The European Commission distinguished between 'advertisements which are merely "informational" or "descriptive" in character and commercial advertisements offering objects for sale'.[94] Only the former were held to be protected by Article 9, and since the adverts relating to the sale of E-Meters were 'more a manifestation of a desire to market goods than the manifestation of a belief in practice', they would not fall within the remit of Article 9(1) of the ECHR.[95]

These decisions can be criticized on a number of grounds. For a start, the approach of the European Commission in the *Arrowsmith* case was

[82] *Arrowsmith* v. *UK*, Application No. 7050/75, 19 DR 5, 19.
[83] Ibid.   [84] Ibid., at 20.   [85] Ibid.   [86] Ibid., at 19.
[87] Ibid.   [88] Ibid., at 20.
[89] C v. *UK* (1983) 37 DR 142.
[90] *Revert and Legallis* v. *France*, Application Nos. 14331/88 and 14332/88, DR 62, 309.
[91] V v. *Netherlands*, Application No. 10678/83, 39 DR 267.
[92] X v. *The Netherlands*, Application No. 2988/66, 10 YB ECHR 472 (1967).
[93] Application No. 7805/77, 22 YB ECHR 244 (1979).
[94] Ibid., 250.   [95] Ibid.

extremely narrow. The fact that *all* of the language used in Arrowsmith's leaflets was not specifically of a pacifist nature[96] led the Commission to hold that her distribution of these materials would not constitute a public manifestation of pacifist beliefs. In dissenting from the majority's view in *Arrowsmith*, Commission member Opsahl argued that even though the leaflets appealed to those other than pacifists,[97] there was no contradiction between Arrowsmith's pacifist beliefs and the views which had been publicly expressed.[98] Instead, he considered that there was a clear link between the applicant's belief and her prosecution for incitement to disaffection.[99] Thus Opsahl advanced a much more flexible test, whereby applicants would be 'entitled to have their acts examined under the Convention in the context of their individual circumstances'.[100] Had it been applied in the *Arrowsmith* case the European Commission would have been forced to accept that the applicant's conduct fell within Article 9(1). Thus, the Commission would have been required to consider the politically controversial question of whether the restrictions on the distribution of Arrowsmith's leaflets were justified under Article 9(2) of the ECHR.[101]

Commissioner Opsahl claimed that another advantage of his wider test was that it would extend beyond what he called 'the more traditional types of manifestation'.[102] This brings us to the second criticism of the European Commission's case-law in this area: a tendency to discriminate against new religious movements when assessing the 'motivation' of applicants. It has been claimed that the ruling in *X and the Church of Scientology* v. *Sweden*[103] case reflects the European Commission's 'bias against non-mainstream religions'.[104] Yet it is difficult to be certain whether the Commission has a latent hostility to, or is merely ignorant of, the practices of many new religious movements.

[96] For example, the pamphlet contained sentences such as: 'what is happening in Ireland is all wrong', and 'a soldier who publicly stated that he refused to serve in Northern Ireland . . . would be setting an example to other soldiers: strengthening their resolve to resist the Government's disastrous policy'.

[97] Presumably Commissioner Opsahl had in mind non-pacifists who wanted British troops to leave Northern Ireland, for *political* and not *pacifist* reasons.

[98] *Arrowsmith* v. *UK*, Application No. 7050/75, 19 DR 5, 26, 27.

[99] Under the Incitement to Disaffection Act 1934, it is an offence maliciously and advisedly to endeavour to seduce a member of the armed forces from his duty or allegiance. Prosecutions, which require the consent of the Director of Public Prosecutions, are rare.

[100] *Arrowsmith* v. *UK*, Application No. 7050/75, 19 DR 5, 27.

[101] It is significant that, unlike Articles 8(2), 10(2) and 11(2), of the ECHR, Article 9(2) does not permit limitations to be placed on the manifestation of a religion or belief on the grounds of 'national security'. This may be one reason why the European Commission adopted such a narrow approach in the *Arrowsmith* case.

[102] *Arrowsmith* v. *UK*, Application No. 7050/75, 19 DR 5, 27.

[103] Application No. 7805/77, 22 YB ECHR 244 (1979).

[104] See T. J. Gunn, 'Adjudicating Rights of Conscience' in J. van der Vyver and J. Witte Jr. (eds.), *Religious Human Rights in Global Perspective* (The Hague, 1996), 327.

For example, the fact that E-Meters were offered for sale by the Church of Scientology was enough to convince the European Commission that the relevant advertisements constituted 'commercial speech' and fell within Article 10, rather than Article 9, of the Convention. However, there have been occasions where the 'mainstream' religions have, in the past, demanded payment for certain services. For example, in addition to the ancient practice of tithing,[105] there is evidence that some Christian churches[106] and Jewish synagogues[107] have charged pew rents for those wishing to reserve a particular seat in a service. Similarly, Mass stipends, paid to Catholic priests in return for performing a service on behalf of the donor, have been described as a form of 'bilateral contract'.[108] And in rejecting the argument that the Church of Scientology's policy towards money meant that it could not be classified as a 'religion', the Italian Court of Cassation referred to the methods employed by the Catholic Church in the past (e.g. the sale of indulgences and Mass costs) to boost its income.[109] Thus, it is argued that in the E-Meter case, as in *Arrowsmith*, the European Commission adopted an unnecessarily narrow approach in determining whether the relevant activities were motivated or inspired by a religion or belief.

It cannot be denied, however, that the European Commission has not acted unreasonably in distinguishing between the *motivation* for and the *manifestation* of religion or belief. No legal system could function properly if individuals were able to extend Article 9 to every action claimed to have been motivated by a religion or belief. Thus, it is not the motivation test per se, but rather the way in which it has been employed, which gives cause for concern. As one commentator has observed, the most important question is not whether an E-Meter is a 'mechanical gimmick or . . . a sophisticated piece of equipment' but the extent to which a court should 'presume that it knows the answer to that question'.[110] Judges tend not to be experts in theology or religious studies, so unless applicants are, to some extent, given the 'benefit of the doubt' when they claim to have been motivated by their faith,[111] there is a danger that Article 9 of the ECHR will be limited to activities which are conventional and orthodox.[112]

---

[105] See e.g. Gen. 14: 20; Lev. 27: 30; Num. 28: 26; and Deut. 14: 28.

[106] See P K Meagher and T. C. O'Brien (eds.), *Encyclopedic Dictionary of Religion* (Philadelphia and Washington, 1979), 2760, as cited by Justice O'Connor in *Hernandez v. Commissioner of IRS*, 490 U.S. 680 (1989).

[107] See J. Feldman, H. Fruhauf, and M. Schoen, *Temple Management Manual* (New York, 1984), ch. 4, p. 10, as cited by Justice O'Connor, *Hernandez v. Commissioner of IRS*.

[108] See *New Catholic Encylopedia, Mass Stipend*, 13 (1967), 715, as cited by Justice O'Connor, *Hernandez v. Commissioner of IRS*.

[109] See *La Corte Suprema di Cassione Repubblica Italiana v. Bandera Fulvio et al.*, Udienza pubblica dell' 8.10.1997, Sentenza n. 1329, Registro Gen. n. 16835/97.

[110] See Gunn, 'Adjudicating Rights of Conscience'.

[111] This point is also made by van Dijk and van Hoof, *Theory and Practice of the European Convention*, 550.

[112] Such an interpretation would fall foul of the Human Rights Committee's interpreta-

In *Goldman* v. *Weinberger*[113] Brennan J warned of 'majoritarian social institutions that dismiss minority beliefs and practices as unimportant, because [they are] unfamiliar'. Thus, when interpreting Article 9 of the Convention, one hopes that British judges will be more aware than their Strasbourg counterparts of the motives which underpin the many different ways in which religion or belief can be manifested in a contemporary Western liberal democracy.

A 'NECESSITY' TEST

Another approach which the courts could take to regulate the manifestation of religion or belief would be to make use of a 'necessity' test. A common characteristic of cases in this area is the contention of applicants that certain activities are 'necessary' for the proper manifestation of their religion or belief. Yet to what extent should the courts accept such claims at face value? Conflicting strategies have been adopted by the Strasbourg human rights organs and the US courts in seeking to answer this question. For example, in *US* v. *Lee*[114] the Supreme Court accepted the submission of an Old Order Amish farmer that the imposition of social security taxes was prohibited by his faith. Its members were reluctant to submit the believer's claim to detailed scrutiny since judges are 'not arbiters of scriptural interpretation'.[115] Accordingly, subject to the caveat that an alleged 'religious' practice is not merely 'bizarre' or 'clearly non-religious in motivation',[116] the US courts have refrained from a detailed examination of every activity which has been accorded the protection of the Free Exercise clause of the First Amendment.

The European Commission on Human Rights, on the other hand, has tended to employ a much more rigorous test in determining the extent to which a certain practice is 'necessary' for an individual to manifest his religion or belief.[117] The relevant Strasbourg jurisprudence has often involved those invoking the ECHR from prison. For example, the European

tion of Article 18 of the International Covenant on Civil and Political Rights 1966, the equivalent of Article 9 of the ECHR. In its General Comment on Article 18 the Human Rights Committee has warned that 'it views with concern any tendency to discriminate against any religions or beliefs for any reason, including the fact that they are newly established' (CCPR/C/48/CRP.2/REV1).

[113] 106 S. Ct 1310 (1986).   [114] *US* v. *Lee* 71 L. Ed. 2d 127.

[115] Ibid., at 132.

[116] *Thomas* v. *Review Board of the Indiana Employment Security Division*, 67 L. Ed. 2d 624.

[117] The European Commission has certainly not accepted, at face value, the claims of applicants that they are manifesting their religion or belief. For example, in *Chappell* v. *UK*, Application No. 12587/86 (1987) 53 DR 241, the Commission rejected the claims of Druids that it was necessary for them to celebrate their midsummer solstice at Stonehenge. Indeed, the European Commission even managed to decide this case without ruling on whether Druidism is a 'religion'.

Commission rejected the complaint of a Buddhist prisoner who had wanted to send out material for publication in a Buddhist magazine, on the basis that he had failed to prove that this was a necessary part of his religious practice.[118] The Commission also denied a prisoner access to a prayer chain on the ground that it was not 'an indispensable element in the proper exercise of the Buddhist religion',[119] but accepted that it would have been appropriate for a Tao Buddhist prisoner to have had access to a religious book, had it not contained a chapter on martial arts.[120] This 'necessity' test has, however, not been confined only to cases involving those in prison. For example, in *Valsamis* v. *Greece*,[121] following the temporary expulsion of two Jehovah's Witness students from school for refusing to attend parades commemorating the outbreak of war between Greece and Italy, the European Court was unable to discern anything 'either in the purpose of the parade or in the arrangements for it, which could offend the applicant's pacifist convictions'.[122] The European Commission has also rejected a Muslim teacher's claim that attendance at Friday prayers, on school days, was a 'necessary part' of his religious practice;[123] refused to accept that visits to Zen Buddhist priories were an indispensable element of a Buddhist applicant's religious worship;[124] denied that a refusal by the Dutch authorities to allow the applicants to adopt Hindu names constituted a violation of Article 9(1);[125] and conceded that, in spite of the inadmissibility of the application, a Quaker's opposition to her income tax contributions funding military expenditure was 'necessary' for the manifestation of her religious beliefs.[126]

In spite of the Commission's endorsement of the 'necessity' test, there are a number of reasons why it should only be used with caution by British judges when they come to interpret Article 9(1) of the European Convention. Firstly, the 'necessity' test presupposes that a religion will

[118] *X* v. *UK* Application No. 5442/72, 1 DR 41.
[119] *X* v. *Austria,* Application No. 1753/63, 8 YB ECHR 174 (1965).
[120] *X* v. *UK*, Application No. 6886/75, 5 DR 100.
[121] See *Valsamis* v. *Greece* (1997) 24 EHRR 294 and *Efstratiou* v. *Greece* (1997) 24 EHRR 294.
[122] See *Valsamis* v. *Greece*, at para. 32.
[123] *Ahmad* v. *UK*, Application No. 8160/78, 22 DR 27. In rejecting Ahmad's request to adduce expert evidence, the European Commission was heavily influenced by the fact that Ahmad had failed to mention, either during his interview for the teaching position or during the six years in which he had been previously employed, that he would require time off from school to attend prayers at the mosque. However, the European Court rejected this 'estoppel' approach in *Sigurdar Sigurjonnson* v. *Iceland* (1993) 16 EHRR 462, a 'closed shop' case which was decided under Article 11 of the ECHR.
[124] *Logan* v. *UK* 86A DR 74, 82.
[125] *Coeriel and Aurik* v. *Netherlands*, [1994] *HRLJ* nos. 11–12, 448.
[126] *C* v. *UK*, No. 10358/83, 37 DR 142. However, the Commission concluded that there had been no interference with Article 9(1) of the ECHR as 'The obligation to pay taxes is a general one which has no specific conscientious implications in itself' (ibid., at 147).

have a clearly discernible text and tenets of belief. This, however, is not always the case, particularly where new religious movements are concerned. Indeed, the diverse ways in which contemporary religious groups express their faith in public has led Bryan Wilson to call for a 'reappraisal of what is understood by worship'.[127] Thus, in the case of religions such as Rastafarianism, where it has been claimed there is 'no set time for rituals or worship [and] no set ways of giving thanks and praises'[128] to God, the courts will inevitably struggle to determine what is 'necessary' for the manifestation of their religion or belief.

Secondly, in the absence of definite holy books or texts, courts may be tempted to call expert witnesses to testify as to whether a particular practice is actually required by a particular faith. The European Commission has, in principle, been prepared to receive submissions from expert witnesses,[129] but a heavy reliance on their opinions usually risks ignoring the fact that religious precepts are usually open to a wide range of different interpretations.[130]

Thirdly, even if such tenets of belief are discernible, the 'necessity' test charges judges, who often have little knowledge or experience of religious matters, with having to take decisions in this area.[131] Judges tend to be cautious about exceeding their jurisdiction and ruling on issues which are essentially matters of doctrine rather than issues of law.[132] Thus, there is perhaps a danger that if British judges are required to examine and pass judgment on the practices of minority religions, they will be perceived as approaching matters from a Judaeo-Christian perspective.

Finally, the 'necessity' test risks focusing on what is necessary for the group at the expense of the interests of the individual. As we shall see, one way of remedying this defect might be for the courts to examine the sincerity of an individual's religion or belief. Yet, in spite of the above reservations, it is difficult to avoid the conclusion that the 'necessity' test has serious limitations and that British judges would be well advised to employ it sparingly, in only the clearest of cases.

---

127 B. Wilson, *The Social Dimensions of Sectarianism* (Oxford, 1990), 276.

128 J. Bones, *One Love. Rastafari: History, Doctrine and Livity*, (Tottenham, 1985), 2.

129 *X v. UK*, No. 8231/78, 28 DR 5, 27 and *X v. UK*, No. 8160/78, 22 DR 27.

130 'Intrafaith differences . . . are not uncommon among followers of a particular creed, and the judicial process is singularly ill-equipped to resolve such differences' (*Thomas* v. *Review Board of the Indiana Employment Security Division*, 67 L. Ed. 2d 624, 631).

131 For example, the vast majority of judges in the United Kingdom will come from, and be most familiar with, the Judaeo-Christian tradition.

132 '. . . it is no business of the courts to say what is a religious practice or activity for one group is not a religion under the protection of the First Amendment' (*Fowler* v. *Rhode Island*, 345 U.S. 67, 70 (1953)).

A 'SINCERITY' TEST

Another strategy for interpreting the rights which will soon be incorporated under Article 9 of the Convention would be for judges to examine the extent to which a particular religious practice is 'sincerely' held. This approach (i.e. of examining the sincerity of a party who claims to have acted out of a religious conviction) has in the past been employed by the US courts as a way of ensuring that only bona fide 'religious' beliefs are entitled to the protection of the religious free exercise clause of the First Amendment.[133] In *United States* v. *Seeger*[134] the US Supreme Court recognised there could be a statutory exemption for conscientious objectors where their religious beliefs were 'sincerely',[135] 'honestly',[136] and 'truly held'.[137] This test was also employed in *US* v. *Kuch*,[138] where a Federal District Court rejected the claims of the Neo-American Church, that they were under a sacred duty to use LSD and marijuana in religious rites, on the ground that the use of drugs was 'the coagulant of this organisation and the reason for its existence'.[139] Similarly, in *Theriault* v. *Silber*, when inmates of a federal prison claimed that they needed steak and wine in order to celebrate their 'religion', their demands were rejected on the basis that the prisoners' 'sole purpose [had been] to cause or encourage disruption of established prison discipline'.[140]

While British judges can legitimately look for assistance in interpreting the Human Rights Act from other jurisdictions, it is undeniable that there would be some problems with employing such a 'sincerity' test in the United Kingdom. For example, the rather unusual facts of a case such as *US* v. *Kuch*,[141] where the 'Church' lacked any tenets of belief and had as its anthems 'Puff the Magic Dragon' and 'Row, Row, Row your Boat', meant that it was almost inevitable that the Court would question its status as a 'religion'. But what of less clear-cut cases, where it is much harder to ascertain 'potentially fraudulent religious beliefs'?[142] There is no objective or scientific way of measuring 'sincerity'. A test which requires a court to gauge the extent to which a particular 'religious' practice plays in a person's life is subjective and might work against those who lack the eloquence or persuasive charms necessary to convince a court of their 'sincerity'. Nevertheless, in spite of these problems, it is suggested that there are four reasons why British judges should consider making use of the 'sincerity' test in this context.

[133] 'Congress shall make no law respecting an establishment of a religion, or prohibiting the free exercise thereof . . .'.
[134] In *U.S.* v. *Seeger* 380 U.S. (1965) 163.			[135] Ibid., at 166–7.
[136] Ibid., at 176			[137] Ibid., at 185.
[138] 288 F. Supp. 439 (D.D.C. 1968).			[139] Ibid., at 444.
[140] 391 F. Supp. 578, 582 (W.D. Tex. 1975), vacated and remanded, 547 F. 2d 1279 (5th Cir.) 1977.
[141] 288 F. Supp. 439 (D.D.C. 1968).			[142] *US* v. *Ballard*, 322 U.S. 78, 84 (1944).

Firstly, it would supplement the previously discussed 'necessity' test, by enabling a court to compare and contrast the actions of the complainant with the key elements of their belief. Secondly, it might compensate for one of the defects of the 'necessity' test by taking account of the interests of the individual believer who, in good faith, dissents from the official line of their religious organization. Thirdly, it would provide an opportunity for a complainant who could demonstrate a willingness to perform alternative (albeit equivalent) duties in conformity with his or her religious duties. And finally, it could be argued that even the European Court of Human Rights implicitly recognized a form of this test in *Kokkinakis* v. *Greece*, when it distinguished between 'bearing Christian witness and improper proselytism'.[143] The former, rather than the latter, would only appear to be synonymous with 'sincerity'.

Therefore, in spite of the difficulties of using it in practice, the 'sincerity' test (as with the previously discussed 'motivation' and 'necessity' tests) may, on occasion, prove useful to British courts when they approach Article 9 of the European Convention. It is suggested that since each of the three 'tests' have various strengths and weaknesses, judges would be well advised to consider them together, in weighing up what constitutes a lawful manifestation of religion or belief.

Conclusion

It is unfortunate that during the Parliamentary passage of the Human Rights Act no real guidance was offered as to how the courts should interpret Article 9 of the European Convention. Rather than focusing on how the incorporation of the ECHR might protect vulnerable religious minorities, debates in Parliament were largely confined to the implications of the Act for the established Church.[144] During one such debate Lord Goodhart, in an effort to reassure those who were concerned that incorporation of the Convention might erode rather than protect their human rights, commented: 'The ECHR is one of the most powerful weapons for the protection of religious freedom which has even been created.'[145] Alas, as yet there is no evidence to support this claim. A deference to Judaeo-Christian norms,[146] a latent suspicion of new religious movements,[147] and

---

[143] *Kokkinakis* v. *Greece* (1994) 17 EHRR 397, at para. 48.

[144] Section 13 of the Human Rights Act was inserted specifically to assuage the fears of a number of churches and religious organizations.

[145] HL Hansard, 5 Feb. 1998, vol. 585, col. 751.

[146] See P. Cumper, 'The Rights of Religious Minorities: The Legal Regulation of New Religious Movements', in P. Cumper and S. Wheatley (eds.), *Minority Rights in the New Europe* (The Hague, 1999), 174, 175.

[147] The latent suspicion of the Court to new religious movements is perhaps illustrated by the fact that in *Kokkinakis* v. *Greece* (1994) 17 EHRR 397, members of the Court appeared to accept unquestioningly the use of terms such as 'brainwashing' (at 17, 35, 36) and termi-

a general reluctance to refer to Article 9[148] are some reasons why the European Commission and Court have traditionally given an 'extremely restrictive'[149] interpretation to this Convention article. However, under the Human Rights Act, UK courts are not bound by the previous rulings of the Strasbourg human rights institutions.[150] Instead British judges will have unprecedented powers to make a 'significant contribution',[151] not merely to the development of the law of human rights generally, but to the protection of religion or belief in particular. Only then, when the courts take account of the diverse and varied ways in which religion or belief is manifested in contemporary Britain, will Lord Goodhart's bold rhetoric actually reflect reality.

nology such as 'unacceptable psychological techniques' (at 37). For a criticism of such an approach see J. Richardson, 'Cult/Brainwashing Cases and the Freedom of Religion', *Journal of Church and State*, 33 (1991), 74.

[148] See e.g. *Hoffman* v. *Austria* (1994) 17 EHRR 293, where the European Court relied on Articles 8 (the right to a family life) and 14 (the prohibition of discrimination) rather than Article 9, in resolving a dispute between warring parents, one of whom was a Jehovah's Witness and the other a non-Jehovah's Witness.

[149] J. Wadham and H. Mountfield, *Blackstone's Guide to the Human Rights Act 1998* (London, 1999), 98.

[150] See s. 2 of the Human Rights Act 1998.

[151] Lord Bingham, HL Hansard, 3 Nov. 1997.

PROFESSIONAL ETHICS AND AUTONOMY: A THEOLOGICAL CRITIQUE

Steven H. Resnicoff

Professional ethics discussions usually focus on the autonomy of the non-professional, such as a client or a patient. Too little attention has been paid to the scope of autonomy afforded the professional. This paper will preliminarily examine and critique, from a theological perspective, the way in which professional ethics codes unduly constrain the professional's freedom of action.

I say 'preliminarily' because, broadly construed, a theological critique of professional ethics and autonomy could easily fill volumes. To place this project within possibly manageable parameters, I will restrict its purview in two ways. First, although the phrase 'a theological critique' may suggest to some a more universal lens, I will explore the topic through the prism of Judaism. In doing so, I rely in part on the title's use of the indefinite article 'a'.[1] Nonetheless, some of my most important observations may be equally valid from other religious perspectives. Second, I will concentrate on two specific professions, law and medicine, as they are regulated in the United States. While somewhat limiting, these cases still provide the basis for interesting contrasts and comparisons.

Section 1 introduces the most prominent concepts of autonomy and describes the roles they play in the leading theories of morality, while Section 2 describes the relevance of autonomy in the context of Judaism. Section 3 provides introductory comments regarding the American regulation of legal and medical ethics, and Section 4 explains how professional ethics rules impinge on Jewish values. Finally, Section 5 explores the implications of this critique at the personal, professional, and policy-making levels and recommends, cautiously, that a particular solution be more thoroughly, and favourably, considered.

1. Competing Concepts of Autonomy

Let us briefly examine three principal versions of autonomy, to which I will refer, respectively, as the Kantian, the identification, and the control

---

[1] We also rely on the fact that the word 'theological' suggests inquiries into the doctrinal application of one or more particular faiths. See Leslie Griffin, 'The Relevance of Religion to a Lawyer's Work: Legal Ethics', (1998) 66 *Fordham Law Review* 1253.

approaches. Kant addresses autonomy as it relates to man's moral character and emphasizes the importance of man's self-sufficiency and imperviousness to external influences. According to Kant, only pure reason is independent of external, or heteronomous, influences, and, therefore, only acts taken according to pure reason are considered autonomous. Pure reason leads man to recognize certain universal duties (categorical imperatives). Man is obliged to obey these categorical imperatives even if the consequences of doing so are unpleasant. For example, Kant maintains that there is a categorical imperative against lying and contends that one may not violate this imperative even to save an innocent person's life.[2] Indeed, he equates morality itself with purposeful compliance with such imperatives. According to Kant, conduct activated by emotions such as loyalty or compassion lack moral value.[3]

One of the difficulties with any attempt to apply the Kantian standard to contemporary conduct, of course, is that each person is bombarded by countless external variables, including those arising out of his religious and socio-economic environments, that affect his psychological make-up. As a result, it may be impossible for a person to know what truly motivates his act. Equally problematic for our practical inquiry, perhaps, is the phenomenon that many, if not most, people seem to reject, rather categorically, the existence of a duty to comply with Kant's imperatives, or at least with some of them. Harmless social lies, for instance, seem to be a widely accepted convention engendering little or no sense of remorse.[4] Interestingly, even more questionable lies are practised by many, although we cannot be confident about how much cognitive dissonance they cause. Illustrative is a recent study published in the *Journal of the American Medical Association* in which a significant minority of physicians surveyed admitted to having deceitfully manipulated reimbursement rules so that insurers would pay for treatments for which, according to the relevant insurance contracts, they would not otherwise be liable.[5]

A second approach asserts that an act motivated by heteronomous forces is nonetheless autonomous if the actor identifies with those heteronomous forces. As Gerald Dworkin writes:

It is the attitude a person takes toward the influences motivating him which determines whether or not they are to be considered 'his'. Does he identify with them, assimilate them to himself, view himself, as the kind of person who wishes to be motivated in these particular ways? If, on the contrary, a man resents his being

---

[2] Sissela Bok, *Lying: Moral Choice in Public and Private Life* (New York, 1999), 38–9.

[3] Grace Clement, *Care, Autonomy, and Justice: Feminism and the Ethic of Care* (Boulder, Colo., 1996), 13.

[4] Bok, *Lying*, 57–72.

[5] Matthew K. Wynia, Deborah S. Cummins, Jonathan B. VanGeest, and Ira B. Wilson, 'Physician Manipulation of Reimbursement Rules for Patients', *Journal of the American Medical Association*, 283/14 (12 Apr. 2000), 1858–65.

motivated in certain ways, is alienated from those influences, resents acting in accordance with them, would prefer to be the kind of person who is motivated in different ways, then those influences, even though they may be causally effective, are not viewed as 'his'.[6]

Nevertheless, others argue that the core of autonomy depends neither on the total absence of external influences nor in a person's identification with such influences but, instead, on a person's ability to control his conduct. From this viewpoint, the external influences merely establish the circumstances in which a person exercises his autonomy. If, however, such pressures are so great that they effectively coerce his action, the action is not autonomous. In arguing for this understanding of autonomy, Thomas May relies in part on Aristotle's analogy to the helmsman of a boat. Just as the helmsman must respond to the many physical forces that confront him, so, too, must every man make choices in the practical circumstances in which he exists. According to Aristotle, a man who does not act under ignorance is morally accountable for his acts so long as the external pressures are not so powerful that it is as if the actor 'were to be carried somewhere by the wind or by men who had him in their power'.[7] May considers an act for which a person is morally accountable an autonomous act, while recognizing, of course, that it is difficult to determine precisely when the level of external pressure is sufficiently great so as to relieve a person of such accountability.[8] Thus, while Kant contends that every autonomous act is a moral one, May—and others that use the control definition of autonomy—argue only that every autonomous act may be characterized as either moral or immoral. Whether an autonomous act is moral or immoral must be determined by using a separate standard.

The primary approaches for assessing morality in which autonomy plays an obvious role may very broadly be described as duty-based or consequentialist.[9] Kantian theory, which centres on duties determined by

---

[6] Thomas May, *Autonomy, Authority and Moral Responsibility* (Dordrecht, 1998), 14.

[7] Aristotle, *Nicomachean Ethics*, cited ibid. 42.

[8] Interestingly, Judaism also recognizes the notion of duress and, on rare occasions, it may not consider a person to be morally responsible for certain consequences. Nevertheless, it seems clear that some of the situations in which Aristotle and May might regard an actor as morally guiltless, Judaism would regard him as morally culpable; the degree of duress in such cases merely operating to mitigate the extent of the guilt. See e.g. *Shulhan Arukh* v. *Yoreh De'ah* 157 (Heb.)(16th cent.). See also Steven H. Resnicoff, 'Jewish Law Perspectives on Suicide and Physician-Assisted Dying', (1998–9) 13 *Journal of Law and Religion* 289, 308–9.

[9] Modern political and ethical discussions often focus on 'rights', rather than on duties or goals. Nevertheless, as one commentator puts it: 'The trouble with rights-based . . . theories is that they are excellent for defining the parameters of personal freedoms but are less helpful in making critical choices within our own area of freedom. We can live an almost totally depraved life in complete accord with the Constitution and laws of the United States. Indeed, it could be argued that we have a legal "right" to lead a depraved life.' See Daniel R. Coquillette, 'Professionalism: The Deep Theory', (1994) 72 *North Carolina Law Review* 1271, 1274. Interestingly, Jewish commentators remark that a depraved or repulsive life could be lived in strict compliance with all specific Jewish law requirements. See R. Moshe

pure reason, represents only one example of a duty-based approach. Others might contend that different kinds of duties, such as those arising from religious or humanistic principles, ought to be obeyed instead. According to such theories, the morality of particular autonomous acts would be assessed according to whether they are motivated by a perceived obligation to comply with such duties.

By contrast, a consequentialist theory categorizes the morality of an act by examining its results.[10] The leading consequentialist theory, utilitarianism, declares that the moral act—among competing choices—is that which maximizes the net positive consequence (i.e. an act that accomplishes the greatest possible good) or, if only negative results are possible, minimizes the net negative results. While early utilitarians may have regarded only happiness or pleasure as positive results, more modern utilitarians have argued that many other values are 'good'. Thus, to the extent that a consequentialist believes that autonomy is a positive result, he would regard acts that foster autonomy to be morally valuable. Of course, reaching agreement on which values count and for how much they count is a source of interminable debate.

According to the control approach to autonomy—and perhaps even the identification approach to autonomy—autonomy is a matter of degree. For example, to the extent that a person has the physical, financial, emotional, or intellectual resources to resist external pressures, that person is often said to enjoy a higher degree of autonomy. Similarly, an act that provides a person with greater flexibility and range of choice would seem to afford the person relatively greater autonomy.

2. The Jewish Approach to Autonomy

Judaism is duty-based.[11] There is a fundamental obligation to emulate G–d (*imitatio dei*)[12] and to obey his laws. An act fulfilling this duty is morally right and an act working at a cross-purpose is morally wrong. As Walter Wurzburger explains:

Jewish monotheism represents a radically different approach to religion. Its novelty consisted not primarily in the substitution of the belief in one G–d for the plurality of G–ds worshiped in polytheism. What was even more revolutionary in the Jewish

---

ben Nahman, *Commentary to Mikrot Gedolot, Leviticus* 19: 2 (Heb.)(13th cent.). Certain overarching Jewish law principles, however, demand *that a Jew do more*, that he strive to be holy by emulating G–d (see e.g. Lev. 19: 2, Deut. 28: 9), and that he do that which is 'good and right' (see Deut. 6: 18). See also R. Samson Raphael Hirsch, *Horeb: A Philosophy of Jewish Laws and Observances*, trans. I. Grunfeld, 4th edn. (New York, 1996), 359–60; Resnicoff, 'Jewish Law Perspectives', 308.

[10] Or, possibly, by its anticipated results at the time one chooses whether to take the action.
[11] Walter S. Wurzburger, *Ethics of Responsibility* (Philadelphia, 1994), 28.
[12] Ibid., 71 (citing various sources, including Maimonides, for this proposition).

conception of monotheism was, as against the pagan emphasis upon divine power, the attribution of moral perfection to G–d.

His moral attributes rather than His absolute power render Him *worthy* of being worshiped and obeyed. In striking contrast to paganism, worship is no longer dictated primarily by self-serving considerations as a device enabling us to get what we want. To serve Him is not a means to the fulfillment of our needs, but an end in itself. Worship of G–d involves commitment to abide by His will and the ethical norms He demands.[13]

Rejecting the need to discern the commandments through pure reason, and with it, Kant's concept of morality, the people of Israel, at the revelation at Mount Sinai, announced, 'All that the Lord has said, we shall do and we shall understand.'[14] We accepted the duty to perform the commandments even before we would understand their respective rationales. As one commentator pointed out, in the story of Creation it was the Serpent who asserted that by eating the forbidden fruit man would 'be as G–d, knowing good and evil'.[15] Jewish tradition rejects this, and believes that, rather than use pure reason to derive a priori rules, we must study G–d's words and learn his reasons.[16]

Central to Judaism is the concept of 'free will', which is what allows man to choose between good and evil and to act on that choice. The value of free will, however, is that through its proper exercise a man can sanctify himself and form a closer and more intense relationship with the Almighty. According to Judaism, there is no positive value to a person's having free will if he exercises it incorrectly. Similar sentiments have been expressed by those espousing other religions.[17]

According to the control definition of autonomy, a person who misuses his free will to do evil behaves just as autonomously as one who uses his free will to do good. Judaism could accept the control definition of autonomy, but, if so defined, it would not necessarily be 'good' that a person acted autonomously. A good result would be where one acts autonomously in a particular way, namely, by using one's free will to do the right thing.

What is the effect of transgression? Judaism posits that man is made in the image of G–d and, as such, his essence, his soul, is holy. Compare the secular and Jewish expressions for one who does more than is minimally required by their respective systems of 'law'. In English, secularists usually say that such a person has gone 'beyond the letter of the law' or has 'gone above and beyond' what is required. This terminology suggests that secu-

---

[13] Ibid., 4.

[14] Exod. 24: 7.

[15] Isaac Breuer, quoted in Hirsch, *Horeb*, p. lxxv.

[16] Wurzburger, *Ethics*, 28.

[17] The Roman Catholic tradition seems to advance a similar position. See Teresa Stanton Collett, 'Speak no evil, Seek no Evil, Do no Evil: Client Selection and Cooperation with Evil', (1998) 66 *Fordham Law Review* 1339, 1343–4.

lar law requires a person to distance himself from his origin. When someone does more than what is required by Jewish law, the Hebrew expression is that he has acted *lifnim mishurat hadin*, 'within the line of the law'. This expression implies that Jewish law establishes a limit beyond which a person is not permitted to stray from his true starting point. The more righteous a person's act, the closer he is to his true, holy essence.[18] By transgressing, a person goes over the line and becomes alienated from himself.

In a society governed by Jewish law, rabbinic leaders would use coercion—including physical force if necessary—to induce an individual to perform a commandment requiring a specific action.[19] Why? Because the consequences of such coercion are deemed more far more beneficial than allowing a person to misuse his free will. Jewish law believes that a person is metaphysically affected by his deeds.[20] Fulfilment of a commandment, even if not done for the right reason, leads a person to performing more commandments and, ultimately, to doing so for the right reason.[21] Failure to comply with a commandment has the opposite effect.[22] Thus, such coercion leads to the coerced individual's ultimate perfection.

But why is one person's perfection the concern of the rest of us? Judaism posits an underlying social relationship not just between man and G–d but also between and among men.[23] Pursuant to this relationship,

---

[18]   Aaron Kirschenbaum, *Equity in Jewish Law: halakhic Perspectives in Law* (Hoboken, NJ, 1991), 38.

[19]   Resnicoff, 'Jewish Law Perspectives', 347–8.

[20]   R. Aharon Ha-Levi, *Sefer Ha-Hinukh* (Heb.) (13th. cent.), Commandment 16.

[21]   See e.g. R. Shlomo Yitzhaki, *Commentary to Babylonian Talmud* (Heb.) (11th cent.) (hereafter *Rashi*), *Nazir* 23*b*. Interestingly, secular writers have long acknowledged that, given the power of habit, proper conduct on one occasion (such as the refraining from doing evil) makes proper conduct easier on future occasions. See e.g. William Shakespeare, *Hamlet*, III. iv. 176–87.

[22]   By doing a forbidden act, one becomes desensitized to its enormity, making repetition of the act increasingly likely. See e.g. *Rashi*, *Yuma* 86*b*, 87*a*, *Mo'ed katan* 27*b*, *Kiddushin* 40*a*, Arakhin 30*b*. See also *Yalkut Shimoni*, *Parshat Be-Har*, *Remez* 661 (Heb.)(13th cent.); Steven H. Resnicoff, 'The Attorney–Client Relationship: A Jewish Law Perspective', (2000) 14 *Notre Dame Journal of Law, Ethics & Public Policy* 349, 366–7; Steven H. Resnicoff, 'A Jewish Look at Lawyering Ethics—A Preliminary Essay,' (1998) 15 *Touro Law Review* 73, 102–3. The social psychology theory of cognitive dissonance arguably addresses this phenomenon. According to that theory, for example, if a person believes certain conduct is bad but, because of various socio-economic pressures, engages in that conduct, the consequential cognitive dissonance that develops causes him to change his attitude about the conduct and regard it as rightful. See, generally, Leon Festinger, *A Theory of Cognitive Dissonance* (Evanston, Ill., 1957); Davida H. Isaacs, ' "It's Nothing Personal"—But should it Be? Finding Agent Liability for Violations of the Federal Employment Discrimination Statutes', (1996) 22 *New York University Review of Law & Social Change* 505.

[23]   See e.g. R. Yehuda He-Hasid, *Sefer Hasidim* 93 (Heb.)(11th and 12th cent.) (Jerusalem, 1957). ('All Jews are responsible for each other. If it were not for this responsibility, a person would not admonish his fellow about his fellow's sins and he would not pay attention to find out who is a transgressor and [take steps to stop him] . . .'). See, generally, Nachum L. Rabinovitch, 'All Jews are Responsible for One Another', in Jacob J. Schacter (ed.), *Jewish Tradition and the Nontraditional Jew* (Northvale, NJ, 1992).

each person owes duties to the other. Man is to love one's fellow as he loves himself.[24] Just as he should seek his own self-improvement, he should seek that of his neighbour. The biblical verse 'Thou shalt not place a stumbling block before a blind man',[25] forbids one from enabling someone who is morally blind to violate Jewish law.[26] Rabbinic law prohibits helping someone to violate Jewish law even if he could have done so without any assistance.[27] Indeed, if a person can prevent another from wrongdoing, he is obligated to do so. A person who could stop someone from sinning but does not do so is responsible, in some sense, for the violation he did not prevent.[28] Even after a wrongdoer acts, a person cannot strengthen a wrongdoer's hand, such as by buying goods from a known thief,[29] and if a person is able to persuade the transgressor to repent, he must do so.[30] When one person does wrong, the entire community, even those who are not present when he acted, bears some blame for the moral climate which contributed to the act.[31] Thus, Jewish tradition provides that each year, on the Day of Judgement, a judgement is issued for the entire community based on the community's collective acts and this judgement affects all of the individual members of the community.[32]

The relationship among community members also affirmatively requires that each person help one another. For example, there is a duty to provide financial assistance through loans and gifts. In addition, there is a duty to protect and rescue others from harm, emotional, financial, or physical.[33] A fortiori, there are prohibitions against the causing of such harms.[34]

Nevertheless, although ensuring compliance with the Commandments is more important than allowing someone to misuse his free will—both to his

---

[24] Lev. 19: 18.

[25] Lev. 19: 14. See also R. Moshe Feinstein, *Iggerot Moshe*, *Yoreh De'ah* 1: 3 (Heb.)(20th cent.).

[26] See, generally, Steven H. Resnicoff, 'Helping a Client Violate Jewish Law: A Jewish Lawyer's Dilemma', in Hannah G. Sprecher (ed.), *Jewish Law Association Studies*, vol. x (New York, 2000), 198–208.

[27] Ibid., 208–27.

[28] *Shulhan Arukh*, *Yoreh De'ah* 157. See also R. Yitzhak Weiss, *Minhat Yitzhak* 5: 14 (Heb.)(20th cent.); R. Eliezer Waldenburg, *Tzitz Eliezer* 15: 15 (Heb.)(20th cent.); R. Moshe Feinstein, *Iggerot Moshe*, *Yoreh De'ah* 1: 72.

[29] *Shulhan Arukh*, *Hoshen Mishpat* 356, 369.

[30] *Shulhan Arukh*, *Orah Hayyim* 608.

[31] *Shulhan Arukh*, *Yoreh De'ah* 157.

[32] Maimonides, *Mishneh Torah*, *Hilkhot Teshuvah* 3: 4 (Heb.)(12th cent.). See also Aryeh Kaplan, *Handbook of Jewish Thought*, vol. ii (New York, 1992), 136–7.

[33] See, generally, Aaron Kirschenbaum, 'The Bystander's Duty to Rescue in Jewish Law', repr. in Martin P. Golding (ed.), *Jewish Law and Legal Theory* (New York, 1993). See also Deut. 22: 2, and *Babylonian Talmud*, *Sanhedrin* 73 (Heb.)(5th cent.).

[34] For example, it is forbidden to damage someone's property (*Shulhan Arukh*, *Hoshen Mishpat* 368: 1); to cause damage indirectly to someone's property (see R. Jacob ben Asher, *Tur*, *Hoshen Mishpat* 368 (Heb.)(14th cent.)), and, a fortiori, to cause someone physical injury (see e.g. *Shulhan Arukh*, *Hoshen Mishpat* 450 :1). See, generally, R. Jacob Y. Blau, *Piskei Hoshen*, *Hilkhot Nezikin* (Heb.) (Jerusalem, 1988–9).

detriment and to the detriment of the community—there remains considerable room within Judaism for man to make decisions that are not required by notions of absolute duty.[35] Such decisions would be deemed 'autonomous' according to the control approach to autonomy described above in Section 1. In countless cases, Judaism neither requires nor forbids particular actions. Instead, Judaism may only encourage or discourage them. For example, in the Sabbatical Year certain financial obligations are legally extinguished. Nevertheless, the Mishnah declares that the sages are pleased with one who repays such debts even though there is no duty to do so.[36] As to other questions that arise in daily life, Judaism may take no particular position at all, allowing a person to decide for himself how to proceed.

More fundamentally, perhaps, the entire process of determining what Jewish law requires involves what has been characterized as an autonomous, vibrant,and creative investment of human energy and intellect.[37] Although the law emanates from G–d, the process of determining its substantive content and applying it to the countless contexts that arise daily was entrusted to man. Indeed, according to Judaism, the revelation at Mount Sinai involved transmission of both a written Torah and an oral Torah. The oral Torah included, among other things, specific exegetical rules (not Kant's pure reason) with which to derive binding laws. The sages' authority to utilize such rules is so great, according to Jewish law, that what they decide is valid even if they unknowingly strayed from what the Creator intended. This notion, 'that Torah is not in heaven', is illustrated in the famous Talmudic narration of the dispute between Rabbi Eliezer and the sages regarding the oven of Akhnai:

On that day, R' Eliezer advanced all the arguments in the world to defend his lenient ruling, but the Sages did not accept his arguments. R' Eliezer said to them: 'If the Halakha accords with me, let this carob tree prove it', whereupon the carob tree was uprooted from its place and moved one hundred amos. And some say it moved four hundred amos. Unconvinced, the Sages said to him: 'You cannot bring proof from a carob tree'. He then said to them: 'If the Halakha accords with me, let the water canal prove it', whereupon the water in the water canal flowed backward. The Sages said to him: 'You cannot bring proof from a water canal' . . . R' Eliezer then said to the Sages: 'If the Halakha accords with me, let heaven prove it', whereupon a Heavenly Echo went forth and proclaimed: 'What argument do you have with R' Eliezer, whom the Halakha follows in all places!' Upon hearing this, R' Yehoshua stood on his feet and declared: 'It [the Torah] is not in heaven.'

The Gemara interjects: What is meant by: 'It is not in heaven?' R' Yirmiyah

---

[35] See, generally, Moshe Sokol, 'Personal Autonomy and Religious Authority', in Moshe Sokol (ed.), *Rabbinic Authority and Personal Autonomy* (Northvale, NJ, 1992), 198–201, who discusses several of the points I proceed to make in this text.
[36] *Mishnah, Shevi'ith* 10: 9 (Heb.)(3rd cent.).
[37] Sokol, 'Personal Autonomy,' 202–3.

said: 'It means that we pay no heed to a Heavenly Echo, because You [G–d] already wrote in the Torah at Mount Sinai: "According to the majority the matter shall be decided." ' And since the majority of the Sages dispute R' Eliezer's position, his position is rejected in practice.[38]

Nonetheless, it is noteworthy that even after a decision of the majority of sages establishes a law, it is possible, under certain circumstances, that the sages of a subsequent generation may disagree with that decision, and, if so, people may rely on the later view.[39]

In addition to the fact that the rules lie in man's hands to apply, the ways in which a particular rule applies to a prospective act depends on the act's *anticipated* consequences. Which consequences are identified and evaluated substantially depends on the knowledge, skills, and perspectives of the individual who performs the assessment.

Even those who are not learned in Jewish law have the opportunity to make certain critical choices. For example, a person has the power to impose upon himself various religious obligations through the taking of oaths or the making of vows. Similarly, simply by choosing to do so, a person may assume the obligation to comport himself in the future with certain, previously voluntary religious stringencies simply by making the conscious decision to do so. Furthermore, as to many specific questions of Jewish law, the normative rule is that an individual has the right to choose among a variety of alternative, recorded authoritative views on what Jewish law requires.[40] In addition, a person can, and indeed should, choose for himself, from among qualified contemporary authorities, the rabbi with whom he would like to consult.[41] He certainly need not accept as binding the views of the rabbi of the synagogue which he attends.

3. American Regulation of Legal and Medical Ethics

Before identifying some of the specific conflicts that professional ethics rules pose to Jewish values, it is useful to make a few observations regarding the evolution of American legal and medical ethics. Each of these professions has had to identify both the interests the professional should promote and the manners in which he is to do so. Each profession began with relatively few specific rules, but is currently regulated through diverse devices, including state and federal statutes, well-established non-statutory doctrines providing for possible private suits, and a variety of ethics codes promulgated by national and local authorities and organizations.

---

[38] *Talmud Bavli* (Schottenstein Edition), *Bava Metzia*, vol. 2 (Brooklyn, 1995), 59b[1].

[39] R. Moshe Isserles, *Commentary on Shulhan Arukh, Hoshen Mishpat* 25: 1 (Heb.) (16th cent.) (following the opinion of R. Asher ben Yehiel).

[40] Steven H. Resnicoff, 'Bankruptcy—A Viable halakhic Option?', 24 *Journal of Halakha and Contemporary Society* (1992), 5, 43–6 (discussing doctrine known as *kim li*).

[41] *Mishnah, Avot* 1:6 (Heb.)(3rd cent.).

Medical practitioners, initially at least, focused on the interests of their immediate patients or clients. As one commentator has explained, 'The first characteristic of the Hippocratic ethic is that it is individualistic; it concentrates only on the benefit to the individual patient.'[42] That ethic directed that the doctor benefit his patient but, above all, the doctor 'do no harm' to his patient. Physicians typically promoted the patient's interests by exercising their own best judgement on how to proceed. Those sympathetic to this approach often characterize it as one of 'beneficence',[43] while those finding it less appealing call it 'paternalism'. In the late 1950s and early 1960s cultural and political changes throughout American society brought about an increased emphasis on an individual's rights. This led to acceptance of the doctrine of 'informed consent', namely, that in order to exercise effectively his right to withhold consent to medical procedures, a client is entitled to be fully informed about relevant facts and alternatives.[44]

Thus, from the beneficence–paternalism model—in which physicians effectively made autonomous decisions based on their perceptions of the patients' best interests—medicine turned to a model of patient autonomy, a transition which some physicians perceived to alter their roles from that of learned professionals to that of technicians. This development, and the simultaneous increase in legal actions against doctors, attenuated the closeness of the patient–physician relationship.

Also contributing to the dilution of this bond, perhaps, was the American Medical Association (AMA)'s promulgation in 1957, and its reiteration thereafter, of principles providing that physicians did not owe duties only to their specific patients. Instead, the AMA's new position was that physicians owed duties not only to patients but to physicians' respective communities and to humanity as a whole.[45] This AMA policy weakened the professional dyad in at least two interrelated ways. Firstly, some physicians understood that, in determining how to proceed with one patient, the AMA felt they should consider the repercussions their decision, particularly regarding the allocation of scarce resources, would have on other patients of theirs, patients of other physicians in the medical facility, and on the community at large. Secondly, physicians who missed the 'autonomy', or discretion, doctors enjoyed during the beneficence–paternalism period might well have found the purported responsibility to persons or constituencies other than the immediate patient to have been an

---

[42] Warren Thomas Reich (ed.), *Encyclopedia of Bioethics*, 4 vols. (New York 1995), iii. 1427. This focus on the individual patient's benefit seems to be preserved in the Declaration of Geneva and in the post-communist 'Solemn Oath of a Physician of Russia', ibid.

[43] This approach might be characterized as a combination of beneficence and non-maleficence.

[44] Charity Scott, 'Why Law Pervades Medicine: An Essay on Ethics in Health Care', 14 *Notre Dame Journal of Law, Ethics & Public Policy* 245, 263–4.

[45] Reich, *Bioethics*, 1428.

attractive idea. Why? These new constituencies were amorphous and could not formulate their own interests and communicate them to the physicians. Consequently, the new approach, by effectively empowering physicians to decide what would best serve these constituencies, returned discretion to the physicians.

Perhaps the fact that the AMA announced that doctors were now responsible to new constituencies also contributed to physician support for legislative permission to refuse to provide treatment, even life-preserving treatment, that doctors deemed to be 'futile'.[46] We should note, however, that Judaism believes that all human life is sacred. This doctrine casts doubt on the appropriateness of characterizing *any* treatment that preserves such life as 'futile', even in those rare instances in which some authorities might not rule that it is absolutely necessary to go forward with the treatment.[47]

Ironically, the most recent manifestation of medical practice, characterized by increased dependence on health maintenance organizations (HMOs) and the like, is one in which both patient and physician agree to limit their ability to control their professional relationship, i.e. to limit their future autonomy. HMO agreements may impose substantial restrictions on the types of advice or treatment particular physicians may provide. This phenomenon may have further alienated physicians, who, in some hospital discussions, are now referred to as 'health care providers', from their patients, who are sometimes simply called 'consumers'.

In contrast to physicians who, at least traditionally, recognized their duty to promote the best interests of their patients, lawyers, or most at least, have always realized they have dual loyalties. Although they are to represent their clients' interests zealously, lawyers, as 'officers of the court', bear some responsibility to the administration of justice. Until recently, there were few formal and unambiguous legal ethics rules. Early principles promulgated by the American Bar Association (ABA), a voluntary organization whose rules lack the force of law, provided relatively vague guidelines. Even the ABA's Model Code of Professional Responsibility, proposed less than thirty years ago, involved more 'ethical considerations', designed to be aspirational in nature, than 'disciplinary rules', which were proposed as binding. Only a few years after recommending its Model Code, the ABA announced a new set of Model Rules of Professional Responsibility. To some, these detailed rules, not aspirations, appear more like a set of guild rules than ethical guidelines. In any event, irrespective of what the ABA proposes, lawyers are legally bound by the rules adopted by authorities in their respective states.

---

[46] For a robust discussion of this topic, see Phillip G. Peters Jr., 'When Physicians Balk at Futile Care: Implications of the Disability Rights Laws', (1997) 91 *Northwestern Univeristy Law Review* 798.

[47] Resnicoff, 'Jewish Law Perspectives', 338–48.

Interestingly, at the same time as medicine moved into the era of increased patient autonomy and patient rights, legal ethics commentators began to question the primacy, at least in some matters, accorded to the rights of clients. Academics began asking whether lawyers should have increased freedom to pursue values other than those of their clients. Unsurprisingly, of course, there has been little agreement on precisely what those other values should be.

Perhaps this division between legal and medical ethics was inevitable. Lawyers are far more likely than doctors to be asked to assist clients to accomplish goals, or employ tactics that clearly, directly, and unfairly harm identified third parties. Indeed, as I will soon discuss in Section 4, it is often easier for doctors than for attorneys to avoid non-professionals with morally troublesome agendas.

4. Professional Ethics and Jewish Values

Professional ethics rules sometimes require professionals to do that which Judaism says is wrong and sometimes forbid that which Judaism says is right. Often the conflict is one based on the ethics rules' concern for autonomy. I will consider just a few examples.

In medicine, for instance, secular rules require doctors, as a general matter, to maintain a patient's confidentiality. It has been argued that this duty is based on the patient's right to autonomy.[48] Despite the existence of limited exceptions to this rule, there are many occasions on which confidentiality is secularly required even when disclosure is necessary to prevent harm to a person other than the patient. For example, perhaps the patient has an infectious disease and, although a statutory exception may authorize a physician to advise the department of health, an innocent, identifiable third party may be infected before the department of health bureaucracy effectively responds. Or perhaps the patient has a condition, such as epilepsy, that causes his use of a car or, in the case of a construction worker, a jackhammer or crane, to place others at risk. Or perhaps the patient has a serious, albeit non-infectious, condition that, were it known to his fiancée, would lead her to break off the engagement to avoid a life of misery.

Similar confidentiality rules apply to lawyers. In California, if a client confidentially tells his attorney that he plans to commit a murder, the attorney is not permitted to disclose this confidence even in an effort to save the prospective victim's life.[49] Although the laws in most states permit

---

[48] See e.g. Patricia I. Carter, "Health Information Privacy: Can Congress Protect Confidential Medical Information in the "Information Age"?', (1999) 25 *William Mitchell Law Review* 223.

[49] See California Business & Professions Code, s. 6068(e): 'It is the duty of an attorney to do all of the following . . . (e) To maintain inviolate the confidence, and at every peril to

disclosure in this case, many states forbid a variety of disclosures even though they would be necessary to avoid devastating financial injury to innocent third persons.[50] By contrast, the Jewish law rule requiring one to protect third parties from harm or the rule against enabling someone, even passively, to violate Jewish law would require disclosure. By the way, it is interesting that most of these same states would allow the attorney to disclose confidential information if doing so were necessary to collect his fee, even if losing the fee in the particular case would not cause the lawyer much real harm.

Does the existence of a 'fiduciary relationship' between the professional and his patient or client make any difference under Jewish law? Generally, the answer is no. Jewish law does not give professionals any special dispensation to do evil. Judaism does not adopt a theology of vocation. Would it matter if the ethics rules were embodied in statutes? Again, the answer is no. Although there are Jewish law doctrines that sometimes make secular law binding in commercial matters,[51] these doctrines do not diminish the moral duties I am discussing. Even if a Jewish professional had taken an oath to abide by the rules, Jewish law provides a mechanism through which he could be released from the oath and it would require the professional to take steps to effectuate this release.[52] Of course, Jewish law is complex and fact-sensitive, and I will leave for other writings a more comprehensive analysis of its application to each of the various dilemmas I identify.[53]

Sometimes, instead of forbidding disclosures that morally ought to be made, secular law conflicts with Jewish dictates by requiring disclosures that ought not be made. Because of a patient's right to make autonomous decisions about his treatment, secular rules require that the physician fully and frankly disclose details regarding his condition and any prospective procedures. Nevertheless, Jewish law authorities believe[54]—and there is secular evidence to sustain this belief [55]—that a patient's condition may worsen should he learn that his doctors have little hope for his recovery. In

himself or herself to preserve the secrets, of his or her client.' This statutory obligation seems to contain no exception. See also Thomas D. Morgan and Ronald D. Rotunda, *2000 Selected Standards on Professional Responsibility* (New York, 2000), 136; Fred C. Zacharias, 'Privilege and Confidentiality in California', (1995) 28 *University of California Davis Law Review* 367.

[50] Morgan and Rotunda, 'Selected Standards', 135–49 (identifying ten states that forbid disclosure of a client's intent to commit a criminal fraud and forty states that prohibit disclosure of a client's intent to commit a non-criminal fraud).

[51] Michael J. Broyde and Steven H. Resnicoff, 'Jewish Law and Modern Business Structures: The Corporate Paradigm', (1997) 43 *Wayne Law Review* 1685, 1765–84.

[52] J. David Bleich, *Contemporary Halakhic Problems*, vol. ii (New York, 1983), 78–80.

[53] See e.g. Resnicoff, 'Jewish Law Perspectives', 330–49.

[54] See e.g. R. Moshe Feinstein, *Iggerot Moshe, Hoshen Mishpat* 2: 74(1).

[55] J. David Bleich, *Judaism and Healing* (New York, 1981), 27–33.

such cases, Jewish law prohibits such a disclosure.[56] Indeed, to protect a patient from harm, the physician might, under certain circumstances, be affirmatively obligated to lie to the patient about his condition.[57]

Another ethical dilemma arises if a nurse or physician is present when a patient—even if a patient of some other doctor—declines life-preserving treatment. Under Jewish law, life is sacred. If treatment would save the patient's life,[58] even if it were administered against the patient's wishes, then Jewish law would generally require that the treatment be administered. Of course, if the treatment would not be effective without the patient's consent, then it should not be given against the patient's wishes.

Sometimes the ethical problem arises from a patient's request for 'treatment'. Euthanasia and, in most instances, abortion, for example, would be forbidden by Jewish law.[59] Non-physician staff members may have a difficult time in avoiding such assignments, although the literature describes some practical and legal steps that may minimize the problem.[60] Physicians, however, may be able to avoid these problems by simply refusing to accept patients as soon as their objectives are identified.

Lawyers may have a much more difficult time with clients with unworthy objectives. Once an attorney enters an appearance on behalf of a client, he usually needs court approval to resign, even if he has cause to do so. Suppose, for instance, that a client lies to the attorney in their initial consultations in order to have the attorney undertake the representation. Somewhere down the line, however, the lawyer learns the truth and does not want to continue to represent him. Under contract law, the client's fraud might be a sufficient reason to enable the lawyer to rescind their agreement. Nevertheless, a court, for any number of reasons, might still refuse to permit the lawyer to terminate the representation. For instance, a court may consider any necessary delay, while the client finds alternative counsel, to be too inconvenient, whether for the other party to the trial or for the court itself. Or perhaps the court simply has a different view of the attorney–client relationship and thinks that the moral bona fides of the client's case should be irrelevant.

Consider, for example, the position taken by the bar authorities in the state of Tennessee. State law permitted a minor to obtain an abortion without parental consent only if the minor could convince a court that she was sufficiently mature to make the decision by herself. Tennessee, as a

---

[56] Bleich, *Judaism and Healing*, 27–33; Basil F. Herring, *Jewish Ethics and Halakhah for our Time* (New York 1984), 47–65.

[57] See nn. 54–6.

[58] Coercion is not compelled, however, when the treatment offers only a speculative, improbable solution. See R. Moshe Feinstein, *Iggerot Moshe, Yoreh De'ah* 4: 24(4) and *Hoshen Mishpat* 2: 73(5). See, generally, Resnicoff, 'Jewish Law Perspectives', 347–8.

[59] Resnicoff, 'Jewish Law Perspectives', 347–8.

[60] Anne M. Dellinger and Ann Morgan Vickery, 'When Staff Object to Participating in Care', 28 (Sept.–Oct. 1995) *Journal of Health Law* 269.

number of other states, requires attorneys to represent indigent parties, from time to time, on a *pro bono* basis. A Tennessee court assigned one of these matters to a Catholic attorney who contended that it was morally wrong for the minor to have an abortion and that assisting her would be a violation of his religious convictions. In an opinion that seems clearly unjust and quite possibly insupportable,[61] the authorities rejected his position and required him to proceed.[62]

On other occasions a client's objective may not offend Jewish law. Nevertheless, a client may want his attorney to employ tactics that, while permitted by secular law, are forbidden by Jewish law.[63] Such tactics might include, for instance, a tough cross-examination to thoroughly undermine the credibility of an adverse witness whom the attorney, based on information given to him by his client, knows to be telling the truth. If the cross-examination would humiliate the truthful witness and cause him substantial emotional distress and the case only involves a dispute over money, Jewish law would not permit it.

If we had more time, I could discuss each of these examples in greater detail, and could adduce additional dilemmas as well. Nevertheless, the issue is clear. There are cases where, ironically, a Jewish professional would want greater autonomy under professional ethics rules so that he can fulfil his duties under Jewish law.

5. Conclusions and Suggestions

Secular professional ethics seems to be in constant turmoil. The questions are serious and, in our culturally diverse and secular society, there is a decreasing commonality of values upon which to reach any consensus.

We have seen that there are a number of specific occasions on which secular professional ethics laws conflict with a Jewish professional's religious responsibilities. On a personal level this should cause religious professionals to seek specific guidance from their religious advisers. At the same time professionals who have strayed from their roots may want to become more acquainted with what their religion has to say about these challenging ethical scenarios. They may be surprised to find that some of the religious messages strike a respondent chord.

On a professional level, assuming that the secular rules are not quickly changed, religious professionals must decide what to do if one of these dilemmas arises. They may engage in quiet or open civil disobedience or they may leave the profession. But civil disobedience is risky, and

---

[61] For a strong criticism of the Tennessee authority's action, see Teresa Stanton Collett, 'The Common Good and the Duty to Represent: Must the Last Lawyer in Town Take Any Case?', (1999) 40 *South Texas Law Review* 137.

[62] Tennessee Board of Professional Responsibility, Opinion 96-F-140 (1996).

[63] Resnicoff, 'A Jewish Look'.

abandoning a profession in which one has invested so much of one's emotional and intellectual energy is difficult.

The policy-making level may offer some relief for the beleaguered religious professional. As to legal ethics, some commentators have discussed, although not necessarily favourably, whether there ought to be ethics rule exemptions for those motivated by religious scruples.[64] Others have considered the incomplete remedy of prudent prosecutorial discretion,[65] which, in any event, would not close the door to potential civil liability.

Another suggestion is to permit religious professionals greater autonomy if they disclose to their patients or clients their intent to exercise such discretion. Although this idea has been criticized, it may well warrant much more serious consideration. Perhaps a Jewish professional should be allowed to announce—in writing, if this be preferred—that he is such and that he is committed to representing his clients, or patients, not only within the law but within his understanding of Jewish law.
While it is true that the clients or patients may not know how the religious professional's conviction would impact every conceivable scenario, the professional could explain how he anticipates it would apply and the clients or patients would have the opportunity to obtain additional information by asking questions. In this way, clients and patients would certainly be placed on notice that the professional's religious orientation may importantly affect the professional services they are to receive.

Such a proposal would represent a balancing of various interests. In today's world, where professionals pursue prospective business more aggressively than ever—through advertising and the like—requiring a religious professional to make such a disclosure would impose a burden on him, while paying what may be adequate attention to the rights of the non-professional. The fact that the non-professional has incomplete information on precisely how the professional's religious views will play out should not preclude implementation of this approach. After all, current ethics regulations do not fully protect non-professionals from the perils of partial information. Clients and patients proceed on limited information all of the time. Neither a lawyer nor a doctor is obligated under ethics laws to tell a prospective client or patient that there is a more experienced or more skilled practitioner down the block. Nor is it necessary for a doctor to tell a prospective patient that the hospital with which the doctor is affiliated is not quite as deep in relevant resources as another alternative. Nor must HMOs vaunt the advantages of their competitors.

Indeed, on some occasions, such as when a client confidentially tells his lawyer that he has committed perjury in an ongoing trial, secular ethics

---

    [64] Griffin, 'The Relevance of Religion'.

    [65] Bruce A. Green, 'Lawyer Discipline: Conscientious Noncompliance, Conscious Avoidance, and Prosecutorial Discretion', (1998) 66 *Fordham Law Review* 1307.

rules may affirmatively require the attorney to disclose this fact to the court. Nevertheless, despite the United State Supreme Court's recent reaffirmation of the Miranda rule requiring that certain warnings be given to interrogated criminal defendants, the ethics rules do not obligate an attorney to give his client any 'Miranda warnings', i.e. he need not advise his client at the outset of the representation that there exist exceptions to the confidentiality rule.

Of course, disparate circumstances in the medical and lawyering contexts might justify differing restrictions or limitations on how, or whether, this proposal should be implemented. Fundamentally, however, the point is that, in today's climate, where multiculturalism of almost every kind is encouraged and nurtured, even though such nurturing involves attendant costs, perhaps it is time for those who have religious convictions to be recognized as groups whose values ought to be protected. Years ago Aaron Twerski lamented the fact that far too many people identify themselves with their professions. After being asked what he does for a living, a person, instead of saying, 'I practise medicine', may reply, 'I am a doctor'. In a similar vein, today's professional ethics rules often seem to regard the professional as a mere technician, taking away his moral accountability for what he does as a professional. The rules accomplish this by broadly and comprehensively imposing duties on the professional, by directing that he subordinate his ethics—including his religious ethics— to his client's interests, and, in the case of lawyers, by declaring that the professional is not responsible for the actions of his clients.[66]

Perhaps it would be best to redefine the professional role, to eliminate the professional's need to subordinate his ethics. In this way, the job would truly be characterized as more limited, and the resultant duties fewer, while the individual holding such a job would be perceived as the independent, morally accountable human being that he really is.[67]

---

[66] American Bar Association Model Rule 1.2(b) states: 'lawyer's representation of a client . . . does not constitute an endorsement of the client's political, economic, social or moral views or activities'. See Morgan and Rotunda, 'Selected Standards', 9.

[67] I express my gratitude to the DePaul University College of Law for the 2000 summer research grant that enabled me to write this and other articles about Jewish law, and to Teree Foster, its dean, for her kind support. I also thank Dr Norton Sokol, who reviewed a draft of this paper and provided insightful suggestions.

CLERGY PRIVILEGE AND CONSCIENTIOUS OBJECTION TO THE PRIVILEGE

J. David Bleich

The Problem

'Can you trust your clergyman?' is the question raised in the minds of many in the wake of a high-profile New York law case. A late 1998 decision of a justice of the New York Supreme Court holding one rabbi liable for damages resulting from the violation of the confidence of a congregant and ordering an evidentiary hearing for clarification of certain disputed facts in the case of a second rabbi has caused consternation in diverse quarters.

Inaccurate and provocative media reports further heightened interest in the case. Many, including the judge, were shocked not so much by the breach of confidence itself but by the argument of the defence protesting that such defendants' actions, at least in the case in question, were mandated by Jewish law. Those more familiar with the applicable provisions of Jewish law were equally shocked not so much at the court's headlong thrust into a quagmire of factual, legal, and constitutional issues as by its wholly improper and injudicious excoriation of the defendants' invocation of 'the protection of the Torah' in defence of their conduct. That conduct, which the defendants unquestionably believe to be not only permitted but mandated by Jewish law, is described by the Court as conduct that 'so transcends the bounds of decency as to be regarded as both intolerable and atrocious'. Remarkably, not a scintilla of proof was adduced charging the defendants either with misrepresentation of Jewish law or with challenging their good faith in its application.

Together with those of many other states, the laws of the state of New York provide that communications to a clergyman are privileged in the sense that the clergyman cannot be required 'to disclose a confession or confidence made to him in his professional character as spiritual advisor'. This provision, incorporated in section 4505 of the Civil Practice Law and Rules of the State of New York (CPLR), is included among statutes regulating admissibility of evidence in legal proceedings, thereby making communications to a clergyman privileged in the same manner that interspousal communications, communications by a client to his or her attorney, and by a patient to his or her physician are privileged. The purpose of granting legal privilege to such communications is to encourage free and open discourse between the individuals to whom the privilege is extended. The New York statute provides that the privilege can be waived only by the person confiding in the clergyman.

On its surface the statute does no more than restrict the admissibility of testimony of the clergyman in a court of law. Nevertheless, in a decision issued on 18 December 1998 in *C.L.* v. *Rabbi Tzvi Flaum and Rabbi David Weinberger*,[1] Justice David Goldstein, sitting in the New York Supreme Court in Queens County, ruled that a woman whose confidence had allegedly been breached by the named clergymen was entitled to sue for damages.

The woman, who had been separated from her husband, was involved in a dispute over which parent should be awarded custody of the couple's four daughters. The husband submitted separate affidavits signed by the two rabbis in which they express the opinion that the spiritual welfare and general well-being of the children would best be preserved by awarding custody to the father. In support of that conclusion the rabbis cited various facts concerning the mother's religious behaviour and comportment that she had disclosed to them, allegedly in confidence. This information was incorporated in a sealed matrimonial file and disclosed only to the Court having jurisdiction over the custody proceeding. Despite those facts, Justice Goldstein, in a separate action, found that, in submitting their affidavits and in discussing the matter with her husband, the rabbis had breached a fiduciary duty of confidentiality owed to the plaintiff.[2]

With regard to the alleged breach of a fiduciary duty in submitting their

[1]   179 Misc.2d 1007, 687 N.Y.S.2d 562 (Sup. 1999).
[2]   The reason underlying Justice Goldstein's ruling that the plaintiff is entitled to compensation for damages sustained as a result of the rabbis' breach of confidence is less than clear. The statute in question establishes a rule of evidence and, at least on its surface, nothing more. The statute does not command a clergyman to respect confidences, does not brand disclosure on the part of the clergyman a breach of contract, and does not declare such breach to constitute an actionable tort. (The sole jurisdiction to impose sanctions for violation of the privilege is Tennessee. Tenn. Code Ann. §24-1-206 (1989) makes violation of the statute a misdemeanour punishable by imprisonment for a period not greater than thirty days and/or a fine not to exceed $50. The penal sanction is apparently imposed only for disclosure 'in giving testimony as a witness in any litigation' but does not apply to breach of confidence in other contexts.) Of course, one might argue that it is an evident condition of the contract between a patient and his physician, a client and his attorney, and a congregant and his clergyman that confidences be held inviolate. Alternatively, one might argue that the duty arising from the professional relationship is fiduciary in nature and hence its breach constitutes a tort. Moreover, those arguments might be made even in the absence of a statute establishing an evidentiary privilege. Were this the Court's reasoning, an appeal to the statute would serve only as evidence of the underlying contractual obligation or fiduciary relationship. The statute, then, serves as evidence of liability but not as the source of such liability. Nevertheless, in ordering a hearing in the case against one of the rabbis for the purpose of determining whether or not a third party was present when the conversation took place, the Court seems to assume that liability can exist only if it is generated by the statute. The presence or absence of a third party is crucial with regard to the privileged nature of the communication in so far as its exclusion from evidence is concerned; contractual and fiduciary responsibilities, however, are generally not affected by the presence or absence of third parties.

affidavit, the Court ruled not only that the plaintiff is entitled to recover damages but that the action of the rabbis

was improper, it was outrageous and most offensive, especially considering the status and standing of these defendants within the community, a standard which they readily abdicated here. From what was done, it is palpably clear why this determination is one of the apparent first impression. No member of the clergy would dare breach the sanctity of his or her office to make public the type of confidential, private disclosures at issue in this case.

Moreover, to do so under the guise of religious necessity, conviction or the protection of the Torah, is not only wrong, it is outrageous . . .

Bearing in mind the sanctity to be accorded such communications between clergy and penitent, and the necessity for confidentiality in conjunction with such spiritual counseling, without the fear of any reprisal or disclosure, it is both outrageous and intolerable that such communications would be revealed, even where, as here, this occurs in part in the context of a judicial proceeding. In my view, the conduct so transcends the bounds of decency as to be regarded as both intolerable and atrocious.

The Court's deprecatory reference to 'the guise of religious necessity, conviction' and 'the protection of the Torah' betrays a profound ignorance of Jewish law. Far from being wrong, much less outrageous, the action of the rabbis (who together with the husband's attorney believed both that their affidavits were admissible as evidence[3] and that their testimony was likely to be persuasive) was both laudable and halakhically mandated.

---

[3] There is indeed strong support for the argument that, despite the unqualified privilege expressed in CPLR 4505, the testimony of clergyman with regard to a privileged communication should be regarded as admissible in a custody proceeding. Although there is no case-law dealing with the clergyman–penitent privilege within the context of a child custody proceeding, New York courts have repeatedly held that the physician–patient, attorney–client, and psychotherapist–patient privileges cannot be invoked in such proceedings.

Some forty years ago, in *People ex rel. Fields* v. *Kaufman*, 9 A.D.2d 375, 377, 193 N.Y.S.2d 789, 791 (1st Dep't 1959), the Supreme Court, Appellate Division, First Department, ruled that confidential psychiatric, psychological, and social welfare reports concerning rehabilitation of a mother following paralytic poliomyelitis must be made available to the opposing party. In refusing to recognize the privileged nature of that information the Court declared: 'Where the welfare of children is concerned and in furtherance of the duty of the State as parens patriae, courts are not so hidebound or limited that they may not depart from strict adversary concepts. By analogy, it appears that so important is the duty of the State deemed to be in its role as parens patriae, so vital is its concern for its infant wards, that from birth to maturity their welfare is paramount even when compared with the rights of the natural parents.' That position was affirmed by the Court of Appeals in *Kessler* v. *Kessler*, 10 N.Y.2d 445, 452, 225, N.Y.S.2d 1, 5 (1962). In *People ex rel. Chitty* v. *Fitzgerald*, 40 Misc. 2d 966, 967, 244 N.Y.S.2d 441, 442 (Sup. Ct. Kings Co. 1963) the Court followed that principle in disregarding the patient–physician privilege on the grounds that 'the right of the petitioner to invoke the patient–physician privilege must yield to the paramount rights of the infant'.

In *Baecher* v. *Baecher*, 58 A.D.2d 821, 396 N.Y.S2d 447, 448 (2d Dep't 1997), *appeal denied* 43 N.Y.2d 645, 402 N.Y.S.2d 1026 (1978), in addition to invoking the parens patriae doctrine, the Appellate Division found yet additional grounds for admitting an otherwise privileged communication. The Court ruled that 'the defendant waived his right to the privilege by

Confidentiality in Jewish Law

Judaism does not recognize a particular fiduciary obligation of confidentiality in association with any professional relationship. Thus, for Judaism, there is no specific physician–patient, attorney–client, or clergyman–penitent 'privilege'. But, at the same time, Judaism binds each and every one of its adherents, laymen as well as professionals, by an obligation of confidentiality far broader than that posited by any other legal, religious, or moral system. Nevertheless, the privilege is neither all-encompassing nor, when it does exist, is it absolute in nature.

Divulging personal information concerning another person is prohibited by Jewish law even when that information is not received in confidence. That prohibition is derived from the biblical verse 'You shall not go as a bearer of tales among your people' (Lev. 19: 16). As formulated by Maimonides, *Mishneh Torah, Hilkhot De'ot* 7: 2: 'Who is a talebearer? One who carries reports and goes from one person to another and says, "So-and-so said this" or "Such and such have I heard about so-and-so." Even if he tells the truth, [the talebearer] destroys the world.' Talebearing activity is forbidden even when it is not accompanied by malicious intent and even if the information is not derogatory in nature. That even non-malicious and non-derogatory talebearing is encompassed within the ambit of the prohibition is evident from the immediately following statement of Maimonides: 'There is a much more grievous sin than this that is included

---

actively contesting custody, thereby putting his mental and emotional well-being into issue'. The notion of automatic waiver in custody proceedings was also employed by the Supreme Court in an unreported case, *Conderre* v. *Conderre*, 1990 WL 312774, 1 (Sup. Ct. Suffolk Co. 1990). In that case, however, the Court required that the medical records be reviewed by the Court and that only those portions deemed to be relevant and material be disclosed. Again in *McDonald* v. *McDonald*, 196 A.D.2d 7, 13, 608 N.Y.S.2d 477, 481 (2d Dep't 1954), the Second Department, citing *Baecher* and *Chitty*, declared that 'it is well settled that in a matrimonial action a party waives the physician–patient privilege concerning his or her physical condition (see CPLR 4504) by actively contesting custody'. See also *Proschold* v. *Proschold*, 114 Misc. 2d 568, 451 N.Y.S.2d 956 (Sup. Ct. Suffolk Co. 1982).

The question of an attorney–client privilege in custody cases was first addressed in New York by the Court of Appeals in *Jacqueline* v. *Segal*, 47 N.Y.2d 215, 222, 417 N.Y.S.2d, 884, 888 (1979), at about the same time as the issue of psychotherapist privilege was being discussed by the Second Department in *Baecher* v. *Baecher*. The Court of Appeals cited precedents establishing that, in so far as the attorney–client privilege is concerned, 'such right ought to depend on the circumstances of each case' in ruling that an attorney may be compelled to disclose the address of his client in order to prevent the unsuccessful litigant from frustrating the court's judgment rendered in the best interests of the child.

The public policy considerations upon which the clergyman–penitent privilege are based are surely no more weighty than the physician–patient or attorney–client privilege. As is the case with regard to those privileges, best interests of minor children should take precedence over the policy considerations underlying the statutory clergyman–penitent privilege. Moreover, as is the case with regard to other statutory privileges, initiation of custody proceedings should be regarded as an automatic waiver of the clergyman–penitent privilege as it pertains to determination of which parent is better qualified to be entrusted with the care of minor children.

in their negative prohibition and that is "evil speech" (*lashon ha-ra*), i.e., speaking derogatorily of one's fellow even though one speaks the truth.' It is clear that, the phrase 'such and such have I heard about so-and-so' does not refer to information divulged by 'so-and-so' about himself whether in confidence or otherwise; the phrase connotes information communicated by a third party. Although disclosure of information revealed by a person concerning himself is certainly subsumed within the prohibition, Maimonides' ruling makes it quite clear that disclosure is prohibited even though no breach of confidence is involved.

Disclosure of a communication of non-personal information not within the public domain is also prohibited by Judaism unless prior permission for such disclosure has explicitly been granted. Thus, in effect, all communications are deemed confidential and hence privileged unless the privilege is waived. Moreover, with regard to derogatory personal information, a waiver does not constitute carte blanche for indiscriminate dissemination of such information.[4] The privilege, it should be noted, is in the nature of a general right of privacy rather than an exclusion from admissible evidence in legal proceedings. Privacy does not serve as a barrier to judicial inquiry. Nevertheless, in most circumstances such communications would not be admissible as evidence on the basis of the hearsay rule, which in Jewish law is far broader in its exclusions than is the case in other legal systems.

However, the privileged nature of a private communication is by no means absolute. Respect for privacy and the inviolability of a confidential communication certainly do not take precedence over preservation and protection of the lives and safety of others. The overriding obligation to protect the lives of others is of sufficient weight to oblige the confidant to take whatever measures may be necessary to eliminate the danger. An oath not to divulge such information when required by Halakha (Jewish law) to do so is regarded as an oath to transgress a commandment and is invalid.[5] Thus, for example, a physician must inform the motor vehicle bureau that his patient is an epileptic and should be denied a driver's licence. The obligation to violate the confidential nature of information entrusted to the physician in such situations is included within the 'law of the pursuer'. A person engaged in an act that will lead to the death of another must be prevented from causing such death even if the consequences of the act are entirely unintended. The eminent eighteenth-century authority R. Elijah of Vilna, *Bi'ur ha-Gra, Hoshen Mishpat* 425: 10, states explicitly that the 'law of the pursuer' applies even in the absence of intention to do harm.

The obligation to divulge information that may preserve a life is not

[4] See *Hafez Hayyim, Be'er Mayim Hayyim, Hilkhot Lashon ha-Ra* 2: 2, and the commentary of R. Binyamin Cohen on *Hafez Hayyim, Helkat Binyamin* (Brooklyn, 5753 [1992–3]), *Bi'urim, Hilkhot Lashon ha-Ra* 2: 61.

[5] See Rema, *Shulhan Arukh, Yoreh De'ah* 239: 7, and R. Eliezer Waldenburg, *Ziz Eli'ezer*, XIII, no. 81, sect. 2.

limited to situations involving a 'pursuer' but extends to all situations in which lack of such information would lead to possible loss of life. Apart from the general principle that preservation of life takes precedence over other religious and personal obligations, failure to disclose such information would constitute a violation of 'You shall not stand idly by the blood of your fellow' (Lev. 19: 16).

Concern for preservation of life is by no means the sole legitimate motive for violation of confidentiality. Even information that is derogatory and personal, and hence subsumed within the prohibition against gossipmongering, must be disclosed if it is necessary to do so in order to prevent serious harm. Maimonides, *Mishneh Torah, Hilkhot Roze'ah* 1: 14, followed by R. Joseph Karo in his authoritative code of law *Shulhan Arukh, Hoshen Mishpat* 426: 1, rules that if an individual hears that others 'are plotting misfortune' for another person, he must bring the matter to that person's attention. Failure to do so, declares Maimonides, constitutes a violation of the commandment 'You shall not stand idly by the blood of your fellow'. The 'misfortune' of which Maimonides speaks includes financial loss as well as bodily harm. This is evident from Maimonides' comments in his *Sefer ha-Mizvot, lo ta'aseh*, no. 297, in which he indicates that the commandment applies in all situations in which an individual is in danger of death or loss. The 'loss' to which Maimonides refers is loss of money or profits, as reflected in the ensuing discussion in which Maimonides cites a statement of the *Sifra*, Leviticus 19: 16, declaring that withholding of testimony in a financial dispute constitutes a violation of the commandment 'You shall not stand idly by the blood of your fellow'. A medieval authority, R. Aaron ha-Levi of Barcelona, *Sefer ha-Hinnukh*, no. 247, makes a more general statement in declaring that when the intent is to 'remove harm and to still the quarrel', the prohibition against gossipmongering does not pertain.

The classic work dealing with Jewish law as it applies to slander, defamation of character, and talebearing is *Hafez Hayyim*, authored by R. Israel Meir Kagan. In *Hilkhot Rekhilut, kelal 9, Hafez Hayyim* emphasizes that disclosure of derogatory information, even when the information is not received in a confidential manner, dare not be lightly undertaken. *Hafez Hayyim* rules that, even when designed to prevent harm or loss, disclosure is justified only when a series of conditions are met: (1) Disclosure may be made only pursuant to careful deliberation in establishing that potential for harm really exists. (2) The information disclosed should be presented accurately without embellishment or exaggeration. (3) The sole motivation prompting disclosure must be the desire to prevent harm. No disclosure may be made when prompted, even in part, by personal animosity.[6] (4) The benefit of the disclosure cannot be achieved

---

[6] When these conditions are fulfilled, disclosure is warranted not as an exception to the prohibition against talebearing, but because the act does not fall within the definition of

in any other way. (5) The disclosure will not lead to any harm or loss to the person who is the subject of the information disclosed other than the liability that would be imposed upon that person by a rabbinic court on the basis of the facts and the available evidence.

Rabbis and the Clergyman–Penitent Privilege

Communications for which a clergy–penitent privilege may be claimed are virtually always of a nature to which the prohibition against talebearing applies. Circumstances in which Jewish law requires a breach of confidence involving such information are quite rare. Even secular law recognizes an exception to the rule of confidentiality when a threat to life or serious physical harm exists.[7] It is little wonder that Jewish law recognizes

---

'talebearing'. Animosity is sufficient to bring the disclosure within the ambit of the prohibition. Accordingly, in *Be'er Mayim Hayyim*, *Hilkhot Rekhilut* 9: 3, *Hafez Hayyim* recognizes that a person who does experience such animus is caught on the horns of a dilemma: he is forbidden to disclose because of the prohibition against talebearing. But in withholding the information he transgresses the command 'You shall not stand idly by the blood of your fellow'. Accordingly, *Hafez Hayyim* declares, 'It is my intention [to say] that at the time of disclosure he [must] force himself to intend benefit and not [disclose] because of animosity.' See also Moshe Bleich, 'Appointing Students as Monitors', (1991) 12 *Ten Da'at*, 12 (Summer 1999), 76–7.

7 Although there is no case-law with regard to the clergyman–penitent privilege (cf., however, n. 19 below, regarding the New Jersey statute), many courts have held not only that the physician–patient privilege is suspended in face of danger to another person but that, at least in some circumstances, the physician has an affirmative duty to disclose a foreseeable harm to an identifiable third party who is at risk. Probably the most widely cited case applying that principle is *Tarasoff* v. *Regents of University of California*, 17 Cal.3d 425 (1976). In *Tarasoff* the California Supreme Court held that when a psychotherapist determines or, pursuant to the standards of his profession, should determine that his patient presents a serious danger of violence to another, the therapist has an affirmative duty to use reasonable care to protect the intended victim against such danger and that the duty may require the physician to warn the intended victim of the danger. See, generally, Williams, Annotation, 'Liability of One Treating Mentally Afflicted Patient for Failure to Warn or Protect Third Persons Threatened by Patient', 83 A.L.R.3d 1201 (1978 & Supp. 1992). For a discussion of *Tarasoff* and its progeny, see Timothy E. Gammon and John K. Hulston, 'The Duty of Mental Health Care Providers to Restrain their Patients or Warn Third Parties', (1995) 60 *Missouri Law Review* 749–97; Peter Lake, 'Revisiting *Tarasoff*', (1994) 58 *Albany Law Review* 97–173; Michael L. Perlin, '*Tarasoff* and the Dilemma of the Dangerous Patient: New Directions for the 1990s', (1992) 16 *Law & Psychology Review* 29–63. See also John C. Williams, Annotation, 'Liability of One Treating Mentally Afflicted Patient for Failure to Warn or Protect Third Persons Threatened by Patient', (1978) 83 A.L.R.3d 1201.

Physicians have also been held liable for failing to warn others about the risk of transmission of communicable disease. See e.g. *Skillings* v. *Allen*, 173 N.W. 663 (Minn. 1919) (negligent failure to disclose risk of transmission of scarlet fever). See also *Gammill* v. *United States*, 727 F.2d 950, 954 (10th Cir. 1984) (physician may be found liable for failing to warn person at risk of exposure of the danger) and *Bradshaw* v. *Daniel*, 854 S.W.2d 865 (Tenn., 1993) (extending liability to include failure to disclose to patient's wife that she was at risk of contracting Rocky Mountain Spotted Fever, a non-contagious disease but which appears in clusters). See, generally, Tracy A. Bateman, Annotation, 'Liability of Doctor or Other Health Practitioner to Third Party Contracting Contagious Disease from Doctor's Patient', (1992) 3 A.L.R.5th 370.

the selfsame exception when a threat to spiritual welfare exists, as was the case in the matter before the New York court.

The applicable New York statute and the laws of other jurisdictions may well exclude as evidence the testimony of a clergyman even in situations in which Jewish law permits breach of confidentiality. But, even assuming that Justice Goldstein is correct in his view that the statute also creates a fiduciary relationship, the fiduciary relationship of a rabbi to his congregant must, by its very nature, be circumscribed by the provisions of Jewish law. A member of the Jewish faith who seek the counsel of a rabbi rather than that of a psychologist, social worker, or marriage counsellor understands quite well that the rabbi's actions will be governed by Jewish law and tradition. The congregant places his faith and trust in the rabbi in anticipation that the rabbi will act in precisely that manner. The uniqueness of a fiduciary relationship recognized as such by the secular legal system is based upon the concept that it is a relationship based upon trust and hence violation of that trust is actionable. If a rabbi is trusted to relate to his congregant on the basis of Jewish law, the rabbi's recognition of the limits that Jewish law places upon confidentiality can hardly be deemed a violation of the fiduciary relationship arising from that confidence. To put the matter quite simply, in situations in which Jewish law requires the rabbi to divulge information, the congregant does not, and should not, have an expectation of confidentiality. Accordingly, the courts should recognize an implied waiver of statutory confidentiality limited to circumstances in which disclosure is required by the faith of the confidant.

Moreover, if a rabbi is bound by a fiduciary duty, his duty is not to his congregant but to a higher authority. In the United States both the Internal Revenue Service (IRS) and the Social Security Administration seem to have an intuitive understanding of this point. The IRS does not demand that congregations withhold income tax from the salaries of their clergy as is generally required of employers. Clergymen serving congregations make contributions to the Social Security system as self-employed individuals. In a very real sense, the members of a synagogue may pay the rabbi's salary but he is not their employee; the rabbi is the employee of the Almighty. Certainly, the rabbi's fiduciary obligation is to the Diety and only through the Diety to the congregant.

Let it be noted that, as will be discussed later in greater detail, clergyman–penitent statutes are directly attributable to the burden placed upon a priest by canon law. The Church requires its priests to hold the sanctity of a confession inviolate even upon pain of incarceration or death. In states in which the priest–penitent privilege is not recognized, were a judge to threaten a priest with citation for contempt for refusing to divulge information revealed to him in the confessional, the priest would feel bound to accept imprisonment despite the requirements of a secular legal system. A rabbi, in some limited circumstances, may be equally obligated by his religious convictions to violate a confidence. His recognition of a religious obligation to do so should not give rise to puzzlement any more so than does the priest's refusal to violate the same confidence.

At the same time a rabbi is under no automatic obligation to reveal that a crime has been committed even if the crime was revealed to him in a context not encompassed within the clergyman–penitent privilege. The obligation to disclose, on the infrequent occasions in which it may exist, is based entirely upon the need to prevent harm and is totally unrelated to society's desire to punish crime. Accordingly, only a well-founded fear of repetition of the criminal act that might be prevented by disclosure of past misdeeds would make such disclosure mandatory.

An absolute clergyman–penitent privilege, if applied to rabbis, would yield results that no Jew could accept in good conscience. Assume, for example, that a butcher afflicted by pangs of conscience, but not yet willing to mend his ways, confesses to a rabbi that the meat he offers for sale is not kosher. For the rabbi to act as if he has no such knowledge is to make a mockery of his fiduciary responsibilities to his other congregants, not to speak of his own religious duties. The rabbi's position—and responsibilities—are analogous to those of a psychiatrist who discovers that a patient is planning to commit mayhem. The rabbi's obligation to prevent sin is no different from the physician's responsibility to prevent bodily harm.

In this regard the obligations of a rabbi and a physician are, from a Jewish law perspective, quite similar and, with regard to the obligations of both, the perspective of Judaism is at variance from that of other legal systems. For Judaism, a physician's obligation does not flow from a contractual or fiduciary obligation vis-à-vis his patient; it flows from an obligation to heal imposed upon him by the Deity. The selfsame obligation to seek healing and to prolong life are imposed upon the patient as well. The patient in seeking medical care and the physician in providing such ministration are together fulfilling an obligation imposed upon them jointly by the Creator of all life. Accordingly, the physician dare not accede to the wishes, or even to the directives, of a patient when they conflict with his duty to God, for it is to the Deity that he owes an overriding fiduciary duty. A person seeking the services of a religiously observant physician, psychologist, attorney, or rabbi should know and respect the moral and professional values of his confidant. Which thief would entrust a policeman with details of a contemplated bank robbery? If a person is so foolhardy as to plan harm to another individual he only compounds such foolhardiness in divulging his intention to any other human being, and all the more so to one whose own moral and professional values require disclosure of the confidence. The congregant in seeking counsel and the rabbi in providing guidance are both engaged in the sacred task of discovering and carrying out the will of God. Each owes a duty to God rather than to the other; to the extent that one owes a duty to the other it is because that duty flows from a duty to God.

It is not at all correct to conclude that rabbis are bound by the decision in *C.L.* v. *Flaum*[8] or by section 4505 of the CPLR on the grounds of *dina de-malkhuta dina* (the law of the land is the law). The finding of the Court in *C.L.* v. *Flaum* that the rabbis were in breach of a fiduciary obligation does not mean they are in violation of either a criminal or civil statute; it means only that the aggrieved party can sue for damages in a civil court.

Moreover, not every civil law is binding in Jewish law as *dina de-malkhuta dina*, i.e. on the basis of the dictum 'The law of the land is the law'. Assuredly, a law requiring violation of a religious precept, even if its purpose is not anti-religious and it is non-discriminatory in nature, e.g. a law requiring all citizens to cast ballots in an election held on the sabbath, is not binding in Halakha and would require an act of civil disobedience on the part of citizens of the Jewish faith.[9] Similarly, a law requiring a Jew to stand idly by while his fellow goes to his death is, from a religious perspective, null and void. A law that requires a person to remain silent in face of spiritual danger to an innocent victim is entirely unworthy of religious respect, much less of enforcement under pain of religious sanction. The only issue that is germane is the severity of the burden that a Jew is obligated to accept in fulfilling a particular religious obligation. Discussion of the threshold level of civil or criminal sanctions that would excuse a Jew from fulfilment of such an obligation is beyond the scope of this endeavour.

Legal Accommodation of Clerical Duty

It is abundantly clear that situations will arise in which, for reasons of conscience, a rabbi will find it impossible to obey the law as announced by the Court in *C.L.* v. *Flaum*. If that interpretation of the clergyman–peni-

---

[8] More generally, there is strong support for the thesis that the principle *dina de-malkhuta* is limited to laws promulgated by a sovereign or by a legislature. According to some authorities, common law, 'judge-made law', or even judicial interpretation of an ambiguous statute is not endowed with the authority of *dina da-malkhuta*. Thus *Teshuvot ha-Rashba*, III, no. 109, writes, 'But the judgments issued by courts are not the law of the realm; rather, courts judge independently in accordance with what they find in judicial works.' See also *Teshuvot ha-Rashba*, VI, nos. 149 and 154, as well as *Me'iri*, *Baba Kamma* 113b, s.v. *kol mah she-amarnu*.

[9] Delineation of the parameters of *dina de-malkhuta dina* is far beyond the scope of this undertaking. Suffice it to say that among early-day authorities there are over half a dozen conflicting theories designed to explain why *dina de-malkhuta* is binding in Jewish law. The ramifications and application of *dina de-malkhuta* vary directly with those theories. According to all authorities, there are areas of *dina de-malkuta* with regard to which Jewish law is entirely neutral, i.e. it neither requires disobedience nor reinforces the binding nature of that law by elevating it to a religious duty. With regard to such laws the Jewish national is no different from his non-Jewish fellow countryman who accepts and obeys the law for reasons entirely divorced from religious duty.

tent privilege prevails, a solution must be found that will render the statute inapplicable in situations in which it creates a conflict between the law and religious conscience. In assessing the policy considerations auguring for or against a 'religious exemption' from the clergyman–penitent privilege it is necessary to identify the rationale underlying the privilege and the purpose it is designed to serve.

The most commonly offered rationale is that the privilege is designed to foster the clergy–penitent relationship much in the same manner as the physician–patient, attorney–client, and spousal privileges are designed to foster particular relationships by shielding communications within those relationships.[10] As the New York Court of Appeals has said: 'It is clear that the Legislature by enacting C.P.L.R. 4505 and its predecessors responded to the urgent need of people to confide in, without fear of reprisal, those entrusted with the pressing task of offering spiritual guidance so that harmony with one's self and others can be realized.'[11] Similarly, the US Supreme Court has recognized that 'the priest–penitent privilege recognizes the human need to disclose to a spiritual counsellor, in total and absolute confidence, what are believed to be flawed arts or thoughts and to receive priestly consolation and guidance in return'.[12]

Some commentators have sought to justify evidentiary privileges, including the clergy–penitent privilege, in terms of privacy interest.[13] Although, on the basis of existing case-law, it is difficult to argue that the constitutionally protected right of privacy includes the right to confidentiality of private information,[14] the concern for privacy is certainly a legitimate rationale for statutory protection of communications for which secrecy is generally anticipated. The intimate nature of interaction between a clergyman and congregant gives rise to a highly personal and private

[10] See Mary Harter Mitchell, 'Must Clergy Tell? Child Abuse Reporting Requirements *versus* the Clergy Privilege and Free Exercise of Religion', (1987) 71 *Minnesota Law Review* 760–77, and J. Michael Kiel, 'Law and Religion Collide Again: The Priest–Penitent Privilege in Child Abuse Reporting Cases', (1997–8) 28 *Cumberland Law Review* 682–3.

[11] 47 N.Y.2d 160, 166, 390 N.E.2d 1151, 1154, 417 N.Y.S.2d 226, 229 (1979).

[12] *Trammel* v. *United States*, 445 US 40, 51 (1980).

[13] See e.g. Richard O. Lempert and Stephen A. Saltzburg, *A Modern Approach to Evidence* (St Paul, Minn., 1977), 614–15; Edward M. Cleary, *McCormick on Evidence*, 4th edn. (St Paul, Minn., 1992), §72; Charles L. Black Jr., 'The Marital and Physician Privileges: A Reprint of a Letter to a Congressman', 751 (1 Mar. 1975) *Duke Law Journal* 48–9; Thomas A. Krattenmaker, 'Testimonial Privileges in Federal Courts: An Alternative to the Proposed Federal Rules of Evidence', (1973) 62 *Georgetown Law Journal* 85–94; David W. Louisell, 'Confidentiality, Conformity and Confusion: Privilege in Federal Court Today', (1956) 62 *Tulane Law Review* 110–11; Stephen A. Saltzburg, 'Privileges and Professionals: Lawyers and Psychiatrists', (1980) 66 *Virginia Law Review* 614–15 and 618–21; Robert Weisburg and Michael Wald, 'Confidentiality Laws and State Efforts to Protect Abused or Neglected Children: The Need for Statutory Reform', (1984) 18 *Family Law Quarterly* 191–3.

[14] See *Paul* v. *Davis*, 424 US 693 (1976), in which the Supreme Court held that the right of privacy does not serve to protect the confidentiality of private information. Cf., however, n. 3 above.

relationship. If privacy is itself an end, rather than an instrumental means to certain goals, and is also worthy of protection as an end, the clergy-man–penitent relationship certainly qualifies as a private relationship.

A third rationale is accommodation of a need that is intrinsically human rather than religious. Human beings have a psychological need to unburden themselves of flaws and deficiencies of conduct. Reassurance that their behaviour is not an aberrant deviation from the norm and/or advice designed to prevent future lapses serve to promote psychological well-being. Accordingly, the religious practice of confession, whether formal or informal, serves a positive cathartic function as part of the process of dealing with feelings of guilt. This rationale for the privilege is reflected in the words of the Supreme Court in *Trammel* v. *United States*: 'The priest–penitent privilege recognizes the *human need* to disclose to a spiritual counsellor, in total and absolute confidence, what are believed to be flawed acts or thoughts and to receive priestly consolation and guidance in return.'[15]

There can, however, be little question that, historically, the privilege was originally designed as an accommodation not of the religious practice of the confiders but of the clergy's religious objection to disclosure.

The legal basis of the priest–penitent privilege is rooted in the Code of Canon Law. Canon 1318 states: 'A confessor who directly violates the Seal of Confession incurs an automatic (*latae sententiae*) excommunication . . .'. There is strong evidence that English law recognized and respected the Seal of Confession from the time of the Norman Conquest in 1066 until the Reformation in the sixteenth century.[16] In the sixteenth century the Anglican Church replaced the Roman Catholic Church as the established Church of England. With the passage of time many changes in church practice were introduced, including a dwindling of emphasis upon, and ultimately elimination of, confession.[17] Since confession was no longer necessary and since the Anglican Church did not have a requirement of secrecy, clerics were no longer in need of protection of the law. Some contemporary historians are of the opinion that the privilege terminated at

---

[15] *Trammel* v. *United States*, 445 US 40, 51 (1980); my italics.

[16] See Scott N. Stone and Ronald S. Liebmann, *Testimonial Privileges* (Colorado Springs, 1983), §1.01; John C. Bush and William H. Tiemann, *The Right to Silence: Privileged Clergy Communication and the Law* (Nashville, 1983), 39–41; and Jacob M. Yellin, 'The History and Current Status of the Clergy–Penitent Privilege', (1983) 23 *Santa Clara Law Review* 96–101.

It is likely that, even in that early period, English law recognized an exception to the privilege in cases of treason. See Bush and Tiemann, *The Right to Silence*, 47. *Garnet's Case*, 2 Howell's State Trials 218, 242 (1606), should probably be understood as an example of the exception. Father Garnet was found guilty, probably of misprision or treason, for refusing to reveal information concerning the Gunpowder Plot, a failed plot to assassinate King James I. Cf. Yellin, 'The History and Current Status of the Clergy–Penitent Privilege', 99–101.

[17] See Bush and Tiemann, *The Right to Silence*, 49–53; and Yellin, 'The History and Current Status of the Clergy–Penitent Privilege', 102.

the time of the Reformation.[18] However, Wigmore, in his classic treatise on evidence, asserts that the privilege survived until the Restoration.[19] In either event it is abundantly clear that during the seventeenth century the privilege was no longer recognized.[20] Thus, the historical record lends support to the view that the privilege was designed as an accommodation of religious practice and was designed for the protection of the cleric.

The history of the privilege in the United States lends even more support to the understanding of the rationale underlying the privilege. Since the privilege was no longer recognized in England, it was not part of the common law imported to the New World. The first known case involving clergy privilege was *People* v. *Phillip*, decided by the New York Court of General Sessions in 1813.[21] The case involved Father Kohlmann, a Roman Catholic priest who had returned stolen goods to their owner but when, in the course of grand jury proceedings, he was called upon to identify the person who had delivered the goods to him, he refused to do so. In the confessional, the defendant, Daniel Phillip, revealed to his parish priest that he had knowingly received stolen goods. The priest insisted that Phillip return the stolen items. Phillip then brought the stolen goods to Father Kohlmann under cover of confidentiality of the Seal of Confession and the priest returned the items to the rightful owner.[22] Father Kohlmann was subpoenaed to appear before a grand jury to identify those responsible for the crime. In refusing to do so, Father Kohlmann testified:

if called upon to testify in quality of a minister of a sacrament, in which my God himself has enjoined on me a perpetual and inviolable secrecy, I must declare to this honorable Court, that I cannot, I must not answer any question that has a bearing upon the restitution in question; and that it would be my duty to prefer instantaneous death or any temporal misfortune, rather than disclose the name of the penitent in question. For, were I to act otherwise, I should become a traitor to my church, to my sacred ministry and to my God. In fine, I should render myself guilty of eternal damnation.[23]

---

[18] Bush and Tiemann, *The Right to Silence*, 53–4; Stone and Liebmann, *Testimonial Privileges*, §6.01; and Yellin, 'The History and Current Status of the Clergy–Penitent Privilege', 103.

[19] James H. Chadbourn, *Wigmore on Evidence* (Boston, 1976), vol. viii, §2394.

[20] Bush and Tiemann, *The Right to Silence*, 120–2; and Yellin, 'The History and Current Status of the Clergy–Penitent Privilege', 103.

[21] The case is abstracted in (1843) 1 *Western Law Journal* 109–14. The records of an attorney who participated in the case are published in Note, 'Privileged Communications to Clergymen', (1955) 1 *Catholic Lawyer* 199–209. That material originally appeared in William Sampson, *The Catholic Question in America* (New York, 1813).

[22] See Michael W. McConnell, 'The Origins and Historical Understanding of Free Exercise of Religion', (1990) 103 *Harvard Law Review* 1410–11, and Sampson, *The Catholic Question in America*, 5.

[23] See McConnell, 'The Origins and Historical Understanding of Free Exercise of Religion', 1411.

The court upheld the priest's right not to testify under the right of 'free exercise of religious profession and worship' guaranteed by the New York Constitution adopted in 1777.[24]

However, four years later in another unreported case, *People* v. *Smith*,[25] a different New York Court ruled that no privilege existed for a Protestant minister, but did not clarify the grounds for the distinction. To be sure, the Catholic Church requires its adherents to confess sins and binds its priests to secrecy. It would, however, be an error to ignore the impact that Father Kohlmann's impassioned testimony must have had upon the Court. There is no doubt that the priest would have indeed accepted 'instantaneous death or any temporal misfortune' rather than violate the sanctity of the confessional.[26]

The spectre of a priest languishing in gaol because he has been sentenced for criminal contempt is not very pleasant. There is always public sympathy for civil disobedience entered into for ideological reasons rather than for personal profit or benefit. Sympathy for civil disobedience in the name of religious liberty is even greater.[27]

In seeking to compel the testimony of a Roman Catholic priest, the law faces a no-win situation. The law must recognize that the testimony will simply not be forthcoming.[28] The law then has the option of holding itself up to ignominy in a futile attempt to enforce its dictates or of pretending that no infraction has occurred and allowing the priest to flout the law. Either way the law will not be obeyed and will be held in disrespect. Far wiser to carve out a religious exemption that is perceived as principled, libertarian, and respectful of religion. Recognition of a priest–penitent privilege allows the law to escape from between the horns of the dilemma and to preserve both religious freedom and respect for the law.

Indeed, although often overlooked, in the United States the free exercise clause of the First Amendment was rooted, at least in part, on precisely that consideration. The framers of the Constitution of the United States

[24] Subsequently, however, with the development of an extensive body of case-law limiting free exercise rights in the face of a compelling state interest, courts were no longer willing to recognize the clergyman–penitent privilege as a constitutionally protected right. Thus, for example, when in *In re Fuhrer* a rabbi contended that both the freedom of religion guaranteed by the Constitution of the state of New York as well as the free exercise clause of the First Amendment protected him against a forced disclosure, the Court applied a balancing test in declaring that 'where it is asserted that governmental action impermissibly treads on one's right to freely exercise one's religion, a balance must be struck weighing the governmental interest to be served against the claimed infringement of one's First Amendment rights' (100 Misc.2d 315, 318, 419 N.Y.S.2d 426, 429 (1979)).

[25] 2 City Hall Rec. (Rogers) 77 (N.Y. 1817). See Note, 'Privileged Communications', 209.

[26] See Seward Reese, 'Confidential Communication to the Clergy', (1963) 21 *Ohio State Law Journal* 81.

[27] Cf. Yellin, 'The History and Current Status of the Clergy–Penitent Privilege', 111–12.

[28] Cf. ibid. 110.

made extensive use of the writings of John Locke, and his influence upon the First Amendment was most direct.[29] Locke recognized that religious intolerance was inconsistent with both public peace and good government and viewed religious rivalry and intolerance as among the most severe political problems of his day. Civil strife and lawlessness, not to speak of war between nations, were regarded by Locke as the product of religious turmoil. In an essay written in 1689 Locke states: 'It is not diversity of opinion, which cannot be avoided; but the refusal of toleration to those that are of a different opinion, which might have been granted, that have produced all the bustles and wars, that have been in the Christian world, upon account of religion.'[30] Elsewhere, decrying the futility of religious coercion, Locke writes, 'let divines preach duty as long as they will, 'twas never known that men lay down quietly under the oppression and submitted their backs to the blows of others, when they thought they had strength enough to defend themselves'.[31] The way to avoid such strife is by assuring toleration and liberty of religious practice for all. Freedom of religious practice also enables a government to govern effectively. A populace that perceives its religious principles to be thwarted by the government will harbour deep resentment and disrespect for the ruling authority. The government will be delegitimized in the eyes of those whose religious liberties are denied; respect for the government and its laws will be compromised.

Thus, there might be strong reason to craft a priest–penitent privilege to be granted to Catholic priests but not to other clergy for whom confidentiality does not rise to the level of inviolability. That distinction was intuitively recognized by the New York court. However, the principle of equality in the eyes of the law demands that a privilege granted to some be granted to all. And so in 1828 the New York legislature enacted the nation's first statute recognizing the clergy privilege.[32] Arguably, the anti-establishment and equal protection clauses of the US Constitution, which are now binding upon the states, would demand no less. In any event, most clergy will not testify concerning confidential communications regardless of whether there is a statutory privilege.[33] Moreover, as one commentator has recently noted:

If the clergyman believes that he has a duty of confidence that is unwaivable by religious doctrine. . . . The clergyman will be guided by the tenets of his faith rather than the rules of evidence, and he will risk contempt of court rather than compro-

---

[29] See documentation supplied by McConnell, 'The Origins and Historical Understanding of Free Exercise of Religion', 1430–1.

[30] John Locke, *Letters on Toleration*, in *The Works of John Locke* (London, 1823), vi. 53.

[31] See H. R. Fox Bourne, *The Life of John Locke* (London, 1876), i. 190.

[32] See N.Y. Rev. Stat. Pt. 3, ch.7, tit. 3, §72 (1828).

[33] See Reese, 'Confidential Communication to the Clergy'.

mise the protection of his ecclesiastic integrity. To compel disclosure would force the clergyman to choose between his religion and the court's wrath. The clergyman will probably be more willing to suffer at the hands of a human judge than at the hand of the Judge of Judges.[34]

It would be paradoxical in the extreme to apply a privilege designed to accommodate religious conscience and practice in a situation in which it would have precisely the opposite effect. Forcing a clergyman to remain silent when his religious conscience demands that he speak out is no less a violation of religious liberty than is coercion in forcing him to violate the Seal of Confession.

If the clergy privilege is designed to obviate the disrespect for law that would flow from inevitable disobedience to the demand for his testimony, it would be anomalous to generate the identical disrespect for law by sealing the clergyman's lips upon threat of either criminal or civil sanctions when he believes that the tenets of his faith require that he disclose information imparted to him in confidence.

Memories of religious oppression of Jews and other religious minorities by government officials acting under colour of law have not yet receded from the collective memory of Western society. Lack of respect, not only for discriminatory laws and oppressive regimes, but for government and civil law in general, persists in the psyche of many of those who experienced discrimination and religious persecution in the past. Scandalous events, of which we have witnessed far too many, serve to underscore how pernicious and infectious such attitudes can be. Forcing clergymen to become lawbreakers in violating the clergyman–penitent privilege when dictates of religious law demand that they do so is inimical both to the interests of the Jewish community and to the interests of society at large. Prudence demands that citizens not be subjected to crises of conscience that will inevitably result in erosion of respect for the law.

A Proposed Remedy

There is, however, a relatively simple legislative solution that would both preserve the benefits of the privilege and accommodate free exercise concerns. The clergy privilege is currently recognized in each of the states and in the district of Columbia as well as in federal courts.[35] At present, in

---

[34] Jeffery H. Miller, 'Silence is Golden: Clergy Confidence and the Interaction between Statute and Case Law', (1998) 22 *American Journal of Trial Advocacy* 64.

[35] This is true for the federal rules of evidence as well. The clergy privilege was first recognized in federal common law in *Totten* v. *United States*, 92 U.S. 165, 107 (1875), and was reaffirmed in *Mullen* v. *United States*, 263 F.2d 275, 276 (D.C. Cir. 1958) (Faby, J. concurring), and is now embodied in Rule 505 of the Federal Rules of Evidence. However, Rule 501 provides that in federal civil actions, when an element of a claim or defence is determined by state law, the existence and scope of a privilege shall be determined by applicable

New York the privilege is held by the communicant, i.e. only the congregant[36] can waive the privilege and authorize testimony by the clergyman.[37] In other states, e.g. Illinois,[38] Ohio,[39] Maryland,[40] and Virginia,[41] the privilege is held by the clergyman.[42] In those states, although the clergyman cannot be compelled to testify, he may voluntarily choose to disclose

state law. In *Eckmann* v. *Board of Education of Hawthorn School District No. 17*, 106 F.R.D. 70, 73 (E.D. Mo. 1985), the Court ruled that the privilege recognized by federal common law belongs to the cleric.

[36] The corollary of this rule is that when the privilege is waived by the congregant, the clergyman may be compelled to testify. See, however, *Pennsylvania* v. *Musolina*, 467 A.2d 605, 611 (Pa. 1983), in which the Court ruled that a priest was not required to testify even though the defendant had disclosed the religious communication in his confession to the State.

[37] Ohio's statute Ohio Rev. Code Ann. §2317.02 (Banks-Baldwin 1996) provides that the clergyman 'may testify by express consent of the person making the communication except when the disclosure of the information is in violation of the clergyman's, rabbi's, priest's, or minister's sacred trust'.

[38] Ill. Comp. Stat. 5/8–803 (West 1992).

[39] Ohio Rev. Code Ann. §2317.02

[40] Md. Code Ann., Cts. & Jud. Proc. §9–11 (1978).

[41] Va. Code Ann., §8.01–400 (Michie 1994). See *Seidman* v. *Fishburne-Hudgin Foundation, Inc.*, 724 F. 2d 413 (4th Cir. 1984).

[42] Many of these statutes, including those vesting the privilege in the communicant, contain language apparently limiting the privilege to confessions made in the course of discipline enjoined by the rules or practices of the denomination. See Reese, 'Confidential Communication to the Clergy', 67–73.

Thus, in *Magar* v. *Arkansas*, 826 S.W.2d 221, 222 (Ark. 1992), the privilege was denied to a minister of the New Life Christian Fellowship who testified that 'confession is not a tenet of his church and keeping evidence of a crime confidential is within the discretion of the pastor'; in *Illinois* v. *Diercks*, 411 N.E.2d 97, 101 (Ill. App. Ct. 1980) the court found that the defendant failed to establish that disclosure of the confession 'would be enjoined by the rules or practices of the Baptist Church' ; and in *Kansas* v. *Andrews*, 357 P.2d 739, 743 (Kan. 1960) *cert. denied*, 368 US 868 (1961), the Court denied the privilege to a Baptist minister under the then governing state statute on the grounds that 'that there was no course of discipline in the Baptist church by which a member thereof was enjoined to confess his sins to a minister of the church'. See also *Johnson* v. *Commonwealth*, 310 Ky. 557, 221 S.W.2d 87, 89 (1949); *Radecki* v. *Schuckardt*, 50 Ohio App.2d 92, 4 Ohio Op. 3d 60, 361 N.E.2d 543, 546 (1976); and Annotation, 'Matters to which the Privilege Covering Communications to Clergyman or Spiritual Adviser Extends', 71 A.L.R.3d 794, 807–8 (1976).

In effect, in these decisions the courts understand the statutes involved as reserving the privilege to Catholics and any others who require confession to a clergyman by virtue of church discipline. See, however, *Scott* v. *Hammock*, 133 F.R.D. 610 (Dist. Ct. Utah 1990), in which a federal magistrate interpreted the relevant language of the Utah statute in a much broader manner. The Federal District Court certified the question to the Supreme Court of Utah, which accepted a broad interpretation of the statute. See *Scott* v. *Hammock*, 870 P.2d 947 (Utah, 1994). It should be noted that the Michigan statute (Mich. Comp. Law Ann. §600.2156) (West 1986) refers specifically to a 'minister of the gospel, or priest of any denomination whatsoever, or duly accredited Christian Science practitioner' in prohibiting disclosure of 'any confession' made 'in the course of discipline enjoined by the rules or practice of such denomination'. Since Christian Science does not require confession to a clergyman or practitioner, inclusion of Christian Science practitioners among the clergy upon whom the privilege is conferred presumably indicates that the terms 'confession' and 'discipline' must be construed broadly.

the content of the communication.[43] Accordingly, the concerns of all religious communities would best be served if states in which the privilege is held by the penitent, including *inter alia* Connecticut, Massachusetts, Michigan, and Ohio, as well as New York, were to amend their codification of the privilege and stipulate that it may be waived by the clergyman.[44] The result would also conform with the original intent and purpose of the privilege which, as has earlier been indicated, unlike the physician–patient privilege or the attorney–client privilege, was designed not so much to encourage free and open communication between clergyman and congregant as it was to protect the religious liberty of priests and penitents.

[43] A number of states, including Georgia (Ga. Code Ann. §24–9–22) (1982), Michigan (Mich. Comp. Law Ann. §600.2156) (West 1986), Missouri (Mo. Ann. Stat §491.060) (West 1996), Vermont (Vt. Stat. Ann. Tit 12, §1607) (1947), and Wyoming (Wyo. Stat. §1–12–01) (1977), also vest the privilege in the clergyman but, if read literally, either declare the clergyman to be incompetent to testify or otherwise employ absolute language negating the possibility of a waiver. Cf., however, *Alpharetta First United Methodist Church* v. *Stewart*, 221 Ga. App. 748, 472 S.E. 532 (1996), which includes dicta in which the Court assumes en passant, without discussion or reference to the language of the statute ('nor shall such minister, priest, or rabbi be competent or compellable to testify'), that, the privilege may be waived by the clergyman. See, however, *Eckmann* v. *Board of Education of Hawthorn School District*, in which a federal court interpreted the Missouri statute as giving the clergyman the right to claim or waive the privilege.

[44] Many states, California (Cal. Evid. Code §1030–1034 (West 1995)) and New Jersey (N.J. Stat. Ann. §2A:84A–23 (West 1994); N.J. R. Evid. 511) among them, provide that the privilege may be claimed either by the communicant or by the clergyman. Those statutes would also require modification to permit disclosure by the clergyman when compelled to do so by reason of religious conscience much as the New Jersey statute presently permits (but does not require) the clergyman to waive the privilege if the communication 'pertains to a future criminal act'.

IS THE JEWISH *GET* ANY BUSINESS
OF THE STATE?

Michael Freeman

Introduction

Whether the Jewish *get*[1] is any business of the state is a subspecies of a much more fundamental question: is religion any business of the state? And, if it is, over what aspects of religion should the state have jurisdiction: faith? doctrine? practice? These are questions deeply rooted in history, in the Reformation and its aftermath, in the Enlightenment and its nineteenth-century legacies, Catholic emancipation, Jewish participation in Parliament, civil marriages, the opening up of university education to non-Anglicans. They are also questions which prick the conscience of the present, when issues like royal marriages (that the law here is incompatible with the Human Rights Act 1998[2] seems to have disturbed no one) or whether religious leaders should continue to occupy seats in the House of Lords[3] (would anyone defend a similar privilege for (say) university vice-chancellors or company chairmen or the chief conductors of the major orchestras?) are debated. The disestablishment question, even in today's largely secular society, is rarely raised: can, we might ask, if we wished to be both mischievous and Kelsenian, the *Grundnorm* change?[4]

These are big issues and they are (unfortunately) beyond the immediate remit of this paper. But the big questions cannot be altogether sidelined. For, if the *get*, a Jewish religious practice, is to be 'the business of the state', what other Jewish religious practices should come within the state's province? Only those which impact on status, thus justifying a control over Jewish marriages?[5] (But how far should this go? Arguably, the ban on *agunot* marrying, upheld by Jewish ecclesiastical authorities, is a breach of the Human Rights Act 1998.[6]) Those which relate to the

---

[1] See Glossary at the end of this chapter.

[2] Bans on marrying a divorcee and marrying a Catholic clearly are incompatible with Articles 8 and 12.

[3] *A House for the Future*, Cm. 4534 (London, 2000). This proposes a reduction (from twenty-six to sixteen) in representation by bishops but would increase religious representation to thirty-one.

[4] Can a just state express neutrality among pluralist conceptions of the good while favouring a particular conception? On the question, see Bruce Ackerman, *Reconstructing American Law* (Cambridge, Mass., 1984), 359.

[5] As in the Marriage Act 1949. This in fact grants Jews privileges and these could, and perhaps should, be removed if the rabbinical authorities refuse to reinterpret Jewish divorce law so as to eradicate its injustices.

[6] This hinges upon whether the rabbinical authorities are 'public authorities' under

'public' realm[7] (conceding that the private–public dichotomy is both illusory and state-constructed)?[8] This would make *brit milah*, a quintessentially private act, none of the state's business and that cannot be right (any practice which could harm must be of concern to the state, though this would have no difficulty in endorsing the practice once it situated it within cultural norms and a broad-based interpretation of what constitutes harm[9]).

Approaches to the *Get*

English law could take a number of different approaches towards the *get*:

- it could recognize it as having the full consequences of a divorce;[10]
- it could refuse to recognize it at all;[11]
- it could recognize it for some purposes but not others;[12]
- it could adopt a laissez-faire policy towards it;[13]
- it could adopt obstructive policies towards it;[14]
- it could seek to assist the process whereby a *get* is given and received;[15]
- it could refuse to assist the *get* process.[16]

section 6(3)(b). The Lord Chancellor (*Hansard*, HL, vol. 583, col. 800) indicated that churches were when they were performing functions 'of a public nature'. This goes beyond *R.* v. *Chief Rabbi, ex parte Wachmann* [1992] 1 WLR 1036 (the case concerned a declaration by the chief rabbi that a rabbi was morally and religiously unfit to hold rabbinical office). It was held that this was non-justiciable because 'the court is hardly in a position to regulate what is essentially a religious function' and that it should 'be wary of entering so self-evidently sensitive an area . . . [as] adjudicating upon matters intimate to a religious community'. While section 13 (on which, see P. Cumper, 'The Protection of Religious Rights under Section 13 of the Human Rights Act 1998' (2000) *PL* 254) might well confirm the *Wachmann* ruling, an argument could certainly be mounted that in banning *agunot* from remarrying a function of a public nature is being carried out and that this is not one protected by section 13. On human rights issues more generally, see E. Tager, 'The Chained Wife' (1999) 17 *Netherlands Q. of Human Rights* 425.

   [7] On public and private, see M. Freeman, 'Towards a Critical Theory of Family Law' (1985) 38 *CLP* 153.

   [8] Well illustrated in Susan B. Boyd, *Challenging the Public/Private Divide* (Toronto, 1997).

   [9] I have argued this: see M. Freeman, 'A Child's Right to Circumcision', *British Journal of Urology International*, 83 (1999), suppl. 1, 74.

   [10] It does this where a *get* can be regarded as effective to dissolve a marriage (as in Israel, provided jurisdictional criteria are satisfied).

   [11] But only on public policy grounds.

   [12] See *Preger* v. *Preger* (1926) 42 TLR 281; *Leeser* v. *Leeser*, *The Times*, 5 Feb. 1955; and *Joseph* v. *Joseph* [1953] 2 All ER 710.

   [13] But this would ignore the interests of the vulnerable and expose them to unfair bargaining and even blackmail.

   [14] This has never been the policy. But if it should be shown that the *get* process is incompatible with the Human Rights Act 1998, it might be argued that this was now the agenda.

   [15] The Family Law Act 1996, section 9(3) was so designed, as is legislation in New York, Canada, and South Africa.

   [16] This was the policy in England before 1996. An attempt to insert a '*get* clause' into the Matrimonial Causes Act 1973 in 1984 thus failed.

My own views on the approach that English law should adopt have changed over the years. Back in the mid-1980s I spearheaded a committee under the aegis of the chief rabbi and wrote a report which examined various models.[17] This recommended that legislation should be passed to facilitate the *get* process where one spouse, usually but not invariably the husband,[18] was recalcitrant. More than ten years later there was legislation passed with this objective in view. It was part of the Family Law Act 1996.[19] The implementation of the relevant part of this Act has been held up for reasons quite unconnected with the *get* provision. As a result, in 2000 there was a private member's bill introduced in the House of Lords (the initiative of Lord Lester of Herne Hill) which seeks to sever the provision in the 1996 Act and pass it as a separate measure.[20] This passed in the House of Lords but failed to make progress in the House of Commons.[21] The provision in the 1996 Act (and the 2000 Bill) is defective in a number of ways. It is accordingly of limited value and may end up as no more than an exercise in symbolic politics. I have expounded on these problems elsewhere[22] and will desist from saying more in this paper than is strictly necessary to my thesis.

My views have changed. The *get* is a deeply flawed institution; it discriminates against women; it has become a vehicle for blackmail and other despicable practices (which the *dayanim* connive at, perhaps even encourage); and the solutions lie within a dynamic interpretation of Jewish law were the halakhic authorities prepared to seek them out. It is sad to reflect upon the dilemma of a religious minority which, having forgotten its liberal heritage, calls upon the dominant culture to bale it out.[23] The world Jewish community, it is clear to me, should not be going cap in hand to the legislatures of the world, but rather rediscovering its own sources, and interpreting these in a principled but creative way to tackle the problem which its halakhic authorities—and not the civil states of the world—have created.[24] The response, so often heard, that these religious authorities can do nothing about the problem, that they are shackled (I

---

[17] 'Divorce and Religious Barriers to Marriage', ms, 1985.

[18] Some wives are known to refuse to accept *gittim*. See Helen Jacobus, 'When a Woman Refuses', *Jewish Chronicle*, 27 Aug. 1999, 22.

[19] Family Law Act 1996, section 9(3): I fully annotated this in M. Freeman, *The Family Law Act 1996* (London, 1996).

[20] Divorce (Religious Marriages) Bill 2000.

[21] See *Hansard*, HL, vol. 614, cols. 1241–63; vol. 615, cols. 505–9; the Bill was talked out by Eric Forth MP when it reached the Commons. The Bill was discussed briefly by David Pannick, 'How to Make a Jewish Divorce a Civil Divorce', *The Times* (Law suppl.), 1 Aug. 2000, 15. On the failure in the House of Commons, see Helen Jacobus, 'Recriminations Follow Failure of Agunot Bill', *Jewish Chronicle*, 28 July 2000, 60.

[22] See Michael Freeman, 'The Jewish Law of Divorce' (2000) *IFL* 58, 59–60.

[23] This statement, first written by me in 1996, was quoted with approval by Wall J in *N v. N (Jurisdiction: Pre-Nuptial Agreement)* [1999] 2 FLR 745.

[24] And see Eliezer Berkovits, *Jewish Women in Time and Torah* (Hoboken, NJ, 1990).

avoid, for obvious reasons, saying 'chained') to laws they cannot change, is simply not true. The laws[25] of the *get* have changed and they can change again. Indeed, I would go further: if the *get* cannot be reinterpreted to create a system where men and women are treated equally, where the opportunities for blackmail are eliminated, where barriers to remarriage are removed, the *get* must, like polygamy a thousand years ago,[26] be abolished. It has no more place in a humane religion than do animal sacrifices (which will, of course, never be restored[27]).

But it may be thought I am getting ahead of myself and should offer an explanation of the *get* itself.

The *Get*

According to Jewish law a marriage cannot be dissolved unless a husband gives his wife and she receives, a bill of divorcement (a *get*). The document is today given under the surveillance of a rabbinical court (a Beth Din), but it is not strictly a religious act, although it takes place in a religious context. The concept was developed by Jews when they ruled themselves. For much of its history the practice of the *get* put Jews ahead of the peoples around them who did not have divorce at all (the small Jewish community in this country did not, with the rest of the population, have to use legislative divorce until 1858 and it would seem their *gittim* were recognized as divorces).[28]

The *get* has always caused problems. These have been exacerbated today with the decline of the tight control of the Jewish *kehilah*, with secularism, and also the decline of marriage. The problem has also come into sharper focus with Jewish acculturation to the norms around them, so that divorce among Jews is much more common than it was only a generation ago.

The problems are mainly caused when a husband refuses to give his wife a *get*. A woman who has been civilly divorced is still regarded, in the eyes of Jewish law, as married. She cannot remarry and if she does so (in a

[25] In this I include both the written law (in the Torah) and the oral law (expounded in the Talmud)

[26] Ze'ev Falk, *Jewish Matrimonial Law in the Middle Ages* (Oxford, 1966) considers this the most important reform ever in Jewish family law. In his view it was influenced by Christianity, which was (rightly) critical of polygyny within Judaism.

[27] There are, however, incredibly *yeshivot* (religious colleges) in Israel 'reclaiming this heritage' in time for the restoration of the Temple.

[28] See M. D. A. Freeman, 'Jews and the Law of Divorce in England' (1981) 4 *Jewish Law Annual* 276, and *Moss* v. *Smith* (1840) 1 Man and G 228. It was only in 1866 that the registrar-general decided that he could not recognize a Jewish divorce as valid. Even so, until 1973 Jews domiciled elsewhere than in the United Kingdom could dissolve their marriage by a *get* (see *Har-Shefi* v. *Har-Shefi* [1953 P 161]). This privilege ended with the Domicile and Matrimonial Proceedings Act 1973, section 16(1); and see now the Family Law Act 1986, section 44(1).

civil ceremony) any children of the new union are *mamzerim* (which trans-
lates roughly as bastards, though the legal discrimination against them
exceeds common law penalties). She is literally chained to her (ex-)husband
(she is an *agunah*). She is a hostage to a dead marriage, and, unfortunately,
like other hostages she can be held to ransom. As I have indicated, it is not
uncommon for women to secure their release by paying large sums of
money extorted from them by acts that amount to blackmail. In one case
reported in June 2000 a *dayan* negotiated a *get* in return for the husband
receiving £30,000:[29] in another widely reported case last year Dayan
Berkovits negotiated a charitable donation in return for a *get*[30] (the document was reproduced in the *Jewish Chronicle* and Berkovits defended his
actions in a subsequent issue[31]). The spectre of *dayanim* participating in
these negotiations is unseemly at best. At worst, it corrupts the whole
process. And, if they only but knew, it alienates. Why should a couple
about to marry agree to a prenuptial agreement, referring any disputes to a
Beth Din, when they become aware of the ways this operates?

The source of the *get* is in the book of Deuteronomy.[32] This takes the
institution of the *get* for granted: it had clearly grown up as a practice.[33]
Deuteronomy codified this custom and introduced a new norm: a man
who had given his wife a *get* was not to be allowed to remarry her upon
the death of her second husband or after that husband, too, had divorced
her. Thus, there is no biblical injunction mandating the giving or receiving
of a *get*.[34] Deuteronomy gives the husband complete discretion. He could
divorce his wife at will, without her consent, and without more than a
semblance of justification. The Talmud subsequently imposed some restrictions upon him. He could not divorce her if she were of unsound mind,
and all husbands who wished to divorce wives had to show fault, although
the minimal nature of this is illustrated by the example given by the school
of Hillel—the burning of his food being apparently sufficient.[35] Concern at

---

[29] *Jewish Chronicle*, 2 June 2000, 1 and 64.   [30] Ibid., 9 July 1999, 27.

[31] Ibid., 16 July 1999.

[32] Deut. 24; 1–4. And therefore post-Mosaic.

[33] It is probable that the concept of the *get* was not known in Israelite society much before
the late days of the Kingdom of Judah. See Yair Zakovitch, 'The Woman's Rights in the
Biblical Law of Divorce' (1981) 4 *Jewish Law Annual* 28, 43.

[34] But there is evidence that a wife could divorce her husband when her basic needs were
not supplied or she was deserted by him. Exodus 21: 7–11 gives Hebrew maidservants this
right, and there is no reason to suppose a free woman's rights would be inferior. See G. R.
Driver and J. C. Miles, *The Babylonian Laws* (Oxford, 1952), i. 292–3, and J. H. Otwell,
And Sarah Laughed (Philadelphia, 1977), 121. This seems to have been totally forgotten by
today's halakhic authorities for within it may lie part of the solution to the problem of the
agunah. Documents from the Cairo Geniza (10th and 11th cents.) indicate that women there
too initiated divorce suits: see M. A. Friedman, 'Divorce upon the Wife's Demand as
Reflected in the Manuscripts from the Cairo Geniza' (1981) 4 *Jewish Law Annual* 103.

[35] There is a difference here between the school of Hillel, which says just this ('even if she
spoiled a dish for him'), and that of Shammai, where the need for the husband to find
'unchastity' in his wife is emphasized (this is consistent with Deuteronomy, where 'some

the unequal distribution of power eventually led rabbinical scholars to take action to mitigate the hardship of wives. In the eleventh century Rabbenu Gershom (c.960–1028) enacted a decree that prohibited a husband from divorcing his wife against her will, subject to specific exceptions. These were wider than what we would understand as the traditional offences.[36] An accompanying decree banned polygamy: this was significant because before this a man could remarry without divorcing his first wife, though if he did not give her a *get* she could not remarry.[37]

The Babylonian Talmud had also given women the power to demand a divorce from their husbands under certain circumstances.[38] These included the possession of certain physical defects, such as a loathsome disease or revolting disfigurement, the husband's involvement in a malodorous occupation, impotence or sterility, refusal to support, habitual unfaithfulness, and apostasy.[39] Further interpretation today would surely extend this list by analogy: one commentator suggested to domestic violence[40] and, if so, then also to sexual abuse of children. But are these interpretations used, since many husbands would surely come within the list? The fiction was also adopted that, although the husband must grant the *get* of his own free will, the Beth Din might apply coercion to him where the wife was entitled, under the interpretation of Jewish law, to a divorce. This was explained by one of the greatest of rabbinical authorities, Moses Maimonides (1135–1204), thus: the recalcitrant husband really desires to comply with Jewish law, but is prevented from so doing by his evil disposition. Maimonides also saw the need to facilitate a divorce for a wife who found her husband repulsive. He wrote: 'they force him to divorce her immediately because she is not like a captive woman who must have sexual relations with one whom she hates'.[41] It is a sad reflection of our times that Jewish law was interpreted more liberally in the twelfth century

---

uncleanness' is stipulated in 24: 1). See, further, I. Haut, *Divorce in Jewish Law and Life* (Hoboken, NJ, 1983), 19. See also James L. Kugel, *The Bible as it Was* (Cambridge, Mass., 1997), 513–18.

[36] The exceptions were (1) physical defects that preclude cohabitation; (2) no children after ten years and he has no other children (this is at issue in the case of *Cheni* v. *Cheni* [1965] P. 85 and is misunderstood in the film *Kadosh* (2000), (3) she causes him to violate a religious precept; (4) she acts immodestly; (5) she dishonours him; (6) adultery.
[37] As to which, see I. Breitowitz, 'The Plight of the *Agunah*: A Study in Halakha, Contract and the First Amendment' (1992) 51 *Maryland Law Review* 312, 323. See also I. Breitowitz, *Between Civil and Religious Law: The Plight of the Agunah in American Society* (Westport, Conn., 1993).
[38] See Haut, *Divorce in Jewish Law*, 25. See also E. S. Nadel, 'New York's Get Laws: A Constitutional Analysis', (1993) 27 *Columbia J. of Law and Soc. Problems* 55, 59.
[39] *Mishnah Ketubot* 70a.
[40] M. Frishtik, 'Physical and Sexual Violence by Husbands as a Reason for Imposing Divorce in Jewish Law' (1991) 9 *Jewish Law Annual* 145 argues for this.
[41] Quoted in Berkovits, *Jewish Women*.

than it is today.[42] Can this be said of any other legal system? It was because of the opinions of Rabbenu Tam, a contemporary of Maimonides, that this liberal interpretation was lost and subsequently forgotten.[43] And the primary objective of Rabbenu Tam was apparently to preserve the institution of marriage and minimize the number of divorces in the intellectual and religious climate of twelfth-century France.

But, these reforms notwithstanding, the position of Jewish women remains inferior to that of men for two important reasons. Firstly, under certain conditions a husband can invoke a procedure known as *heter me'ah rabbanim* (the permission of 100 rabbis), enabling him to circumvent Gershom's decree, which bans polygamy and requires the wife's consent to a divorce. No such procedure is available to the wife, who can never remarry according to Halakha without a *get*.[44] There are modern, if infrequent, examples of the *heter*.[45] Secondly, the consequences of violating Jewish law and remarrying without first complying with the *get* requirement are much more severe for the wife than the husband. A 'wife' without a *get* is still 'married' to her husband—despite a civil decree of divorce. This means that, according to Jewish law, she cannot remarry. If she remarries civilly (or in a synagogue which has relaxed the *get* rules) or if she cohabits, she and her partner are guilty of adultery. She forfeits (in Jewish law only, of course) her alimony rights and, even if her 'husband' subsequently delivers to her a *get*, she is barred from marrying her partner. But the husband, who is separated from his wife without granting her a *get*, is not similarly stigmatized. So, if he remarries in a civil ceremony (or a non-Orthodox synagogue) or cohabits, he does not commit adultery. He is technically 'guilty' of polygamy. And if he has children by his new partner, they are not regarded as *mamzerim* (as hers inevitably would be). Furthermore, if he subsequently delivers a *get* to his wife, he can marry the woman whom he has civilly married or with whom he has been cohabiting. Thus, the consequences of failing to obtain a *get* can be disastrous for a religious Jewish woman: the consequences for a man in similar circumstances are relatively minor in comparison.

Jewish law can be reformed by creative and dynamic interpretation. Further rights could be given to women. Again I have argued this elsewhere, as have others, and these arguments, which are internal to the

[42] My view to this effect was cited by Lord Lester of Herne Hill: see *Hansard*, HL, vol. 614, col. 1244.

[43] According to Berkovits, *Jewish Women*. S. Riskin, *Women and Jewish Divorce: The Rebellious Wife, the Agunah and the Right of Women to Initiate Divorce in Jewish Law: A Halakhic Solution* (Hoboken, NJ, 1989), p. xi, argues that Rabbenu Tam's approach was always a minority position.

[44] And see Breitowitz, 'The Plight of the *Agunah*', 325.

[45] An example formed the basis of *Singer v. Union of Orthodox Rabbis of the United States and Canada* (New York Supreme Court; see www.jlaw.com/Recent/singer/html). The husband paid a $50,000 bribe to the UOR to obtain a *heter*.

halakhic system, are outside the scope of this paper.[46] It has to be said, though, that the rabbinical authorities—a self-perpetuating male elite over whom the Jewish community has no control—are resistant to reform. Indeed, insistent that reform is impossible. They refuse to resort to fictions, though Maimonides had no difficulty in doing so, and they themselves have no difficulty when the problem is one they wish to solve. If they have found ways round carrying on the sabbath (the *eruv*) and retaining their whisky over Passover (the sale of *chametz*)—and for both fictions are employed—they could find solutions to the plight of the *agunah* as well (even if again fictions have to be used). Instead, they resort to expedients like the prenuptial agreement. Some have approved 'naming and shaming procedures'. Meanwhile, the chief rabbi claims the problem is exaggerated (there are, he says, only fifteen *agunot* in the country[47]) and prefers to tackle the problem case by case rather than by getting to its causes. The individualistic approach would be hopeless if there were only fifteen cases: no one knows how many there are, and many never surface, but estimates put the figure at least ten times this suggested number.

Using the Ordinary Law of the Land

So, how is the state to respond? What are the arguments for invoking state assistance to alleviate the problem? The courts first tried to assist in 1969. In *Brett* v. *Brett*[48] a wealthy husband had made it clear to his wife, who was divorcing him not long after their marriage, that he would not give her a *get*. Phillimore LJ made the point that the husband's refusal was motivated by his desire to use it as a bargaining counter against the wife's maintenance demands. Mrs Brett was lucky to find a bench of English judges: the *dayanim*, as we have seen, might have reacted differently. The Court used its power to award financial provision to coerce the husband into granting a *get*. What they did was to increase the sum payable in the event that the husband did not grant his wife a *get* within a stipulated period. They offered no clear justification for this: the reason was just 'obvious'—justice demanded that he not be allowed to treat his wife in this

---

[46] M. Freeman, 'The Dayanim Must Act', *Jewish Chronicle*, 17 Dec. 1999, 27. For other solutions, see J. David Bleich, 'Modern-Day Agunot: A Proposed Remedy' (1981) 4 *Jewish Law Annual* 167. 'Modern' debates can be traced back to I. Epstein, 'The Problem of the Agunah: An Attempted Solution', *Jewish Chronicle*, 31 Jan. 1936, which provoked a leading article headed 'A Public Scandal' on 7 Feb. 1936.

[47] *London Jewish News* (28 Apr. 2000). Jack Nusan Porter, *Women in Chains* (Northvale, NJ, 1995), believes about 5% of all Orthodox marriages in the United States 'end in the *agunah* stage' (p. xiii).

[48] [1969] 1 All ER 1007. Roman courts in Roman Judaea were involved in compelling Jews to carry out decisions of Jewish courts. See Aharon Oppenheimer, 'Jewish Penal Authority in Roman Judaea' in Martin Goodman (ed.), *Jews in the Graeco-Roman World* (Oxford, 1998), 181, 186–7.

way. It was as if the courts saw the *get* as part of a holistic process of divorce. Questions of jurisdiction and the scope of the Court's powers were not debated. The ruling was acceptable to the British rabbinical authorities in 1969, but they no longer accept it. Although a Beth Din may apply coercion where a *get* is required by Jewish law, they do not accept that a secular court may force a husband to give his wife a *get*. If they do so, the *get* which results is *me'useh* (given under duress and accordingly void). The rabbinical authorities now say that a *get* granted in similar circumstances to those in *Brett* would be *me'useh*. Indeed, they have been saying this since the mid-1980s (when I first became involved with the chief rabbi's committee) and probably for some time before. Whether the change of attitude is retrospective has not been vouchsafed. If retrospective, it is also not clear to when. But, even if the *Brett* solution were acceptable to today's interpretation of Jewish law in England—and note how swiftly changes can come—it would only be of limited value. Not all recalcitrant husbands are wealthy, and some might pay the additional sum seeing it as a burden like tax and their wives would be no better off.

Since *Brett* v. *Brett* the courts have involved themselves on a couple of other occasions. Thus, it has been made clear that if a husband wants a divorce based on two years' separation, the wife can make her consent conditional on the granting of a *get*.[49] And, further, in *N* v. *N*[50] Wall J expressed the view that courts have the power to refuse to permit a decree nisi of divorce to be made absolute on the application of a spouse who is refusing to cooperate in the grant and receipt of a *get*. This *per curiam* remark became the basis for a well-publicized refusal by Judge Viljoen, sitting in the Watford County Court in December 1999, to make a decree absolute where the husband was refusing to give his wife a *get*.[51] These judges are to be applauded, but their humanity and inventiveness reckons without the dogmatism and conservatism of those who interpret Jewish law in England today. I understand that the husband in the Watford case has now given his wife a *get*, but I wonder what the *dayanim* will make of it. Could not the husband say that he only gave his wife the *get* because of duress applied to him by a County Court judge? Is not the *get* therefore *me'useh*?

The courts have been unwilling to refuse divorces on the ground that dissolution of the marriage will cause the respondent grave hardship and that in all the circumstances it would be wrong to dissolve the marriage.[52] This defence only applies to one type of divorce (that based on the fact of five years' separation[53]) and, so far as is known, has never been raised by a

---

[49] *Beales* v. *Beales* [1972] Fam. 210. [50] At 757.
[51] *O* v. *O* (*Jurisdiction: Jewish Divorce*) [2000] 2 FLR 147.
[52] *Rukat* v. *Rukat* [1975] Fam. 63; *Banik* v. *Banik* [1973] 1 WLR 860. Cf *N* v. *N*, 757 (Wall J envisages 'circumstances' in which refusal to initiate the *get* procedure could amount to hardship).
[53] The Matrimonial Causes Act 1973, section 5, only applies to section 1(2)(e) divorces.

potential *agunah*. But it is doubtful if it would bite anyway, since the grave hardship is not caused by the civil divorce but by a refusal to give a religious divorce.[54] When the divorce provisions of the Family Law Act 1996 come into operation (if they ever do), the gravity standard will be lowered: it will only be necessary to show 'substantial' hardship and it will apply to all divorces.[55] *Agunot* will clearly suffer 'substantial' hardships, but again this will not be attributable to the civil divorce order, and therefore it may be doubted whether a court would be right to refuse a divorce to a recalcitrant husband.

These examples of judicial (or potential judicial) intervention all use the ordinary law of the land. They extend no special privileges to the Jewish population.

In the United States—which has, of course, a much larger Jewish population—other judicial strategies have been employed. That these have been successful despite claims that they infringe the First Amendment[56] suggests a fortiori that they should succeed in England. Although I do not think they will, I will briefly discuss them.

First, attempts have been made specifically to enforce civil agreements to cooperate in religious divorce proceedings. These failed initially (usually on the grounds that the contract was too vague[57]), but by 1977 the courts were granting specific performance,[58] even in one case where the husband was prepared to give a *get*, albeit not one from the religious authorities of the wife's allegiance.[59]

A second strategy has been to seek to enforce the *ketubah*. This sets out the obligations that a Jewish husband undertakes with respect to his wife, and is presented by the groom to the bride during the marriage ceremony. One of his promises (the *ketubah* is standardized, and he has no choice) is to pay his wife a certain sum of money upon divorce. The courts have

---

[54] I owe this point to Rhona Schuz, 'Divorce and Ethnic Minorities', in M. Freeman (ed.), *Divorce: Where Next?* (Aldershot, 1996), 131, 135.

[55] Family Law Act 1996 s. 10. It is looking increasingly likely that this Act will never be implemented. It was announced by the lord chancellor in Jan. 2001 that the divorce provisions of the Act will not be implemented, and will be repealed. Ironically, had it been implemented, the English law of divorce would have looked more like the Jewish! (See M. Freeman, 'Divorce Gospel Style', (1997) 27 *Family Law* 413.)

[56] See J. H. Choper, 'The Religion Clauses of the First Amendment: Reconciling the Conflict', (1980) 41 *Univ. of Pittsburgh LR* 673; M. J. Perry, *Love and Power: The Role of Religion and Morality in American Politics* (New York, 1991).

[57] For failures, see *Koeppel* v. *Koeppel* 138 N.Y.S. 2d 366 (Sup. Ct. 1954); *Margulies* v. *Margulies* 344 N.Y.S. 2d 482 (App. Div. 1973) (in this case the husband was nevertheless fined for contempt of court in refusing to carry out his promise); *Rubin* v. *Rubin* 348 N.Y.S. 2d 61 (Fam. Ct. 1973) (where the 'clean hands' doctrine was used).

[58] *Waxstein* v. *Waxstein* 394 N.Y.S. 2d 253 (App. Div. 1977).

[59] *Scholl* v. *Scholl* 621 A. 2d 808 (1992) (Delaware Family Court). The husband was prepared to give his wife a Conservative *get*, but she wanted an Orthodox one. The marriage had been celebrated in an Orthodox synagogue and he said he wanted her to suffer 'since she had made him suffer' (p. 813).

regularly enforced the contract. Husbands have raised First Amendment arguments, but these have been dismissed, the courts accepting expert testimony that the delivery of a *get* is not a religious act, merely the severance of a contractual relationship.[60] In the leading case of *Avitzur* v. *Avitzur*[61] the highest court in New York enforced the *ketubah* in a 4–3 decision, and ordered the husband to appear before a Beth Din. It saw the *ketubah* as analogous to an arbitration agreement, the enforceability of which could be decided on the application of 'neutral principles of contract law, without reference to any religious principle'.[62] It saw the relief sought as 'simply to compel the defendant to perform a secular obligation to which he has contractually bound himself'.[63]

Thirdly, some courts in the United States have construed a husband's refusal to give his wife a *get* as tortious. The claim is that failure to deliver a *get* prevents the wife from remarrying and constitutes as a result an intentional infliction of emotional distress. Courts were initially unwilling to agree to this, but a court in New York in 1990 held that the wife's claim stated a valid cause of action.[64]

Australian courts have employed yet another strategy, that of the injunction. Australia's Family Law Act 1975 gives the courts the power to grant an injunction where it is just or convenient to do so, and to do this unconditionally or upon terms and conditions considered appropriate.[65] As in the United States, in Australia Church and State are constitutionally separated,[66] but this has not prevented Australian courts from granting mandatory injunctions ordering recalcitrant spouses to appear before a Beth Din. In *In the Marriage of Shulsinger*[67] it was said to be 'contrary to all notions of justice' to allow the husband to seek and obtain a civil divorce while refusing to relieve his wife from their Jewish marriage and 'to say that a court can do nothing'.[68] In *In the Marriage of Gwiazda* all

---

[60] *Minkin* v. *Minkin* 434 A. 2d 665 (N.J. Super. Ct. Ch. Div. 1981). Adultery was alleged by the husband in this case which, said the court, required him to deliver a *get*. In *Burns* v. *Burns* 538 A. 2d 438 (N. J. Super. Ct. Ch. Div. 1987) this was extended to a case where adultery was not alleged. (Courts in other US jurisdictions have followed this, though not the Court of Appeals in Arizona (*Victor* v. *Victor* 866 P. 2d 899 (1993)).

[61] 446 N.E. 2d 136.   [62] Ibid. 138.

[63] Ibid. The *ketubah* in this case was a Conservative one, which contains an additional clause in which the parties agree to recognize the authority of the Beth Din of the Rabbinical Assembly. A New Jersey court more recently followed the minority opinion on *Avitzur*: *Aflalo* v. *Aflalo* 295 N.J. Super. 527 (1996).

[64] *Weiss* v. *Goldfelder* N.Y.L.J. Oct. 26 1990, 21. Courts were initially unwilling to agree to this tortious claim: see *Perl* v. *Perl* 512 N.Y.S. 2d 372 (App. Div. 1987). S. D. Gluck, 'The Agunah in the American Legal System: Problems and Solutions', (1993) 31 *J. Fam. L.* 885, 906–13 discusses this.

[65] Family Law Act 1975, s. 114(3).

[66] Commonwealth Constitution, s. 116. A wide-ranging new article is Kent Greenawalt, 'Religious Law and Civil Law: Using Secular Law to Assure Observance of Practices with Religious Significance', (1998) 71 *S. California LR* 781.

[67] (1977) 2 Fam. L. R. 11, 611.   [68] Ibid. 617.

the court was asked to do, said the judge, was to ensure a party (in this case a recalcitrant wife) submitted to the jurisdiction of a tribunal 'set up well beyond time immemorial . . . by the religion of which that party is a professed adherent'.[69]

So far as is known none of these strategies has been employed in this country. Would any of them succeed? Should they do so? There can be no objection to invoking a tort remedy. The contractual remedies may cause greater problems. Although the American courts have overcome the difficulties, English courts might find contractual obligations of the *ketubah* couched in vague language, for example requiring a husband to act 'in accordance with the manner of Jewish men' too uncertain to merit enforcement. English courts might also have problems in upholding prenuptial agreements to appear before a Beth Din. On this, hitherto, there is only a first instance ruling. Wall J in *N* v. *N*, held that 'an agreement made prior to marriage which contemplates the steps the parties will take in the event of divorce or separation is . . . contrary to public policy because it undermines the concept of marriage as a life-long union'.[70] I find this persuasive, though it uses a concept of marriage (a lifelong union) which is embedded within Christianity rather than Judaism. And Wall J did concede that agreements had 'evidential weight when the terms of the agreement are relevant to an issue before the court in subsequent proceedings to the divorce'.[71] It was argued that clauses in the agreement could be severed, in particular that the husband's agreement to attend a Beth Din and comply with their instructions was specifically enforceable against the husband as a matter of contract. But the judge held that 'Even if one divides up the prenuptial agreement in this case, and looks at the individual clauses separately, one cannot avoid the fundamental proposition that each is part of an agreement entered into before marriage to regulate the parties' affairs in the event of divorce. The public policy argument, therefore, continues to apply.'[72] The mandatory injunction runs up against the objection that the spouse to whom it is directed is being required to meet religious obligations. It is the clearest example of the state imposing religion on an individual. But Australia, as we have seen, has had no problem with it. And it has to be said that those who refuse to cooperate with the *get* requirement of Jewish law are rarely motivated by religious beliefs (in which I include anti-religious sentiments). As Breitowitz is surely right to notice:

---

[69] Unreported. No. M10631 of 1982 (23 Feb. 1983). My source for this is an unpublished paper by A. Strum, 'Jewish Divorce: What can the Civil Courts Do?' His article 'Jewish Divorce in Australian Family Law: The Enforceability of Jewish Nuptial and Prenuptial Contracts', (1991) 17 *Monash Univ. LR* 182 is most helpful on Australian sources and practice.

[70] At 752.   [71] Ibid.   [72] Ibid. 754.

The unwilling spouse's claim that the *get* law violates his free exercise rights [a reference in the US First Amendment] is further refuted in the vast majority of cases, where his refusal to give a *get* is not motivated by religious beliefs, but out of spite, or as a means of obtaining valuable concessions. Indeed, it is precisely because the husband knows that a *get* is needed that he is able to use it as a bargaining chip.[73]

Perhaps then only the tort strategy would succeed, and success here would depend on surmounting a number of barriers. As indicated already, there can be no objection to an action in tort: the *agunah* is as entitled to protection from intentionally inflicted injury as anyone else. The other remedies, however, raise, as legislative intervention does, the whole question of propriety. The American and Australian courts were not particularly troubled by this; at least the American courts were not once they had convinced themselves that entanglement in religious matters was not in violation of the First Amendment. In the leading case of *Avitzur* v. *Avitzur* the *ketubah* was seen as analogous to an arbitration agreement, the enforceability of which could be decided on the application of 'neutral principles of contract law, without reference to any religious principle'.[74] I doubt whether the analogies are all that close. Most *ketubot* (though not I think the one in *Avitzur*[75]) are in Aramaic, which virtually no spouses will understand. The terms are standard, vague, and archaic. And, most significantly, it is a strange contract where, as here, only one party is a party to it. The Australian court does at least adduce a reason to justify intervention: the denial of a *get* was, said the Court in *Shulsinger*, 'contrary to all notions of justice';[76] the injunction, said the Court in *Gwiazda*, would ensure that 'the court's dissolution of the marriage would be fully effective, not only in theory but in fact'.[77]

So we can return to the question already posed. Is the plight of the *agunah* any business of the state? Is it within the state's remit at all. What arguments are there to justify state entanglement in what appears to be a parochial issue?

The State's Business?

There are a number of arguments.

First, it is indisputable that we are a multicultural society, a people of different religions and none. There is an established religion, but ironically fewer of its supposed adherents worship in its churches than is the case with several of the minority religions (including Judaism and Islam). Within a pluralistic society mutual toleration and acknowledgement of

[73] Breitowitz, 'The Plight of the *Agunah*', 395.   [74] At 138.
[75] It was a Conservative one.   [76] At 617.
[77] n. 69 above.

difference is preferable to the enforcement of a single standard of morality in those areas of life which do not harm others.[78] Those who posit this standard of liberalism envisage the 'others' to be outside the community of the practice in question. But here the flourishing of the lives of members of the community itself, in particular women, are frustrated by rules they have not made and cannot influence. The argument, as developed, says that Parliament and the courts should support the religious institutions of minorities. But there are distinctions to be drawn between non-interference and active support, and also between toleration and endorsement.[79] The case for tolerating the *get* process is strong, though arguments can be adduced against it. It is more difficult to justify upholding what many believe to be a tottering and discredited institution by using state machinery to support it. It is even more difficult to make out a case for endorsement, since that would amount to according legitimacy to the institution and practice of the *get*.

Secondly, it may be argued that the law allows Jews to marry according to their own marriage customs and practices. If, the argument goes, the state assists in the creation of marriages according to Jewish usages, then it should also offer assistance to those engaged in dissolving a Jewish marriage.

A further stage in this argument is that, since Jewish marriages are recognized, so should their divorce rules. This would enable those who marry 'according to the law of Moses and Israel'[80] to divorce according to the law of Deuteronomy (as interpreted or misinterpreted). As in Israel, a *get* would dissolve a marriage:[81] a civil decree of divorce would be otiose. It would follow (and this is not a slippery slope argument) that, since we allow Muslims to marry according to the tenets of their faith, we would also have to recognize the *talaq*.[82] If Jews were to be exempted from the civil laws of divorce, so would Muslims and any other groups with special provision for marriage (Quakers could create their own divorce machinery[83]). There is commendable logic to this argument and Rhona

---

[78] See Bhikhu Parekh, *Rethinking Multiculturalism* (Basingstoke, 2000). A good introduction to the debate is Susan Moller Okin, *Is Multiculturalism Bad for Women?* (Princeton, 1999).

[79] See Joseph Raz, *The Morality of Freedom* (Oxford, 1986); *Ethics in the Public Domain* (Oxford, 1994).

[80] The words of the *ketubah*.

[81] As in *Berkovits* v. *Grinberg (A-G Intervening)* [1995] Fam. 142: we did not recognize it since the proceedings had started in England. That a *get* in England does not dissolve a marriage was confirmed in *Maples (formerly Melamud)* v. *Maples* [1988] Fam. 14.

[82] Even the bare *talaq*, at least where the parties were domiciled in a country where this was sufficient.

[83] They are lumped together with Jews in the Marriage Act 1949, and accordingly section 9(3) of the Family Law Act 1996 applies also to them. Of course, this is merely a quirk of legislative drafting.

Schuz supports it.[84] Does this mean that the *get* would really become no business of the state? Is this laissez-faire solution one that can sensibly be contemplated? I think not. True, it would solve the *agunah* problem at a stroke and all uncertainties about status would go. But the *get* process can only be initiated by the husband. The legitimization of such a discriminatory practice would be unacceptable even if it were lawful. Nor can a particular group in the population be denied access to the courts of the land. With the implementation of the Human Rights Act 1998 the laissez-faire model is ruled out completely.[85] It would have been completely unacceptable anyway to all but a small section of the Jewish population: most of the rest would have no confidence in the Batei Din.

This still leaves the argument that the state allows Jews to marry according to its rules, in its ceremonies, and in accordance with its practices. If it does this, should it not also assist the full dissolution of such marriages? The argument is superficially attractive but it ignores (1) the distinction between creating a facility and assisting an additional remedy; and (2) the real difference between marriage and divorce, the former of which is to be encouraged, the latter discouraged. English law, in common with other systems, has always taken a more liberal attitude to marriage than to divorce: there is no rule of private international law more firmly established than that a marriage will be recognized if it complies with local form[86] (provided the parties have capacity by their personal law[87]). A tighter rein is kept on dissolution of status. There is a pronounced reluctance to refuse to recognize marriages, but public policy[88] (and other grounds[89]) can be invoked to refuse recognition to foreign divorces, separations, and annulments.

A third argument is that where there is a civil divorce but no *get*, a 'limping' marriage is created. The undesirability of this is not contested. It is, of course, a fundamental principle of private international law that a status conferred by a party's personal law should be universally recognized.[90] So, as Schuz puts it, 'the civil law, by its willingness to dissolve marriages which were contracted under Jewish religious law, other than in accordance with that law, exacerbates the problem inherent in the consensual nature of

---

[84] See Schuz, 'Divorce and Ethnic Minorities', 144. Less 'radical' is B. Berkovits, 'Jewish Divorce', (1989) 19 *Family Law* 115 and '*Get* and *Talaq* in English Law: Reflections on Law and Policy', in C. Mallat and J. Connors (eds.), *Islamic Family Law* (London, 1993).

[85] Both because it would discriminate (see Art. 14) and because it would deny access to the courts (see Art. 13).

[86] *Berthiaume* v. *Dastous* [1930] AC 79. The rule can be traced back to *Scrimshire* v. *Scrimshire* (1752) 2 Hag. Con. 395.

[87] The law of the antenuptial domicile of each party.

[88] See Family Law Act 1986, s. 51(3), as interpreted in *Kendall* v. *Kendall* [1977] Fam. 208. Of especial interest is *Chaudhary* v. *Chaudhary* [1985] Fam. 19, 45.

[89] See Family Law Act 1986, s. 51.

[90] See the famous dissent of Scott LJ in *Re Luck's Settlement* [1940] Ch. 864.

Jewish divorce'.[91] In effect, the civil courts, when they dissolve a marriage celebrated according to Jewish rites, grant an incomplete divorce. This was why Emery J in the Australian case of *Gwiazda*[92] issued a mandatory injunction to the wife to appear before the relevant Beth Din. The blame can hardly be attributed to the civil courts: the problem is not one of their creation. The solution favoured by some (including myself in the mid-1980s) which has now found its way into legislation (as yet unimplemented) and was embodied in the failed 2000 Bill is to deny a dissolution where it will be incomplete. That this is incompatible with the Human Rights Act 1998 seems to have been noticed by no one, not even initially by the proposer of the 2000 Bill, who is the country's leading human rights lawyer.[93]

A fourth argument for intervention is that the law relating to the *get* offers a potentiality for blackmail by the unscrupulous. A husband can use the threat to withhold a *get* as a bargaining inducement to get an agreement relating to the children[94] or to financial or property arrangements.[95] He can also make the granting of a *get* dependent on the payment to him of a large sum of money. There has been a tendency in the past to hush up these transactions. Women in particular have kept quiet for fear that they will lose their *get* and join the ranks of *agunot*. A B'nai Brith report in Canada in 1987 documented 311 cases where the *get* had been used as a bargaining tool to obtain financial and custodial gains.[96] Evidence has emerged in this country several times recently and the practice is known to be prevalent. Worse still it is connived at, even assisted, by *dayanim*. The argument that the state should intervene to protect the victims of these extortionate practices is compelling, though it is both sad and salutary to report that, if the Family Law Act 1996 is implemented, the scope for such

[91] Schuz, 'Divorce and Ethnic Minorities', 144.

[92] n. 69, above.

[93] Possible incompatibility with Article 14 was referred to in the Second Reading debate in the House of Lords (by Lord Lester of Herne Hill, *Hansard*, HL, vol. 614, cols. 1245–8 and by Lord McIntosh of Haringey at col. 1261). As a result, at the Third Reading amendments were passed which purport to rule out such incompatibility: see *Hansard*, H.L. vol. 615, cols. 505–6. I do not believe they achieve this objective. Nor am I convinced that incompatibility with Article 14 is the only problem: it is distinctly possible that the Bill was incompatible with Articles 6, 9, and 12 as well. If the 1996 Act is ever implemented, section 9(3) will be similarly open to challenge.

[94] In *O* v. *O* and in *N* v. *N* the husband's refusal was linked to a contact issue. In *N* v. *N* Wall J did hold that there was a residual discretion not to entertain an application for contact by a husband who was refusing his wife a *get* (see 758–9). But this is only tenable where the refusal was so affecting the child that contact would not be in the child's best interests until the issue was resolved: the child's welfare is the paramount (that is the only) consideration.

[95] But such an agreement would be overturned by a court, were this duress or undue influence to come to its attention. Unfortunately, a woman desperate for a *get* is not likely to disclose this.

[96] B'nai Brith, *The Use of Get as a Bargaining Tool in Jewish Divorce Proceedings* (Toronto, 1987).

practices within English jurisdiction will increase.[97] But does the state need to become involved in the *get* process as such to protect vulnerable women? There are Augean stables in urgent need of cleansing, and if the Jewish community cannot do this, perhaps the state should. I should be surprised if the criminal offence of blackmail has not been committed in at least one of the cases in which a woman has paid out a large sum to receive her *get*. Let the husband be prosecuted. And if it can be shown that the participation of the *dayan* concerned was other than benign, prosecute him too as an accessory.

Finally, there is another possible argument for state intervention, particularly if this takes the form of legislation. A law is an unequivocal declaration of public policy: the symbolic importance of law cannot be underestimated. The educative effect of law, its social engineering potential, is part of the modern experience of law reform.[98] Critics will say this optimism rests upon a 'hollow hope',[99] and the reasons for optimism may not be as great as perhaps they were when law stood in the vanguard of the battle to create equal opportunities. Using law as an instrument of social change tends to work best where there is a readily identifiable victim—there could not be a better example than the *agunah*.[100] Against this it may be said that the authority of a state legislature may not have the impact upon the men involved in these situations that the 'rival' authority of a Beth Din has (Massell's work on Bolshevik legislation and its impact upon the lives of the people of Soviet Central Asia is instructive[101]).

Conclusion

There is a sixth argument. I excluded it deliberately because it is both weak and insulting. But it is one often heard. The state, it is said, must do something to solve the problem of the *agunah* because the rabbinical authorities either cannot or, worse, will not do anything. Whether it is impotence (as they perceive it), complacency, or lethargy (or a combination), almost no progress is being made. An early initiative of Jonathan Sacks's chief rabbinate was a women's committee.[102] It achieved very little. He has now established a task force and given the job, apparently, to

---

[97] See M. Freeman, 'Family Values and Family Justice', (1997) 50 *CLP* 315, 348–54.

[98] See Harry V. Ball and Lawrence M. Friedman, 'The Use of Criminal Sanctions in the Enforcement of Economic Legislation', (1965) 17 *Stanford LR* 197. The classic juristic source is Karl Olivecrona, *Law as Fact* (Copenhagen, 1939).

[99] Gerald N. Rosenberg's thesis in *The Hollow Hope* (Chicago, 1991).

[100] See Troy Duster, *The Legislation of Morality* (New York, 1970), 26–7.

[101] Gregory Massell, 'Law as an Instrument of Revolutionary Change in a Traditional Milieu: The Case of Soviet Central Asia', (1968) 2 *Law and Society Review* 179.

[102] This was reported in June 1994 (see *The Times*, 1 July 1994). Frustration at the lack of progress since is reflected in Helen Jacobus, 'For the Sake of our Community', *Jewish Chronicle*, 12 Nov. 1999, 35.

a woman who knows little about the subject.[103] The current approach is individualistic, the solving of problem cases as they arise. This does nothing to get to the root of the problem. Prenuptial agreements may[104] coax the potentially recalcitrant spouse into the jurisdiction of the Beth Din. But the Beth Din itself loses more of its claim to legitimacy every time a negative story about its activities or those of one of its *dayanim* is published, and this is worrying often. It is predicted that the number of couples agreeing to a prenuptial agreement will decline.[105] That the rabbinical authorities cannot or will not reform the *get* law is no argument for state intervention.

But does the *get* serve any useful purpose at all today? I doubt it. In cases (fortunately the majority) where it is willingly given and received it adds another layer of bureaucracy to the divorce process. It is neither very expensive nor very time-consuming, though it is a drain on both time and money. The actual ceremony itself borders on the comic, but entertainment value is not proffered as a justification! In cases where one of the spouses obstructs the process, it causes distress. It discriminates against women. It gives a spiteful spouse an additional and unnecessary divorce weapon. It exposes the vulnerable to unseemly negotiation, even to blackmail. Some (men in particular) claim it is a way of evening up a divorce process which they believe at civil level is weighted against them. Even were this true, it would not exonerate or excuse callous behaviour.

The time has come to admit that the days of the *get* are over. They were days when the Jewish *kehilah* was self-governing and when Jews, liberally, recognized divorce, and those around them did not. The *get* could be reformed, but the preferable solution would be an acknowledgement that a divorce granted by the secular authorities of a legal system having jurisdiction of the parties is all that is necessary to dissolve a marriage.[106] Provision could be made to this effect in the *ketubah*. Attempts by the state to get involved will no more solve the problem than sticking plaster will solve cancer. And the *get* is a real cancer in the body of the Jewish world.

---

[103] Mrs Judy Nagler (the appointment is announced in *Jewish Chronicle*, 9 June 2000, 64).
[104] There is a full (if partial) discussion of this by Kenneth Auman and Basil Herring, *The Prenuptial Agreement: Halakhic and Pastoral Considerations* (Northvale, NJ, 1996).
[105] We are told that 70% of couples about to marry agree to a prenuptial agreement.
[106] Rabbi Michael Weil of Paris suggested this as long ago as 1884. See Moshe Meiselman, 'Jewish Woman in Jewish Law: Solutions to Problems of Agunah', in Porter, *Women in Chains*, 61.

GLOSSARY

agunah (pl. *agunot*)	chained woman
Beth Din (pl. Batei Din)	rabbinical court
brit milah	circumcision
chametz	leavened (expanded and interpeted to mean not usable during Passover)
dayan (pl. *dayanim*)	judge
eruv	fictional creation of walled city
get (pl. *gittim*)	bill of divorcement
Halakha (adj. halakhic)	Jewish law
heter me'ah rabbanim	permission of 100 rabbis
kehilah	community
ketubah (pl. *ketubot*)	marriage contract
mamzer (pl. *mamzerim*)	bastard (but not exactly translatable)
me'useh	void for duress
talaq	Muslim divorce

THE INTERSECTING WORLDS OF RELIGIOUS AND SECULAR MARRIAGE

Perry Dane

Introduction

The topic of this paper is the legal encounter between the religious and secular institutions of marriage. I want to approach the question obliquely, however, and indeed postpone it until the last part of this paper. Instead, I will dwell on a close examination of two official texts—one civil and one religious—that figure in the current struggle in both spheres over the possibility of marriage, or some related status, for samesex couples. The civil text is a statute of the state of Vermont enacted at the end of April 2000. The statute allows same-sex couples to enter into, and have legally certified, something called a 'civil union',[1] which the statute explicitly distinguishes from a marriage.[2] The religious text is a decision of the Permanent Judicial Commission of the Presbyterian Church USA.[3] That decision, which by chance the Commission issued only about a month after the passage of the Vermont bill, authorizes ministers and congregations under its jurisdiction to perform ceremonies called 'holy unions' for samesex couples, ceremonies that the Commission, much like the State Legislature of Vermont in its definition of 'civil union', emphatically distinguishes from marriage.[4]

---

[1] Act 91, 2000 Vt. Acts & Resolves (available at <http://www.leg.state.vt.us/docs/2000/acts/ACT091.HTM>) (hereafter Act 91).

[2] Ibid., §1(10).

[3] Remedial Case No. 21211, *Benton v. Presbytery of Hudson River*, Report of the Permanent Judicial Commission to the 212th General Assembly of the Presbyterian Church, USA (22 May 2000) (available at <http://horeb.pcusa.org/ga212/rga/12pjc.htm>) (hereafter *Hudson River*).

[4] Ibid., at paras. 12.185, 12.191-4. Both the Vermont statute and the Presbyterian judicial ruling have obviously been controversial. And, as has only become clearer since I first presented this paper, each is in at least some danger of being undone. In Vermont several of the legislators who voted in favour of the civil union statute have lost subsequent primary elections. See *New York Times*, 14 Sept. 2000, p. A24, col. 1 ('In a sign that voters in Vermont remain divided over the state's new civil union law, five Republican state legislators who supported the gay-rights law were defeated in Tuesday's primary, while four other Republicans and one Democrat who backed the law won. The primary was largely seen as a referendum on civil unions, with many challengers campaigning on the issue'). And the General Assembly of the Presbyterian Church, USA, narrowly voted to send to the Church's 173 presbyteries a proposed amendment to the Church's constitution that would flatly

Civil Union

The Vermont civil union statute was a legislative response to the decision of the Vermont Supreme Court in *Baker* v. *State*.[5] Interpreting the Common Benefits Clause of the Vermont State Constitution,[6] the Court in *Baker* held that Vermont could not constitutionally deprive same-sex couples of the 'statutory benefits and protections afforded persons of the opposite sex who choose to marry'.[7] It explicitly declined, however, to require that Vermont make marriage itself available to same-sex couples, as long as the state created a legal framework for allowing such couples to share the benefits and protections that are incident to marriage.

Taking up this invitation, the Vermont civil union statute reaffirms what the Court in *Baker* had held was already implicit in Vermont law[8]— that marriage in the legal contemplation of the state of Vermont is the 'legally recognized union of one man and one woman'.[9] The statute goes on, however, to establish a parallel category called 'civil union', the parties to which 'shall have all the same benefits, protections and responsibilities under law, whether they derive from statute, administrative or court rule, policy, common law or any other source of civil law, as are granted to spouses in a marriage',[10] including rights and duties in domestic relations law, property law, tort law, and tax law. Vermont civil unions can be certified by judges, justices of the peace, members of the clergy, and certain religious congregations, which is to say by the same secular and religious officers who solemnize marriages.[11] Such unions can only be dissolved by divorce or annulment, subject to the same rules that apply to marriages.

A civil union, in other words, has—with the possible exception of its interjurisdictional effects, which I will discuss below—essentially the same practical legal incidents as a marriage.[12] In this respect, it is different from

---

prohibit any form of same-sex union. See Jerry L. Van Marter, 'Assembly Sends Same Sex Union Ban Amendment to Presbyteries: Measure Passes by 268–251 Vote,' (30 June 2000) (available at <http:horeb.pcusa.org/ga212/news/ga00150.htm>).

[5] *Baker* v. *State*, 744 A.2d 864 (1999).   [6] Vt. Const., ch. I, art. 7.
[7] *Baker*, 744 A.2d, at 867.   [8] Ibid., at 868–9.
[9] Act 91, §3, codified at Vt. Stat. Ann., tit. 15, §1201(4).
[10] Act 91, §3, codified at Vt. Stat. Ann., tit. 15, §1204(a).
[11] Compare Act 91, §5, codified at Vt. Stat. Ann., tit. 18, §5164 (persons authorized to certify civil unions) with Vt. Stat. Ann., tit. 18, §5144 (persons authorized to solemnize marriages). It might bear emphasis, particularly to readers more acquainted with other legal systems, that religious functionaries and institutions are under no *obligation*, either in general or in particular cases, to conduct civil union ceremonies or certify civil union relationships, just as they are under no obligation, either in general or in particular cases, to conduct marriages. Indeed, imposing such an obligation would, in the American constitutional scheme, be unthinkable.
[12] The statute goes so far as to include the following rule of construction: 'This act shall be construed broadly in order to secure to eligible same-sex couples the option of a legal status with the benefits and protections of civil marriage, in accordance with the requirements of the Common Benefits Clause of the Vermont Constitution. Parties to a civil union shall have all

other socalled 'domestic partnership' statutes, enacted in various jurisdictions, that grant to couples a more limited, precisely defined, set of rights.[13]

This, though, inevitably raises several related questions. What is this statute trying to accomplish? Is there any genuine difference between marriage and civil unions? If so, is there any genuine rationale for that difference? And, if not, is the statute engaging in a semantic sham? These questions are important both theoretically and practically. Some opponents, and defenders, of the statute have treated it as authorizing same-sex marriage, in reality or in effect. But this is not the dominant view. The law's margin of passage might have been provided by legislators who understood civil union to be something short of marriage. And some gay couples and gay rights activists argue that the statute, even though it benefits same-sex couples, falls objectively short of their goal of civil recognition of gay marriage.[14]

At one level, it is apparent what Vermont is trying to do: grant to gay and lesbian couples the right to enjoy the legal incidents of marriage without extending to them the right to marriage itself. In fact, this is so obvious that working so hard to make sense of it, as I am about to do, might seem bullheaded. Nevertheless, what Vermont is doing is, at the least, jurisprudentially mysterious. Arguably, marriage—like other legal categories—just is the sum of its legal incidents, and nothing more. To that extent, any institution with the same legal incidents as marriage is, by definition, marriage. The problem is roughly analogous to the philosophical principle of the identity of indiscernibles. Entities 'cannot merely differ (full stop), but must necessarily differ in some respect. If what are ostensibly distinct

---

of the same benefits, protections and responsibilities under state law, whether derived from statute, administrative or court rule, policy, common law or any other source of civil law, as are granted to spouses in a marriage. Treating the benefits, protections and responsibilities of civil marriage differently from the benefits, protections and responsibilities of civil unions is permissible only when clearly necessary because the gender-based text of a statute, rule or judicial precedent would otherwise produce an unjust, unwarranted, or confusing result, and different treatment would promote or enhance, and would not diminish, the common benefits and protections that flow from marriage under Vermont law' (Act 91, §39(a)).

[13] See e.g. Cal. Family Code §§297–299.6. The Vermont civil union statute itself contains a littlenoticed set of provisions authorizing the creation of 'reciprocal beneficiaries relationships' among family members related by blood or adoption, such as brothers and sisters, or children and parents. These 'reciprocal beneficiaries relationships' confer a narrow, specifically enumerated, and explicitly limited set of rights regarding, for example, medical decision-making and the disposition of remains. See Act 91, §29, codified at Vt. Stat. Ann., tit. 15, §§1301–6 and elsewhere. But nobody would confuse this relationship with marriage.

[14] See e.g. Andrew Sullivan, 'Why Civil Union isn't Marriage', *New Republic*, 8 May 2000, 18. I do not mean to suggest, of course, that all gay and lesbian activists put same-sex marriage on their agenda in the first place. For an argument that effectuating an institution of same-sex marriage would only perpetuate the shame attached to non-monogamous, unmarried sex, see Michael Warner, *The Trouble with Normal: Sex, Politics and the Ethics of Queer Life* (New York, 1999).

items differ in no respect, then, we may legitimately conclude that the items are two "in name only", i.e., that we have to do with one and only one item.'[15]

For myself, I do not think that we need to be so narrow in our jurisprudence as to think that legal incidents exhaust legal meaning. Even so, however, the challenge, if the difference between marriage and civil union is to be thought genuine, is rigorously to identify some property, or essential quality, other than a legal incident, that makes it real. Merely saying so is not enough. Nor is it enough to posit some ghostly difference that we cannot pin down.

To be sure, some observers have argued that the failure to give sames-ex unions the label of 'marriage' by itself confers a 'second-class' status on homosexual relationships. But this conclusion is too simple. Both the legislative findings enshrined in the statute and the Vermont Supreme Court's opinion in *Baker* are, on their face, respectful of gay persons and their bonds. If the distinction between the terms 'civil union' and 'marriage' stigmatizes, that cannot be merely because the terms are *different*. It must, rather, be because of some extra meaning attached to the term 'marriage'. And it should be possible, unless this is all a mere play of effect, to identify that extra meaning with some precision. So we are back to the original question.

Some clues to the inquiry do appear both in the *Baker* opinion and in the civil union statute itself. As noted, the Vermont Supreme Court in *Baker* held that the Common Benefits Clause of the Vermont Constitution required that same-sex couples have available to them the 'statutory benefits and protections afforded persons of the opposite sex who choose to marry'.[16] But, in writing that this requirement could, at least presumptively,[17] be met by conferral of a right short of marriage, it also insisted that while 'many have noted the symbolic or spiritual significance of the marital relation, it is plaintiffs' claim to the secular benefits and protections of a singularly human relationship that, in our view, characterizes this case'.[18] Along similar lines, the legislative findings in the statute propose that

While a system of civil unions does not bestow the status of civil marriage, it does satisfy the requirements of the Common Benefits Clause. Changes in the way significant legal relationships are established under the constitution should be

---

[15] Jay Rosenberg, 'The Identity of Indiscernibles: Some Tractarian Reflections', *Acta Analytica*, 21 (1998), 12.

[16] *Baker*, 744 A.2d, at 867.

[17] Ibid., at 886 ('While some future case may attempt to establish that—notwithstanding equal benefits and protections under Vermont law—the denial of a marriage license operates per se to deny constitutionally—protected rights, that is not the claim we address today').

[18] Ibid., at 888–9.

approached carefully, combining respect for the community and cultural institutions most affected with a commitment to the constitutional rights involved.[19]

Put another way, civil union—as contemplated by the court and enacted by the legislature—seeks to confer the legal incidents of marriage without the 'symbolic', 'spiritual', or 'cultural' meaning of the institution. In this light, it seems particularly evocative that, under the statute, while marriages are 'solemnized', civil unions are merely 'certified'.

This account, however, is also at best incomplete. To begin with, it clarifies but does not eliminate the jurisprudential problem of the identity of indiscernibles. Admittedly, laws have symbolic and cultural meanings. But it is not clear that a statute, simply by the choice of operative terms, can confer, or refuse to confer, such meaning. Symbolic and cultural meanings arise out of a complex, collective, process; they cannot just be arbitrarily legislated.

Even if laws could themselves confer symbolic and cultural meaning, the real question here is precisely what symbolic or cultural meaning is at stake in the difference between marriage and civil union. If that meaning is, at root, religious, then some would argue that, general jurisprudential considerations aside, the religion clauses of the First Amendment to the United States Constitution[20] specifically disable Vermont from playing in that arena. In fact, one of the arguments that proponents have made in favour of same-sex marriage statutes to begin with is that civil marriage, properly understood, is nothing more than the grant of certain secular rights and responsibilities, which should have nothing to do with either the vocabulary of religious marriage or the dictates of religious doctrine. I find this view too simplistic, for reasons I will elaborate. But it would be perilous, or at least odd, to imagine that as a matter of the positive law of Vermont, the difference between marriage and civil union is that one is sacred and the other is not.

In any event, even if this were Vermont's intention, the civil union statute seems ill fitted to sustain that distinction. After all, as noted, a Vermont civil union can be certified by a member of the clergy in a religious ceremony, much as a marriage can. For that matter, it could presumably be certified through a ceremony that used all the trappings and vocabulary of a religious marriage. Conversely, a marriage under Vermont law can be solemnized in a purely civil ceremony with a bare minimum of symbolic, spiritual, or cultural overtones, with parties whose main interest is to take advantage of the secular legal incidents of marriage.

Consider, though, another cut at the problem. Some American cases, especially older ones, treat marriage as an institution grounded, not only in

---

[19] Act 91, §1(10).

[20] 'Congress shall make no law respecting an establishment of religion, or prohibiting the free exercise thereof' (U.S. Const. Amend. 1).

statute, but in 'natural law'.[21] Such language has fallen out of style, but the Supreme Court of the United States has, in more recent years, also declared marriage to be a 'fundamental right' in American constitutional jurisprudence.[22] Perhaps, then, it could be said that, whatever civil union *is* under Vermont law, we know what it is *not*. It is *not* the institution of marriage that the law has recognized as a subject of natural law or a species of fundamental right.[23] Thus, the Court in *Baker* was careful not to rely on fundamental rights jurisprudence, but on the tamer analysis of 'common benefit'.[24] Indeed, one might even go so far as to argue that, *if* same-sex couples had a constitutionally protected fundamental right to marry, then Vermont would still be depriving them of that right, despite its enactment of a civil union statute.

This account seems, at one level, correct. But it does not solve the puzzle. What, after all, is the content of either the natural law of marriage or the constitutional right to marriage? It cannot embrace the entire set of detailed, mundane, and varied positive legal incidents attached to marriage. Neither natural law (if we take it seriously) nor constitutional doctrine could be read to require, for example, a specific property regime or a particular set of tax benefits or the like.

Maybe the basic definition of marriage, as understood in natural law or constitutional law, lies in a subset of indispensable legal incidents, to which the other rights and obligations of the positive law of marriage are merely appended. But civil union in Vermont encompasses all the legal incidents of marriage, including any arguably essential subset. Or maybe the natural or constitutional definition of marriage rests in some property apart from any specific legal incidents at all. But that would just return us—again—to the puzzle with which we began.

To see the issue more clearly, consider the following thought experiment. To date, the United States Supreme Court has upheld a fundamental right to marry only in cases involving efforts to close marriage to certain

[21] See e.g. *Sharon v. Sharon*, 16 P.345, 346 (Cal. 1888) ('though marriage is a contract, its rights and obligations are fixed by society in accordance with the principles of natural law, and are beyond and above the parties themselves'). Several American decisions have quoted the striking language of Lord Stowell in *Dalrymple v. Dalrymple* (Eccl. 1811) 161 Eng. Rep. 665, that 'Marriage, in its origin, is a contract of natural law; it may exist between two individuals of different sexes, although no third person existed in the world, as happened in the case of the common ancestors of mankind. It is the parent, not the child of civil society. In civil society it becomes a civil contract, regulated and prescribed by law, and endowed with civil consequences.'
[22] See e.g. *Turner v. Safley*, 482 U.S. 78 (1987); *Zablocki v. Redhail*, 434 U.S. 374 (1978); *Loving v. Virginia*, 388 U.S. 1 (1967).
[23] This is, indeed, part of Andrew Sullivan's objection to the Vermont statute in Sullivan, 'Why Civil Union isn't Marriage'.
[24] Cf. *Baehr v. Lewin*, 852 P.2d 44 (Haw. 1993) (holding that, though there is no 'fundamental right' to same-sex marriage, denial of the status and benefits of marriage to same-sex couples constituted impermissible discrimination under the Hawaiian Constitution).

categories of persons, such as interracial couples or incarcerated persons. The right itself, however, is not merely comparative; it is a basic entitlement.[25] What, then, would it take for a state actually to deprive *all* its citizens of the right to marry? That is to say, what exactly does it mean to say that persons have a fundamental constitutional right to participate in an institution such as marriage that is so much the creature of, and so minutely defined by, a complicated configuration of positive law?

Presumably, a state could shave off some legal incidents of marriage—this tax benefit or that property rule—without violating the Constitution. But there might come a point when the state had stripped enough legal consequence to hit the bone. That point might define, as in the natural law account, the legal core of marriage, as distinct from its contingent attributes.

Actually identifying the content of the core of marriage—the exact legal incident without which marriage would not be marriage—might be difficult. Rather than going down that path, however, imagine now that a state abolished marriage entirely, but replaced it with a regime, such as civil union, with the same legal incidents as marriage, that it made available to couples, perhaps *both* homosexual and heterosexual. This, by the way, is not a mere fantasy; the Law Commission of Canada, for example, has toyed with this idea as a way of fine-tuning the civil treatment of close personal relationships, separating secular law from religious doctrine, and sidestepping the gay marriage debate.[26] Indeed, the idea fits comfortably with the claim that the term 'marriage' is only shorthand for a set of legal incidents that might be reshuffled almost at will. But would an effort by an American state to abolish marriage, and replace it with something else, abridge the constitutional right to marry? The answer is not clear. But the question is related, at least roughly, to the puzzle of whether Vermont's civil union is really different from marriage.

[25] See *Turner* v. *Safley*, 482 U.S. 78 (1987); see also *Zablocki* v. *Redhail*, 434 U.S. 374, 395–7 (1978) (Stewart J concurring in the judgment) ('The problem in this case is not one of discriminatory classifications, but of unwarranted encroachment upon a constitutionally protected freedom'). This point is doctrinally crucial in American constitutional law because, absent the use of a 'suspect' class such as race, only encroachment on a 'fundamental right' can trigger the 'strict scrutiny' of a classification challenged under the Equal Protection Clause.

[26] See Law Commission of Canada Discussion Paper, *Recognizing and Supporting Close Personal Relationships between Adults* (Catalogue No. JL2–10/2000, May 2000) (available at <http://www.lcc.gc.ca/en/forum/cpra/paper.html>) ('As an alternative to developing its own definition of marriage to deal with claims for equality of status, Parliament could decide simply to delete the words marriage and spouse from all its statutes and regulations. If it had previously made its various policies and programmes dealing with close personal relationships between adults dependent on a new concept that identified the factual properties of targeted relationships, no substantive consequences would flow from such a deletion. After dispensing with the legal concept of marriage, Parliament would then be in a position to establish a new formal status applicable to a broad range of close adult personal relationships'); see also Mindelle Jacobs, 'Compromise would Take Sex out of the Equation', *The Edmonton Sun*, 4 June 2000, SE16.

I suggested earlier that the there might be one important way in which the legal incidents of a Vermont civil union differ from that of a marriage. That possible exception relates to whether, or how, civil unions would be recognized by other jurisdictions, including the federal government and other states. This could potentially be the hard distinction we have been looking for. Again, however, it will be hard to reach a definitive resolution.

The civil union statute does not seek to restrict its extraterritorial effect. It does, however, assert that 'the General Assembly recognizes that it does not have the jurisdiction to control federal laws or the benefits, protections and responsibilities related to them'.[27] More specifically, it assumes that federal law will not respect Vermont civil unions, and even adjusts some of the technical details of its estate tax provisions accordingly.[28] And the statute establishes a review commission, one of whose tasks is to 'collect information about the recognition and treatment of Vermont civil unions by other states and jurisdictions, including procedures for dissolution'.[29]

It is important to be exact here, however. The legislature's doubts about the extrajurisdictional effect of civil unions largely arises out of the resistance of other jurisdictions to recognizing *any* legally enshrined homosexual union, marriage included, or marriage in particular. The issue, very briefly put, is this: Traditionally, marriage has been considered a portable status, which is to say that a marriage validly celebrated in one place will, subject to certain important exceptions, be recognized everywhere, though subject, perhaps, to different legal incidents in different places.[30] With regard to the celebration of a fullfledged same-sex *marriage* valid according to the law of the place where it is celebrated, other jurisdictions might refuse to recognize the marriage either on definitional grounds—positing that marriage is, necessarily, the bond between a man and a woman[31]—or on an argument from public policy.[32] Such strategies, which remain to be

[27] Act 91, §39(b).
[28] Act 91, §22, codified at Vt. Stat. Ann., tit. 32, §7401(a).
[29] Act 91, §40(d)(1).
[30] For my own recent discussion of some of the complications relating to the choice of law of marriage, see Perry Dane, 'Whereof One cannot Speak. Legal Diversity and the Limits of a Restatement of Conflict of Laws', (2000) 75 *Indiana Law Journal* 511. I argue in that article that, at least according to some traditional formulations, fundamental prescriptive jurisdiction over the validity of marriages is actually vested, not in the place of celebration, but in the domicile(s) of the parties. For the sake of simplicity, however, I will leave that important complication out of my discussion here.
[31] For opposing views on this question, compare David Orgon Coolidge, 'Same-Sex Marriage? *Baehr v. Miike* and the Meaning of Marriage', (1997) 38 *South Texas Law Review* 1, and John Finnis, 'Law, Morality, and "Sexual Orientation" ', (1994) 69 *Notre Dame Law Review* 1049, with William N. Eskridge Jr., *The Case for Same-Sex Marriage* (New York, 1996) and Andrew Koppelman, 'Is Marriage Inherently Heterosexual?', (1997) 42 *American Journal of Jurisprudence* 51.
[32] See Larry Kramer, 'The Public Policy Exception and the Problem of Extra-Territorial Recognition of Same-Sex Marriage', (1996)16 *Quinnipiac Law Review* 153; L. Lynn Hogue,

constitutionally tested, have in the last several years been inscribed in statutes such as the federal Defense of Marriage Act[33] and parallel legislation recently enacted in more than thirty states.[34]

For our purposes, though, the relevant question is whether the status of *civil union* poses *distinctive* issues of interjurisdictional recognition, apart from the general debate over the recognition of samesex marriage. With respect to this more specific and technical issue, one might imagine a forum outside Vermont taking several different approaches to a Vermont civil union. The other forum might identify civil union with marriage and treat it the same way it would treat a fullfledged putative same-sex marriage, which is to say treat it as either a valid or an invalid marriage depending on considerations of choice of law doctrine, statutory law, and constitutional law. Or it might reject the identity between marriage and civil union, which would in turn suggest several possibilities. The foreign forum might try to enforce civil union as best it could by assimilating it to one or more of its own legal institutions. Thus, for example, one might imagine a state treating the parties to a Vermont civil union as entitled, not to the same rights and obligations as a married couple, which they would be in Vermont, but to the benefits of the forum's own, more limited, domestic partnership statute. Or the forum might try to enforce the legal incidents of civil union, one by one, as best it could consistent with its own private law, such as the law of contracts or fiduciary responsibility. Or, to the contrary, the forum might conclude that the notion of a civil union is just too unfamiliar to its own legal vocabulary to enforce. Or, finally, a forum outside Vermont might avoid the issue by deciding that civil unions, unlike marriages, create—in the parlance of choice of law—purely 'local' rather than 'transitory' or portable legal rights. In this account, a civil union would be an administrative category, not a 'status' in the deepest and most historically resonant meaning of the term.

'State Common-Law Choice-of-Law Doctrine and Same-Sex "Marriage": How will States Enforce the Public Policy Exception?', (1998) 32 *Creighton Law Review* 29.

[33] The federal Defense of Marriage Act, Pub. L. No. 104–99, 110 Stat. 2419 (1996), purports both to limit recognition of same-sex marriages for purposes of federal law and to authorize states to refuse to recognize such marriages solemnized in other states. Its operative provisions are codified at 1 U.S.C. §7 ('In determining the meaning of any Act of Congress, or of any ruling, regulation, or interpretation of the various administrative bureaus and agencies of the United States, the word "marriage" means only a legal union between one man and one woman as husband and wife, and the word "spouse" refers only to a person of the opposite sex who is a husband or a wife') and 28 U.S.C. §1738C (1996) ('No State, territory, or possession of the United States, or Indian tribe, shall be required to give effect to any public act, record, or judicial proceeding of any other State, territory, possession, or tribe respecting a relationship between persons of the same sex that is treated as a marriage under the laws of such other State, territory, possession, or tribe, or a right or claim arising from such relationship').

[34] For a state-by-state report, see the Lambda Legal Defense and Education Fund AntiMarriage Legislation Map, <http://www.lambdalegal.org/cgibin/pages/states/antimarriagemap>.

To put the matter simply, looking to the extraterritorial consequences of civil union to obtain a deeper understanding of its legal character is, at least partly, putting the matter backwards. A forum outside of Vermont trying to make sense of the extraterritorial consequences of Vermont civil unions will, to some degree, have to ask itself exactly the same question that we have been asking: is the distinction between civil union and marriage real or illusory? Nevertheless, this discussion has been useful in emphasizing that the relationship of civil union to marriage is not merely an abstract issue, but has likely operational consequences. It has also suggested some deeper puzzles. Why, for example, do we assume that conventional heterosexual marriage creates transitory, and not merely local, legal rights? That is to say, what makes conventional heterosexual marriage a portable 'status' to which different jurisdictions attach different specific legal incidents, rather than an administrative regime peculiar to any given jurisdiction?

The discussion so far has reached no definitive conclusion. Every path it has taken seems to return to the original, elementary, question: Is there a genuine difference between marriage and civil union? Nevertheless, one thing is becoming clear. All the considerations addressed so far—including the religious or symbolic character of marriage, its place in accounts of natural law and fundamental right, and its aspiration to universal recognition as a portable status—are, in a deep sense, of a piece. They suggest that, *if* there is an extra ingredient that separates marriage from potential marriagelike institutions, that ingredient does not merely transcend the positive legal incidents of marriage. It also transcends, in very specific ways, the very boundaries of any particular legal system seeking to fashion a law of marriage. Indeed, that ingredient might inhere, very precisely, in the threads that connect legal systems one to another.

Holy Union

For a legal pluralist, the notion of a 'legal system' embraces both the laws of nation-states and their subdivisions and other normative systems, including the discourse of religious law.[35] I want, therefore, to turn now to the recent decision of the Permanent Judicial Commission of the Presbyterian Church, USA, in an adjudication captioned *Benton* v. *Presbytery of Hudson River*,[36] which, as noted earlier, that Commission released almost exactly one month after the Vermont legislature enacted its civil union statute.

The *Hudson River* decision arose out of the claim by several

---

[35] See generally Perry Dane, 'Maps of Sovereignty: A Meditation', (1991)12 *Cardozo Law Review* 959.
[36] See n. 3 above.

Presbyterian congregations and individuals that the Hudson River Presbytery, one of the Church's regional divisions, had 'committed an irregularity' by adopting a motion affirming 'the freedom of any session to allow its ministers to perform ceremonies of holy union (within or outside the confines of the church sanctuary) between persons of the same gender, reflecting our understanding at this time that these ceremonies do not constitute marriage as defined in the Book of Order'.[37] The Judicial Commission reaffirmed the Church's view that marriage is limited to the union of a man and a woman, but also dismissed the complaint against the Hudson River Presbytery. It held that 'some same-sex ceremonies could be the equivalent of a marriage ceremony, and therefore would contravene the *Book of Order*, and some might not'.[38] A service of 'holy union', celebrating the committed relationship of a samesex couple, was not a marriage, and would be allowed, so long as the appropriate theological and liturgical distinctions were maintained.[39]

The parallels between this text of the Presbyterian Church and the texts of Vermont are striking, particularly in how both explicitly try to transcend the simple choice of embracing same-sex marriage or rejecting any formal recognition of same-sex couples.[40] But about the question that has perplexed this paper so far—the difference between marriage and other forms of same-sex union—the language of the Presbyterian Permanent Judicial Commission is actually much clearer than that of either the Supreme Court or legislature or Vermont. Indeed, the Commission's account of the matter might illuminate, if sketchily, what is going on in Vermont.

According to the Permanent Judicial Commission, the 'distinction

---

[37] *Hudson River*, 12.170.   [38] Ibid., 12.191.

[39] The Judicial Commission's decision in the *Hudson River* adjudication did not necessarily conclude the issue among Presbyterians. During its 212th General Assembly, held from 24 June to 1 July 2000, the Church considered a resolution that would amend its Book of Order to include the following language: 'Christian marriage between a man and a woman is the only form of personal union sanctioned by the church. Special unions between persons of the same gender or others wishing to live together outside of wedlock, but in a physical union, shall not be sanctioned, encouraged, or condoned in the church. Ministers or other approved persons in the PC(USA) shall not perform such ceremonies and sessions shall not permit such ceremonies to take place on church property.' See <http://horeb.pcusa.org/ga212/overtures/ovt0054.htm>.

[40] For example, compare *Baker*, 744 A.2d, at 886 ('Although plaintiffs sought injunctive and declaratory relief designed to secure a marriage license, their claims and arguments here have focused primarily upon the consequences of official exclusion from the statutory benefits, protections, and security incident to marriage under Vermont law. While some future case may attempt to establish that—notwithstanding equal benefits and protections under Vermont law—the denial of a marriage license operates per se to deny constitutionally-protected rights, that is not the claim we address today') with *Hudson River*, 12.191 ('Both parties erred in applying the Authoritative Interpretation categorically and without distinction. Said Authoritative Interpretation clearly assumes that some same-sex ceremonies could be the equivalent of a marriage ceremony, and therefore, would contravene the Book of Order, and some might not').

between a permissible same-sex ceremony and a marriage ceremony is that the latter confers a new status whereas the former blesses an exiting relationship'.[41] To understand this distinction, consider the following analogy.

My daughter is now 11 years old. Some time after her twelfth birthday she will participate in a service that many of our friends and family will probably refer to as her 'bat mitzvah'. In serious Jewish usage, however, the term 'bar' or 'bat mitzvah' is not, strictly speaking, a noun referring to an event, as in 'I had a bar mitzvah'. Even less is it a verb, as in 'I was bar mitzvahed'. Rather, the term refers to the status of an individual who has reached the age of Jewish religious adulthood, with the rights and obligations that attach thereto. Becoming a 'bar' or 'bat mitzvah' does not require a service, or a ceremony. It happens automatically when a boy turns 13 or a girl turns 12. The event we often call a 'bar' or 'bat mitzvah' celebrates that change in status, and gives the new Jewish adult an opportunity to perform ritual acts for which he or she would previously have been too young. But it does not confer a new status.

The Presbyterian ceremony of holy union seems to serve a similar function. In the words of the Judicial Commission, it 'celebrates a loving, caring, and committed relationship'.[42] But it is not, theologically, a speech act; it does not change the religious status of the parties.

This account of a Presbyterian holy union does not transfer directly to explaining Vermont's idea of civil union. A civil union does more than celebrate a relationship; it confers a new set of rights and obligations. Nevertheless, the notions resonate. Marriage under Vermont law creates a new status, to which the law then appends a comprehensive set of legal predicates. Civil union, on the other hand, if it really is distinct from marriage, confers those legal predicates in themselves. Here, by the way, is another explanation for the statute's use of the term 'certified' rather than 'solemnized' to describe entry into a civil union. The term 'certified' might not imply, as I earlier suggested, a secular rather than spiritual act. After all, civil unions can be 'certified' by a religious official. Rather, the term might reflect an understanding that a civil union authoritatively identifies—certifies—a pair of persons entitled to the same benefits as a married couple, but does not, in itself, fundamentally change their status.

The difficulty in this comparison between holy union and civil union, of course, is the same one that we have been facing all along. A theological system can assert that there is a distinct metaphysical quality to the marriage bond. But what, if anything, does it mean for a secular legal system to assert the same thing? And, in the United States in particular, can a government even claim to impart metaphysical meaning to a relationship?

The Presbyterian decision on the permissibility of ceremonies of holy

---

[41] *Hudson River*, 12.191.   [42] Ibid., 12.193.

union is, as noted, refreshingly clear in one important respect. But it contains its own riddles. In particular, note the following passage regarding the prerequisites for a legitimate holy union ceremony:

ministers and sessions should take special care to avoid any confusion of such services with services of Christian marriage. Ministers should not appropriate specific liturgical forms from services of Christian marriage or services recognizing civil marriage in the conduct of such ceremonies. They should also instruct same-sex couples that the service to be conducted does not constitute a marriage ceremony and should not be held out as such.[43]

The intriguing phrase here is that proscribing the use of liturgical forms 'recognizing civil marriage'. In the Presbyterian Church's liturgical vocabulary, a 'service recognizing civil marriage' is a ceremony in which the community of faith blesses the union of a couple that has already had a civil wedding with a judge or other secular official. The 'service recognizing civil marriage' is not itself a marriage ceremony, because the Church recognizes the efficacy of civil marriage, and understands marriage to be a civil contract that is also, for Christians, a covenant before God. In the context of same-sex couples, holding a 'ceremony recognizing civil marriage', in a state that recognized same-sex civil marriage and in which the parties had already entered into such a civil marriage, would impermissibly blur the theological line between marriage and holy union. And in a state that did not recognize same-sex marriage as a civil status, the appropriation of such a liturgy would be either confusing or dishonest.

There is a deeper point lurking here, though. In a state that recognized samesex marriage as a civil status, could a Presbyterian minister conduct a ceremony that was, religiously, merely a 'holy union' and not a covenant of marriage, but which would also be understood to fulfil the state's requirements for the solemnization of a marriage? The answer, one supposes, is no. The Church would view such an effort to bifurcate the religious and civil meanings of marriage as artificial and inconsistent with its own view of what marriage is.

For Presbyterian churches and ministers in Vermont, the problem gets more complicated, however. Could a minister in Vermont, consistent with the decision of the Permanent Judicial Commission, conduct a ceremony that both certified a civil union (from the state's point of view) and celebrated a holy union (from the Church's point of view). The answer, I am told, would probably be no, but might depend on whether a civil union could fairly be characterized as merely a civil contract, as distinct from something like a marriage. So we are back to the question that has plagued us all along. The Church, in this sense, is in the same position as a foreign judicial forum. But even if the Church did conclude that civil unions were

[43] Ibid., 12.192.

not marriages, and could be certified as part of the celebration of a holy union, the effect would be interesting. For, if holy unions are meant to grant symbolic recognition to an existing relationship, but without a change of status, and civil unions are meant to grant a set of legal entitlements, but without the symbolism of marriage, then what, precisely, is produced when these two innovations, each born of compromise, are merged?

The Encounter of the Civil and the Holy

This last question finally returns the discussion to its ostensible topic: the encounter of the civil and religious meanings of marriage. Of course, that topic has been lurking here all along, and the extended discussion of civil union and holy union has only been a way to cast it in relief. We have seen in that discussion how Church and State look over their shoulders, each at the other. But the evolving formulations of fledgling institutions such as civil union and holy union, though they are compromises born of the current debate, also suggest that it might have been possible, under different historical and cultural circumstances, to have kept the meanings of civil marriage and religious marriage separate and distinct all along. Indeed, they pose the puzzle of why civil and religious marriage should have anything to do with each other at all.

Consider again the bar or bat mitzvah. When my daughter becomes a bat mitzvah at the age of 12, she will under Jewish law have the rights and responsibilities of an adult. Yet the state in which we live will not then treat her as having reached her majority, nor would she expect it to. And even though Jewish law in principle treats a 12-year-old girl as competent to marry and contract and the like, the civil state will not punish my daughter for masquerading as an adult; it knows that, in practice, the different religious and secular meanings of adulthood will not conflict or confuse. Conversely, we would not consider postponing treating our daughter as a bat mitzvah until she reaches the age of majority under secular law. Simply put, the secular and religious accounts of minority and majority, in today's culture, neither interact nor compete.

Marriage is a different story, however. Historians have documented how, in Western Christendom, marriage—once conceptualized in largely worldly terms—was increasingly claimed by the Church as a sacrament, and then, hundreds of years later, reclaimed by modern secular states as part of their regulation of family, property, and sexuality.[44] The competition over control over the institution of marriage was played out not only in the majority culture, but also between the state and minority religious

---

[44] See e.g, John Witte Jr., *From Sacrament to Contract: Marriage, Religion, and Law in the Western Tradition* (Louisville, Ky., 1997); Mary Ann Glendon, *State, Law and Family: Family Law in Transition in the United States and Western Europe* (Amsterdam, 1977).

communities. Thus, for example, when Napoleon, pondering the legal emancipation of the Jews of France, convened an Assembly of Jewish Notables in 1806, many of the questions put to the Assembly—to which it carefully drafted obsequious replies—involved Jewish attitudes to polygamy, civil divorce, and mixed marriage.[45]

This paper is not a historical study. But today the complex play of divergence and convergence, competition and recognition, between the religious and secular meanings of marriage, continues to be apparent. And I want to spend some pages surveying aspects of these interactions, from the view of both State and Church. Among nation-states on the contemporary scene, some, including those influenced by historical anticlericalism such as France and Mexico, come as close as they can to separating the religious and secular meanings of marriage. Other nations, including those such as Israel influenced by the millet system of the Ottoman empire, largely leave questions of marriage and divorce directly to the religious authorities of the various religious communities in the State. For my purposes, however, I am most interested in nations such as the United States where the dynamic interaction of the two realms is most directly, if complexly, acknowledged by the State.[46]

Every state in the United States recognizes that civilly effective ceremonies of marriage can be conducted, not only by civil functionaries, but also by members of the clergy. It is possible, to be sure, to read this authority as a mere delegation of secular authority, grounded in mere convenience, but having no deeper meaning. But it is not quite that simple. For example, while state law typically prescribes certain types of formality before religious ceremonies will be recognized as having civil effect, many states explicitly accommodate those faiths, such as the Society of Friends (Quakers), Mennonites, Baha'i, and to some extent Jews, whose religious practices don't always fit the standard model.[47] Moreover, in many states, if a couple goes through a religious marriage ceremony without complying with the formalities required by secular law, they have committed an offence, but their marriage is nevertheless recognized as valid.

---

[45] See generally Paula E. Hyman, *The Jews of Modern France* (Berkeley, 1998), 41–4; Paul R. Mendes-Flohr and Jehuda Reinharz (eds.), *The Jew in the Modern World: A Documentary History* (New York, 1980), 116–21.

[46] See generally Carol Weisbrod, 'Family, Church and State: An Essay on Constitutionalism and Religious Authority', (1987–8) 26 *Journal of Fam. Law* 741. Cf. Symposium, *The Intersecting Institutions of Marriage*, 4 *Tex. Wesleyan L. Rev.* 143 (1998). Some of my observations in this subsection are drawn from a paper titled 'The Varieties of Religious Autonomy' that I delivered at the Second European/American Conference on Religious Liberty at the University of Trier, Germany, and which is due to be published in the proceedings of that conference.

[47] See e.g. Ala. Code, §30–1–7(c); Ark. Stat. Ann., §9–11–213(b); Fla. Stat., §741.07(2); Maine Rev. Stat., §658; Mich. Stat. Ann., §25.13; Minn. Stat., §517.18; Nev. Rev. Stat., §122.150; N.H. Rev. Stat., §457:37; N.Y. C.L.S. Dom. Rel. §12; N.C. Gen. Stat., §51–1; 43 Okl. St., §7(D); R.I. Gen. Laws, §15–3–6; Tenn. Code Ann., §36–3–301(b).

At least at the edges, this recognition of the inherent jurisdiction of religious communities over marriage is not merely procedural but substantive as well. In Rhode Island, for example, Jewish uncles and nieces may marry, as allowed by Jewish law, even though such marriages are ordinarily proscribed.[48] More interesting is a well-known case in New York in which the state's highest court upheld the validity of a marriage celebrated in Rhode Island between an uncle and his half-niece who were domiciled in New York. The Court concluded that the marriage 'solemnized, as it was, in accord with the ritual of the Jewish faith in a State whose legislative body has declared such a marriage to be "good and valid in law", was not offensive to the public sense of morality to a degree regarded generally with abhorrence and thus was not within the inhibitions of natural law'.[49] Years later the same Court, in a purely domestic case, faced another uncle and his half-niece who were married in a Jewish ceremony.[50] The Court held that the marriage itself was incestuous and void under New York law. But it also held that the couple's antenuptial agreement—which would generally be held unenforceable in the absence of a valid marriage— remained binding.

In the regulation of divorce, jurisdictions in the United States and Canada have tried to avoid the dilemma that arises when a Jewish couple goes through a civil divorce, but one party refuses to participate in the ritual of Jewish divorce, without which an observant Jew will not feel free to remarry. These jurisdictions, in at least some cases, make the willingness to participate in a Jewish religious divorce a prerequisite to obtaining a civil divorce,[51] or treat an unwillingness to participate in a Jewish religious divorce as relevant to the division of marital property.[52]

The point of these examples is not that secular law will always respect religious law, but only that it cognizes it as a genuine normative discourse, coexisting with that of the State and worthy of attention. Indeed, even more interesting in some ways than these examples of state deference to religious law are instances in which the state recognizes, and integrates, the religious nomos for the sake of penalizing those who participate in it.

Consider, for example, the prosecution of Mormon polygamy in the nineteenth century. When Mormons entered into 'plural' marriages in purely religious ceremonies, without (particularly in the later years of the institution) necessarily claiming the civil legal incidents of marriage, the federal government nevertheless prosecuted them for bigamy, treating their religious rites as sufficiently real, in secular terms, to constitute a crime.[53]

---

48 R.I. Gen. Laws, §15–1–4.
49 *In re May's Estate*, 305 N.Y. 486, 114 N.E.2d 4 (1953).
50 *In re Simms*, 26 N.Y.2d 163, 257 N.E.2d 627 (1970).
51 See e.g, NY CLS Dom. Rel., §253(3).
52 See e.g. NY CLS Dom. Rel., §236(B)(5)(h).
53 See *Reynolds v. United States*, 98 U.S. 145, 166–7 (1879).

That is to say, the Mormons were prosecuted not merely for engaging in a religious rite, but for participating in a ceremony to which the government accorded genuine, *though negative*, secular significance. Thus, while the civil state would not imagine prosecuting my daughter for masquerading as an adult after she marks reaching the age of bat mitzvah, it took as unproblematic the prosecution of polygamous Mormons for masquerading as married.

A more recent case from Georgia both echoes these prosecutions of Mormon plural marriage and reflects the dark undercurrent of the contemporary debate over same-sex marriage. The AttorneyGeneral of Georgia informed Robin Shaha, a young woman lawyer, that he was withdrawing his offer of employment to her because she had participated in a same-sex religious wedding ceremony. He argued that taking her on would conflict with Georgia's opposition to same-sex marriage and his office's enforcement of the State's sodomy statutes. Shaha sued in federal court, arguing in part that her wedding ceremony was a purely religious act, and that she never held herself out to be married in a civil sense and even disavowed any secular legal rights as a result of her marriage. The court's majority disagreed, however. Though Shaha's religious marriage was not recognized as such by secular law, it was enough of a marriage in civil and public contemplation that it justified the Attorney-General's concern.[54]

As I have been emphasizing, I am not arguing that civil cognizance of religious marriage, or the religious meaning of marriage, is automatic or uncomplicated. I am only making the weaker, but still important, claim that religious categories are visible, and meaningful, to the secular gaze. The same can be said when we look at how religious communities understand the meaning of civil marriage, or the civil meaning of marriage.

Just as various countries respect the religious aspect of marriage to different degrees, and in different ways, various religious traditions respect the civil aspect of marriage to different degrees, and in different ways. Most Protestants, for example, as illustrated in the Presbyterian doctrine noted earlier, mainly treat marriage and its legal incidents, including procedures for dissolution, as subject to the civil authority, even though marriage also has religious significance. More interesting, however, is the view of, say, the Roman Catholic Church, which has notably retained a strong jurisdictional claim over the character and significance of marriage.

The current formulation of the Catholic Church's Code of Canon Law provides that

The marriage covenant, by which a man and a woman establish between themselves a partnership of their whole life, and which of its very nature is ordered to the well-being of the spouses and to the procreation and upbringing of children,

---

[54] *Shaha v. Bowers*, 114 F.3d 1097 (11th Cir. 1997) *cert. denied*, 118 S.Ct. 693 (1998).

has, between the baptised, been raised by Christ the Lord to the dignity of a sacrament.[55]

The essential properties of marriage are unity and indissolubility; in Christian marriage they acquire a distinctive firmness by reason of the sacrament.[56]

In the Church's view, these canons apply to all marriages, inside and outside the Church, whether among Catholics, other Christians, and even non-Christians. In that sense, the Church claims a universal jurisdiction. At the same time the Church recognizes a role for civil authority, though to different degrees depending on the identity of the parties. Marriages contracted by unbaptized persons are not subject to the direct juridical authority of the Church. 'Hence the civil authorities have a right to make reasonable regulations, not contrary to the divine law, establishing impediments to these marriages and determining the formalities to be observed in entering them.'[57] Even for baptized non-Catholics, among whom marriage is a sacrament whether or not they acknowledge it to be one, the Church leaves to others regulation of the 'form of marriage'.[58]

The consequence of the Church's recognition of authority outside itself, however, combined with its fundamental claim to define the nature of marriage itself, produces a result that might, to an outsider, seem at first surprising. If two non-Christians marry in a civil ceremony, and then divorce in a secular court, that does not in itself terminate the marriage in the eyes of the Church. Thus, if one member of that couple wants to marry a Catholic under the auspices of the Church, he or she will have to go through the Church's processes for adjudicating the original marriage a nullity according to the Church's own understanding.[59] Indeed, a major portion of the docket of the Church's tribunals is concerned with the evaluation of marriages that were originally contracted by parties who at the time of their marriage had no connection to the Church.

For Catholics, the situation is more complicated. As to Catholics, the Church does claim direct juridical authority over the form and procedure, as well as the substance, of marriage. Thus, at one time, Catholics who married outside the auspices of the Church were subject to automatic excommunication. And while this is no longer true, the Church still considers such marriages profoundly defective, even invalid.

Even for Catholics who marry in a purely civil ceremony, however, such a civil marriage is not meaningless in the eyes of the Church. It will not, for example, simply be ignored if the parties divorce and one wants to remarry in the Church.[60] Pope John Paul II wrote in a 1981 apostolic

---

[55] Canon 1055(1).   [56] Canon 1056.

[57] 9 *New Catholic Encyclopedia* 281.   [58] Ibid.

[59] In rare cases, the Holy See can also exercise an extraordinary power to dissolve such marriages.

[60] See James A. Coriden, 'Not Null and Void, but Invalid', *New Theology Review*, 12 (Feb. 1999), 67, 68 ('invalid marriages can cause the existence of the impediment of prior

letter that such couples are not 'people living together without any bond at all' because 'there is at least a certain commitment to a properly defined and probably stable state of life'.[61] As one scholar of Church law explains, 'The Pope recognized that these Catholics who are married outside the Church are married, even though the Church judges their marriage to be invalid for lack of canonical form. In other words, there is a distinction between a marriage which is invalid and no marriage at all, a nullity.'[62] A civil marriage is 'juridically inefficacious'.[63] But it is 'not nonexistent, and it represents much more than concubinage or cohabitation'.[64] The upshot of all this is that the Catholic Church's view of civil marriage in many respects mirrors the view of most secular legal systems to marriages conducted outside their auspices. Thus, the less direct the connection between the Church and the parties to a marriage, the more easily it will recognize the right of a 'foreign' authority to govern aspects of the marriage. Nevertheless, a 'foreign' marriage is still a real marriage, not an alien or unfamiliar institution, and when such a marriage comes into the Church's legal purview, the Church will draw its own legal consequences from that reality. The Church, much like a secular state, most strictly enforces the full sweep of its own norms against parties with whom it has the deepest connection from the start. But, again much like a civil state, it will, even in those instances, admit that when parties are 'married' in a manner contrary to its own norms and jurisdiction, it must hesitate before treating that 'marriage' as entirely meaningless.

Just as important as the juridical interpenetration of the religious and secular meanings of marriage is the influence that each realm has on the other's attitudinal and cultural imagination. Beyond a doubt, the religious traditions of marriage have influenced the secular state's account of the institution, and that influence continues, however elliptically coded or deeply submerged. Just as striking, however, has been the flow of influence in the other direction. Thus, American Catholics, having in large measure internalized the secular acceptance of divorce, have lost much of their confidence in the formal Catholic doctrine of indissolubility. The result, which the Catholic hierarchy laments but also, to some extent, facilitates, has been the development of a 'culture of annulment', in which a remedy once thought extraordinary has become the Church's way of reducing the

---

bond. . . . Even though they were not canonically valid, they were marriages; they were not simply nullities'). The complex status of civil marriages entered into by Catholics does produce the result, less ironic than it seems, that Catholics who marry in a civil ceremony have, at least in theory, a stronger argument for annulment by a Catholic tribunal than nonCatholics who marry in a civil ceremony.

[61] *Familiaris consortio*, 15 Dec. 1981, para. 82, quoted in Coriden, 'Not Null and Void', 68.

[62] Coriden, 'Not Null and Void', 68.   [63] Ibid.   [64] Ibid.

gap between formal doctrine and lived reality.[65] I do not mean to suggest that the Catholic view of the indissolubility of marriage must, either normatively or descriptively, surrender to the larger cultural consensus recognizing that marriages do dissolve. But it is part of the dynamic of encounter that the Church's view will not just stand in majestic isolation, but will find itself in dialogue with larger, contradictory, trends.

Existential Encounter and the Two Faces of Marriage

The complex interplay of the religious and secular realms of marriage is largely the product, as I have already suggested, of a long, specific and contingent, history of both competition and cooperation between the institutions of Church and State. But it is also the consequence, and remains so, of the dynamic of legal pluralism itself. As I have written elsewhere, the impulse to appreciating legal pluralism arises, not merely out of theoretical commitments, but out of a process of existential encounter, as each normative system asks itself precisely what is going on outside the reach of its most solipsistic concerns.[66]

Marriage, in both secular and religious traditions, has been regarded as vitally important because it defined the norms of acceptable sexual bonding, the boundaries of family, and the allocation of material and symbolic resources. So a secular state faced with marriage in another secular state, or by a religious marriage, must ask itself what is going on in that other system of norms out there. It must ask itself, 'Is what those folks call marriage merely playacting, of no juridical consequence? Is their relationship lawless? Are they merely cohabiting? Are their children illegitimate? And even if we disapprove of what they call a marriage, can we imagine that nothing whatsoever is going on?' And, similarly, a religious tradition faced with marriage in another religious tradition, or by a secular marriage, must ask itself exactly the same questions. The answers in both cases will be complex and varied. Each party to this existential encounter of legal and normative systems might defer to, or incorporate, or be influenced by, or reject and punish, or some combination of all these, the meanings articulated by the other parties. But it will be unlikely to ignore them. Hence, for example, the acknowledgement by the state of New York that a marriage consistent with Jewish law will not be a nullity for all purposes. And hence the acknowledgement by the canon law that civil marriage between Catholics, however defective and improper, is not simply cohabitation.

---

[65] This development actually has a doctrinal, and not merely sociological, explanation in Catholic practice: to the extent that the surrounding culture has influenced individual Catholics not to appreciate fully the sacramental, indissoluble, character of the bond into which they are entering, that in itself can be a factor in granting a declaration of nullity.

[66] See Dane, *Maps of Sovereignty*.

The consequence of the juridical and cultural interaction between civil and religious meanings of marriage, and between civil and religious marriage, is that marriage, in both realms, has two faces. In one respect, it is an institution governed by very precise, often technical, requirements and consequences. At the same time, though, it is an institution that participates in a larger legal and cultural project—an ongoing conversation about ends and means. These two faces coexist. Neither face should be reduced to the other, or deemed irrelevant.

It would still be possible, I suppose, to sever religious and secular marriage. In such a dispensation the two institutions would stand in a relation of mere homonymy, understood to be incommensurate and invisible to each other. Indeed, there might come a time when the prevailing religious and secular understandings of the meaning, prerequisites, and consequences of marriage diverge so radically that such a break would make sense. For the time being, however, two sets of considerations make that unlikely and probably undesirable. The first consideration is practical, and obvious. The second consideration is the imperative of existential encounter itself, an imperative that can be resisted, but cannot simply be willed or legislated away. Here, I suggest, is the key to the puzzle of the Vermont civil union. If there is an increment of meaning that distinguishes civil union from marriage, it is in the imperative of encounter. The Vermont court and legislature, it seems to me, recognize that the state's law of marriage participates in a complex, pluralistic, web of meaning and juridical consequence, cognizing and being cognized by other laws of marriage. Some of those other laws of marriage belong, like Vermont's, to 'secular' legal systems, thus raising all the questions of interjurisdictional recognition that have recently perplexed scholars and legislators.[67] But what gives this web of meaning particular resonance, and import, is that it also involves religious and quasi-religious normative realms. And that, it seems to me, is the key. In creating civil union as something separate from marriage, Vermont was trying to opt out of that larger legal and cultural conversation, a conversation born of the coexistence and interpenetration of normative systems that have long been historically and existentially enmeshed with each other. It was trying, as much as it could while still complying with the constitutional requirement of 'common benefit', to avoid either drawing meaning from that conversation or projecting meaning into it.[68] To be sure, Vermont could not entirely disentangle itself from the larger conversation; simply by legislating on questions relating to the sexual bond and the legal construction of homosexual relations, it was

---

[67] See nn. 30–2 above and accompanying text.
[68] The Presbyterian effort to distinguish 'holy union' from marriage seems in this respect similar to Vermont's effort to distinguish 'civil union' from marriage. The Presbyterians, however, are also emphasizing an internal theological distinction that, as I noted earlier, is less clearly available to Vermont.

saying something about the assumptions underlying most Western laws of marriage. But the effort to opt out *as much as possible* was, right or wrong, at least coherent, neither empty nor hopelessly obscure.

Seen in this light, the various iterations of the problem that I discussed earlier appear now as aspects of this most basic effort to distinguish between marriage and civil union. Thus, Vermont's claim that, in creating civil union alongside marriage, it is bypassing the 'spiritual' or 'symbolic' meanings of marriage, and attuning itself to the sensitivities of 'community and cultural institutions', is jurisprudentially meaningful. Moreover, it is not a violation of the establishment clause, but an effort to speak to the facts of a pluralistically understood normative world.

Consider also the earlier discussions of marriage in the discourse of natural law and fundamental constitutional right. The natural law aspect of marriage can be understood, at least in part, anthropologically, as a crosscultural statement about the universality of something like the marriage relation in all human societies. And the constitutional right to marry, as articulated by the United States Supreme Court, can be understood as a guarantee that positive law will allow access to the larger, transjurisdictional, legal and cultural project of marriage.

Finally, my observations about the difficulties that Vermont civil union might face in being recognized by other states now seems, in the light of the discussion here, only one piece of the larger dynamic by which Vermont is seeking—to an ambiguous degree and with uncertain consequences—to opt out of the legal and cultural project by which jurisdictions, both secular and religious, try to understand each other's claims regarding the nature, incidents, and consequences of marriage.

Epilogues

Two questions remain. The first is whether, assuming the possibility that Vermont could genuinely distinguish civil union from marriage, it has succeeded in doing so. The second is whether it should have felt the need to try.

Regarding the first question, the answer must necessarily remain uncertain. To be sure, it now appears possible, in principle, to distinguish between civil union and marriage. But if the increment of meaning that might distinguish marriage from civil union concerns the place of marriage in an interjurisdictional encounter, then Vermont can only provisionally determine the terms of that encounter. Whether Vermont is successful in crafting a form of legal entitlement with the same legal incidents as marriage, but genuinely different from marriage, will depend in part on whether other jurisdictions—including both other states and the Presbyterian Church—understand the distinction, accept it, and draw their own appropriate conclusions.

The second, normative, question is beyond the scope of this paper. Suffice it to say that nothing in my argument here *required* Vermont to close the possibility of marriage to same-sex couples. To say that the norms of marriage of any specific legal order need to be understood as participating in a larger, transjurisdictional, pluralistic, conversation is not to say that those specific norms must be beholden to a larger consensus. The Catholic Church, after all, stands almost alone in its view that marriage is indissoluble, but though this view is under pressure, it remains. Nothing would stop Vermont, if it saw fit, from standing lonely in the view that marriage is a relationship open to samesex couples. The project of defining marriage might be common, but it is neither seamless nor unchanging. Maybe including the right to same-sex union in a law of marriage would break the chain in the larger legal and cultural conversation about marriage, so that such a radically revised law of marriage would only have a relationship of homonymy to other versions of the institution.[69] But I doubt it.

---

[69] Such, for example, was the classic English view of legal systems that permitted polygamous marriage. Not only did English law refuse to recognize *second* marriages entered into under such regimes, it even refused to recognize *first* marriages, positing that the allowance of polygamy rendered marriage under the foreign system too alien to be recognized, at least for many purposes, as marriage under English law. One classic case is *Hyde v. Hyde and Woodmansee* (1866) L.R. 1 P. & D. 130.

JUDICIAL APPROACHES TO RELIGIOUS DISPUTES

Mark Hill

The attitude of the English legislator to racing is much more akin
to his attitude to religion . . . it is something to be encouraged but not
the business of government.

R. v. *Disciplinary Committee of the Jockey Club, ex parte Aga Khan*
[1993] 1 WLR 909, 932G-H *per* Hoffman J

The debate on Church and State within the United Kingdom in recent
years has largely been limited to the constitutional ramifications of the
disestablishment of the Church of England.[1] However, elsewhere in
Europe and in the United States there is a sophisticated jurisprudence
concerning the treatment of religious organizations. In much of Europe the
law of Church and State is recognized as a discrete academic discipline,
known as *Staatskirchenrecht* in Germany. The purpose of this paper,
however, is not to fill this lacuna but instead, by reference to the litigation
of the last decade, to examine the manner in which the judiciary in
England approaches disputes concerning religious organizations, established and non-established, Christian and non-Christian. This nascent
jurisprudence is of particular interest with the coming into force of the
Human Rights Act 1998[2] whereby, for the first time, freedom of thought,
conscience, and religion[3] became directly justiciable in domestic courts.

Supervision by the Courts

Disputes are not uncommon in religious organizations and may take
different forms. There may be factional disagreement between members or
groups of members; an individual may have a grievance against the organization; or the organization may itself may come into dispute with an organ

[1] Rare, but notable, exceptions to this general rule include D. McClean 'State and Church
in the United Kingdom', in G. Robbers (ed.), *State and Church in the European Union*
(Baden-Baden, 1996); and N. Doe, 'The Citizen, the Believer and the Law in the United
Kingdom: England and Wales', in *European Consortium for Church State Research* (Milan,
1999). See also M. Hill, 'Church Autonomy in the United Kingdom', in G. Robbers (ed.),
Church Autonomy in Europe and America (University of Trier, forthcoming).

[2] The Act came into force in England on 2 Oct. 2000. For a general discussion, see M.
Hill, 'The Impact for the Church of England of the Human Rights Act 1998', (2000) 5 *Ecc.
LJ* 431, and P. Cumper, 'The Protection of Religious Rights under Section 13 of the Human
Rights Act 1998', [2000] *PL* 254.

[3] Art. 9 of the European Convention on Human Rights.

of the State or some public or private authority. Central to these disputes, usually, is the manner in which religious organizations choose to run their affairs. As with non-religious organizations, such as professional bodies and trade associations, judicial supervision of their internal regulation is a matter which lies at the boundary of public and private law and has given rise to some vigorous academic discussion in recent years.[4] The court will only intervene if a 'public law function' is being exercised.[5] This test has evolved into the 'government interest' test, since its first articulation by Simon Brown LJ in *R. v. Chief Rabbi of the United Hebrew Congregations, ex parte Wachmann*,[6] which, as its name suggests, concerned what may be classified as a religious dispute. The judge stated that 'to attract the court's supervisory jurisdiction there must not be merely a public but potentially a governmental interest in the decision making power in question'.[7] Questions of judicial supervision therefore fall to be resolved by posing the hypothetical question, 'but for the regulatory body, would the government regulate?'[8] If the answer is yes, then the court will intervene. Since, as a general rule, there is no governmental interest in the functioning of religious organizations, judicial supervision is rare. This is not the case, however, for the Church of England.

The Problem of Establishment

The general principle that decisions of religious organizations lack the element of government interest necessary for judicial supervision can be of no application to the Church of England by dint of its established status. Historical accident has created at the heart of the English Constitution a Church which is regulated by central government through primary or delegated legislation,[9] whose archbishops and bishops are appointed by Her Majesty on the advice of the prime minister,[10] whose internal affairs are

---

[4] See J. Black, 'Constitutionalising Self-Regulation', (1996) 59 MLR 24.
[5] See, by way of example, *R. v. Panel on Takeovers and Mergers, ex parte Datafin plc* [1987] 1 All ER 564; *Law v. National Greyhound Racing Club* [1983] 3 All ER 300; and *O'Reilly v. Mackman* [1982] 3 All ER 1124.
[6] [1993] 2 All ER 249.
[7] *R. v. Chief Rabbi of the United Hebrew Congregations, ex parte Wachmann* [1993] 2 All ER 249, 254.
[8] The test has been applied in *R. v. Football Association, ex parte Football League* [1993] 2 All ER 833; *R. v. Disciplinary Committee of the Jockey Club, ex parte Aga Khan* [1993] 2 All ER 853. It is criticized, however, in Black, 'Constitutionalising Self-Regulation', 35.
[9] See M. Hill, *Ecclesiastical Law* (London, 1995), 7–9. All Church of England measures require parliamentary approval, which is not always forthcoming. The Ecclesiastical Committee of Parliament has in recent years rejected a draft measure concerning episcopal appointments and caused the General Synod of the Church of England to reconsider provisions in the draft Churchwardens Measure.
[10] See Hill, *Ecclesiastical Law*, 235.

adjudicated in consistory courts, being courts of the realm[11] presided over by ecclesiastical judges about whose appointment the lord chancellor must be consulted.[12] Parish priests in the Church of England are legally obliged to baptize,[13] marry[14] and bury[15] all their parishioners in accordance with the rites of the Church of England regardless of the religious allegiance or practice of the parishioner.

It follows, therefore, that when one is considering the affairs of the Church of England, one is not looking at the constitution, rules, and regulations of a members' club (as with other religious organizations) but with the law of the land.[16] Ecclesiastical law is part of English law. As a subject it sits beside 'easements' in volume xiv of *Halsbury's Laws of England*. The Church of England is a manifestation of the State. Thus, for example, the public element of the Church of England renders its processes liable to judicial review, whereas those of other churches are not.[17] Furthermore, because the Church of England is governed by primary legislation, the challenges over the change of doctrine upon the ordination of women priests were less easily sustainable. An interesting contrast may be made between the *Williamson* litigation[18] and *Varsani and others* v. *Jesani and others*.[19] In the latter, a *cy-près* scheme was approved to divide the assets of a religious organization between two competing factions which had arisen out of an irreconcilable schism. No such indulgence was granted to Mr Williamson, whose contention was that ordination of women amounted to a departure from a historical doctrine of the Church such as to disentitle the continuing Church to some or all of the benefactions given

[11] Ecclesiastical Jurisdiction Measure 1963. For an example of a consistory court applying the Human Rights Act 1998 even before it had come into force, see *Re Durrington Cemetery* [2000] 3 WLR 1322 *per* Hill Ch. This concerned the exhumation of the remains of a Jew who had been buried in part of a municipal cemetery consecrated in accordance with the rites of the Church of England for reburial in a Jewish cemetery under Jewish law.

[12] Ecclesiastical Jurisdiction Measure 1963, s. 2(1A).

[13] Canon B 22.

[14] See Hill, *Ecclesiastical Law*, 305.

[15] A common law right extended to non-parishioners on the electoral roll and also to cremated remains. See the Church of England (Miscellaneous Provisions) Measure 1976, ss. 3 and 6.

[16] See *Attorney-General* v. *Dean and Chapter of Ripon Cathedral* [1945] 1 Ch 239 *per* Uthwatt J, at 245: 'The law is one, but jurisdiction as to its enforcement is divided between the ecclesiastical courts and the temporal courts.'

[17] See M. Hill, 'Judicial Review of Ecclesiastical Courts', in N. Doe, M. Hill, and R. Ombres, *English Canon Law* (Cardiff, 1998), and compare and contrast *R.* v. *Exeter Consistory Court, ex parte Cornish* (1999) 5 Ecc LJ 212 with *R.* v. *Provincial Court of the Church in Wales, ex parte Williams* (1999) 5 Ecc. LJ 217.

[18] Prior to his declaration as a vexatious litigant, the Revd Paul Williamson brought a series of cases against various component parts of the Church of England. The common feature of his actions both at first instance and on appeal was his singular lack of success. See, by way of illustration, *R.* v. *The Archbishops of Canterbury and York, ex parte Williamson* (1994) 1 Mar. (unreported) CA (Bingham MR, Evans and Rose LJJ), repr. in Hill, *Ecclesiastical Law*, 77–81.

[19] [1998] 3 All ER 372 CA (Sir Stephen Brown P, Morritt and Chadwick LJJ).

to it while its former doctrine persisted.[20] Before turning to the wider
question of how the judiciary in England approach religious disputes in
both established and non-established churches, it is helpful to draw upon
the experience of the courts in America.

The American Approach

The United States has no established Church. Indeed, the First Amendment
to the United States Constitution states, 'Congress shall make no law
respecting an establishment of religion or prohibiting the free exercise
thereof.' The Supremacy Clause of the Constitution (Article VI) provides
that all constitutional provisions are superior to all non-constitutional
laws, whether adopted by the federal government or by one of the state
governments. Thus all labour, property, tax, education, and other laws are
subject to constitutional constraints. Accordingly America's courts, including the Supreme Court, have been much occupied (and her lawyers much
enriched) by litigation concerning the constitutionality of the affairs of religious organizations and their relationship with the State.

In adjudications concerning the internal disputes of religious organizations over a good many years, the United States Supreme Court has
considered three approaches, each subtly different from the other. First,
the *departure from doctrine* approach. This course involved considering
which party to the dispute most closely adhered to the doctrinal tenets
held by those who set up the Church. This analysis was ultimately rejected,
as it necessarily involved the courts in detailed analysis of doctrine.[21]
Second came the *deference to polity* approach, whereby the secular courts
deferred to the decision of the recognized source of authority of the religious organization in question. This approach, however, was not without
problems since it too required an examination of the functioning of the
Church where doctrinal issues had a part to play. A third approach, therefore, is that enunciated in what has become a seminal decision,[22] namely
the *neutral principles* approach. To the extent that religious organizations
have framed 'normal' legal documents like deeds, wills, contracts, and
trusts that spell out what is to happen in the case of a dispute, the secular
courts will interpret those documents as they would any private documentation and render a decision accordingly.

The superficial attraction of the neutral principles approach—which
likens any religious organization to a golf club or similar—is not without
its own difficulties. First, it may well be that the lawyers (or non-lawyers)

[20] See *Williamson* v. *Archbishop of Canterbury* (1994) *The Times* 25 Nov. *per* Lightman J,
affirmed (1996) 5 Sept. (unreported) CA.
[21] See *Presbyterian Church in the United States* v. *Mary Elizabeth Blue Hull Memorial
Presbyterian Church* 393 US 440 (1969).
[22] *Jones* v. *Wolf* 443 US 595 (1979).

who drafted the documents concerned did not do so in ways which reflected ecclesiastical realities. Secondly, no documents may have been drafted in the first place. Thirdly, there may be documents and these may have been accurate when written but the doctrines and polity of the religious organization may have shifted over time so that they no longer reflect the realities of life in the religious community.[23]

What has developed in America since the *Jones* case is a refinement of the neutral principles approach identifying secular (i.e. religiously neutral) governing principles which the court considers itself free to apply.

Courts can decide secular legal questions in cases involving some background issues of religious doctrine, so long as they do not intrude into the determination of the doctrinal issues ... In such cases, courts must confine their adjudications to their proper civil sphere by accepting the authority of a recognised religious body in resolving a particular doctrinal question, while, where appropriate, applying neutral principles of law to determine disputed questions which do not implicate religious doctrine ... 'Neutral principles' are wholly secular legal rules whose application to religious parties does not entail theological or doctrinal evaluations.[24]

It may therefore be that the breadth of the autonomy of religious organizations is more restricted that the bald wording of the First Amendment of the Constitution might suggest since the variable yardstick of neutrality may, in certain judicial hands, serve to restrict or curtail neutrality.

The Position in England

Whereas the First Amendment to the US Constitution prohibits Congress from making laws respecting the establishment of a religion,[25] England has done completely the reverse.[26] Accordingly, none of the expressions 'departure from doctrine', 'deference to polity', or 'neutral principles' finds itself articulated in the English cases. Instead one sees a reluctance to interfere. This reluctance is in the nature of a self-denying ordnance—a variable yardstick of neutrality.

[23] A full discussion of this subject may be found in C. Durham, 'The Right to Autonomy in Religious Affairs: A Comparative View', Paper prepared for the Second American/European Conference on Religious Freedom held at Trier, Germany, on 27–30 May 1999, upon which much of this summary is based.

[24] *South Jersey Catholic School Teachers Association* v. *St Teresa of the Infant Jesus Church Elementary School* 290 NJ Super 359, 675 A.2d 1155 (App. Div. 1996), a decision of an intermediate appellate court in New Jersey. See also *Elmora Hebrew Centre Inc* v. *Fishman* 125 NJ 404, 414–15 (1991).

[25] For an interesting discussion on the real effect of the First Amendment with particular reference to institutionalized anti-Semitism, see S. Feldman, *Please don't Wish me a Merry Christmas: A Critical Study of the Separation of Church and State* (New York, 1997), reviewed by M. Hill, (1999) 26/4 *Journal of Law and Society* 561.

[26] Thus the generalization of Simon Brown LJ, quoted above, is not entirely accurate.

As Smith J stated in *Gill v. Davies and others*[27] when entertaining an application to prevent the carrying out of an ordination service which did not have the approval of the diocesan bishop,

[the Defendant] submits that matters which affect the Church of God should not be litigated in this Court. That is an argument which seems to me to have some force and for my part I would be reluctant to interfere with the right of any person's wish to go through a form of Service in accordance with his or her own religious beliefs.[28]

Sir Thomas Bingham, Master of the Rolls (as he then was), had previously stated,

I hope it is unnecessary to say that the merits of this religious controversy [the ordination of women] are a matter on which this court is not entitled to hold any opinion. Just as day by day the courts hear cases touching on political issues, and in doing so do their best to decide the legal question before them without being drawn into any partisan position on those political issues, so here it is plainly the duty of the court to adjudicate on the legal questions raised in argument without taking up any position at all on the fundamental underlying issues.[29]

When considering the question of public policy in *R. v. Chief Rabbi of the United Hebrew Congregations of Great Britain and the Commonwealth, ex parte Wachmann*,[30] Simon Brown LJ stated:

the court is hardly in a position to regulate what is essentially a religious function—the determination whether someone is morally and religiously fit to carry out the spiritual and pastoral duties of his office. The court must inevitably be wary of entering so self-evidently sensitive an area, straying across the well-recognised divide between church and state. One cannot, therefore, escape the conclusion that if judicial review lies here, then one way or another this secular court must inevitably be drawn into adjudicating upon matters intimate to a religious community.[31]

Further, in *R. v. The Provincial Court of the Church in Wales, ex parte Williams*[32] Latham J stated,

the Church in Wales is a body whose legal authority arises from consensual submission to its jurisdiction, with no statutory or (*de facto* or *de jure*) governmental function. It is analogous to other religious bodies which are not established as part of the State. This court has consistently declined to exercise jurisdiction over such bodies.[33]

---

[27] (1998) 5 *Ecc. LJ* 131.   [28] See transcript (unapproved) at 8H–9A.
[29] *R. v. Archbishops of Canterbury and York, ex parte Williamson* (1994) 1 Mar. CA (unreported). The transcript is reproduced in Hill, *Ecclesiastical Law*, 77–81. The extract is at p. 78.
[30] [1992] 1 WLR 1036.   [31] At pp. 1042H–1043A.
[32] (1999) 5 *Ecc. LJ* 217.   [33] See transcript at p. 8.

In an example drawn from outside the Anglican Communion, Morritt LJ in *Versani and others* v. *Jesani and others*[34] stated,

the Attorney General and the court are agnostic in the sense that all religious charities are treated alike irrespective of the nature of the faith they are established to profess.

This statement, however, runs contrary to a widely held opinion that the law of religious charities in England and Wales, whether by accident or design, continues to discriminate against the Roman Catholic Church.[35] All of these examples illustrate that, in the main, religious disputes are not justiciable in the secular courts, since they concern the expression and manifestation of private or collective spiritual beliefs which are not amenable to adjudication by the State.

But establishment brings a degree of special treatment to the Church of England. This is to be seen in challenges to its internal regulation and derives, in the main, from its ability to alter its doctrine and functioning by primary legislation. Thus, even if a court were minded to entertain a challenge founded on a religious dispute, it is precluded from doing so by the doctrine of parliamentary sovereignty. As Morritt LJ stated in *Williamson* v. *The Archbishops of Canterbury and York*,[36] 'The Church of England is and at all material times has been the established church. As such its doctrines and government were and are susceptible to change by the due processes of law.'[37] It may well be that the judiciary is uneasy with the special status afforded the Church of England. An interesting example is *Gill* v. *Davies and others*[38] in which Smith J granted an *ex parte* injunction of very limited duration to prevent the taking place of an ordination service which did not have the sanction of the acting bishop, in order that the matter could be resolved upon the newly appointed diocesan bishop taking up office. While the judge's decision cannot be criticised as a proper exercise of judicial discretion, her reasoning was in one particular highly questionable. Acknowledging that the vicar would be acting in breach of canon law by permitting the ordination service to take place in the church, Smith J declined to injunct him on this basis since he was an adult and intelligent man and it was for him to decide how to behave in accordance with his own conscience. While accepting that the judgment was *ex tempore*, delivered after limited argument when only one party was represented and in circumstances when the status quo was being preserved for three months, the reasoning is highly suspect because of the refusal to

---

[34] [1998] 3 All ER 273 at pp. 280a *per* Morritt LJ.

[35] See Rickett, 'An Anti-Catholic Bias in the Law of Charity?', (1990) *The Conveyancer & Property Lawyer* 34.

[36] (1996) 5 Sept. (unreported) in whose judgment Simon Brown and Phillips LJJ concurred.

[37] See transcript at p. 15C–D.   [38] (1998) 5 *Ecc. LJ* 131, Smith J.

grant a *quia timet* injunction to prevent a breach of the law of England. To the extent that this decision appears to mark a departure from the existing practice relating to the legal treatment of the Church of England, then this part of the reasoning must be regarded as *per incuriam*. The result, however, would be unchanged.

It is also instructive that in *R. v. Ecclesiastical Committee of the Houses of Parliament, ex parte the Church Society*,[39] counsel for the archbishops of Canterbury and York specifically argued that the Divisional Court lacked jurisdiction to entertain an application to declare invalid a measure of the Church of England. Her point, summarized by McCowan LJ, was that if the Court were to accept jurisdiction the courts and not the Church would become the arbiters in doctrinal disputes. Due to the shortage of time (the matter being due to be debated in the House of Commons on the following day) the Court did not resolve the question of jurisdiction but, instead, considered and rejected the merits of the application. One issue which arose in argument was who might determine changes in doctrine. 'I have every confidence', said McCowan LJ, 'that if this task were thrust upon the courts they would find it possible to form a view on what was fundamental, though with very great reluctance, particularly in the area of doctrine.'[40]

This, to a certain extent, is at variance with what was said by Morritt LJ in *Williamson v. Archbishops of Canterbury and York*:[41]

It emerged in the course of argument this morning that Mr Williamson's concern in bringing each of those three applications for leave to apply for judicial review was to obtain by one means or another an order of the court compelling the Archbishops, or other respondents to those applications, to answer his (Mr Williamson's) questions so as to demonstrate to his satisfaction that the ordination of women is authorised by Holy Scripture. That is not a proper function of the court and demonstrates that, not only is Mr Williamson's case unarguable, but that it is also an abuse of process of the court.[42]

On occasions the courts do give special regard to the religious nature of an organization in certain circumstances. The inquiry into the sacking of the organist of Westminster Abbey considered whether in defining the scope of the employee–employer relationship regard should be had to the spiritual nature of the employment. Contrary to the contention of leading counsel for the organist, Lord Jauncey of Tullichettle held that it did. He stated that charging 'fixing' fees for the choir's salaried duties 'neither accorded with the prior practice at the abbey nor with the usual practice in similar ecclesiastical institutions'. Lack of openness and the deriving of

---

[39] (1993) 28 Oct. CA McCowan LJ and Tuckey J (unreported). The judgment is reproduced in Hill, *Ecclesiastical Law*, 72–7.

[40] See the judgment reproduced in Hill, *Ecclesiastical Law*, 76.

[41] (1996) 5 Sept. (unreported) CA.   [42] See transcript at p. 20C–E.

secret profits 'was such as fatally undermined the relationship of trust and confidence which should have subsisted between [the organist] and the abbey'.[43] Equally in the employment field, the nature of a priest's vocation as a servant of Christ has been considered to have been of much importance.[44] In relation to criminal law, the Divisional Court demonstrated a surprising degree of indulgence in entertaining submissions from a clergyman who had been convicted of an offence of criminal damage that he had a defence of lawful excuse in that he was carrying out the instructions of God and acting with God's consent.[45] Less surprisingly, each of the submissions was roundly rejected.

However, no account was taken of the religious dimension in cases such as *Harries and others* v. *Church Commissioners*,[46] where the ethical investment policy of the Church Commissioners was considered as with any other charity with no regard given to the religious element of the organization. Equally, in *Gatherer* v. *Gomez*[47] the matter was resolved on the basis of the pension provisions of Barbados without reference to the religious nature of the priestly ministry involved. In *Brown* v. *Runcie and Habgood*[48] both Hoffmann J at first instance and the Court of Appeal gave detailed consideration to the internal procedural requirements of General Synod in relation to special majority voting, but no particular regard was given to the fact that this was a religious organization. Further, *R.* v. *Ecclesiastical Committee of the Houses of Parliament, ex parte the Church Society*[49] turned on a simple matter of statutory interpretation based upon the plain and ordinary meaning of English words with no special account given to the religious organization concerned.[50] Little regard was given to religious matters in a notorious planning case which went all the way to Strasbourg.[51] The Commission was required to examine the balance achieved in English law between planning regulation and the right to freedom of religion of a Hindu sect.[52]

---

[43] *Neary and another* v. *Dean of Westminster* (1999) 5 Ecc. LJ 303.

[44] *Diocese of Southwark* v. *Coker* [1998] ICR 140 CA. A comparison may usefully be made with *R.* v. *Bishop of Stafford, ex parte Owen* (2000) 14 Aug. (unreported) CA Schiemann, Thorpe, and Rix LJJ.

[45] See *Blake* v. *DPP* [1993] Crim. LR 586. A fuller transcript of the judgment is reproduced in Hill *Ecclesiastical Law*, 13–17 per Otton J.

[46] [1992] 1 WLR 1241, Sir Donald Nicholls V-C. The judgment is reproduced in Hill, *Ecclesiastical Law*, 63–8.

[47] [1992] 1 WLR 727.

[48] (1991) 13 Feb. CA Dillon, Leggatt, and Nolan LJJ (unreported). The judgment is reproduced in Hill, *Ecclesiastical Law*, 68–72. [49] Ibid.

[50] The same approach was adopted in *R.* v. *Archbishops of Canterbury and York, ex parte Williamson* (1994) 1 Mar. Bingham MR, Evans and Rose LJJ (unreported). The judgment is reproduced in Hill, *Ecclesiastical Law*, 77–81.

[51] *International Society for Krishna Consciousness* v. *United Kingdom* (1994) 76-A Dec & Rep 90.

[52] For a full discussion, see S. Poulter, *Ethnicity, Law and Human Rights: The English Experience* (Oxford, 1998), 243–76.

Simon Brown LJ, in dismissing all of five applications before him
brought to the Court of Appeal by the Revd Paul Williamson, stated,
perhaps more out of exasperation than anything else, 'With regard to these
applications as a whole, I express no view whatever on what the Applicant
contends to be the theological heresies arising. I say with confidence,
however, that his submissions to this court were full of legal heresies.'[53]

The Human Rights Act 1998

On 2 October 2000 the Human Rights Act 1998 rendered the provisions
of the European Convention on Human Rights directly applicable in the
domestic courts of England. Article 9 of the Convention, which is entitled
'Freedom of Thought, Conscience and Religion', provides as follows:

(1) Everyone has the right to freedom of thought, conscience and reli-
    gion; this right includes freedom to change his religion or belief and
    freedom, either alone or in community with others and in public or
    private, to manifest his religion or belief, in worship, teaching, prac-
    tice and observance.
(2) Freedom to manifest one's religion or beliefs shall be subject only to
    such limitations as are prescribed by law and are necessary in a
    democratic society in the interests of public safety, for the protec-
    tion of public order, health or morals, or for the protection of the
    rights and freedoms of others.

In responses to concerted lobbying from various religious organizations
within the United Kingdom, a statutory concession—the value of which is
doubtful—was introduced into the Act, section 13 of which now reads

(1) If a court's determination of any question arising under this Act
    might affect the exercise by a religious organisation (itself or its
    members collectively) of the Convention right to freedom of
    thought, conscience and religion, it must have particular regard to
    the importance of that right.
(2) In this section 'court' includes a tribunal.

It remains to be seen how this section, which appears to create a statutory
hierarchy of rights, will, in practice, affect the balancing of freedom of religion against, say, freedom of expression.[54] For example, the provisions of
the Ecclesiastical Courts Jurisdiction Act 1860, pursuant to which Peter
Tatchell was arrested in Canterbury Cathedral on Easter Day 1998 and in
due course prosecuted to conviction, may fall for reconsideration in the
light of Article 10.

[53] *Williamson* v. *Archbishops of Canterbury and York* (1996) 5 Sept. (unreported) CA.
[54] Art. 10 of the Convention.

For what it is worth, the home secretary at the committee stage of the bill said:

The intention is to focus the courts' attention in any proceedings on the view generally held by the Church in question, and on its interest in protecting the integrity of the common faith of its members against attack, whether by outsiders or by individual dissidents. That is a significant protection . . .

If a case is brought against a charity, and the charity can show that what it is doing is to maintain and practise the religious beliefs which it shares with its parent Church, we consider that [section 13] would come into play so as to ensure that due consideration was given to those beliefs . . .[55]

Few believe that section 13 will have any significant effect upon the adjudication of cases concerning religious organizations.[56] It is at best an articulation and codification of the present position, broadly described as judicial deference or neutrality.

Conclusions

In the light of the general observations made in the body of this paper, the following broad conclusions may be ventured.

- As a general rule, the English judiciary is reluctant to enter into a detailed examination of the internal affairs of religious organizations (*Gill, Wachmann, Williamson*).
- When the judiciary is called upon to make such an examination, it applies secular legal principles irrespective of the religious nature of the dispute (*Gatherer, Brown, Cheesman, Varsani, Harries, Blake*).
- In certain circumstances, the judiciary will take into account the religious nature of a dispute (*Neary, Coker*).
- The Church of England 'enjoys' a unique status, being the established church in England and regulated by primary and secondary legislation.
- There is thus a preparedness on the part of the judiciary to enter into the affairs of the Church of England when they would not do so in relation to other religious organizations (*Williamson*, cf. *Varsani*; *Cornish*, cf. *Williams*; *Cheesman*, cf. *Wachmann*).
- Such preparedness, wrongly, may be on the decline (*Gill*).
- The Human Rights Act 1998 places a positive duty on the judiciary to have regard to Article 9 of the European Convention on Human Rights, which provides a right to freedom of thought, conscience, and religion (*Durrington*).

[55] See *Hansard*, HC 20 May 1998, col. 1020.

[56] For a speculative overview, see M. Hill, 'The Impact for the Church of England of the Human Rights Act 1998', (2000) 5 *Ecc. LJ* 431. See also Cumper, 'The Protection of Religious Rights under Section 13 of the Human Rights Act 1998', and *Re Durrington Cemetery* [2000] 3 WLR 1322 *per* Hill Ch.

- Such right will fall to be interpreted in the light of section 13 of the Act, which requires the judiciary to have particular regard to the importance of the importance of the right to freedom of thought, conscience, and religion.
- In all likelihood the effect will be to favour a religious organization collectively rather than an individual member of such church (*Williamson, Church Society, Brown, Williams*).

JUSTIFICATIONS FOR RELIGIOUS AUTONOMY

Norman Doe and Anthony Jeremy

The achievements in contemporary scholarship dealing with the State, religion, and society in the United Kingdom have included, over recent years, not only a renewed vigour in the practical exposition of substantive laws, but also a sharpened, critical analysis of the aims and effects of those laws. These have occurred from the perspectives of both the State (and its laws) and religious organizations (and their laws), and each makes claims to a fundamental right to freedom of religion, as the basis of their dealings one with another. Indeed, the freedom which the State may recognise and protect for both individuals and religious organizations within society, its terms and limits, is always profoundly conditioned, needless to say, by religious laws, the laws of religions, and their institutional manifestations. Yet, one obvious subject which seems to have been neglected in contemporary scholarship is the respective justifications advanced by the State and by religious organizations for the freedom they each claim.

Firstly, therefore, the following aims to identify and classify those secular ideas which the State, through its many institutions, articulates to justify freedom of religion. These ideas surface in very many forms, and an attempt is made to illustrate them with reference to those particular, practical arrangements and decisions appearing in legislative, executive, and judicial settings. Such arrangements seek to effect, on the one hand, the right of individuals to practise religion freely, and the collective autonomy of religious organizations, as well as, on the other hand, limits upon their exercise. Secondly, the following aims to identify and classify those ideas which the major religions—Judaism, Christianity, and Islam—articulate to justify, from their own particular perspectives, their autonomy from the State to practise faith freely. Finally, an attempt is made to relate the two groups of justifications, one with another, in order to identify similarities and differences.

Secular Justifications for Religious Autonomy

From the secular perspective, the regulation and protection of religious freedom in society are understood primarily as the responsibility of, and in the keeping of, the State. The ordinary means which the State employs to express and implement its approach to religion is law. The law of the State defines the freedom of individuals to practise religion, the collective autonomy of religious organizations, and the relationship of religious organizations and their members to the State.[1] The State, through its law, regulates religion in the distribution of entitlements (in the form of liberties, rights, or privileges of religious organizations and their members), and it does so through the imposition of limits on their exercise (in the form of prohibitions, conditions, and duties). The quest for secular justifications of religious freedom, therefore, involves identifying the reasons for the benefits and burdens of the law of the State on religion.[2] Two preliminary points may be made.

Firstly, this section seeks to elucidate and to classify (but not to evaluate) justifications for State law on religion employed in England and Wales: that is, those *practical reasons* which are actually articulated and employed by the governmental institutions of the State, legislative, judicial, and executive, in their decisions on religion. Some reference is also made to *theoretical justifications*, reasons articulated and employed by commentators to justify religious freedom. Generally, practical justifications for the benefit of religious freedom, advantages which the beneficiary receives under the law, are rather more conspicuous than the justifications for the burdens, for others, arising as a result of the benefit legally given. Sometimes practical reasons coincide with or are based on theoretical reasons and vice versa. Both classes of justification may be in the form of large political or moral reasons which legitimize and underlie state law on religion, or else they may take the form of legal reasons used as the basis of or causative of particular decisions and arrangements about religious autonomy and its limits.

Secondly, there is considerable diversity in terms of both the incidence or practice of giving reasons for religious freedom and autonomy, and in the nature of reasons employed. This is due, in part, to the complexities, ambiguities, and, sometimes, contradictions which characterize the general framework of state law on religion in England and Wales.[3] It is a system which discloses a bewildering spectrum of stances: from *identification* of Church and State (surfacing in England as one of the incidents of establishment),[4] to *separation* of State and religion (illustrated by the disestablishment of the

---

[1] *Re South Place Ethical Society* [1980] 1 WLR 1565: for Dillon J the 'two essential attributes of religion are faith and worship; faith in a God and worship of that God'; 'religion is concerned with man's relations with God, and ethics are concerned with man's relations with man'. See T. Macklem, 'Faith as a Secular Value', (2000) 45 *McGill LJ* 1, 10 ff., for the idea that legal definitions of religion are not a fruitful source of ideas about justifications for freedom of religion.

[2] Needless to say, justifications for religious freedom, in the sense of reasons for the terms of state law on religion, are, therefore, relative to the legal system in question. In what follows, however, many of the reasons described have the characteristics of universal justifications, not least in their general congruence with justifications appearing in international instruments on freedom of religion.

[3] See, generally, N. Doe, 'National Identity, the Constitutional Tradition and the Structures of Law on Religion in the United Kingdom', in *Religions in European Union Law*, Proceedings of the European Consortium for Church–State Research (Milan, 1998), 93.

[4] See e.g. N. Doe, *The Legal Framework of the Church of England* (Oxford, 1996), 7 ff.

Church of England in Wales);[5] from the existence of legal *liberties* to practise religion,[6] through positive legal *rights*,[7] to *exemptions* or *privileges*.[8]
Yet, as has been said by the courts, 'the starting point of our domestic law
is that every citizen has a right to do what he likes, unless restrained by the
common law . . . or by statute'.[9]

TOLERANCE AND RESPECT AS JUSTIFICATIONS FOR RELIGIOUS FREEDOM

In the instruments of international law the values of tolerance and respect
command a central position as justifications for religious freedom, itself
associated fundamentally with 'the dignity and equality inherent in all
human beings'; international instruments stress that 'it is essential to
promote understanding, tolerance and respect in matters relating to freedom of religion',[10] intolerance,[11] in the form of discrimination on grounds
of religion, is 'an affront to human dignity'; moreover, 'religion or belief,
for anyone who professes either, is one of the fundamental elements in his
conception of life' and 'freedom of religion or belief should be fully
respected and guaranteed'.[12] Historically, the value of tolerance has played
a prominent role in the practical development of domestic state law on
religion, both explicitly and implicitly,[13] as well as in, needless to say, the
works of political theorists.[14] In the practical sphere of government the

---

[5] However, while the Church of England in Wales was disestablished (in 1920) as a result
of the Welsh Church Act 1914, a number of vestiges of establishment continue (such as the
duty to solemnize the marriages of parishioners and the right to burial) (see T. G. Watkin,
'The Vestiges of Establishment: The Ecclesiastical and Canon Law of the Church in Wales',
(1990) 2 *Ecclesiastical Law Journal* 110.

[6] For the legal liberty of Jehovah's Witnesses to be considered as suitable people to adopt
children, see R. Terrell, 'Religious Considerations in Custody and Adoption', (1979) 9 *Family
Law* 198.

[7] e.g. those of Quakers and Jews to conduct marriages in accordance with their own rites
when also the civil requirements of marriage are satisfied (Marriage Act 1949, ss. 26 and 47).

[8] See e.g. Motor-Cycle Crash Helmets (Religious Exemption) Act 1976.

[9] *AG v. Guardian Newspapers Ltd (No 2)* [1990] 1 AC 109, 178, *per* Donaldson MR;
see also *Malone v. MPC* [1979] Ch 344, 357. Once the Human Rights Act 1998 is fully in
force, by which religious freedom becomes a formal, civil right, it is not unlikely that the
courts in particular will develop their own distinctive jurisprudence about justifications.

[10] United Nations Declaration on the Elimination of All Forms of Intolerance and of
Discrimination Based on Religion or Belief (1981), proclaimed by the General Assembly of
the United Nations on 25 Nov. 1981 (Resolution 36/55); hereafter UN Res. 36/55.

[11] UN Res. 36/55, Art. 2: ' "intolerance and discrimination based on religion or belief"
means any distinction, exclusion, restriction or preference based on religion or belief and
having as its purpose or as its effect nullification or impairment of the recognition, enjoyment
or exercise of human rights and fundamental freedoms on an equal basis'.

[12] Ibid.

[13] For discussion of the Toleration Act 1689 and associated legislation, see C. Hamilton,
Family, Law and Religion (London, 1995), ch. 1.

[14] See e.g. John Locke, 'A Letter concerning Toleration', in *Works of John Locke*, vol. vi
(Aalen, 1963), 3: the principal justification for tolerance, and non-intervention of the State in
matters of religion, is that the State lacks the capacity to compel religious belief. For a discus-

concept of religious toleration surfaces in both judicial decisions,[15] and in government policy, which from time to time claims that proposed legislation 'is based on religious tolerance', which itself is 'an important and vital part of our society';[16] in the promotion of draft legislation reference is commonly made to the idea that the legislation is designed to give 'expression to our own values of tolerance and respect for religion'.[17] The notion of equality appearing in international instruments is echoed occasionally by the courts in the idea of impartiality: the courts refer to the *neutrality* of the State as between religions,[18] though this is treated by some commentators as mythical,[19] and, indeed, some judges consider that 'there may be good reason why groups are treated differently, for instance, out of respect for religious convictions'.[20] Judicial impartiality in matters of religion exists 'for the reason that it has as a court no evidence, no knowledge, no view as to the respective merits of the religious views of various denominations'.[21]

DEFERENCE TO RELIGIOUS LAW AS A JUSTIFICATION FOR RELIGIOUS FREEDOM

The value of respect is developed in the form of deference to religious law. Historically, that the State and religion function in separate realms, the one temporal and the other spiritual, each enjoying their own sovereignties, has supplied a justification for religious freedom.[22] There is some evidence to suggest that the vestiges of this idea linger in contemporary justifications for religious freedom. It is found particularly when institutions of government justify legal arrangements because of their deference to the binding force of religious law, the internal law of religious organizations and communities. Pressure to reconsider the statutory exemptions

---

sion as to whether an intolerant sect has a title to complain if it is not tolerated, and whether a tolerant sect has a right to tolerate intolerant sects, see J. Rawls, *A Theory of Justice* (Oxford, 1972), 217.

[15] For judicial reluctance to defeat religious conditions in trusts on grounds of public policy see e.g. *Clayton* v. *Ramsden* [1943] AC 420; *Blaythwayt* v. *Lord Cawley* [1975] 3 All ER 625.

[16] Report of HC Standing Committee 'F', 3 June 1976, col. 11: this concerned the bill to exempt Sikhs from the wearing of motorcycle crash helmets: see S. Poulter, *Ethnicity, Law and Human Rights* (Oxford, 1998), 295; see also HL Debs. 512, cols. 78–9, 84 (concerning exemption of Sikhs from wearing protective helmets in the construction industry).

[17] HL Debs., 512, cols. 79 (concerning Sikhs and the construction industry); see Poulter, *Ethnicity, Law and Human Rights*, 317.

[18] See e.g. *Neville Estates Ltd* v. *Madden* [1961] 3 All ER 769, 781, *per* Cross J: 'As between different religions the law stands neutral.'

[19] See, generally, A. Bradney, *Religions, Rights and Laws* (Leicester, 1993), 7, 156 ff.

[20] Mackay LC, 'The Role of the Profession in Securing Access to Justice', in *Conference Papers of the Ninth Commonwealth Law Conference* (Auckland, 1990) 59.

[21] *Re Caroll* [1931] 1 KB 317 *per* Scrutton LJ (CA).

[22] See e.g. P. R. Beaumont (ed.), *Christian Perspectives on Human Rights and Legal Philosophy* (Carlisle, 1998), 32 ff.

enjoyed by Muslims and Jews under the slaughter of animals legislation led the minister responsible to state: 'The religious communities have made clear that elements of their slaughter requirements are fundamental obligations, forming part of their religious law which it is not open to them to alter'; as to proposed changes in the law, the minister explained, therefore, that 'We do not believe that we would be justified in imposing such a burden on these communities.'[23] The idea of the 'duty to religion' of a person who is to be the beneficiary of proposed legislation is also used to justify government action.[24] The concept of deference has been used implicitly by the courts.[25] In contrast with other legal systems,[26] the courts, however, have not generally employed as a justification for decisions the idea that religious freedom is a natural right.

PUBLIC UTILITY AS A JUSTIFICATION FOR RELIGIOUS FREEDOM

A justification for religious freedom which commonly appears in legal theory is the value in society of faith.[27] The State promotes and protects religious liberty because of the value that religious faith and activity contribute to the human well-being of society; this provides a moral justification for religious liberty.[28] Whatever the theoretical justifications for religion in society,[29] at the practical level, the notion of public utility of religion is often invoked by governments; typically, 'The Government fully

---

[23] HC Debs., 121, col. 406; as to the legal status within the Jewish community of dietary requirements, the Jewish community stressed that 'the detailed rules relating to the method of slaughter of shechita form a basic and integral part of the corpus of Jewish law. The rules are not merely general "traits", "principles" or "religious categories" . . . but constitute binding legal prescriptions' (*Comments by the Jewish Community on the FAWC Report* (1985), 4); see Poulter, *Ethnicity, Law and Human Rights*, 137.

[24] As part of debates concerning the exemption of Sikhs from wearing protective headgear in the construction industry, Lord Boyd-Carpenter stated: 'They [Sikhs] have apparently weighed this up and have come to the conclusion that their duty to their religion, their faith in it, demands that they should not wear a helmet. The Government are right to accept that view' (HL Debs., 511, col. 740).

[25] *Buckley* v. *Cahal Daly* [1990] NIJB 8: rules contained in the Code of Canon Law (1983) of the Roman Catholic Church were enforced to justify the decision of the High Court that a priest had no *locus standi* to upset a disciplinary decision by the bishop; for deference to the Roman Catholic canon law, see also *Daly* v. *Commissioners for Inland Revenue* (1934) 18 Tax Cas 641.

[26] See e.g. the US case of *Re Santos* 278 App. Div. 373, 105 NYS 2d 716: 'children have a natural and legal right [to their religious faith] of which they cannot be deprived by their temporary exposure to the culture of another religion prior to the age of reason'.

[27] This section seeks to elucidate, of course, justifications employed by institutions of government; as to the value of religion: sociologists have argued that religion provides an agreed way of looking at the world; anthropologists have argued that the value of religion is that it unites people in a shared experience, or that it binds society as a moral community; others have suggested that religion provides a pattern for human behaviour.

[28] See T. Macklem, 'Faith as a Secular Value', (2000) 45 *McGill LJ* 1, 27 ff.

[29] See the studies in P. Oliver, S. D. Scott, and V. Tadros (eds.), *Faith in Law: Essays in Legal Theory* (Oxford, 2000).

recognises the benefits that derive from the maintenance of religious . . . traditions among ethnic minority communities.'[30] State legislation requiring the provision of religious worship and education in schools, the result of effective lobbying from Christian pressure groups in particular, is an obvious expression of the legislative acceptance of the public benefit of religion.[31] The justification is employed in a dogmatic fashion: government statements do not elucidate, beyond the general claim, the actual benefits.

Evaluative justifications for religious freedom, in the form of general moral propositions, may also be implicit in the conditions which must be satisfied in the exercise of particular legal freedoms or rights. Religious organizations and their members have a general legal liberty to establish trusts for the advancement of religion, which enjoy charitable status provided the trust in question effects a public benefit. The requirement of public benefit itself serves as both the precondition for charitable status and the justification for endorsing the religious activity as charitable. Recognition of its charitable status, and therefore freedom to establish the trust, are justified on the basis of judicial acceptance of the value of religion to society at large. The courts admit the scheme as charitable if, and they permit the religious activity prescribed by it because, that activity benefits the public. In short, charitable trusts for the advancement of religion are justified as such because the courts recognize the utility of religion to society at large: typically, the courts are 'entitled to assume that some benefit accrues to the public from the attendance at places of worship of persons who live in this world and mix with their fellow citizens', and the law 'assumes that any religion is at least likely to be better than none'.[32]

Indeed, while public policy may be an elusive concept as the basis of religious freedom, it is commonly invoked to justify judicial decisions about the rights of religious organizations: there is no 'offence to English public policy in allowing a Hindu religious institution to sue in our courts for the recovery of property which it is entitled to recover by the law of its own country. Indeed, we think that public policy would be advantaged.'[33]

SPIRITUAL NEED AS A JUSTIFICATION FOR RELIGIOUS FREEDOM

Religious need, collective and individual, in society is another obvious justification. Commentators not uncommonly relate the need of human beings to engage in shared activities to justify laws which enable or protect

---

[30] Home Office, *Criteria for the Administration of Section 11 Grants* (made under the Local Government Act 1966 as amended) (1990), 3.

[31] See D. Harte, 'Religious Education and Worship in State Schools', in N. Doe, M. Hill, and R. Ombres (eds.), *English Canon Law* (Cardiff, 1998), 115.

[32] *Neville Estates* v. *Madden* [1962] Ch 852 *per* Cross J, 583.

[33] *Bumper Development Corp Ltd* v. *Commissioner of Police of the Metropolis* [1991] 4 All ER 638, 648, *per* Purchas LJ.

the collective character of religious practices or collective participation in religious institutions.[34] The concept of need has been used by the European Commission of Human Rights.[35] In the practical sphere spiritual need is sometimes used to override other values, such as public health and safety, which tends to suggest the legislative acceptance of religion as a superior claim. In consequence, religious freedom itself, without any ulterior purpose, may be the sole justification for particular rules of state law. The instances of religious freedom being used to outweigh safety considerations are well known: Parliament has specifically exempted turbaned Sikhs from the statutory requirement that all motorcyclists must wear crash helmets;[36] a similar privilege is accorded to Sikhs working on construction sites,[37] as well as to Sikhs carrying a ceremonial dagger (*kirpan*) for 'religious reasons'.[38] The notion of equality of opportunity would seem to have been the justification for the statutory prohibition against discrimination on religious grounds in both the public and the private spheres of employment in Northern Ireland.[39]

The justification of spiritual need commonly surfaces in practice, by implication at least, in rules designed to protect religious activity blocked as a result of the incapacity of its beneficiaries. Laws confer rights to religious ministrations because their beneficiaries are unable freely to effect access to them; the State makes provision because incapacitated individuals are unable to do so. The justification of incapacity seems to underlie the duty of prisons to appoint chaplains, the right of prisoners to the visits and ministrations of ministers, the provision of religious services and books in prisons, and the right of prisoners to comply, within reason, with the tenets of their faith in matters of dress and diet.[40] Incapacity would seem to justify the meeting of spiritual needs of the hospitalized, for which the State makes provision in the form of guidance governing spiritual care in hospitals.[41] The State also has legal provisions designed to enable religious instruction and practice for children in residential homes.[42]

---

[34] See Macklem, 'Faith as a Secular Value', 28.

[35] *Sunday Times* v. *UK* (1979) 2 EHRR 245 at 107: 'It is in any event clear from the terms of the Inspector's report and the decision letter of the Secretary of State that considerable weight was attached to the religious needs and interests of the members of ISKON and to the importance of the Manor in relation to the religious activities of the members'; see Poulter, *Ethnicity, Law and Human Rights*, 268.

[36] Motor-Cycle Crash Helmets (Religious Exemption) Act 1976.

[37] Employment Act 1989, s. 11. [38] Ibid., s. 139(5)(b).

[39] Fair Employment (Northern Ireland) Act 1989.

[40] Prison Act 1952 and Prison Rules 1964 SI 1964 No. 388.

[41] See e.g. HSG(92)2: 'the NHS should, where necessary, make every effort to provide for the spiritual needs of patients and staff'.

[42] For duties to provide religious instruction and provisions as to dress and diet, see Children's Homes Regulations 1991, SI 1991/1506, r. 11.

SOCIAL JUSTICE AND PEACE AS JUSTIFICATIONS FOR RELIGIOUS FREEDOM

Consequentialist justifications are very prominent. An idea which appears in international instruments is that freedom of religion contributes to the attainment of the goals of peace, social justice, and friendship among individuals.[43] Laws seeking to promote religious freedom are designed to prevent religious discord from becoming a source of conflict or dispute in society: religious freedom promotes political stability and harmony.[44] Domestically, harmonization and integration of immigrant minority religious groups into society is commonly perceived as a justification for religious freedom.[45] A number of legal provisions may be regarded as being based on integrationist justifications: local authorities[46] and adoption agencies[47] must give due consideration to the religious persuasion of any child whom they are looking after; the Independent Television Commission must endeavour to ensure every due responsibility with respect to the content of religious programmes, and that these do not abuse religious views and beliefs of those belonging to a particular religion or religious denomination.[48] Similarly, at the political level, religious freedom as an aspect of integration in a pluralistic society is justified as necessary for social justice.[49]

Consequentialist justifications for non-intervention by the state courts in internal religious matters occasionally appear in the decisions of state institutions. Decisions to allow religious freedom are sometimes justified explicitly on the basis of ideas about the harm, economic and social, which may result were the State to disallow religious freedom or to intervene in the affairs of religious organizations. The legal exemption for Sikhs from wearing helmets in the construction industry was considered by the government, as part of the value of integration, as necessary not only on

[43] UN Res. 36/55: 'the disregard and infringement of human rights and freedoms, in particular of the right to freedom of [*inter alia*] . . . religion . . . have brought, directly or indirectly, wars and great suffering to humankind'.

[44] See e.g. K. Boyle and J. Sheen (eds.), *Freedom of Religion and Belief: A World Report* (London, 1997), 12; for historical studies about the nature of the confessional state, its built-in tendency for religious conflict and civil war, the replacement of the confessional state with the secular state, and its development of concepts of religious freedom as effecting peace, see D. Saunders, *Anti-Lawyers: Religion and the Critics of Law and State* (London, 1997).

[45] See Poulter, *Ethnicity, Law and Human Rights*, ch. 2.

[46] Children Act 1989, s. 25(5)(c); see also Children (Private Arrangements for Fostering) Regulations 1991, SI 1991 2050, r. 2(2)(c).

[47] Adoption Act 1976, s. 7.

[48] Broadcasting Act 1990, s. 6(1)(d).

[49] Home Office, *Policy Criteria for the Administration of Section 11 Grants*, 2: 'The Government's fundamental objective is that Britain should be a fair and just society where everyone, irrespective of ethnic origin, is able to participate freely and fully in the economic, social and public life of the nation while having the freedom to maintain their own religious and cultural identity.'

economic grounds,[50] but also 'in the longer term for our diverse society and its harmony and cohesion'.[51] In legal proceedings seeking state intervention in the internal affairs of religious organizations, consequentialist justifications may lurk somewhere beneath the surface in the principle, commonly used, that 'The court must inevitably be wary of entering so self-evidently sensitive an area, straying across the well-recognised divide between church and state.'[52] For some commentators, special law on religious freedom may be necessary because other freedoms (such as freedom of expression, association, and assembly) cannot adequately cover all the ground guaranteed by freedom of religion law.[53] While normally legislation itself does not contain statements justifying its own provisions,[54] legislation may present factual justifications for rules about religion which are contained in it.[55]

PRIVACY AS A JUSTIFICATION FOR RELIGIOUS FREEDOM

Reasons for religious freedom may also be the by-products of other justifications for state law. The effect of legislation or judicial decisions may be religious freedom, but the justification for the law or decision will be something other than religious freedom. Litigation entertained by the state courts relating to disputes between authorities within a religious organization and members of that organization provides a useful illustration. In cases concerning internal disciplinary religious processes against members and officers of religious organizations, technical, legal reasons justify the decision of the state court in disposing of the litigation. In these cases the technical, legal reason for the judicial decision generates indirectly collec-

---

[50] HL Debs., 512, cols. 77–8: 'it is estimated that there are up to 40,000 Sikhs working in the construction industry who would be dismissed if they felt unable to comply with the requirement . . . the effect on the Sikh communities themselves . . . would be a severe economic blow and cause unnecessary damage to their perceptions of British society and its laws'.

[51] Ibid.

[52] R. v. *Chief Rabbi, ex parte Wachmann* [1992] 1 WLR 1036, 1043, per Simon Brown J; see also R v. *Provincial Court of the Church in Wales, ex parte Revd Clifford Williams* (1998) C0/2880/98 per Latham J: 'the Court is likely to be very slow to interfere in a case such as this, where the judgment has been made within an area of religious faith and discipline'; and R. v. *Ecclesiastical Committee of Both Houses of Parliament, ex parte Church Society* (1994) Admin LR 670.

[53] See Macklem, 'Faith as a Secular Value', 8 ff.

[54] Laws are cast descriptively as precepts, prohibitions, or permissions, and not as justifications; see e.g. The Ecclesiastical Exemption (Listed Buildings and Conservation Areas) Order 1994 SI 1994 No. 1771, Art. 4: 'Ecclesiastical exemption is retained for . . . buildings within the faculty jurisdiction of the Church of England . . . buildings held in trust by the diocesan trustees of a diocese of the Roman Catholic Church.'

[55] See e.g. Education Act 1996: the role of Christianity in religious education is justified on the basis of 'the fact that the religious traditions in Great Britain are in the main Christian'; syllabuses must reflect this fact while taking into account the teaching and practices of the other principal religions represented in Great Britain (s. 375).

430   *Norman Doe and Anthony Jeremy*

tive freedom of religion for the religious organization against which the
aggrieved member proceeds. Privacy is the by-product justification for religious freedom, and, of course, a view commonly held today is that in the
United Kingdom religion is in the main a private affair.[56] Indeed, even
when the legislative intent to privatize may be understood as based on
punitive reasons, the result may be religious freedom.[57]

In some cases the state court declines jurisdiction because religion is a
private matter: when a cleric of the Church in Wales sought judicial review
of a decision of the Provincial Court of the Church, the High Court justified non-intervention because the Provincial Court was a domestic tribunal
exercising private (rather than public law) functions; moreover, the cleric's
voluntary submission to the constitution of the Church and the jurisdiction
of its courts meant that the cleric could not have 'a legitimate sense of
grievance'.[58] The same applies to disciplinary decisions of the chief rabbi:
'his functions are essentially intimate, spiritual and religious—functions
which the government could not and would not seek to discharge in his
place were he to abdicate his regulatory responsibility'.[59] Similarly, the
state courts' technical understanding that ministers of religion are not in
law employees (by virtue of the incompatibility of spiritual functions and
the existence of a contract of employment) has been used as the reason for
their lack of jurisdiction in many disciplinary cases; this technical legal
reason, again, effects disciplinary freedom for the religious organization in
which the minister functions, and, in turn, it enhances the notion of
privacy.[60] Other technical, legal reasons may result in religious freedom: a
right of parishioners at common law has been used by state courts to
justify admission to Holy Communion in the established Church of
England.[61]

---

[56] See e.g. A. Bradney, 'Faced by Faith', in Oliver, Scott, and Tadros (eds.), *Faith in Law*,
89: in this the author explores the proposition that 'Within Great Britain religion is now
largely a private matter.'
[57] The Welsh Church Act 1914, enacted for political reasons which are often understood
as punitive, had a liberating effect for the Church in Wales in its separation from the State:
see T. G. Watkin, 'Disestablishment, Self-Determination and the Constitutional Development
of the Church in Wales', in N. Doe (ed.), *Essays in Canon Law* (Cardiff, 1992), 25.
[58] *R. v. Provincial Court of the Church in Wales, ex parte Revd Clifford Williams* (1998)
CO/2880/98 *per* Latham J: as a result of the disestablishment of the Church of England in
Wales in 1920, by virtue of the Welsh Church Act 1914, the Church was organized on a
contractual basis; the Welsh church courts were contrasted with the public law status of the
courts of the established Church of England; a further reason for non-intervention was that
an appeal against the cleric's deposition was pending to the Provincial Synod of the Church.
[59] *R v. Chief Rabbi, ex parte Wachmann* [1992] 1 WLR 1036, 1042, *per* Simon Brown J.
[60] See E. Brodin, 'The Employment Status of Ministers of Religion', (1996) 25 *Industrial
Law Journal* 211.
[61] *R. v. Dibdin* [1910] P 57 (CA) and [1912] AC 533 (HL).

JUSTIFICATIONS FOR LIMITATIONS ON RELIGIOUS AUTONOMY

Consequentialist justifications are the most commonly used reasons for limitations on the exercise of religious freedom. Here the consequence of harm to society is used to justify the limitation: the courts do not accept that religiously motivated activity justifies breaches of state law governing criminal damage—however sincere the conviction may be, 'they do not amount and *cannot amount* to a defence in English law'.[62] The same concept has been applied with regard to manslaughter, in the case of Jehovah's Witness parents withholding medical treatment from a child, by reason of religious convictions, resulting in the death of the child.[63] Indeed, the paramount welfare of the child has been invoked to justify injunctive relief against infant baptism.[64]

The consequences for public health and hygiene have also been invoked to justify limitations: rules forbidding the wearing of beards in a chocolate factory, a confectionery factory, a bakery, and an ice-cream factory have been justified on these grounds.[65] Public order is sometimes used as a justification.[66] Similarly, protection of the fundamental rights and freedoms of others has been employed to justify limitations; rules which fall into this category may include prohibitions against the electrical amplification of the Muslim call to prayer, or limits on the practice of Hindus and Sikhs to scatter human ashes in rivers.[67] Floodgate arguments are also perceived as justifications to limit the enjoyment of religious freedom.[68]

---

[62] See e.g. *Blake* v. *DPP* (1992): M. Hill, *Ecclesiastical Law* (London, 1995), 13: a priest of the Church of England 'was given a mandate from God and he felt compelled to do what he did . . . and I would not wish Mr Blake to think that my conclusions in any way reflect any disrespect for them'; 'I accept for my part that this was a belief honestly and deeply held' (Otton J).

[63] *R* v. *Senior* [1899] 1 QB 283; see also *Jane* v. *Jane* (1983) 4 FLR 712, 13 Fam. Law 209: 'If there is a conflict between honouring the mother's religious belief and the interest of the child in continuing life, it is perfectly plain that in such a conflict the interests of the child and its welfare are paramount and the mother's religious beliefs have to be overridden in order to save the child' (*per* Cumming-Bruce LJ).

[64] See Canon Law Society, *Newsletter*, no. 96 (1993) 17, 'Exercise of Parental Role of a Muslim Father over Christian Baptism of Daughter', extract from *Independent*, 24 July 1993 (the action was under the Children Act 1989); see also UN Convention on the Rights of the Child, Art. 3(1): 'In all actions concerning children . . . the best interests of the child shall be a primary consideration.'

[65] *Panesar* v. *Nestlé Co Ltd* [1980] ICR 144 (chocolate); *Singh* v. *Rowntree Mackintosh Ltd* [1979] IRLR 199 (confectionery); *Kabal Singh* v. *RHM Bakeries (Southern) Ltd*, EAT 818/77 (bakery); *Singh* v. *Lyons Maid Ltd* [1975] IRLR 328 (ice-cream); see also *Singh* v. *British Rail Engineering Ltd* [1986] ICR 22 (meat).

[66] For litigation concerning the use of property as a Hindu temple and training institute, *Hertsmere BC* v. *ISKON Ltd* (18/4/1986), unreported, and *ISKON* v. *Sec of State for the Environment and Hertsmere BC* (1992) 64 P&CR 85, see Poulter, *Ethnicity, Law and Human Rights*, ch. 7.

[67] S. Poulter, *Asian Traditions and English Law* (Trentham, 1990), 116, 125.

[68] See e.g. *Ahmad* v. *ILEA* [1978] 1 All ER 574 and *Ahmad* v. *UK* (1982) 4 EHRR 126; see also P. Cumper, 'Religious Liberty in the United Kingdom', in J. D van der Vyver and J.

Hard and soft notions, about the lack of public utility, and of harm, not infrequently come to the fore in charity law. Trusts for the advancement of religion may not be accepted as charitable if the utility of the religious activity, its public benefit, cannot be established or is otherwise in doubt. Court decisions which deny charitable status, on the basis of lack of public benefit, also indicate judicial conceptions about the boundaries of religious utility. In consequence, these decisions both establish and justify the limits of religious freedom. The cases are well known: activities directed predominantly to the social and not to the religious well-being of beneficiaries do not constitute charitable trusts for the advancement of religion;[69] religious activity with an intangible public benefit may fail, as with the spiritual benefit derived by members of the public from intercessory prayer offered by cloistered nuns, which sought to provide edification of members of the public by the example of lives devoted to prayer.[70] In turn, evaluative justifications are used when religious activity is treated as detrimental to the moral welfare of society,[71] or as 'adverse to the foundations of all religion and ... subversive of all morality', or as being unacceptable on grounds of public policy;[72] the same applies to the propagation of religious belief which is considered judicially to be 'dangerous material' or 'pernicious nonsense'.[73] Sometimes, the notion of lack of 'appropriateness' is used to justify blocking claims to religious freedom.[74]

Justifications for intervention by state courts in property disputes of religious organizations are more difficult to discern. Sometimes parliamentary legislation expressly confers jurisdiction in cases of this sort,[75] and sometimes the judges consider such temporal matters to be legitimately within the purview of the temporal courts in order to protect civil rights.[76] Free submission of members to the internal rules of voluntary religious organizations, having the status of terms of a contract in secular law, may in addition provide both a technical, legal, and a moral reason for secular

---

Witte (eds.), *Religious Human Rights in Global Perspective: Legal Perspectives* (The Hague, 1996), 231: 'The floodgates fear that hundreds of minority faith teachers might disrupt the teaching week by taking work off to pray obviously influenced both the Court of Appeal and the European Commission.'

[69] *IRC v. Baddeley* [1955] AC 572.

[70] *Gilmour v. Coats* [1949] AC 426.

[71] *Charity Law and Voluntary Organisations*, The Goodman Report (Bedford, 1976), 24.

[72] *Re Watson* [1973] 1 WLR 1472, 1482–3, *per* Plowman J following *Thornton v. Howe* (1862) 31 Beav 14.

[73] *Church of Scientology v. Kaufman* [1973] RPC 635, 658, *per* Goff J.

[74] For government reactions to proposals to introduce Muslim personal law, see Poulter, *Ethnicity, Law and Human Rights*, 210: 'The proposal appears to have been rejected out of hand on the ground that the suggested legislation would not be "appropriate".'

[75] See e.g. Welsh Church Act 1914, s. 3: this provides that the domestic law of the church on property is enforceable in the temporal courts.

[76] *Forbes v. Eden* (1867) LR 1 SC & Div 568: 'A Court of Law will not interfere with the rules of a voluntary association unless to protect some civil right or interest which is said to be infringed by their operation.'

intervention to enforce those rules.[77] The public nature of some religious activities also justifies the possibility of state intervention: the legal reason for state court competence over decisions of the Rabbinical Commission is that it exercises public, statutory licensing functions.[78] Finally, one reason employed by the State in conferring a religious freedom is to enable a religious organization to carry out functions which would otherwise be carried out by the State. Failure of a religious organization to discharge a devolved responsibility properly may justify termination of the freedom; for example: 'If the State is to continue to treat the faculty jurisdiction [of the Church of England] as a basis for the ecclesiastical exemption, it must be satisfied that the jurisdiction is effective.'[79]

Religious Justifications for Religious Autonomy

While it is a fundamental responsibility of secular society to protect religious liberty and the autonomy of religious communities, for the reasons and in the manner articulated in the first part of this paper, it is necessary to consider three related, but quite separate, questions: What justifications for religious autonomy does religion advance? To what degree is religion a source of the rights of humankind? and To what extent does the secular state need a religious justification? Ultimately, a religious apologia rests on the divine law, as revealed in Judaism, Christianity, and Islam, and the shared perception that truth originates not from man but from God. Therein lies the genesis of the idea that religious rights are independent of state provenance and control, and the notion that in its conception the secular state is limited in its governmental functions to temporal affairs. In consequence, from this general outlook there developed the classical concept of the neutrality of the State towards the religious and non-religious, to the intent that no benefit should be derived nor burden imposed by reason of religion. Arguably the most sophisticated development and application of this approach is to be found in the government of the United States—and, as has been seen, there are glimpses of it in the United Kingdom. It follows that the authority of the State should be restricted to temporal matters not spiritual, rooted in civil law not divine law, and that the authority of religion should be restricted to spiritual matters not temporal, and rooted in divine law not civil law. By parity of reasoning, the concept of the secular state is completely at variance with the idea of a religious state. Since the very essence of religion is that it involves voluntary personal acts of faith, and voluntary association in a religious organization, the idea of imposing faith is antithetical to authentic religion.

---

[77] In the Church in Wales, for example, undertakings are made to be bound by the constitution of the Church.
[78] R. v. *Rabbinical Commission, ex parte Cohen* (1987) unreported.
[79] *Re All Saints, Eccleshall* (1998) 5 Ecc. LJ 135.

THE JUDAEO-CHRISTIAN TRADITION

Judaic and Christian thought had a significant influence on the process which led to the conviction that the State must permit religious freedom. In particular, the notion that all people are created equally in the image of God was inextricably bound up with the concept of human autonomy and human responsibility, which found expression in the Universal Declaration of Human Rights in 1948, a crucial step in the recognition of the individuals as a legal subject of international law: 'All men are born free and equal in rights and dignity.'[80] This assertion is founded in the Jewish and Christian belief that all persons are created in the image of God. Of course, while the Declaration expresses the ideal position of every human being in any juridical system, and presents an objective for the progressive realization of the ideals expressed within it, there is no acknowledgement within the Declaration itself either of religion as the basis of the fundamental principle of equality and dignity, or of religion as a source of human rights. In the aftermath of the horrors perpetrated in the Second World War it is understandable why the United Nations wished to avoid association with or attribution to religious tradition which in the broad sweep of history had generated so much intolerance and suppression of religious liberty. Indeed, the failure of the Declaration to address human duties and duties to God, as stressed in the Bible, has been the subject of much critical comment.[81]

The secular character of the Declaration, however, disguises the importance of religion as a primary source of human rights, as appears from the teachings and tenets of Judaism and Christianity, in each of which traditions tolerance for other religious views is expressly laid down as a basis for legal provision in both municipal and international law. After all, the thrust of the Declaration that all individuals have inalienable rights and are fundamentally equal in dignity by the simple fact of being human is founded upon the equality of all human beings taught in the Judaic and Christian tradition. Thus the principle of basic human reciprocity, replete with rights and duties, is recorded in the Talmud, in the passage where Hillel the Elder responds to a request to state the Torah succinctly, and his responses 'what is hateful to you do not do to your fellow'.[82] And in the Gospel Jesus is recorded as saying, 'Do unto others what you would have them do unto you.'[83]

---

[80] Universal Declaration of Human Rights, Art. 1.

[81] Carl Henry, 'The Judeo-Christian Heritage and Human Rights', in C. H. Esbeck (ed.), *Religious Beliefs, Human Rights and the Moral Foundations of Western Democracy* (Columbia, 1986), 29, and the official message of Paul VI to the Tehran Conference on the thirtieth anniversary of the Declaration, in Doc. Kath. 1517 (19 May 1968), 881–4.

[82] Babylonian, *Shabbat* 31a.

[83] Matt. 7: 12.

Such teachings suggest that these religions regard the terms of the Declaration of Human Rights as setting out a minimal standard. Their theology is a permanent and dynamic challenge to the provision for constitutional and legally enforceable religious rights both in municipal and international law. In Judaism God chose his people, entered into a covenant with them, and made them his own—but at the same time Judaism explicitly acknowledges God's love to be for all people.[84] The intrinsic worth of every human being and respect for other faiths is expressly set forth in the Talmud, and the Mishnah contains the celebrated passage 'therefore was a single person created to teach that if anyone destroys a single soul . . . scripture challenges him as though he had destroyed a whole world, and who so ever rescues a single soul . . . scripture credits him as though he has saved a whole world'.[85]

The Christian tradition also teaches that the whole of humanity is created 'in the image of God'.[86] Throughout the New Testament the universality of God's approach to humankind, with implicit tolerance and respect for the religious convictions of others, is the subject of frequent teaching: 'Truly I perceive that God shows no partiality, but in every nation everyone who fears him and does what is right is acceptable to him.'[87] For St Paul, between Jews and Gentiles God shows no partiality;[88] and 'I say to you, love your enemies, do good to those who hate you.'[89] The principle that freedom is the essential characteristic of religious faith is aptly expressed by the World Council of Churches: 'God's redemptive dealing with men is not coercive. Accordingly, human attempts by a legal enactment or by pressure of social custom to coerce or eliminate faith are violations of the fundamental ways of God with men. The freedom which God has given . . . implies free response to God's love.'[90]

THE ISLAMIC TRADITION

In Islam the Qur'ān states: 'There shall be no compulsion in religion.'[91] Moreover: 'Proclaim, O Prophet, this is the truth from your Lord; then let him who will, believe, and let him who will, disbelieve.'[92] On this principle, that a person is free to choose his faith and indeed that such freedom is a precondition of faith, the Qur'ān also expressly requires tolerance towards other religions from its own followers, so that non-Muslims, though living in a Muslim state, must be free to follow their own faith and

---

[84] See e.g. Gen. 12: 3: 'all the families of the earth are to be blessed'.
[85] *Sanhedrin* 4: 5.   [86] Gen. 1: 27.
[87] Acts 10: 34–5.   [88] Rom. 2: 11.
[89] Matt. 5: 44.
[90] 'Statement on Religious Liberty', in the New Delhi Report: *The Third Assembly of the World Council of Churches 1961* (New York, 1962), 159.
[91] Q. 2: 256.   [92] Q. 18: 29.

belief without coercion. The teaching of the Qur'ān further emphasizes that God will judge human beings not on the basis of what they profess but on the basis of their belief and righteous conduct: 'those who believe [in the Qur'ān] and those who follow the Jewish scriptures and the Christians and the Sabians, any who believe in God and the Last Day, and work righteousness, will have their reward saith the Lord; on them shall be no fear, nor shall they grieve'.[93] And the prohibition against compulsion applies both to non-Muslims and also to Muslims who have renounced their faith or failed to profess it. Given the status of the Qur'ān as the most authoritative statement of norms in Islam, it is not surprising that it holds a unique status as an expression of human rights in general and of protection of religious freedom in particular.[94]

The Universal Islam Declaration of Human Rights, adopted by the Islamic Council in 1981, states that 'human rights decreed by the Divine Law aim at conferring dignity and honour on mankind and are designed to eliminate oppression and injustice'. The Declaration provides that everyone has the right to freedom of conscience and worship in accordance with religious beliefs (Article 13). The Declaration provides, moreover, that: 'the Quranic principle [that] there is no compulsion in religion shall govern the religious rights of Non-Muslim Countries. In a Muslim Country religious minorities shall have the choice to be governed in respect of their civil and personal matters by Islamic Law or by their own Laws' (Article 10).[95] It follows that from a strictly Islamic religious perspective, freedom of belief (since it goes to the root of religious belief) is clearly established in the authoritative norms as divinely willed.

It is a common perception that the Islamic corpus of divine law and theological principle, as expressed in the Declaration, is sharply at variance with the repressive approach of some militant Muslim regimes. The fundamentalist approach which negates freedom of thought conscience and religion and punishes dissent has increasingly come to be associated with some Islamic states, although the extent to which such policies are truly expressions of the people at large, rather than a small controlling elite, clearly varies from state to state. The diversity of schools of interpretation in the varying traditions of Islam (particularly Sunni, Shīʿī and Ṣūfī Muslim schools) makes generalization extremely difficult, and probably accounts for the theoretical sanctions attending apostasy contained within the Sharīʿa scheme of religious rights. This contemplates forfeiture of property and capital punishment for repudiation of the faith. But that interpretation

---

[93] Q. 33: 34.
[94] See the discussion by Riffat Hassan in 'Rights of Women within Islamic Communities', in J. Witte and J. D. van der Vyver (eds.), *Religious Human Rights in Global Perspective: Religious Perspectives* (The Hague, 1996).
[95] For the text, see e.g. C. G. Weeramantry, *Islamic Jurisprudence: An International Perspective* (London, 1988), 176.

does not command universal support among Islamic scholars, and a more liberal approach is practised within other traditions of Islam.

THE IMPACT OF RELIGIOUS FREEDOM IN PRACTICE

Christian justifications for religious liberty have been conditioned, needless to say, by historical developments. What follows is an outline background to these. History, of course, has revealed a sad disparity between doctrine and practice in the matter of tolerance and respect for religious human rights, on the part of all the major world religions but more sharply discernible in the case of Christianity, whose historical record in the treatment of other religions has been patently adverse to its doctrines of peace and rejection of coercion of religious dissenters on the grounds of heresy. On the other hand, there were many Fathers of the early Church who repudiated the repressive approach to non-Christian religion. After all, Constantine himself, in acknowledging and endorsing the Christian Church, was careful to express toleration to all other religions 'so that every man may worship according to his own wish'.[96] In the ensuing history of the Church the case for the defence of religious freedom was rarely without distinguished advocates. In the third century Lactantius attacked the pursuit of so-called heresy and proclaimed the rights of conscience: 'It is religion alone in which liberty has established her dwelling place. Beyond everything else, religion is a matter of free choice, nor can anyone be compelled to worship what he dislikes.'[97]

Following the twelfth century, itself a period of renewal of life and thought in general, Christian natural rights theorists were beginning to place an emphasis on the individual human person. This profoundly affected the development of canon law in relation to the juristic place of individual conscience, individual intent, and individual consent. In applying this approach throughout the ecclesiastical courts of Western Christendom the canonists adumbrated and developed doctrines based upon individual conscience, good faith, and intent, assessing the obligations of parties on the basis of Christian ethical conduct and the demands of conscience. The doctrinal basis of the substantive law applied by the ecclesiastical courts throughout Western Europe was founded in the general jurisdiction of the Church over sins. Whether a recalcitrant had sinned was a moral issue that could be resolved only by reference to canon law and in particular those components of it derived from divine and natural law. Throughout the Middle Ages there were large parts of Western Europe in which the rules of civil law were not obeyed, whereas throughout the same territory the canon law was being enforced on a uniform basis under the authority of the Pope.

---

[96] Constantine, Edict of Milan 313.   [97] Lactantius, *Epitome* 54.

Thus, during the Middle Ages the Canon Law exercised similar but a wider influence than the Civil Law in securing, firstly, the permanence of those intellectual and political ideas by which this period is distinguished; and secondly, the spread of those more enlightened legal ideas upon such matters as the machinery by which the law should be administered, the form in which its rules should be expressed and the substance of some of its rules, all of which it had inherited in close and continuous association with the Civil Law.[98]

The impact of canon law and the procedure of its courts upon the developing legal systems of Europe was significant. The moral and ethical principles, which canonists believed should regulate Christian society, were bound to have a significant impact on secular law and procedure. The Roman Curia and the itinerant papal legates carried the authority of the Pope to all corners of Western Christendom grounded in a comprehensive and universal canon law, the effect of which upon the nascent legal systems of Europe was to be substantial and beneficial. Thus the emphasis on the making of amends in the course of penitence, in the interest of one's soul and good conscience, was reflected in the willingness of the ecclesiastical courts to enforce promises for which there was no remedy in the secular courts, a procedure which required that the aggrieved party had to establish not only its claims but that the defendant was in bad faith. The decree required the defendant to 'go out of his sin'. So out of the penitential system of the tenth and eleventh centuries the canonists developed the principle of conscience in adjudication, the notion that the duty of the judge was to discern by interrogation the moral conduct of the sinner and indeed to try and identify himself with the accused. They exercised a profound influence upon the development of secular law in transmitting fundamental moral concepts of the Church. Its jurisprudence has been neatly summed up:

The rights of direct legal representation by professional lawyers and the procedure for interrogation by the judge according to carefully worked out rules were among the new institutions created to implement the principle of Conscience. Conscience was associated with the idea of the equality of the law, since in conscience all litigants are equal; and from this came equity—the protection of the poor and helpless against the rich and powerful, the enforcement of relations and trust and confidence, and the granting of so called personal remedies such as injunctions . . . and so the church sought both to legalise morality and to moralise legality: it took legal jurisdiction over sins, and it influenced the secular law to conform to moral principles.[99]

The most serious difficulty, however, in the way of developing a true doctrine of religious liberty was the problem of heresy, which medieval jurists, clerics, and commentators judged to be not only sinful but wrong-

---

[98] Holdsworth, *History of English Law*, 4th edn., vol. ii (London, 1936), 143.
[99] See H. J. Berman, *The Interaction of Law and Religion* (Nashville, 1974), 60.

ful, notwithstanding the efforts of leading theologians who developed the concept that the law of Christ was a law of liberty which the contemporary Church had disregarded by the imposition of regulations which were creatures of man-made, not divine, law. Such theologians argued for the application of St Paul's doctrine of Christian liberty with the emerging concepts of natural rights, to the intent that a Christian was obliged to accept a divine law of Scripture and the natural law of reason and conscience, rights which could not be removed by any oppressive authority, secular or clerical.

Given its pre-eminence throughout the Middle Ages, as a multinational institution with its own governmental structures, the Church (as distinguished legal historians such as Maitland have pointed out) was a State holding Western Christian society together with the bound of a common religion. Just as the modern secular state treats treason with great severity and denies a defence to a traitor who pleads good intentions and conscience, so heretics in the Middle Ages were regarded as traitors whose errors and dissent must have had Satanic, not divine, origins. In other words, heretics were perceived to be guilty of treason to God and had to be restrained and if necessary excised albeit by the persecution of the Inquisition.

The writings of natural lawyers and philosophers in the sixteenth century, applying the principles of rationalization, were to have a substantial and beneficial effect upon the theory and practice of municipal and international law. Much of the principle of conscience and good faith propounded by the natural lawyers was plainly derived from divine law and canon law: 'Fides formed the basis for justice. Hence promises must be kept whether they have been couched in a specific form or not. Even God would be acting against His nature if He did not keep His word . . .'.[100] As the Reformation took hold, in Western Europe freedom of conscience and of religion were perceived to represent limits beyond which the secular state should have no authority, and also as sources from which sprang basic secular rights. The Protestant Reformation may not have actually espoused the principle of religious rights or religious liberty, but it did establish a clear resistance to religious and political authority. From the sixteenth century onwards the idea that the human person is too sacred to be violated by religious conformity underpinned the development of 'liberty of conscience'. The notion that all persons have religious rights is, for Christians, founded in the principle that humans are created in the image of God and that conscience cannot be violated by coercion, concepts alien to totalitarian regimes, such as Marxism and Nazism, which promoted deification of the State and the exclusion of religion.

By the mid-twentieth century Christianity had appropriated religious

---

[100] H. Grotius, *De Iure Belli ac Pacis* (1625), bk. 2, ch. 11, para. 1.

toleration and freedom and the acknowledgement of a human being's right to believe or not to believe a religious dogma, or to worship one God or many gods or none at all, and to be in membership of a religious organization or of none. The point is given prominence in the documents of the Second Vatican Council. Several conciliar documents affirm the right to religious freedom and connect it with other human rights, committing the Roman Catholic Church to defend all of the freedoms necessary to protect human dignity.[101] In *Gaudium et Spes*, for instance, the Council addresses the theological basis for defending human rights and setting clear limits on the competence of the secular state in regard to religion. It identifies the fundamental justification for personal dignity and autonomy of the human person as the call to communion with God, since the fulfilment of human nature can be understood only in terms of the risen Christ. The ministry of the Church in human rights is expressed to be part of its mission. The present pontiff is celebrated for his commitment to this ministry, literally travelling the world to preach a theological vision of the individual whose religious liberty is grounded in Christian principles. In short he has taken up the role for the Church in the secular realm of public affairs which was identified in the Second Vatican Council: the Church's role was to stand as 'A sign and to safeguard the transcendence of the human person'.[102] Indeed, the Pope has defined the person as 'the way for the Ministry of the Church'.[103]

It is during this pontificate that we have witnessed struggles for the recognition of human rights in which the Church has been prominent and indeed sometimes the only protagonist, offering pastoral, material, and moral support. This trend coincided with the rise of authoritarian regimes attended by the suppression of the organs of freedom of conscience and expression, including the press, Parliament, the universities and trade unions, and sometimes the Church itself. It brought the Church into direct confrontation with government. The clearest illustrations of this engagement were in Latin America from 1960, and throughout the 1980s, and then in central and eastern Europe, where the repression had subsisted throughout the cold war. The impact of John Paul II throughout the 1980s was such that history will probably judge him to have been an essential participant in the collapse of the Soviet Union and its satellites.

---

[101] In *Dignitatis Humanae* (1965), 13, the Church seeks the right to enjoy 'that freedom of action which her responsibility for the salvation of men requires'; in particular the Church claims an autonomy which will confer genuine freedom 'to practise the faith, to proclaim its teaching about civil society, to carry out her task without hindrance, to pass moral judgments relating to politics, whenever the fundamental rights of man or the salvation of souls requires it'.

[102] *Gaudium et Spes* (1965), pt. I.

[103] John Paul II, *Redemptor Hominis* (1979), 44.

Conclusions

Secular justifications for religious freedom are characterized by their diversity and generality. Firstly, needless to say, in the United Kingdom there is no official compendium of secular justifications; they have developed pragmatically, not programmatically, though they coincide generally with those justifications implicit in instruments of international law. Secondly, however, secular justifications, as expressed by the various organs of government, fall into fairly distinct but associated categories: ideas of respect, tolerance, and spiritual need are, broadly, rationalistic, moral justifications; ideas of social peace and public benefit are consequentialist, utilitarian justifications; and ideas of deference to religious law and privacy justify religious freedom as an implicit recognition of the inherent limits of the capacity or competence of the State. Thirdly, secular justifications differ in their historical pedigree: while tolerance, social harmony, and deference to religious law are ancient concepts, that of respect is a product particularly of human rights thinking (about human equality and dignity) characteristic of international law, whereas privacy, spiritual need, and public benefit justifications are perhaps the most recent to enter domestic secular jurisprudence.

In contrast with this obvious diversity, religious justifications are far more homogeneous than those found in secular jurisprudence. Religious justifications tend to coalesce around the notion that personal freedom and the dignity of the individual cannot be separated from duties to and communion with God, since the fulfilment of the human person can be realized only in divine terms. The central justification therefore, one shared by all three major religions represented in British society—Judaism, Christianity, and Islam—is that the State must facilitate freedom of religion because religious freedom is an indispensable precondition to religious faith itself. Religion is necessarily concerned with the free response of the individual to God. There can be no true religion unless humankind practises it freely. The State must not be the source either of obstruction or of coercion in its treatment of religion, for this would be the antithesis of religion. In short, without autonomy and true religious liberty the religious and their communities will not realize that full communion with God to which they are called by divine law.

Indeed, a truly secular state which has no commitment in the realm of belief and religion, and in which religion enjoys complete independence from the State, may be more likely to act as a guarantor of religious freedom. The very conflict or tension between religious organizations on the one hand and the State on the other may be beneficial. Religion without law loses its social effectiveness, but on the other hand when traditional religious concepts are repressed, reduced, or eliminated so that the link between law and religion is broken, then society itself becomes demoralized. Without belief in it, the law will not work, and in the end religious rights are classically concerned with considerations of social order and social justice, and perceived to be dimensions of God's love and grace.[104]

One obvious difference between secular and religious justifications is that the latter postulate religious freedom as a requirement of divine law; the State does not. Judaism, Christianity, and Islam justify religious liberty because this is willed by God. However, the two sets of justifications meet around the concept of human rights. The norms of human rights are founded in the values and visions of human society, and the source of such values and visions is most commonly to be found in religion. The texts, teachings, and canons of the great religions represent the highest moral tradition of humankind, providing a comprehensive statement of basic religious human rights. The religious systems of law and procedures to protect such rights have significantly affected secular legal systems. The medieval canon law of the Western Catholic Church perhaps provides the most striking example. And this 'legal transplantation' of religious laws into secular laws is plainly in evidence today.

[104] See Berman, *The Interaction of Law and Religion*, 130.

RELIGIOUS REMNANTS IN THE COMPOSITION OF THE UNITED KINGDOM PARLIAMENT

Peter W. Edge

The most powerful law-making body in the United Kingdom is Parliament, which can make or unmake any law within the United Kingdom jurisdictions by Act of Parliament. The most important element of Parliament is the directly elected House of Commons, but membership of Parliament, and a role in legislation, extends to the House of Lords and the sovereign.

In this paper I wish to consider briefly the religious elements remaining in the composition of Parliament, arguing that the current position includes a number of features which are susceptible to critique, particularly under the provisions of the European Convention on Human Rights. A number of important issues relating to religion and Parliament are not discussed here, notably the religious commitment of members whose offices are not bound by religious affiliation, the extent to which religious ideas feed into legislative policy, and the role of religion in the ceremonial of Parliament.

Membership of the House of Commons

The House of Commons consists of freely elected[1] representatives of their constituents.[2] Once elected, MPs take their place upon making an oath or affirmation concerning their duties. Formerly the oath was crafted to exclude members of some religious groups from the House,[3] and, although it no longer has a sectarian content, some elected MPs feel unable to take the oath and thus their places.[4] The most important restriction on membership of the Commons for our purposes relates to some ministers and clergy.

Under the House of Commons (Clergy Disqualification) Act 1801, which was stated as removing doubts as to the law,[5] no person ordained

---

[1] See Bill of Rights 1688, s.1; 3 Edw. I, c. 5 (1275).
[2] See *Report of the Royal Commission on the Constitution 1969–73*, Cmnd. 5460 (1973), para. 1236.
[3] Affirmation was introduced by the Oaths Act 1888, s. 5.
[4] On the procedure, see C. J. Boulton (ed.), *Erskine May's Treatise on the Law, Privileges, Proceedings and Usage of Parliament* (London, 1989), 229–31.
[5] For the background to the Act, and historical instances of clergy being excluded from the House of Commons, see the argument by Shawcross, Gage, and Parker in *Re MacManaway* [1951] A.C. 161 (P.C.) at 163–4.

as priest or deacon, or minister of the Church of Scotland, may be elected
to serve as an MP, or continue to serve as an MP if they take on this role
after their election.[6] The Act arose as a reaction to the radical politics of
John Tooke, an Anglican clergyman who had previously been imprisoned
on a charge of seditious libel and charged with high treason.[7] The only
significant case to discuss the Act came before the Privy Council in *Re
MacManaway*.[8] In that case MacManaway had been ordained by a
Church of Ireland bishop. The principal question was whether the terms
'priest or deacon' were limited to the Church of England. Strong arguments were put forward limiting the Act to clergy of the Church of
England and the Church of Scotland, based partly on the policy of the Act,
its legislative history, and a section of the Act dealing with proof which
suggested that only members of those bodies were envisaged as falling
within the Act.[9] Lord Radcliffe delivered the report of the Privy Council,
and found that a Church of Ireland priest fell within the restriction. An
analysis of the judgment suggests that, although the exact scope of the
restriction remains unclear, not every dedicated adherent of every religion
is included.

Firstly, the Church of Ireland is part of the Anglican communion, and
at the time of the 1801 Act had been part of a United Church of England
and Ireland, 'bound by statute to observe the doctrine, worship, discipline
and government as by law established for the Church of England'.[10]
Episcopal ordination within the Church of Ireland could provide the basis
for any ecclesiastical promotion or dignity in the Church of England, as
well as the performance of religious rituals. At the time of the case the
Church of Ireland was no longer an established Church, but 'disestablishment does not seem to have led to any divergence in doctrine or practice'.[11] Additionally, in dealing with the evidential point raised by counsel,
Lord Radcliffe stressed that 'it looks . . . to a person's active ministry in a
Church observing the English rite whatever the source of his orders'.[12]
Thus, the narrowest reading of this case suggests that it extends only to
priests and deacons within a member of the Anglican communion—which
would include the Scottish Episcopalian Church—and ministers within the
Church of Scotland.

Secondly, there is some evidence for a wider interpretation which still
limits the range of clergy affected. Lord Radcliffe referred to the variety of
ordinations which would be accepted by the Church of England as creat-

    [6] House of Commons (Clergy Disqualification) Act 1801, s. 1, 2.
    [7] See further Boulton, *Erskine May's Treatise*, 45–6.
    [8] *Re MacManaway*.
    [9] House of Commons (Clergy Disqualification) Act 1801, s. 4.
    [10] *Re MacManaway*, at 173 *per* Lord Radcliffe.
    [11] Ibid., at 175 *per* Lord Radcliffe.
    [12] Ibid., at 176 *per* Lord Radcliffe.

ing a priest or deacon, citing with approval a passage showing that the Church of England accepted any episcopal ordination, including those made within Roman Catholicism, or the Greek Orthodox Church.[13] Later, Lord Radcliffe noted that

Their Lordships cannot accept without some reservations the conception that a priest or deacon is ordained in, or into, any particular Church: a conception which, indeed, conflicts with the prevailing doctrine of ecclesiastical law. Such a phrase may conveniently denote the source from which a person derives his status in holy orders, but it is one of the complications inherent in this subject that a person may derive his orders from one Church, even though he ministers in another.[14]

Thus, priests and deacons of any episcopal body, even those falling outside the Anglican communion, may be subject to the restrictions of this Act. It is probable, however, that this would not extend to every body with officials named as bishops, priests, and deacons. The Church of Jesus Christ of Latter-Day Saints, for instance, practises ordination, but its offices are not recognized by the Church of England. The Act may be limited to ordinations recognized as such by the Church of England.[15]

Thirdly, the widest reasonable interpretation of the Act would include every individual identified as a priest or deacon within their religious system. Such a wide interpretation may best accord to the spirit of Lord Radcliffe's judgment, which rejected all arguments for restricting the interpretation put before the Privy Council. It does not accord well with the history of the legislation, however, nor with the constitutional argument that access to the House of Commons should be as broad as possible. Even if this interpretation is accepted, however, religious systems which do not have a distinction between clergy and laity, or which use sufficiently different titles for their clergy, should not be covered by the Act.

This unclear piece of legislation has been supplemented by an express provision applying these provisions to those 'in holy orders in the Church of Rome'.[16] It may be possible to argue that this explicit clause suggests that the first, and narrowest, of my possible meanings should be given to the 1801 Act, as such individuals would already be covered by the other meanings. Against this, the provision occurred as part of a broader scheme of emancipation for Roman Catholics, and contains a specific evidential clause which undoubtedly added to the law. Although we can add Roman Catholic priests to those who are definitely excluded from the House of Commons, the existence of this provision is not decisive as to the meaning of the general restriction.

---

[13] Ibid., at 173 *per* Lord Radcliffe.
[14] *Re MacManaway*, at 174 *per* Lord Radcliffe.
[15] This would have the consequence of allowing the internal law of the Church of England to determine whether an elected MP was entitled to take his or her seat in the legislature.
[16] Roman Catholic Relief Act 1829, s. 9.

There was some pressure for reform of this law, to allow excluded clergy to become MPs.[17] Reform suddenly became a pressing issue in 2001, when it was realized that a prospective parliamentary candidate would be excluded by the legislation. At the time of writing the House of Commons (Removal of Clergy Disqualification) Bill 2001, which would repeal these provisions but continue to exclude the Lords Spiritual from the House, seems very likely to become law.

Membership of the House of Lords

Turning to the House of Lords, this chamber of Parliament no longer has authority equal to the House of Commons. The Lords do not have the authority to amend, reject, or delay money bills, and most other legislation may receive the royal assent without the consent of the House of Lords, if the Commons is determined to put the legislation through.[18] The House of Lords is currently in the process of being reformed, although its final composition remains to be determined. The current House contains a number of Lords spiritual. The Lords spiritual are all members of the Anglican hierarchy. Originally, all bishops of the Church of England sat in the Lords, but the increase in the number of bishoprics was not met by an increase in the number of seats.[19] Today, both archbishops, the bishops of London, Westminster and Durham, and the twenty-one most senior of the remaining bishops sit in the House of Lords.[20] They retain their position so long as they hold their bishopric, effectively retiring from both roles before the age of 70.[21]

It is possible for other religious organizations to gain a voice in the national legislature, through the appointment of a life peer with strong links to the organization.[22] Although these are sometimes seen as being appointments of religious representatives, in a recent review Weller identified them as having 'been solely on the basis of a recognition of the individual concerned, rather than as part of an explicit attempt to reflect the wider range of religious traditions and communities now present in our increasingly pluralising society'. [23] Even if it is possible to have religious

---

[17] See V. Elliot, 'Plea to Let Clerics Give up the Pulpit for Parliament', *The Times*, 2 Oct. 1998.   [18] See Parliament Act 1911; Parliament Act 1949.

[19] See *Halsbury's Laws of England*, 4th edn. (London, 1973–), vol. xiv, para. 528.

[20] See Bishoprics Act 1878. This excludes the Bishop of Sodor and Man, who has a seat in the legislature of the Isle of Man; and the bishop of Gibraltar in Europe. See P. Goodrich, 'A Bishop in the House of Lords', [1997] *Law and Justice* 63.

[21] Ecclesiastical Offices (Age Limit) Measure 1975; Bishops (Retirement) Measure 1986.

[22] 'Other ecclesiastical groupings may be represented through the nomination of Life Peers. The Roman Catholic Archbishop of Westminster is not included, and only recently the Chief Rabbi, head of the Jewish faith, has been made a Life Peer' (J. F. McEldowney, *Public Law* (London, 1994), 55).

[23] P. Weller, 'Submission to the Royal Commission on the Reform of the House of Lords', ms, 29 Apr. 1999, para. 6.5.

representation through this mechanism, however, there are significant differences between this peer and a Lord spiritual. Life peers effectively retain their position for life, so remain in the Lords even if they cease to be a member of their original religious organization or community, while Lords spiritual who cease to hold their position in the Church of England hierarchy lose their place in the Lords. The appointment of a Lord spiritual is effectively automatic, and as of right to the most senior bishops, while appointment of life peers to function as religious representatives is ad hoc and at the discretion of the political figures recommending the creation of life peers. It follows that the selection of a religious figure as a representative of a religious organization or community can be contentious. In discussing the chief rabbinate, Newman notes:

the extent to which the 'host society' has welcomed the intervention of successive chief rabbis in politics—even to the extent of awarding one of them a seat in the House of Lords—might well in itself have weakened the status of the chief rabbinate within the Jewish community itself. And the extent to which the State has turned to the chief rabbinate and regarded it as the official spokesman of the community has further alienated those groups within the community who are unhappy about many of its aspects.[24]

The White Paper on reform of the Lords[25] concentrated primarily on the position of hereditary peers, the number of which has been radically reduced,[26] leaving any changes to the position of the Lords spiritual to the Royal Commission.[27] The Commission accepted that part of its role was to consider whether the reformed second chamber should include a formal religious element, and in its public hearings a number of witnesses raised issues pertaining to the representation of other religious groups, and the proper role for the Lords spiritual in the Lords.[28]

The Commission noted that a reformed second chamber should include people capable of articulating moral and philosophical viewpoints.[29] A minority of the Commission felt that neutrality between religions, including atheisms, precluded additional mechanisms for representing religious organizations and communities.[30] The majority, however, felt that the Church of England should continue to receive representation due to its public role and contribution of a spiritual viewpoint to the legislative process;[31] and that other faiths should be represented. Christian representation would be

---

[24] See A. Newman, 'The Office of Chief Rabbi: A Very English Institution', in N. Aston (ed.), *Religious Change in Europe, 1650–1914* (Oxford, 1997).
[25] *Modernising Parliament: Reforming the House of Lords*, Cm. 4183 (1998).
[26] House of Lords Act 1999.
[27] *Modernising Parliament*, Cm. 4183 (1998), para. 7.21.
[28] See *Reform of the House of Lords: A Consultation Paper*, Royal Commission on the Reform of the House of Lords (London, 1999). See also the transcripts of evidence given at the public hearings on the Commission's web pages <www.lords-reform.org.uk>.
[29] Wakeham Report, *A House for the Future* (London, 2000), paras. 15.1–6.
[30] Para 15.7. [31] Paras. 15.8–9.

structured along organizational–congregational lines, with the twenty-six seats currently occupied ex officio by the Anglican bishops being divided among the Christian communities according to baptismal numbers. Responsibility for appointing these representatives would remain with the Appointments Commission,[32] although it was anticipated that Anglican nominations would always be accepted,[33] and nominations from the Churches Together in England and similar organizations in the other nations of the United Kingdom would normally be accepted.[34] Although it was felt impossible to create organizational entitlements for non-Christian faiths, the Appointments Commission would aim to ensure that at least five members had been 'specifically selected to represent the various non-Christian faith communities',[35] and 'would be perceived as broadly representative of the different faith communities'.[36] In marked contrast to the Christian representatives, and particularly those from the Church of England, the Appointments Commission would be 'open to receive nominations' from the non-Christian communities, but would 'make its own decisions on the basis of individual nominees' personal standing'.[37]

The Crown

Although originally the sovereign enjoyed considerable personal power, since the seventeenth century this power has increasingly shifted to other actors within the Constitution, most notably to Parliament, and then to the prime minister and Cabinet. Nonetheless, the sovereign retains a number of residual powers, including de jure assent to all Acts of Parliament, and thus membership of the legislature. There are strong links between the Crown and the Church of England.

The sovereign is the supreme governor of the Church of England,[38] although not *ipso facto* a minister of that Church.[39] The control of the sovereign over the Church of England was declared[40] by the Act of Supremacy 1558, which united and annexed all ecclesiastical powers of visitation, reformation, and correction of the Church of England with the Crown.[41] The sovereign also possesses very wide powers of appointment to offices within the Church of England.[42] Although the sovereign is responsible for a range of functions within the life of the Church of England, there is no provision for delegation of these functions in the event that the sovereign should be of a different denomination or religion, as is

---

[32] Paras. 15.18–23.   [33] Paras. 15.20–1, Recommendation 112.
[34] Paras. 15.21–3, Recommendations 112, 113.   [35] Para. 15.16.
[36] Para. 15.15. The mechanisms are detailed in paras. 15.16–17.
[37] Para. 15.17.   [38] See Act of Supremacy 1558, s. 9.
[39] Articles of Religion 37.
[40] *Caudrey's Case* (1591) 5 Co.Rep. 1a, 8a.
[41] Act of Supremacy 1558, s. 8.
[42] See *Halsbury's Laws of England*, vol. xiv, para. 358.

the case for, for instance, the lord chancellor.[43] Rather, there are absolute limits on the religion of the sovereign.

In 1688 the Protestant Parliament offered the Crown to the Protestant William and Mary, prince and princess of Orange. As part of the Bill of Rights 1688, which confirmed this constitutional change, Parliament provided:

whereas it has been found by experience that it is inconsistent with the safety and welfare of this Protestant kingdom to be governed by a popish[44] Prince or by any King or Queen marrying a papist[45] the said Lords and Commons pray that it may be enacted that all and every person that is are or shall be reconciled to or shall hold communion with the see or church of Rome or shall profess the popish religion or shall marry a papist shall be excluded and be forever incapable to inherit possess or enjoy the crown and government . . . or to have use or exercise any regal power authority or jurisdiction.[46]

This provision of the Bill of Rights, although far-reaching, is primarily negative. Although it serves to bar Roman Catholics or those who choose to marry them from inheriting or occupying the position of sovereign, it does not positively state the religion of the sovereign. It should be remembered, however, that the Bill of Rights was enacted in a context where the only realistic faiths of a sovereign were Roman Catholic or Protestant, although it should be noted that the latter covered a range of possibilities.

The Bill of Rights also contains, by implication, a positive requirement that the person becoming sovereign should be a Protestant at that time. In the event of a person being excluded from the sovereignty as a result of the section reproduced above, the Crown descends to the next Protestant person in line to inherit.[47] Strictly speaking, this does not cover the position of a non-Catholic, non-Protestant inheriting from a sovereign who was not barred from succession or office by the Bill of Rights, but the provision was supplemented by a requirement that the sovereign take an oath, normally at coronation, renouncing certain aspects of Roman Catholic doctrine.[48] Again, strictly speaking, a non-Christian could have honestly taken this original oath, but it was replaced in 1688 by an obligation to protect the Protestant religion,[49] and in 1910 by a shorter form containing a positive declaration that the sovereign was 'a faithful Protestant'.[50] In 1700 the succession to the Crown was laid down by statute, and limited to Protestants.[51] The same Act reaffirmed the relevant provisions of the Bill of Rights,[52] and provided that 'whosoever shall here-

---

[43] See Lord Chancellor (Tenure of Office and Discharge of Ecclesiastical Functions) Act 1974 ss. 1, 2.
[44] i.e. Roman Catholic.   [45] i.e. Roman Catholic.
[46] Bill of Rights 1688, s. 1 (the spelling has been modernized).
[47] Ibid.   [48] Ibid.
[49] Coronation Oath Act 1688.   [50] Accession Declaration Act 1910, Schedule.
[51] Act of Settlement 1700, s. 1.   [52] Ibid., s. 2.

after come to the possession of this Crown shall join in communion with the Church of England as by law established'.[53]

The effect of these provisions can be summarized as follows. Only Protestant Christians can inherit the Crown, and they must affirm this faith at their coronation. Protestants may not inherit the Crown if they are married to a Roman Catholic, and may be barred from inheriting if they have been married to a Roman Catholic, although that marriage is no longer in existence. Reigning sovereigns who convert to Roman Catholicism, or marry a Roman Catholic, lose the Crown, which passes to the next Protestant in line by force of law. Reigning sovereigns who convert to any faith other than Roman Catholicism, or who marry anyone of any other faith, retain the Crown so long as they have joined 'in communion with the Church of England'.

Commentary

There are three groups of actors whose place in the legislature depends, to some extent, upon their religious status. Firstly, ministers of religion, who are excluded thereby from membership of the House of Commons. Secondly, the Lords spiritual in the House of Lords, whose legislative position depends upon their position within a particular religious hierarchy. Thirdly, the sovereign, whose position is hedged around with both positive obligations towards Anglican Christianity, and negative obligations concerning Roman Catholicism.

It would be possible, if ahistorical, to construct these religious remnants in the legislature as evidence of a coherent policy by Anglican Christianity to retain not only its position as a state Church, but as a hierarchical religious organization. I think this approach is of limited value: the relationship between the Church of England and the State is neither simple, nor deliberate, nor reflective of a single paradigm. A better approach is to consider the impact of these religious remnants separately.

Policy arguments about the qualifications of a hereditary head of state may seem surreal. Although non-discrimination is an important principle, to retain the hereditary principle while removing the religious differentiation seems analogous to retaining the rights and privileges of hereditary peers, while ensuring that men and women are not discriminated between when considering to whom the title descends.[54] The range of individuals directly affected by any such reform is tiny, even when including all those who might be affected by the right to adopt a non-Protestant, or non-Christian, spirituality. Nonetheless, I would argue that this bundle of laws, the most important dating from the cusp of the seventeenth and eighteenth

---

[53] Act of Settlement 1700, s. 3.
[54] As was suggested in the Hereditary Peerages Bill 1994.

centuries, carry with them the remnants of a potent political message. The drafters of the 1688 Bill of Rights had a clear vision of a Protestant state, ruled by a Protestant sovereign. Constitutional developments since then have considerably reduced the practical authority of the sovereign, but she remains a figurehead and central symbol of the United Kingdom Constitution. The current laws concerning the beliefs of the sovereign are not only a potential infringement of their religious interests, but a powerful affirmation that the legal United Kingdom is not a truly pluralist state. If the laws discussed in relation to the sovereign have any importance, they represent the United Kingdom as primarily a Protestant, and thus Christian, state; if they have no importance, they are an unnecessary remnant of anti-Catholic prejudice.[55]

Turning to the House of Lords, it might be argued that the Lords Spiritual could be expected to bring certain values into the Lords. Given the career structure of the Church of England, we might expect them to be men of some maturity, with experience of running complex, but non-commercial, organizations; and with a considerable track record in relatively poorly paid public service. They might also be expected to have a core of values not necessarily associated with loyalty to any particular political party, giving them a degree of insulation from normal political life. Finally, they might be expected to be Christians of some moral courage, willing to express themselves on points more commonly constructed as private, than public, morality. It seems to me that if these values are important within the Lords, it is possible for the executive to ensure their presence by its selection of appointed members.[56] If the individual characteristics of the Lords spiritual justify their presence, it seems more appropriate to select these individuals on the basis of those characteristics, rather than a conceptually distinct place in the Church of England—particularly one which, while female priests cannot become bishops, includes selection by gender.

It seems at least possible, however, that the Church of England has a voice in the legislative process not simply because the Lords spiritual are likely to be individuals capable of contributing to the debate, but because the voice of the Church of England is seen as a special voice within United Kingdom society. The Church of England is seen as providing religious input into an otherwise secular legislative process. This input is seen as

---

[55] I have argued elsewhere that an analysis based on establishment and disestablishment is of restricted value. Within this discourse, however, unless we treat the religious identity of the constitutional monarch as a touchstone of establishment, it is possible to remove these limits on the sovereign without *ipso facto* disestablishing the Church of England. See further P. W. Edge, 'Reorienting the Establishment Debate: From the Illusory Norm to Equality of Respect', [1998] *Anglo-American Law Review* 265–84.

[56] See the evidence of Phillip Daniels, of the Catholic Union, to the Royal Commission on Reform of the House of Lords, London, 12 May 1999.

important to the quality of the process, rather than, as would have been the case in earlier periods, a beneficial entitlement of the Church itself.

I would identify two problems with prioritizing the religious voice of the Church of England in this way. Firstly, it is troublesome to view a single religious organization as providing undifferentiated religious input. Some defenders of the Lords spiritual have argued that non-Anglicans, and even non-Christians, view their input into debate as essential, and as ensuring that a 'religious' perspective is always kept before the otherwise secular legislature. I would doubt whether a homogenization of all religious traditions, and belief systems, does justice either to their diversity, or to their different social missions. In particular, this may require the Lords spiritual to raise issues concerning religious beliefs or practices they find difficult to accept; for instance, would we require the Lords spiritual to advocate an exemption for animal sacrifice to Satan during a debate on cruelty to animals legislation? Secondly, legislators do not leave their own religious beliefs at the doorway to the legislating chamber. Although believers in some traditions may feel that specialist clergy are the appropriate individuals to formulate and voice their religious doctrines, this is not to say that only such clergy would be expected to adhere to them. In a society which is predominantly Anglican, we would expect a sizeable number of the legislators to be Anglican. If the society is not predominantly Anglican, we might query why the Anglican input should be given special status.

This brings me to my third area of concern: the exclusion of some ministers of religion from the House of Commons. So far, the general thrust of my paper might appear as, not merely a secularization of the legislative process, but an establishment of secular humanism in the place of the Anglican Church. Such a project would require the positive silencing of non-secular voices in the legislature, and would be compatible with the exclusion of religious officers from the House of Commons. I would argue, however, that the current law is problematic, not least for its incompatibility with the European Convention on Human Rights.

Article 9 provides the primary guarantee of freedom of religion. Convention organs have generally been reluctant to allow individuals to rely upon Article 9 in relation to employment or office, preferring to construct freedom of religion as the freedom to leave an office which imposes restrictions upon religious rights.[57] In the recent case of *Buscarini* v. *San Marino*,[58] however, the applicants were elected to the Parliament of San Marino, and asked permission to take their oaths of office without reference to 'the Holy Gospels'. This was refused, and the applicants even-

---

[57] See P. W. Edge, 'Religious Rights and Choice under the European Convention on Human Rights', (2000) 3 *Web Journal of Current Legal Issues*.

[58] *Buscarini and Others* v. *San Marino* (1999) HUDOC (European Court of Human Rights, Grand Chamber).

tually took the oath under protest.[59] The Court found that this requirement 'did indeed constitute a limitation within [Article 9], since it required
them to swear allegiance to a particular religion on pain of forfeiting their
parliamentary seats'.[60] As this was 'tantamount to requiring the elected
representatives of the people to swear allegiance to a particular religion', it
was not a limitation acceptable under the Convention.[61] The Court opted
for a more pluralistic vision: 'it would be contradictory to make the exercise of a mandate intended to represent different views of society within
Parliament subject to a prior declaration of commitment to a particular set
of beliefs'.[62]

The emphasis on the democratic mandate in this case may limit its
applications to attempts to exclude elected representatives from office
because of their beliefs. Even with this narrow reading, however, if elected
representatives are denied their place in the House of Commons because of
their ministry, a claim under the European Convention on Human Rights
would stand a good chance of success. This indicates that the statutes
imposing such restrictions are prima facie contrary to the Convention. It
may be possible to invoke the Human Rights Act 1998 in order to interpret the statutory provisions narrowly, especially as the Act requires
particular regard to be given to the religious interests of religious organizations.[63] Given the clarity of the provisions, however, this may serve only to
exclude non-Anglican clergy, contrary to even the narrowest reading of *Re
MacManaway*. In relation to Anglican priests or deacons, and ministers of
the Church of Scotland, a declaration of incompatibility seems the more
likely outcome.[64]

Conclusions

Only a small number of individuals are likely to be directly interested in
the processes described here. Very few people are likely to be in a position
where the limits on election to the House of Commons directly affects
them; fewer still by the composition of the House of Lords, or the limits
on freedom of conscience of the sovereign. Nonetheless, these constitutional issues are significant to all citizens of the United Kingdom.

Firstly, constitutional rules can effectively limit full participation in the
political life of the State. For instance, the United Kingdom constitution of
the early nineteenth century restricted the political activities of Jews,
Roman Catholics, and atheists. On the whole, the British constitution does
not impose excessive restrictions on the rights of adherents of particular

---

[59] The legal requirement of referring to the Holy Gospels was later removed for these
offices, but not all offices in San Marino.
[60] *Buscarini and Others* v. *San Marino*, para. 34.   [61] Ibid., para. 39.
[62] Ibid.   [63] Human Rights Act 1998, s. 13.
[64] Ibid., s. 4, 10.

religions to become involved in politics, to seek to use the political system to achieve what they see as a better state of affairs, or to stand for political office. The exclusion of some clergy from the House of Commons is a noticeable exception to this general state of affairs. The limits on the religion of the sovereign, while the harshest within the Constitution, are of such narrow application that they may be seen as unimportant.

I would argue, however, that all these limits are significant. It would be simplistic, and both unduly cynical and naive, to assume that political figures from a particular background will represent the special interests of their community. I have already alluded to concerns within the Jewish community over the role of a chief rabbi in the political life of the state. Nonetheless, it may be fair to assume that a political figure from a particular religious community will have some knowledge and understanding of some of the concerns and values of that community. Exclusion of religious adherents from office represents a stilling of valuable voices, and an impoverishment of pluralism. The importance of exclusion goes beyond even this practical aspect. A constitution which allows the active, official involvement of individuals of religious groups would be preferable to a constitution which excluded members of a particular community, even if no members of that community were so involved.

Secondly, constitutional rules can seek to support a particular religion, sometimes as part of a state ethnicity. The debate on religious education in state schools, resolved in the Education Reform Act 1988, appeared to structure the United Kingdom as a primarily Christian country.[65] The emphasis given to the Church of England in the House of Lords, and to Protestantism in succession to the Crown, would suggest that England should be structured as a primarily Protestant country.

This special treatment of a dominant religious organization, whether dominant in terms of traditional links with the state's territory or demographics, can be seen as a positive recognition of the role of the organization in the life of the state. In other words, this seemingly preferential treatment is no more than recognition of the de facto situation within the state. I think the problem here is that this view concentrates on the experience of those who are members of the dominant religious community, and thus included within the construction of ethnicity. Respect for your religious identity by the state is crucial for a feeling of full belonging to that state. By making use of constitutional rules to support the linkage between particular religious communities and the state there is a danger that those who exclude themselves from those groups will feel at least partly excluded from full citizenship in the state. If Christianity, and particularly Protestant Christianity, occupies a special constitutional position because

---

[65] C. Hamilton and B. Watt, 'A Discriminating Education: Collective Worship in Schools', (1996) 8(1) *Child and Family Law Quarterly* 28.

of national history and culture, there is at least a danger that non-Christians and non-Protestants will be constructed as less than full participants in the state, because of their less than full participation in that part of national history and culture.

The symbolic importance of these constitutional rules does not necessarily depend upon practical impact, or the extent of the rules. I would argue that the limits on the religious beliefs of the sovereign, because of the symbolic power of the sovereign as head of state, are significant. Although a non-Protestant may not be in a position to succeed to the throne in the foreseeable future, the exclusion of this possibility still sends an important symbolic message.

RELIGIOUS DENOMINATION OR PUBLIC RELIGION? THE LEGAL STATUS OF THE CHURCH OF ENGLAND

Augur Pearce

'The Churches' and the Human Rights Act 1998

A number of contributions to this volume understandably focus on the implications of the Human Rights Act 1998 for religious bodies and structures in the United Kingdom. In the early Lords debates on the bill attention focused particularly on the potential status of these or their functions as 'public', and the possibility that it might therefore be unlawful for their actions to be incompatible with Convention rights.

The attempts of the bill's champions and of government spokesmen to allay ecclesiastical fears basically sought to portray 'the churches' as 'private' bodies exercising certain 'public' functions; bodies, in other words, which were caught only by subsection (3)(b) of the public authorities section, and which therefore benefited from the exemption, under subsection (5), of their 'acts of a private nature' from the compatibility requirement. The comments of the home secretary on 20 May 1998 were typical, distinguishing activities 'essentially private in nature . . . for example, the regulation of divine worship, the administration of the sacrament, admission to church membership or to the priesthood and decisions of parochial church councils about the running of the parish church' from any activity—he instanced marriages and the provision of education in church schools—'which is also carried out by the state, and which, if the churches were not engaged in it, would be carried out directly by the state'.[1]

Given such an understanding of the role of the churches, much of the debate was concerned with the identifying side of the public–private line on which particular collective activities of believers might be thought to fall. Adoption agencies were instanced as a case where the decision might be crucial. Lord Alton and Earl Russell found themselves arguing the question of the priest's role at a Roman Catholic marriage.[2]

---

[1] *Hansard*, HC, 1015–18 (Mr Secretary Straw).
[2] *Hansard*, HL, 19 Jan. 1998, cols. 1325–6 (Bishop of Ripon); 1338–9 (Alton, Russell).

This paper will focus on aspects of the English domestic law of religion, past and present, which suggest that the blanket treatment of the churches' by the bill's supporters, based on an insufficiently long historical perspective, may prove to have been misleading. I shall suggest that while the character of a private association assuming occasional public functions is correctly ascribed to any of the voluntary churches (meaning both the Free Churches commonly so called and the Roman Catholic), it is quite wrongly ascribed to the Church of England.

In an earlier analogy the lord chancellor distinguished a private security company's activities managing a contracted-out prison from its guarding of commercial premises.[3] The argument of this paper is that while the Methodist Church might legitimately be compared to such a company, history shows the correct parallel for organs of the Church of England to be the Prison Service itself, whose acts can never be of such a 'private nature' that it can ignore convention rights with impunity.

The Christian Commonwealth and the Establishment of a National Form of Religion

My starting point in this contention is the concept of the Christian commonwealth, widely accepted in the late Middle Ages and inherited by Henrician England. The revolutionary developments of the 1530s equated this *corpus Christianum* with the nation instead of with Western Christendom, and by emancipating the laity in church government they removed the need to conceive its law as having two sources, one clerical and one lay.[4] The logic of this second development was perhaps only fully realized following the Civil War and Glorious Revolution, which together made it clear that religious affairs were no exception to the general principle of government by consent.[5]

But they remained undoubtedly a matter of *government*. The liturgy, ministerial doctrinal standards, arrangements for pastoral ministrations, and ecclesiastical government and discipline, which we call those of the Church of England, were forms and structures for which the law had provided to give practical expression to the nation's Christianity. It was

---

[3] *Hansard*, HL, 24 Nov. 1997, col. 811 (Lord Irvine of Lairg LC).

[4] Compare the preambles of the Ecclesiastical Appeals Act 1532 and Ecclesiastical Licences Act 1533. The former Act indicated the English national focus which the law of religion has never abandoned (save briefly and partially under Mary I); but at least so far as law-making was concerned, its continuing distinction between temporal and spiritual spheres must be seen as a transitional phase, superseded by the later Act's unitary approach.

[5] Hence not only the abolition of the High Commission, associated in the popular mind (justly or not) with royal and episcopal autocracy, but also the establishment of the principle that the convocations of the clergy could not make canons more widely binding than their own constituency (16 Car. I, c. 11 (1640), 13 Car. II, st. 1, c. 12 (1661); *Middleton v. Crofts* (1736) 2 Atk 650).

primarily these forms and structures that were 'established'; one speaks of an 'established *Church*' only as a derivative shorthand. All religious bodies are established by something: one could speak of the Methodist Church as established by its Basis of Union, a document of private law significance. What differentiates the national religious structure is its establishment directly by the public law of the land.

'Establishment by law' is not entirely the work of statute, nor—at least in the modern law's retrospective view—was it a novel development of the Reformation. Those received rules of the continental *jus commune* that had 'established' the worship and discipline of the English Church before the Reformation continued, as 'the King's ecclesiastical law', in full effect thereafter until legislation should alter them. Lord Blackburn in 1881 made a very helpful distinction between two senses of 'the common law': the narrower sense, meaning the law governing the remedies of Westminster Hall, and the wider, in which the canon law was not separate but itself a part of the common law.[6]

The Concept of the Church of England as a Distinct Body

It will be clear already that I have serious reservations about dicta like that of Hoffmann LJ that the English legislator sees religion as 'something to be encouraged but not the business of government',[7] and about the explanation of 'establishment' as an arm's length relationship between two distinct entities, 'Church' and 'State', offered by Phillimore J in *Marshall* v. *Graham*.[8] Hoffmann LJ was not directing his mind particularly to the Church of England, while Phillimore J's high theology of the Church could occasionally colour his legal perceptions. The European Human Rights Commission too, noting in 1994[9] that 'the Church of England is structurally a separate entity from the state', was frankly fumbling with an unfamiliar English situation on which neither party had an interest in presenting full arguments. I find the true position to have been summarized much earlier by the Supreme Court of the United States, looking back shortly after independence at the former status of Prayer Book religion in the colonies: 'The phrase "Church of England" is nothing more than a compendious expression for the religious establishment of the realm considered in aggregate.'[10]

---

[6] Submission of the Clergy Act 1533, s. 7; *Caudrey's case* (1591) 5 Co Rep 1; *Mackonochie* v. *Lord Penzance* (1881) 6 App Cas 424, 446–7. See also A.-G. v. *Dean and Chapter of Ripon* [1945] Ch 239, 245.

[7] R. v. *Disciplinary Committee of the Jockey Club, ex parte Aga Khan* [1993] 1 WLR 909, 932.

[8] [1907] 2 KB 112.

[9] *Tyler* v. *United Kingdom* (1994) 77 DR 81, 86.

[10] *Town of Pawlet* v. *Clark* (1815) 13 US 292, 325. See C. C. A. Pearce, 'Public Religion in the English Colonies', (2000) 5 *Ecclesiastical Law Journal* 440.

The point can, of course, be made that to find such clear and authoritative statements of my case one needs to delve fairly far back, and to part company with many modern popular assumptions. But English law being what it is, this is not necessarily a refutation. If Tudor statute unequivocally stated England to be a nation holding the essentials of Christian doctrine—which it did[11]—and if the law supported Elizabeth I in treating religion as the business of government—which it did—then either later legislation, or a revolutionary breach in legal continuity sufficient to warrant judicial reinterpretation of the past, must be adduced to account for any change. The last such revolution was that of 1688, and while this put the seal on shifting concepts of *how* public religion was administered, it was far from being a revolution against all public religion.

It is therefore to legislation that we must look if the concept of the Church of England as a membership organization distinct from the society around it is to be supported. Two categories call for special attention: the legislation passed for the relief of various forms of religious dissent, and the concession of an independent initiative in matters of English public religion to a body representative of active conformists.

From 1688 onwards a gradual legislative shift could be seen from a Christian nation directly regulating the practice of religion for all its inhabitants to a nation predominantly Christian, tolerating any form of religious practice or none, and leaving those most closely concerned by the public religious provision to frame alterations to it. Even at the latter end of this development, however, there was no express disclaimer of the nation's Christian character, nor of national organs' ultimate responsibility for public religion. Concessions to those who rejected the whole idea of such responsibility were in the nature of practical compromises, defusing resentment without making any wholesale surrender.

This view of what the legislative shift since 1688 has, and has not, achieved is confirmed when we distinguish various classes of legal provision.

The Relaxation of Religious Burdens

LITURGICAL AND DOCTRINAL

The field of worship and doctrine was the only field in which the law was relaxed selectively. The post-Reformation law had modified the offence of heresy so that very few who made any pretence to Catholic Christianity would be guilty of it,[12] and prescribed no further doctrinal tests for the general laity, except as preconditions of specific rites (e.g. the catechism

---

[11] Ecclesiastical Licences Act 1533, s. 13.
[12] Act of Supremacy 1559, s. 20; *Case of Heresy* (1601) 12 Co Rep 56.

before confirmation and Communion). It had also provided a moderate reformed liturgy which it was hoped all would feel able to attend. Initially, and for their unreasonable stubbornness or for their disloyalty, rather than their wrong belief as such, it penalized those who failed to do so, or whose conventicles rivalled the public provision.[13] In some ways we may compare proposals to outlaw private medicine or independent schools.

Subsequently it was realized that Christian society would hold together even if individuals were permitted to express their dissent from this public liturgy and to worship in their own fashion. Trinitarian dissenting Protestants qualifying by appropriate oaths were the first to be allowed to do so; Roman Catholics followed, and later the oaths for Protestants were replaced by the confinement of services to registered buildings. The emancipation of Unitarians, the ending of oaths for Catholics, and then the repeal of virtually all laws against alternative worship completed this process.[14]

Sunday absence from church was a slightly different issue, and change took longer. Although the more draconian penalties were repealed early for Protestant Dissenters who went to their own services, the underlying statutory obligation remained until abolished altogether for Roman Catholics in 1844, and for Protestant Dissenters usually attending alternative Sunday worship in 1846.[15]

OTHER BURDENS

By contrast, the law's religious burdens in fields outside the strictly liturgical have been relaxed with no distinction between conformist and Dissenter. Both together benefited from the de facto obsolescence of the episcopal courts' moral control in the nineteenth century; both were emancipated from episcopal jurisdiction over defamation, wills, and divorce;[16] both were given the choice of marrying in register offices.[17] Financially, both together were freed from enforceable obligations to support parochial

---

[13] e.g. Act of Uniformity 1551, s. 2; 35 Eliz. I, c. 1 (1592).

[14] Toleration Act 1688; Roman Catholic Relief Act 1791; Places of Religious Worship Act 1812; 53 Geo. III, c. 160 (1813); Roman Catholic Relief Act 1829; Religious Disabilities Act 1846.

[15] Toleration Act 1688, s. 16; Roman Catholic Relief Act 1791; 7 & 8 Vic. c. 102 (1844); Religious Disabilities Act 1846. The obligation remained, though without penalty, for all Protestants not attending dissenting services, or dissenting on grounds neither doctrinal nor liturgical, until the repeal of the 1551 Act by the Statute Law (Repeals) Act 1969. Until then Roman Catholics were the only class which the law did not require to attend worship of any sort.

[16] 18 & 19 Vic., c. 41 (1855) (defamation); Probate Act 1857; Matrimonial Causes Act 1857. Both alike were freed from episcopal disciplinary jurisdiction altogether, when the procedure for its application to laymen was abolished by the Ecclesiastical Jurisdiction Measure 1963.

[17] Marriage Act 1836.

ministry[18] and benefited from the ending of ecclesiastical provision from general taxation. None of these changes supported a concept that 'members of the Church of England' were being distinguished from non-members; the impression given was rather that the religious obligations of the Christian commonwealth were becoming matters for individual conscientious decision.

Where there has been no change for conformists, there has been none for dissenters either. Any person may still be summoned as a witness or condemned in costs by an episcopal court;[19] notaries of all creeds need the Archbishop of Canterbury's faculty to practise;[20] the law on which the Lords spiritual deliberate in Parliament applies to all.

Religious Rights and the Enabling Act

A third class of provision encompasses the religious rights, rather than burdens, stemming from membership in the Christian commonwealth. Here again no distinction between conformist and dissenter was made throughout the nineteenth century: all parishioners, irrespective of their general conformity, remained entitled at any time to attend parish worship,[21] or to demand pastoral ministrations, the solemnization of their marriages,[22] the baptism of their children, and churchyard burial.[23] They can still claim an interest in faculty proceedings[24] and vote in the election of churchwardens.[25] Entitlement to the burial service depends upon baptism rather than conformity; and a confirmed dissenter has the right to be admitted to Communion, while an unconfirmed conformist does not.[26]

A significant inroad into this culture of parity was made, however, by the Rules for the Representation of the Laity annexed to the constitution

---

[18] Compulsory Church Rate Abolition Act 1868; Tithe Act 1936.

[19] Ecclesiastical Jurisdiction Measure 1963, s. 81, preserves an older power.

[20] Courts and Legal Services Act 1990, s. 57, assumes and supplements the basic jurisdiction of the Archbishop of Canterbury's Master of the Faculties, which derives from the Ecclesiastical Licences Act 1533, s. 3.

[21] *Cole* v. *Police Constable 443A* [1937] 1 KB 316.

[22] The authority from which a prima facie duty of parish clergy to solemnize the lawful marriage of parishioners, both by licence and a fortiori after banns, is derived is *Argar* v. *Holdsworth* (1758) 2 Lee 515; although the duty has since been affirmed by implication in the 1857 and subsequent Acts, as well as by the House of Lords in *Thompson* v. *Dibdin* [1912] AC 533. Recent doubts as to whether a duty to solemnize after banns was indeed to be deduced from the original judgment of Lee DA rest upon the doubtful premiss that a common licence could ever be thought to *command*, rather than permit, solemnization. See e.g. Michael G. Smith, 'An Interpretation of *Argar* v. *Holdsworth*', (1998) 5 *Ecc. LJ* 34.

[23] *R.* v. *Taylor* (1721) unreported, but cited in Robert Phillimore, *Ecclesiastical Law*, 2nd edn. (London 1895), 653; *Kemp* v. *Wickes* (1809) 3 *Phil. Ecc.* 264.

[24] Faculty Jurisdiction Rules 1992, r. 15(2)(a).

[25] Churchwardens (Appointment and Resignation) Measure 1964, s. 3.

[26] Sacrament Act 1547, s. 8; Rubrics to the Orders for Confirmation and Burial in the Book of Common Prayer 1662.

of the Church Assembly in 1919. In conferring a significant role in religious legislation upon this body,[27] Parliament indirectly approved a religious franchise confined to active conformists—those baptized parishioners who sought entry on a separate roll, declaring themselves 'members of the Church of England' and—initially—denying membership of any alternative religious body. These restrictions were at the time a matter of considerable controversy: while High Churchmen like Charles Gore fought for a stricter 'confirmation franchise' (Gore ultimately resigned his see when his campaign failed), others condemned provisions which they felt would 'turn a national church into a denomination'.[28]

But three points should be noted. Firstly, the exclusive nature of the church electoral roll proved a temporary feature, and since 1973 any baptized parishioner, regardless of links to Nonconformist bodies, has been eligible for enrolment.[29] Secondly, the role of the Assembly (now the General Synod) is simply to *frame* primary religious legislation, which still needs the approval of Parliament, representative of the whole commonwealth, to become law.[30] And thirdly, the role of such legislation is concurrent with that of Acts, by which the Houses still occasionally take direct religious initiatives.[31]

The Relative Status of the Church of England and its Alternatives

Church Government

It is instructive to contrast with the Church of England the legal status of the structures of alternative religion. The Toleration Act 1688 recognized 'congregations of dissenting protestants' and the concept of 'belonging' to these.[32] But such bodies are viewed in English law as aggregates of their

---

[27] Church of England Assembly (Powers) Act 1919.

[28] e.g. Letter of Bishop Herbert Hensley Henson to *The Times,* 16 Apr. 1917.

[29] Church Representation Rules (Amendment) Resolution 1973.

[30] The Enabling Bill was presented to Parliament not as a principled transfer of legislative authority from 'State' to 'Church', but as an efficiency measure, enabling religion legislation to receive consideration elsewhere by those with more time and relevant learning, so that when it came before the legislature its consideration would require considerably less parliamentary time; see David M. Thompson, 'The Politics of the Enabling Act of 1919', in David Baker (ed.), *Church, Society and Politics* (Oxford, 1975). A proposal recently refused assent was the first draft of the Clergy (Ordination) Measure 1990 (*Hansard*, HC, 17 July 1989, cols. 174–93). The position of such measures as primary legislation, to be construed in accordance with the Convention and on which a section 4 declaration of incompatibility can be made, is quite clear from definitions in the Human Rights Act 1998. The fact that the accelerated procedure for ministerial amendment is not applicable to them (s. 10(6)) does not alter the principle of compatibility, and simply leaves the onus of corrective legislation with Parliament if the General Synod fails to act. See, however, the assurance given by the bishop of Ripon on 29 Jan. 1998; *Hansard*, HL, col. 397.

[31] Examples of post-1919 Acts affecting the Church of England directly and specifically (albeit affecting the 'denominations' also, in less specific fashion) are the Matrimonial Causes Act 1937 and the Sharing of Church Buildings Act 1969.   [32] ss. 8, 14.

members. They, and any structures above them such as a General Assembly or a circuit meeting, derive their existence not directly from public law but from the agreement of individuals, express or tacit, to join together for the exercise of religion; to which agreement (once rendered lawful by the Act) *private* law attaches the same consequences as to any other contract for a common undertaking.[33] The Crown claims no role in their government; Parliament does not concern itself with their internal business except when asked to assist through the private bill procedure.[34] The courts will take such notice of their constitution as is necessary to enforce trusts of property and safeguard private rights; but no more.[35] The recent issue of an injunction restraining the performance of a Church of England ordination by a retired bishop in Newcastle, where he had no standing to officiate,[36] would have been unthinkable in the context of a voluntary religious body.

LAND AND BUILDINGS

This sharp contrast between the structures of public and voluntary religion has generally been accentuated by statutory language, though exceptions should be recognized. The greater the political influence of dissenters on legislation, the more likely it has been to treat the Church of England as just another denomination. An early terminological success of the Dissenting Deputies was the Places of Religious Worship Act 1812, which instead of taking the existence of the national Church as its starting point, made it an exception after referring generally to 'the religious worship of protestants'.[37] The Religious Disabilities Act 1846 was the first to penalize even-handedly the disturbance of *any* meeting 'of persons lawfully assembled for religious worship'.[38] Nonetheless, the fact that the registration of sacred buildings, even after this became wholly advantageous and ceased to have any connection to the restriction of alternative worship, never applied to the national Church, while episcopal consecration and licensing for public worship retained direct common law and statutory significance, emphasizes a continuing difference of approach.[39]

---

[33] The authority of a Roman Catholic bishop derives from the agreement of Roman Catholic worshippers in the same way; see *Brown* v. *Curé of Montréal* (1874) LR 6 PC 157, 204.

[34] The first English example being the Methodist Church Union Act 1929 (19 & 20 Geo. V, c. lix).

[35] *Forbes* v. *Eden* (1867) LR 1 Sc & Div 568.   [36] *Gill* v. *Davies* (1997) 5 *Ecc. LJ* 131.

[37] ss. 2, 13; this approach was taken also in the Places of Worship Registration Act 1855, ss. 2 ('Religious Worship of any Body or Denomination of Persons'), 10.

[38] s. 4.

[39] Places of Worship Registration Act 1855, s. 10; compare the treatment of parts of private cemeteries consecrated for burial with Church of England rites and 'set apart' by the cemetery company for other burials, in Cemeteries Clauses Act 1847, ss. 23, 35–6.

IDENTIFICATION AND PRIVILEGES OF MINISTERS

References in criminal statutes to ministers and places of worship made no distinction between the national and other churches,[40] nor (in recent times) has the exemption of ministers of religion from jury service or conscription. However, the law has always acknowledged a special status for clerks in holy orders. How such orders are transmitted is a question of public law, contrasting with the factual or private law issue of a non-episcopal minister's status.[41]

MAINTAINED EDUCATION

The hard-won 'Cowper-Temple clause' in the Elementary Education Act 1870 gave a hint of parity, ranking the characteristic emphases of Prayer Book and Articles of Religion alongside alternative tenets in its requirement that board (now community) schools provide religious education 'not distinctive of any particular religious denomination'.[42] It should be borne in mind, though, that neither these, nor what are now voluntary schools, are official emanations of the national Church at all. Church school promoters are in principle individuals, as are the trustees of their sites, and can be considered private individuals with public functions without affecting the principle regarding the organs of public religion themselves.[43]

If a diocesan board of education steps into these roles, it does so simply to replace individuals, and equal treatment with the representatives of alternative religion is only to be expected. However, that board's position as a body which such individuals *must* consult is a statutory one having no counterpart in other denominations.[44] A distinction appears again in decision-making on the 'agreed syllabus' for county school religious education under the Education Act 1944: the committee representing for this purpose 'such religious denominations as ought to be represented, with regard to the circumstances of the area' is a *separate* committee from that 'representative of the Church of England'.[45]

---

[40] Malicious Damage Act 1861, s. 1 ('Arson of Place of Worship'), Offences Against the Person Act 1861, s. 36 ('Assault on Minister').

[41] See *A.-G.* v. *Glasgow College* (1846) 2 Coll 665, *per* Knight Bruce LJ. The significance which orders (including Roman Catholic ones) carried per se was once concerned with marriage (*R.* v. *Fielding* (1705) 5 St Tr 610; *R.* v. *Millis* (1844) 10 Cl & Fin 534, 861, 906). A relic of their special treatment can be seen in an exclusion from the House of Commons capable of covering both Church of England and Roman Catholic clergy, and those ordained by Protestant bishops elsewhere: House of Commons (Clergy Disqualification) Act 1801 and see *Re MacManaway* [1951] AC 161.

[42] s. 14(2).

[43] The same applies a fortiori to church adoption agencies.

[44] Diocesan Boards of Education Measure 1991.

[45] Sch. 5, para. 2(a), (b), and proviso.

CHARITY LAW—THE GREAT EXCEPTION

This brings us to the great exception to the law's special treatment of the Church of England. The 'repair of churches' provision in the preamble to the Charitable Uses Act 1601 was extrapolated by the courts to create the 'head of charity' which now appears in the textbooks as 'the advancement of religion'.[46] Decisions on charitable status, and the benefits and restrictions that it imposes, have paid no special attention to the national Church but treated all lawful Christian practice, and later all religious practice, equally.[47]

As with the schools provisions just considered, though, this can be explained by the fact that the law of charity is (in its positive aspects) essentially a series of privileges designed to encourage *private* individuals to do good and so relieve the burden on public authority; it is the antithesis of public provision. Its benefits were coterminous with religion conforming to the national provision only so long as this was considered the only tolerable form of religious expression even for individuals. But once alternative religion was considered allowable, this could also be recognized as laudable.

EXCURSUS: NON-CHRISTIAN RELIGIONS

This development is easier to explain in relation to Christian nonconformity than to non-Christian religion. The precondition for a public regulation of religion was that England itself was Christian; as such the nation could *be* the Church, and their organs, once the link between spiritual jurisdiction and holy orders was cut, could be one and the same. All inhabitants fell under the jurisdiction of episcopal courts, which included the power to punish for breaches of Christian morality, as well as for blasphemy and what was left of heresy.[48] The requirement of conformity to a particular mode of expression of Christian faith was a temporary phenomenon, but the assumption of Christian faith itself went deeper and survived the Toleration Acts.[49]

This remained theoretically the case despite the return of the Jews in the Commonwealth and Restoration periods, and initially it was only the repeated royal *nolle prosequi* that prevented Jewish gatherings from being prosecuted as conventicles.[50] Before 1846 statute law turned a blind eye to

---

[46] *Commissioners for Special Purposes of the Income Tax* v. *Pemsel* [1891] AC 531, 583.

[47] See e.g. *A.-G.* v. *Cock* (1751) 2 Ves Sen 273 (bequest to support Baptist ministers), *Thornton* v. *Howe* (1862) 31 Beav 14 (Joanna Southcott's Sealed Writings), *Gilmour* v. *Coats* [1949] AC 426, 457, *Neville Estates* v. *Madden* [1962] Ch 832, 853 ('any religion likely to be better than none').

[48] The jurisdiction was saved by the statute abolishing the writ for burning heretics; 29 Car. II, c. 9 (1677).

[49] The statement of England's adherence to 'the very articles of the catholic faith of Christendom' in Ecclesiastical Licences Act 1533, s. 13, remains on the statute book today.

[50] H. S. Q. Henriques, *The Jews and the English Law* (London, 1908).

English Judaism or tacitly assumed its existence rather than expressly sanctioning it: in the very year of his Act exempting Jewish marriages from the new solemnization rules, Lord Hardwicke LC remarked: 'The Jewish religion . . . is not taken notice of by any law, but is barely connived at by the legislature.'[51]

However, the express recognition that a Christian nation did not have to compel its subjects to worship alike was followed by a tacit recognition that it need not compel them to believe alike, and could even support them in their legal arrangements for the furtherance of practice expressing alternative belief.[52] The reinterpretation of blasphemy as requiring an element of vilification, and the practical obsolescence of the heresy law, prevented either from interfering with moderate non-Christian utterance. Both continued as features of the legal system; both remained Christian;[53] but de facto they did not impede the collective exercise of other faiths once the conventicle laws finally disappeared in 1846.

The majority speeches of the House of Lords in *Bowman* v. *Secular Society*[54] concerning the lack of any Christian presuppositions in the common law were therefore rather widely expressed, neither the heresy jurisdiction nor the implications of the church-governmental role of national institutions being considered. But there is no reason to question the decision as regards the field with which the House actually had to deal, namely the legality of non-Christian purposes for the purpose of Supreme Court remedies; and its consequence was that there was no further question as to the 'advancement of religion' privileges covering non-Christian religious purposes.

MARRIAGE SOLEMNIZATION

From 1898 it has been possible for marriage to be solemnized in buildings registered for alternative worship without a registrar present. It is significant, though, that while the presence of a person competent by virtue of his orders (the minister) suffices in a parish church, the essential presence at dissenting ceremonies (apart, possibly, from a registrar) is that of a person, not defined by any role in the dissenting religious polity, but authorized by the 'trustees or governing body' of the registered building—a definition easily given meaning by private law.[55]

---

[51] *De Costa* v. *De Paz* (1753) 2 Swans 532 n.; Religious Disabilities Act 1846, s. 2.

[52] Prior to the 1846 Act a bequest to provide Passover meal ingredients was held lawful in *A.-G. ex rel. Strauss* v. *Goldsmid* (1837) 8 Sim 614.

[53] As to the Christian assumptions of the law of blasphemy, see *R.* v. *Chief Metropolitan Stipendiary Magistrate, ex parte Choudhury* [1991] 1 QB 429.

[54] [1917] AC 406, e.g. *per* Lord Sumner at 464.

[55] This provision dates from the Marriage Act 1898, s. 6(3). It is fair to say that since 1836 there has been statutory recognition as such of local synagogue and meeting officials certified

MINISTERS' EMPLOYMENT STATUS

Finally, a long line of cases beginning in 1912 has looked at the employment status of ministers of religion. The reasoning common to all these decisions has been that the nature of a minister's duties and the understanding of his stipend rule out an employment relationship for both national insurance and employment protection purposes.[56] But a significant extra factor has featured in the judgments concerning Church of England curates, namely that '[the curate's] relationship with the bishop is governed by the law of the established church which is part of the public law of England, and not by a negotiated contractual agreement . . . There is no private law contract transforming him into an employee.'[57]

The Church of England as a Membership Association

One further argument in support of the 'public authority' status of the organs and officers of the Church of England is that their powers and functions are not confined to any particular 'membership'. The distinction between an inhabitant of England and a member of the national Church has never been anything but hazy.

A few nineteenth-century statutes envisaged 'non-membership of the Church of England'. In 1847, for example, the Cemeteries Clauses Act allowed the allocation of land 'for the bodies of persons not being members of the established church';[58] while the university reforms relaxing religious tests contained safeguards for offices previously 'confined to members of the Church of England'.[59]

It is arguable, though, that the cemetery provision meant no more than 'not conforming to the established church'. The complementary provision for the 'Church of England portion' did not confine that land to the burial 'of members', but rather confined it to burials 'according to the rites' of the national Church, for which most dissenters could opt if they chose.[60] The context of the university Act provisions made it clear that the offices

---

by 'the Recording Clerk of the Society of Friends called Quakers at their Central Office in London' and by 'the President for the time being of the London Committee of Deputies of British Jews'; Births and Deaths Registration Act 1836, s. 30. But the difficulties of treating a private law association as though it were a public body are illustrated by the Sharing of Church Buildings Act 1969, s. 11, which still applies the Act to religious bodies acceding by notice to 'the General Secretary of the British Council of Churches', an officer who no longer exists!

[56] e.g. *Davies v. Presbyterian Church of Wales* [1986] 1 WLR 323.
[57] *Diocese of Southwark v. Coker* [1998] ICR 140, 148, *per* Mummery LJ; see also *Re Employment of Church of England Curates* [1912] 2 Ch 563.
[58] s. 35; and see, for public cemeteries outside London, Burial Act 1853, s. 7
[59] Oxford University Act 1854, s. 44; Cambridge University Act, s. 45; Universities Tests Acts 1871, s. 3.
[60] Cemeteries Clauses Act 1847, s. 23.

in question would be open only to those willing to make the doctrinal declarations and oaths formerly required of graduands (or, in the case of the Cambridge Act, a declaration of '*bona fide* membership of the Church of England'); which cannot be considered a universal membership criterion.

The Local Government Act 1894 made special provisions for trusteeship of a charity whose endowment was held 'for the benefit of any particular Church or denomination, or of any members thereof as such'. Four years later Stirling J held a charity where eligibility for benefit depended on worshipping habits and godly conduct to be 'for members of the Church of England as such' within the meaning of the Act. However, he was clear that, while he might hold certain attributes to identify beyond doubt and *as such* a 'member of the Church of England', he was not attempting to give a strict legal definition of what was necessary to constitute such membership.[61]

Since the church electoral roll appeared in 1919, it has always been accepted that this is not a membership roll; for one thing it excludes the clergy and there is no register which could determine the 'membership' status of a cleric teetering on the brink between conformity and Roman Catholicism.[62] A spectrum of views on membership criteria has been expressed in churchgoing circles, in which baptism has generally been the lowest common denominator; but it must be recognized that many of the religious rights considered earlier are enjoyed by parishioners irrespective of whether they are baptized.

The modern decision in *Re Allen deceased*, whereby a bequest conditional on 'membership of the Church of England and adherence to its doctrine' was held not to be void for uncertainty, is less pertinent since the issue there was not to impose an objective test but to interpret what the testator meant. Even so, two of the four judges concerned in the case found the condition to lack precise meaning.[63]

Conclusion

Modern office-bearers in the Church of England often speak of expressing or following 'the mind of the Church', which they conceive to be an entity

[61] *Re Perry Almshouses* [1898] 1 Ch 391, 400.

[62] The roll now serves a number of other functions besides defining the lay franchise and eligibility for office. A person on the roll of a parish can marry and be buried in that parish even when not otherwise qualified, be heard in faculty proceedings, and join in a complaint against a parish minister. (Marriage Act 1949, s. 6(4); Church of England (Miscellaneous Provisions) Measure 1976, s. 6; Faculty Jurisdiction Measure 1964, s. 9(1); Ecclesiastical Jurisdiction Measure 1963, s. 20). But a person not on any roll can do all of these things as of right in his own parish, except lodge a disciplinary complaint which he can do as a person authorized by the bishop.

[63] [1953] Ch 810.

distinct from the wider community in which it operates. Some regard the notion of the Christian commonwealth as misguided ecclesiology from the start; others recognize the weight of support given to it by Richard Hooker[64] and prefer to contend that the factual basis from which Hooker reasoned has now changed. Clearly the religious complexion of the country is indeed very different from that of the sixteenth century, though today's concepts of what is 'Christian' are also broader.

The concern of this paper was not, however, to justify the modern religious constitution so much as to describe it—offering an alternative approach to that of earlier writers on ecclesiastical law, especially of the Tractarian school, whose large claims for the national Church on historical and doctrinal grounds did not essentially distinguish it from voluntary bodies so far as its constitution was concerned.

To sum up: despite the existence of an electoral roll of active conformists, and a massive shift in popular perceptions and lawyers' terminology over the past 150 years, the institutions of the Church of England still carry on that public administration of English Christianity which was once unequivocally 'the business of government', and has never unequivocally ceased to be so. The rules of public religion are as much the law of the land as the law of mental health, but have been revoked altogether in many areas so as to make active participation in religious observance a matter of conscience rather than legal obligation for all concerned. The continuing religious rights of the whole populace, the contrasting treatment of alternative religious bodies, and the lack of any clear concept of Church of England 'membership', all testify to the national and official nature of the activities performed in English parish churches.

Other members of the Council of Europe may no longer regard the ordinances of religion as something which it is the task of public authority to secure to its subjects. The concept of what is 'public' is a flexible one; education, after all, was once a wholly private matter. In many former colonies, in Ireland, and (save as regards marriage) in Wales the national regulation of religion has now ceased.[65] But so long as a particular form of religious practice remains a public matter in England—and historic resources (derived from an era of national compulsory contribution) are devoted to its support—it is not unreasonable to expect its conformity with whatever the national conscience, itself informed by a broadly Christian outlook, may recognize to be fundamental human rights.

---

[64] *Of the Lawes of Ecclesiastical Polity*, 8 vols. (London, 1593–1648) (leading modern edn. Folger Library, Binghamton, NY, 1993).

[65] Irish Church Act 1869; Welsh Church Act 1914, s. 3, as qualified by Welsh Church (Temporalities) Act 1919, s. 6.

DEFINING THE LEGAL BOUNDARIES OF ORTHODOXY FOR PUBLIC AND PRIVATE RELIGION IN ENGLAND

David Harte

Introduction

This paper is concerned with a central dilemma in the relationship between religion and the modern State. Liberal democratic states seek to accommodate a great range of cultures and ideological beliefs, and the law has been progressively shaped to make such accommodation by requiring equal treatment for all citizens. However, concentrating on individual rights fails adequately to take account of the way that people identify with structures and organizations. In particular, a person's religious affiliation may be more important to them than their affiliation to the State itself. If the claims of religious bodies are taken seriously, a person's religion should be more important to him or her than the State. The State is limited in time and space, whereas a religion claims to have universal implications.

In the past, states have identified with particular religious traditions and have sought to impose a uniform code of belief as part of their own system of control. The Church of England was an obvious example of an established national Church used in this way.[1] Modern states which are avowedly secular, in practice, support a materialist orthodoxy which threatens individual choice in a similar manner to the old confessional states. In extreme cases, as with Marxist states, the enforcement of materialist orthodoxy can involve outlawing or severely limiting religious bodies. However, even states which stress the importance of human freedoms for individual citizens may be essentially materialist. They may apparently give individuals extensive freedom to practise their religion but they may quite considerably restrict the autonomy of the religious organizations to which people belong by excluding such organizations from certain areas of life or by forcing them to comply with a secular canon of values.

---

[1] The Orthodox churches of Greece and of post-Soviet Russia may to some extent be seen as modern examples. For the way in which an established Church may be protected from potential rivals though the use of ostensibly anti-discriminatory legislation, see *Kokkinakis* v. *Greece* (1994) 17 EHRR 397.

In Britain the confessional State came to tolerate extensive nonconformity in a range of Christian denominations and then in other faiths, all outside the established Church. The confessional State still survives in the remaining constitutional role of the Church of England, but, in practice, if there is a uniform ethos which underlines modern British society, it would seem to be essentially materialist. This ethos may rely on some shared humanitarian principles which particularly emphasize the equal right of all citizens to share in the material benefits of society. However, the very concern to treat all citizens equally means that it is difficult for the State to treat their beliefs seriously because that would be likely to involve discrimination, giving priority to certain beliefs over others.

In the secular Western world, generally, the tendency has developed of treating religion as an essentially private matter which should be seen as an aspect of individual human rights. The legal framework by which the modern State relates with religious organizations is typically that of contract law. Religious organizations are seen as private contractual associations of their members. This makes them vulnerable to secular interference by a secular State which imposes uniform standards, notably for contracts of employment. In any event, the State can be involved in internal disputes between a Church or other religious body and its members when the courts are called upon to adjudicate on such contracts. By contrast, the Church of England is formally part of the State because of the remaining bonds of 'establishment'. Its decisions may therefore be subject to judicial review as an aspect of public law.

The subject of disestablishment is an aspect of the contemporary debate on the Constitution. The future of the monarch as governor of a national Christian Church causes problems for some in a multi-faith society.[2] The place of bishops in the House of Lords is under review as part of the general reform of the House of Lords.[3] Among members of the Church of England there is some resentment both towards interference by Parliament in the making of new church law, when measures are in effect vetoed,[4] and also towards the perceived cost of running a special system of courts and the faculty system to protect church buildings and so keep them free of secular listed building control.[5] Disestablishment is a complex issue, but its

[2] For a review of the current relationship between the British monarchy and the Church of England, see Vernon Bogdanor, *The Monarchy and the Constitution* (Oxford, 1995), ch. 10.

[3] The Wakeham Committee, Royal Commission on the Reform of the House of Lords, *A House for the Future*, Cm. 4534, Jan. 2000, 150–9.

[4] The often quoted example of Parliament overruling the will of the elected representatives of the national Church was its rejection of the proposed authorization of the 1928 Prayer Book. More recently Parliament has rejected two successive draft churchwardens' measures designed to enable bishops to suspend churchwardens from office. For further discussion of these, see below.

[5] Under Planning (Listed Buildings and Conservation Areas) Act 1990, s. 60.

essential effect would be to privatize what is at present a public institution and to transform its internal legal framework into a complex series of private contractual relationships. This has happened already with the Church in Wales, which was disestablished in 1920.[6]

This paper is not concerned with arguments for or against the establishment of the Church of England. Rather, it seeks to question how far a private law model is adequate for the proper recognition of major religious bodies within the State and whether wider provision could be made for treating religious bodies as subjects of public law. A major consideration for modern British society is whether it is to be avowedly secular or genuinely plural. If it is to be genuinely plural, the law needs to be framed so as to provide a public rather than merely a private role for religion. The impact of the Human Rights Act 1998 gives an urgency to identifying the extent to which religion is to be a dimension of public life, rather than simply a matter of individual rights. It is significant here that the Act incorporates European Convention rights into United Kingdom law by means of imposing a duty on public authorities not to act in any way which is incompatible with a convention right.[7] Further urgency is added by proposed European Community legislation aimed at outlawing discrimination on religious grounds in employment law.[8]

This paper considers, first, how religious associations have been shown to be vulnerable if they rely on the traditional private law regime of contract law. This is illustrated by a discussion of state intervention in contracts of employment by anti-discrimination legislation. It is argued that although the State has a proper concern in ensuring fair treatment of employees of religious organizations, it is important for the integrity of such an organization to be respected, particularly in allowing it to insist that its employees conform with its own belief systems. It is suggested that a public law model inspired by that which applies to the Church of England could strike a better balance.

Machinery for regulating belief may affect a range of rights within a religious body. Thus, admission to full membership is likely to depend on some test of doctrinal orthodoxy. Membership may, in turn, involve rights to choose or stand as office-holders and, there, defined beliefs are likely to be considered an essential requirement both for appointment and for retaining office. The paper suggests that if a religious body is to assume a public role in society, it may be appropriate for the State to exercise some degree of supervision in respect of offices which do not involve employment and indeed in respect of decisions over who is or is not a member of the relevant body.

---

[6] Welsh Church Acts 1914 and 1919. [7] Human Right Act 1998, s. 6.

[8] Proposal for a council directive establishing a general framework for equal treatment in employment and occupation; EC 1999, 599 pc0565, subsequently approved as Council Directive 2000/78/EC, OJ L 303, 02/12/2000, pp. 16–22.

Interference with the Autonomy of Religious Bodies in their Contracts of Employment

Religious bodies in England, other than the Church of England, are largely treated in law as private associations whose members are voluntarily bound together by contract. However, such contracts are not simply private matters for their members. In particular, modern employment law has greatly restricted freedom of contract, notably to eliminate discrimination and to prevent unfair dismissal on the grounds of race or gender.[9] Here the likely impact of the Human Rights Act 1998 is a subject of wide-ranging debate. In assimilating the rights prescribed by the European Convention on Human Rights into UK law, a crucial issue is whether the Act will lead to new restrictions which will prevent employers from requiring particular religious affiliations of their employees.

The European Convention on Human Rights does not specifically confer rights in respect of employment law. However, Article 14 of the Convention, on prohibition of discrimination requires that 'The enjoyment of the rights and freedoms set forth in the Convention shall be secured without discrimination on any grounds such as sex, race, colour, language, religion, political or other opinion, national or social origin, association with a national minority, property, birth or other status.' Article 9, which guarantees freedom of thought, conscience, and religion, has been treated in case-law on the Convention as applying to the right to be free not to practise any religion.[10] Thus it can be argued that a person who is not considered for a job because he or she either does or does not belong to a particular faith is being denied their religious freedom by being discriminated against on the grounds of their religion.

The debate over how this principle may be applied in national employment law turns on section 6 of the Act, which makes it unlawful 'for a public authority to act in a way which is incompatible with a Convention right'. As public authorities specifically include a court or a tribunal,[11] there is an imperative for the general law of employment to be interpreted so as to prohibit discrimination on religious grounds. Although this does not itself prohibit such discrimination in private contracts of employment, public authorities also include 'any person, certain of whose functions are functions of a public nature'. Any act by such a person which is not private[12] and which is discriminatory can be directly attacked by a 'victim' bringing legal proceedings.[13] There would seem to be no doubt that the Church of England would be a public body for these purposes, although it is much less clear which of its acts would be considered of a public nature.

---

[9] See Sex Discrimination Act 1975 and Race Relations Act 1976.
[10] *Kokkinakis* v. *Greece* (1994) 17 EHRR 397.
[11] Human Rights Act 1998, s. 6 (2)(a).
[12] s. 6(5).   [13] s. 7(1).

Its legislation and its courts are part of the state system and are subject to the Act.[14] It is also unclear as to what extent other religious bodies may be public for this purpose.

If churches and other religious bodies were prohibited from making appointments on the basis of belief, their integrity would be substantially undermined. It would be a major threat to a church if it could not advertise for a verger or a caretaker who was a practising Christian and to a mosque if it could not advertise for a Muslim cleaner. Concerns of this sort led to the inclusion of section 13 of the Human Rights Act, which provides at (1): 'If a court's determination of any question arising under this Act might affect the exercise by a religious organisation (itself or its members collectively) of the Convention right to freedom of thought, conscience and religion, it must have particular regard to the importance of that right.' This safeguard for religious organizations is considered to be unnecessary by some commentators.[15] In particular, the Convention rights to freedom of religion are subject to a rider which does allow limitations to be prescribed by law which are 'necessary in a democratic society in the interests of public safety, for the protection of public order, health or morals or for the protection of the rights and freedom of others'. However, those who are prevented from discriminating against others are inevitably going to be restricted in their own freedom. Where the line is drawn is bound to be uncertain without more guidance in legislation or case-law.[16]

Further uncertainty has been introduced by proposed European Community intervention in the freedom of employers to discriminate in their choice of employee.[17] The proposal is in a draft directive which would set a general framework for equal treatment in employment and occupation. This would require member states to prohibit discrimination in employment on various grounds. Some, such as race, are already covered by national legislation, but the proposed directive would also include religion. Different treatment would be justified in national legislation made under the directive on the basis of a genuine occupational qualification.

[14] Church of England Measures are specifically identified as primary legislation under Human Rights Act 1998, s. 21.

[15] e.g. Jason Coppel, *The Human Rights Act 1998; Enforcing the European Convention in the Domestic Courts* (Chichester, 1999), 70–2.

[16] Conflicts over religious rights are particularly likely to arise in respect of the manifestation of belief in seeking to proselytize. The scope of the Convention Right to religious freedom which is discussed more fully below does not specifically include proselytizing, and it is apparent that one person seeking to witness to another may be seen by that other as a threat to their rights; *Kokkinakis* v. *Greece*. Conflict may also arise where a statement on a religious subject may be interpreted by others as blasphemous; *Choudhury* v. *UK* Appl. 17439/90 Commission (5 Mar. 1991).

[17] Proposal for a council directive establishing a general framework for equal treatment in employment and occupation; EC 1999, 599pc0565, subsequently approved as Council Directive 2000/78/EC, OJ L 303, 02/12/2000, pp. 16–22.

Such an exception could be made 'in the case of public or private organisations which pursue directly and essentially the aim of ideological guidance
in the field of religion or belief with respect to education, information and
the expression of opinions' for the particular occupational activities within
those organizations which are directly and essentially related to that aim.

The final form of the directive remains to be resolved, but unless the
exception for a religious qualification were widened substantially, religious
individuals would be severely hampered in forming associations to carry
out ordinary activities, such as medical or legal work or providing housing
services, which maintain the principles and ethos of a particular faith.

The proposed exception would extend to both public and private organizations. If a wider exception were given, it is possible that it might be
confined to private associations, but that would, for example, leave vulnerable a charity run by the Church of England or a voluntary-aided confessional school. Although such a school would be able to require religious
commitment from teachers of religious education, it would be impossible
for a religious school to pursue a general policy of appointing staff of the
relevant faith. So far as European Community law is concerned, the
Church of England would appear to be an emanation of the State subject
to vertical direct effect. An individual may rely directly on a European
Community directive in legal proceedings against such a state Church, and
the principle has been applied to a voluntary-aided church school.[18] The
proposed fair treatment directive, as initially drafted, seems to threaten the
substantial activity of many faith bodies as partners with the State in
providing a wide range of social services.[19]

The example of a church being unable to advertise for a Christian
verger or a mosque for a Muslim caretaker could be affected by both the
Human Rights Act 1998 and the proposed EC directive. Such cases might
seem of little practical concern, since it might be supposed that only
members of the relevant religions would be interested in such a job.
However, that is not necessarily the case. An atheist enthusiast for ancient
buildings could well establish that he or she was a very well qualified
candidate for a post of church verger apart from their lack of belief.

English statute law has already recognized the special nature of certain
types of public contract such as those for teachers in state schools.
Religious schools are provided for within the state system, as 'voluntary
schools'.[20] Most of these are Church of England or Roman Catholic,

---

[18] N.U.T. v. Governing Body of St Mary's Church of England (Aided) Junior School
[1997] 1 ICR 334.

[19] J. D. C. Harte, 'Establishment and Autonomy: The Church of England as a Voluntary
Body', in Alison Dunn (ed.), The Voluntary Sector, the State and the Law (Oxford, 2000). As
eventually approved as Council Directive 2000/78/EC, the Directive makes significant concessions at Article 4 in respect of occupational requirements relating to churches and other
public or private organizations 'the ethos of which is based on religion or belief'.

[20] School Standards and Framework Act 1998, ss. 20 and 21.

although a few are Methodist, Jewish, and, now, Muslim. There are quite elaborate provisions concerned with religious education and worship in ordinary non-religious, particularly community, schools, but there is a required interdenominational and multi-faith emphasis. In religious schools, by contrast, the religious education and worship is expected to be appropriate to the denomination or faith to which the school belongs.[21] In voluntary-aided schools, where the religious affiliation is strongest, priority in appointments may be given to those whose religious opinions are in accordance with the tenets of the relevant religion, to active worshippers and to those willing to teach in accordance with the tenets of the relevant faith.[22] In voluntary-controlled schools, which are more substantially subject to state control, specific provision is made for the appointment of a limited number of teachers on the same basis who are reserved to teach religious education.[23] A head teacher in a voluntary-controlled school may be selected with 'regard to that person's ability and fitness to preserve and develop the religious character of the school'.[24]

All this may be seen as striking a balance between those parents who want their children to be educated within a particular religious ethos and those who do not or are indifferent. However, a significant rule which applies even to voluntary-aided schools is that 'no person shall be disqualified by reasons of his religious opinions, or of his attending or omitting to attend religious worship, from being employed for the purposes of the school otherwise than as a teacher'.[25] It may seem appropriate that in a state school, even though it is attached to a particular faith, ancillary staff should not be expected to belong to a particular faith, although in practice the people who gravitate towards such jobs may well belong to the same faith in any event. However, if a school with a religious ethos is serious about maintaining that ethos, even a ban on insisting that cleaners or cooks should belong to the relevant religion would seem to be inconsistent with the liberty of the religious body with which the school is associated. If the ban were extended to teachers apart from those specifically appointed to teach religious studies, the character of confessional schools would be very vulnerable.

The idea of prohibiting religious discrimination in employment raises

---

[21] The rights of individual parents to ensure that the education and teaching of their children is in conformity with the parents' own religious and philosophical convictions is guaranteed by Article 2 of the First Protocol to the European Convention on Human Rights (1952). At an individual level this is partly met by the rights of withdrawal from religious education and worship under School Standards and Framework Act 1998, s. 71. This section envisages that withdrawal may allow parents to make suitable arrangements for alternative religious education and worship. However, the convention right may suggest a more substantial right to education in accordance with a particular religious ethos and therefore of adequate provision of schools which provide such ethos.

[22] School Standards and Framework Act 1998, s. 60(5).   [23] s. 60(3).
[24] s. 60(4).   [25] s. 60(6).

fundamental issues where members of a particular faith wish to work together in whatever way, for example in a Christian retail business, in a Jewish medical practice, or in a Muslim law firm. It remains to be seen whether the Human Rights Act or the proposed EC directive would discourage such associations by tending to outlaw them. Such religious associations could be seen as discriminating against those who were not members of the same religion, or they could be seen as enabling those who set them up to enjoy their own religious liberty. It is not intended to explore these issues further here but simply to note that such associations cannot be regarded simply as ordinary subjects of private contract law. It may be appropriate for them to be covered by special concessions which allow them to discriminate in favour of co-religionists. However, some such relationships are of more public significance than others, notably where they involve a public service or a monopoly of certain activities. In such cases the balance may need to be struck differently between the rights of those who are excluded and those who wish to associate for their work with those sharing the same religious ideals. Striking such a balance cannot be regarded simply as a matter of individual liberties but must take adequate account of the belief systems of the religious organizations to which the individuals belong.

The Position of Ministers of Religion

The position of ministers of religion in relation to employment law is a peculiar one. On the one hand, clergy of the Church of England are considered to be office-holders, which may give them a stronger position than employees. On the other hand, clergy of all denominations and faiths are treated by the law as having a distinctive status, which means that they are not employees of the religious organization to which they belong or of anyone else, unless, nominally of God.[26] Instead, they are technically self-employed.

It is a basic rule of contract law that contracts to provide personal services will not be enforced against either party, because of their intimate nature, but that a breach will be compensated for by damages. By contrast, a person who is wrongly dismissed from a public office may obtain a declaration that they are still in possession of the office. The reasoning behind this would seem to be that an office is a property right which will be protected by real remedies. Because of the public nature of the office there is not the same degree of intimacy which would make enforcement objectionable. Where a minister of the Church of England enjoys a freehold

[26] *Powell* v. *Representative Body of the Church in Wales* [1957] 1 All ER 400; *Baker* v. *Jones* [1954] 2 All ER 553; *Davies* v. *Presbyterian Church in Wales* [1986] IRLR 194; *President of the Methodist Conference* v. *Parfitt* [154] ICR 176.

office, even today, he or she will therefore enjoy significant independence.[27]

However, many clergy of the Church of England have only minimal security, and that would seem to be the case with ministers of other religious bodies. A recent example involved the dismissal of an assistant curate in the Southwark diocese in London, south of the Thames.[28] There was an implied complaint that the curate had been treated unfairly because of his racial background. He complained to an industrial tribunal that he had been unfairly dismissed and the tribunal accepted jurisdiction on the basis that he was for practical purposes an employee of the bishop or the diocese. On appeal, however, the traditional view was affirmed that there was no jurisdiction because a minister of religion licensed to serve in a parish is not an employee.[29]

The idea of the office of a minister of religion as a property right may seem singularly inappropriate in the twenty-first century. There is pressure from some that all clergy should, instead, be given contracts of employment and be enabled to claim the normal rights of employees. Such arguments have been advanced particularly by clergy who have joined trade unions. However, to many members of churches and of other religious bodies, treating ministers of religion as employees of clerical organizations is even less appropriate than treating their offices as pieces of property, which at least may give them independence in pursuing their vocation. The alternative is to accept that ministers of religion generally are a distinct legal category because of the nature of their work and of the bodies in which they minister. In that case, public law may provide a better framework for regulating their position in a manner which is fair both to them and to the integrity of their religious associations. That would not prevent religious organizations from choosing to use contracts of employment for

---

[27] The principal benefit of the incumbent's freehold is security in occupying the parsonage house. The assured stipend which will now largely be paid for from a pool of parish contributions to the diocese, and pension rights, which are underwritten by the Church Commissioners, are also significant, even though stipends are modest by today's standards of income.

[28] *Diocese of Southwark* v. *Coker* [1996] 140.

[29] The same principle was taken for granted in the case of the Revd Anthony Freeman, which is discussed below. Freeman was a clergyman licensed as priest in charge of a parish and jointly as a diocesan officer in the diocese of Chichester. He was removed by his bishop after publishing a book which rejected orthodox Christian belief. In the Church of England such appointments, like those of an assistant curate, lack any significant security. In practice notice of a period of months has been given before such dismissal, and the ecclesiastical authorities have arguably demonstrated good practice in giving warnings and opportunities to make representations. In other cases, particularly in team parishes and in cathedral chapters, posts are now often on a leasehold basis for a number of years, continuing the property model for appointment. Here senior clergy are now vulnerable to removal at the end of the set term. A recent controversial example was the removal of the team rector of Hanley by the Bishop of Stafford, which was unsuccessfully challenged in the High Court, *Church Times*, 18 Aug. 2000.

ministers where that is mutually agreeable and, if the organization preferred, in all cases.[30]

A Public Framework for Religious Ministry

Religious bodies are but one form of a wide range of public or quasi-public associations which, at present anomalously, tend to be treated as private associations under English law, although they fulfil important public functions. There is a well-known body of case-law concerned with the powers of sporting organizations controlling particular sports at a national level. Notoriously, even though these have powers to license participants and the places where events are held, with considerable influence on individual livelihoods and on public enjoyment of sport, they cannot be challenged by way of judicial review.[31] This gap in the public law has been criticized both judicially[32] and academically.[33] In Scotland the Court of Session does have power to oversee such bodies. There, even if powers to make decisions affecting individuals are conferred merely by a contract between members of an association, they may be policed by the courts within a public law framework.[34]

Most relevantly, in Scotland judicial review has been held appropriate to regulate abuses of power in a religious setting. This is of considerable value where the person concerned does not have a contract of employment, as in the case of a member of a religious order.[35] In England judicial review has been declined in comparable religious disputes.[36] What may be particularly valuable about the Scottish approach is that it envisages third-party rights in such proceedings. The existence of a 'tripartite relationship' has been relied upon, that is between the body making the power, the

---

[30] Within the Church of England many posts are filled by ordained as well as by non-ordained persons under contracts of employment, for example diocesan posts such as education or youth or mission officers. The title 'officer' in many such posts reveals a shift in the understanding of that term.

[31] *Law v. National Greyhound Racing Club Ltd.* [1983] 1 WLR 1302; *R. v. Disciplinary Committee of the Jockey Club Ltd., ex parte Aga Khan* [1993] 1 WLR 909; *R. v Football Association Ltd., ex parte Football League Ltd.* [1993] 2 All ER 833.

[32] *McInnes v. Onslow-Fane* [1978] 1 WLR 15520; *Nagle v. Feilden* [1966] 2 QB 633; *R. v. Jockey Club, ex parte Massingberd-Mundy* [1993] 2 All ER 207.

[33] For example, by Sir William Wade and Christopher Forsyth, *Administrative Law*, 7th edn. (Oxford, 1994), 665–6. See too P. P. Craig [1991] PL 538. The separation of public and private law in such circumstances was compounded by *O'Reilly v. Mackman* [1983] 2 AC 237, where private law procedures for a declaration or an injunction were held by the House of Lords not to be available in what was clearly a public law context, there, prisoners in Hull Prison claiming that the prison rules had been violated in refusing them visits.

[34] *St Johnstone Football Club Ltd. v. Scottish Football Association* 1965 SLT 171; and see *Finnegan v. New Zealand Rugby Football Union Inc (No. 2)* [1985] 2 NZLR 181.

[35] *M'Donald v. Burns* 1940 SLT 325. In Ireland see *Buckley v. Cahal Daley* (1990) 8 NIJB.

[36] *R. v. Imam of Bury Park Jami, ex parte Dulaiman Ali* [1991] and *R. v. Chief Rabbi, ex parte Wachmann* [1991] 1 WLR 1036.

party exercising the power and individuals whom the exercise of the power, affects.[37] Implicit in this is the possibility that members of a religious body who may be indirectly affected by an important decision, for example about the suitability of another individual for office, may have standing in proceedings challenging the decision in the courts.

A characteristic of major religious bodies is that they hold services and other ceremonies which are open to the public. Churches, mosques, temples, and other religious buildings may be public places for a variety of legal purposes. The public status of religion may be beneficial from the point of view of both the State and the religion and its adherents. Thus religious teaching is generally supportive of public order and of structures which make for the stability of society, even if the State identifies with another religion or seeks to be neutral.[38] Some religious groups are essentially private in their outlook and wish to maintain a distance from the State. For them, a private law model may be entirely appropriate, although freedom from public interference in their contracts, notably in whom they choose to employ, may be an important aspect of their autonomy and of the religious freedom of their individual members. However, if a religion is to grow and to play a part in shaping the development of society in accordance with its own tenets, it must operate openly in the public arena. Thus, for most major religious traditions and certainly for the main Christian denominations and for Islam a public identity expressed in public law relations with the State is crucial.[39]

It could therefore be appropriate to enable individual organizations and their members to opt for a status which is essentially either private or public. They could rely either on a private contractual model for regulating their affairs within the State or a public law model, for which the Church of England provides a precedent. Put another way, rather than a single religious denomination established by law, a range of genuine public religious bodies whose members so wish would be entitled to special public law machinery establishing their relationship with the State. Such machinery could, in particular, provide the framework for resolving disputes

[37] *Naik* v. *University of Stirling* [1993] *The Times* 5 Aug. Generally, see *West* v. *Secretary of State for Scotland* 1992 SLT 636.

[38] This is certainly true of Christianity and draws on standard biblical passages such as Rom. 13, Titus 3: 1, and 1 Pet. 2: 13–14. In modern Britain national representatives of major religions, such as Judaism and Islam, are supportive of the democratic institutions of society, while often contributing effective criticism of specific policies. This is not to deny the numerous examples where religious differences have been a focus for disorder. Rather, it underlines the desirability of such differences being discussed openly and in a mutually respectful manner within a public framework.

[39] Examples in English law include the special role accorded to religious voluntary schools in the state education system, and provision for religious education and worship in state schools, generally, statutory provision for religious broadcasting, facilities for recognition of religious marriages of various types, and the special arrangements for the conservation of ecclesiastical buildings in use outside secular listed building controls.

between would-be members or members and the religious body concerned, including disputes over office-holding or employment.[40]

A function of such machinery would be to allow for the resolution of disputes within the relevant body over issues of doctrine, faith, and orthodoxy, so as to protect the interests of individuals, while respecting the integrity of the religion and reducing the risk of fragmentation. Internal disputes may have a profound effect on an ordinary member who is excluded from the religious community and on aspiring members who are refused admittance. By defining such matters as essentially private, the State both declines to protect individuals who are at loggerheads with a body which they may regard as central to their identity and it may deny a genuinely public identity to key social organizations.

In a plural society, where the State abjures any part in enforcing a structure of religious conformity, fragmentation may reduce the effectiveness of all religions and undermine the positive contribution which they can make to the quality of life of their members and of society as a whole. If groups wish to split off from a publicly organized religious body of the form suggested here, they would be entirely free to do so. The public religious framework supported by the State would not be an instrument of oppression as it could all too unhappily be in previous eras. Rather, it would serve as a safeguard against polarization and especially against the exclusion of individuals, save in clearly defined circumstances and subject to procedural safeguards.

Merits of a Public Law Framework for Determining Religious Orthodoxy

The point where a public–private distinction between religious bodies may be particularly relevant to the freedom of operation by such bodies is where issues arise over orthodoxy of belief. Here, the State may be reluctant to judge between differences of opinion, but this may result in members who control a religious body imposing their views on others by means which would not be tolerated in a secular context. On the other hand, if the State does intervene, to protect what it sees as a superior individual right, it may threaten the integrity of the religious body concerned. There is no simple solution to such a dilemma, and if a religious body chooses to insulate itself from public interference, it may be that its

---

[40] Rights under the European Convention on Human Rights may, in any event, be called in aid by religious bodies and organizations, even if they are essentially private, since they may be afforded standing as victims in their own right (*X and Church of Scientology* v. *Sweden* Appl. No. 7805/77, (1979) 16 D&R; *Chappell* v. *UK* Appl. No. 12587/86, (1987) 53 D&R 241). An approach similar to that envisaged here appears to be identified with the 'mini-establishments' described by Julian Rivers in 'From Toleration to Pluralism: The UK Human Rights Act', in Rex J. Ahdar (ed.), *Law and Religion* (Dartmouth, 2000).

members, including paid ministers, may prefer to risk injustice at the hand of their own internal decision-makers than to submit to state adjudication.[41]

However, if a major faith body purports to be a public institution, seeking to witness and minister to the public on a national basis, it would seem desirable that its decision-making procedures, especially those affecting the individual rights of its members, should comply with the highest standards of natural justice as are recognized in the public administrative law of the State. If such a body is afforded some status as a partner in carrying out state functions, it will be subject to the Human Rights Act 1998 and to the convention rights under the Act. Thus, a Roman Catholic diocese or a Jewish, Muslim, or Methodist organization which is in the position of laying down policies, such as admission policies for a voluntary school, must submit to scrutiny in that context under the public law of the State. It would be invidious if it failed to observe similar standards in its dealings with its members and ministers.

The tradition of the Church of England is to submit to judicial scrutiny, but only as a last resort. Clergy are subject to disciplinary proceedings in the public consistory courts of each diocese, although these powers are extremely rarely invoked and the whole idea of criminal-type professional disciplinary procedures has for some time been under anxious review.[42] There are alternative powers under pastoral provisions which may enable a bishop to remove an unsatisfactory clergyman more easily, but these are not without danger to the rights of the ministers concerned.[43] What is significant is that those who argue for new, simplified procedures appear, in practice, to be concerned mainly with the high cost of the present disciplinary proceedings and by the unseemliness of church scandals being made public. It may be that such objections actually demonstrate the merits of the present arrangements.

The courts of the Church of England have a much more active jurisdiction, in dealing with faculty applications for changes to church buildings and their contents and to churchyards.[44] Despite the cost of running such a system, it is generally recognized that it does give the Church much greater flexibility in looking after its own buildings and in altering them to fit modern liturgical needs than if the decisions were made by secular planning authorities. The ecclesiastical exemption from listed building control which is enjoyed by the Church of England is shared with the other major Christian denominations, and to ensure that it is not removed they have

---

[41] There is certainly biblical authority for this view: 1 Cor. 6: 1–6.
[42] General Synod Working Party reviewing Clergy Discipline and the working of the Ecclesiastical Courts, *Under Authority: Report on Clergy Discipline* (London, 1996).
[43] Incumbents (Vacation of Benefices) Measures 1977 and 1993.
[44] G. H. and G. L. Newsom, *Faculty Jurisdiction of the Church of England*, 2nd edn. (London, 1993).

put in place their own administrative systems which have had to pass the scrutiny of governmental critics.[45]

The experience of the Christian churches and of other faith bodies with regard to their schools and their historic buildings provide precedents, where the State claims an interest in overseeing their activities but allows them substantial autonomy within a legal framework which is designed to protect the rights of the individuals who are involved in these major religious institutions. In both schools and historic buildings problems may arise over doctrinal differences of opinion. There, the present arrangements can deliver solutions which take account both of individual rights and of the integrity of the religious bodies themselves.[46]

Disputes over doctrinal orthodoxy are most likely to arise over the disciplining of ministers or other officers and the admission or exclusion of ordinary members. The argument of this paper is that there are advantages in such rules being provided for in the public sphere, as they are at present under the ecclesiastical law of the Church of England. If any faith wishes to operate in the public sphere, it should be possible for it do so openly and to articulate the terms of its faith in a manner which is clear to the public. If its adjudicative procedures are consistent with generally accepted good practice, the religious body should then be able to determine and uphold orthodoxy in the forms which it considers right.

Disputes involving orthodoxy may relate to differences between individuals and a religious body over the ordering of the religion, that is its ecclesiology, over rules of morality, or simply over belief in the truth of fundamental dogmas. These are all areas where belief in absolute values or truths may be at issue and where the religious body is likely to demand freedom of judgement. The argument of this paper is that religious bodies must be free to determine their own criteria for office, but it may be necessary for them to reach consensus with the State on the procedures and material consequences of depriving individuals of office. Satisfactory criteria for membership and procedures for expressing, developing, and applying those criteria to individuals may also need to be worked out between religious bodies and the State.

The Orthodoxy of Religious Associations and their Officers

Conflicting views of orthodoxy held by individuals and by the central

---

[45] Planning (Listed Building and Conservation Areas) Act 1990, s. 60(5), grants powers to the Secretary of State for the Environment, Transport, and the Regions to withdraw the exemption. It is at present safeguarded in an Order under this section which circumscribes its present extent and limits it to the churches of major Christian denominations which have provided satisfactory systems (Ecclesiastical Exemption (Listed Buildings and Conservation Areas) Order 1994, SI No. 1771).

[46] Cf. *Board of Governors of St Matthias Church of England School* v. *Crizzle* [1993] IRC 401 and *St Stephen Walbrook* [1987] Fam. 146.

body to which they belong can give rise to considerable tension. If a religious body is allowed genuine freedom, it must be able to determine the beliefs which are central to its existence. Realistically, it must also be able to require a level of belief, or at least public adherence to a set of beliefs, on the part of those who hold any office in the body. However, if office-holders depend upon their office for their livelihood, the State has an interest in their protection. In a plural democratic society the notion of requiring certain beliefs of a prospective employee would normally be considered inappropriate. The tendency has been to sidestep the dilemma by categorizing office-holders of religious bodies as something other than employees, even where they are paid and from a purely secular perspective do seem to be employees.

Alternatively, where a person is employed in circumstances where their religious beliefs are relevant, these may be treated in effect as a matter of professional qualification or competence or as an aspect of professional ethics. There a different standard may be required of a professional person than of a lay person because of the power which the professional person wields and because of the expectations of the public with whom they work. As we have seen, in appointing, paying, or promoting teachers in church voluntary-aided schools or reserved teachers in voluntary-controlled schools, preference may be given to those 'whose religious opinions are in accordance with the tenets of the religion or religious denomination' relevant to the school, or 'who attend religious worship in accordance with those tenets, or who give, or are willing to give, religious education at the school in accordance with those tenets'.[47] This presupposes expertise in the tenets of the faith and a commitment to them such as might be required of a lawyer, a doctor, or an engineer in their respective spheres, although the reference to holding 'opinions' in accordance with such tenets would be strange in a non-religious setting.

In terminating the employment of such a teacher, 'regard may be had ... to any conduct on his part which is incompatible with the precepts, or with the upholding of the tenets, of the religion or religious denomination'.[48] Here the requirement as to conduct parallels what might be required in a secular context of, say, a doctor who abuses his or her position by becoming personally involved with a patient in entering into a relationship which would normally be considered an entirely private affair.

In practice, disciplinary proceedings against religious office-holders are often for misbehaviour which would readily be recognized as such in secular employment. If the standards demanded are higher than in other contexts, that may be considered entirely appropriate because of the nature of the work. Disciplinary cases brought under the public ecclesiastical law of the

[47] School Standards and Framework Act 1998, s. 60(5)(a).
[48] s. 60(5)(a).

Church of England have generally been for such offences, including financial[49] or sexual impropriety,[50] or for failure properly to carry out professional work.[51] Sometimes an offence has involved a breach of church
order which again would be recognizable in a secular context as a major
disruption of the organization.[52] Indeed a disciplinary offence by a clergyman may be a straightforward criminal offence under the general law.
There, as in other professional contexts, such as medical disciplinary
proceedings, a conviction in the ordinary courts provides the jurisdiction
for ecclesiastical proceedings and proof of the conviction avoids the need
to prove the offence again.[53]

In practice, in modern Britain religious organizations, or at any rate the
major Christian denominations, tolerate a substantial diversity of opinion
among their official ministers. This contrasts strongly with bitter litigation
in the ecclesiastical courts late into the nineteenth century over what now
seem trivial doctrinal matters, such as whether it is permissible to have
candles on a Communion table and various other sorts of church orna-
ment. Nevertheless, major doctrinal disputes can still arise in any denomination or faith body. In such cases, those in conflict may feel equally
strongly that right is on their side. For that very reason, if the matter is
dealt with by the religious body itself, there may be a real danger that
procedural safeguards may be dispensed with for what is considered a
higher good. There may be a strong pressure to save money for what are
believed to be worthier purposes. Disputes may involve personal conflicts
where it is difficult, objectively, to identify the real issues and to what
extent matters of doctrinal difference are really fundamental. For example,
it may be unclear whether a person who has a different belief on a particular matter is really a threat to the integrity of the institution because of
that belief or is actually no more than a threat to the power or feelings of
other individuals.

For justice to be done and to maintain the intellectual validity of the
doctrinal position of a religious body, it is therefore desirable that any
disputes between ministers and such a body over doctrine should be dealt
with under public and objectively fair procedures. The resolution of a matter
of doctrine by a Church or other religious body may be considered analogous to the policy of a public decision-making body, such as a local authority or a government department. The courts will not question the policy or
the discretion required in balancing it against other policies, but they will
require it to be applied in accordance with high procedural standards and
will require the policy to be articulated coherently and applied consistently.

[49] *Beneficed Clerk* v. *Lee* [1897] AC 226; *Fitzmaurice* v. *Hesketh* [1904] AC 266.
[50] *Sweet* v. *Young* [1902] P. 37.
[51] *Bland* v. *Archdeacon of Cheltenham* [1972] Fam. 157.
[52] *Bishop of St Albans* v. *Fillingham* [1906] P. 163.
[53] Ecclesiastical Jurisdiction Measure 1963, s. 55.

Religious doctrines and their imposition can be tested in this way in the ordinary courts in various circumstances. They may be tested where a minister is disciplined and in an extreme case removed for denying a matter of doctrine, or they may be tested where a minister challenges the doctrinal orthodoxy of his or her superiors. As with administrative law cases concerned with the policies of public bodies, the courts have been chary about fundamental issues of doctrine but have nevertheless illuminated the points of difference in a public setting by treating the disputes in terms of procedure.

Such disputes can arise over different views on church order, as with the ordination of women, different views on personal morality, such as the propriety of homosexual relationships, and different views over fundamental issues of belief, such as the nature of God. Three recent examples relating to clergymen in the Church of England are the Williamson litigation, the case of *Gill* v. *Davies*, and the Freeman affair.

The Revd Paul Williamson was rector of Hanworth in Surrey and a firm opponent of the ordination of women. Ordination of women to the priesthood in the Church of England was authorized in 1993.[54] In *R.* v. *Archbishops of Canterbury and York, ex parte Williamson*,[55] Mr Williamson sought a declaration by way of judicial review that canons which were drafted to implement the Measure were unlawful. Popplewell J refused leave, and his renewed application was refused by the Court of Appeal in a judgment by Sir Thomas Bingham MR[56] on the ground that a Measure had the same force and effect as an Act of Parliament.[57] A canon made within the authority of a Measure was similarly not open to challenge in the courts. In a later case, Mr Williamson failed to obtain an injunction from Arden J to prevent the first service for the ordination of women priests in London.[58]

In *Gill* v. *Davies*,[59] the Revd Kenneth Moulder, the vicar of a parish in Newcastle, and his parochial church council had publicly rejected the oversight of the newly appointed bishop of Newcastle on the grounds of the bishop's reported refusal to formally condemn as sin 'homosexuality

---

[54] Priests (Ordination of Women) Measure 1993.

[55] 16 Apr. 1994, unreported. I am indebted to Chancellor Mark Hill for enabling me to see a transcript of this case and other material relating to the Williamson litigation.

[56] Unreported, 1 Mar. 1994. An edited version may be found in Mark Hill, *Ecclesiastical Law* (London, 1995). A previous unsuccessful attempt was made to challenge the endorsement of the measure itself by the Ecclesiastical Committee of Parliament (*R.* v. *Ecclesiastical Committee of the Houses of Parliament, ex parte Church Society*, 28 Oct. 1993; Hill, *Ecclesiastical Law*, 72. It was unsuccessfully argued that the ordination of women was a fundamental matter and was therefore outside the powers granted to the Church of England's internal legislature by the Church of England Assembly (Powers) Act 1919.

[57] Church of England Assembly (Powers) Act 1919, s. 4.

[58] *Williamson* v. *Bishop of Willesden*, unreported, 16 Apr. 1994.

[59] Unreported, 19 Dec. 1997.

within a loving permanent relationship'. The acting bishop, Bishop Gill, then postponed the ordination as deacon of a curate at Mr Moulder's church for the dispute to be resolved. Mr Moulder arranged his own rival ordination service to be conducted by Bishop Davies, a retired bishop from Africa. Bishop Gill successfully obtained an injunction from Smith J to prevent the rival ordination from proceeding.

The case of the Revd Anthony Freeman, by contrast, did not come to court or involve formal legal proceedings. Mr Freeman, who was a priest in charge of a small parish in the diocese of Chichester, and also held a diocesan teaching post, was dismissed by the bishop of the diocese, Dr Kemp, after publishing a book which asserted that God was no more than a human invention. The case was taken up by the press as an example of orthodox theology being enforced simply at the discretion of the diocesan bishop.

These cases between them provide examples of disputes over church order, morality, and pure theological belief. In the Williamson cases an ordinary church minister sought to challenge a change in church order which he believed involved an unacceptable shift in doctrine. In *Gill* v. *Davies* the boot was on the other foot. The church authorities invoked the secular courts to prevent disorder where a congregation objected to what the congregation perceived as a change in the moral rules taught in the Church. In the Freeman case, a clergyman who simply denied fundamentals of belief was effectively disciplined without any recourse to the courts by either side.

It is not the purpose of this paper to argue the merits of ordination of women, traditional views on homosexual behaviour, or the nature of basic Christian belief. The judges involved in these three court cases were at pains to emphasize that matters of doctrine are to be decided by the Church itself. A passage in the first Williamson case by Sir Thomas Bingham MR is significant. He is dismissing an argument that it must be possible to challenge a provision by the General Synod of the Church of England which made possible a fundamental change in doctrine 'such as would effect a radical alteration in the nature of the Church', for example, 'permitting a change which would substitute some central figure other than Jesus Christ' in its worship. He went on:

For such an absurd result to occur it would mean that the majority of members in the three Houses of the Synod, perhaps of the legislative Committee, certainly the Ecclesiastical Committee, and of both Houses of Parliament should take leave of their senses or in any event of their faith. That is, I think, something so unlikely as to be disregarded for practical purposes. I, for my part, can see nothing absurd about entrusting decisions on matters of doctrine and faith to a body of church people, including the Bishops and the Clergy, with overall control reserved to a majority in Parliament.

Some may doubtless ask, if the Church can be left to make its own decisions on doctrine, then why should Parliament or the state courts be involved at all? However, what these cases suggest is that a formal public law structure can ensure that decisions are made fairly and openly. The elaborate legal hurdles needed to introduce the ordination of women have, so far, enabled that to be achieved with relatively small damage to the Church of England. The public courts are still there to demonstrate that the procedures have been followed properly and fairly. Similarly, the courts are not being used to enforce a particular pattern of sexual morality. However, where differences arise on topics such as homosexuality, the courts will support the maintenance of order but leave it to the religious authorities to determine the moral rules themselves.[60] In the Freeman case, the procedural correctness of the bishop's decision to dismiss a clergyman was not tested, but it may be significant that the minister was given a cooling off period of a year in which to dissociate himself from his book.

Although cases over orthodoxy which have or could have reached the courts have tended to involve paid ministers, the legal position of unpaid office-holders also provides a measure of the extent to which the organization to which those office-holders belong can be taken seriously as responsible public bodies. It is particularly significant that, here, most religious bodies are treated by the ordinary courts as private clubs. They may dispose of their officers with minimal supervision and certainly would probably be given considerable leeway in removing them if the views of the officers happened to disagree with those of the relevant governing body of the organization. It is here that recent efforts by the Church of England to change the law concerning churchwardens may be instructive.

Churchwardens are public office-holders, elected to hold office for a year. Parishes always have two, sometimes more. In past centuries they had extensive responsibilities for social welfare in the parish. Today all those resident in the parish on the local government electoral roll, as well as those who worship at the church and are on its electoral roll, have a right to take part in the election of churchwardens.[61] They play a significant roll in looking after parish church buildings and churchyards, an aspect of the law of the Church of England where the State has a major interest in the activities of the Church because of its concern to protect the national heritage for all citizens.

The Church of England has been trying for several years to provide a

---

[60] Since *Gill* v. *Davies* an analogous dispute arose between the bishop of Worcester, Dr Peter Selby, and the Revd Charles Raven, vicar of Kidderminster. The vicar organized a confirmation service with an outside bishop in defiance of Dr Selby. Although a unilateral confirmation service may be less significant than an ordination, it would seem to be a clear infringement of canon law. The bishop did not seek to invoke the secular law but did publicly rebuke the vicar.

[61] Churchwardens (Appointment and Resignation) Measure 1964, s. 2.

simple means of removing churchwardens. The ostensible reason is to cope with persons suspected of crime, such as child abuse or financial irregularity, pending its investigation. However, there have been fears that such a power could be used to remove a churchwarden with whom clergy disagree on matters of doctrine. As churchwardens are elected public officers, a summary power to remove them is seen as intrinsically undemocratic. Twice a draft Churchwardens Measure has been passed by the National Synod but rejected as 'inexpedient' by the Ecclesiastical Committee of Parliament. The second of these, the Draft Churchwardens Measure 1999, would have allowed for suspension by the bishop in very controlled circumstances, as where the warden concerned was ill or had been convicted of a criminal offence.[62] What was most controversial would have been a power to suspend where the warden was charged with an imprisonable offence. Such a power would be commonplace in many professions and was agreed upon by the democratically elected synod of the Church. Nevertheless, it was rejected by the Ecclesiastical Committee.

This conflict between Church and State has been presented by some in the Church of England as unwarranted interference by the State in internal disciplinary matters. It is not intended here to debate whether this provision in the draft Measure was desirable or not. However, what is clear is that because of the public law dimension the position of churchwardens is being subject to the closest of scrutiny before any changes are made which could affect their role and independence. There may be state interference, but it has nothing to do with principles of doctrine and it may be seen as protecting the public character of religion at the local parish level.

Orthodoxy and Public Interest in Admission to Membership and Exclusion

Ministers and employees of a religious body and other office-holders, even if they are unpaid, are likely to be the focus for disputes over orthodoxy. However, disputes may also affect ordinary members. They may affect whether a particular person is admitted in the first place or whether he or she may be removed.

Freedom of the individual to live his or her life in a manner which is fully consistent with his or her religious beliefs and aspirations must include freedom to do so in association with others of like belief. The right to freedom of assembly and association in Article 11 of the European Convention on Human Rights would seem to encompass such a right of association, although the article itself and the fairly sparse case-law emphasize the right 'to form and to join trade unions' for the protection of the individual's interests. The primary article of the Convention concerned

---

[62] Clause 9.

with religion, Article 9(1), also envisages freedom for individuals to express their faith in association with others and to do so publicly. Article 9(1) states: 'Everyone has the right to freedom, thought, conscience and religion; this right includes the right to change his religion or belief and freedom, either alone or in community with others and, in public or private, to manifest his religion or belief, in worship, teaching, practice and observance.'

The right to join a religious organization raises difficult considerations for private law. If the organization is legally based on a network of contracts involving its members, those who have not yet become members cannot be contractual parties. How a person becomes a member is legally problematical. In practice, religious bodies will usually welcome aspiring applicants, but not always. Problems may arise with regard to admission to a denomination or on transfer between congregations, but more fundamental questions may arise over whether a person belongs to a major faith irrespective of particular denominations. Thus the canon law of the Church of England[63] recognizes as a Christian anyone who has been baptized with water in the name of the Holy Trinity. A baptized person then has a number of public law rights to the ministrations of the Church of England[64] and to participation in its government.[65]

More fundamentally, as a citizen, an individual has rights to become a Christian through baptism into the Church of England. The canons of the Church of England impose duties on the clergy including the duty to baptize and these may be enforced either through disciplinary proceedings against recalcitrant clergy in the church courts[66] or by judicial review in the ordinary courts. Canon B 22.4 of the Church of England provides in terms that 'No minister shall refuse or, save for the purpose of preparing or instructing the parents or godparents, delay to baptise any infant within his cure that is brought to the church to be baptised, provided that due notice has been given and the provisions relating to godparents in these Canons observed.'

Under Canon B 23 there must be three godparents, two of the same sex as the child and one of the opposite sex. They must be baptized and, unless the minister makes an exception on grounds of need, must also be confirmed. They must also be persons 'who will faithfully fulfil their responsibilities both by their care for the children committed to their charge and by the example of their own godly living'.[67] However, if the parents can find three such suitable people, there is clearly a duty on the

[63] Canon B 15A. For the basic law of the Roman Catholic Church, see the minimalist description of baptism in Code of Canon Law 1983, c. 849.
[64] For marriage, Canons B 30–5; for burial, Canon B 38.
[65] Synodical Government Measure 1969, and the Church Representation Rules therein.
[66] *Bland* v. *Archdeacon of Cheltenham* [1972] Fam 157.
[67] Canon B 22.2.

incumbent of a parish to baptize a child resident in the parish and there is little doubt that this duty could be enforced by the courts.

Canon B 24, which is concerned with the baptism of those who are of riper years, does not explicitly impose a duty to baptize but it does impose a duty to instruct the applicant in the principles of the Christian religion and there may well be an implied public law duty to perform the baptism unless there are reasonable grounds for not doing so.[68] In any event, baptism was and still is valid in terms of the law of the Church of England, even if it is carried out by someone other than an ordained Anglican minister, whether a minister of another Trinitarian denomination or simply a lay person.[69] Therefore, a person who secured their own baptism and ensured that this could clearly be proved would be entitled to claim membership of the Church of England.[70]

Like the old notion of an incumbent's living being a right of property, the idea of a right to baptism enforceable in secular courts may seem an anachronism, and it may be distasteful to those who are Christians and who take exception to the views of a person who wishes to join them as members of the Church. The historical explanation is, of course, that until the nineteenth century there was no distinction between a citizen and a Christian, so that all citizens were entitled to the full membership of society which baptism into the Church entailed. However, in a plural society the right to belong to the religion of one's choice may be no less important to the individual than the right to belong in a confessional society which subscribes to a single faith. If a faith body chooses to operate nationally and publicly, it may appropriately submit to a legal obligation to accept as members those who choose to join it, just as the State may be obliged to accept as citizens those who are born within its boundaries.[71]

If a religious association chooses to operate as a public body, and certainly if it wishes to act as a partner with the State in such public functions as running state schools or celebrating marriages, it may be arguable that Article 11 of the European Convention on Human Rights will oblige it to accept as members those who wish to belong to it. Certainly, the article would seem to mean that the religious association must allow any of its members to transfer freely to another religion or simply to leave. From a theological perspective, a person may not be able to remove the indelible identity of membership of a particular faith. They may be apostate, and by

---

[68] See too canon B 28.1 on reception of unbaptized persons,

[69] *Kemp* v. *Wickes* (1809) 3 Phillimore 264.

[70] Confirmation would be a prerequisite for certain further rights such as membership of the higher elected offices, churchwarden in the parish or membership of the deanery, diocesan or national synods. Even for confirmation it is not clear that the bishop would be in a position to insist on a candidate's orthodoxy provided a candidate can recite the requisite credal statements. See Canon B 27.

[71] The test for the right to citizenship of course varies between states and is not necessarily dependent on the place of birth.

the teaching of their religion may be considered as dead. However, the State certainly claims the authority to prevent the religion from punishing a person who chooses to withdraw, by any action which will interfere with their civil rights.

A test of whether a religious body is genuinely public and so a fit partner for the State in various public activities may be whether it is prepared to allow scrutiny by the courts of the State over whom it admits or expels from membership. It may be that stricter criteria for belief than are imposed by the Church of England are entirely appropriate and should be left to religious bodies to determine freely for themselves. However, decisions as to whether an individual meets those criteria either on admission or even more on expulsion may nevertheless be a matter where the public courts could appropriately exercise a supervisory jurisdiction.

Conclusion

It has been argued in this paper that religion is an area of public importance which is an appropriate subject for public law. Public law may the best forum for supervising contentious issues such as the defining of the boundaries of orthodoxy. Religious bodies are important not merely as associations of individual members but as vessels for major traditions and structures of belief which underlie society. For those within these broad traditions fully to influence national life there need to be effective and publicly recognizable religious communities which relate with the State at a national and at a local level. The history of religion shows that the identity of faith communities is vulnerable to fragmentation. Such fragmentation may pose a greater threat to the effective life of faith communities than unorthodox views which are contained within them.

Paradoxically, it may be that a religious association which strives to ensure its permanent orthodoxy by operating in the private sphere is at least as vulnerable to state action which can cause it to ossify as the body which chooses to operate in the public sphere and accepts a more discriminating supervision by the civil courts. The important Scottish case of *The Free Church of Scotland* v. *Lord Overtoun*[72] provides an object lesson. The Free Church of Scotland was set up in 1843 by a large proportion of the ministers and members of the established Church of Scotland who objected to the selection of ministers under a system of patronage rather than by congregations. The new Church was based on foundation documents which included the early seventeenth-century Westminster Confession of Faith. This contained a statement which was considered to affirm belief in double predestination, that is the belief that certain people

---

[72] *Assembly of the Free Church of Scotland* v. *Lord Overtoun* [1904] AC 515.

are predestined by God for damnation.[73] At the end of the nineteenth century a large majority of members of the Free Church of Scotland wished to recombine with another Presbyterian offshoot of the Church of Scotland. Part of the agreement was that the Westminster Confession was not to be interpreted in this manner.[74]

The merger was challenged successfully by members of the Free Church who claimed that the Church was bound by its foundation documents and was unable to develop its doctrine. Even a large majority who wished to do this must leave the Church and do so as individuals in a new association. The speeches of those who decided the case in the House of Lords reveal very different attitudes to the nature of a religious body. The majority held that if it was set up under a clear private law constitution, a religious association would be prevented from evolving from that constitution. Typical is a passage from the speech of the Lord Chancellor, the Earl of Halsbury LC,

My Lords, apart from some mysterious and subtle meaning to be attached to the word 'Church,' and understanding it to mean an associated body of Christian believers, I do not suppose that anybody will dispute the right of any man, or any collection of men, to change their religious beliefs according to their own consciences; but when men subscribe money for a particular object and leave it behind them for the promotion of that object, their successors have no right to change the object endowed.[75]

By contrast, Lord Macnaghten appeared to think more in catholic terms of a single Church within which different denominations should be free to evolve:

The question, therefore, seems to me to be this. Was the Church thus purified—the Free Church—so bound and tied by the tenets of the Church of Scotland prevailing at the time of disruption that departure from those tenets in any matter of substance would be a violation of that profession or testimony which may be called

---

[73] 'Chap. III. Of God's Eternal Decree. Sect. III. By the decree of God, for the manifestation of his glory some men and angels are predestinated unto everlasting life, and others foreordained to everlasting death. Sect. IV. These angels and men, thus predestinated and foreordained are particularly and unchangeably designed; and their number is so certain and definite that it cannot be either increased or diminished.'

[74] Act (Declaratory Act) anent Confession of Faith made 26 May 1892 (1): 'That this Church also holds that all who hear the Gospel are warranted and required to believe to the saving of their souls; and that in the case of such as do not believe, but perish in their sins, the issue is due to their own rejection of the Gospel call. That this Church does not teach, and does not regard the Confession as teaching, the fore-ordination of men to death irrespective of their own sin.'

[75] *Assembly of the Free Church of Scotland* v. *Lord Overtoun*, at 626. See also Lord Alverstone CJ at 721: 'I am unable to support a judgement which would deprive the persons forming a minority of their rights simply upon the grounds that they are unwilling to become members of a body which has not only abandoned a fundamental principle of the Church to which they belong, but supports a principle essentially different from that on which that Church was founded.'

the unwritten charter of her foundation, and so necessarily involve a breach of trust in the administration of funds contributed for no other purpose but the support of the Free Church—the Church of the Disruption? Was the Free Church by the very condition of her existence forced to cling to her subordinate standards with so desperate a grip that she has lost hold and touch of the supreme standard of her faith? Was she from birth incapable of all growth and development? Was she (in a word) a dead branch and not a living Church?[76]

With a suitable constitution a religious association can doubtless be set up in the private sphere in a manner which will enable it to evolve with considerable freedom. However, the concept of a national religion provides a comprehensive framework for enabling those citizens who wish to align themselves within a particular faith tradition. By contrast, in a secular state, where religions are not incorporated in the general law, they may show a greater tendency to fragment. The Macnaghten approach may suggest a rather Anglican outlook on life. However, it does not necessarily presuppose the present establishment of a single religion or even any formal preference for Christianity by requiring the head of state to be a Christian.

As a national Church operating within a public law framework, the Church of England has struggled, not without some success, to maintain its comprehensive character to which any Christian may belong. Notably, the contentious debates over whether women could or should be ordained resulted in a solution designed to maintain within one Church the 'two integrities' of those who did and those who did not believe that the ordination of woman was doctrinally right. This resolution of specific tensions between beliefs through parallel legal arrangements suggests models for containing future contention, notably over whether women are to be consecrated as bishops, whether divorcees should more freely be enabled to remarry, and how stable homosexual and lesbian relationships are to be treated. If such matters are dealt with publicly in a forum which articulates with the civil courts and tribunals, it may be that religious freedom will be better served than by a proliferation of mutually suspicious splinter denominations.

There are those within the faith traditions who may well be appalled at the prospect of the State being called on to adjudicate in religious matters. However, the State has done so in the past and always will. The practical aim must be to ensure that the law is framed as far as possible so as to ensure that the oversight of the State is exercised in the interest of religious freedom and not oppressively. This paper has suggested that a public law model may best serve this purpose. It may ensure openness and fair procedures which can be accepted as generally applicable while allowing for matters of faith and doctrine to be judged by the faith bodies themselves.

---

[76] Ibid. 630.

INTERNATIONAL LAW AND PEACE BETWEEN THE NATIONS: THE CONTRIBUTION OF THE BAHA'I FAITH

Danesh Sarooshi

1. Introduction

The attainment of peace between nations is a long-cherished ideal. The Baha'i Scriptures contain much guidance on the principles that humanity should implement in order to reach and maintain a lasting peace. Important among these is the concept of collective security.

This concept of collective security is also today an important part of international law's approach to imposing legal limitations on the use of force by sovereign states against one another. It is this concept that is the focus of this discussion. In particular, I will examine what the concept of collective security means, provide a brief description of how it currently operates under the auspices of the United Nations, and, finally, turn to discuss what are some of the proposals for reform of the concept that may be suggested by Baha'i Scripture.[1]

2. An Ideal of Collective Security

The concept of collective security institutes a system where a collective measure is taken against a member of a community of states that has violated certain community-defined values. In the ideal of the system there are three constituent elements. First is the determination by a community of states of the core values which are sought to be maintained as part of the status quo of the community. Second is the determination by an authorised representative of the community that a core value has been violated in a particular case. And third is the determination by the authorized representative of what the response of the community should be to the violation by the recalcitrant state.

---

[1] The Baha'i International Community has been an active participant at the United Nations (UN) and has, as discussed below, suggested specific reforms that should be made to the workings of the Security Council more generally. This paper, however, goes beyond these to discuss all reforms suggested by Baha'i Scripture that can be made to the concept of collective security as currently practised by the UN. It should be emphasized that the views set forth in this paper are solely those of the author and should not therefore be taken as necessarily being those of the Baha'i International Community.

These three elements are in existence in the system constituted by the United Nations Charter. However, the earlier, and in fact the first, attempt by states at implementing the concept of collective security when they established the League of Nations after the First World War was not so advanced.

3. The League of Nations and Collective Security

In 1919 the nations of the world established the League of Nations by conclusion of the League of Nations Covenant, a treaty between states. This Covenant constituted a system of collective security that in the area of taking military action against an aggressor state was decentralized in its application. Thus although the League of Nations Council was given the ability to decide that a certain state had committed, for example, aggression, the decision, however, to take military action against a rogue state was left entirely up to each state. In other words, there was no compulsory requirement to take military action against an aggressor state. This was the major weakness of the League's collective security system. Nonetheless, the League of Nations Council could require states to impose economic sanctions (trading and financial measures) against a recalcitrant state. But even where these economic sanctions were in practice imposed against an aggressor state, they were only partial and thus were not effective. For example, the determination by the Council that Italy had resorted to an illegal war against Abyssinia (now Ethiopia) within the meaning of Article 16 of the League of Nations Covenant led the Council only to impose temporary, partial, and thus ineffective economic sanctions against Italy.[2] The collective security system of the League was not used by states in favour of a policy of appeasement, and the world descended into the Second World War.

Despite, however, the failings and ineffectiveness of the League's system of collective security, it did mark a crucial stage in the evolution of the idea that the nations of the world should act collectively in order to deal with a rogue nation. The importance of this has been described by Shoghi Effendi, a central figure of the Baha'i faith, in the following words:

That no less than fifty nations of the world, all members of the League of Nations, should have, after mature deliberation, recognized and been led to pronounce their verdict against an act of aggression which in their judgment has been deliberately committed by one of their fellow-members [Italy], one of the foremost Powers of Europe; that they should have, for the most part, agreed to impose collectively sanctions on the condemned aggressor, and should have succeeded in carrying out, to a very great measure, their decision, is no doubt an event without parallel in human history. For the first time in the history of humanity the system of collective

---

[2] See also Y. Dinstein, *War, Aggression and Self-Defence* (Cambridge, 1994), 278.

security, foreshadowed by Bahá'u'lláh and explained by 'Abdu'l-Bahá, has been seriously envisaged, discussed and tested. For the first time in history it has been officially recognized and publicly stated that for this system of collective security to be effectively established strength and elasticity are both essential—strength involving the use of an adequate force to ensure the efficacy of the proposed system, and elasticity to enable the machinery that has been devised to meet the legitimate needs and aspirations of its aggrieved upholders. For the first time in human history tentative efforts have been exerted by the nations of the world to assume collective responsibility, and to supplement their verbal pledges by actual preparation for collective action.[3]

The international organization which superseded the League of Nations was the United Nations (UN).[4] With the horrors of the Second World War and in particular the Holocaust fresh in their mind, the founders of the UN stated in the UN Charter that the primary object and purpose of the organization is to maintain 'international peace and security, and to that end: to take effective collective measures for the prevention and removal of threats to the peace, and for the suppression of acts of aggression or other breaches of the peace'. The legal mechanism that the UN was to use to attain this objective was to be its collective security system.

This discussion now proceeds by examining briefly how the UN has sought to maintain international peace and security using its collective security system and then by examining what innovations Baha'i Scripture suggests for the way in which collective security is currently being applied by the UN.

4. The United Nations and Collective Security

The renewed determination after the Second World War to prevent a recurrence of the scourge of war saw states establish a UN Charter with a relatively advanced collective security system in order to maintain world peace. In particular, Chapter VII of the UN Charter gives the UN Security Council, an important component organ of the UN, broad powers to take action to deal with threats to world peace.

The UN Security Council can *require* states as a matter of legal obligation to take certain action against, for example, an aggressor state. Recall from above that this was a failing of the League of Nations system of collective security, and as such the UN system represents a significant improvement in this regard. The Security Council has the competence under Article 25 of the Charter to impose a binding obligation on UN member states to comply with its decisions. This includes, of course, decisions under

---

[3] Shoghi Effendi, *The World Order of Bahá'u'lláh* (Wilmette, Ill., 1938), 191–2.

[4] For a description by the International Court of Justice of how the UN took over certain of the functions of the League of Nations, see *International Status of South West Africa* case, *International Court of Justice Reports* (1950), 128.

Chapter VII of the Charter that deal with world peace. In other words, UN member states are under a legal obligation to carry out measures against a rogue state that have been determined by the UN Security Council. The one exception to this position is that states are not obligated to send forces to fight against an aggressor. The reason for this exception is the non-implementation of the Charter provisions that provided for the compulsory contribution by members to a standby UN force.

When the Security Council orders the taking of collective security measures to restore peace under Chapter VII, there is a two-stage process that is envisaged. The first is that the Security Council has the power to make a determination under Article 39 of the Charter that specific action by a state constitutes 'a threat to the peace, breach of the peace or act of aggression'. The Council has, in other words, been given by states the power to determine the content of the community values that are to be maintained by the UN collective security system, and, moreover, the power to decide when a state is violating these values. This Article 39 determination is a legal prerequisite for the Council to be able to use its other powers under Chapter VII: it is the doorway through which the Council must walk before it can have access to its other Chapter VII powers. The Council has made a large number of such Article 39 determinations in respect of a number of issues ranging from widespread human rights abuses within a state (for example in Somalia, Resolution 794 (1992); and East Timor, Resolution 1272 (1999)) to Iraq's invasion of Kuwait (Resolution 660 (1990)). Once this determination has been made, the second stage of the collective security process is the prescription by the Security Council of what measures should be taken by the international community of states to restore the observance by the recalcitrant state of the community value that it is presently violating. The Security Council has the power under Chapter VII to order two main types of measure to be taken against a state to ensure that it respects community values: it can impose economic sanctions and military sanctions.

The Security Council can, under Article 41 of the Charter, impose economic sanctions against a state. The Security Council has imposed economic sanctions against a number of UN member states in response to their actions that the Council had decided was a threat to international peace. For example, the Security Council imposed economic sanctions against Iraq in Resolution 661 in response to that country's invasion of Kuwait.

When imposing economic sanctions the Security Council will, for example, often require that all the world's states must stop trade with, and investment in, the target state. As a result, the population of the country will often suffer shortages of essential food and medical supplies that were being imported into the country before sanctions were imposed. The effect of economic sanctions particularly affects the poorer sections of a country's population, while the members of the government whose actions caused the imposition of the economic sanctions are usually not affected. This problem is exacerbated in the case of a dictator of a country, whose actions have often led to the imposition of economic sanctions against the country, in the first place, but who will in no way be affected by the sanctions. The case of Saddam Hussein, his family, and his allies in Iraq is a case in point here.

The imposition of economic sanctions is, however, useful in most cases since it will often provide diplomatic and other processes of conflict resolution the time they need to try and resolve a situation before the next step of the use of military force is used by the Security Council against the recalcitrant state. However, where economic sanctions are not—or do not look as if they will be—successful, then the use of military force is an important, final, collective security measure. This is the two-stage process that the Security Council employed against Iraq. When the economic sanctions imposed against Iraq looked as if they were not going to force Iraq to withdraw from Kuwait, the Security Council as a final measure in Resolution 678 authorized UN member states to use military force against Iraq.

The Security Council is given the power under Article 42 of the Charter to use a military force to fight against an aggressor. However, the cold war saw member states unwilling to give the Security Council and its military organ, the Military Staff Committee,[5] a power of command over their armed forces, an undertaking that by definition required cooperation and a unity of purpose. The end of the cold war has not yet seen a change in policy by states concerning this issue. The result is that the Security Council has had to delegate its Chapter VII powers to member states acting under their own command in order to ensure that military action could be taken to maintain or restore peace. Thus, for example, in responding to the 1990 Iraqi invasion of Kuwait, the Security Council did not itself form a 'UN force' to fight against Iraqi forces, but it did authorize UN member states to form an ad hoc coalition to use force against the occupying Iraqi forces.[6] As a result, states contributed troops to a coalition that repulsed Iraqi troops from Kuwait. This combined force was not under UN command and control, but was, by common choice of the states concerned, under the command and control of the United States. It has been explained in more detail elsewhere that this process of the Security Council delegating its Chapter VII powers to UN member states to carry

---

[5] The Military Staff Committee is composed of the chiefs of staff of the five permanent members of the Security Council (Article 47(2) of the Charter), the permanent members being the United States, United Kingdom, France, China, and Russia.

[6] For further examples of such delegations, see D. Sarooshi, *The United Nations and the Development of Collective Security* (Oxford, 1999), ch. 5.

out military action on its behalf does not violate the letter[7] or the spirit of the UN collective security system.[8]

Having examined the core elements of the present UN system for maintaining peace, let us now turn to discuss the innovations to this system suggested by Baha'i Scripture.

5. Baha'i Innovations to the UN System of Collective Security

The Baha'i writings contain a clear statement of its ideal collective security system; and it is inextricably linked to the Baha'i concept of world peace. Bahá'u'lláh, the founder of the Baha'i faith, stated in a Tablet to the Sovereigns and Rulers of nations in 1867:

hold ye fast unto this . . . Peace, that haply ye may in some degree better your own condition and that of your dependents. Be reconciled among yourselves, that ye may need no more armaments save in a measure to safeguard your territories and dominions . . . Be united, O kings of the earth, for thereby will the tempest of discord be stilled amongst you, and your peoples find rest, if ye be of them that comprehend. Should any one among you take up arms against another, rise ye all against him, for this is naught but manifest justice.[9]

This is a clear affirmation of the principle that collective action should be taken against an aggressor state. Abdu'l-Bahá, the son of Bahá'u'lláh and the sole appointed interpreter of His writings, subsequently went on to elaborate, more than eighty years ago now, the details of Bahá'u'lláh's principle of collective security in the following terms:

True civilization will unfurl its banner in the midmost heart of the world whenever a certain number of its distinguished and high-minded sovereigns . . . shall, for the good and happiness of all mankind, arise, with firm resolve and clear vision, to establish the Cause of Universal Peace. They must make the Cause of Peace the object of general consultation, and seek by every means in their power to establish a Union of the nations of the world. They must conclude a binding treaty and establish a covenant, the provisions of which shall be sound, inviolable and definite. They must proclaim it to all the world, and obtain for it the sanction of all the human race. This supreme and noble undertaking—the real source of the peace and well-being of all the world—should be regarded as sacred by all that dwell on

---

[7] There are, however, important limitations which the Security Council must observe when delegating its Chapter VII powers for these delegations to be lawful; see Sarooshi, *The United Nations*, ch. 4.

[8] In fact, some states see such delegations of power—or authorizations—as a novel way to ensure that the Charter system of maintaining or restoring international peace and security remains effective. See e.g. the statement by the Federal Chancellor of Austria, Mr Vranitzky, in the Security Council Summit Meeting in 1992 (S/PV.2981, 63, 64–5). See also A. Miller, 'Universal Soldiers: UN Standing Armies and the Legal Alternatives', (1993) 81 *Georgetown Law Journal* 773, 776; and T. Weiss, 'Overcoming the Somalia Syndrome: Operation Rekindle Hope?', *Global Governance*, 1/2 (1995), 177.

[9] Bahá'u'lláh, as quoted in Shoghi Effendi, *The World Order*, 192.

earth. All the forces of humanity must be mobilized to ensure the stability and permanence of this Most Great Covenant. In this all-embracing Pact the limits and frontiers of each and every nation should be clearly fixed, the principles underlying the relations of governments towards one another definitely laid down . . . the size of the armaments of every government should be strictly limited, for if the preparations for war and the military forces of any nation should be allowed to increase, they will arouse the suspicion of others. The fundamental principle underlying this solemn Pact should be so fixed that if any government later violate any of its provisions, all the governments on earth should arise to reduce it to utter submission, nay the human race as a whole should resolve, with every power at its disposal, to destroy that government. Should this greatest of all remedies be applied to the sick body of the world, it will assuredly recover from its ills and will remain eternally safe and secure.[10]

It is thus clear that the Baha'i concept of collective security is only one element, albeit important, of the Baha'i approach to maintaining peace. The role of collective security is to enforce the provisions of some future type of world constitution adopted by states and their peoples.[11] This is the first important innovation that the Baha'i principle of collective security would suggest: that states should conclude a binding treaty (the 'Most Great Covenant') which incorporates the issues that Abdu'l-Bahá has expressly mentioned in the passage quoted above. Reaching agreement on these matters will not be easy in practice, and will require a great deal of political will by states. However, it is Baha'i belief that the peace and security of the world depends on it. Once such an agreement is concluded, then collective security can act as the mechanism to ensure enforcement of the agreement's provisions. The body exercising such collective security powers could well be a revamped version of the Security Council.

This approach of specifying in express terms the community values that collective security is to maintain is a significant improvement on the current system where the UN Security Council determines on an ad hoc— and often very selective—basis what constitutes a threat to or breach of

---

[10] Abdu'l-Bahá, as quoted *ibid*.

[11] Interestingly, the view has already been expressed that the present UN Charter can be characterized in many ways as a 'constitution'; see e.g. the statement by the representative of the US government in the oral proceedings in the *Expenses* case, *Pleadings, Oral Arguments, Documents* (1962) 413, 427; J. Crawford, 'The Charter of the United Nations as a Constitution', in H. Fox (ed.), *The Changing Constitution of the United Nations* (London, 1997), 3; B. Simma, 'From Bilateralism to Community Interest in International Law', 250 *Recueil des cours* (The Hague, 1994-VI), 209, 258–62; T. Franck, 'The "Powers of Appreciation": Who is the Ultimate Guardian of UN Legality?', (Editorial Comment) (1992) 86 *American Journal of International Law* 519, 521; W. M. Reisman, 'The Constitutional Crisis in the United Nations', (1993) 87 *American Journal of International Law* 83; B. Fassbender, *UN Security Council Reform and the Right of Veto: A Constitutional Perspective* (The Hague, 1998), 89–115; and M. Herdegen, 'The "Constitutionalization" of the UN Security System', (1994) 27 *Vanderbilt Journal of Transnational Law* 135, 150. But cf. G. Arangio-Ruiz, ' "The Federal Analogy" and UN Charter Interpretation: A Crucial Issue', (1997) 8 *EJIL* 1.

the peace or act of aggression and thus what types of state action will trigger a collective security response. The greater certainty provided by the Baha'i approach can only provide a greater sense of security for states than that which currently exists.

Another innovation that the Baha'i concept introduces to collective security as it is currently understood is that the government of the rogue state should be removed from power and not just be made to cease its violation of a fundamental community value. Under current international law—in particular the law of the UN—this is clearly not an essential objective of a collective security response by states. This is evidenced by the response of the UN and its member states to the invasion of Kuwait by Iraq. In responding to the Iraqi invasion, the allied troops only forced Iraqi troops to withdraw from Kuwait. The allies did not go on and remove from power the Iraqi government. This left in power a government that continued to violate international law and the decisions of the Security Council. The subsequent response of the Security Council to this Iraqi government action was to reimpose economic sanctions on Iraq. These sanctions have not to date effected any change in the policy of the government, but they have, as noted above, had an adverse effect on the poorer sections of the Iraqi population. Moreover, several UN member states have launched unilateral air strikes against the Iraqi government in an effort to compel compliance.[12] This also met with little or no success. This example does highlight the problem with leaving in power a government that has no respect, or even possibly disdain, for fundamental norms of international law such as, for example, the principle of non-aggression against other states.

However, the measure of removing the government of a state from power would not be appropriate in the context of the present UN collective security system. It would only be appropriate as part of the broader set of Baha'i proposals that the states and peoples of the world conclude and accept the 'Most Great Covenant' and provide therein their consent to such a final measure. It is this consent which would give the collective security system the authority and legitimacy to remove from power the government that violates the terms of this Covenant, since this government no longer has any legal or moral basis to govern its state. It has shown a flagrant disregard for international law and also the considered view of the majority of its peoples who affirmed the Covenant. The latter is the case since we recall that, according to Abdu'l-Bahá, the Covenant should be ratified by all the peoples of the world: it must obtain the 'sanction of all the human race'. Accordingly, an international force would be acting with

---

[12] For the legal considerations relating to this action, see e.g. D. Kritsiotis, 'Legality of the 1993 US Missile Strike on Iraq', (1996) 45 *International & Comparative Law Quarterly* 162.

international and local legitimacy were it to remove from power a government that had transgressed any of the fundamental provisions of the Covenant, since the force would have received a mandate to act in such a manner from all the peoples of the world as well as, importantly, the peoples of the nation concerned.

The removal of a government from power as a collective security response has in any case already occurred in the case of the Security Council's response to the overthrow within Haiti of the democratically elected president, Aristide, in September 1991. The Security Council decided in 1993 to authorize states to use force to restore back to power the democratically elected government of President Aristide.[13] This mandate was carried out by a multinational force spearheaded by the United States in an action known as Operation Uphold Democracy.[14] Despite the positive outcome in the case of Haiti, there were serious concerns expressed over the operation's international legitimacy.

What we mean by international legitimacy in this context is that the UN, when it takes action to deal with threats to world peace, can be said to be acting on behalf, and with the support, of the majority of the world's nations and peoples. It is clear that not every action by the Council under Chapter VII would in the light of this test be seen as being legitimate,[15] even where strictly speaking that action may be lawful. A lawful position is not always a legitimate one.[16] The main issue concerning legitimacy that

[13] Security Council Resolution 940 in 1993 provides in part: '4. *Acting* under Chapter VII of the Charter of the United Nations, [the Security Council] authorizes Member States to form a multinational force under unified command and control and, in this framework, to use all necessary means to facilitate the departure from Haiti of the military leadership . . . the prompt return of the legitimately elected President and the restoration of the legitimate authorities of the Government of Haiti, and to establish and maintain a secure and stable environment . . .'.

[14] On the legal considerations relating to this operation, see D. Malone, *Decision-Making in the UN Security Council* (Oxford, 1999); and D. Sarooshi, 'The United Nations Collective Security System and the Establishment of Peace', (2000) 53 *Current Legal Problems* 621, 628–32.

[15] Cf. the view that because the UN is not responsible to individuals but only states, it has no legitimacy at all to use force. In other words, there is no constituency from which the UN could draw such a mandate or authority. For a Baha'i response to this problem, see text that follows n. 17, below.

[16] See also I. Claude, 'Collective Legitimization as a Political Function of the UN', (1996) 20 *International Organization* 367. A collective security system maintains the status quo of a particular community. It is thus of considerable importance that the values which the system maintains are those which the majority of states in the world are dedicated to upholding. In other words, the system must be 'legitimate'. The legitimacy of action by the Security Council under Chapter VII of the UN Charter has been the source of considerable academic discussion. On the issue of the legitimacy of collective enforcement measures by the Security Council, see J. Alvarez, 'Judging the Security Council', (1996) 90 *American Journal of International Law* 1; I. Brownlie, 'The Decisions of Political Organs of the UN and the Rule of Law', in R. St J MacDonald (ed.), *Essays in Honour of Wang Tieya* (Dordrecht, 1993), 91; D. Caron, 'The Legitimacy of the Collective Authority of the Security Council', (1993) 87 *American Journal of International Law* 552, 556–88; T. Franck, 'Legitimacy in the

was contested by states in the case of Haiti was whether the removal of a government from power is a legitimate objective of a collective security response.[17] This is where the Baha'i approach of expressly providing in a treaty the principles and values that collective security is to maintain together with the agreement of the nations and peoples of the world that a collective security response can involve the removal of the government is of importance, since it provides a degree of legitimacy for such action that currently does not exist. Moreover, the incorporation into the 'Most Great Covenant' of the community values that collective security is to maintain has the further advantage in terms of legitimacy that these will have been agreed to by all states that have ratified the agreement, while under the current UN system it is only the fifteen member states of the Security Council who decide what are the community values.

There is also a more general issue of legitimacy concerning the present use of collective security by the UN. This issue relates to the legitimacy of the decision-making processes of the Security Council when exercising its collective security powers. The main point that arises here concerns the veto power that the five permanent members of the Security Council possess over, among others, decisions relating to collective security made by the Council. The five Great Powers that emerged from the Second World War—the United States, the United Kingdom, the former Soviet Union (now replaced on the Council by Russia), China, and France—have been designated by Article 23(1) of the UN Charter as 'Permanent Members of the Security Council'. In addition to having the right to permanent representation on the Security Council—the other ten members of the Security Council being elected on a two-yearly basis—Article 27(3) of the Charter gives the permanent members the power to veto decisions of the Security Council. This power of veto of the five permanent members means that they exercise greater weight than the ten non-permanent members in the decision-making processes of the Council. This is borne out by the private consultations that take place between the permanent members on a matter before it is taken to the wider membership of the Security Council. The practice is now such that the permanent members will often agree, or agree to disagree, on a particular matter in their private consultations. Subsequently in the full Security Council meeting which takes place in public the ambassador of each state simply reads out a

International System', (1988) 82 *American Journal of International Law* 705; S. Murphy, 'The Security Council, Legitimacy, and the Concept of Collective Security after the Cold War', (1994) 32 *Columbia Journal of Transnational Law* 201; and B. Weston, 'Security Council Resolution 678 and Persian Gulf Decision Making: Precarious Legitimacy', (1991) 85 *American Journal of International Law* 516.

[17] See e.g. the statements in the Security Council made by the representatives of Brazil (S/PV.3413, 9–10); Mexico (S/PV.3413, 4–5); Uruguay (S/PV.3413, 7); and New Zealand (S/PV.3414, 21–2).

prepared speech with no substantive discussion taking place among the wider membership of the Council. This process does not sit easily with the Baha'i administrative principle of consultation, which suggests that persons who are part of a decision-making organ should have an equal right to participate, set forth their views, and vote when making a decision as part of a decision-making body. This principle is contained in part in the following statement by Abdu'l-Bahá:

members [of a group that are consulting] . . . must take counsel together in such wise that no occasion for ill-feeling or discord may arise. This can be attained when every member expresseth with absolute freedom his own opinion and setteth forth his argument. . . . The shining spark of truth cometh forth only after the clash of differing opinions. If after discussion, a decision be carried unanimously, well and good; but if . . . differences of opinion should arise, a majority of voices must prevail.[18]

Application of this principle to our case may suggest that every state in the Security Council should have an equal right to participate in the decisions of the Council. In addition to ensuring a full and frank debate on the substance in the Security Council, the current processes of decision-making would have to be changed to ensure that no one state possesses the power to veto decisions that were acceptable to a majority of the Council. Such innovations are also important for the long-term legitimacy of action by the Security Council, since the Security Council must be perceived by states to be acting to ensure international peace and not just the achievement of their own individual interests. The abolition of the veto power—if it were to take place—would assist greatly in reassuring states who are not members of the Security Council that the Council was genuinely acting 'on their behalf', in the words of Article 24 of the Charter, and not just in those cases where the permanent members agreed. The Baha'i International Community—a body with Observer Status to the UN granted by a subsidiary organ of the General Assembly—itself made such a proposal first in 1955 and more recently in 1995 when it stated concerning UN reform that there should be gradual elimination of the concepts of 'permanent membership' and 'veto power'.[19]

6. Concluding Remarks

The operation of an effective collective security system is one of the most urgent needs facing our world today. We have been reminded recently of

[18] Abdu'l-Bahá, as quoted in Shoghi Effendi, *Baha'i Administration: Selected Messages 1922–1932* (Wilmette, Ill., 1998), 21.
[19] See *Proposal for Charter Revision Submitted to the United Nations by the Baha'i International Community* (Wilmette, Ill., 1955), 6; and Baha'i International Community, *Turning Point for All Nations* (New York, 1995), 11.

what happens when the system does not operate: for example, the genocide of an estimated 800,000 people in Rwanda in the space of less than
four months in 1994.[20] However, the establishment of an effective collective security system—or for that matter peace—does not just depend on
the conclusion of treaties alone.[21] It depends on the political will of
nations, and this in turn depends, largely, on the peoples of the world
wanting such a system to work.

In a document issued in Haifa in 1985 the governing body of the Baha'i
world community, the Universal House of Justice, stated the following:

The Great Peace towards which people of good will throughout the centuries have
inclined their hearts, of which seers and poets for countless generations have
expressed their vision, and for which from age to age the sacred scriptures of
mankind have constantly held the promise, is now at long last within the reach of
the nations. For the first time in history it is possible for everyone to view the entire
planet, with all its myriad diversified peoples, in one perspective. World peace is
not only possible but inevitable. It is the next stage in the evolution of this planet . .
. Whether peace is to be reached only after unimaginable horrors precipitated by
humanity's stubborn clinging to old patterns of behaviour, or is to be embraced
now by an act of consultative will, is the choice before all who inhabit the earth.[22]

An important precondition for this act of 'consultative will' to take place is
a genuine acceptance by nations and their peoples of the organic unity of
the world. In the illuminating words of Bahá'u'lláh: 'The well-being of
mankind, its peace and security are unattainable unless and until its unity
is firmly established.'[23] An essential part of this unity, Bahá'u'lláh explains,
is the following: 'It is not for him to pride himself who loveth his own
country, but rather for him who loveth the whole world. The earth is but
one country, and mankind its citizens.'[24] It is this more inclusive loyalty of
persons as citizens of the world that will ensure the effective operation of a
future collective security system and is the surest guarantor of peace
between the nations. The Baha'i approach of concluding a 'Most Great
Covenant' will allow full expression to be given to the considered view of
the peoples and governments of the world, and it will also give a body
such as a future UN Security Council the legitimacy and limited authority
to take effective collective security measures.

---

[20] G. Prunier, *The Rwanda Crisis: History of a Genocide* (London, 1995), 265.
[21] Universal House of Justice, *The Promise of World Peace* (Haifa, 1985), 12.
[22] Ibid., 1.
[23] Statement by Bahá'u'lláh contained in Shoghi Effendi, *The World Order*, 203.
[24] Ibid., 198.

A VOYAGE IN GOD'S CANOE:
LAW AND RELIGION
IN MELANESIA

Reid Mortensen

Introduction

A sense of the sacred permeates the cultures of Melanesia: a region among the world's most Christian but, at the same time, noted for the continuing influence of its indigenous beliefs and practices. Indeed, the religious has an honoured place in the political rhetoric of the region and is promoted as an agent of state-creation in all of its independent states: Papua New Guinea (PNG), Solomon Islands, Vanuatu, and Fiji. Early nationalists in these countries considered that effective decolonization would involve the inculturation of political institutions, civil law, and social obligation with Christian principles and custom. As Vanuatu's founding prime minister, Fr. Walter Lini, urged in his independence speech in 1980, 'God and custom must be the sail and steering paddle of our canoe.' For Lini, these would be central to national unity, state-creation, and development in multicultural Vanuatu.[1]

Lini's metaphor would be incomprehensible in Melanesia's most densely populated provinces in the New Guinea Highlands. It nevertheless encapsulates the central theme of any discussion of law and religion in the region: how the modern civil law can be reconciled with the deep religiosity of Melanesian peoples, expressed publicly in a commitment to both Christianity and custom. I intend to consider this question in light of the extensive cultural pluralism of the region. This requires an initial review of the political thinking about the role of religion in the development of a Melanesian jurisprudence, especially as this thinking has been expounded since these countries became independent in the 1970s. The relationship between religion and the civil law in Melanesia is then considered, and involves questions of constitutional symbolism, religious freedom, enforcement of custom, and, a different thing, custom as civil law—specifically, its appropriation in the sorcery laws. This allows a reconsideration of Melanesian thought about Church, custom, and civil law, and how religious freedom can be maintained in what has become a turbulent period for the independent Melanesian states.

[1] W. Lini, *Beyond Pandemonium: From the New Hebrides to Vanuatu* (Wellington, 1980), 62.

Religious, Cultural, and Political Context

Christians comprise more than 95 per cent of the population in PNG, the Solomons, and Vanuatu. In 1986 the figure in Fiji was 53 per cent, but Fiji's general pattern of cultural pluralism and its political institutions differ from that of western Melanesia. It is more 'polyethnic', in Kymlicka's sense of a state that has become multicultural through immigration.[2] The geographic and economic hub of the South Seas, Fiji is more urbanized, wealthy, and Anglicized than the other countries. Its polyethnicism has nevertheless been a significant source of political instability since the 1987 military coups. In 1997 a multiracial Constitution restored institutions of democratic governance. However, while in May 2000 a small group of Taukeists (ethnic Fijian nationalists) held Cabinet ministers hostage, an interim military government revoked the Constitution.[3] After the safe release of the hostages an interim civilian administration initiated further constitutional review, pledging a return to democracy but committed to reserving the prime ministership to ethnic Fijians. The future of liberal institutions in Fiji remains uncertain. Fijians constitute just over half the population and show a higher degree of cultural unity than other indigenous Melanesian nationals do. There are strong provincial loyalties and differences in dialect and social structure, especially between the more Tongan-influenced east and the western islands. However, Fijians share a common language (a British-sponsored Bauan) and have developed common social hierarchies: families, land groups, clans, and provinces, the latter three being under different grades of chiefs. As regards religion, 99.5 per cent of Fijians are Christian and 75 per cent are Methodist, putting the Methodist Church in a prominent position in national life but one that closely identifies with Fijian interests. In contrast, people of Indian descent comprise the other large ethnic grouping (about 42 per cent). In 1986 about 80 per cent of Indians were Hindu, 16 per cent Muslim, and only 4 per cent Christian. Thus religion adds to the sharp cultural bipolarism of Fiji, and has been a destabilizing agent in Fiji's ethnic traumas since 1987. As large numbers of Indians emigrated after the coups, the current position of Christians in Fiji is undoubtedly stronger.

The other countries have weaker government than Fiji but, though poorer and increasingly unstable, have been more settled democracies. Solomon Islands became the exception in 2000, when democratic government was paralysed by civil war between Guadalcanalese and Malaitan militia around the capital, Honiara.

In contrast to Fiji's polyethnicism, the western Melanesian states are

---

[2] W. Kymlicka, *Multicultural Citizenship: A Liberal Theory of Minority Rights* (Oxford, 1995), 6, 10–26.

[3] Fiji Constitution Revocation Decree 2000 (Fiji), s. 2.

also better classified as 'multi-nations'. Immigration has been insignificant, but each country embraces a large number of cultures that, before European annexation, were largely self-sufficient, localized, and mutually suspicious. PNG, with more than 800 distinct language groups, could be the most culturally pluralized country on the globe. The western Melanesian peoples are almost entirely Christian, but in no country does one Church dominate indigenous peoples' adherence like the Methodist Church does in Fiji. Presbyterians are the largest group in Vanuatu (37 per cent), Anglicans in Solomon Islands (34 per cent), and Roman Catholics in PNG (28 per cent). The Lutheran Church in PNG is also large (23 per cent) and, as in the other countries, Protestants altogether account for more than 70 per cent of the population. There are strong regional concentrations in church affiliation, reinforcing the cultural distinctiveness of different islands and districts. For example, Anglicans represent more than 96 per cent of the population in the Solomons' Isabel and Temotu Provinces, but are a minority in Western Province, where the United Church (a union of Methodists and Congregationalists) is dominant.

The numbers who hold only custom beliefs or belong to cargo cults are small, and dwindling. In Fiji they are extinct. Elsewhere they are territorially concentrated: Malaita in the Solomons; Tanna in Vanuatu—the stronghold of the John Frum Cargo Cult. In the late 1980s Vanuatu had the highest proportion of traditional religionists, at 4.5 per cent.[4]

Malinowski famously denied that indigenous Melanesian belief was *religion*, preferring to locate it in a pre-religious state called *magic*.[5] The Eurocentrism of this distinction is well known, and more recent approaches to religion as the organization of life around a sense of transcendence dismiss it. These approaches not only expand the realm of the religious, they include as religious practice some pragmatic rituals: repeated, stylized actions that represent or claim to appropriate the supernatural.[6] In these terms, Melanesian custom is religious. Furthermore, its religious world-view is pervasive as it does not distinguish the sacred and the profane, and ritual inevitably has a practical end. Invocations, spells, pig-slaughtering, and the use of charms are usually directed at something material: a successful hunt, fertile garden, reconciliation, healing, killing. To a large extent, this integrated *Weltanschauung* has been brought into Christian belief and practice. Christian converts have often accepted the new religion without disbelieving in ancestral ghosts, *tabus*, and the power

---

[4] Fiji, *Report on Fiji Population Census 1986* (Suva, 1989), 15; Papua New Guinea, *Report on the 1990 National Population and Housing Census in Papua New Guinea* (Port Moresby, 1994), 171–80; Solomon Islands, *1986 Population Census* (Honiara, 1989), 171–7; Vanuatu, *National Population Census* (Port Vila, 1991), 38.

[5] B. Malinowski, *Argonauts of the Western Pacific* (London, 1922), 392–407.

[6] W. King, 'Religion', and E. Zeusse, 'Ritual', both in M. Eliade (ed.), *Encyclopedia of Religion*, 16 vols. (New York, 1987), xii. 286, 405.

of sorcerers. Especially outside Fiji, the practices of later generations of Christians have shown high degrees of syncretism, and since the 1970s this has helped Churchmen to incorporate custom rituals into Christian worship. The Melanesian is also much more likely than the Western Christian to invoke God for good weather, business success, healing, or, according to a recent review in the *Fiji Times*, a favourable bounce of the ball in a rugby game.[7] These societies certainly carry powerful secularizing agents like urbanization, the cash economy, and deeper contact with the West. Protestantism itself will almost inevitably promote further secularization. However, at present the pervasiveness of the religious in Melanesian life remains striking.[8]

High Melanesian Thought on Law and Religion

In each of the Melanesian countries independence raised expectations that its cultural distinctiveness could be rediscovered by indigenizing its civil institutions. No nationalist spelt out whether civil institutions were to be harmonized with those of pre-contact Melanesia, or with the contemporary custom of rural Melanesia, and for the most part these were assumed to be the same. An important precondition for the indigenization of the law was the recognition in western Melanesia of custom as an independent source of law, although no indication of how custom could be used in civil courts was given. The beginnings of this post-independence movement lay in 'the Pacific Way', expounded in the early 1970s by Fiji's prime minister, Ratu Sir Kamisese Mara. He claimed to be articulating a unique Pacific approach to governance: peaceful decolonization, tolerance, environmentally and culturally sustainable development, concern for Christian morals.[9] There was nothing unique in these principles, and Melanesia has often lacked them. However, Ratu Mara's rhetoric of a Pacific distinctiveness was narrowed and consolidated in western Melanesia, especially after PNG's Bernard Narokobi began systematically to promote 'the Melanesian Way'. It would return to Fiji, but in an undemocratic form, in the cultural assertiveness of the Taukei Movement.

Indigenizing policies were espoused by early nationalist politicians like Fr. John Momis, Fr. Walter Lini, and Solomon Mamaloni. But it was the lawyer Narokobi, a law reform commissioner, judge, and legislator, who elaborated the detail of 'high Melanesian' political ideas and who oversaw a substantial programme of law reform that still awaits implementation. Narokobi aimed to develop some correspondence between 'classical' and modern Melanesia. This required a profound understanding of custom

---

[7] *Fiji Times* (FT), 5 May 2000, 7.
[8] G. Trompf, *Melanesian Religion* (Cambridge, 1991), 241–8.
[9] R. Crocombe, *The Pacific Way* (Suva, 1976), 4–7, 24–5.

and, then, that lawmakers adopt the assumptions underlying it as and into the civil law. Custom is simply the 'way of life or the fashion of the people': how a village community does things. As such, it is all that Westerners differentiate as law, religion, morality, and social habit. Narokobi consequently emphasized how significantly classical Melanesia was organized around the transcendent, and how custom therefore grounded 'a total cosmic vision of life'. No Western treatise on law would recognize, as his *Lo Bilong Yumi Yet* does, the territorial habitation of ghosts and tree-fairies; the normative relations between a man and his dead ancestors; kinship created by common descent from animals or plants; or the use of dreams, sixth-sense, and bird, animal, or plant communication in determining disputes. However, the cosmic vision that informed these would have to be incorporated into the civil law: 'for Melanesians at least, the active participation of the "spirit" in human affairs will continue to dominate their perceptions of the law'. For example, 'any development of Melanesian jurisprudence will have to give full cognizance to the interaction between living persons and the spirits of the dead'. This has implications for the ascription of blame. 'In assessing the value of human conduct, pre-ordained conduct [compelled by ghosts] is more often than not, excused.' Narokobi's ambition was therefore normative wholeness or, as he referred to it, 'integrated integrity'.[10] If realized, his programme would invest the civil law with assumptions and methods that are only explicable by reference to the supernatural. It demands a sacralizing of the civil law.

High Melanesian thinking outside Fiji has been a philosophy of decolonization, dichotomizing the content of indigenized institutions and those left by the British, French, and Australian metropoles. In polyethnic Fiji it was more partisan, pitched against Indian communities, and overtly Christian. The Taukei Movement was responsible for the social destabilization that led to the 1987 coups, and agitated strongly for the maintenance of the Fijian ascendancy afterwards. Taukeism revived on the formation of the Chaudhry government in 1999, and Taukeists who took the government hostage in May 2000 forced the recent revoking of the multiracial Constitution. Though factionalized, Taukeism generally emphasizes the exercise of chiefly power, particularly through the Great Council of Chiefs; traditional landholding; the revival of custom; and a guarantee of ethnic Fijian government. It is firmly centred in conservative Methodism, and supported the establishment of a Christian state during the Fijian ascendancy. It still calls for the state to adopt Christian principles.[11]

---

[10] B. Narokobi, *Lo Bilong Yumi Yet: Law and Custom in Melanesia* (Goroka, 1989), 9, 74; *The Melanesian Way* (Port Moresby, 1983), 8, 17, 67.

[11] *FT*, 26 Apr. 2000, 3; R. Norton, *Race and Politics in Fiji*, 2nd edn., (Brisbane, 1990), 137–40.

An ample anthropology now exists showing how high Melanesians have romanticized pre-contact Melanesia, inventing custom to deal with problems of national identity in states that had never been nations.[12] There may be nothing wrong with this as a political endeavour, unless—as with the Taukeists—the invention of tradition is used unjustly to marginalize other peoples. The weakness in the high Melanesian project lies elsewhere. First, Narokobi recognizes that his description of custom is incompatible with Christian thought.[13] Despite the PNG Constitution's equal commitment to custom and the 'Christian principles that are ours now', he offers no means of integrating, at times, competing religious world-views. It is plainly one reason why many of Narokobi's law reform proposals are unacceptable to Papua New Guineans. Secondly, the high Melanesian project ignores, or grossly underestimates, the significance of cultural pluralism throughout the region. In general, its aim of normative wholeness idealizes the homogeneous village as the model for the state. Taukeists recognize the cultural difference brought by the Indian presence in Fiji, but openly deny its right to be there. Indigenous Polynesians on outlying islands in PNG, the Solomons and Fiji, and smaller migrant communities throughout the region, are also disregarded. Even in its understanding of Melanesian peoples, the High Melanesian project has not properly addressed the pluralism of traditional cultures. Of the early nationalists, Solomon Islands' Mamaloni recognized that his country was an artificially bordered, multi-nation state, but his proposals for a federal polity with powerful state governments were unsuccessful.[14] Narokobi also maintained the need for a stratified federalism that approximated the settlement patterns of classical Melanesia, but has not indicated how village custom is to be adapted as the laws of the heterogeneous provinces and nation-state. He actually suggested that custom as civil law should override borrowed institutions that do address cultural pluralism, like the Bills of Rights.[15]

If cultural pluralism is to be addressed properly, these countries urgently need some institutional objective other than the national village. Ethnic conflict in the region is serious: Bougainville, Guadalcanal, and the political crisis in Fiji show that it is worsening. Inter-group violence has also followed religious lines. At independence Vanuatu was torn by two rebellions motivated by religion. Nagriamel, a custom religious movement on Espiritu Santo, and the John Frum Cargo Cult on Tanna both tried to secure the secession of their islands, but were defeated by armed force.[16] In

---

[12] See M. Jolly, 'Spectres of Inauthenticity', *Contemporary Pacific*, 4/1 (1992), 49.

[13] Narokobi, *Lo Bilong Yumi Yet*, 73.

[14] S. Mamaloni, 'The Road to Independence', in R. Crocombe and E. Tuza (eds.), *Independence, Dependence, Interdependence* (Honiara, 1992), 7, 10, 18.

[15] Narokobi, *Lo Bilong Yumi Yet*, 87, 140.

[16] W. Miles, *Bridging Mental Boundaries in a Postcolonial Microcosm* (Honolulu, 1998), 105–6.

Fiji the 1987 coups led to the rise of a crusading Taukei Methodism that, between 1988 and 1990, targeted mosques and temples for arson and vandalism. In October 1989 the burning of Indian temples and a mosque in Lautoka by the Methodist Youth Fellowship saw the firebombing of the Wesley Church in retaliation.[17]

This resort to violence has been used as a cruel satire on 'the Melanesian Way': when negotiations failed in inter-village disputes in classical Melanesia, only a raid or warfare could solve them.[18] It should at least be recognized that either there is an insufficient body of common tradition to bring to the nation-state, or the common tradition lacks pacific ways of organizing cultural diversity. However this problem is conceived, high Melanesians must either invent a tradition that, first and foremost, accommodates pluralism, or abandon the programme of normative wholeness altogether.

Constitutional Symbolism

The preambles to the western Melanesian Constitutions all declare, one way or another, that the state is founded on Christian principles and worthy custom.[19] The preamble in Fiji's revoked Constitution is both more evangelical and less emphatic about the role of custom than the others, but Fiji has experienced larger political developments since independence and, again unlike the other countries, has dealt with its ethnic troubles in its constitutive documents. However, even the multiracial 1997 Constitution recalled 'the conversion of the indigenous inhabitants of these islands from heathenism to Christianity through the power of the name of Jesus Christ; the enduring influence of Christianity in these islands and its contribution, along with that of other faiths, to the spiritual life of Fiji'.[20]

These preambles are non-justiciable, so only rarely give assistance in legal reasoning. For instance, when having to determine whether mandatory sentencing laws violated the PNG Constitution's prohibition on cruel, degrading, and inhuman punishments, Kapi Dep CJ said this about the ban: 'This section seeks to protect the dignity of the human person ... This special protection under the *Constitution* is given only to mankind and not other animals ... In my view, the dignity of the human person stems from the Christian philosophy of mankind. These Christian principles are a

17 *FT*, 16 Oct. 1989, 1, 2, 6; 17 Oct. 1989, 1, 3; 19 Oct. 1989, 2; 20 Oct. 1989, 3.

18 C. Filer, 'The Bougainville Rebellion, the Mining Industry and the Process of Social Disintegration in Papua New Guinea' in R. May and M. Spriggs (eds.), *The Bougainville Crisis* (Bathurst, NSW, 1990), 73, 84–7.

19 Preamble, Constitution of the Independent State of Papua New Guinea (Constitution (PNG)); Preamble, Constitution of Solomon Islands (Constitution (SI)); Preamble, Constitution of the Republic of Vanuatu (Constitution (Van)).

20 Preamble, Constitution Amendment Act 1997 [Constitution (Fiji)].

foundation upon which our nation has been built'.[21] The judge then
warned against any government that acts to undermine human dignity,
and that 'treats its people like animals'. He did not think that the PNG
sentencing laws did that.[22] PNG judges have also pondered, but not too
seriously, whether the Constitution's Christian principles import a principle of mercy into sentencing practice.[23]

That is as far as the Christian preambles have affected the substantive
civil law. Thus, although Fiji's 1997 Constitution recognized 'that worship
and reverence of God are the source of good government and leadership'
this was subordinate to the general principle that 'religion and the State
are separate'.[24] Nowhere in the Commonwealth does separatism have the
meaning that it does in the United States, but in Fiji the phrase was
included as an explicit rejection of calls that Fiji be declared 'a Christian
state'. Those calls paralleled proposals throughout the region for substantive legal preferences to be given to Christian churches, all of which raised
concerns about religious freedom.

Religious Freedom

The Melanesian Bills of Rights incorporate religious freedom guarantees
that override other laws.[25] However, somewhat surprisingly for religious
and pluralized countries, there is no reported adjudication on the religious
freedom guarantees. To an extent, this can be attributed to the dominant
position of mainstream Christian churches in the region. Litigation involving religion tends to come before the civil courts as a question of custom.
The churches generally have the political influence to ensure that Christian
practices are accommodated by legal or administrative arrangements with
government. There are also cases that suggest that lawyers and judges are
limited by an older common law mindset, and are less sensitized than, say,
Americans to Bill of Rights questions. For example, in the Solomons case
of *Talosui* v. *Tone'ewane*[26] a claim that constitutional rights of religious
freedom had been violated would probably have succeeded, if it had been
raised. An expatriate English judge felt that the petitioners' religious beliefs
deserved legal protection, but apparently neither he nor the lawyers before
the court were aware of the Bill of Rights. The same occurred in *Talasasa*
v. *United Church*,[27] where Muria ACJ relied on common law principles in

---

[21]   *Special Constitutional Reference No. 1 of 1984: Re Minimum Penalties Legislation*
[1984] PNGLR 314, 326.   [22]   Ibid.
[23]   *Hane* v. *The State* [1984] PNGLR 105, 113; *Kalabus* v. *The State* [1988] PNGLR 193,
199.
[24]   Constitution (Fiji), s. 5.
[25]   Constitution (Fiji), s. 35; Fundamental Rights and Freedoms Decree 2000 (Fiji), s. 6;
Constitution (PNG), s. 6; Constitution (SI), ss. 3, 11; Constitution (Van), s. 5(1)(f).
[26]   [1985/86] SILR 140, 144.
[27]   Unreported, High Court of Solomon Islands, 26 Feb.1993.

assuming that a court could determine whether the Church had complied with the rules of natural justice, in a case involving the discipline of a minister for an extramarital relationship. No consideration was given to the question whether, in Solomon Islands, the Bill of Rights immunized internal matters of church discipline from judicial review as, for example, the US Bill of Rights does.[28] Still, it should be recognized that, even in the absence of judicial enforcement, governments have generally been conscious of the limits that rights of religious freedom place on them, and have a good practical record of respecting them. There are exceptions, and all relate to claims of legal privilege for either Christian belief in general or, where this is not perceived as being under threat, the larger mainstream churches.

FIJI: THE SUNDAY BAN

While proposals for the formal declaration of a Christian state have arisen throughout Melanesia, they have had more political force in Fiji, where large Hindu and Muslim populations enabled Taukei Methodists to argue that Christian Fiji required constitutional protection. They only succeeded in part, in the maintenance of Fiji's Sunday ban (or Siga Tabu). After the Taukeist Revd Manasa Lasaro secured control of the Methodist Conference in September 1989, the Methodist Church began to call for Fiji to be declared 'a Christian state to the end of time'. This was also pursued by the Great Council of Chiefs and the government party, the Soqosoqo ni Vakavulewa ni Taukei (SVT). Little content was given to Christian statism, although church and SVT submissions to the Constitution Review Commission (CRC) in 1995 conceptualized it in distinctly Fijian and Methodist terms: involving the maintenance of ethnic Fijian political supremacy, and bans on Sunday activities and gambling. The CRC was intent on dismantling the Fijian ascendancy, and from 1996 a new moderate Methodist leadership lent its support.[29]

The centrepiece of Fijian Christian statism was the Sunday ban, and this was successfully implemented. Colonel Sitiveni Rabuka, leader of the military coups, issued the Sunday Observance Decree after the second coup in September 1987. This was an explicitly religious measure, banning all activities on Sunday so that it would 'be observed in the Republic of Fiji as a sacred day and day of worship and thanksgiving to Christ the Lord'. The ban was so complete that exceptions had to be stated for worship, use of private vehicles, essential services, and backyard barbecues. Even picnics were forbidden.[30] It met unrestrained criticism from the Fiji Council of

[28] *Serbian Eastern Orthodox Diocese* v. *Milivojevich* 426 US 696, 712–20 (1976).
[29] I. Tuwere, 'The Church–State Relation in Fiji', and P. Niukula, 'Religion and the State', in B. Lal and T. Vakatora (eds.), *Fiji in Transition*, 2 vols. (Suva, 1997), i. 44, 53.
[30] Sunday Observance Decree 1987 (No. 20) (Fiji), ss. 2, 4–5.

Churches (FCC), in which Revd Josateki Koroi, president of the Methodist Conference, joined. Conscious of the effect that the Decree would have on the Indian community, the FCC accused the government of dishonouring its responsibilities to maintain religious freedom, crossing the limits of state authority, and imposing worship 'by threat of punishment and force of arms'.[31] Tourism and sugar industries suffered, but the Decree also burdened poorer Fijians, who had to walk to church because public transport was unavailable.

The interim government that succeeded Rabuka eventually introduced a revised Sunday Observance Decree in 1989. This prohibited general trade and business more directly: allowing Sunday worship, essential services, sugar-milling, barbecues, picnics, private sports, public transport, and limited restaurant hours.[32] While the FCC also objected to the 1989 Decree, the now Taukei-controlled Methodist Church organized demonstrations against any relaxation of the 1987 Decree. Lasaro consistently articulated the Sunday ban as a Fijian tradition, demonstrating the conflation of Methodism, Taukeism, and Fijian political supremacy. He denied that it violated the religious freedom of Indian Hindus or Muslims, and argued that his 'common ground for compromise' with non-Christians was that he would not ask them to believe what he believed, and they must observe Sunday as Methodists required.[33] In this light it is unsurprising that Taukeists interpreted any dilution of the Decree as undermining Fijian rights, despite its widespread unpopularity and its evident economic cost. The end came in 1995, by which time a politically maturing Rabuka was the elected prime minister. In February 1995 Lasaro organized 12,000 Methodists to march against Rabuka's plan to repeal the Decree, and this was sufficient to persuade the Senate to postpone the passage of the repealing legislation. However, the Senate was effectively only stalling and, by this time, political arrangements in Fiji were again liberalizing. The Senate passed the repealing legislation in October.[34]

WESTERN MELANESIA: CHURCH SURVEILLANCE LAWS

In western Melanesia, where inter-faith challenges to Christianity are minuscule, more concern has been expressed about the threat that new Protestant (especially Pentecostal) and quasi-Christian missions present to the older mainstream churches. The earliest measures to limit new missions were taken in PNG, where members of Parliament privately sponsored a Religious Movements (Control) Bill in 1981. Although this would

[31] 'Fiji Council of Churches' Statement on the Sunday Decree, March 11, 1988', *Pacific Journal of Theology*, 2nd ser., 1 (1989), 46–7.
[32] Sunday Observance Decree 1989 (No. 13) (Fiji), ss. 4–6.
[33] *Pacific Islands Monthly* (*PIM*) (Sept. 1989), 16.
[34] Sunday Observance (Repeal) Act 1995 (Fiji), s. 3; *PIM*, Apr. 1995, 14–16.

have allowed government monitoring of all churches, new groups entering the country would be placed under probation. The bill made no reference to non-Christian groups, revealing that it was principally intended to protect the larger churches from the proselytism of new Christian groups. Strangely, this would have placed restrictions on the churches that the small communities of Muslims, Hindus, Buddhists, and Baha'i would escape. However, the example modelled by Christian statists in Fiji in the early 1990s led at least two MPs to propose that non-Christian groups be prohibited in PNG. Despite this, the members of the PNG Council of Churches have generally warned against the use of coercion to maintain a Christian country or any compromise of the religious freedom guarantees that, they point out, also protect the mainstream churches. Robert Fergie of the Evangelical Alliance expressed the more common view of speakers at the Council's conference on religious freedom in 1994: 'There seems little doubt that there is a need for action with regard to the influx of various sects and non-Christian religions into PNG. However, the most needed change is for inner renewal of the Church rather than an external change of the Constitution.'[35]

The Solomon Islands Christian Association (SICA) and the Vanuatu Council of Churches (VCC) have shown less concern for religious freedom than their counterparts in PNG and Fiji, and both have lobbied to restrict the entrance of new religions to the country or to member churches' spheres of geographic influence. In a review of the Solomons Constitution in 1987 the Mamaloni Committee reported widespread support for SICA's position and received a submission from the world's most Anglican community, Temotu, that it be constitutionally declared an Anglican province. The Committee recommended that parliaments be able to prohibit the conversion of Christians, but nothing came of it.[36]

In the 1980s the VCC also began to propose restrictions on other religious groups, including Mormons, Jehovah's Witnesses, and Baha'i. However, the VCC's main concern has been Neil Thomas's Holiness Fellowship. In 1989 this group feuded with Presbyterians and Anglicans, upset by its rebaptism of converts. Later, accusations were made that the Fellowship was a front for Thomas's Gudfala stores. In the early 1990s he was implicated in TV-evangelist business collapses in Vanuatu and Australia.[37] However, it was the government that initiated church surveillance laws, and these ironically met immediate objections from two

---

[35] R. Fergie, 'Perspectives from an Evangelical', in T. Aerts (ed.), *Religious Freedom in Papua New Guinea* (Port Moresby, 1994), 46, 54.

[36] Constitutional Review Committee, *Report*, 3 vols. (Honiara, 1987), i. 290–4, 580–3, 587; iii. 2, 16, 18.

[37] *Vanuatu Trading Post (VTP)*, 5 Mar. 1997, 1; 22 Mar. 1997, 2; *Vanuatu Weekly Hebdomadaire (VWH)*, 14 Apr. 1989, 9; 5 May 1989, 8; 7 July 1989, 8; 14 July 1989, 7; 21 July 1989, 4, 7; 28 July 1989, 6; 6 Oct. 1989, 9; 3 Nov.1989, 6.

members of the VCC: the Presbyterians and Churches of Christ. Prime
Minister Maxime Carlot introduced the Religious Bodies (Registration)
Bill to the Parliament, which passed it, in July 1995. It required all religious bodies in Vanuatu to register with the government, and made it illegal for a religious body to preach, teach, or maintain its doctrines and
observances in Vanuatu without being registered. The Holiness Fellowship
was plainly in view, as registration could be refused if the group's 'opera-
tions' were inconsistent with a religious purpose, or if its leader was bank-
rupted.[38] Carlot claimed that the Act was not meant to limit religious
freedom, but would merely allow the government to monitor new groups.
However, it was never enforced as President Jean-Marie Léyé thought it
invalid and refused his assent. Fr. Lini, then Opposition leader, was also
aware of the constitutional problems but suggested that the Bill of Rights
be amended first, and the Act then be reintroduced. Most non-VCC
churches objected to the Act precisely because of Carlot's reasons for it,
and refused to register because they thought it would put them under VCC
control. It was a dead letter and was repealed in 1997.[39]

The main concern expressed about current missionary activity in
Melanesia is that new religions bring division to small, traditional communities. Emphasis has been placed on a common religion for sustaining
village cohesion. This has led to some representation of religious freedom
as a group right, held only by citizens. For the most part, it is suggested
that the right should be exercised through the village chiefs or bigmen,
who could veto the entry of new religious groups. The corollary is that
village leaders could also place internal restrictions on religious life in the
village. In Vanuatu this been refined as cultural policy by the
Malvatumauri (the national council of chiefs), which warns against the
admission of new religions, proposes government screening of missionar-
ies, and obliges chiefs to protect the churches they belong to.[40] However,
as President Léyé's response to church surveillance laws exemplifies, religious freedom is more generally understood as an individual right to
choose, and a group's right to preach. It is only when we turn to custom as
law that we find some opportunity for internal restrictions on the religious
life of a village community possible.

Custom-Based Claims

In most respects, custom remains more important than the civil law for the
average Melanesian, particularly in rural villages and in western

---

[38]   Religious Bodies (Registration) Act 1995 (Van), ss. 1, 3–5, 11.
[39]   *VTP*, 22 June 1996, 2; 15 June 1996, 6; 1 Mar. 1997, 3; *VWH*, 5 Aug. 1995, 1; 7
Oct. 1995, 3; 21 Oct. 1995, 3, 5; 25 Oct. 1995, 2; Religious Bodies (Repeal) Act 1997 (Van),
s. 1.
[40]   L. Lindstrom and G. White (eds.), *Culture, Kastom, Tradition* (Suva, 1994), 241.

Melanesia, where institutions of civil government may have no presence in some communities. Custom is also civil law capable of recognition in courts throughout the region, although its status differs from country to country. In PNG it is ranked below constitutional and statute law, but above the common law.[41] In the Solomons and Vanuatu it is also subordinate to constitutional and statute law, but its relationship with the common law is unclear.[42] This was also the case in Fiji under the 1990 Constitution but, the CRC thinking that this was merely another privilege of the Fijian ascendancy, the 1997 Constitution abandoned custom as an independent source of law. This is probably still the case under the present interim administration. There remains a power to adopt custom into statute.[43] But, despite all the hopes that a distinctive Melanesian jurisprudence immersed in custom would develop after independence, it has not happened. This is not the place to explain the failure of Melanesian courts to decolonize the civil law, except to the extent that it affects religious claims rooted in custom. However, the proof of custom as a question of fact in litigation means that it is conceptually denied any role in developing the law.[44] Furthermore, this makes it more likely that courts, already culturally disinclined to recognize custom, will deny individual claims on technical evidential grounds.

The sacred dimension of custom has already been discussed, and its recognition as law is therefore the most important means by which indigenous religion comes before the civil courts. Land and ocean rights rely significantly on custom. In establishing the intensity of a people's association with the land or sea, courts consider tribal mythology, stories of the supernatural origins of landscapes and islands, and sacred uses of land.[45] In other claims the technical problems of proving custom have meant that courts have generally refused to accommodate traditional religious obligations.[46] However, the Solomons case of *Talosui* v. *Tone'ewane* deepened these problems considerably. *Talosui* was mentioned in showing how lawyers schooled in the older common law tradition seemed unaware of the Bill of Rights. It shows the same problem for a claim based on custom.

[41] Constitution (PNG), Sch. 2.1, 2.2; *Supreme Court Constitutional Reference No. 4 of 1980; In the Matter of Somare* [1981] PNGLR 265, 285–6.

[42] Constitution (SI), s. 76(c); Constitution (Van), s. 95(3).

[43] Constitution 1990 (Fiji), s. 100(3); P. Reeves, T. Vakatora, and B. Lal, *The Fiji Islands: Towards a Unified Future* (Suva, 1996), 610.

[44] *Aisi* v. *Hoala* [1981] PNGLR 199, 203; *Sukutaona* v. *Hauanihoa* [1982] SILR 12, 13; *K* v. *T & Ku; In re Custody Application* [1985/86] SILR 49, 51; *Banga* v. *Waiwo*, unreported, Supreme Court of Vanuatu, 17 June 1996.

[45] *Fugui* v. *Solmac Construction Company Limited* [1982] SILR 100; *Iti* v. *Kvaragkiri*, unreported, Supreme Court of Vanuatu, 22 Sept. 1986, pt. IV; *Nangia* v. *Naukae*, unreported, Vanuatu Magistrate's Court, 7 Oct. 1994, 3–4.

[46] e.g, *Fugui* v. *Solmac Construction Company Limited* [1982] SILR 100, 111–12 (religious use of land); *Sipe* v. *Malaita Customary Land Appeal Court* [1985/86] SILR 255 (Polynesian bereavement rites).

The member for Ward 9 of the Malaita Provincial Assembly won the seat in 1985 by three votes. Twenty-two registered voters—Toabaita men— were nevertheless prevented from voting, as they believed that they would be ritually defiled if they entered any room (like the polling station) that a menstruating woman might have been in earlier that day. In Toabaita culture this has serious consequences: ghosts would wreak vengeance on men who suffered contamination. Malaitan authorities were aware that this belief prevented the men from voting unless they could do so in a place where women had not been beforehand. No special arrangements were made in Ward 9. It was therefore argued that the recognition of 'customary law' in the Constitution required electoral procedures to accommodate Toabaita belief, and failure to do so for a critical number of voters rendered the election void. Wood CJ rejected this, despite thinking that these beliefs were worthy of accommodation. The question was only addressed as one of statutory interpretation. Parliament had not provided for the accommodation of custom in the electoral law, so it could not be allowed. In itself, this is doubtful. It is unlikely that parliamentary sanction is needed before custom can be recognized. But, much more seriously, the judge questioned whether the objection to entering the polling station was 'customary law' or just 'custom'. He then asked whether the objection was based on 'customary law' or was 'merely a religious tenet or belief'.[47] The latter did not qualify as custom.

Talosui shows an expatriate judge with an extremely poor understanding of the structure of custom, segregating it into legal, religious, and other 'merely custom' components that are unknown to Toabaitans or, for that matter, Melanesian villagers generally. Extraordinarily, the recognition that the men's refusal to vote was motivated by belief in the supernatural disqualified the classification of this norm as *law*. If followed consistently, this approach could remove custom from the legal universe altogether. However, the immediate effect of Wood CJ's reconstruction of Toabaita culture was to deny a proven and well-known custom the place preserved for it in the Solomons Constitution.

Inexpertise on the part of civil judges can be partly addressed by using assessors in the civil courts or referring questions to specialists in custom. In Vanuatu the courts send questions to the Malvatumauri when a decision involving custom is required.[48] The procedure, though imperfect, has the advantage of limiting the court's unconscious entanglement in sensitive religious issues. Where custom is law, entanglement cannot be avoided completely. But, as the *Nagol Jump* case illustrates, the procedure can balance the court's obligation to recognize custom as civil law and yet to have decisions made in the *forum conveniens*. The land dive on South

[47] [1985/86] SILR 140, 143, 144.
[48] *M v. P* (1988) 1 Van LR 33, 35; *G v. L* (1990) 2 Van LR 486, 487.

Pentecost is one of Melanesia's most lucrative tourist attractions, but this can mask its religious significance. It re-enacts the story of a Sa ancestor, Tamlie, who dived to his death from a banyan tree while chasing his wife. She had survived the leap, as vines tied to her ankles broke her fall. The land dive now takes place most Aprils, with young men jumping from a timber tower with vines of a suitable strength and flexibility to restrain them at ground level. The women dance below: they cannot approach the tower until the dive occurs, or else Tamlie's ghost, which inhabits the tower, might take a diver's life. The dive is also an important grade-taking and agrarian fertility rite, coinciding with the yam harvest. There is a symbolic association between the yam and the male penis: if the young men dive successfully, there will be a good harvest and a healthy community.[49]

Understanding the intimate relationship between the Pentecost land dive and the myths, calendar, and food production of the Sa helps to explain why an attempt by two Pentecost men to conduct a land dive in urban Luganville, on neighbouring Santo, met strong resistance from the chiefs of both islands. Even though it would make the dive more accessible to tourists, the island chiefs and the Malvatumauri disapproved its export to Santo on the ground that the custom should remain local.[50] An application was made to the Supreme Court for orders allowing the men to conduct the land dive on Santo, on the ground that constitutional rights like freedom of movement enabled them to take it anywhere in Vanuatu. D'Imécourt CJ's solution was to postpone the constitutional question and adopt the chiefs' response, relying on the constitutional requirement that his judgment be compatible with custom. So, the judge required traditional procedures to be exhausted before a claim could be made in the civil courts. For a custom-based claim, only once the Malvatumauri had ruled on the question could constitutional rights be considered. D'Imécourt CJ refused the application and declared that, if the land dive were ever to leave Pentecost, all local chiefs and the Malvatumauri would have to agree.[51] The possible deferral of the enforcement of constitutional rights in *The Nagol Jump* obliges villagers to respect customary procedures and the authority of chiefs. D'Imécourt CJ was vaguely aware that Tamlie was haunting the diving tower,[52] and may well have enforced a *tabu* that supernatural agents had placed on moving the ritual. However, his method ensured that the question was dealt with by experts—the chiefs—and avoided any involvement in questions like the significance of the custom,

---

[49] M. Jolly, 'Kastom as Commodity', in Lindstrom and White (eds.), *Culture, Kastom, Tradition*, 131, 133–6.

[50] VWH, 23 May 1992, 1–2; 30 May 1992, 7.

[51] *In the Matter of the Nagol Jump; Assal v. The Council of Chiefs of Santo* (1992) 2 Van LR 545, 552.

[52] (1992) 2 Van LR 545, 547.

its amenability to export, whether it was one that could be appropriated by other peoples, and whether it could be adapted by Christians.

While *Nagol Jump* shows that, to a small degree, custom has penetrated the constitutional law, it simultaneously retains the condition that any internal restrictions on communities maintain Bill of Rights standards. This is a larger limitation on communal autonomy than is found in, say, the United States, where judicial review of Native American custom in the federal courts is generally unavailable.[53] In practice custom will nevertheless have a greater influence in village life than the civil law. Thus, despite the religious freedom guarantees, chiefs do effectively impose churchgoing obligations on villagers. There is no reported civil enforcement of religious freedom rights against custom churchgoing obligations, as there is in Polynesia,[54] although there is some evidence that custom courts themselves have adopted religious freedom guarantees.[55] However, as a matter of civil law, human rights limitations on custom restrictions are generally uncontroversial, especially where religious beliefs continue to motivate violence. These include prohibitions on practices like cannibalism, which, though now extremely rare, has been undertaken by *sanguma* (sorcerers) as a rite of preparation for killing others by magic.[56] Also, the more widespread problem of payback killing often has supernatural motives and sanctions, as it is commonly believed that ancestors' ghosts will punish those who do not avenge the killing of kin.[57] In none of these cases will civil courts recognize that the practice should be accommodated merely because, in a broad sense, it is religious.

Custom as Civil Law: The Case of Sorcery

Anthropologists now believe that European contact has increased the incidence of sorcery in Melanesia. Pacification led to the conduct of inter-village warfare by less visible means. Fewer external threats to village cohesion also allowed greater tolerance of sorcerers, usually regarded as misfits. The practice is still common throughout the region, particularly in PNG, and belief in its efficacy is widespread. Belief in sorcery is also not limited to custom religionists. Christians, though occasionally sceptical, often still understand sorcery in traditional terms, or recast it as a use of demonic powers.[58]

In general, sorcery is understood as the appropriation of powers—like

[53] Kymlicka, *Multicultural Citizenship*, 38–9.
[54] *Tuivaiti* v. *Faamalaga*, unreported, Supreme Court of Western Samoa, 17 Dec. 1980.
[55] *VTP*, 22 June 1996, 2.
[56] *The State* v. *Feama* [1978] PNGLR 301, 304;
[57] *Loumia* v. *DPP*, unreported, Solomon Islands Court of Appeal, 24 Feb. 1986; *Hane* v. *State* [1982] PNGLR 390.
[58] *VWH*, 3 June 1995, 8.

gods, ghosts, or other unseen forces—and the effective redirection of those powers against other people or evils. These can be meant for good or ill, and take different forms. The most feared, especially in PNG, is *vada*: assassination by a paid sorcerer, known widely as a *sanguma* man. The victim is drugged and beaten, and needles may be inserted into his body. This brings on a slow death after the victim is returned to his village, with little consciousness of his assailants or their identity. *Vada* can involve long preparatory rites (including cannibalism) and, it is believed, shape-changing. Cassowaries are often thought to be *sanguma* men.[59] The *sanguma* man killed in the *Wanosa* case[60] held a leaf to make himself invisible.

The social disruption caused by sorcery (especially *vada*) in Melanesian communities can be immense. As a consequence, the practice is often thought to deserve death. Highlanders tried to incinerate three suspected sorcerers as recently as April 2000.[61] *Tabus* on sorcery are still dealt with by bigmen or chiefs, or in custom courts.[62]

However, throughout the region sorcery is also an offence under the ordinary criminal law.[63] It was introduced in the Fiji Penal Code as late as 1969, before then having only been an offence for ethnic Fijians. The last colonial government's efforts to remove special restrictions on Fijians led it to generalize the offence to all in Fiji, although this met objections and ridicule from the Indian Opposition. The deputy speaker alone suggested that, as sorcery was rooted in belief in the supernatural, prosecutions would meet religious freedom defences based on the Bill of Rights. His suggestion that the offence be tied to the perpetration of violence was not adopted, and the offence in Fiji does not require intent to cause harm.[64] Elsewhere it does, although—like Fiji—governments in Vanuatu and Solomon Islands are apparently too embarrassed about the offence to prosecute.[65]

Not so in PNG, where there is long experience in civil prosecutions for sorcery. The current Sorcery Act dates from the later Australian adminis-tration, and states its agnosticism in dealing with religious beliefs in section 5. 'Even though this Act may speak as if powers of sorcery really exist . . . nevertheless nothing in this Act recognizes the existence or effec-tiveness of powers of sorcery in any factual sense . . . or denies the

---

[59] M. Patterson, 'Sorcery and Witchcraft in Melanesia', *Oceania*, 45 (1974), 132, 141–6.
[60] *Wanosa* v. *R* [1971–2] PNGLR 90.
[61] *Post-Courier*, 11 Apr. 2000; W. Yak, D. Tibu, T. Mionzing and K. Kara, 'Four Customary Law Cases', (1975) 3 *Melanesian Law Journal* 151, 160–4.
[62] PNG Law Reform Commission, *Sorcery* (Port Moresby, 1977), 1.
[63] Penal Code (Fiji), s. 232; Sorcery Act 1971 (PNG); Penal Code (Van), s. 151.
[64] Criminal Offences Code 1948 (Fiji), r. 19; Fiji, *Legislative Council Debates*, 1 May 1969, 788–803; 5 May 1969, 815, 836–9.
[65] Miles, *Bridging Mental Boundaries*, 167.

existence or effectiveness of such powers.'[66] The offence is explicitly based on the harm principle: 'it is just as evil to do or to try to do evil things by sorcery, as it would be to do them, or to try to do them, in any other way'. It prohibits evil (but not 'protective or curative') sorcery and making false accusations of sorcery, prescribing a maximum penalty of two years' imprisonment.[67] In *The State* v. *Magou*[68] Narokobi AJ held that the punishment could not account for any injury caused to the sorcerer's victim. Nor could it, without accepting that the sorcerer actually had the power to cause the injury. PNG law also accommodates belief in sorcery in other important respects. A premeditated killing of a supposed sorcerer can be treated as manslaughter.[69] Sorcerer-killings are also considered a special class of murder for sentencing decisions, and six years' gaol has been a common sentence.[70]

Following independence there was some resistance in PNG to the Sorcery Act's secular themes. In the *Aumane* trial in 1980 a believing judge accepted that a woman had killed twenty people in an Engan village through sorcery, and thought her execution by a firing squad of three archers to be 'honourable'. He gave the murderers only three months' gaol.[71] In contrast Kapi DepCJ adopted a sceptical position in *The State* v. *Kwayawako*, holding that the effect of section 5 of the Sorcery Act was that 'the law does not permit nor encourage the customary belief in the power of sorcery'. He therefore rejected the idea that there was a special class of sorcerer-killings for determining sentence, and imposed relatively long terms of twelve to fifteen years' imprisonment.[72] In both cases the Supreme Court corrected these departures from the official agnosticism towards sorcery, increasing the *Aumane* and reducing the *Kwayawako* sentences.[73]

Narokobi has argued through the Law Reform Commission for further indigenization of the Sorcery Act, incorporating a believer's perspective on sorcery and sorcerer-killings. These include punishment commensurate to the injury caused, longer terms in gaol, and banishment as an alternative sanction. He also wanted to use divination in inquiries to detect sorcery, and to supplement empirical methods of proof in trials.[74] While this has not become law, custom methods of proof are certainly used in lower

---

[66] Sorcery Act 1971 (PNG), s. 5.
[67] Preamble, ss. 6, 10, Sch. 1 Sorcery Act 1971 (PNG).
[68] [1981] PNGLR 1, 3.   [69] Sorcery Act 1971 (PNG), s. 16.
[70] PNG Law Reform Commission, *The Punishment for Wilful Murder* (Port Moresby, 1976), 11.
[71] *Acting Public Prosecutor* v. *Aumane* [1980] PNGLR 510.
[72] [1988] PNGLR 174, 176–7.
[73] *Acting Public Prosecutor* v. *Aumane* [1980] PNGLR 510; *Kwayawako* v. *The State* [1990] PNGLR 6.
[74] PNG Law Reform Commission, *Sorcery amongst the East Sepiks* (Port Moresby, 1978), 2–10.

courts. In March 2000 a District Court in the Highlands dismissed a prosecution for making a false accusation of sorcery, accepting that the pros-
ecutrix actually was a sorceress on the basis of the evidence of a New
Britain medium who used divination to establish that.[75]

The appeal judges in *Kwayawako* identified a distinction between the
existence of powers of sorcery (which is not officially recognized) and the
existence of *belief* in powers of sorcery (which is recognized as widespread).[76] In this sense the sorcery laws can be interpreted merely as an
adaptation of the harm principle in communities that believe the supernatural is immanent, and accessible. Sorcery must be controlled because
people *believe* it causes injury, and that *belief*, coupled with the payback
obligation, itself leads to social disorder. But even in this light it seems that
the State cannot maintain the agnosticism it professes. PNG's response to
sorcery effectively amounts to a partial appropriation of custom into the
criminal law. A serious *tabu* on sorcery has become a rational proscrip-
tion, and a traditional obligation to kill an evil sorcerer has become a civil
duty to make concessions in sentencing. To an extent, villagers do interpret the sorcery laws as the State's enforcement of a custom *tabu*.[77] The
success of this partial inculturation of the civil law nevertheless remains
limited. The trend before independence was a decline in the incidence of
sorcerer-killings, but even at that point the Law Reform Commission
thought that the capacity of the civil law to deter sorcery itself was
restricted.[78] It begs the question whether liberal agnosticism can be maintained rigorously, in societies that remain profoundly sacralized.

Conclusion

In the 1990s there was an emerging interest in Fijian theology in the consequences of the contraction of the *vanua* (which encompasses the chiefly
system, provincial identity, and custom) in Fijian life after European
contact. In contrast to Taukeism, which generally wanted to impose the
vanua on all aspects of political, social, and religious life in Fiji, moderate
Methodist theologians began to articulate the importance of a range of
differentiated, semi-autonomous institutions. Paula Niukula saw overlapping, mutually supportive, and simultaneously competing roles for the
vanua, the *lotu* (church), the *matanitu* (civil government), the *bula
vakailova* (money economy), and cultural pluralism.[79] This account
certainly needs refining: pluralism is more a setting for civil institutions

---

[75] *Post-Courier*, 14 Apr. 2000. [76] [1990] PNGLR 6, 8, 11.
[77] M. Zelenietz, 'Sorcery and Social Change: An Introduction', *Social Analysis*, 8 (1981),
1, 12.
[78] PNG Law Reform Commission, *Wilful Murder*, 6; *Sorcery*, 11.
[79] P. Niukula, *The Three Pillars: The Triple Aspect of Fijian Society* (Suva, 1994),
15–18, 122–3; Tuwere, 'The Church–State Relation', 44, 47–8.

than an institution itself. Niukula's institutions are also described generally, and themselves encompass many different institutions that are simultaneously supportive and competitive. Thus, tensions between those supporting the Sunday ban in Fiji and those supporting religious freedom were found within the *lotu* (Taukei Methodists as against moderates and the Fiji Council of Churches) and the *matanitu*. However, the theory does provide a point of departure for a more accurate description of how institutions in a modern Melanesian state work, and how the role of law can be reconciled with the deep religiosity of these countries.

The integration of the civil law with religious world-views has been restrained by considerations as varied as parliaments uninterested in high Melanesian ideals, the professional habits of common lawyers, legal institutions themselves, and political action of religious groups. Therefore, despite supportive constitutional rhetoric, periodic efforts of some churches to establish a Christian state or protect existing religious oligopolies have been contained by the existence of guarantees of religious freedom. Interestingly, while the letter of those guarantees has barely been mentioned in the civil courts, the liberal values they carry have been promoted with explicit reference to the Bills of Rights by different churches, church councils, parliaments, the Vanuatu presidency, and, even, custom courts. This promises a long-term commitment to religious diversity from significant public institutions. Independent Melanesia has now entered a period of unprecedented political instability, and the recent past has shown that, especially in Fiji, this can lead to religious oppression. The security against this lies in the increasing extent to which churches and civil government have absorbed values of religious freedom.

The churches' place in state-creation in Melanesia is critical, and often more important than civil government in remote areas where government has little presence and provides no services. This can still be maintained when the churches understand their role as that of critical participants in pluralized states with a mix of secular, Christian, and custom-based institutions, but with paramount responsibility for the spiritual well-being of the people. The place of indigenous religion is different as it lacks the organizational structures that Christianity has to participate in public life, and the custodians of custom, like the councils of chiefs, are overwhelmingly Christian. Its practice is declining and, in losing the indigenous sense of transcendence that informed it before contact, custom will either become a shell of secularized traditions or, perhaps more likely, replace indigenous world-views with the Christian. The anxieties inherent in this development are already evident in the administration of the sorcery laws. However, there is little question that custom-based claims could be made easier without compromising Church or State, and indeed, as examples like the *Nagol Jump* case show, Melanesia's peculiar blend of liberal and indigenous institutions would probably be strengthened if this were to happen.

CHRISTIAN PERSPECTIVES ON THE LAW: WHAT MAKES THEM DISTINCTIVE?

Paul Beaumont

Introduction: A Clear World-View does not Lead to a Clear View of what Modern Law Should Be

At least among Christians who hold to an orthodox position there is a shared belief that people need to have the opportunity to come to know Jesus Christ as the person who can bring meaning and purpose to life: indeed who can enable men and women to enter into a right relationship with God the Father, be filled with the presence of God by his Holy Spirit and enjoy eternal life with God. Christians have a strong commitment to be guided by God on how to live their lives and see the Bible as the key guide to knowing what God intends for his followers. So Christians will agree on the need to argue for laws that give people freedom to choose to follow Jesus Christ and to live lives according to the teaching laid down in the Bible. This is true even though they disagree among themselves over the detail of how the biblical teaching should be applied today.

Even though there is a clear world-view about the need for personal salvation, it is hard to discern what is the distinctive core of Christian perspectives on the law, but at least three propositions are worth examining:

(1) Christianity does tolerate a wide range of views on what the law in a given modern society should be because Jesus did not prescribe a set of laws by which society should be governed but rather sought to bring about changed lives in his followers which would live up to higher standards than external laws can impose and be salt and light in the wider community (Matt. 5: 13–16).

(2) Christians should be free to live their lives in accordance with Christ's teaching and therefore it is legitimate to argue for such freedom in a democratic society.

(3) Christians are called by Christ to be salt and light in the wider community and therefore it is reasonable for Christians to advocate the benefits of the Christian life for society as a whole. Much of this will be done by seeking to persuade individuals to become Christians but there can also be a role for seeking to influence the law-making process. Here Christians will be cautious because they

are aware that the Bible does not provide a template for modern law and because they are passionate advocates of giving people freedom of conscience. Nonetheless, there may be norms which can be agreed with and adhered to by people who are not Christians which Christians may wish to advocate.

Diversity over how Christian Principles should be Applied in Modern Law

The first point to make is that there are several different perspectives on the law taken by Christians. This is reflected in the division of views about whether it is advantageous to have compliance with human rights as a key test of the validity of laws. Matthijs de Blois argues that there are three values which are at the core of human rights: dignity, equality, and freedom. He makes the case that these three values can be founded in Christian morality.[1] The dignity of all human beings, regardless of sex, race, disability, etc. is founded on the biblical idea that man is unique among God's creation on earth in being made in God's image.[2] This justifies human rather than animal rights. God's image is not destroyed by mankind's fall, merely marred. The possibility of all people to experience reconciliation with God through Jesus' saving work on the Cross is good reason to treat all people with dignity. De Blois posits that this emphasis on dignity as a foundation for human rights is a useful counterbalance to the modern emphasis on self-determination. The dignity of human life points towards protecting the unborn rather than the self-determination of the pregnant mother, of preventing euthanasia rather than allowing people to ask others to terminate their life.

The notion of the 'equality' of all human beings can be supported by biblical teaching.[3] However, de Blois is conscious that not all forms of discrimination are necessarily wrong. He cites the Netherlands General Act on Equal Treatment which came into force in 1994 as potentially going too far in not preserving the opportunity for religious groups to discriminate on grounds of sex or sexual orientation. In the context of the clash between the 'equality' right to non-discrimination and the 'freedom' right to live in accordance with particular religious beliefs de Blois comes down firmly on the side of the latter. He regards freedom of religion as 'the most

---

[1] 'The Foundation of Human Rights: A Christian Perspective', in Paul Beaumont (ed.), *Christian Perspectives on Human Rights and Legal Philosophy* (Carlisle, 1998), 14–27.

[2] Gen. 1: 26–7. For an extended treatment of the idea that a Christian foundation for human rights is found in the 'dignity' of mankind, see John Warwick Montgomery, *Human Rights and Human Dignity* (Dallas, 1986).

[3] But the passages cited by de Blois, 'The Foundation of Human Rights', 19, seem more convincing as regards the equality of all people who have accepted Christ (e.g. Gal. 3: 28) than they do about the equality of all human beings.

fundamental freedom'[4] given that it is the only freedom that takes account of mankind's eternal destiny. On the other hand, de Blois argues that the equality principle should have some bearing in the context of economic and social rights in that the State should give some minimum guarantee of social security for all people.

In conclusion de Blois is an advocate of human rights and a firm believer in the primacy of freedom of religion over equal treatment. He is concerned that some people are making 'human rights' their god, and warns Christians against doing so. One of the problems of adopting a rights-based formulation is its limited value when rights clash. Presumably de Blois's concerns for human dignity would mean that he would find it difficult to give priority to the religious freedom for a group to choose to assist each other to commit suicide together. Religious freedom may be the most fundamental right, but can it always take priority over other rights. Perhaps a less systematized approach to the development of law and public policy has its attractions. Some of these were considered by Julian Rivers in his argument against the United Kingdom adopting a bill of rights that would take primacy over primary legislation.[5]

Rivers makes five observations: '(*a*) Humanity has no rights against God . . . (*b*) All human relations are ultimately reflections of relationships with God: rights are therefore not primary . . . (*c*) Some aspects of morality cannot be cast in terms of rights . . . (*d*) Rights prejudice against communitarian benefits . . . (*e*) Legal rights are not necessarily the best means of enforcing morality'.[6] In Christian terms Rivers argues that rights are 'at root reflections of our duty to God, not the source of duties'. In other words, Christians cannot just view the world in terms of relationships between human beings but rather in terms of the duties God imposes on mankind to love each other. The duty to forgive someone who has wronged you if he or she asks for forgiveness cannot be recast as a right to forgiveness. An emphasis on duties rather than rights makes it easier to promote the common good, whereas an emphasis on individual rights means that promotion of the common good has to be justified as a derivation from those rights. The emphasis on rights rather than duties or responsibilities may reinforce the fallen nature of mankind and promote self-interested behaviour. The Christian acknowledges the fallen nature of mankind and the value of protecting individuals from unwarranted state interference, but the Christian is also anxious to help to create a more moral society.[7]

---

[4] Ibid., 22.
[5] See 'A Bill of Rights for the United Kingdom?', in Paul Beaumont (ed.), *Christian Perspectives on Law Reform* (Carlisle, 1998).
[6] Ibid., 42–4.   [7] Ibid., 36–41.

Here again we see the classic tension between (2) and (3) in the introduction. The promotion of (2) might lead to an emphasis on traditional civil liberties and the freedom seen in the First Amendment to the US Constitution.[8] However, as Rivers points out, there is a tendency for judges to expand the scope of constitutional rights beyond these minimal freedoms.[9] The desire of (3) above might be to promote what is good, and this might not be fully achievable by a rights-based mechanism but rather by a route which is duty-based. However, such desire to promote the good solution runs up against the Christian desire to preserve freedom for non-Christians to choose a bad solution. So the Christian vision of law reform is split between freedom to allow Christians and others to choose how to live their lives within constraints of not harming others and encouraging people to behave in a moral way at some expense to their freedom to choose to do otherwise. The rights debate to some extent is just a reflection of that split.

The law of blasphemy in England does seek to prevent people from sinning by making extremely offensive statements about the Christian God which are not couched in decent and temperate language.[10] In that sense it can be seen as a law which promotes morality. On the other hand, it is a law which denies freedom of conscience to non-Christians in not permitting them to speak intemperately about the fundamentals of the Christian faith. However unwise and indeed sinful it might be for non-Christians to act in this way, those Christians who emphasize the fundamental nature of religious liberty, like me, will tend to support the abolition of blasphemy laws.[11] On the other hand, there is a school of thought which would like to see the blasphemy laws extended to cover all major religions.[12] The loss of freedom of expression is justified by advocates of this approach on the basis that offence to Christians or Jews or Muslims is enough to warrant some restrictions on free speech or that the possible breakdown in public order caused by the reaction of members of the offended religious group is enough to do so. So the 'harm' justification for restricting free speech is either the hurt feelings of the hearers[13] or the physical harm which may ensue from the adverse reaction of the hearers.

[8] 'Congress shall make no law respecting an establishment of religion or prohibiting the free exercise thereof; or abridging the freedom of speech or the press or the right of the people peaceably to assemble, and to petition the Government for a redress of grievances.'

[9] Rivers, 'A Bill of Rights', 32–6.

[10] For a more detailed definition and analysis of blasphemy law in England and Wales, see Ian Leigh, 'Towards a Christian Approach to Religious Liberty', in Beaumont (ed.), *Christian Perspectives on Human Rights and Legal Philosophy*, 52–9.

[11] Abolition was favoured by Leigh , ibid. 59.

[12] See ibid. 53 n. 60 for some references.

[13] See e.g. Julian Rivers, *Blasphemy in the Secular State*, Cambridge Papers, vol. i. no. 4 (Cambridge, 1992), arguing for the introduction of a new offence of incitement to religious hatred applicable to all religions, whose purpose would be to protect believers' feelings. It would require threatening, abusive, or insulting words or behaviour used with intent to

The range of Christian perspectives on law is also seen in how far the fallenness of man or alternatively the fact that man is made in God's image is emphasized when discussing what contract law should be: a relational or good faith approach[14] leans towards the latter, whereas an emphasis on the terms of the contract[15] leans towards the former. Christians have differences of view on whether employment practices should reflect a long-term commitment in the form of some kind of tenure,[16] and whether divorce law should be modelled on the high standards set by Jesus for Christians.[17]

Freedom for Christians and Christian Groups to Act Differently

Christians want to have the freedom to live lives in accordance with the patterns laid down in the Bible. This involves not only allowing the individual to worship God but also allowing groups of people to meet in Christian communities not only to worship but to live out all aspects of their lives in accordance with Christ's teachings. Thus there is a strong urge to ask the State to allow religious schools[18] and to resist efforts seen in the proposed EC Directive establishing a general framework for equal treatment in employment and occupation to impose non-discrimination on the ground of religion and sexual orientation even on explicitly Christian schools, medical practices, hospices, etc.

The Commission proposal for a Council Directive establishing a general framework for equal treatment in employment and occupation[19] was made on 25 November 1999. It has Article 13 of the EC Treaty as its legal basis. The Commission proposal seeks to outlaw direct and indirect discrimination on grounds of 'racial or ethnic origin, religion or belief, disability, age or sexual orientation'.[20] The material scope of the Directive

outrage, or likelihood of outraging, the feelings of a significant number of a recognized religious group. Rivers would also retain the existing narrowly drawn blasphemy law in England—a point criticized by Leigh, 'Towards a Christian Approach', 56.

[14] See Stephen Copp, 'Developing a Relationally Based Law of Contract: A Question of Good Faith', in Paul Beaumont and Keith Wotherspoon (eds.), *Christian Perspectives on Law and Relationism* (Carlisle, 2001).

[15] Ewan McKendrick, 'The Contracting Society: A Misplaced Faith', in Paul Beaumont (ed.), *Christian Perspectives on the Limits of Law* (Carlisle, 2001).

[16] See Thomas Watkin, 'The Concept of Commitment in Law and Legal Science', in Beaumont (ed.), *Christian Perspectives on Human Rights and Legal Philosophy*.

[17] See Lord Mackay of Clashfern, 'Family Law Reform: A Personal View', in Beaumont and Wotherspoon' (eds.), *Christian Perspectives on Law and Relationism*, and Paul Beaumont, 'Christianity and Law Reform: A Living Tradition?', in *The Law and Christian Ethics* (Edinburgh, 2001).

[18] See de Blois, 'The Foundation of Human Rights', 27, and David Harte, 'The Legal Framework for Religion in Schools: Enforcement or Enablement?', in Beaumont (ed.), *Christian Perspectives on the Limits of Law*.

[19] COM (1999) 565 final. An earlier version of my treatment of the draft Directive is published in Beaumont, 'Christianity and Law Reform: A Living Tradition?'.

[20] Art. 1.

extends beyond employment to self-employment and membership of professional bodies.[21] The Commission proposes that member states should have the discretion to create two exceptions to the prohibition on discrimination. The first exception would permit discrimination based on one of the discriminatory characterisitics (religion etc.) if 'by reason of the nature of the particular occupational activities concerned or of the context in which they are carried out, such a characteristic constitutes a genuine occupational qualification'.[22] This provision, if utilized by the relevant member state, may make it possible for a firm of Christian lawyers to insist that being a Christian 'constitutes a genuine occupational qualification' because of the Christian 'context' in which the work is carried out. The firm would find it harder to argue that a requirement that the person is not a practising homosexual is a genuine occupational qualification unless it could convince the court to give a very broad construction to the 'context' in which the occupational activities are carried out. The argument would be that the firm was made up of only those who are not practising homosexuals and offered legal services on that basis. The second exception proposed by the Commission is that

Member States may provide that, in the case of public or private organisations which pursue directly and essentially the aim of ideological guidance in the field of religion or belief with respect to education, information and the expression of opinions, and for the particular occupational activities within those organisations which are directly and essentially related to that aim, a difference of treatment based on a relevant characteristic related to religion or belief shall not constitute discrimination where, by reason of the nature of these activities, the characteristic constitutes a genuine occupational qualification.[23]

This exception, if adopted by the relevant member state, would allow a church to employ only Christians as ministers and Christian schools to employ only Christians as teachers of religious education. However, the church or school might not be allowed to insist on their other staff being Christians unless they had some kind of role in disseminating information or expressing opinions about the 'ideological guidance' offered by the church or school. It is difficult to see what the second exception adds to the first exception, and therefore one fears that it might be construed as placing a limit on the scope of the first exception. This concern is reinforced by the response made by the commissioner responsible for the draft Directive to a question in the European Parliament. Her reply suggested that it would be appropriate for a Roman Catholic School to insist that a teacher is a Roman Catholic but not to insist that he or she is not a practising homosexual or lesbian.[24]

---

[21] Art. 3.   [22] Art. 4(1).   [23] Art. 4(2).
[24] See Commissioner Diamantopoulou's reply to a question by Michael Cashman MEP in 20000118EN.doc, Verbatim Report of Proceedings, 81.

The proposal has caused anxiety among some Christians, and the Christian Institute launched a campaign in June 2000 to try to persuade the British government not to vote for the present text of the Directive in the Council.[25] Some of my own concerns about the proposal relate to three issues: subsidiarity, human rights, and external competence.

Paragraph 4 of the Protocol on Subsidiarity and Proportionality requires that 'the reasons for concluding that a Community objective can be better achieved by the Community must be substantiated by qualitative or, wherever possible, quantitative indicators'. Recital 22 of the draft Directive gives no quantitative indicators and asserts subsidiarity compliance rather than giving qualitative indicators of such compliance. Admittedly the explanatory memorandum goes a little further in paragraph 3.1, but even here the quantitative data relate only to gender discrimination. No clear justification is given for two of the most controversial parts of the Directive: discrimination on grounds of sexual orientation and on grounds of religious belief. If the Directive comes into force, it will apply in the vast majority of cases to disputes which involve parties who live in the same member state with no 'transnational aspect'.[26] Very few people moving across frontiers to work are being denied jobs on the grounds of their sexual orientation or religious belief. There is a very strong case for saying that these decisions should be taken as 'closely as possible to the citizen' (Article 1 of the Treaty on European Union). Decisions about the balance between the rights of particular groups in society to preserve their rights to group identity (e.g. Christians, Jews, Muslims, political parties) and thereby to discriminate against people who want to work for the group but will not accept some or all of the group's core values should be taken much closer to the citizen than in Brussels. This is a matter to be decided in Edinburgh or London, where the decision-makers can take account of the delicate balancing needed between conflicting rights (e.g. the right to freedom of religion and belief, Article 9 of the European Convention on Human Rights (ECHR); the right to freedom of association, Article 11 ECHR; and the right to non-discrimination, Article 14 ECHR).[27] If it is wise at all for the European Union to legislate in this area, it should remember its own commitment to minimum harmonization and only deal with those cases which have a cross-border dimension, i.e. involving citizens of more than one member state of the European Union. Even in such cases it must be more aware of the importance of allowing religious groups to positively discriminate in favour of members of that group.

---

[25] The Christian Institute, *European Threat to Religious Freedom* (Newcastle, 2000).
[26] See para. 5 of the Protocol on Subsidiarity and Proportionality.
[27] Cf. s. 13 of the Human Rights Act 1998 which emphasizes the 'importance of the right' in Article 9 of the ECHR in balancing any clashes of rights.

It would seem that the draft Directive does not leave enough scope for the balancing of conflicting rights and starts from the premiss that non-discrimination is the priority because this is the particular right which has been given concrete expression in the EC Treaty. This could be categorized as 'liberal fundamentalism', which makes it difficult or impossible for a Christian medical practice only to hire Christian doctors, for a Jewish hospice only to hire Jews, for a Muslim society only to appoint heterosexuals to office, etc. Such fundamental value judgements should not be made for the whole of the European Union in Brussels given its remoteness from the full democratic processes and the limited capacity of citizens to effectively influence the outcomes.[28] Indeed, the chairman of the House of Commons Foreign Affairs Select Committee, Donald Anderson MP, in a debate in the House of Commons on 15 June 2000 expressed his concerns about the draft Directive in the context of paying insufficient attention to the principle of subsidiarity:

Although Opposition Members have talked about debate, it is sadly difficult to have a rational debate on Europe when everything they say is wholly negative. That negativity will no doubt increase as we approach the general election. I still believe in subsidiarity, but it does not end in London. Therefore, I support its extension to the Scottish Parliament and the Welsh Assembly, and—if there is demand for it—to the English regions as well. It is subsidiarity to move decisions as close to the people as possible. There should be no block in London, and that is where the argument for subsidiarity from the Opposition stops in its tracks.

However, old habits die hard in the Commission, and attempts are still being made to meddle in areas that it should leave alone. I had brought to my attention yesterday the proposal for a Council directive that would establish a general framework for equal treatment in employment and education. That sounds good, but the effect could be very serious for religious organisations. Professor Ian Leigh of Durham, who specialises in the issue, has said:

This directive has all the potential to seriously undermine freedom of association for religious people. It places the modern concept of "equality" over and above religious liberty. By requiring religious organisations to radically alter their recruitment practices, it will make it difficult, or impossible, for them to maintain a distinctive religious ethos.

Professor Paul Beaumont, the co-author of 'EU Law', has said:

This is a kind of liberal fundamentalism which makes it difficult or impossible for a Christian medical practice to only hire Christian doctors, for a Jewish hospice to only hire Jews, for a Muslim society to only appoint male heterosexuals to office.

---

[28] For a thorough critique of the sort of liberal fundamentalism which elevates non-discrimination above religious liberty, see Leigh, 'Towards a Christian Approach', 31–52. For a more tolerant vision of liberalism which is rooted in Christian principles, see Julian Rivers, 'Liberal Constitutionalism and Christian Political Thought', in Beaumont (ed.), *Christian Perspectives on the Limits of Law*.

I cannot believe that it is right that Brussels seeks to override religious liberties in member countries. That is wrong and meddlesome, but unfortunately the proposal has had little publicity in this country . . . The directive will come before the Council of Ministers in September, but so far there has been no debate. The issue is an example of the criticisms that I am open enough to make of Brussels, where necessary. I hope that my right hon. Friend the Foreign Secretary will consider the implications of the directive, and various legal opinions that I shall put to him, and seek to counter the liberal fundamentalism that threatens to override deeply held rights in this country.[29]

Elevating the right to non-discrimination above other human rights may be unlawful under Community law. The European Court of Justice can strike down Community legislation on the grounds that it is contrary to fundamental rights. The Court has recognized freedom of religion as a fundamental right.[30] In order to make the rights to freedom of religion, association, and expression meaningful it should be possible for groups of people in society to explicitly set themselves up as offering a service based on a particular set of beliefs and to ensure that the people who work for those groups adhere to the common values which are at the heart of the group. Therefore a Christian medical practice should be able to employ only people that adhere to Christian teachings—including the teaching that homosexual practice is sinful and should be able to exclude non-Christian doctors or Christian doctors that are practising homosexuals. Yet such a Christian medical practice may not be protected by either of the possible exceptions in Article 4 of the Directive and the exceptions may not be utilized by all the member states. The rights of these Christians to associate as Christians and provide a specialist medical service based on a clear Christian ethos could be removed in Brussels unless the European Court of Justice is careful to give a very broad construction to the exceptions in Article 4 in order to protect rights to association and freedom of religion. If the member states do not take advantage of these exceptions then the Court of Justice may need to be persuaded to build in some minimal protection for these rights in its interpretation of the Directive or to go further and declare the Directive invalid for not guaranteeing such minimum protection.[31]

In policy terms one has to question the wisdom of giving the Commission a mixed competence with member states in external relations in this delicate field of the balance between the right to non-discrimination and the right to allow groups of people to have a distinctive identity which

---

[29] See <http://www .publications. parliament. uk/pa/ cm199900/cmhansrd/vo000615/deb text/ 00615–24.htm 00615–24–spnew2>.

[30] See Case 130/75 *Prais* v. *Council* [1976] ECR 1589.

[31] See Stephen Weatherill and Paul Beaumont, *EU Law*, 3rd edn., (London, 1999), 284–90, for a brief discussion of the European Court of Justice's doctrine of fundamental human rights which can be used by that Court to strike down Community legislation which does not conform with those rights.

means their focus is based on their religious beliefs and these beliefs conflict with the liberal consensus about non-discrimination on grounds of religion or sexual orientation. The creation of external competence is a by-product of adopting the Directive and should be kept to a minimum by passing only the non-controversial aspects of the Directive. The Commission is not an elected body and has a recent track record of taking on too many things and not accepting responsibility for dealing with them.[32]

The final version of the Directive was adopted on 27 November 2000 (2000/78/EC, OJ 2000 L303/16). Recital 37 deals with subsidiarity and shows no improvement on the Commission's draft. It asserts that the objective of the Directive, 'namely the creation within the Community of a level playing-field as regards equality in employment and occupation, cannot be sufficiently achieved by the Member States'. However, it brings no quantitative data to bear on this proposition. Furthermore, Article 13 of the EC Treaty, the legal basis for the Directive, is not about creating level playing-fields but rather about taking 'appropriate action to combat discrimination' 'within the limits of the powers conferred by' the EC Treaty. One would expect a more systematic analysis of the powers conferred by the EC Treaty and why, within that sphere, the particular anit-discrimination measures are appropriate. No justification is given for dealing with discrimination in cases that are purely internal to a member state.

Article 4 of the Directive was changed quite markedly and this must be least partly attributable to the campaign by Christian groups including extensive correspondence with UK ministers and Members of Parliament. UK ministers agreed to fight for at least the right of religious schools to hire staff of the same religious ethos. Article 4(1), the general operational requirement exception (see note 22 above), was amended by changing 'genuine occupational qualification' to 'genuine and determining occupational requirement'. Article 4(2), the special religious occupational requirement exception, was amended to make it slightly broader than Article 4(1) in that 'a person's religion or belief' only needs to 'constitute a genuine, legitimate and justified occupational requirement'. Thus a Christian school might find it difficult to argue that it is a 'determining' requirement that a maths teacher be a Christian but might find it easier to argue that it is a 'legitimate and justified' requirement in order to maintain and promote the ethos of the school. The sting in the tail is that the difference of treatment based on a person's religion or belief 'should not justify discrimination on another ground'. This would seem to prevent a Christian organization from making it clear that it would not employ practising homosexuals or

---

[32] See the Committee of Independent Experts Report of 15 Mar. 1999, noted in Weatherill and Beaumont, *EU Law*, 1059–64.

lesbians. However, the Christian organization could legitimately argue that the reason why such a person is not being employed is because of their 'belief' that it is not sinful to engage in homosexual or lesbian acts rather than because of their sexual orientation. Some support for Christian organizations that believe in the sinfulness of homosexual practice being able to discriminate against a practising homosexual who does not share that belief, even though the person claims to be a Christian, may be found in the new closing paragraph of Article 4(2):

Provided that its provisions are otherwise complied with, this Directive shall thus not prejudice the right of churches and other public or private organisations, the ethos of which is based on religion or belief, acting in conformity with national constitutions and laws, to require individuals working for them to act in good faith and with loyalty to the organisation's ethos.

There is still much to be decided in the national laws implementing the Directive before 2 December 2003.

Gary Watt[33] and Alison Dunn[34] in two separate articles have identified the problem of the duties on trustees to prioritize financial considerations over ethical considerations when investing trust funds unless the beneficiaries would all agree to the potentially lower financial return of the ethical investment.[35] Watt argues from a relational perspective against this automatic prioritization of wealth maximization. He hints that it should be enough if the trustees would have the backing of a majority of the beneficiaries for a decision to make an ethical investment. Watt would like to see the relationship between the trustees and the beneficiaries strengthened by requiring beneficiary representation among the trustees and consultation by the trustees of the beneficiaries. He is not concerned only or even primarily with trusts that have a Christian purpose. However, drawing on the earlier work of Nobles,[36] Watt points out the ridiculous nature of the current law in England which permits a Christian charitable trust to give away its money to promote Christian values but not to make an investment, which might yield a lower return than another investment, that is designed to promote the same Christian values.

Dunn analyses the law on ethical investments by trustees in great detail and helpfully adds some empirical research on the investment policies of the trustees for the main Christian denominations in the United Kingdom.[37] Her conclusion is that the courts should develop the law by

[33] 'Relationism and the Law of Fiduciaries and Trusts', in Beaumont and Wotherspoon (eds.), *Christian Perspectives on Law and Relationism*.

[34] 'Between a Rock and a Hard Place: Law's Dilemma over Trustees' Ethical Investment', in Beaumont (ed.), *Christian Perspectives on the Limits of Law*.

[35] See *Cowan v. Scargill* [1985] 1 Ch. 270; *Harries v. The Church Commissioners for England* [1992] 1 WLR 1241.

[36] 'Charities and Ethical Investment' (1992) 56 *Conv.* 115.

[37] This reveals how ethical investment policies can be pursued within the constraints of

moving away from the notion of financial considerations as the 'sole' crite-ria for investment decisions by trustees because the current law tends to 'polarise ethical investment into stark questions which divide profit from principle'. She goes on to argue that

The Christian duty of love requires trustees not to polarise issues, but to pay atten-tion to the concerns of their beneficiaries as well as question the source of the bene-ficiaries' income, at the same time as pursuing a solid investment return. In terms of resolving the law's dilemma, the trustees' duty of care as it revolves around the notion of prudence could usefully be drawn more widely to take into account not just financial criteria but also other factors which inform a balanced investment strategy.

Christians also wish to have conscience clauses in legislation to prevent them from having to do things which they regard as inconsistent with biblical teaching,[38] for example, so that they are not required to perform abortions or to subject their children to religious education which they might find unsuitable. They want to have freedom to bring their children up in accordance with Christian teaching.[39]

Promotion of Christian Ideas to be Considered by Society with Respect for the Consciences of All

Historically Christians have been in the vanguard of some law reform measures, e.g. the abolition of slavery, and the improvement of working conditions and of prison life.[40] In doing so Christians have combined with non-Christians to advocate changes to the law to correct injustice. In modern times Christians are arguing along with non-Christians for appro-priate protection of the environment which reflects the fact that mankind owes a duty of stewardship to the rest of creation,[41] for freedom for

---

the existing law, and Dunn concludes by drawing out four key features of the policies adopted by the Christian churches: 'the need for strict monitoring of investment policies and of company practices; the importance of balancing interests of all parties, not least in order to secure fairness; the need to foster an environment of mutual respect with the companies invested in so as to open and maintain constructive channels of communication; and finally, the recognition that whatever policy is pursued, ethical or not, it will be open to criticism'.

[38] See Article 7.681, para. 2(e) of the Dutch Civil Code referred to by de Blois, 'The Foundation of Human Rights', 27.

[39] See de Blois, 'The Foundation of Human Rights', 27, and in much greater depth, Rex Ahdar, 'Parental Religious Upbringing in a Children's Rights Era', in Beaumont and Wotherspoon (eds.), *Christian Perspectives on Law and Relationism.*

[40] See Teresa Sutton, 'Christians as Law Reformers in the Nineteenth and Twentieth Centuries', in Beaumont (ed.), *Christian Perspectives on Law Reform.* She highlights the lives of William Wilberforce, Anthony Ashley-Cooper (seventh Earl of Shaftesbury), and Elizabeth Fry.

[41] See David Harte, 'A Christian Approach to Environmental Law', in Beaumont (ed.), *Christian Perspectives on Law Reform*; and Thomas Watkin, 'Can the Law Ensure Proper Stewardship of Land?', in Beaumont (ed.), *Christian Perspectives on the Limits of Law.*

trustees to engage in ethical investment,[42] and that the goal of corporations should move away from maximization of profit to profit optimization within a framework of social responsibility.[43] Christians of all denominations are concerned with such issues of social and economic justice. In charting this welcome fact, Teresa Sutton correctly points out that it is not a new phenomenon.[44]

What is new is that Christian academic lawyers are attempting to place questions of what the law ought to be more explicitly within a Christian framework of reference. Sometimes this leads to advocacy of law reform, as in some of the examples just discussed. On other occasions it means that a vigorous defence of the present law is mounted. Hilaire McCoubrey shows that the international law outlawing aggression and requiring humanitarian treatment of prisoners of war and of civilians is consistent with Jesus' teaching on the need to love our enemies.[45]

John Warwick Montgomery argues that a continued prohibition on assisted suicide (euthanasia) is the best way to uphold the sanctity of life which reflects the Christian view that God, not men or women, gives life and takes it away.[46] The issue of euthanasia highlights a very real tension for Christians in their advocacy of what the law should be. Christians would like to see all people according a high value to human life consistent with the fact that all men and women are made in the image of God. This leads Christians to wish to have laws that will not put any pressure on individuals to feel that at a certain stage in their life they are no longer of value to society or their families and friends and that they should do the decent thing and ask to be put to death. The best way to avoid such pressure is probably to have a law banning assisted suicide. On the other hand, Christians want people who are made in God's image to have the freedom to reject God. If two people who have rejected God agree together to take actions to enable one of them to die, should not their freedom of conscience be respected? In other words, should Christians not allow non-Christians to play God at least where there is no doubt that this choice is based on consent, made freely, and without spoken or unspoken pressure to cease to be a burden on others?

Different Christians will give different answers to this question. Some will say that one of the limits that Christians can reasonably impose on

---

[42] See the chapters by Dunn, 'Between a Rock and a Hard Place', and Watt, 'Relationism and the Law of Fiduciaries and Trusts'.

[43] See Stephen Copp, 'A Christian Vision for Corporate Governance', in Beaumont (ed.), *Christian Perspectives on Law Reform*, esp. 144–7.

[44] 'Christians as Law Reformers', 9–13.

[45] See Matt. 5: 44 and Hilaire McCoubrey, 'A Christian Approach to International Laws of Armed Conflict', in Beaumont (ed.), *Christian Perspectives on Human Rights and Legal Philosophy*.

[46] 'Whose Life Anyway? A Re-Examination of Suicide and Assisted Suicide', in Beaumont (ed.), *Christian Perspectives on Law Reform*.

freedom of conscience is the limit of taking the life of another human being even when that human being has freely consented to having his or her life taken by that individual. The removal of life removes the freedom of conscience and prevents the individual from ever exercising that conscience to decide to become a Christian. The person assisting the suicide may later regret his or her actions and carry the emotional scars for a long time. The family and friends of the person who has died may be devastated. So while human autonomy in the form of freedom of conscience is a very high value, it is legitimate for Christians to place limits on it in the context of assisted suicide because the act ends irrevocably the freedom of conscience of the person who dies and because it may bring lasting harm to the other participant in the act and/or the dead person's family and friends. It is 'relational' considerations of this kind which have prompted some Christians to try to come up with a new litmus test for public policy which is not driven by economic growth and increased personal wealth, nor by an entirely individualistic model.

Michael Schluter, a Christian economist, is the prime mover in what he has christened 'Relationism'.[47] This is a complex notion, but lying at the root of it is the idea that society should make policies and laws which help to promote close relationships between people through the notion of 'relational proximity'.[48] This value-neutral language is designed to be attractive to policy-makers in a pluralist society. However, Schluter and Lee acknowledge the limitations of value-neutrality in accepting that one of the presuppositions lying beneath Relationism is that it wishes to promote not just 'close relationships', but 'good relationships' with the latter having an inevitable 'moral' context.[49] Thin, value-neutral relationism is an interesting idea for humanizing public policy. However, when it comes to tough policy choices of a morally sensitive nature only a thicker value-laden form of relationism can give answers. An attempt to form such a thicker relationism, firmly rooted in Christian principles, is necessary. A start has already been made.[50]

One of the distinctive features of the Christian view of God is the notion of the Trinity. The Godhead reflects the concept of perfect relationships. So close are the three persons of the Trinity, the Father, Son, and Holy Spirit, that they are in fact one life as well as being three persons.

---

[47] He is the director of the Relationships Foundation. Some of the key books on the subject are: Michael Schluter and David Lee, *The R Factor* (London, 1993); J. Burnside and N. Baker (eds.), *Relational Justice Repairing the Breach* (Winchester, 1994); and N. Baker (ed.), *Building a Relational Society* (Aldershot, 1996).

[48] Schluter and Lee, *The R Factor*, 276, define 'relational proximity' as 'A closeness of relationship between two individuals, through which each is able to recognise the other more fully as a complete and unique human being'.

[49] Ibid., 267.

[50] See Beaumont and Wotherspoon (eds.), *Christian Perspectives on Law and Relationism*.

The closeness is rooted in selfless love and perfect justice demonstrated in the means by which people are able to enter into a right relationship with God through Jesus' self-sacrificing death on the Cross paying the price for the sin of men and women.[51] So self-sacrificing high-quality relationships are the ideal which Christians should aim for. However, this is a long way from a prescription for public policy and law. Some big ideas can be sold using relational thinking. One is a major shift away from imprisonment towards community-based solutions based on the idea that the offender should put things right in relation to the victim and in turn will be enabled to remain free to maintain or create good relationships with his or her own family and friends. Putting things right will involve a mixture of repentance, paying compensation, and serving the individual and/or the wider community. Imprisonment is a necessary last resort but should be used sparingly because it is destructive of the offender's relationships.[52] Sometimes relational thinking may only offer a small piece of a complex jigsaw. One example of this is the measurement of 'seriousness' of criminal offences.[53]

Where a 'Christian' standard is adopted as the law, care must be taken to respect the consciences of non-Christians and of Christians who take a different view from the one set down in the law.[54] At the moment in England and Wales religious education is a core part of the curriculum and some public worship must take place in schools. David Harte is a vigorous defender of both legal requirements, but also defends the right of parents to withdraw children from either or both activity.[55]

An interesting issue is whether children, at least from a certain age, should have the right to absent themselves from religious education or school worship. This concerns the extent to which children should have a right to choose their religious beliefs independent of the preference of their parents. The Christian is faced with the tension between the command to children to obey their parents[56] and the clear welcoming of little children

---

[51] Michael Schluter, 'Three Relational Dimensions of Justice: Defining the Moral Order, Upholding the Moral Order and Putting Things Right', in Beaumont and Wotherspoon (eds.), *Christian Perspectives on Law and Relationism*.

[52] 'Introduction', by the editors and Schluter, 'Three Relational Dimensions', in Beaumont and Wotherspoon (eds.), *Christian Perspectives on Law and Relationism*.

[53] Jonathan Burnside, 'Justice, Seriousness and Relationships', in Beaumont and Wotherspoon (eds.), *Christian Perspectives on Law and Relationism*.

[54] For the importance of respecting the freedom of conscience of the non-Christian, see Julian Rivers, 'Liberal Constitutionalism and Christian Political Thought', in Beaumont (ed.), *Christian Perspectives on the Limits of the Law*, and Beaumont, 'Christianity and Law Reform: A Living Tradition?', in his *The Law and Christian Ethics*.

[55] 'The Legal Framework for Religion in Schools: Enforcement or Enablement?', in Beaumont (ed.), *Christian Perspectives on the Limits of Law*. I would prefer to make religious education optional after primary school and for there to be no public worship in normal state schools. Of course, religious schools should be free to have worship.

[56] See Eph. 6: 1.

by Jesus as capable of putting their faith in God and having a relationship with God.[57] My own instinct, as someone who became a Christian when I was 6 years old, is towards recognizing that a child can make free choices about which religion to follow. However, it may not be appropriate to give a child a legal right to make choices about religious education or attendance at worship in school until they are of the appropriate age and maturity. This will vary from child, to child but in a normal case may be when the child is at least 12. Rex Ahdar is more concerned with the 'collective' good of the family.[58] He does not want the State to interfere in an intact family by allowing the child to insist on a legal right to depart from the religious beliefs of his or her parents. This is a relational approach which values the parent–child relationship more than child autonomy. Of course, Rex Ahdar would admit that a prudent parent would want to preserve their relationship with their child by respecting the child's religious choices as they get nearer to the age of majority. He just wants the law to stay out of what should, in his view, be a family matter. As Matthijs de Blois states: 'the realm of the law should be restricted in order to leave room for human beings to live in accordance with their own moral opinions'.[59] De Blois argues that the 'freedom' principle owes much to the Reformation, in particular its peaceful Anabaptist wing, which advocated the separation of Church and State, and the later writings of Roger Williams.[60] The problem in this context is whether one should emphasize the religious freedom of a child, or of a teenager, or only of an adult.

Conclusion

What are some of the distinctive features of Christian perspectives on the law?

1. Christianity does not offer a corpus of law which should be applied as the law in a State. Rather it offers people a relationship with God which empowers them to seek to live in accordance with God's very high moral standards.

2. Christians will want to live their lives in accordance with the very high moral standards exemplified in the Sermon on the Mount and more generally in the New Testament. This will mean that Christians will argue

---

[57] See Matt. 19: 13–15.

[58] 'Parental Religious Upbringing in a Children's Rights Era', in Beaumont and Wotherspoon (eds.), *Christian Perspectives on Law and Relationism.*

[59] 'The Foundation of Human Rights', in Beaumont (ed.), *Christian Perspectives on Human Rights and Legal Philosophy*, 12.

[60] Ibid., 23–4. The writings of Roger Williams are analysed at greater length by Julian Rivers, 'Liberal Constitutionalism and Christian Political Thought', in Beaumont (ed.), *Christian Perspectives on the Limits of Law.*

for the liberty as individuals and as groups of Christians in churches or other Christian organizations to be able to live their lives in accordance with biblical standards. This can lead to clashes with the State if it seeks to impose values which are not consistent with what many Christians would regard as the highest biblical standards, e.g. requiring a Christian organization to employ a person who is a practising homosexual.[61] Christians will often argue for the right to offer distinctive services to people based on their Christian ethos, e.g. education, health, legal services, and social work. Christians would not wish to be monopoly providers in any of these areas.

3. Christians will take their duty to act as salt and light in the world seriously. This will mean that some Christians will spend some of their time advocating ideas about the sort of laws that will make the state a better place to live in. Christians will have different views on what the law should be. However, they will be influenced in arriving at their viewpoint by biblical principles. One strand of such thinking is to emphasize solutions which build up good relationships, another strand emphasizes the need to look after God's creation, and another emphasizes giving directors and trustees freedom to act ethically rather than always making financial considerations paramount.

4. Christians will wish to respect the freedom of conscience of non-Christians to live their lives rejecting Christianity. This means that the promotion of the 'good' law must be carefully balanced with the need to give appropriate freedoms to non-Christians. As we have seen above, this is not an easy balance to strike in the area of assisted suicide, nor is it easy to do if the Christian lawyer seeks to make the divorce law consistent with the New Testament's high standards for Christians (divorce on grounds of adultery and desertion only).[62] So the more the law of the land is in conformity with biblical principles, the greater the intrusion into the freedom of conscience of the non-Christian. Conversely, the greater the law of the land departs from biblical principles, the greater the difficulty for Christians to live their lives in accordance with biblical principles. This last point can be illustrated by the fact that no-fault divorce leaves a Christian vulnerable to being divorced when under biblical standards of adultery and desertion a divorce would not be possible. The difficulty for the Christian law reformer is to find the middle way that leaves as much room as possible for Christians to live distinctive Christian lives in accordance with the law and allows non-Christians to live lives following many different value systems in accordance with the law. Of course, no law reformer can achieve perfection in this middle way, so some loss of freedom of

---

[61] Some Christians would focus on Rom. 1: 18–32 in this context.

[62] See Lord Mackay of Clashfern, 'Family Law Reform'; and Beaumont, 'Christianity and Law Reform: A Living Tradition?'.

conscience or ability to live in accordance with Christian teaching may be inevitable. The alternative may be the very un-Christian solution of requiring non-Christians to take all the restrictions on their freedom of conscience and their capacity to live their lives in accordance with their strongly held views.

RADICAL CHANGE IN THE LEGAL REGULATION OF RELIGIOUS AFFAIRS IN POST-COMMUNIST POLAND

Piotr Mazurkiewicz

The Round-Table Agreements between the communist authorities and the Solidarity-led opposition signed in Warsaw on 5 April 1989 triggered a process of political transformation, not only in Poland, but throughout central and eastern Europe as well. Political scientists immediately set about developing theories seeking to explain radical systemic change. The difficulty they encountered stemmed from the uniqueness of the process of transition from communism to democracy, from a centrally planned economy to a free market. Never before had mankind had the opportunity to watch the collapse of a communist regime. The development of a theoretical model became problematic also because in general one constructs 'stationary' models in reference to stable political systems. In this instance, however, the object of theoretical interest was the transition from one system to another. That involved grasping the logic of the deterioration of the old system's functioning and the emergence of a new one to take its place. The subject of research was therefore the period of what might be called 'intersystemic suspension'.[1] In effect, the constructed theories could only be medium-range ones, i.e. applicable solely to a certain finite period of time and a clearly defined space. Today, after ten years of natural social experimentation, we already have at our disposal a plethora of theoretical works devoted to the actual mechanics of the economic and political changes being discussed. However, proper models of changes in religious affairs law, describing the external framework within which religious communities function in the new reality, have yet to be constructed. It therefore remains an open question whether those changes came about coincidentally or whether there too one can speak of certain regularities permitting the formulation of at least a fragmentary theory.

The undertaking of such an attempt necessitates having at one's disposal experiences that permit a comparison of the events being described with similar processes taking place under analogous conditions

---

[1] E. Wnuk-Lipiński, *Demokratyczna rekonstrukcja: z socjologii radykalnej zmiany społecznej* ('Democratic Reconstruction: The Sociology of A Radical Social Change') (Warsaw, 1996), 18.

elsewhere. One could go back to the changes that occurred in the Roman empire during the transition from paganism to Christianity. Other possibilities include the French and Russian Revolutions, where attempts to implement an opposite process were launched. One could investigate native Polish events from the period of Poland's acceptance of Christianity. The point is that no historical examples provide instances of the transition from the functioning of religion and the Church within a totalitarian system to its functioning under democratic conditions. At first glance, the situation of other central and east European countries abandoning communism might appear to provide such examples, but none of them could claim a religious organization whose size and influence compared with that of Poland's Roman Catholic Church. The fact is that process of change cannot be understood outside its historical, cultural, and systemic context.

The Church in Poland had played an exceptional role under communism, different from that of the remaining eastern bloc countries, and has continued to maintain an exceptional position. The moment those changes began, it already bore a greater similarity to the churches of western Europe than those in the eastern part of the continent. Seeking analogies between the changes in Poland, the Czech Republic, and Romania may therefore turn out to be not too productive a pursuit. Since authorized comparisons can only be fragmentary in nature, it seems, then, that also in this area we lack the possibility of creating any long-range theory.[2]

Therefore, nothing stands in the way of accepting as our point of reference, for instance, the transition from paganism to Christianity that took place in the Roman empire in the fourth century AD. That is a justified choice inasmuch as it marked the first radical change of religious law in favour of Christianity. Nevertheless, it should be remembered that other smaller Christian states were already in existence at that time. After nearly three centuries of persecution Christianity eventually achieved a reversal of roles. From 15 June 313, following Licinius' decree, the Church of the East enjoyed full and complete freedom of religion and regained all its confiscated assets.[3] Additionally, Constantine granted the Catholic clergy privileges such as monetary subsidies and tax breaks. In 315 the first Christian symbols appeared on coins, and in 323 the last pagan emblems vanished. The Catholic Church achieved legal status. The State recognized the verdicts of episcopal courts in purely secular matters as binding. The Church was granted the right to accept bequests. Outstanding Christian personalities began holding the highest offices: the consulate in 323, the

---

[2] Comprehensive comparative studies have been conducted for several years now by a group led by Prof. Paul Zulehner. The project is entitled Aufbruch ('Breakthrough').

[3] Many decisions were made to secure tolerance, i.e. decrees issued by Galerius (311), Constantine, Licinius, and finally Maximus Daia. In the West tolerance was proclaimed by a decree of Maxentius (306) under which the Christian cult was permitted.

prefecture of Rome in 325, and the prefecture of the Praetorium in 329. Almost at once decrees restricting pagan practices were issued. In 318 private sacrificial offerings, magic, and fortune-telling in private homes were banned. In the years 341–56 Constantine's sons on five separate occasions issued legal acts banning pagan cults under pain of death and ordered pagan temples closed. State policy changed for several months under the rule of Emperor Julian the Apostate (361–3), who attempt to revive a brand of paganism, modified through the incorporation of Neoplatonic elements. His successor, Valentinius, briefly restored equality of conscience for all. But in 381 Theodosius the Great again banned sacrificial offerings during the day or at night as well as visits to pagan temples, although the penalty (deportation) was less severe. In 392, however, he issued a law amounting to the death penalty for paganism. Anyone engaging in any form of pagan religious practice faced a fine of 25 pounds of gold. In 435 Theodosius II ordered the destruction of pagan temples.

In attempting to put the above-mentioned events into some ordered scheme of things, one might distinguish the following stages:

- period of persecution of Christians;
- period of toleration of Christians and restitution of plundered assets;
- period of privileges for Christians and the removal of pagan symbols from public life; Christians achieve the highest offices in the land;
- ban on pagan practices under pain of death;
- pagan reaction;
- renewed ban on pagan practices amid less severe punishment and orders to destroy pagan temples.

The fact that such a radical initial ban proved insufficient, and successive rulers, without even referring back to it, kept issuing new legal acts, appears to indicate that such measures attested to the ruler's intentions rather than describing the existing state of affairs. At that very same time pagans continued to predominate in the army, and the emperors themselves continued to appoint pagan Roman senators to the post of consul. We are therefore dealing with a kind of transition period in the empire, in which the emperor's policy towards pagans was becoming increasingly intolerant as Christianity consolidated its position. That is not surprising if one remembers that late antiquity was not known for its tolerance on either side: Christian or pagan. Much was said and written about tolerance, but always from the position of the weaker side that was demanding its due rights. The arguments were almost exclusively instrumental rather than being based on merit.[4] When Roman aristocrats presented through

---

[4] M. Simon, *Cywilizacja wczesnego chrześcijaństwa* ('Early Christian Civilization') (Warsaw, 1981), 228–32; J. Daniélou, *Od początków do końca trzeciego wieku* ('From the Beginning to the End of the Third Century'), in J. Daniélou and H. I. Marrou, *Historia Kościoła: od początków do roku 600* ('History of the Church: From the Beginnings to the

Senator Symmachus a petition to Emperor Valentinian II demanding the restoration of the image of the goddess Victoria, dear to all Romans, they did not mention that everyone, Christians included, would then be forced to make offerings to her.[5] At that time clashes occurred not only between Christianity and paganism, but also within the womb of the Church itself. An example was the conflict with the Donatists as well as the story of Athanasius of Alexandria, whose episcopal service included a total of seventeen and a half years in exile, or five successive instances of banishment during the reigns of four emperors. One may even get the impression that conflicts among Christians sapped more of their energy than did clashes with the slowly withdrawing pagans.[6] During the transition period from paganism to Christianity in the Roman empire a sudden rift with the pagan form of statehood, pagan-style exercise of power, and perceived relations between politics and religion did not occur. Instead, these forms persisted at least partially; consequently religious intolerance also continued.[7]

Let us now move to the twentieth century. During the period of the State's political transformation there occurred in Poland an abrupt shift from a legal system in the service of an atheistically programmed state to one marked by world-view neutrality. A desire on the part of the government to establish dialogue with the Church occurred as a result of the social changes launched in 1980, when Solidarity, the Soviet bloc's first independent trade union was set up. They led to the reactivation of the Government–Episcopate Joint Commission. During the martial-law period a draft law on the State's relationship towards the Catholic Church was formulated, as was a document on religious ministry in the armed forces. In 1984, when the government side felt a bit more confident, an impasse in the work of the Commission occurred. The initialled draft law was not submitted to normal legislative proceedings. It was not until 1987, when the authorities again felt threatened by public unrest, that the talks resumed with renewed haste. In January communist strongman General Jaruzelski paid a visit to the Vatican, during which he raised the issue of diplomatic relations. In October, after the visit of John Paul II to his native land, the Joint Commission accepted the concept of concluding a convention with

---

Year 600') (Warsaw, 1984), 188–9; E. Wipszycka, *Kościół w świecie późnego antyku* ('The Church in the World of Late Ancient Times') (Warsaw, 1994), 85–9.

[5] Ambrose, *Epistola* 17.3, in J. P. Migne, *Patrologiae Cursus Completus*, Series Latina (Paris, 1844–55), 16, 962 B. This problem recurs many times: in 382, 384, 389, 392, 402–3, and also later it is mentioned in *Saturnalia* by Macrobius, which proves how long pagan elites revolted against the new faith and new customs (Daniélou, *Od początków do końca trzeciego wieku*, 227).

[6] Daniélou, *Od początków do końca trzeciego wieku*, 191–6.

[7] In this context Oswald Spengler used the term *pseudomorphosis*, which is taken from crystallography. It denotes the state of a mineral in which, changing chemical composition, it conserves a previous crystal form instead of crystallizing logway axes, angles, and facets of the new substance (O. Spengler, *Der Untergang des Abendlandes. Umrisse einer Morphologie der Weltgeschichte* (Munich, 1924), ii. 227).

the Apostolic See and the preparation of legislation to work out its details and regulate the legal situation of other churches functioning in Poland. Ultimately, at the start of April 1989, three pieces of draft legislation were sent to Parliament. Following minor corrections, they were passed on 17 May of that year. That took place within the context of talks between the communist authorities and the Opposition, under way since autumn 1988, in which the Church played the role of mediator ahead of the 4 June elections to what was known as the contractual Sejm (lower house). Further work on the draft convention with the Apostolic See, bearing the date of 4 May 1988, could formally resume after diplomatic relations with the Apostolic See had been restored in 1989. The first stage in the change of legislation regulating religious affairs therefore took from 1980 to May 1989. As a result of nearly nine-year-long negotiations with the communist regime, in which the authorities alternately adopted a hard or soft line depending on the country's social situation, laws were adopted guaranteeing individual religious freedoms, freedom for the Catholic church's activities and the restitution of confiscated property. The three 'May laws' laid down new principles regulating the Church's functioning within a reformed communist system. But they were little more than a concession by the regime, which had decided to adjust its laws to the international conventions ratified earlier by the Polish People's Republic. In exchange, the deteriorating authorities hoped to receive certain 'security guarantees' from the Church, which enjoyed great esteem within the Solidarity opposition. Neither the communists nor the Church negotiators had yet envisaged the prospect of the regime's collapse. Unlike the conventions, the 'May laws' conceived the right to freedom not as a human right which man is entitled to by virtue of his inherent dignity, but as a civil right granted by the State.[8]

The collapse of the communist system necessitated a thorough regulation of the principles by which the Catholic Church would function in an emerging democratic and law-abiding State. The law had to be urgently supplemented with two issues of cardinal importance for which there had not been a favourable atmosphere in 1987–9: an entry pertaining to church marriages and one on religious instruction in schools. The law was duly amended in 1991.

In autumn 1989 diplomatic relations between Poland and the Apostolic See resumed. Archbishop Józef Kowalczyk was appointed the apostolic nuncio, and the Polish government designated Jerzy Kuberski as Poland's

---

[8] J. Krukowski, *Kościół i Państwo: podstawy relacji prawnych* ('State and Church: Foundations for Legal Relations') (Lublin, 1993), 215–21; W. Góralski, *Konkordat polski 1993: od podpisania do ratyfikacji* ('The Polish Concordat: From Signing to Ratification') (Warsaw, 1998), 13–20; W. Adamczewski and B. Trzeciak, *Ustawa o stosunku Panvstwa do Kościóła katolickiego w Rzeczypospolitej Polskiej* ('The Law on Relations of the State towards the Catholic Church in the Republic of Poland') (Warsaw, 1995), 22–5.

ambassador extraordinary and plenipotentiary to the Apostolic See. The fruit of that second stage of systemic changes was the signing in 1993 of a concordat between the Apostolic See and the government of Poland.

At that time sharp political disputes involving the Church, i.e. the hierarchy and the lay faithful, erupted. The basic dispute centred round the legal permissibility of abortion. That topic had been 'planted' by communist groups during a session of Parliament in March 1989. One can only speculate that the purpose of that legislative initiative was to bring about a rift in the Solidarity camp ahead of the approaching elections. The attitude to conceived life did in fact divide the Solidarity camp, but—contrary to the intentions of the initiators—not until after the June elections. Following a dramatic political struggle, on 7 January 1993 a compromise law on family planning, protection of the human foetus, and conditions warranting the termination of pregnancy was passed. It ensured protection to the conceived child but also legalized abortion in four specific cases: if the mother's life was endangered or her health was seriously threatened as well as criminal or eugenic situations. The termination of pregnancy for social reasons remained beyond the pale of legality.[9] The legislation stated that the mother of the conceived child was not subject to punishment. The possibility of waiving punishment by the court was also envisaged. In addition, citizens were guaranteed free access to contraceptives, and the introduction of courses on human sexuality in schools was recommended. The Church had maintained an unwavering stand throughout the dispute, but the new law was accepted by its representatives as 'a step in the right direction', which appeared to end the public conflict over the issue.[10]

Another disputed world-view issue was the introduction of optional religious instruction in public schools and the 'decreeing' of Christian values in the educational law and the law on radio and television. In the preamble to the education law the following statement was included: 'Instruction and upbringing, whilst respecting the Christian value system, accept as their basis the universal principles of ethics.'[11] Article 18, point 2, of the radio and television law reads: 'Programming should respect the religious feelings of the audience and in particular respect the Christian value system.' Article 21, point 6, states: 'The programming of public radio and television should . . . respect the Christian value system, accepting the universal principles of ethics as its basis.'[12] A protest against the law was lodged to the Constitutional Tribunal by MPs of the Democratic Left Alliance, who charged that it was contrary to the Constitution. In its verdict of 7 June 1994 the Tribunal ultimately rejected the charges.

---

[9] *Journal of Laws*, 1 Mar. 1993, no. 17, item 78.

[10] J. Glemp, 'Godność osoby ludzkiej jako wartość chrześcijańska' ('Human Dignity as a Christian Value'), *Circular of the Episcopate*, 12 (1993), 1307.

[11] *Journal of Laws*, 25 Oct. 1991, n. 95, item 425, preamble.

[12] Ibid., 29 Jan. 1993, n. 7, item 34.

The second stage of transformation lasted therefore from 1989 to 1993. The elimination of communist restrictions led to a virtual 'eruption of Catholicism'. The Church, which had earlier been shunted off into the sacristy, now began developing successive new areas of public life. Christians, including clergymen, began turning up in prisons, hospitals, schools, and the media. They became involved in evangelization, educational efforts, and charitable activities. They also became active in politics. The Church was seeking a new place for itself in the public arena and made a few blunders in the process. That stage in the transformation indisputably came to an end with the signing of the concordat, in which the legal model of the Church's presence was worked out in detail. In essence, it described the relations between the State and Church as they actually existed in that period with only minor changes. The purpose of that agreement was to ultimately close the period of transformation in that particular field. That was important, since the relationship towards the Church and Christianity had often been politically instrumentalized in the period under discussion. Such attempts had been encountered both in certain Christian communities, which claimed the exclusive right to represent the Church and act in its interests, as well as in atheist circles. On the basis of anticlerical moods, some political groups exploited existing attitudes towards the institutional Church, abortion, and the concordat as one of the ways of mobilizing their electorates. They intimidated voters with the vision of a theocratic state, and sought to pass themselves off as defenders of democracy and human rights. In actuality, 96 per cent of Poland's clergy favoured developing State–Church relations on the basis of autonomy and cooperation. Only 3 per cent believed that the Catholic Church should be entitled to certain privileges and attempt to defend democracy and human rights.[13]

In 1993 post-communist groups returned to power. Tensions between the State and Church began to escalate. The provisions of the concordat were questioned by the new post-communist government coalition as incompatible with the 1952 Constitution, amended in 1992. Ratification of the concordat was postponed until later. A number of conflicts erupted over detailed matters which—it seemed—had been legally regulated once and for all. But the post-communist coalition disrupted the compromise solutions achieved with such difficulty, attempting to restore the previous legal situation in some matters and regain the territory it had lost in its world-view struggle. The abortion law was liberalized—something later rejected by the Constitutional Tribunal as incompatible with the very principle of a democratic law-abiding state.[14] Other conflicts erupted over

[13] L. Kolarska-Bobińska (ed.), *Duchowieństwo polskie wobec perspektywy integracji europejskiej* ('Polish Clergy and the European Integration Process') (Warsaw, 1998), 57.

[14] Ruling by the Constitutional Court of 28 May 1997, sign. K. 26/96, in *Trybunał Konstytucyjny w sprawie życia: dokumenty* ('Constitutional Court Rulings on the Issue of Life: Documents') (Częstochowa, 1997), 98.

attempts to relegate religious instruction classes in schools to the first or last hours and the way in which the Marxist-rooted education minister introduced sex education into school curricula. There were controversies over chaplains in the armed forces and, finally, clashes occurred over the ethical foundations of the State in the new Constitution then being drafted. During that period there arose what might be termed 'a pagan reaction'. It requires deeper analysis, however, since the return to power of representatives of the former regime took place as a result of democratic elections. The direction of changes in the Church's position in public life was in a sense questioned by society itself—a society declaring itself to be 90 per cent Catholic. At the same time, throughout the entire period of transformation no major change in the religiosity of Poles was noted. What, therefore, were the reasons behind that anti-Church and anticlerical 'reaction'.

A kind of dual misunderstanding appears to have been at the root of it. In the first place, an unfamiliarity with diversified European standards prompted some to acknowledge communist era solutions as the norm for the Church's presence in public affairs, and attempts to change the status quo were regarded as clericalization of the State. The above-mentioned questions, whose proposed solutions had been based on those binding in Germany, Austria, and other Catholic countries of Europe, were most often regarded as manifestations of clericalization. The only solutions deviating from those accepted in the non-religious states of the European Union were the above-mentioned entries on the obligation of respecting the Christian system of values.

Another reason for the accusations levelled at the Church was a strategic manoeuvre by post-communist circles which led to 'an error of substitution' committed by some leftist post-Solidarity groups. The consciousness of a considerable part of society had been shaped in an atmosphere of an omnipotent institution ruling people's lives. It decided every aspect of life, and those subject to its authority were deprived of any real way of influencing it. In the Polish People's Republic that institution was the communist party, known as the Polish United Workers' Party (PZPR). It was in the political interest of post-PZPR groups for the vacant space in the public awareness to be filled as soon as possible. Therefore, there emerged the thesis that the 'red dictatorship' had been replaced by a 'black dictatorship'. Thanks to that approach, post-communist formations could abandon the uncomfortable position of an heir to the once-ruling, externally imposed party and assume the role of a would-be defender of human rights.[15] The characteristic thing was that many Western journalists and politicians succumbed to such manipulation, since they referred to solutions similar to those functioning in their countries as clericalization.

---

[15]	E. Wnuk-Lipiński, 'Recydywa PRL: z naszą pomocą',*Gazeta Wyborcza*, 5 July 1994.

The struggle for moral authority in society was essential to former PZPR activists. At stake was the moral rehabilitation of the PZPR, which would allow them to become a 'normal' player on the political stage. The Church, meanwhile, was stressing the importance of defending historical memory and the truth about the communist era. The failure to settle accounts with communist crimes and national amnesia would—in the bishops' view—mean building a new democratic political system on a foundation of falsehoods and understatements. That could pose a threat to the State's future, since it could become an alibi for successive generations of politicians. The bishops therefore urged a path that, while avoiding disdain and the spirit of revenge, would not forget the nation's past and made reconciliation contingent on a readiness to make amends.

That is not to imply that the Church was free from error. During the communist period the Church performed many substitute functions in society and took on responsibility for representing it in relations with the state authorities, for maintaining the nation's sense of identity, etc. When the process of political transformation began and society was given a say in its own affairs, there emerged the hope that the Church would now be able to divest itself of its ersatz functions and concentrate on its main function: evangelization. Well-educated and organized lay Catholics were expected to assume responsibility for the shaping of the State. In fact, only insignificant ecclesiastical circles held the view that the time had not yet come for the Church to withdraw from its substitute functioning and that that should occur only with the conclusion of the Solidarity revolution.[16] As a result of the weakness of Catholic associations and political representations of believers, more than once the church hierarchy had to speak up in their behalf on vital issues. Whereas in the Polish People's Republic the hierarchy had exercised many ersatz functions in behalf of society, after 1989 it undertook similar functions in place of the laity, creating the impression of excessive political involvement. The episcopate took a clear stand in favour of withdrawing from a direct political role following their *ad limina* visit to the Vatican in January 1993.[17] 'The Church is not a political party and does not identify with any political party,' stated the document *A Word from the Polish Bishops on Parliamentary Elections.* 'It is above parties and open to all people of goodwill. Neither does any political party have the right to represent the Church . . . Bishops and priests are not to engage in party-political discussions, stand for Parliament or

---

[16] W. Chrzanowski, in W. Zdaniewicz (ed.), *Znaczenie Kościoła w pierwszych latach III Rzeczypospolitej* ('The Importance of the Church in the Early Years of the Third Republic') (Warsaw, 1994), 198.

[17] John Paul II, 'Ojciec Święty . . . do biskupów polskich w Rzymie, ad limina, 15 stycznia 1993' ('The Holy Father . . . to the Polish Bishops in Rome, ad limina, 15 January 1993'), *Wiadomości Archidiecezjalne Warszawskie*, 1 (1993), 21.

take part in election campaigns . . .'.[18] It remains an open question to what extent that influenced the outcome of the September 1993 elections.

The Polish Church rather quickly realized that its methods of influencing public life must be changed in view of the newly emerging way of organizing public affairs. Quite early attempts were made to activate the laity and to re-establish associations disbanded in the communist era. But, owing to the considerable passivity of the laity, it must be stated that to this day they remain poorly organized and have only a limited impact. Only the anti-abortion movement has assumed mass proportions, demonstrating the possibility of the Church appealing to institutions of civil society. The establishment of certain Catholic associations could have created the impression of an attempt to build 'a parallel Catholic world'.

Another problem was the language used in discussions on vital public issues. Often a vocabulary constituting the legacy of the previous period was employed. That was one of the reasons why extremist groups emerged both on the Catholic and on the anticlerical side. The autocratic option in Poland, which constituted a marginal development both in society and in the Church, is of both secularist (anti-Church) as well as pro-Church coloration, with only a slight predominance of the latter.[19]

The above disputes boil down to the question: does the principle of religious freedom mean restricting religion to the private sphere or does it mean allowing religion to have free access to public life? Does the right to silence on religious matters take precedence over the right to manifest one's faith? In my view, that problem should be perceived within the context of a broader dispute taking place within the framework of Euro-Atlantic civilization. The presence of many Christian religious symbols, behaviour, and institutions, including the legal protection of Sunday, had for centuries been something entirely natural in that region. In recent years, however, numerous attempts to desacralize or even 'decontaminate' public space have been launched.[20] Whereas that process is a rather recent

---

[18] *Słowo Biskupów Polskich w sprawie wyborów do parlamentu, Olsztyn, 19 czerwca 1993* ('A word from the Polish Bishops concerning Parliamentary Elections, Olsztyn, 19 June 1993'), Circular of the Episcopate, 25 (1993), 1320.

[19] J. Marianvski, 'Autorytet moralny Kościoła w II Rezeczypospolitej', in Zdaniewicz (ed.), *Znaczenie Kościoła*, 167; 'I belong among those people who sincerely deplore the declining prestige of our Church. I deplore it for many reasons but the most important one is social: as a matter of fact, in Poland there is no alternative to Catholicism. This means that anyone who abandons the Church will find for himself a substitute in a shape of "tramline atheism", to quote Anna Morawska, or a zoological anticlericalism, more and more popular in this country' ('Religia to poważna sprawa: z Adamem Michnikiem rozmawia ks. Adam Boniecki', *Tygodnik Powszechny*, 26 July 1992).

[20] The dispute about the presence of the crosses broke out in Bavaria in 1998. In a small town near Karlsruhe a clock on the church tower was stopped because it chimed *Ave Maria*. In another town a traditional voluntary Christmas meeting was cancelled because of the protest of a parent of one of the children. In summer 1987, in the county court in Charlestown, SC, somebody discovered an old and almost illegible plaque inscribed with the Decalogue and sued the town councillors (J. Salij, 'Przestrzeń światopoglądowo neutralna?',

development in the West and is carried out in the name of democracy, in the East a similar large-scale 'decontamination' was conducted in the name of atheism and through the use of brutal methods. The question remains whether a lack of violence justifies such efforts.

The subsequent, fourth stage of the systemic transformation occurred on the 2 April 1997, when a new Constitution was adopted. Representatives of the Roman Catholic Church were among those who participated in shaping the chapter on religious freedom and State–Church relations. Solutions concordant with the spirit of the Second Vatican Council, developed in detail in the concordat, were accepted therein. In the same year the post-communist coalition lost power. Within several months the concordat was finally ratified. This would appear to mark the end of radical changes in religious affairs legislation. In the meantime, in the years 1991–7, in accordance with the principle of equality of 'churches and religious organizations', Poland's Parliament adopted eleven laws guaranteeing other religious communities rights analogous to those enjoyed by the Roman Catholic Church.[21] With the exception of the 1991 legislation regulating the status of the Eastern Orthodox Church, they were all patterned on solutions adopted by the concordat. Although the period of reconstructing State–Church relations has ended, that is not to suggest that no conflicts or antagonisms will ever emerge in this area in future. These are normal elements in the functioning of democratic societies, in which the will of the majority often confronts absolute ethical norms. But the basic issues may be regarded as settled once and for all in the spirit of the Second Vatican Council. Procedures for settling potential future misunderstandings also appear to have been put into place. The question remains whether post-communist groups have permanently abandoned the instrumentalization of religious and world-view issues. One should not forget that tensions in this area not only stem from passing controversies but are ideologically rooted in fundamentally divergent visions of the world. The proof is that the dividing line does not exactly coincide with the former division into the authorities and the opposition.

The sum up, the period of transformation of religious affairs legislation can be broken down into the following phases:

in A. Dylus (ed.), *Europa: zadanie chrześcijańskie* ('Europe: A Christian Responsibility'), (Warsaw, 1998), 154).

[21] This refers to the following: the Polish Autocephalous Orthodox Church, Lutheran Church, Polish Catholic Church, Old Catholic Church of Mariavites, Pentecost Church, Church of Adventists, Baptist Church, Methodist Church, Reformed Church, Catholic Church of Mariavites, Jewish Religious Communities, Muslim Religious Union, Eastern Old Rite Church, and the Karaim Religious Union, which operate under the laws of the Second Republic of Poland.

- talks between the communist authorities and the Church when the regime was in a period of decline, ending with the adoption of what have come to be known as 'the May laws';
- the period in which the Church regained the ground usurped by the atheist authorities, ending with the signing of the concordat;
- the period of 'pagan reaction' following the return of post-communist groups to power, when attempts were made under new conditions to reduce the Church's influence to a minimum;
- adoption of a new constitution, the fall of the post-communists from power and ratification of the concordat.

In spite of the considerable time difference, certain similarities between the process I have been discussing and events in the Roman empire of late antiquity may be noticed. But the differences between them are significant, making this a rather remote analogy. During the times of Constantine, Christians accounted for a mere 10 per cent of the empire's population, whereas in Poland the figure was 96 per cent. During the transformation period no attempts by either side to employ physical violence in religious or world-view disputes were encountered. Even when the antagonism was significant, the arguments remained purely verbal. Each side, the post-communists included, had accepted democratic procedures as binding. When engaging in the dispute, the Church accepted as its point of departure the teaching of the Second Vatican Council, including the principle of religious freedom, the autonomy of the state and its world-view neutrality or public pluralism. To be sure, representatives of the Church also had to 'learn democracy', but they nevertheless turned out to be the group that most swiftly adapted their activities to the new conditions. To invoke Spengler's terminology, one can state that this time mental changes in the Church were synchronized with changes in the external structures in which it had to function. As a result thereof, a new model of the Church's presence in the public arena seems to have developed in the course of the nearly ten years in which the Third Polish Republic has been in existence. That model situates Poland among countries quite different from highly secularized France, closer to Ireland, Italy, Spain, or Germany. An eloquent symbol of such 'friendly separation' was the visit of Pope John Paul II to Poland's Parliament.

INDEX